Pharaohs of the Bible
(Mizraim to Shishak):
A Unifying High Chronology of Egypt
based on a High View of Scripture

Front cover pharaohs left to right are Khafre (of Abram's time in Egypt; photo by José-Manuel Benito Álvarez), a pectoral of Ahmose I (the pharaoh who made Joseph second in command), Amenhotep III (of Moses' early life in Egypt), and Rameses I (of the exodus). The sand dune background photo was by Wing-Chi Poon. Peter Engelbrite put it together.

The back cover picture of the wall at Karnak of Thutmose III's history of Egypt's long period of division was based on a drawing by Lespius which was enhanced and uploaded by Peter Lundstrom to Wikimedia.

Pharaohs of the Bible (Mizraim to Shishak)
© July 31, 2012 Eve Clarity

I have created charts and a dozen maps in this book. I have added data to most other maps, and, if not public domain, I have included the name of the original map maker in accordance with Wikimedia licenses. I have included public domain Biblical art, much of which was found at http://www.biblical-art.com/index.htm. Most other art was obtained through Wikimedia Commons, and attributions given in accordance with licenses if not in public domain. A few photos and drawings have been used with permission, and are stated as such. Some photos were obtained from websites which did not have copyright notices.

All rights reserved. No part of this publication may be reproduced without the prior permission of the author, except for cited brief quotations in printed reviews and papers.

All Scripture quotations are from the American King James Version of the Holy Bible which is in the public domain. It is available for free at www.crosswire.org. Scripture has been *italicized,* and is often indented as a block quotation. **Bold lettering** and <u>underlining</u> have been added for emphasis. Occasionally original language words and meanings are placed within brackets [ ].

Foreign language words and titles of books are also *italicized*, but it should not be difficult to distinguish them from Scripture quotations.

Library of Congress Cataloging Number: 2012908646

Clarity, Eve, 1960-
    Pharaohs of the Bible (Mizraim to Shishak): A Unifying High Chronology of Egypt based on a High View of Scripture / by Eve Clarity
    ISBN-13: 978-1477447291 (paper binding)
    ISBN-10: 1477447296 (paper binding)

Dedicated to the Truth

Jesus said to him, I am the way, the truth, and the life: no man comes to the Father, but by me. (John 14:6)

However, when he, the Spirit of truth, is come, he will guide you into all truth: for he shall not speak of himself; but whatever he shall hear, that shall he speak: and he will show you things to come. He shall glorify me: for he shall receive of mine, and shall show it to you. (John 16:13-14)

If any of you lack wisdom, let him ask of God, that gives to all men liberally, and upbraides not; and it shall be given him. (James 1:5)

So that you incline your ear to wisdom, and apply your heart to understanding; Yes, if you cry after knowledge, and lift up your voice for understanding; If you seek her as silver, and search for her as for hid treasures; Then shall you understand the fear of the LORD, and find the knowledge of God. For the LORD gives wisdom: out of his mouth comes knowledge and understanding. (Proverbs 2:2-6)

But God has chosen the foolish things of the world to confound the wise; and God has chosen the weak things of the world to confound the things which are mighty . . . But of him are you in Christ Jesus, who of God is made to us wisdom, and righteousness, and sanctification, and redemption: (I Corinthians 1:27+30)

    I praise YaHWeH (halleluYaH) for His Son YaHshua/Yeshua (Jesus in English) and His Holy Spirit who guide me into all truth because I asked and sought for wisdom and understanding. Elohim has enabled a lowly middle school teacher to figure out how Egyptian history fits into Biblical history. I think He has done so to prove the historic accuracy of His Word and to substantiate Israel's legal ownership of their land. As with all attempts to interpret the Holy Bible and the archaeological facts, there will be human errors; but overall, this book should bolster the faith of Jews and Christians, and give Egyptologists real solutions to ponder. I have attempted to simplify enough of the data so that anyone could follow the chronology; yet I have added plenty of footnoted details for Egyptologists.
    I thank all the archaeologists and their crews who have uncovered the hard evidence cited in this book. I thank my husband for enabling me to stay home these last three years to research and to write this book; it has been a marvelous adventure.
    Since Kenneth Kitchen's chronology is referred to as chronology K, and David Aston's chronology is referred to as chronology A; if you choose to refer to my chronology, refer to it as chronology C or Clarity chronology.

    Visit the website time-line at www.PharaohsOfTheBible.com.

Contents

	Page #
Introduction	vii

CHAPTER TITLE
1.	Presuppositions	11
2.	Chronology Overview	31
3.	Shem's Pharaohs	71
4.	Abraham's and Isaac's Pharaohs	85
5.	Jacob's Pharaohs	115
6.	Joseph's Pharaohs	147
7.	Moses' Pharaohs	177
8.	Joshua's Pharaohs	213
9.	Pharaohs of Israel's Judges	227
10.	Pharaohs of Saul and David	265
11.	Pharaohs of Solomon and Rehoboam	293

APPENDICES
Appendix A: Revised stratigraphy of Israel's cities	327
Appendix B: Calculations of pharaonic regnal dates	367
Appendix C: Late Rameside Letters and Time-lines	455

(planned for Volume 2)
12. Pharaohs of the Divided Kingdom
13. Pharaohs of the Prophets
14. Pharaohs of Ezra and Nehemiah
15. Pharaohs of Esther
16. Pharaohs Prophesied in Daniel 11
17. Pharaohs of the Maccabees
18. Egypt during Jesus' Life

Introduction

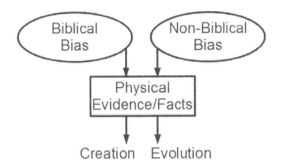

My bias and premise is that the Holy Bible is true and factual as the inspired words of Creator God, *Elohim*, as originally written by men in Hebrew, Aramaic, and Greek. When there is a discrepancy between a fact in the Bible and man's understanding of it, I accept the following possibilities of why man is misunderstanding that Biblical fact:
- Mistranslation or poor translation of the original texts
- Bible fact was removed from its clarifying scriptural, historical or cultural context
- Man is purposely or inadvertently falsifying or suppressing supporting data
- Man lacks the spirit and/or knowledge to understand the Bible fact
- Man has either not found or recognized the supporting data

Though I suspect all of these possibilities have had a part in the continued struggle to rectify Egyptian chronology to the Bible, I believe it is the last one which has caused the most difficulty, and which I plan to remedy. I hope to encourage believers and interest unbelievers in the chronological facts of the Bible, both historically and prophetically. We analyze facts based upon our biases and presuppositions. According to my interpretation of the Holy Bible, I have several presuppositions which will be lightly supported in the first chapter, as many great scientists have already provided full treatments of the issues:
- Ancient universe ("*in the beginning*") and 'recently' (6015 years) populated Earth
- Noah's world-wide flood created our fossil and geologic records
- Only one ice age after Noah's flood during which the Tower of Babel occurred
- Neanderthals and Cro-magnons were highly intellegent post-flood humans
- Shortening of mankind's longevity and age of procreation
- People lie and hide and/or change truth and facts
- North Africa and the Levant were verdant prior to Joseph's 7-year drought

How my Egyptian chronology differs from others

The Bible's 4,000 years of human history prior to Christ's birth encouraged me to consider more dynasties were concurrent with each other. Pyramids were built between Faiyum and the base of the Nile delta during the following dynasties: 3rd and 4th (Memphis), 5th and 6th (Nen-Nesu), 8th (Thinis) and 9th (Herakleopolis Magna), 12th (Itjtawy), and 13th (Thebes). Why weren't pyramids built during the 7th (Thinis) and 11th (Thebes and south) except for Intef II? The Turin King List and Karnak history of Thutmose III helped me realize that some dynasties were consecutive at a certain location while being concurrent with other dynasties. "Pharaoh of two lands" didn't mean north and south, but the red desert and the black fertile soil of the Nile; so there could be several pharaohs simultaneously. The Nile flows from the higher elevations in the south (Upper Egypt=UE) to the lower elevations of the northern delta (Lower Egypt = LE).

The 1st dynasty ruled over a united Egypt, but the 2nd dynasty had a civil war between north and south in which the south (UE) was victorious under Khasekhemwy, whose monuments describe the war against the northerners. Sanakhte of the 3rd dynasty maintained the fragile united Egypt, but Djoser moved his capital to Memphis (LE) leaving a fledgling Thinite 7th dynasty behind. Djoser's pyramid complex was built as a food storage facility prior to the first famine of the Bible recorded in Genesis 12:10.

The first Biblical drought and famine occurred for two years beginning 1921 BC which effected Abram and Sarai. I suggest three years for the next famine (Gen. 26:1) and place it in 1856-1853 BC and effecting Isaac and Rebekah, and ending my First Intermediate Period (cFIP) and immediately starting my Second Intermediate Period (cSIP).

My cFIP and cSIP encompass more concurrent dynasties based in different locations. My cFIP is composed of the 4th, 5th, 8th, 10th, first three pharaohs of 12th, the Theban half of the 13th, 14th, and the Hyksos pre-15th dynasties during the time of great pyramid building. The 4th dynasty of Memphis established the reigns of their children as the 5th dynasty in Henennesut Nen-Nesu ('house of royal child') while the 12th dynasty of Itjtawy established their children as the 13th dynasty in Thebes and established the Kushite 14th in the delta, while the weak 8th dynasty continued at Thinis. The Phoenician entrepreneurs of the delta (pre-15th) briefly stepped into authority at the end of the 4th dynasty in Memphis. The 9th-10th dynasty was based out of Asyut, and linked the Nile trade port of Herakleopolis Parva with Nen-Nesu, renamed Herakleopolis Magna, which is located 5 miles west of Beni Suef.

My cSIP is composed of dynasties following the second Biblical famine: the 6th, 9th, 10th, Theban 11th, rest of 12th, UE 13th, pre-15th alongside the 6th in Memphis, the end of the 14th followed by the Hyksos 15th in the delta, the 16th of El-Kab and Edfu, and the victorious 17th. The Theban 17th dynasty battled with the 15th dynasty for supremacy, and Thebes gained victory led by Ahmose who began the 18th dynasty. The 18th, 19th, and 20th dynasties reigned over a united Egypt, and were comprised of some of the most famous pharaohs.

I include a fifty-five year period of anarchy between the 19th and 20th dynasties. Some of these 55 years can later be attributed to any new pharaohs or new longer regnal dates which are discovered. For now, they conveniently fill a gap. Gap-filling is a practice widely used by Egyptologists. I recognize the reign of king Herihor and the other priest-kings of dynasty

21A during the 21st dynasty by keeping the records of "rebirths" to when one pharaoh died and another's reign began, as was applied to Seti I. The high priests of Amun (HPA) did not constitute a separately numbered dynasty until the 23rd dynasty.

Dynasty 21A of UE is concurrent with 21 of LE. Dynasty 22 of LE is concurrent with 23 of UE. Dynasty 25 of UE is concurrent with dynasty 24 proceeding to dynasty 26 of LE. Then the Persians took over in 525 BC who were conquered by the Greeks (Ptolemies as pharaohs) in 330 BC, who were conquered by Rome in 30 BC. At the time of Messiah's birth in 3 BC, Augustus Caesar ruled Rome and Egypt. At the time of Messiah's death in 33 AD, Tiberius Caesar ruled Rome and Egypt.

Clarity Chronology of Egyptian Dynasties

When one dynasty progresses linearly in time to the next, I use an arrow; when they are connected by an ampersand, the dynasties are concurrent. Thinis is near Tunis, just north of Sohag. Tunis is about 40 miles north of the necropolis at El Araba el-Madfuna (Abydos).

2330-1978	$1^{st} \rightarrow 2^{nd} \rightarrow 3^{rd}$ & 7th Mizraim to Huni in **Thinis to Memphis**
1978-1861	cFIP during the **great pyramid builders**
1861-1720	cSIP with **Hyksos** 15th who lost to 17th dynasty at the end
1738-1378	$18^{th} \rightarrow 19^{th}$ of **famous pharaohs** (Hatshepsut, Tut, and Rameses II)
1378-1323	anarchy
1322-1199	20th with **Rameses** III-XI
1199-1052	**High Priests** of Amun in Thebes and 21st in Tanis
1055-757	22nd **Sheshonks & Osorkons** in Tanis and 23rd high priests in Thebes
787-525	cTIP of 25th in Thebes, & $24^{th} \rightarrow 26^{th}$ in **Sais**

Clarity Chronology of Israel's Divided Kingdom and Shishak

I disagree with Ussher and Dr. Floyd Jones in their use of Nisan to determine Israel's regnal dates based upon rabbinic rules written in the Mishnah in 200 AD. The rabbis incorrectly deduced that since the exodus and entrance into Canaan both occurred in Nisan, that Solomon also counted his regnal years from Nisan (I Kings 6:1, Talmud book 2, p. 2). The *"memorial of trumpets"* when Joseph was released from prison and inaugurated as second to pharaoh was celebrated at the festival of the new moon on the 1st of Tishri and is a Biblical precedent (Gen. 41:39-46; Ps. 81:3-5; and Lev. 23:24) for dating Israelite kings.

I disagree with the traditional assumption that Sheshonk I of the 22nd dynasty was the Shishak of the following verse. I will delineate how Sheshonk IIa fits the data better.

> *And it came to pass, when Rehoboam had established the kingdom, and had strengthened himself, he forsook the law of the LORD, and all Israel with him. And it came to pass, that in the fifth year of king Rehoboam Shishak king of Egypt came up against Jerusalem, because they had transgressed against the LORD . . . (2 Chronicles 12:1-2)*

Shishak is the first named pharaoh in the Bible. This book will explore reasons and explanations for how he and unnamed pharaohs of the Bible fit into the Bible's chronology.

Presuppositions

> *". . . the Laws of Nature and of Nature's God . . .*
> *We hold these truths to be self-evident,*
> *that all men are created equal,*
> *that they are endowed by their <u>Creator</u>*
> *with certain unalienable Rights,*
> *that among these are Life, Liberty*
> *and the pursuit of Happiness."*
> *(Declaration of Independence)*

Originally "the pursuit of Happiness" was "property" under the "Laws of Nature" detailed in John Locke's 1690 *Two Treatises of Government* in which Creator God, *Elohim*, bequeathed the Earth to Adam and Eve as its stewards.[1] What was "self-evident" in the 1700's all but disappeared by the 1800's.

Ancient Universe and 'Recently' Populated Earth

I interpret Genesis 1:1-2a to mean the "*heavens and earth*", the universe, are ancient, and the earth was "*without form [tohu] and void [bohu]*"; it was a water planet covering an earthen core. The first day of terraforming the earth did not begin until ". . . *the Spirit of God moved on the face of the waters.*" (Gen. 1:2b). This interpretation is known as 'Old Universe/Young Earth' theory. I do NOT believe in the current "Gap theory" which purports that the earth had human inhabitants prior to Elohim's creation of Adam and Eve, and the destruction of that world left our current fossil record. I think our current fossil record was the result of Noah's flood. I do believe in a 'millions of years' time gap in which the Earth remained "*void*" of inhabitants between Elohim's creation of the universe and His terraforming the Earth in six literal days in 4004 BC. For a scientific synopsis of this theory and 6-day creation, please read Michael Engelbrite's "Windows of Heaven".[2]

> *And Adam called his wife's name Eve; because she was the mother of all living. (Genesis 3:20)*

---

1 "Primacy: the Declaration of Independence," http://batr.org/autonomy/111804.html accessed 6/14/11
2 Engelbrite, Michael Peter, "Windows of Heaven," http://www.kneelingmedia.org/windowsofheaven/

Eve is *chavvah* in Hebrew meaning "life or life-giver". *Newsweek's* 1988 article referring to "mitrochondrial Eve" as the mother of all living humans made quite a buzz, but the scientists were emphatic she had nothing to do with the Biblical Eve, since this woman lived in Africa among lots of other people 200,000 years ago. Rebecca Cann convinced 147 pregnant women to donate their placentas to science, and "All the babies' DNA could be traced back, ultimately, to one woman. . . . a well-established outcome of the laws of probability."[3]

> "They looked at the most distant branches of the family tree -- the DNA types most different from one another -- and worked backward to figure out how many steps it would have taken for Eve's original DNA to mutate into these different types. They **assumed** that these mutations occurred at a regular rate -- <u>a controversial assumption that might be wrong</u>, but which has been supported by some studies of humans and animals. Over the course of a million years, it appears that 2 to 4 percent of the mitochondrial DNA components will mutate. By this molecular calculus, Eve must have lived about 200,000 years ago."[4] [emphasis mine]

Another group of scientists agree with the date, but not the origin.

> "Wallace's data suggests that Eve can be traced to southeast China, but he cautions that this is <u>only one possible interpretation of the data</u>. "If we make other **assumptions**, we can run our data through a computer and come up with a family tree starting in Africa," he says. "So I'm not ruling out Africa. I'm just saying that we can't yet decide whether it's Asia or Africa.""[5] [emphasis mine]

Tierney continued, "the rival geneticists agree that she lived relatively recently, and this is what provokes anthropologists to start arguing."

> "[Anthropologists] rightly point out that the <u>geneticists' molecular clock could be way off</u> -- change a few **assumptions** and Eve's birthday could move back hundreds of thousands of years."[6] [emphasis mine]

I have used this one article to make a point about the assumptions of scientists effecting data and conclusions. Sciences which involve history are based upon assumptions. Tierney went on to note the possible "Noah's Ark theory," and added, "Eve herself might have been our immediate ancestor, an archaic Homo sapiens, and therefore brawnier, with a large, protruding face and a forehead receding behind prominent brow ridges."[7]

---

3 Tierney, John, "In Search of Adam & Eve", *Newsweek* 1992 based upon *Newsweek III* (Jan. 11, 1988), pp. 46-52; http://www.virginia.edu/woodson/courses/aas102%20(spring%2001)/articles/tierney.html
4 Ibid.
5 Ibid.
6 Ibid.
7 Ibid.

Other scientists have concluded that all living humans on all continents share a recent common ancestor who lived about 5,000 years ago.[8] This would be a Most Recent Common Ancestor (MRCA) which traces ancestry of specific organisms, like humans, as opposed to Mitochondrial Eve and Y-chromosomal Adam which trace ancestry of individual genes which could occur in humans, apes, or chimpanzees.

Scientists agree that human DNA went through a cataclysmic bottleneck which reduced the population severely, limiting our DNA diversity. But instead of attributing it to the world-wide flood of Noah, they'd rather find another more distant reason.

People Lie and Hide/Change Facts and Truth

After the scandal of global warming emails, I don't know how anyone can trust the scientific world. Scientific misconduct includes fabrication, falsification, obfuscation, and making unsupported claims. Archaeological forgeries have produced fame and fortune. But some have committed fraud to give credence to evolution by providing 'missing links'. Such was the case of Archaeoraptor, the kludged 'missing link' fossil of some land animal and bird made in China. *National Geographic* published it in 1999 and retracted it the next year.[9] The Piltdown man was in textbooks for over a generation as an ape-man, but it was a 1912 hoax created from an orangutan's jawbone and human skull undiscovered until 1953.[10] "Lucy" *Australopithecus* is a fossilized 3.5 foot tall chimpanzee discovered in 1974 and touted as a 3.2 million year old missing link. But then "Ardi", at 4 feet tall and 4 million years old, topped that discovery in 1994, and became a new species, *Ardipithicus ramidus*.[11]

In 1829 Charles Lyell heard that the Niagara Falls "receded about 45 metres (150 feet) during the 40 years" a resident had lived there[12] — which was an average of 3.75 feet a year; which would make the gorge 9,333 years old. Charles Lyell visited Niagara Falls in 1841 and noted the gorge from the Falls to Queenston was seven miles or about 35,000 feet long. In Lyell's book, *Principles of Geology*, he claimed the gorge was 35,000 years old[13] (an average of one foot per year of recession). The actual average is between 1.5 to 2 meters per year,[14] or 4.9 to 6.6 feet per year; placing the gorge between 5,303 and 7,143 years old if the rate of erosion was constant, which it wasn't after the flood. Because of Lyell's falsification and theory of uniformitarianism, today's geologists have no problem assigning millions of years to various geologic strata.

---

8   Rhode DL, Olson S, Chang JT, "Modelling the recent common ancestry of all living humans," *Nature* 431, September 2004, pp. 562–566
9   Mayell, Hillary, "Dino Hoax was Mainly Made of Ancient Bird, Study Says," *National Geographic* November 20, 2002 http://news.nationalgeographic.com/news/2002/11/1120_021120_raptor.html
10 "Piltdown Man is revealed as fake" 1953 http://www.pbs.org/wgbh/aso/databank/entries/do53pi.html
11 "Ancient Human Ancestors Found", Canada and the World, November 2010
    http://www.canadaandtheworld.com/ancienthumanancestor.html
12 Pierce, Larry, "Niagara Falls and the Bible", *Creation ex nihilo* 22(4):8–13 September 2000,
    http://www.answersingenesis.org/creation/v22/i4/niagara_falls.asp
13 Lyell, C., *Principles of Geology*, 11th edition, D. Appleton and Co., New York, NY, USA, 1:354–358, 1873
14 "Erosion at Niagara Falls supports the biblical time-scale" with same article as footnote #12.

Since people lie, facts must always be verified by those who can't gain from doing so.

In hope of eternal life, which God, that cannot lie, promised before the world began . . . (Titus 1:2)

*For the wrath of God is revealed from heaven against all ungodliness and <u>unrighteousness of men, who hold the truth in unrighteousness</u>; Because that which may be known of God is manifest in them; for God has showed it to them. For the invisible things of him from the creation of the world are clearly seen, being understood by the things that are made, even his eternal power and Godhead; so that they are without excuse: Because that, when they knew God, they glorified him not as God, neither were thankful; but became vain in their imaginations, and their foolish heart was darkened. Professing themselves to be **wise**, they became fools, And changed the glory of the incorruptible God into an image made like to corruptible man, and to birds, and four footed beasts, and creeping things. Why God also gave them up to uncleanness through the lusts of their own hearts, to dishonor their own bodies between themselves: <u>Who changed the truth of God into a lie, and worshipped and served the creature more than the Creator</u>, who is blessed for ever. Amen. (Romans 1:18-25)*

The serpent deceived Eve into believing that God could lie and was withholding wisdom from her, and so she ate of the forbidden tree of knowledge of good and evil, and gave some to Adam who also ate (Genesis 3:1-6). They tried to 'cover up' their misdeed and hide from Elohim, and then they played the blame game. Their sin separated them from Elohim and eternal life (the other tree in the garden), and brought great violence into the earth. Archaeologists acknowledge many monuments are propaganda pieces and not reliable history. Some people deceive others intentionally; while others deceive themselves. That's why basing all other knowledge upon the Holy Bible is wisdom.

Now I beseech you, brothers, mark them which cause divisions and offenses contrary to the doctrine which you have learned; and avoid them. For they that are such serve not our Lord Jesus Christ, but their own belly; and by good words and fair speeches deceive the hearts of the simple. (Romans 16:17-18)

*Let no man deceive himself. If any man among you seems to be **wise** in this world, let him become a fool, that he may be wise. For the wisdom of this world is foolishness with God. For it is written, He takes the wise in their own craftiness. (I Corinthians 3:18-19)*

Presuppositions

A Pre-flood Earth Year was 360 days, and a Month was 30 days

The year has only lengthened by 5.24 days since before the flood. Noah calculated 30 days to a month[15] in the ark until the skies cleared enough for him to see the phases of the moon, and determined the moon was no longer in sync, and so he gave counts of days only. Pre-flood years were 360 days[16] long, but after the cataclysm were 365.24 days long with a moon cycle of 29.5 days instead of 30 days. Dr. Henry Morris stated, "There is even a possibility that the earth's rotation speeded up by about 1.5 percent if the year was really 360 days long."[17] The exact mathematical calculations are provided by Dr. Walter Brown,[18] who theorizes Earth mass was lost at the breaking up of the abyss, and accounts for many comets, asteroids and meteors; some of which hit the moon, slowing it.[19] According to the Egyptian's Osiris myth, the calendar was first 360 days long. After the Tower of Babel, cultures on every continent erected an observatory atop a ziggurat in order to establish a new calendar based on the new revolutions of the earth and moon.[20] Besides the pyramids of Egypt, there are pyramids in Central and South America, Europe, China, and Russia.[21]

Maya Calendars

The Maya arrived at the most precise calendar by using several calendars to check and balance each other. They had a lunar year of 354 days. The Maya solar *tun* was a period of 360 days plus 5/6 intercalary days. The Maya *katun* was a period of twenty years which is roughly the interval of when Jupiter and Saturn have a conjunction.[22] The Maya *tzolkin* was a sacred year of 260 days. The Maya also had a Venus calendar of 584 days based on the appearance of Venus in the same place in the sky as viewed from Earth.

> "As 5 X 584 is equal to 8 X 365, the Maya considered five Venus years equal to eight solar years. And as 365 X 104 is equal to both 146 X 260 and 65 X 584, the solar, sacred, and Venus calendars become coincident every 37,960 days, or 104 years, which was two Mesoamerican centuries of 52 years. . . .
> The Mesoamericans had figured out correctly
> that 260 X 18 is the same as 360 X 13,
> that 260 X 7 is the same as 364 X 5,
> that 260 X 73 is the same as 365 X 52 and
> that 260 X 1461 (the Egyptian Sothic cycle) is the same as 365.25 X 1040."[23]

---

15 See Gen. 7:11 and 8:3-6 in which 5 months = 150 days, but a couple months later, they say "40 days".
16 360 days for a year of 30 day months continued to be used in the Bible for prophetic years (Rev. 11:2-3).
17 Morris, Henry, *The Genesis Record*, Baker Book House, 1976, p. 212
18 Brown, Walter, Ph.D., *In The Beginning: Compelling Evidence for Creation and the Flood*, Center for Scientific Creation, www.creationscience.com, 2008, pp. 430-432
19 Ibid., pp. 263-313
20 Velikovsky, Immanuel, chapter "The Year of 360 Days" in *Worlds in Collision*, NY, Doubleday, 1950, p. 330-359 which cites 360 day writings from Egypt, China, South America, and the Middle East.
21 See http://www.world-pyramids.com/
22 Every 800 years (Great Mutation Cycle), Saturn and Jupiter return to within one degree of starting point.
23 Tompkins, Peter, *Mysteries of the Mexican Pyramids*, Harper & Row Publishers, 1976, p. 290

Pharaohs of the Bible

Pre-flood and Post-flood Man were more advanced than Modern Man

There are Maya legends of the "Naacal, or 'the exalted' who were reported to have set out across the world to teach others their language, architecture, and astronomy."[24] The Mayan and Egyptian alphabets have several similar characters and similar words.[25]

Astronomy

Because pre-flood people lived roughly 900 years, they acquired an amazing understanding of practical science, mathematics, and astronomy.

> "God afforded them a longer time of life on account of their virtue and the good use they made of it in astronomical and geometrical discoveries, which would not have afforded the time of foretelling [the periods of the stars] unless they had lived six hundred years; for the Great Year is competed in that interval."[26]

Nabta Playa is 100km west of Abu Simbel

According to NASA, the stones at Nabta Playa marked the summer solstice.[27] They may have been arranged by (K)Ham, the father of all K(h)emmites (Africans) and Cush.

The Egyptians noted the "dog star" Sirius, in Canis Major, had its heliacal rising (after a 70-day absence, about a month before the inundation of the Nile and the summer solstice. Summer solstice occurs at Earth's maximum axial tilt to the Sun. Because of Earth's wobble on its axis (precession), the rising of most stars slip through the calendar but Sirius does not, and was likely chosen because of this stability. The Sothic year's average duration was exactly 365.25 days during Egypt's first dynasties to the end of my Second Intermediate Period when Thuban of the constellation Draco was the pole star (3942 to 1793 BC).[28] During that period the Sothic rise would return to the same calendar day each 1461 calendar years. Kappa Draconis in Draco was closest to the North Celestial Pole visible to the naked eye from 1793 BC to approximately 1000 BC,[29] and the Sothic cycle dropped to about 1456 calendar years during that time.[30]

---

24 Tompkins, Peter, *Mysteries of the Mexican Pyramids*, Harper & Row Publishers, 1976, p. 169
25 Ibid., pp. 116 and 169
26 Josephus, *Antiquities of the Jews*. The Great Year of 600 years is called the Neros cycle when the sun and moon are in conjunction at the spring equinox. See Godwin's *Theosophical Enlightenment*, 1994, p. 82
27 "Egyptian Stonehenge," NASA, http://sunearthday.nasa.gov/2005/locations/egypt_stone.htm
28 "Thuban,", *Wikipedia*
29 "Kappa Draconis," *Wikipedia*
30 "Sothic year," *Wikipedia*

Mathematics

Petrie measured the dimensions of the Great Pyramid at Giza: length of one side of the base, 755.733 feet; height, 481.33 feet; angle, 51°51'59"; approximation to pi based on the measurements, 3.14017.[31] Engineer and stone/metal craftsman Christopher Dunn has examined the precise measurements of Egypt's pyramids and statues. Evidence of advanced mathematics in Egyptian architecture and sculpture abounds: metrology (the science of exact measurement), Cartesian grids, the 3-4-5 right triangle, Fibonacci spirals, the golden ratio, pi and overlapping circles, and elliptical geometry.[32] Dunn has verified the conclusions of Flinders Petrie that the ancient Egyptians had powered, fixed jewel-point saws which were able to cut the hardest and most brittle stones.[33] A trench at Abu Roash could once have held a 37 foot diameter megasaw for cutting granite, limestone, and basalt. And a similar trench at the Giza Plateau has steps into it for easier waste removal.[34]

Metallurgy

> . . . Jubal: he was the father of all such as handle the harp and organ. And Zillah, she also bore Tubalcain, an instructor of every artificer in brass and iron: and the sister of Tubalcain was Naamah. (Genesis 4:21-22)

Lavaur supposed the name of the Greek and Roman smith-god *Vulcan* was derived from (Tu)balcain, the son of Lamech.[35] Tubalcain was born about 450 years after Adam. That means metallurgy had 1800 years to develop before Noah began building the ark. I suggest they developed metals and steel with a hardness modern man has yet achieved, and that Noah used some of those tools in building the ark and brought them into the ark. They may have also brought simple iron tools.

Upon clearing the southern air-channel to the King's Chamber at the Great Pyramid of Giza by blasting, a piece of wrought iron was discovered "embedded in the cement in an inner joint."[36] Petrie noted "it has a cast of nummulite on the rust of it, proving it to have been buried for ages beside a block of nummulitic limestone, and therefore to be certainly ancient."[37] Egypt is primarily known for its bronze, and there is a bronze battle axe head engraved with the name of Senusret I (1934-1889 BC). Bronze is a metal alloy of about 88% copper and 12% tin. The world's oldest copper mine is in the Negev desert 25km north of Eilat, Israel in the Timna Valley, and produced "22-lb. copper ingots that were 97% to 98% pure, a degree of purity not exceeded until modern times."[38]

---

31 Petrie, Flinders, *Pyramids and Temples of Gizeh*, 1883
32 Dunn, Christopher, *Lost Technologies of Ancient Egypt*, Bear & Company, 2010
33 Ibid., pp. 197-339
34 Ibid., pp. 283-289
35 Lavaur, M. Dr., *Conference de la Fable avec l'Histoire Sainte*, 1730
36 Toth, Max, *Pyramid Prophecies*, 1988, pp. 208-209
37 Petrie, Flinders, *Pyramids and Temples of Gizeh*, 1883, p. 85
38 "The Oldest Mine?" *Time*, January 13, 1975, p. 65

Pharaohs of the Bible

Noah's Ark and World-wide Flood (2348 – 2347 BC)

"It has long been known that legends of a great flood, in which almost all men perished, are widely diffused over the world ..."[39]

In fact, there are over 270 different world-wide flood legends in cultures all around the world.[40] Most of them have similarities to the Biblical saga, and warn against causing another disaster by making the gods angry.

*And God looked on the earth, and, behold, it was corrupt; for all flesh had corrupted his way on the earth. And God said to Noah, The end of all flesh is come before me; for the earth is filled with **violence** through them; and, behold, I will destroy them with the earth. Make you an ark of gopher wood; rooms shall you make in the ark, and shall pitch it within and without with pitch. And this is the fashion which you shall make it of: <u>The length of the ark shall be three hundred cubits, the breadth of it fifty cubits, and the height of it thirty cubits</u>. (Genesis 6:12-15)*

Noah's Ark

For measurements, I am using the following conversions:
1 royal Egyptian cubit = 0.52325 meters = 1.7167 feet = 20.6 in.
1 meter = 3.281 feet

If Noah used the royal Egyptian cubit to build the ark which was 300 X 50 X 30 cubits (Genesis 6:15), then it would have measured 156.975 X 26.1625 X 15.6975 meters, or 515.01 X 85.835 X 51.501 feet. A boat-shape 515 feet long was discovered by Ron Wyatt in 1977 near the "Valley of Eight" (Noah and his wife, and Noah's sons and their wives total eight persons). But it exceeds the ark's width, and has been determined to be a natural formation from earthquakes and lava flows.[41] I think Wyatt was self-deceived on that, yet in 1978, Ron Wyatt discovered the Red Sea crossing at Nuweiba beach and King Solomon's pillars of commemoration placed there and on the Arabian side, and he discovered Mounts Sinai and Horeb (Jebel Maqla and Lawz); and these discoveries were verified by other archaeologists.

As for Noah's ark, the Bible placed its landing in the "*mountains of Ararat [arrt]*" which was in the ancient lands of Urartu which now includes Armenia and northern Iran. The city of Ararat, Armenia is 25 miles NE of *Agri Dagh* (Mt. Ararat) in Turkey today, but it was a part of Armenia until the Turks conquered it in the 10th century. In 1724, Sir John Chardin reported that the Armenian natives told him the Ark was situated on the northeast side of Mount Ararat, and he drew a sketch of its position.[42]

---

39 James George Frazer, *Folk-Lore in the Old Testament*, Vol. 1, London: Macmillan Publishing Co., 1919, p. 105, http://www.nwcreation.net/noahlegends.html
40 Gish, Duane Dr., *Dinosaurs by Design*, Master Books, 1992
41 http://www.answersingenesis.org/-creation/v14/i4/report.asp#ark5
42 Chardin, Sir John, *Sir John Chardin's Travel in Persia*, 1724, introduction

Five miles west of the city of Ararat is the town Yeghegnavan on the Araxes River which can be seen from the northeastern slopes of Mt. Ararat, and it is the closest descent to water at 20 miles. From Yeghegnavan, sixty miles south along the river is *Nakhchivan*, which translates to "first resting-place", where Noah's family established their new home on a wide plain across from a lake.[43]

[Hovhannes Aivazovsky, *Descent of Noah from Mount Ararat*, 1889. National Gallery of Armenia, Yerevan.]

When the pressurized aquifers that had watered the earth for over a thousand years were compromised, "*all the fountains of the great deep* [were] *broken up*"[44]. Dr. Walter Brown gives an excellent scientific explanation of these aquifers rupturing in his hydroplate theory.[45] William Whiston theorized a comet was responsible for the rupture of earth's crust causing Noah's flood.[46] Breaks in the earth's crust which allowed water to erupt, also allowed magma to erupt during Noah's flood. Sediments were deposited vertically with the larger and heavier rocks on the bottom and the smaller and lighter rocks on top,[47] though we observe the horizontal lines of strata and fossils according to their density when deposited.[48]

Since the flood waters were upon the earth for almost a year, many unique deposits and inland lakes were left as the flood waters abated. Some inland lakes burst through at their

---

43 Lanser, Richard, mDiv, "An Armenian Perspective on the Search for Noah's Ark", Associates for Biblical Research, 2008; article available at http://noahsarksearch.com/ararat.htm

44 Genesis 7:11

45 Brown, Walter Dr., Brown, Walter, Ph.D., *In The Beginning: Compelling Evidence for Creation and the Flood*, 2008, pp. 105-141; also at www.creationscience.com, "Hydroplate theory of the Flood", hydroplate video at http://www.youtube.com/watch?v=zKO-vTwYCo8&feature=related

46 Whiston, William, *A New Theory of the Earth*, 1696, London. See further notes in appendix.

47 Piu, Hou, *et al.*, *Experiment Study on Sediment Deposit in High Pressure Water Conveyance Pipe*, China. "whatever the operating condition is, at the beginning of the pump running, the distribution of the sediment concentration along the vertical line in the pipe's cross section is fairly uniform, The grain size of the sediment along the vertical line is a little larger near the bottom than that near the top."

48 Sungenis, R. *Dialogue on Evolution vs Creation*, at http://www.catholicintl.com/scienceissues/dialogue-evolution3.htm

weakest points, cutting giant canyons into the new soft earth and making the spectacular canyons we have today. The speed at which canyons are made can be deduced from the formation of modern canyons; like the one created by Mount Saint Helens' eruption in 1980;[49] and Burlingame Canyon near Walla Walla, Washington which is 1500 feet long and up to 120 feet deep and 120 feet wide and formed in less than six days.[50]

No 'Pre-History' of Mankind

Genesis does not explain the timing of Elohim's creation of the universe, except to place it "*in the beginning*" preceding His terraforming of Earth, and creating Adam and Eve on the sixth day. The Holy Bible contains mankind's ancient history along with the "*great whales [tanniyn],*" which can also be translated 'monsters' or 'dragons', created one day prior. There was only a 24-hour gap between the first sea dinosaurs and man, not millions of years. Adam walked with land dinosaurs, and Noah brought young ones on the ark.[51] Noah and his family disembarked with the animals, seeds and seedlings, metal tools; and vast knowledge of their Creator and mankind's past in written form. They understood astronomy, metallurgy, mathematics, engineering, construction, farming, and animal husbandry.

'Stone-Age' People Groups Have Always Been, and Are Now, Present

There was no 'Stone-age' with grunting cavemen, though there are stone-age people groups throughout mankind's history to present day due to isolation. Elohim created Adam and Eve as adult humans with full language capabilities. The unique Son of God, Yeshua, taught the first physical son of God, Adam, how to write the first human language which may have been Sumerian with its cuneiform writing, or, more likely, proto-Hebrew.

Like any good teacher who personalizes assignments, Yeshua taught Adam the signs beginning with those for 'brother'[52], and then included 'brother' several times at exciting points of His simplified creation account:[53]

And God created, <u>brother</u>, huge stretched-out monsters; oh, <u>brother</u>, all breathing, living crawlers which spawn in water according to their kind. And, <u>brother</u>, every flapping bird according to their kind. And God saw it was good. (Genesis 1:21)[54]

---

49 Austin, Stephen Dr, "Mt. St. Helens and Catastrophism" at http://www.icr.org/article/mt-st-helens-catastrophism/ and also http://www.nwcreation.net/mtsthelens.html

50 Morris, John Dr., "How long does it take for a canyon to form," http://www.icr.org/article/how-long-does-it-take-for-canyon-form/

51 Gish, Duane T., Dr., *The Amazing Story of Creation from Science and the Bible*, Institute for Creation Research, 1990

52 The Hebrew word "ach" is translated over 400 times as "brother" in the Old Testament, and is clearly present in the Hebrew version of Genesis 1, but is omitted in English translations.

53 Beechick, Ruth, *Genesis: Finding Our Roots*, Arrow Press, Canada, 1997. Yeshua's creation account is Genesis 1:1-2:4a. Adam's account is Genesis 2:4b-5:1a. These plus the accounts of Noah, Shem, and Terah were later compiled and edited by Moses into the book now called Genesis.

54 Genesis 1:21 retranslated from the Hebrew with help from Steven L. Ross, author of *Genesis Said It First*, self-published, 1992, p. 21

1800's New Sciences of Geology, Archaeology, and Evolution

When American colonists were writing the *Declaration of Independence* (1776) and crying, "No king but King Jesus,"[55] James Hutton in England was contemplating a geologic time of tens of thousands of years[56] contrary to roughly 6,000 years of human history interrupted by a cataclysmic flood. Instead of postulating that volcanic activity accompanied Noah's flood which produced the flows of magma between other strata, he decided the volcanic activity must have preceded a flood by tens of thousands of years with periods of erosion between,[57] and he even went on to suggest natural selection of species.[58] This began a "scientific" revolution in the 1800's. In 1830 Charles Lyell's *Principles of Geology* espoused the idea that the great canyons were produced by consistent erosion over periods of thousands of years (uniformitarianism) instead of at the cataclysm of Noah's flood. That book and *Vestiges of the Natural History of Creation* published in 1844, paved the way for people to believe Charles Darwin's theory of evolution in *On the Origin of Species* in 1859, though it was Anaximander (c. 610 – 540 BC) who first wrote ". . . originally, humans were born from animals of a different kind . . ."[59] In 1847, Edouard Collomb was the first to suggest there was more than one ice age.[60] In 1848 a Danish historian published *A Guide to Northern Antiquities*, in which he divided prehistory into three ages based upon the materials most often used: stone, bronze, and iron.[61] Thus the fledgling science of archeology was born into an anti-Bible culture. These 1800's "scientists" continued to attack every historical fact of Holy Scripture as some continue to do today. The root of the word "science" is "to know" in Latin, which is *ginosko* in Greek.

> . . . *avoiding profane and vain babblings, and oppositions of <u>science</u> [gnosis] falsely so called: Which some professing have erred concerning the faith. (1 Timothy 6:20b-21a)* [hence, a-gnostics do 'not know' of God]

Not heeding Paul's command has led many away from the faith to follow their error. Yet in the last two decades there has been an increase of scientists who, due to faulty and/or missing old evidence and new research, no longer believe in uniformitarianism or evolution, and now pursue science based upon Intelligent Design. There are also more archaeologists who are challenging the three ages, and are giving more credence to the historic accuracy of the Bible.[62] Today's Intelligent Design scientists often lose their jobs or grant money when

---

55 Manuel, David, and Marshall, Peter and Fischel, Anna, *The Light and the Glory for Children*, 1995
56 Hutton, James, *Considerations on the Nature, Quality and Distinctions of Coal and Culm*, 1777
57 Hutton, James, *Concerning the System of the Earth, its Duration and Stability*, 1785
58 Hutton, James, *An Investigation of the Principles of Knowledge and of the Progress of Reason, from Sense to Science and Philosophy*, volume 2, 1795
59 Barnes, Jonathan, *Early Greek Philosophy*, Penguin Classics, Harmondsworth, 1987, p. 73
60 Oard, Michael J., *An Ice Age Caused by the Genesis Flood*, Institute for Creation Research, 1990, p. 136
61 Chalcolithic, meaning 'copper'-'stone', was also squeezed in between stone and bronze ages.
62 Wood, Bryant, "In what ways have the discoveries of archaeology verified the reliability of the Bible?", 1995 at http://www.christiananswers.net/q-abr/abr-a008.html

they give up on the agnostic ('against knowledge') science of the 1800's.[63]

Concurrent with the theories of Hutton and Lyell were the studies of Johannes Walther who studied sedimentary deposits that advanced from land toward the ocean. He observed something unique about the horizontal bands (fasciae/facies) of the drilled core samples which is now termed "Walther's Law of Facies".

> "He found that the various facie from the test sample were in the same order as the leading edge of the advancement into the ocean. He reasoned that the facie were being laid side-by-side. Walther did the same testing in the bay of Naples. He found that after drilling-out a vertical column of sediment it had the same sequence of facies arrangement as the sediments laying horizontally. He soon reasoned that the previous theory that facies on the top were forming later than the facies on the bottom was wrong. Instead, he found that the facies were being formed simultaneously . . ."[64]

Unlike the false theories of Hutton and Lyell, Walther's experiments were repeated by American geologist Edwin McKee and French geologist Guy Berthault with the same results to designate it to be a scientific law.[65] Real science is observable and reproducible.

Remains of Post-flood (anti-deluvian) People

Jack Cuozzo's book, *Buried Alive: the startling truth about Neanderthal Man*, first opened my eyes to the scientific evidence of 'cavemen' which supports the long lives recorded in the Bible. Dr. Cuozzo, an orthodontist, was allowed to x-ray the actual skulls and jaws of the Neanderthals and Cro-Magnons discovered in Europe. What he uncovered almost got him killed. When these skulls are on display, the jaws were jutted forward so that the top and bottom teeth met, or the bottom teeth protruded in front of the upper teeth. When he properly placed the condyle, back hook of the jaw, into the TM fossa of the zygomatic arch of the skull, the lower teeth naturally went into position behind the upper teeth, and worn groves meshed between the top and bottom teeth producing centric occlusion, a good bite. I believe that if it had not been for the brave report and photos of his discovery, the scientific world would still be promoting Neanderthals and Cro-Magnons as ape-men instead of fully human beings. But Dr. Cuozzo also proved those skulls were of people who lived for hundreds of years.

> ". . . many of the 'archaic' features of some strains of 'early man' are very likely due to delayed maturation in early post-flood people who still had (as the Bible record indicates) significantly longer lifespans than today."[66]

---

63 Stein, Ben, *Expelled, No Intelligence Allowed*, movie documentary, 2008
64 Sungenis, R. *Dialogue on Evolution vs Creation*, at http://www.catholicintl.com/scienceissues/dialogue-evolution3.htm; also see http://en.wikipedia.org/wiki/Facies
65 Ibid., see video on Walther's Law at http://www.youtube.com/watch?v=1XvbbE_VwC8& 21-32+ minutes
66 Cuozzo, Dr. John (Jack), "Neanderthal Children's Fossils: Reconstruction and Interpretation Distorted by Assumptions," *Technical Journal*, August 1994, http://creation.com/neandertal-childrens-fossils

Presuppositions

The 'archaic' features are the pronounced supraorbital (above the eye) brow ridges, and longer and thicker skulls with angled nasal bones. Contrary to popular understanding, the skull continues to grow throughout life. Just looking at elderly people today, one notices larger noses and ears, the possibility of dentures, and an enlarged brow ridge. The enlarged brow ridge is due to years of the pressure of chewing being transferred into the buildup of the bones of the face. Dr. Cuozzo made the analogy of the bones around our eyes being like flying buttresses which enabled large stain-glassed windows to be placed in cathedrals; ". . . the flying buttresses of the face and head absorb the forces of chewing."[67]

The first post-flood generations lived several hundred years and developed enlarged brow ridges. Nimrod's kingdom began in Shinar/Sumer,[68] and interesting cuneiform tablets described their schoolmasters as having big, thick, or heavy brows.[69]

This is the key which Jack Cuozzo discovered: "The first point is that early maturity must be related to the process of loss of longevity."[70] Neanderthals were "uniquely slow-developing and long-lived humans."[71] As an orthodontist, he had to wonder how their teeth could last for hundreds of years. He found Neanderthal teeth had more enamel folds than modern man, and likely had better or thicker 'enamel pellicles', which Job referred to as "*the skin of my teeth*"[72]. The enamel pellicle is a membrane on teeth which repairs them and fills in scratches.[73]

Dr. Henry Morris emphasized the mutations caused by inbreeding after the Tower of Babel, and the fallacies of uniformitarianism and radiocarbon dating methods.

> "As far as the drop in longevity is concerned, it was apparently just before Peleg's birth that the Dispersion took place, as we have seen. This was an extremely traumatic experience for the entire human race, and it is not surprising that it would have severe physical effects on mankind in general. In addition to the difficulty of mere survival under the new conditions of living in small tribal communities, the effects of the genetic mutations that had been accumulating for several generations since the Flood were much aggravated by the necessity of close inbreeding. In general, it does not seem at all necessary to assume a gap in the genealogy in order to account for the drop in longevity at this time. The only real reason for wanting to stretch the chronology here, therefore, is to deal with the opinion of archaeologists that early civilizations must be dated earlier than the Ussher chronology (which is based on the assumption of complete genealogical lists in Genesis 5 and 11) will allow. This opinion, however, is based mainly on uniformitarian methods of dating, especially the radiocarbon method; and one should not base his Biblical exegesis on some latter-day scientific theory. There are no actual, indisputable written historical records in Egypt, Sumeria, or any other ancient

---

67 Cuozzo, Dr. Jack, *Buried Alive: the startling truth about Neanderthal Man,* MasterBooks, 1998, p. 217
68 Genesis 10:9-10
69 Cuozzo, Dr. Jack, *Buried Alive: the startling truth about Neanderthal Man,* 1998, pp. 246-248
70 Ibid., p. 262
71 Ibid., p. 244
72 Job 19:20 Job is the oldest book of the Bible
73 Cuozzo, Dr. Jack, *Buried Alive: the startling truth about Neanderthal Man,* MasterBooks, 1998, p. 222

nations, which force the insertion of any gaps in these genealogies. The uniformitarian premises in radiocarbon and other dating methods have been seriously questioned in recent years, and there is no firm evidence that the Flood needs to be dated significantly earlier than about 2350 B.C., which is the traditional Ussher date."[74]

Presupposition of Shortening of Longevity and Earlier Onset of Puberty

The days of our years are three score years and ten; and if by reason of strength they be fourscore years, yet is their strength labor and sorrow; for it is soon cut off, and we fly away. . . . So teach us to number our days, that we may apply our hearts to wisdom. (Psalm 90:10 and 12 written by king David c. 1030 BC)

For the last three thousand years, man's expected life-span has been 80 years though some rare individuals have survived until 120. In 1491 BC, Moses robustly led the children of Israel out of Egypt at 80 years old, and died at age 120 after climbing a mountain. In 1451 BC, Joshua robustly led the Hebrews into battle for several years beginning at age 85 conquering Canaan, and died at 110 years. The physical abilities of Moses and Joshua at 80 and 85 are significantly different to the weakness people experience today.

Prior to Noah's flood in 2348 BC, people lived for hundreds of years with Methuselah almost reaching 1,000 years at 969 (Genesis 5:27); the average age at death of Seth and his next four descendants was <u>916.8 years</u>. They matured and gave birth much later in life, starting at age 100 for Seth to have a son down to age 65 when Enoch begat Methuselah.[75] They were procreating at younger ages, but still living about 900 years. Between the birth of Seth's son Enos (3769 BC) and Enoch's son Methuselah (3317, 6th generation from Seth) is 452 years, so the average rate of decline in the age at which a man could procreate was 7.74% each generation.

After the flood, Shem at age 100 begat Arphaxad (2346 BC), and at age 35 Arphaxad begat Salah (2311 BC). Between Salah begetting Eber (2281 BC) and Nahor begetting Terah (2126 BC) the average age for a man to procreate had leveled out to 30 years. The three generations after Shem: Arphaxad (438), Salah (433) and Eber (464), lived an average of <u>445 years</u> (half of the pre-flood people); then the next three generations lived an average of <u>236 years</u> (almost half of the post-flood people). Terah, father of Abraham, lived 205 years. The next three generations: Abraham (175), Isaac (180), and Jacob (147) lived an average of <u>167.3 years</u>; a decline of 30% from the previous three. The three generations born in Egypt: Kohath (133), Amram (137), and Moses (120) averaged <u>130 years</u>; a decline of 22% from the previous three. After Noah's flood, earlier maturity stabilized, but the loss of longevity accelerated. Today twelve year olds have sex and give birth, and girls as young as five and six have given birth.[76]

---

74 Morris, Dr. Henry M., *The Genesis Record*, Baker Book House, 1976, p. 285; Ussher's date was 2348 BC
75 Genesis 5
76 Wikipedia's "List of Youngest Birth Mothers" and "Precocious Puberty"

Abraham bought a cave in Hebron to bury his wife Sarah, and later Isaac and Rebekah and Jacob and Leah were also buried there; so it should be no surprise to find several generations of ancient people buried in caves. The surprise was finding people between 400-500 years old buried above people between 100-200 years old; but it shouldn't have been because Eber outlived Abraham by 4 years. Scientists have defined these skeletons and skulls as "hominids" as they searched for their "missing link" of an ape-man to prove their theory of evolution; but their fossils always "prove" to be an ape, a human, or a fraud. No fossil of a transitional creature has ever been found,[77] as was noted by Charles Darwin.

> "The number of intermediate varieties, which have formerly existed on the earth, (must) be truly enormous. Why then is not every geological formation and every stratum full of such intermediate links? Geology assuredly does not reveal any such finely graduated organic chain; and this, perhaps, is the most obvious and gravest objection which can be urged against my theory."[78]

God Gave National/Tribal Boundaries at Peleg's Birth (2247 BC)

Remember the days of old, consider the years of many generations: ask your father, and he will show you; your elders, and they will tell you. When the Most High divided [nachal] to the nations their inheritance, when he separated [parad] the sons of Adam, he set the bounds [gebulah] of the people according to the number of the children of Israel. (Deuteronomy 32:7-8)

Peleg and *palag* both derive from a root which means a rill, a small channel of water used in irrigation. (Elohim gave each nation a drinking water source.)
Nachal means to bequeath as to divide an inheritance.
Parad is from a root to break through, and means to spread or scatter abroad, and is used in Genesis 10:5 "*By these were the isles of the Gentiles [goy] divided in their lands; every one after his tongue, after their families, in their nations [goy].*" *Goy* means Gentile and nation.
Gebulah means boundaries or borders to distinguish territories (*gebul*).

And to Eber were born two sons: the name of one was Peleg; for in his days was the earth [erets] divided [palag]. . . (Genesis 10:25a)

Erets is used for the planet Earth as well as its land.

And Canaan begat Sidon his first born, and Heth, And the Jebusite, and the Amorite, and the Girgasite, And the Hivite, and the Arkite, and the Sinite, And the Arvadite, and the Zemarite, and the Hamathite: <u>and afterward were the families of the Canaanites spread abroad [puts]</u>. And the border [gebul] of the Canaanites was

---

77 Various articles at www.icr.org (Institute for Creation Research) and Dr. Jack Cuozo's pictures of teeth and skulls at http://creation.com/neandertal-childrens-fossils.
78 Darwin, Charles, *On the Origin of Species*, 1859

from Sidon, as you come to Gerar, to Gaza; as you go, to Sodom, and Gomorrah, and Admah, and Zeboim, even to Lasha. (Genesis 10:15-19)

Puts is to dash into pieces, to disperse or to scatter abroad.

And they said, Go to, let us build us a city and a tower, whose top may reach to heaven; and let us make us a name, <u>lest we be scattered abroad [puts] on the face of the whole earth [erets]</u>. (Genesis 11:4)

Canaan was Ham's fourth born son, and it wasn't until after Canaan's eleventh son was born that Elohim divided the land to the clans and established boundaries for the nations. This was one hundred years after Noah's family descended from Mt. Ararat (2347 BC), when Peleg was born (2247 BC) and Elohim set boundaries for nations. Since Canaan was cursed, he and his eleven sons (a total of twelve according to Deut. 32) would inhabit the land which would become the promised land of Israel; and God would later use the twelve tribes of Israel to destroy the Canaanites. Some clans were given clear boundaries around lands they currently occupied, but YHWH told others to move to new areas, and gave them a period of time to do so. From Gen. 11:4, it seems Nimrod's clan was asked to move. But Nimrod had already spent about sixty years establishing his kingdom, and so his people built a tower in defiance of God's command to inhabit the boundaries which Elohim set.

"Around 2300 BC, a major disaster in the Near East wiped out hundreds of Early Bronze Age sites in Mesopotamia, the Levant, Israel and Egypt. Of the 350 Early Bronze Age sites in ancient Greece, more than 300 were destroyed, many others <u>abandoned</u>. While most archaeologists and paleoclimatologists generally agreed that a major disaster occurred at that time, there is no consensus as to what may have triggered it in the first place." - Benny J Peiser

Gophna wrote regarding Canaan, ". . . it is suggested that the EBI period ended with a major socio-spatial crisis . . . Many settlements were <u>abandoned</u>, implying that their inhabitants became immigrants and nomads."[79] My EBII (2200-2100 BC) is when the many cities were abandoned as Earth's precipitation patterns shifted to primarily snow at the poles. Most clans just moved to where God told them. Elohim's set period of time to move must have been long enough for Nimrod to think he could outsmart YHWH, possibly 40-50 years. That way some clans could build an entire fleet to transport themselves and their goods over the oceans. Nimrod used the time to build a water-proof tower to withstand another flood, (even though Yahweh promised He would never flood the Earth again) which would later be called the Tower of Babel.[80] Yahweh may have patiently warned Nimrod and his people for another couple of decades before He decided to end their disobedience, and forestall the rebellion of other nations, by confusing the languages of the world.

---

79 Gophna, Ram, "Early Bronze Age Canaan," The Archaeology of Society in the Holy Land, Facts on File, 1995, p. 273
80 Genesis 11:1-9 For water-proofing Noah used pitch, and Nimrod used bitumen ("*slime*").

(c. 2174 BC) Tower of Babel and Glacial Maximum of the Ice Age

Elohim gave each of the seventy nations[81] a different language, and scattered Nimrod's people to those other countries. The 70 nations were comprised of 30 from Ham, 26 from Shem, and 14 from Japheth. The seventy nations include the thirteen sons of Peleg's brother, Joktan.[82] If Joktan was born in 2246 BC, and had his first son at age thirty (2216 BC), and we allow 42 years in which his thirteen sons and unknown daughters to be born; this would place the confusion of languages regarding the Tower of Babel at 2174 BC.

The cooling of the earth brought about by Noah's flood combined with a warm ocean "would result in a snowblitz, or a rapid ice-age".[83] The year 2174 BC would be the peak of glacial maximum of the ice age when the sea level would be at its lowest,[84] thus exposing land bridges. God supernaturally transported Nimrod's people, and some would have sailed by ships, but I think the majority walked to their new domains as directed by YHWH. The major ice sheets would have melted within 250 years by 1924 BC,[85] thus raising sea levels and isolating some people and animals on islands, and also submerging some coastal cities, which may be a reason Terah and Abram left Ur which was once a coastal city.

Job Lived During the Ice Age and the Tower of Babel

*God thunders marvelously [pala - extraordinary, <u>separate</u> by distinguishing action] with his voice; great things does he, which we cannot comprehend. For he said to the **snow**, Be you on the earth; likewise to the small **rain**, and to the great rain of his strength. <u>He seals up the hand [yad - side (of land), part, portion] of every man</u>; that all men may know his work. Then the beasts [chay - living] go into dens, and remain in their places. Out of the south comes the whirlwind [suphah - hurricane]: and **cold** out of the north [mezareh – <u>scatterer</u>, from zarah which is to scatter, spread, or disperse]. By the breath of God **frost** is given: and the breadth of the waters is straitened [mutsaq]. Also by watering he wearies the thick cloud: he scatters his bright cloud: <u>And it</u> [Tower of Babel?] <u>is turned round about by his counsels: that they may do whatever he commands them on the face of the world in the earth.</u> He causes it to come, whether for correction [shebet - from an unused root probably meaning to branch off; a stick (for punishing, writing, fighting, ruling, walking, etc.) or (figuratively) a clan: usually translated tribe.], or for his land, or for mercy. Listen to this, O Job: stand still, and consider the wondrous [pala] works of God. Do you know when God <u>disposed</u> them, and caused the light of his cloud to shine? (Job 37:5-15, spoken by Elihu)*

---

81 Genesis 10:1-32
82 Cooper, Bill, *After the Flood*, 1995, p. 174. Joktan's sons settled in Arabia.
83 Oard, p. 188
84 Oard, Michael J., *An Ice Age Caused by the Genesis Flood*, Institute for Creation Research, 1990, p. 173 and 190. The range for maximum glaciation after the flood is between 174 to 1,765 years, and I chose the earliest possible. 2348 – 174 = 2174 BC
85 Oard, p. 116 Oard placed ice sheets melting between 250 and 287 years, and I chose the earlier.

> *Yes, surely God will not do wickedly, neither will the Almighty pervert judgment. Who has given him a charge over the earth? or who has <u>disposed</u> the whole world? (Job 34:12-13, spoken by Elihu)*

'Disposed' is *sum (soom)* meaning to set, ordain, establish, appoint, determine, station, put, or to set in place. Elihu seems to link the glacial maximum to God's command from a cloud of glory to men to disperse, and that He justly destroyed the Tower of Babel and scattered the disobedient people to remind Job that Elohim is in control of the nations and the weather.

Job lived during the ice age in the land of Uz. Uz was Shem's grandson[86] who located his city in northern Arabia, possibly near Jabal Unazah in northern Saudi Arabia.[87] The book of Job described ice and snow (6:16), snow water (9:30), cold (24:7), and hoary frost (38:29). Job also may have described glaciers as water with "*straightness*" (36:16) which God had "*straightened*" (37:10) [*mutsaq*, which means narrow, from *yatsaq* which means to flow; so a narrow flow]. There are verses in Job which can be translated with that meaning.

> *For God speaks once, yes twice, yet man perceives it not. . . . If there be a messenger with him, an <u>interpreter</u>, one among a thousand, to show to man his uprightness (Job 33:14 and 23 spoken by Elihu)*

If an interpreter is needed, then God has already confused the languages at the Tower of Babel; so the reference to God speaking "*once*" could be that command to each nation to accept His boundaries for them, and "*twice*" to confound human languages to impede human ingenuity in their rebellion.

> *Behold, he breaks down, and it cannot be built again: he shuts up a man, and there can be no opening. . . . He leads princes away spoiled, and overthrows the mighty. <u>He removes away the speech of the trusty, and takes away the understanding of the aged.</u> He pours contempt on princes, and weakens the strength of the mighty. . . . He increases the nations, and destroys them: he enlarges the nations, and **straitens** them again. He takes away the heart of <u>the chief of the people of the earth</u>, and causes them to wander in a wilderness where there is no way. (Job 12:14-24 spoken by Job)*

'Straitens' is *nachah* meaning to put, guide, or transport. It is Elohim who increases the people of a nation, or destroys them; enlarges their boundaries or transports them to new boundaries. Possibly, "*the chief of the people of the earth*" was a reference to Nimrod.

It is interesting that out of roughly 7,000 languages, about 70 are unique;[88] and they include Sumerian[89] cuneiform and Egyptian hieroglyphs.

---

86 Genesis 10:22-23
87 Cooper, Bill, *After the Flood*, New Wine Press, England, 1995, p. 173
88 Unique languages without relationships to other languages.
    See http://en.wikipedia.org/wiki/Language_isolate
89 The Sumerians had a calendar that divided the year into twelve 30-day months, divided the day into twelve

Presupposition of Lush, Green, Forested Levant and North Africa

The deserts of the Middle East and the rest of the globe did not exist immediately after Noah's flood;[90] the lands were lush and green with varied flora and fauna. According to Micahel Oard, strong anticyclone and downglacier winds would dry the air near the ice sheets, with strong winds blowing dust below them.[91] From cores drilled in Egypt, Dr. Fekri Hassan found evidence of a generation of windblown dust beginning about 2200 BC. Also at 2200 BC at Tell Leilan in Mesopotamia, about 100 years of windblown dust ended that vibrant city.[92] During deglaciation, after initial drought, Egypt and the Middle East would have experienced much more precipitation than they do today.[93]

In southwest Egypt, near the border with Libya, lies the Cave of Swimmers, so called because of the rock art of people swimming. Other ancient rock art of the current Sahara Desert depicts giant buffalo, elephant, giraffe, rhinoceros, and hippopotamus which haven't lived in the area for at least 2,500 years. Scientists call it the Green Sahara period. Archaeology agrees with the Bible that the lands of the Levant and North Africa were once verdant, wooded habitats of abundant and varied flora and fauna.

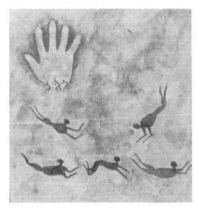

Cave of Swimmers

The Levant includes the eastern Mediterranean countries of Jordan, Israel, Lebanon, and Syria. Egyptologist James Breasted derived the term "fertile crescent" which depicted the shape of the nutrient rich lands from Egypt's Nile through Canaan to Mesopotamia, "the land between two rivers".

---

periods from dusk to dusk, and had a sexagesimal (base 60 = 12 X 5) numbering system.
90 Patten, Donald Wesley, *The Biblical Flood and the Ice Epoch*, Pacific Meridian Pub. Co., 1966, p. 199
91 Oard, pp. 111 and 114
92 "Why Ancient Egypt Fell," *Discovery Channel* program, a spike in dolomite was found at 2200 BC
93 Oard, p. 111

Historical Sciences are not Hard Sciences

"No result of <u>real</u> science ever contradicted Theology; nor do men of real science."[94]

Real science is observable and reproducible according to the scientific method. Though ancient humans have left us their accounts of their observations during their lifetimes, we do not have time machines to observe and to verify their claims for ourselves. Creation and evolution theories must remain scientific theories because people can not reproduce the universe and all the creatures upon earth. Historical 'scientists' arrive at the best scenarios which incorporate all the accounts and artifacts at hand. Breakthroughs of understanding often come from considering the accounts and artifacts from a different perspective.

Presupposition of Multiple Pharaohs during Life of Biblical Individual

A major breakthrough in this Egyptian chronology was in recognizing that Joseph and Moses both lived during the reigns of several pharaohs, not just one. During the 18th dynasty in which Joseph and Moses lived, the average reign was about 15 years; and Joseph and Moses lived 110 and 120 years respectively. The last third of Moses' life was during the 19th dynasty. Though Rameses II had a reign of 66 years, the average reign of the other pharaohs during the 19th dynasty was only seven years.

Presupposition of Incorrect Chronologies

Another breakthrough in this book was recognizing the early dynasties did not move their capitals or rule one after the other, but were reigning simultaneously from different locations in a very divided Egypt as represented by the relief engraved at Karnak in the festival hall of Thutmose III. Egypt was more like the United States of America during the cFIP and cSIP, with its national capital at Itjtawy overseeing several nomes, each with its own 'state' capital. This aspect will be examined in the next chapter.

Bishop Ussher carefully went through the Holy Bible's begats to arrive at 1491 BC for the exodus, which makes 1451 BC the year of Joshua's first campaign into Canaan. Archaeologists dismiss this year because their Canaanite chronologies are based upon incorrect Egyptian chronologies, and they have chosen 1200 BC for the exodus instead. Then when they didn't find evidence of Joshua's campaigns in 1200 BC strata, they blamed the Bible for being historically inaccurate, yet they used the Bible to locate the dig site they excavated in the first place. They look for evidence of kings Saul and David in the 10th century BC instead of the 11th. This book provides a unifying high chronology of Egypt while maintaining a high view of Holy Scripture, and the correlations are amazing.

---

94 Pusey, E. B., "Un-science, not Science, Adverse to Faith," sermon in 1878, p. 65

Chronology Overview

"These are the families of the sons of Noah, after their generations, in their nations: and by these were the nations divided in the earth after the flood."
(Genesis 10:32)

This is the book [sepher] of the generations [toledah] of Adam. In the day that God created man, in the likeness of God made he him; Male and female created he them; and blessed them, and called their name Adam, in the day when they were created. And Adam lived an hundred and thirty years, and begat a son in his own likeness, and after his image; and called his name Seth: And the days of Adam after he had begotten Seth were eight hundred years: and he begat sons and daughters: (Genesis 5:1-4)

Adam means red or ruddy, which may refer to the color of dirt Elohim used in creating them. Adam and Eve's first sons, Cain and Abel, would have married their sisters. This Scripture has the first mention of "*book*" in the Bible; akin to the word 'cypher'. Genesis contains the written records of origins and of generations called *toledah* (*toledoth*[95], singular) in Hebrew, with a form of Hebrew being the original language of mankind. These *toledah* were handwritten accounts of the years at births and deaths.

    The origins of creation written by pre-incarnate Jesus and given to Adam (Gen. 1:1-2:4)
    The generations and history of Adam and Eve written by Adam (Gen. 2:5-5:1)
    The generations and history before the flood written by Noah (Gen. 5:2-6:9)
    The history of the flood written by Shem (Gen. 6:10-10:1)
    The generations & history of nations and languages written by Shem (Gen. 10:2-11:10)
    The generations and sojourns of Terah written by Terah (Gen. 11:11-27)
    Abraham did not sign off "*these are the generations of*" on his history, so . . .
    The generations and history of Abraham and Isaac written by Isaac (Gen. 11:28-25:19)[96]
    The generations and wealth of Esau written by Esau/Edom (Gen. 36:1-8)
    The generations of Edomites written by an unnamed Edomite (Gen. 36:9-42)
    The generations and history of Jacob written by Jacob (Gen. 25:20-35:29; 37:1-2a)
    The generations and history of Jacob's children written by Joseph (Gen. 37:2b-50:25)

---

95 Morris, Dr. Henry M., *The Genesis Record*, Baker Book House, 1976, p. 27
96 This includes Ishmael's brief genealogy in Gen. 25:12-16, so Isaac outlived Ishmael.

Pharaohs of the Bible

The genealogies/*toledah* were kept safe by Joseph[97], and most likely discovered in Joseph's coffin during the exodus and then combined into one book, Genesis, by Moses.

Biblical chronology is superior to traditional Egyptian chronology

Moses (1571-1451 BC) was born 250 years after the death of the Hebrew patriarch, Abraham. Moses lived in Egypt and wrote extensively about his conversations and interactions with the pharaoh of the Hebrews' exodus from Egypt; thus providing a primary source. The history of the Hebrews continued to be written by contemporaries for the next thousand years. These books (scrolls) were accurately copied and widely disseminated. The Dead Sea Scrolls contained 2,000 year old copies of every book of the Bible, except Esther, and the high accuracy of these copies to today's copies in original languages is truly astonishing. For example, the book of Isaiah is 95% accurate: "The five percent of variation consisted primarily of obvious slips of the pen and spelling alterations."[98]

In 1650AD, Archbishop James Ussher of Ireland used all the "begats" from Adam to the regnal dates and release of Jehoiachin in the winter of 562 BC at Nebuchandnezzar's death (dated by Ptolemy) and published a time-line in *The Annals of the World*. Using available documents, Ussher aligned histories of other cultures, including Egypt, with the Bible.

Herodotus and Manetho

Herodotus wrote an Egyptian history in the 5th century BC, but most Egyptologists use the list of pharaohs created by the Egyptian priest Manetho, who wrote a 2,000 year linear history of Egypt around 240 BC, long after the facts. Manetho's dynasties were based on geographic location or a new genealogical shift. No copies remained by 75 AD when Josephus tried to piece it back together from other writings (some particularly anti-Jewish) which quoted Manetho. No copies of Josephus' epitome of Manetho remain, but only translations made 200 years later. Even if Josephus had managed to recreate Manetho's original work, only third-hand altered copies remain upon which the foundation of conventional Egyptian history rests. Manetho's dynasties were grouped by Egyptologists:

Conventional Chronology	Dynasties	**Dynasties in Clarity Chronology**
Old Kingdom	1-6	1-3, and 7
First Intermediate Period	7-10	4, 5, 8, 9, 10, ½ 12, ½ 13, and pre-15
Middle Kingdom	11-13	none; cFIP followed by cSIP
Second Intermediate Period	14-17	6, 9, 10, 11, ½ 12, ½ 13, 14, pre-15, 15, pre-16, 16, and 17
New Kingdom	18-21	18-21 and 21A (Theban high priests)
Third Intermediate Period	22-26	22 and 23, followed by 24-26 combined
Late Period	27-31	27-31

---

97 Joseph may have arranged to have the genealogies placed inside his coffin, which could be the reason Joseph made his brothers swear an oath to take his bones with them when God led them out of Egypt.

98 Archer, Gleason, *A Survey of Old Testament Introduction* Chicago: Moody 1974, p. 25

Chronology Overview

These designations were concocted based upon the concept that Egypt's dynasties followed each other in numerical order, and they provided terms for easier communication amongst Egyptologists. The conventional periods were not based upon archaeological evidence. In fact, evidence supports that a Middle Kingdom period never existed. In her surveys of Old Kingdom (OK) sites in the Nile delta, Dr. Sarah Parcak discovered lots of OK pottery sherds from 27 sites which suddenly dropped to 4 New Kingdom sites, and declared, "There are no Middle Kingdom potsherds at all."[99] Hence there's not really a FIP or SIP either, but dynasties 8-17 were concurrent with dynasties 4-6. I will use the terms cFIP and cSIP (**c**larity) to distinguish my concurrent dynasties during those periods.

Turin King List on Papyrus

In the 1800's, an Italian discovered a list of kings on the back of a tax roll along with several papyrus fragments, and it was placed in the Egypt Museum in Turin, and dubbed the Turin King List (TKL). Ryholt wrote, ". . . the Turin King-list proceeds chronologically throughout, except that contemporary dynasties are recorded one at a time in order not to mix kings of different dynasties . . ."[100] It has discrepancies and many additions to those kings found in Manetho's list, but it is "the only genuine king-list from ancient Egypt."[101] The TKL included years, months, and days of reigns for most pharaohs from the 1st through 17th dynasties, but only round years for kings of the 3rd - 6th, and the 11th dynasties; which intimates the list was a compilation of copies,[102] and a clue as to changes of royal residence.

Dynasties	Reign in TKL	Royal Residence
1-2	Years, months, days; king's age	Thinis
3-4	Years only	Memphis
7-10	Years, months, days	7-8 Thinis; 9-10 delta+
11	Years only	Thebes
12-16	Years, months, days	12 Itjtawy; 13-16 various

The king's age is given during the dynasties of a more united Egypt in Thinis. Dynasties 3, 4, and 6 ruled from Memphis, with dynasty 5 ruling in *Hwt-Nen-Nesu* ('house of royal child') as the offspring of dynasty 4.[103] Dynasties 7-8 ruled in Thinis while the Herakleopolitan dynasties 9-10 ruled in Asyut, Herakleopolis Magna, and the delta ports as the main traders. Dynasty 12 had a royal residence at Itjtawy/Lisht. Dynasty 13's TKL heading reads "Kings who came after the King of [Upper and] Lower Egypt [Sehet]epibre . .

---

99 "Why Ancient Egypt Fell," *Discovery Channel* program
100 Ryholt, K.S.B., *The Political Situation in Egypt during the Second Intermediate Period*, CNI Publications 20, Museum Tusculanum Press, 1997, p. 164
101 Ryholt, K.S.B., *The Political Situation in Egypt during the Second Intermediate Period*, p. 9
102 Ibid, p. 18-19, and 31-32. Roughly five base copies called 'vorlages' in German: the text before a translator or copyist reconstructs it by working backwards from the original.
103 "A *hwt* is a planned royal foundation as opposed to a general settlement." [Atzler 1972, pp. 17-44]

."[104]   Thus it is very clear that the dynasty 13 kings came right after (Sehetepibre) Amenemhat I, with most being his sons, and that they were concurrent with dynasty 12. Dynasty 13 initially ruled from Thebes, but retreated to outlying nomes when dynasty 11 took over Thebes with dynasty 16 ruling Edfu and El-Kab. Dynasty 14 ruled from the delta followed by dynasty 15. The Turin King List also includes dynasties which are usually dismissed by chronologists: the pre-15th dynasty of twelve kings (X/1-12), the pre-16th dynasty of nine kings (X/22-30), the Thinis dynasty of six kings (XI/10-15) placed by the 13th dynasty, and the 16+ kings of the Abydos dynasty (XI/16-31) placed there by kings of the 14th dynasty. (I use Gardiner's Roman numeral columns instead of Ryholt's.)

Lepsius' Karnak King List drawing enhanced by Peter Lundstrom

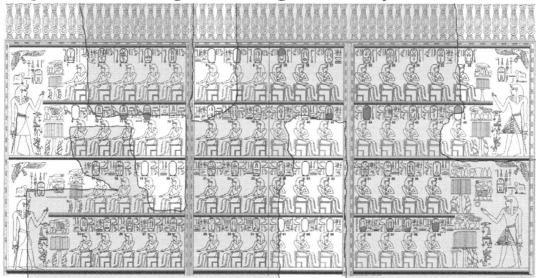

Karnak, Abydos, and Saqqara King Lists in Stone

Three king lists were chiselled in stone at Karnak, Abydos, and Saqqara during the reigns of Thutmose III, Seti I, and Ramesses II respectively. Since Seti I and Rameses II were father and son, those very different lists were not created to prove ancestry; and the hodge-podge of the Karnak king list certainly wasn't. They were created with obvious clues to help future generations understand the complexity of overlapping dynasties especially during the tumultuous 12th dynasty which spans my cFIP and cSIP.

The Karnak king list is located in the jubilee festival hall of Thutmose III and lists 61 kings in two sets of two horizontal rows split down the middle facing opposite directions which screams a divided Egypt occurred after the more united 1st - 3rd dynasties had ended. Thutmose III lived only 100 years after the end my cSIP, and he had the names of the concurrent pharaohs of this history carefully inscribed. Not all the names survived, but it seems each row is to be read left to right. The Karnak king list supports my cFIP and cSIP.

---

104 Kinnaer, Jacques, "Turin Kinglist" translation at http://www.ancient-egypt.org/index.html

Chronology Overview

Karnak King List: Left Side with Clarity dates BC

Neferkare 7th Thinis 2000 BC	Sneferu 4th Memphis 1977-1953	Sahure 5th NenNesu 1965-1953	Niuserre Ini 5th NenNesu 1935-1922	Djedkare Isesi 5th 1914-1886	—	—	Djehuti 16th Edfu 1820-1817
—	Intef I? 11th Thebes 1878-1866	In...	Mon...	Intef III? 11th Thebes 1817-1815	Teti 6th Memphis 1856-1815	Pepi I? 6th Memphis 1842-1817	Nemtyemsaf I 6th Memphis 1817-1804
—	Amenemhat I 12th Itjtawy 1954-1924	Amenemhat II 12th Itjtawy 1890-1852	—	—	AmenemhatIV 12th Itjtawy 1770-1761	SobekNeferu 12th Itjtawy 1914-1910	Intef IV? 11th Thebes 1799-1798
Senusret I 12th Itjtawy 1934-1889	Tao II 17th Thebes 1746-1742	Ahmose/Tao I 17th Thebes 1747-1746	Bebiankh 16th Ombos 1771-1759	Intef VI 17th Thebes 1761-1756	Montuhotep II 11th Thebes 1815-1764	MontuhotepIII 11th Thebes 1764-1761	—

The left top row indicates that the end of the 7th dynasty was concurrent with the 4th and 5th dynasties which came to an end about the same time Djehuty left the delta to begin the 16th dynasty. The second row indicates the 11th dynasty was concurrent with the 6th dynasty. The third row indicates the 12th dynasty ended about the time of Intef IV or Intef V (1754-1752). Maybe Senusret I should have been placed in the third row, and then the rest of the fourth row were leaders at the end of my cSIP.

Karnak King List Right Side with Clarity dates BC

Senusret III 12th Itjtawy 1847-1808	SobekHotepIV 13th Thebes 1845-1835	Neferhotep I 13th Thebes 1850-1839	SobekHotepIII 13th El Kab 1865-1861	SobekHotep II 13th Thebes 1925-1921	Amenemhat V 13th nome 1 1938-1935	Nebiriau I 16th Edfu 1799-1733	...kaure
Sobekhotep I 12th El Kab 1933-1931	Sobekhotep 6 13th 1824-1822	Senefer...re 14th TKL, IX/7	....re	Sobekhotep 8 16th 1817-1801	Sobekhotep 7 13th 1820-1818	NeferhotepII 13th 1823-1821	—
Rahotep 17th Thebes 1761-1757	—	—	Wegaf 13th ? 1940-1938	Sobekhotep V 13th ? 1825-1820	Senebmiu 13th ? ?	Khety II 10th Asyut 1870-1861	
....re	Senefer..re 14th TKL, IX/7	Sewadj..re 13th, 14th or 16th	Sekhem..re 14th, 16th or 17th	—	—	—	

Brothers Neferhotep I and Sobekhotep IV in the top right row were concurrent with Senusret III and Sobekhotep III. In the second row, Sobekhotep I is the earliest of the other Sobekhoteps. A group of six reigned in the 1800's: Sobekhotep V, VII, and VIII, Senebmiu, Khety II, and Neferhotep II. The rest seem to be a catch-all for other dynasties.

The Abydos king list is located in the temple of Seti I and consists of three rows with 38 cartouches on each row, but the third row merely repeats Seti I's name. Listed between a 3rd dynasty and a 7th dynasty pharaoh, is 'Sedjes' ('erased' TKL III/2). The Abydos list only records Mentuhotep II and III of the 11th dynasty, and omits the 13th - 17th dynasties; and omits Hatshepsut, Akhenaten, Smenkhkare, Tutankhamen, and Ay of the 18th.

The Saqqara king list is located in the tomb of Tjuneroy who was a priest and official during the reign of Rameses II. It contains 58 kings in two horizontal rows written from left to right, and begins in the bottom row with Anedjib, the sixth pharaoh of the 1st dynasty. Other dynasties begin with the first pharaoh and end with the last pharaoh except for the 12th dynasty pharaohs which are listed in reverse order. This supports my cFIP and cSIP in which the 12th dynasty rules the minor 8th - 17th dynasties (along with the 4th - 6th dynasties) in an upside-down Egypt. The Saqqara king list does not include the 7th - 10th dynasties or the 13th - 17th dynasties, and it only records Mentuhotep II and III of the 11th dynasty.

The existence and regnal lengths of pharaohs not included in these king lists are based upon archaeological finds. Manetho's list and the Turin King List coupled with the kings lists chiseled at Abydos and Saqqara have been the basis for conventional chronology of Egypt's kings. Yet this Egyptian chronology became the standard chronology, with indifference to Karnak's list; and the chronologies of all other cultures were aligned to it.

Aligning Egypt's kings to Ussher's Bible chronology

When Ussher aligned Egypt's chronology with the Bible, hieroglyphs had not yet been successfully deciphered. Napoleon's discovery of the Rosetta Stone in 1799 led to Jean-Francois Champollion's linguistic breakthrough in the 1820's; and eight years later when he saw the Canaanite conquest in Karnak of Hedjkheperre Sheshonk I, he declared him to be the Biblical Shishak. (The first named king/pharaoh of Egypt in the Bible is Shishak; all others prior are simply called king or pharaoh.) Much more information on Egypt's kings has been unearthed since then. Biblical details and descriptions of each pharaoh can be linked to details and descriptions on monuments, papyrus, and other works.

Ussher's Bible Chronology

<u>Total Years</u>
1656 years   from creation of Adam and Eve to Noah's flood (Genesis 5)
2083 years   from Arphaxad's birth (Shem 100) to Abram entering Canaan at 75 (Gen. 11)
2513 years   from promise given to Abram (at 75) to Exodus is 430 years (Gal. 3:17)
2992 years   479 from Exodus to beginning of Temple in Solomon's 4th year (1 Kings 6:1)
                (480th year occurs after the completion of 479 years; Septuagint had 440th)
3029 years   from start of Temple to division of kingdom (1 Kings 11:42) 40-4+1 = 37
3417 years   388 years from kingdom division to destruction of Jerusalem (Ezek. 4:4-6)
                (~390=388 whole years plus two partial years during the divided kingdom)
4004 years   Destruction of Jerusalem in 588 BC: 588 - 1 + 3417 = 4004
                [subtract 1 because there's no year zero; I prefer 390 years ending in 586 BC]

Chronology Overview

Backtracking from Nebuchadnezzar II's death in (Jan.-Feb.) 562 BC, Ussher arrived at the creation of Adam and Eve in 4004 BC and Noah's flood at 2348 BC. People lived for hundreds of years prior to the flood. After the flood, lifespans gradually shortened. It is through Noah's son, Shem, that the Hebrew patriarchs were born; listing Ussher's birth years <u>b</u>efore <u>C</u>hrist (B.C., also BC in this book). Semites came from Shem. The Levant is composed of Syria, Lebanon, Israel and Jordan; and the Arabic language spoken in the Levant is called *Shami*. The 'fertile crescent' also includes Mesopotamia and lower Egypt.

	Semite lineage		**Then judges ruled Israel.**
2448	Shem	1409	Othniel
2346	Arphaxad	1369	Ehud (overlap with Shamgar)
2311	Salah	1366	Shamgar (until 1340?)
2281	Eber	1339	Deborah
2247	Peleg	1291	Gideon
2217	Reu	1251	Tola
2185	Serug	1228	Jair
2155	Nahor	1206	Jepthah
2126	Terah	1200	Ibzan
1996	Abram	1193	Elon
1896	Isaac	1183	Abdon
1836	Jacob	1175	Samson
1765	Levi and 1745 Joseph	1155	Eli
1735	Kohath	1115	Samuel (anointed first king)
1646	Amram	-----	**Then kings ruled Israel.**
1571	Moses	1095	Saul
1491	**Exodus** from Egypt	1055	David
1451	Hebrews enter Canaan	1015	Solomon
-----	Joshua died in 1426	1011	**Temple** construction began
		975	Divided kingdom

From the oldest state archives of 15,000 clay tablets at the great Syrian city Ebla (Tell Mardikh), an ancient ruler named Ebrum, likely Eber, ruled over Syria and Canaan. The tablets name Hazor, Akko, Megiddo, Gaza, Lachish, Urusalima, and the Sinai. From Eber came the name Hebrew, likely because his clan spoke the Hebrew language after the tower of Babel. Not all Semites are Hebrew, descended from Eber.

(K)Ham's Lineage

"Israel also came into Egypt; And Jacob sojourned in the land of Ham." (Psalm 105:23)

Pharaohs of the Bible

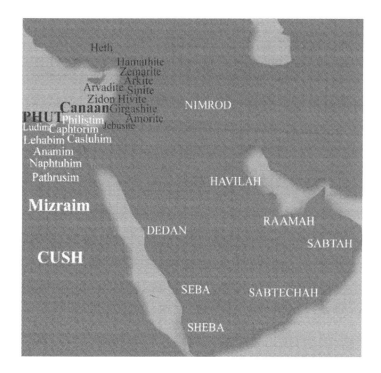

Egypt, Nubia, Cush

On old maps, the land of Africa is labeled 'Kham' (Hebrew pronunciation of Noah's son, Ham); its people 'khemet'. The Bible is not as detailed regarding Ham's lineage: *"And the sons of Ham; Cush, and Mizraim, and Phut, and Canaan."*[105] Ham's grandsons are listed except for those of Phut. The children of Cush spread over the Arabian Peninsula and Mesopotamia, though Cush himself lived between the third and sixth cataracts of the Nile. Mizraim's sons lived north of the first cataract, but Ludim and Lehabim (Libya) joined uncle Phut and lived west of Egypt. Canaan's son Jebus lived around Salem; and Canaan's son Heth became the Hittites of Anatolia,[106] though some settled near Hebron (Gen. 23:1-3).

Cush established his kingdom between the third and sixth cataracts with its capital of Kerma near the third cataract; his empire is also called Kerma and Kush/Cush. The land of Nubia was between the first and third cataracts. Mizraim's kingdom, Egypt, was north of the first cataract to the Mediterranean Sea. Eventually a kingdom of Meroe claimed land between the fifth and sixth cataracts to Khartoum, Sudan.

Noah planted a vineyard and became drunk one night, and Ham went into his father's tent and looked upon his nakedness. Ham was Noah's youngest son, and Noah pronounced a curse upon Ham's youngest son, Canaan.[107] So it is likely Ham's four sons were born soon after they left the ark in 2347 BC.

---

105 Genesis 10:6
106 Cooper, Bill, *After the Flood*, New Wine Press, 1995, p.195 and maps and amazing research
107 Genesis 9:18-29; 10:21 The birth order is Japheth, Shem, and Ham.

Mizraim, the Scorpion King

Banque Misr (Bank of Egypt) was founded in 1920. The Turks still call Egypt, Mitzir. Mizraim ('im' makes the noun plural in Hebrew) is also a word describing the people of Mizra (Egypt) who largely settled along the Nile; but the Philistim moved toward the land of their uncle Canaan, and established the cities of Gaza, Ekron, Ashkelon, and Ashdod.[108] The eastern border of Egypt often extended across the Sinai into the land of Canaan.

Several Egyptian king lists begin with nine gods of Egypt: Ptah, Ra, Shu, Kronos, Oriris, Set, Horus, Thoth, and Maat. These are followed by thirty kings who ruled for roughly 1700 years prior to Noah's flood. (Manetho's chronology implied 40 kings spanning 2,140 years ruled before the flood.) Then a group of names is listed which I think all refer to Mizraim: Scorpion I, Iry-Hor, Ka, King Scorpion, and Narmer. These may refer to differences throughout his reign, or to different aspects of his name. Menes was his nebty name and Narmer was his horus name.

Gunter Dryer excavated tomb U-J at Umm el-Qaab near Abydos and found an ivory crook and 70 jars with scorpion symbols, and dubbed it the tomb of the Scorpion King. There were also 180 ivory tags with early hieroglyphs of city names, which he surmised was in order to record taxes received.[109]

A block depicting the Scorpion King was found at el-Lahun near tomb of Senusret II.[110] Mizraim's daughter had bracelets of gold, amethyst, turquoise, and gold strung on a gold wire with a large gold 'Babylonian' rosette in the center.[111]

". . . the beginning of Egyptian history is now generally dated to about 3000 B.C.E."[112] I start Egypt's history after Noah's flood (in 2348 BC) in 2330 BC when Ham's son Mizraim was about 16 years old and likely guided by his father. It is considered a 'high' chronology.

> "Ambiguity means one can make plausible calculations in favour of any of the high, middle, or low Egyptian chronologies. Again, it is reassuring that the available evidence does roughly mesh together, but an attempt to offer a firm sequence relies on making unproven assumptions, or taking the low New Kingdom chronology as a given. It is also worth remembering that the all important Sothic and lunar data from the Middle Kingdom are unsatisfactory, and that the entire Sesostris III year date hangs on an assumption (since the pharaoh is not actually named in the key texts)."[113]

---

108 Joshua 13:3
109 *Egypt Unwrapped: Scorpion King* episode on the History Channel
110 AFP (French Press Agency), "Prehistoric fishing gear, sewing equipment found in Egypt," *The Daily Star*
111 Sayce, A.H. Prof., *The Homiletic Review*, Volume 43, June 1902, pp. 484-5
112 Depuydt, Leo, *Civil calendar and lunar calendar in ancient Egypt*, Peeters Publishers & Department of Oriental Studies, Belgium, 1997, p. 69
113 Manning, Sturt, *A Test of Time: The Volcano of Thera and the chronology and history of the Aegean and east Mediterranean in the mid second millennium B.C.*, Oxbow Books, 1999, p. 411

Pharaohs of the Bible

Archaeologists and Egyptologists have provided enormous amounts of well-researched materials slanted by their own biases and commonly accepted unprovable assumptions like Sothic dating. Many have largely based their chronologies on assumptions which have denied the genealogies and historical accuracy of the Holy Bible and the overwhelming evidence of Noah's world-wide catastrophic flood.

Clarity's Biblically aligned Egyptian chronology

Clarity's Old Kingdom

1st Dynasty   166 years from Thinis

2330-2298	Mizraim/Menes (Narmer)
2298-2296	Hor-Aha
2296-2284	Djer
2284-2261	Djet
2261-2229	Den
2229-2219	Anedjib
2219-2210	Semenkhet
2210-2184	Qa'a

2nd Dynasty   122 years

	Thinis	Memphis
2184-2146	Hotepsekhemy	
2146-2137	Raneb (Kakaw)	Weneg (Wadjnes) ruled 8y?
2137-2097	Nyetjer	Senedj ruled 20y?
2097-2089	Sekhimib-Peremaat	Seth-Peribsen (Aaka) ruled 17y?
2089-2062	Khasekhemwy	Neferkasokar (TKL, reigned 8y)
		'Erased' (TKL, reigned 1y, 8m, 4d)

3rd Dynasty	85 years mostly in Memphis	Thinis 7th Dynasty
2062-2043	Sanakhte/Nebka [Thinis]	
2043-2014	Djoser-It (Netjerykhet) [Memphis]	Netjerikare/Netiqerty 30y?
2014-2007	Sekhemkhet (Djoser-Ti)	Menkare (Neferka/Neferkare I) 25y?
2007-2001	Khaba (TKL, 6y)	Neferkare II (Nefer) (TKL, reigned 2y)
2001-1977	Huni	Neferkare III (Neby) (TKL, 4y)
		Djedkare Shemai (TKL, 2y)
		Neferkare Khendu IV (TKL, 1y)

Clarity's First Intermediate Period (cFIP)

4th, 5th, 8th, Thinis and Abydos, 9th and 10th, early 12th, Theban 13th, Kushite 14th, and Hyksos pre-15th dynasties of Great Pyramid Builders of my cFIP

The 9th and 10th dynasties constitute the Herakleopolitan dynasty of Herakleopolis Magna east of the Fayyum on the Nile, and two Mediterranean ports: Herakleopolis Parva on the Pelusiac eastern branch, and another port on the westernmost branch of the Nile delta which was originally called Herakleotic, but is now named Canopic. Asiatics were employed by Egyptians "from the Old Kingdom on for their seagoing navy."[114]

The primary source of cedar wood was Lebanon, and their main port was Byblos. Pharaoh Sneferu of the 4th dynasty was the first to record "bringing of 40 ships filled with cedar wood."[115] To assure his own supply, Amenemhat I brought Nubian mercenaries (14th dyn.) and Canaanite seamen to Avaris. According to Bietak, "Soldiers of Asian and Nubian origin were also in service during the First Intermediate Period assisting in the unification attempts by various nomarchs and by the kings of the 10th and 11th Dynasties."[116] I suggest Queen Khentkaus I asked her trading partners in Byblos to send representatives (pre-15th dyn.) to Memphis to oversee shipments which came through Herakleopolis Parva, and the pre-15th continued to rule under the 6th dynasty pharaohs in Memphis. Byblos was thoroughly Egyptianized during the 12th dynasty and had trade with the 13th dynasty also.[117]

With the exception of Salitis (15th) conquering the Nile delta and Djehuty (14th) fleeing south to realms of the 16th dynasty, there is no concrete evidence of transition of power from one dynasty to the next from the end of the 4th dynasty to the 17th dynasty; thus these dynasties become my cFIP and cSIP with the 12th dynasty as the 'Residence' of the high pharaoh at Itjtawy/Lisht.

> Manetho's concurrent dynasties by Eusebius are noted in the Armenian translation:
> "If the number of years is still in excess, it must be supposed that perhaps several Egyptian dynasties ruled at one and the same time; for they say that the rulers were kings of This, of Memphis, of Ethiopia, and of other places at the same time. It seems, moreover, that <u>different kings held sway in different regions, and that each dynasty was confined to its own nome; thus it was not a succession of kings occupying the throne one after the other, but several kings reigning at the same time in different regions.</u>"[118]

---

114 Bietak, Manfred, *Avaris, The Capital of the Hyksos: Recent Excavations at Tell el Dabᶜa,* London, p. 20
115 Breasted, James, *Ancient Records of Egypt, volume 1*, 1907, translation of Palermo Stone line 146, p. 66
116 Bietak, Manfred, *Avaris, The Capital of the Hyksos: Recent Excavations at Tell el Dabᶜa,* British Museum Press, London, 1996, p. 14
117 Ryholt, K.S.B., *The Political Situation in Egypt during the Second Intermediate Period*, 1997, p. 86
118 Williamson, G.A., translator, Eusebius: *The History of the Church*, England: Penguin Books, 1984, p. 9

Pharaohs of the Bible

Clarity's First Intermediate Period (cFIP)

First Intermediate Period   [▲= pyramid built]   [/▲\= unfinished pyramid]

14th Dynasty in Nile Delta	4th Dynasty in Memphis	5th Dynasty in Nen-Nesu	12th Dynasty in Itjtawy	13th Dynasty in Thebes	8th Dynasty in Thinis
[1956-1886 Khety of 9th]	1977-1953 Sneferu ▲	1972-1965 Userkaf ▲	[1956-1886 Khety of 9th]	1951-1949 Wegaf '49-'44 Sonbef	5y Merenhor 5y Neferkamin I
1954-1933 'Ammu	1953-1930 Khufu ▲	1965-1953 Sahure ▲	1954-1924 Amenemhat I ▲	1944-1938 Nerikare; -Seth I	1974-1950 Qakare Ibi ▲
1934-1894 Yakbimu	1930-1919 Djedefre ▲	1953-1943 ▲ Neferirkare Kaki	1934-1889 Senusret I ▲	3y Amenemhat V 4y Sobekhotep I	1950-1945 Khuiqer
	1919-1895 Khafre ▲	& queen ▲ Khentkaus II	>1914-1910 NeferuSobek	1931-1925 ▲ Ameny-Qemaw	1 lost, Pantjeny, Wepwawemsaf,
1894-1884 Ya'ammu	1895-1893 Baka /▲\	1943-1936 ▲ Shepsekare Isi	[20y Nikare of 9th] {10th in Asyut} Meryhathor (10th)	-Siharnedjheritef -Amenemhat VI 4ySobekhotep II	Snaib {5 prior placed by 13th}
1884-1874 Qareh	1893-1865 Menkaure ▲	1936-1935 Neferefre /▲\	1890-1852 Amenemhat II ▲	1921-1915 Khendjer ▲	Abydos Dynasty placed by 14th
1874-1821 Sheshi	1865-1861▲ Shepseskaf	1935-1922 Niuserre Ini ▲	1886-1883 (10th) Neferkare V	1915-1891 Aya ▲ ?	(Woser...re) (Woser...re)
1860-1856 I... (p15)->	1861-1859▲ Khentkaus I	1922-1914 ▲ Menkauhor	1883-1873 (10th) Meribre Khety I	1891-1889 Merhotepre Ini	8 lost
	1856-1854 Seth II (p15)	1914-1886 ▲ Djedkere Isesi	1873-1870 (10th) Senenh...	[1889-1878 11th Montuhotep I]	(...hebre) 3 names lost
	1854-1850 Sunu.. (p15)	1886-1856 ▲ Wenis/Unas	1870-1861 (10th) Wahkare Khety II	-Hor I, Khabaw, -Djedkheperew	(...heb?re) (...webenre)

Pre-15th Dynasty

TKL	Name		
X/1	I...	X/7	Nib... (Nob...)
X/2	Seth... II	X/8	Mer?en?
X/3	Sunu...	X/9	(Penensetensepet)
X/4	Hor...	X/10	Shepesu (Kheretheb)
X/5-6	lost	X/11	(Khut... hemet)
		X/12	lost

Chronology Overview

Clarity FIP and SIP Maps

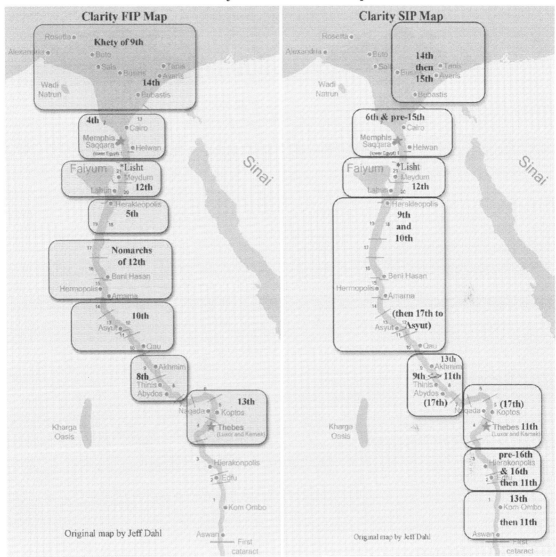

1978 – 1861 BC   1861 – 1720 BC

During my cFIP and cSIP, the 12th dynasty capital of Itjtawy/Lisht was recognized as the king's residence in which the most powerful pharaoh dwelt.

> "Horus, avenger of his father, gave me a commission to the **Residence**, . . . the good office of **Itjtawy in the presence of the king himself**."[119] - Horemkhauef of the 13th dynasty on a stela at his Hieraconpolis' tomb

---

119 Shaw, Ian, *The Oxford history of ancient Egypt*, p. 186

Clarity's Second Intermediate Period (cSIP)

6th, 9th, 10th, 11th, rest of 12th, 13th, 14th, pre-16th, 16th and 17th dynasties with Hyksos pre-15th and 15th in my cSIP.

The Kushite 14th dynasty was loyal to the pharaohs of Egypt and protected their shipments in the delta, beginning with chieftains 'Ammu, Yakbimu, Ya 'ammu, and Qareh. Sheshi and his son Nehesy brought trade to its height at the end of the cFIP and recovered from the Ethiopic War at the beginning of cSIP, and were followed by Nehesy's son, Djehuty. These seven leaders made up the 14th dynasty with the other 50+ 'kings' representing them throughout Egypt and the Levant protecting trade. The 40+ other 'kings' of the 13th dynasty provided administration of trade and towns in Egypt. Djehuty, fled and began the 16th dynasty when Salitis, first pharaoh of the 15th dynasty, conquered Avaris. The 16th dynasty were 'kings' south of Thebes governing cities of El-Kab and Edfu. Those who had ruled south of Thebes prior to Djehuty were the pre-16th dynasty comprised of three lost kings, Zeket..., Ar..., and ...nia... . Montuhotep I (1889-1878 BC) began the 11th dynasty in Thebes, and Montuhotep II (1815-1764 BC) reunited middle and southern Egypt.

The left two columns are in Lower Egypt (LE) in the Nile Delta. The middle two columns are in Middle Egypt (ME). The right two columns are in Upper Egypt (UE) which is basically Thebes and south to Nubia. So from left to right is going from north to south.

[14th] & 15th Dynasty (Hyksos) in Delta	6th Dynasty in Memphis (pre-15)	12th Dynasty in Itjtawy/Lisht	9th & 10th Dynasties in Herakleopolis Magna	11th Dynasty in Thebes 13th Dynasty various cities	16th Dynasty in El-Kab & Edfu
[1874-1821 Sheshi]	1856-1844 Teti ▲		1861-1856 Merikare▲	1878-1856 Intef I (11th)	[Ankhtifi of Mo'alla]
[Sheshi to Nehesy; Nehesy to Djehuty]	Hor... 3 lost	1858-1839 Senusret II ▲	1861-56 Khuy▲ 1856-1845 Neferkare VII ▲	1866-1817 Intef II (11th)▲	1850-1840 Zeket... 1840-1830 Ar...
[1821-1820 Nehesy] [Djehuty fled south]	1844-1842 Userkare, usurper	1847-1808 Senusret III ▲	1845-1825 Shed...+ H... 1845-1830 Neferkahor	11y Neferhotep I, Sihathor 9y Sobekhotep IV, 5y Hori	1830-1820 ...nia... 1820-1817 Djehuty
	1842-1817 Pepi I ▲	1827-1779 ▲ Amenemhat III	1830-1825 (Neferkare) Pepiseneb VIII (9th)	Montuhotep V, Dedumose 10y Sobekhoteps III, V-VII	1817-'01 Sobekhotep VIII 1801-1800 Neferhotep III
1820-1815 Salitis15th 1815-1810 Beon	Nib... Mer?en		1825-1815 (Wankhare) (10th) Khety III	Nebnun, Renseneb, Neferhotep II, Nedjemibre	1800-1799 Montuhotepi 1799-1773 Nebiriau I
1810-1805 Sakir-Har	Penensetensepet		1825-'15 Neferkamin II	Seb,Kay, 3y Amenemhat VII	-Sobeknakht II El-Kab
1805-1765 Khyan	Shepesu (Kheretheb) (Khut... hemet) lost		1815-1801 (Nebkaura) (10th) Khety IV	2y Imyremashaw, 3y Ined, 11y Wahibre Ibiau; Ibi	1773-1772 Nebiretawe 1772-1771 Nebiriau II
	1817-1804 Nemtyemsaf I ▲		1815-1805 Kaukara 1805-1795 Neferkaure 2	3y Sewadjtu; Senebmiu, Sankhptahi {13th ends 1780}	1771-1759 BebiAnkh 1759-1758 Shedwaset
1765-1731 Apepi	1804-1760 Pepi II ▲	1781-1772 /▲ \ Amenemhat IV	1795-1790 (9th) Neferkauhor Khu Hepu	1817-1815 Intef III (11th) 1y (Sehotepkare) Intef V	Montemsaf at Edfu Dudimose I + II Edfu
	1760-1759 Nemtyemsaf II	[1772-1764 Montuhotep IV]	1790-1785 Neferirkare II	1815-1772 Montuhotep II (Upper Egypt only) (11th)	Senusret IV 17th Dyn. N. of Thebes
(Apepi conquered Memphis in 1754.)	1759-1754 (Netjerikare) Siptah	(1772-1761 by 11th dynasty)	(1785-1761 by 11th dynasty)	1772-1764 Montuhotep II Middle and Upper Egypt	1761-1757 Rahotep 5y Nub Intef VI ▲
				> Montuhotep IV at Lisht 1764-1761 Montuhotep III	1757-1754 Sobekemsaf I 2y wep Intef V
1731-1720 Khamudi	(1754-1720 15th dyn)	(17th dynasty)	(then 17th dynasty)	(then 17th dynasty)	> Intefs VII + VIII

Chronology Overview

17th Dynasty in Thebes during cSIP

1761-1757 Rahotep
1757-1754 Sobekemsaf I
1754-1747 Sobekemsaf II
1747-1746 Ahmose [formerly Tao I]
1746-1742 Tao [formerly Tao II]
1742-1738 Kamose (last year co-reign with his brother Ahmose)

18th → 19th dynasties of famous pharaohs in the **New Kingdom**

18th Dynasty 245 years (capital began in Luxor)

1738-1712	Ahmose I, who defeated the Hyksos in 1720, reuniting Egypt
1712-1702	Amenhotep I (Ahmose-Nefetari, mom)
1702-1688	Amenhotep I
1688-1674	Thutmose I
1674-1672	Thutmose II (with Hatshepsut; Thutmose III designated successor in 1674)
1672-1651	Hatshepsut (with Thutmose III)
1651-1618	Thutmose III (1651-1622 sole reign; last 4 years as co-reign)
1622-1596	Amenhotep II (first 4 years as co-reign)
1596-1588	Thutmose IV
1588-1550	Amenhotep III (one year co-reign with his son)
1551-1534	Amenhotep IV/Akhenaten (capital in Akhenaten - Amarna)
1534-1531	Smenkhkare (Nefertiti maintained royal status and function)
1531-1530	Nefertiti/Neferneferuaten
1534-1524	Tutankhamun (Tut usurped regnal years; his first attestation is in his 4th year)
1524-1520	Ay (moved his capital back to Thebes)
1520-1493	Horemheb

19th Dynasty 115 years (delta capital at Qantir)

1493-1491	Rameses I
1491-1480	Seti I
1480-1414	Rameses II
1414-1394	Merenptah
1394-1388	Seti II
1394-1390	Amenmesse, a rival
1388-1381	Merenptah Siptah
1381-1378	Tausret
1378-1323	(anarchy)

Pharaohs of the Bible

20th Dynasty of **Rameses**, 124 years

1323-1318	Setnakhte
1318-1286	Rameses III
1286-1279	Rameses IV
1279-1275	Rameses V
1275-1266	Rameses VI
1266-1258	Rameses VII
1258-1256	Rameses VIII
1256-1237	Rameses IX
1237-1228	Rameses X
1228-1199	Rameses XI

High Priests of Amun in Thebes and 21st pharaohs in Tanis

High Priests ruling in Thebes, 147 years, with		21st dynasty ruling in Tanis	
1199-1169	Herihor (with Pinedjem as HPA)	{1195-1171	Smendes, treasurer}
1169-1148	Pinedjem I	1169-1146	Smendes I
1148-1099	Menkheperre	1146-1142	Amenemnisu
		1146-1100	Psusennes I
1099-1097	Smendes II	1100-1091	Amenemope
1097-1075	Pinedjem II	1091-1085	Osorkon, elder
		1085-1066	Siamun
1075-1052	Psusennes III	1066-1052	Psusennes II (III)

It was thought at one time that Psusennes II and Psusennes III were two different men, but there was just one person who ended up ruling all of Egypt.

When pharaohs/kings have a duplicate name of a predecessor, subsequent Roman numerals are added to the name. When a High Priest of Amun (HPA) has a duplicate name of a predecessor, a subsequent alphabetical letter is added. Several HPA's of the 23rd dynasty became pharaohs just as Herihor did in dynasty 21A above. When an HPA becomes a king as well, their letter is changed to a corresponding Roman numeral, and then they normally appoint someone else to be HPA; hence the reason for a middle column in the following chart. Since Iuput A did not become a king; Iuput B became the first king by the name Iuput I. HPA's have been italicized for easier recognition. Sheshonks V and VIa were simultaneously pharaohs and HPA's.

Chronology Overview

Clarity's Third Intermediate Period (cTIP)

22nd **Sheshonks & Osorkons** in Tanis and 23rd high priests in Thebes

22nd Dynasty in Tanis/Bubastis		concurrent with	23rd Dynasty in Thebes	
1055-1022	Sheshonk I		1052-1024	*Iuput A*
1022-988	Osorkon I		1024-994	*Sheshonk C*
988-979	Takelot I		994-984	*Iuwelot*
979-970	Sheshonk IIa		984-970	*Smendes C*
970-965	Sheshonk IIb		970-950	Smendes III
965-960	Sheshonk IIc	[960-950 *HarSiEse A*]	950-928	HarSiEse I
960-928	Osorkon II		947-935	... *dju* ...
928-889	Sheshonk III	[935-910 Takelot F/II]	930-901	*HarSiEse B*
			928-905	PedubastSiEse
889-874	Sheshonk IV	[886-881 *Sheshonk VIa*]	914-901	Iuput I (co-reign)
			901-890	*Takelot B*
874-863	Pami		890-871	*Osorkon B*
863-834	Osorkon III		866-840	*Takelot C*
		[863-834 *Shepenupet I*]	840-826	Takelot III
834-796	*Sheshonk V*	[834-827 Amenirdas I]	826-788	Pedubast SiBast
796-790	Sheshonk VI	[834-811 Kashta]	803-788	*Takelot D*
790-772	Osorkon IV	{790 Tefnakhte became general in **Sais**}		
772-767	Shepseskare-Imere (placed by Tefnakhte I)			
767-757	Sekhemkare (Tanis only)			

24th → 26th in **Sais** and 25th in Thebes

24th Dynasty in Sais		concurrent with Kushite 25th Dynasty in Thebes	
787-759	Tefnakhte I	780-745	Piye
759-743	Bakenrenef	745-729	Shabako
741-718	Padinemti	729-713	Shebitku
718-702	Tefnakhte II	713-687	Taharqa

26th Dynasty in Sais/Tanis			
702-688	Nekauba		
688-678	Necho I (placed by Sennacherib)	687-678	Tantamani (25th ends)
678-663	Psammetichus I	678-663	12 kings
663-624	Psammetichus I	663-624	Psammetichus I
624-605	Necho II (delta only)		
605-595	Necho II	605-595	Necho II

Pharaohs of the Bible

595-589	Psamtik II
589-570	Hophra
570-526	Amasis
526-525	Psamtik III (defeated by Cambyses II of Persia)

Clarity's Late Period

27th Dynasty — First Persian Period
525-522   Cambyses II
522-486   Darius I
486-466   Xerxes
465-424   Artaxerxes I (Longmanus)
424-404   Darius II

28th Dynasty
404-399   Amenirdis (Amyrtaios)   Pedubast III (Seheribre SiBast)

29th Dynasty
399-393   Nepherites (Baenre merynetjeru)
393-393   Psammuthis (Userre stepenptah)
393-380   Hakoris (Khnemmaatre)
380-380   Nepherites II

30th Dynasty
Nectanebo I (Kheperkare)
Teos (Irmaatenre)
Nectanebo II (Senedjemibre setpenanhur)

31st Dynasty — Second Persian Period
343-338   Artaxerxes III Ochus
338-336   Arses
335-332   Darius III Codoman

32nd Dynasty — Ptolemaic Period
333-323   Alexander the Great
323-317   Philip Arrhidaeus
317-310   Alexander IV

Chronology Overview

33rd Dynasty Ptolemaic Period

305-285	Ptolemy I Soter I
285-246	Ptolemy II Philadelphius
246-221	Ptolemy III Euergetes I
221-205	Ptolemy IV Philopater
205-180	Ptolemy V Epiphanes
180-145	Ptolemy VI Philometor
145	Ptolemy VII Neos Philopater
170-116	Ptolemy VIII Euergetes II
116-107	Ptolemy IX Soter II
107-88	Ptolemy X Alexander I
88-80	Ptolemy IX Soter II (restored)
80	Ptolemy XI Alexander II
80-51	Ptolemy XII Neos Dionysus (Auletes)
51-30	Cleopatra VII Philopater
51-47	Ptolemy XIII
47-44	Ptolemy XIV
44-30	Ptolemy XV Caesarion (son of Julius Caesar, co-reign with Cleopatra VII)

End of pharaonic dynasties by
30 BC – 14 AD Octavius/Octavian (born Gaius Octavius Thurinus, later Caesar Augustus)

"Neither in Egypt nor in Babylonia has any beginning of civilization been found. As far back as archeology can carry us man is already civilized, building cities and temples, carving hard stone into artistic form, and even employing a system of pictorial writing. And of Egypt it may be said that the older the culture the more perfect it is found to be. The fact is a vary remarkable one in view of modern theories of development and of the evolution of civilization out of barbarism. Whatever may be the reason, such theories are not borne out by the discoveries of archeology. Instead of the progress we should expect we find retrogression and decay; where we look for the rude beginnings of art, we find an advanced society and artistic perfection. <u>Is it possible that the Biblical view is right after all, and that civilized man has been civilized from the outset? . . . In any case, the culture and civilization of Egypt and Babylonia appear to spring into existence fully developed</u> . . ."[120]

---

120 Sayce, A. H., *The Homiletic Review*, Volume 43 #6, June 1902, p. 487

Egypt's Calendar and Regnal Years

Egypt had a calendar of twelve months containing thirty days each, and appended five days for a total of 365 days in a year. Their calendar recognized three seasons of four months each: Akhet ("inundation", roughly August – November), Peret ("winter", roughly December – March), and Shemu ("summer", roughly April – July). The new year beginning in Akhet was heralded by the appearance of Sirius. Because they didn't add a day every four years, this calendar was unreliable, and so they also had agricultural calendars.

According to the *Handbook of Oriental Studies of Ancient Egyptian Chronology*, pharaohs from the 16th dynasty onward dated their regnal years from New Year's Day on the first day of the first month of Akhet. Pharaohs from the 18th dynasty onward counted their first day as year one and added years on that anniversary. Pharaohs from the 26th dynasty onward counted their first New Year's Day as regnal year 2 regardless of accession date.

Pharaoh Names

A pharaoh's title (titulary) is composed of five names: nomen or birth-name, prenomen usually followed by *nsw-bit* (sedge and bee glyphs), Horus (upon coronation), Nebty (*neb* is a basket glyph for 'lord'; *ty* is two) represented by a vulture and cobra, and golden Horus represented by a falcon. The name he was given at birth is called his 'nomen', which in lists is followed by Roman numerals to distinguish those with the same name, like Sheshonk I. To differentiate, the nomen or prenomen can become quite long; like Sheshonk Meryamun Si-Bast Netjerheqawaset/Netjerheqaon is the nomen of Sheshonk IV. A pharaoh's throne name is called the 'prenomen' which usually includes an epithet of Re, like Set-epen-re ("elect/chosen of Re"), written Setepenre for Sheshonks I, IIa, III, IV, and VI. The prenomen of Sheshonks I, IV, and VIa also include Hedj-Kheper-Re ("bright is the manifestation of Re"), written as Hedjkheperre. The prenomen and nomen are each placed in an oval called a 'cartouche' which signified royalty. A pharaoh might also have a Horus name, a Nebty name, and a golden Horus name, but not always.

Only consonant sounds are represented in Egyptian hieroglyphs, though Egyptologists have agreed to allow a few glyphs to also represent vowel sounds. The vowels in pharaohs' names prior to Akhenaten are random guesses, but with the correspondence from other countries which did include vowel sounds, other names of pharaohs are better approximations. There are many different spellings of the pharaohs' names. The following are interchangeable: e=a, i=y, u=w, and c=k. Thus the sun god can be written Re or Ra. Since spellings are flexible and the Bible refers to 'Shishak', I prefer Sheshonk to Shoshenk. The glyph for 'n' is not in the oldest names, making it Shishak, like the Bible reference.

King of Upper and Lower Egypt

Upper Egypt (UE) refers to the source of the Nile coming through Thebes and flowing to the delta which was Lower Egypt (LE). The first pharaoh to establish 'kings' in UE and LE was Den, the fifth pharaoh of the 1st dynasty. During Den's thirtieth year celebration (sed festival in 2231 BC), he recorded the appearances of the kings of UE and LE separately. So only 100 years after Mizraim established the nation of Egypt, two underling kings were needed to help Den administrate the growing population which he further divided into nomes.[121] Upper Egypt was represented by the sedge plant glyph and the white crown. Lower Egypt was represented by the bee glyph and the red crown. Den constructed a new title *nj-sw.t-bj.t* meaning literally "he of the sedge and the bee" which became known as "King of the Two Lands" of Upper and Lower Egypt, and later shortened to *nsw-bit*. *Nsw* came to mean king or royal. After another 100 years, both UE and LE had a full time pharaoh during the 2nd dynasty. Sanakhte temporarily reunited them, but then a more permanent split occurred with the 3rd dynasty ruling LE and the 7th dynasty ruling UE. Most pharaohs still used the signs *nsw-bit* whether Egypt was divided into two dynasties or several. "King of the Two Lands" became a title, not a definition.

> "The title *htmty-bit* is often incorrectly translated as 'Seal-bearer of the King of Lower Egypt', but *bit* evidently does not mean 'King of Lower Egypt' despite the conventional and unfortunate translation of *nsw-bit* as 'King of Upper and Lower Egypt'. The absurdity of the translation 'Seal-bearer of the King of Lower Egypt' is well illustrated by the fact that this title also was used by the high-ranking officials of the Sixteenth and Seventeenth Dynasty during the wars with the Hyksos who, in fact, were the kings of Lower Egypt. It may further be noted that a title *htmty-nsw is non-existent. Similarly, the offspring of the kings of the Fourteenth and Fifteenth Dynasties were designated *s3-nsw/s3t-nsw*, although the two dynasties were seated in Lower Egypt. These two titles do obviously not mean 'Son/daughter of the King of Upper Egypt', but simply 'King's Son/daughter'."[122]

Pharaoh

Pharaoh means 'great house' and describes the royal residence. In order to expedite trade outside of Egypt, quasi-kings were created by the 12th dynasty who could use a royal seal with their own name and 'pharaoh' in order to do business. 'Pharaoh' did not become a king's title until after Ahmose I reunited Egypt, and began the 18th dynasty. When Rameses XI died without an heir at the end of the 20th dynasty, his high priest, Herihor, took over administrative and military responsibilities without assuming the title pharaoh immediately. During this interim he sent Wenamun to Byblos to purchase cedar. Wenamun recounted how leaders there made him wait several months, reminding him about the envoys of Khamweset (part of Rameses' IX name, and name of his vizier) who were delayed 17 years until they died. The Byblite leaders derisively used the word 'pharaoh', whereas Wenamun neither used the term 'pharaoh' or 'king' of any man. They refused Wenamun until he

---

121 Breasted, J., *Ancient Records of Egypt, volume 1*, 1907, translation of Palermo Stone lines 105-6, p. 59
122 Ryholt, K.S.B., *The Political Situation in Egypt during the Second Intermediate Period*, CNI Publications 20, Museum Tusculanum Press, 1997, p. 109, footnote 361

returned with a letter and funds from the treasurer Smendes.

Israel's Calendars and Feasts

When Moses led the children of Israel out of Egypt, the LORD established a new religious calendar for them to follow with several feasts, the first being Passover. The civil calendar still began in the fall in the seventh month of Tishri. Since chronology is based upon calendars, it is important to understand the Hebrew calendar which was lunar and solar. The first of each lunar month was determined by the new moon, so Hebrew months actually straddle two Gentile months.

Gezer calendar, about the time of Solomon, described a farmer's year.

Civil calendar	*Feasts*	Gezer Calendar
Tishri & Cheshvan	Trumpet, Atonement, Booths	Two months gathering (Sept.-Oct.)
Kislev & Tebeth		Two months planting (Nov.-Dec.)
Shevat & Adar		Two months late sowing (Jan.-Feb.)
Nisan	Passover, Bread, First Fruits	One month howing flax (March)
Iyyar		One month barley harvest (April)
Sivan	Weeks (Pentecost)	One month wheat harvest (May)
Tammuz & Ab		Two months pruning grapes (June-July)
Elul		One month summer fruit (August)

The Hebrews numbered the days of their months and called the seventh day of each week *Shabbat* (Sabbath), a day of rest, as Creator God rested from His work on the seventh day. The 14th of the month would always be a full moon. A Hebrew day is from dusk to dusk, so one Hebrew day is parts of two Gregorian days.

Spring and Summer Feasts

On the 10th of Nisan a family would take an unblemished lamb into their home and begin to rid the home of leaven. At twilight at the beginning of the 14th day the lamb was to be slain and its blood applied with hyssop to the doorpost's sides and top, so that the angel of death would "*pass over*" the home: Passover. The lamb would be roasted and eaten with unleavened bread. The Feast of Passover would also begin the Feast of Unleavened Bread. Passover was celebrated on the 14th, but Unleavened Bread continued seven more days. Depending upon when the Sabbath fell during the Feast of Unleavened Bread, the Feast of First Fruits would be celebrated on the morning after that Sabbath, offering the first sheaves of barley in thankfulness to God for the harvest. First Fruits was always on a Sunday.

From the Sunday of the feast of First Fruits, the Hebrews were to count seven sabbaths, and celebrate the "*morrow after the seventh sabbath*" (Lev. 23:15), the fiftieth day (so later called Pentecost), which would be another Sunday. The Feast of Weeks is similar to the jubilee celebration of the fiftieth year after seven sabbaths of years. It is the only summer feast, and it celebrated the wheat harvest.

Fall Feasts

All the fall feasts are held during the seventh month of Tishri. Feast of Trumpets is the only feast on the first day of a month; the new moon. It is a *"memorial of blowing of trumpets"* (Lev. 23:24) recalling the day of Joseph's inauguration as second unto pharaoh (Genesis 41:15-16, 39-46). It also celebrates the civil New Year (*Rosh Hashanah*). But the trumpet was to be blown at every new moon and on other holidays (Numbers 10:10).

On the 10th of Tishri is the Day of Atonement (*Yom Kippur*) in which a fast of repentance unto the LORD is observed. No labor is allowed during any of the feasts. So after Yom Kippur, everyone finishes bringing in the harvest of grapes and other fruit. Feast of Tabernacles or Booths (*Succoth*) is seven days of feasting beginning on the 15th of Tishri in which everyone lives in booths outside like a big camp-out, followed by a day of rejoicing in Torah, the Law. Succoth recalls the 7-day trek across the Sinai during the exodus.

Sabbath Year

Every seventh year after the children of Israel entered into their promised land, they were commanded to let their land rest. God would provide them with bumper crops in the sixth year with plenty to store for food through the seventh year, much like He allowed them to gather double the manna on the sixth day in the wilderness (Exodus 16:12-27).

> *And the LORD spoke to Moses in mount Sinai, saying, Speak to the children of Israel, and say to them, <u>When you come into the land which I give you, then shall the land keep a sabbath to the LORD</u>. Six years you shall sow your field, and six years you shall prune your vineyard, and gather in the fruit thereof; <u>But in the seventh year shall be a sabbath of rest to the land, a sabbath for the LORD</u>: you shall neither sow your field, nor prune your vineyard. (Leviticus 25:1-4)*

If any of their kinsmen had sold themselves into slavery to another Israelite, those kinsmen were to be set free on the Sabbath year (Exodus 21:2) and allowed to reap the fields (Ex. 23:10-11). Also, during the Feast of Tabernacles (Booths – *Succoth*) of the Sabbath year, the Law (first five books of the Bible written by Moses) were to be read and taught to all those living in Israel, young and old and foreigners, so all might obey it.

> *And Moses commanded them, saying, <u>At the end of every seven years, in the solemnity of the year of release, in the feast of tabernacles</u>, When all Israel is come to appear before the LORD your God in the place which he shall choose, you shall <u>read this law before all Israel in their hearing</u>. Gather the people together, men and women, and children, and your stranger that is within your gates, that they may hear, and that they may learn, and fear the LORD your God, and observe to do all the words of this law: And that their children, which have not known any thing, may hear, and learn to fear the LORD your God, <u>as long as you live in the land</u> where you go over Jordan to possess it. (Deut. 31:10-13)*

Some have stated that Israelites were only to keep the Sabbath years while they lived in the land, but this phrase refers to being gathered together for the teaching. The Sabbath rests were for the land and would be kept whether Israelites remained in the land or not, or whether the land was sown six years prior or not (Lev. 25:2). In this I differ from Ussher who based his understanding of jubilees upon first century AD letters.

Joshua and the children of Israel entered into Canaan in spring of 1451 BC. From fall 1451 to fall 1445 they tilled the soil between fighting their enemies, and then Joshua ended his conquest and they celebrated the first sabbath year from fall 1445 to fall 1444 BC. The Sabbath year released land and slaves, and returned focus to God as provider.

Jubilee

A Jubilee is celebrated on the 50th year according to Leviticus 25:8-13 which is celebrated on Yom Kippur (10th of Tishri) with the blowing of the silver trumpets to release the land and its people from all indebtedness. The 48th year must have been an abundant crop so as to sustain the people through the next two years of not sowing the land and again through to the harvest of the year after the jubilee. Then after the seventh sabbath (49th) year, the Hebrews were commanded to celebrate another special sabbath year called the year of jubilee. Any lands that had been sold were returned to the original owner or the ownership of their tribesmen. Those who had sold themselves into slavery were freed. All debts were canceled. All farmers took another 'sabbatical' from working the fields.

> *And you shall number seven sabbaths of years to you, seven times seven years; and the space of the seven sabbaths of years shall be to you forty and nine years. <u>Then shall you cause the trumpet of the jubilee to sound on the tenth day of the seventh month, in the day of atonement shall you make the trumpet sound throughout all your land.</u> And you shall hallow the fiftieth year, and proclaim liberty throughout all the land to all the inhabitants thereof: it shall be a jubilee to you; and you shall return every man to his possession, and you shall return every man to his family. <u>A jubilee shall that fiftieth year be to you</u>: you shall not sow, neither reap that which grows of itself in it, nor gather the grapes in it of your vine undressed. (Leviticus 25:8-11)*

Upon a pharaoh's attainment of his 30th regnal year (and sometimes every third year thereafter), he held a heb-sed festival and cancelled payment of taxes. The Anatollian Hittites made decrees called *misarum* in which debts were cancelled and slaves were freed.

The Hebrew Year

A twelve lunar month calendar will fall eleven days short of a solar year, as does the Islamic calendar of 354 days. A solar calendar of 365 days has to add an extra day every four years because the earth's orbit around the sun takes 365.24 days. The Hebrews had a combined lunar-solar calendar which included a 13th month (Adar II) every six years until reaching the 36th year when an extra month was added to the 40th year. Every forty years this ancient Hebrew calendar was in sync with the modern 365-day calendar. Observing the moon, the number of days of Hebrew month vasciate between 29 and 30 days, so that they average out. The Sanhedrin had strict parameters to declare the new moon of a month.

This month [khodesh – new moon] shall be to you the beginning of months: it shall be the first month of the year to you. (Exodus 12:2)

A land which the LORD your God cares for: the eyes of the LORD your God are always on it, from the beginning [reshiyth - firstfruits] of the year even to the end of the year. (Deuteronomy 11:12)

The first month when the Hebrews left Egypt was Nisan, also called Abib in Ex. 13:4. It was Spring when the *"first fruits"* of the land were ripened for harvest. Just as we recognize different years within our twelve month calendar: school year, fiscal year, campaign year, and so on; so did the Hebrews. They had their religious year which began the 1st of Nisan, and the king's regnal year and New Year celebration which began the 1st of Tishri. They also recognized the 1st of Elul as the cattle-tithe, and the 1st of Shevat as the summer fruit-tithe, and the end of the agricultural year after the Feast of Tabernacles (Exodus 23:16). The Hebrew months in numerical order are as follows:

1 Nisan/Abib	7 Tishri
2 Iyar	8 Cheshvan
3 Sivan	9 Kislev
4 Tammuz	10 Tevet
5 Av	11 Shevat
6 Elul	12 Adar I
	13 Adar II (for 'pregnant' years)

Biblical Famines

Though Job 30:3 mentions famine in the *"former time"* before Noah's flood, this book will focus on Biblical famines after the flood. Moses wrote an account of his own history in Egypt, and he compiled the first-hand accounts of Egypt from Shem/Imhotep, Abraham, and Jacob, and Joseph. These men were involved in the famines of the Bible. Shem built Djoser's Food Complex long before the first famine which occurred during Abram's life.

First Biblical Famine (1921-1920 BC) of Abram - Drought

*And there was a famine in the land: and **Abram** went down into Egypt to sojourn there; for the famine was grievous in the land. (Genesis 12:10)*

Abram and Sarai returned to Canaan in 1919 BC, so the first famine probably lasted about two years. This famine has a clear beginning year when Abram was 75 years old. The famine itself may have only last one year, and they remained in Egypt a second year.

Second Biblical Famine (1856-1853 BC) of Isaac - Deluge

*And there was a famine in the land, beside the first famine that was in the days of Abraham. And **Isaac** went to Abimelech king of the Philistines to Gerar. And the LORD appeared to him, and said, Go not down into Egypt; dwell in the land which I shall tell you of . . . (Genesis 26:1-2)*

Isaac was told specifically NOT to go to Egypt during this second famine, but to go to the Philistines. My guess is that this second famine lasted about three years. The Egyptians were not well prepared for it, as is evidenced by the emaciated Egyptians depicted in several tombs. This famine has neither a clear beginning nor ending year, but there are clues.

Third Biblical Famine (1707-1700 BC) of Jacob/Israel and Joseph - Drought

*They said moreover to Pharaoh, For to sojourn in the land are we come; for your servants have no pasture for their flocks; for the famine is sore in the land of Canaan: now therefore, we pray you, let your servants dwell in the land of Goshen. . . . And **Joseph** brought in **Jacob** his father, and set him before Pharaoh: and Jacob blessed Pharaoh. (Genesis 47:4-7)*

This famine has a clear beginning and ending year ascertained from the Holy Bible.

Fourth Biblical Famine during rule of Gideon[123]

*Now it came to pass in the days when the **judges** ruled, that there was a famine in the land. And a certain man of Bethlehemjudah went to sojourn in the country of Moab, he, and his wife, and his two sons. (Ruth 1:1)*

Fifth Biblical Famine during King David (3 years) 1023-1020 BC

*Then there was a famine in the days of **David** three years, year after year; and David inquired of the LORD. And the LORD answered, It is for Saul, and for his bloody house, because he slew the Gibeonites. (II Samuel 21:1)*

Sixth Biblical Famine during Elijah and King Ahab (3.5 years) - Drought

*And it came to pass after many days, that the word of the LORD came to **Elijah** in the third year, saying, Go, show yourself to **Ahab**; and I will send rain on the earth. And Elijah went to show himself to Ahab. And there was a sore famine in Samaria. (I Kings 18:1-2)*

This famine lasted for three and a half years according to Luke 4:25 and James 5:17.

---

[123] Ussher, *The Wall Chart of World History*, first published in 1890

Seventh Biblical Famine during Elisha and King of Syria (7 years)

*Then spoke **Elisha** to the woman, whose son he had restored to life, saying, Arise, and go you and your household, and sojourn wherever you can sojourn: for the LORD has called for a famine; and it shall also come on the land seven years. (II Kings 8:1)*

Famines within cities also occurred. Elisha noted a local famine in Gilgal (II Kings 4:38). The famine in the city of Samaria was caused by Syrian Benhadad besieging it (II Kings 6:24-25), but it was followed by a seven year famine throughout Israel. Jerusalem experienced famine when king Zedekiah rebelled against Nebuchadnezzar who then besieged the city (Jer. 52:4-6).

Dating Methods

Some Egyptian chronologists used Sothic dating based upon the rise of the star Sirius (Sothis) as cited in the Ebers and Illahun papyri. But since neither document mentioned the name of the reigning pharaoh, a true synchronism could not be found.

Pottery dating methods can ascertain a general period, and can help determine which cultures were involved in international trade in the ancient world. Syrian pottery was found in 1st dynasty tombs at Abydos, Egypt and incorrectly termed 'Abydos ware'.

Geological dating dismisses Noah's one-year world-wide flood in favor of millions of years depositing strata (which often show no signs of erosion, or have a vertical tree through several strata). Then a fossil is dated to the level/stratum in which it is found using circular logic. Real flood deposits create vertical layers with heavier, larger material on the bottom and lighter, smaller things on top; the strata are not chronological but based upon mass.

As to the false assumptions upon which a cornucopia of radiometric dating methods are placed, please read John Woodmorappe's *The Mythology of Modern Dating Methods: Why million/billion-year results are not credible.*

Let no man deceive you by any means: for that day shall not come, except there come a falling away first . . . with all power and signs and lying wonders, And with all delusion of unrighteousness in them that perish; because they received not the love of the truth, that they might be saved. And for this cause <u>God shall send them strong delusion, that they should believe a lie</u>: . . . God has from the beginning chosen you to salvation through sanctification of the Spirit and belief of the truth: . . . brothers, stand fast, and hold the traditions which you have been taught . . . (2 Thessalonians 2:3-15)

This "*strong delusion*" began in the 1800's with a "*lie*" from <u>Ly</u>ell. Repeating for clarity, in 1830 Charles Lyell's *Principles of Geology* espoused that the great canyons were produced by erosion over periods of ten thousands of years instead of in one year after Noah's flood. So if human remains were discovered beyond 10,000 years, that would indicate the Bible's teaching that mankind began in 4004 BC was wrong, and God was not mankind's Creator. This conclusion was the basis of *Vestiges of the Natural History of Creation* published in 1844, and Charles Darwin's theories of evolution in *On the Origin of Species* in 1852. The "*strong delusion*" is evolution, which has caused a great "*falling away*" from the Christian faith. This dating of fossils by the geologic strata (now dated to millions of years) is not the same as archaeological stratification of non-fossils.

Archaeological stratification is based upon the law of superposition in which older layers of human activity are buried beneath newer ones. This is helpful but it's not an exact science as assumptions must be made as to whether the site was ever abandoned or saw continual use, whether items are heirlooms or are contemporary with the level, and whether fires and other damage were caused by war or nature. Archaeology includes scientific research and discovery of hard evidence, but it also involves interpretation of the evidence, which incorporates world-view and bias.

I interpret the hard evidence in light of the Holy Bible, totally biased that Creator God has observed history and directed His people to write it down as eyewitnesses. Throughout the ancient world, it is only the Hebrews who consistently recorded their moral and military defeats. Therefore assigning absolute chronological dates to other ancient empires is impossible, but I've provided a rough estimate based upon Biblical synchronisms. For those who think there are contradictions in the history of the children of Israel, please read Dr. Floyd Jones' *The Chronology of the Old Testament*.

Other Major Civilizations

"In Mesopotamia no less than five different chronologies result from different datings of the First Dynasty of Babylon and Hammurabi . . ."[124]

"The key underlying assumption is that the Babylonian (Kassite), and via this, the core Assyrian, chronological data are totally secure. However, this is far from the case."[125]

"Brinkman (1970:34) did in fact conclude by observing, with reference to his preferred minimum chronology, that 'in general, it may be said that, with the exception of possible revisions from the Assyrian side, most adjustments in dates for Babylonian events and reigns here set between 1374 and 1155 should be expected to be upward'."[126]

---

124 Niemeier, Barbara and Wolf-Dietrich, *Tel Kabri: The 1986-1993 Excavation Seasons*, Tel Aviv, 2002, p. 262

125 Manning, Sturt, *A Test of Time: The Volcano of Thera and the chronology and history of the Aegean and east Mediterranean in the mid second millennium B.C.*, Oxbow Books, 1999, p. 380

126 Ibid., p. 382

Chronology Overview

Rewriting one chronology means adjustments to all of them; they all needed to be adjusted "upward" by a couple hundred years. My research has been focused on Egypt, and so the following king lists are rough estimates. If there was documentation of the king's regnal years, I have noted it to the right of his name; or used an 'x' for a digit mark now lost. In absence of data I have made a guess. I have noted important synchronisms in brackets.

Clarity Assyrian Kings List

2300-2290	Tudiya	{23rd c. BC, contemporary of Ibrium of Ebla}
2290-2285	Adamu	
2285-2280	Yangi	
2280-2275	Suhlamu	
2275-2270	Harharu	
2270-2265	Mandaru	
2265-2260	Imsu	
2260-2255	Harsu	
2255-2250	Didanu	
2250-2245	Hanu	
2245-2240	Zuabu	
2240-2235	Nuabu	
2235-2230	Abazu	
2230-2225	Belu	
2225-2220	Azarah	
2220-2215	Ushpia	{possible founder of the temple of Ashur in Assur}
2215-2210	Apiashal, "*son of Ushpia*"	
2210-2205	Hale, "*son of Apiashal*"	
2205-2200	Samani, "*son of Hale*"	
2200-2195	Hayani, "*son of Samani*"	
2195-2190	Ilu-Mer, "*son of Hayani*"	
2190-2185	Yakmesi, "*son of Ilu-Mer*"	
2185-2180	Yakmeni, "*son of Yakmesi*"	
2180-2175	Yazkur-el, "*son of Yakmeni*"	
2175-2170	Ila-kabkabu, "*son of Yazkur-el*" 5	
2170-2168	Aminu, "*son of Ila-kabkabu*" 2	
2168-2164	Sulili, "*son of Aminu*" 2	
2164-2159	Kikkiya 5	
2159-2154	Akiya 5	
2154-2149	Puzur-Ashur I 5	
2149-2144	Shalim-ahum/Shalim-ahhe 5	
2144-2139	Ilu-shuma 5	{contemporary of Samu-abum of Babylonian}
2139-2099	Eru-shum I 30-40	
2099-2094	Ikunum x	

Pharaohs of the Bible

2094-2089	Sargon I x	
2089-2084	Puzur-Ashur II x	
2084-2079	Naram-Sin x	
2079-2074	Erushum II x	
2074-2041	Shamshi-Adad I 33 (also called Atamar-Ishtar)	
2041-2001	Ishme-Dagan I 40	
2001-1996	Mut-Ashkur	
1996-1991	Remu . . .	
1991-1986	Asinum	
1986-1976	Ashur-dugul	
1976-1966	Ashur-apla-idi	
1966-1956	Nasir-Sin	
1956-1946	Sin-namir	
1946-1936	Ipqu-Ishtar	
1936-1926	Adad-salulu	
1926-1916	Adasi {drove Babylonians and Amorites from Assyria}	
1916-1906	Bel-bani, "son of Adasi" 10	
1906-1889	Libaya, "son of Bel-bani" 17	
1889-1877	Sharma-Adad I 12	
1877-1865	Iptar-Sin 12	
1865-1837	Bazaya 28	
1837-1831	Lullaya 6	
1831-1817	Shu-Ninua 14	
1817-1814	Sharma-Adad II 3	
1814-1803	Erishum III 13	
1801-1795	Shamsi-Adad II 6	
1795-1749	Ishme-Dagan II 16	
1749-1733	Shamshi-Adad III 16	
1733-1707	Ashur-nirari I 26	
1707-1683	Puzur-Ashur III 24 {contemporary of Burna-Buriash I of Bablyonia}	
1683-1670	Enlil-nasir I 13	
1670-1658	Nur-ili 12	
1658	Ashur-shaduni (1 month)	
1658-1653	Ashur-rabi I x	
1653-1648	Ashur-nadin-ahhe I x	
1648-1642	Enlil-nasir II 6	
1642-1626	Ashur-nirari II 7-16	
1626-1608	Ashur-bel-nisheshu 9-18	
1608-1391	Ashur-rim-nisheshu 8-17	
1600-1580	Ashur-nadin-ahhe II 10-20	
1580-1552	Eriba-Adad I 27-28	

Chronology Overview

1552-1506	Ashur-uballit I 36-46 {El Amarna letters #15-16 to **Akhenaten**}
1506-1496	Enlil-nirari 10
1496-1484	Arik-den-ili 12
1484-1452	<u>Adad-nirari I</u> 30-32{Sought iron from Hittite king Mursili II (1532-1506)}
1452-1432	Shalmaneser I 29-30
1432-1395	Tukuti-Ninurta I 36-37{contemporary of Hittite Suppiluliuma II}
1395-1391	Ashur-nadin-apli 3-4
1391-1385	Ashur-nirari III 6
1385-1380	Enlil-Kudurri-usur 4-5
1380-1366	Ninurta-apal-Ekur 3-14
1366-1320	Ashur-Dan I 46
1320	Ninurta-tukulti-Ashur and Mutakkil-nuska
1320-1302	Ashur-resh-ishi I 18
1302-1363	Tiglath-Pileser I 39
1363-1361	Asharid-apal-Ekur 2
1361-1343	Ashur-bel-kala 18
1343-1341	Eriba-Adad II 2
1341-1337	Shamshi-Adad IV 4
1337-1318	Ashur-nasir-pal I 19
1318-1296	Shalmaneser II x2
1396-1390	Ashur-nirari IV 6
?	
1013-972	Ashur-rabi II 41
972-967	Ashur-resh-ishi II 5
967-935	Tiglath-Pileser II 32
935-912	Ashur-Dan II 23
912-891	Adad-nirari II 21
891-884	Tukulti-Ninurta II 7
884-859	Ashur-nasir-pal II 25
859-824	Shalmaneser III 35 {battle of Qarqar 853 BC}
824-811	Shamshi-Adad V 13-18
811-807	Queen Shammuramat (Semiramis in Greek) until son matured
807-783	Adad-nirari III 28 {solar eclipse 791}
783-773	Shalmaneser IV 10 {1st Olympiad 776}
773-755	Ashur-Dan III 18 {solar eclipse 763}
755-745	Ashur-nirari V 10
745-727	Tiglath-Pileser III 18
727-722	Shalmaneser V 5
722-705	Sargon II 17 {720 victory at Qarqar; 717 victory at Carchemish}
717-681	Sennacherib 36 {co-reign 717-705; ruled Babylon 688-681}
681-668	Esarhaddon 13 {Ptolemy gives him 13 years; others only 12}

668-627	Ashurbanipal 41	
631-627	Ashuretil-ilani 4	
626	Sin-shumu-lishir	
627-612	Sin-shar-ishkun 15	{612 Nineveh defeated by Medes and Babylonians}
612-609	Ashur-uballit II 3	{governor over Harran defeated by Nabopolassar}

Clarity Babylonian Kings List

And the beginning of his kingdom was Babel, and Erech, and Accad, and Calneh, in the land of Shinar. Out of that land went forth Asshur, and built Nineveh, and the city Rehoboth, and Calah, And Resen between Nineveh and Calah: the same is a great city. (Genesis 10:10-12)

Nimrod founded several cities in Shinar/Sumer. From Nimrod's Sumerian-Babylonian empire, the Assyrian empire came. Nimrod built a tower in Babel in rebellion against God's command to spread out over the whole earth. I am choosing 2174 BC as the year when God changed their languages and scattered the people; hence Babel was not fit to be a capital, and the capital became Erech for a generation of 40 years before returning to Babel, renamed Babylon. Different kings of the various city-states ruled throughout Mesopotamia simultaneously, and Babylon did not always maintain dominance.

2260-2174	Nimrod	
2174-2135	Lig-Bagas of Erech/Uruk	
2135-2094	Dungi of Babylon	
2094-2081	Sumu-Abum 13	{contemporary of Ilushuma of Assyria}
2081-2045	Sumu-la-el 36	{contemporary of Erishum I of Assyria}
2045-2031	Sabium(Sabum) 14	
2031-2013	Apil-Sin 18	
2013-1994	Sin-muballit 19	
1994-1952	Hammurabi 42	{cont. of ZimriLim, and Siwe-palar-huppak of Elam}
1952-1916	Samsu-iluna 38	
1916-1888	Abi-eshuh(Abieshu) 28	
1888-1851	Ammi-ditana 37	
1851-1831	Ammi-saduqa(Ammisaduqa) 20	
1831-1800	Samsu-Ditana 31	{sack of Babylon by Mursili I about 1800 BC}
1800-1740	various Kassite and Sealand kings	
1740-1720	Agum II(Agum-Kakrime) 20	
1720-1700	Burnaburiash I	{treaty with Puzur-Ashur III of Assyria}
1700-1680	Kashtiliash III	
1680-1660	Ulamburiash	{conquered the first Sealand dynasty}

Chronology Overview

1660-1640	Agum III	
1640-1620	Karaindash	{contemporary of Amenhotep III of Egypt}
1620-1600	Kadashman-harbe I	
1600-1580	Kurigalzu I	{mentioned in Burnaburiash's II EA#9}
1580-1555	Kadashman-Enlil	{cont. of Amenhotep III in Amarna letters}
1555-1530	Burnaburiash II	{cont. of **Akhenaten** and Ashur-uballit I}
1530-1505	Kara-hardash	{grandson of Ashur-uballit of Assyria}
1505-1480	Nazi-Bugash(Shuzigash)	
1480-1455	Kurigalzu II	{son of Burnaburiash II; fought Battle of Sugagi with Enlil-nirari of Assyria}
1455-1430	Nazi-Maruttash	{contemporary of Adad-nirari I of Assyria}
1430-1405	Kadashman-Turgu	{contemporary of Hattusili III of the Hittites}
1405-1380	Kadashman-Enlil II	{contemporary of Hattusili III of the Hittites}
1380-1355	Shagarakti-Shuriash	
1355-1330	Kashtiliashu IV	{contemporary w Tukulti-Ninurta I of Assyria}
1330-1305	Enlil-nadin-shumi	{Assyria installed governor}
1305-1280	Kadashman-Harbe II	{Assyria installed governor}
1280-1255	Adad-Shuma-iddina	{Assyria installed governor}
1255-1230	Adad-shuma-usu	
1230-1205	Marduk-apla-iddina I	
1205-1180	Zababa-shuma-iddin	
1180-1155	Enlil-nadin-ahi	{defeated by Shutruk-Nahunte of Elam}
1155-1146	Marduk-kabit-ahheshu 9	
1146-1132	Itti-Marduk-balatu 14	
1132-1126	Ninurta-nadin-shumi 6	
1126-1103	Nabu-kudurri-usur 23 (Nebuchadnezzar I)	
1103-1100	Enlil-nadin-apli 3	
1100-1080	Marduk-nadin-ahhe 18	
1082-1069	Marduk-shapik-zeri 13	
1069-1046	Adad-apla-iddina 23	
1046	Marduk-ahhe-eriba (less than a year)	
1046-1033	Marduk-zer-X 13	
1033-1025	Nabu-shum-libur 8	
1025-1008	Simbar-shipak 17	
1008	Ea-mukin-shumi (less than a year)	
1008-1004	Kashu-nadin 4	
1004-987	Eulma-shakin-shumi 17	
987-985	Ninurta-kudurri-usur 2	
985	Shiriqti-shuqamunu (less than a year)	
985-979	Mar-biti-apla-usur 6	
979-943	Nabu-mukin-apli 36	

Pharaohs of the Bible

943	Ninurta-kudurri-usur (less than a year)
943-923	Mar-biti-ahhe-iddina 23
920-900	Shamash-mudammiq 20
900-888	Nabu-shar-ishkun I 12
888-855	Nabu-apal-iddin 33
855-819	Marduk-nadin-shum 36
819-814	Marduk-balatsu-iqbi 5
814-812	Bau-akh-iddin 2
812-801	(5 kings) 11
801-791	Ninurta-apla-X 10
791-781	Marduk-bel-zeri 10
781-773	Eriba-Marduk 8
773-760	Nabu-shum-ishkun II 13
760-746	Nabu-nasir(Nabonassar) 14
746-734	Nabu-nadin-zeri 10
733-732	Nabu-shum-ishkun III 1
732-729	Nabu-mukin-zer 3
729-727	{Babylon ruled by Assyrian Pul/Tiglath-pileser III}
727-722	{Babylon ruled by Assyrian Shalmanesar V}
722-710	Merodach-baladan I 12
710-702	{Babylon ruled by Assyrian Senacherib}
702	Marduk-zakir-shum (1 month)
702	Merodach-baladan II (9 months)
702-700	Bel-ibni 2
700-694	Ashur-nadin-shum 6 {Assyrian}
694-693	Nergal-ushezib 1
693-689	Mushezib-Marduk 4
688-669	{Babylon ruled by Assyrians Senacherib and Esharaddon}
668-648	Shamash-shum-ukin 20
648-626	Kandalanu 22
626	Ashur-etil-ilani-ukin
625-605	Nabopolassar 20
607-562	Nebuchadnezzar II 45 (20 months viceroy, 43 years sole king - Eusebius)
562-560	Evil-Merodach 2
560-556	Neriglissar 4 (brother-in-law)
556	Labosoarchad
555-554	Nabonidus 1
554-537	Belshazzar 7

Cyrus conquered Babylonia in 537 BC.

Clarity Hittite Kings List

The Hattians lived in Anatolia for roughly 100 years, and called it the land of Hatti. Anatolia covered much of central Turkey today. Northwest Turkey is where Troas and the city of Troy were located. The Hattian people were conquered by Sargon of Accad, one of the cities built by Nimrod.[127] Sargon's people intermarried with the Hattians and continued to call it the 'land of Hatti', but they became known as Hittites.

2230-2175	Sargon of Akkad	
2175-2135	Naram-Sin of Akkad	
2135-2105	Hermeli	
2105-2075	Harpatiwa	
2075-2045	Inar	
2045-2015	Warsama	
2015-1990	Anum-Herwa/Anum-Herbi	{contemporary of Zimri-Lim of Mari 8 years}
1990-1985	Pithana	
1985-1975	Piyusti	
1975-1965	Anitta	
1965-1955	Pamba	
1955-1945	Pithana	
1945-1935	Piyuti	
1935-1916	Anitta	
1916-1891	Tudhaliya	{likely "Tidal, king of nations" Gen. 14:1,9 - Abram}
1891-1861	Pu-Sarrumu	
1861-1831	Papadilmah	
1831-1811	Hattusili I, Labarna (ruling title) 20	{cuneiform tablet of year 6}
1811-1781	Mursili I 30	{deposed Samsu-Ditana in Babylon, victory at Aleppo}
1781-1751	Hantili I 30	
1751-1741	Zidanta I 10	
1741-1721	Ammuna 20	
1721-1716	Hazziya I 5	
1716-1691	Telipinu 25	
1691-1688	Alluwana 5	
1686-1683	Hantili II 3	
1683-1680	Tahurwaili 3	
1680-1660	Zidanta II 20	{30 Idrimi of Alalakh raided Hittite lands}
1660-1618	Huzziya II 42	
1618-1597	Muwatalli I	{treaty with Amenhotep II}
1597-1589	Tudhaliya 5	{Mitanni treaty with Amenhotep II (1622-1596 BC)}
1589-1574	Arnuwanda I 15	

---

127 Genesis 10:10

Pharaohs of the Bible

1574-1554	Tudhaliya II 20	{contemporary with Shausatar of Mitanni}
1554	Tudhaliya III	{prince Zita/Zikar wrote El Amarna letter EA #44}
1554-1532	Suppiluliuma I 22	{conquered Mitanni; EA #41 to **Ahkenaten**}
1532-1506	Mursili II 26	{10th year solar eclipse of 6 min. on April 20, 1522}
1506-1483	Muwatalli II 23	
1483-1476	Mursili III 7	{contemporary with Adad-nirari I (1484-1452 BC)}
1476-1436	Hattusili III 40	{peace treaty with Rameses II in 1459 BC}
1436-1408	Tudhaliya IV 28	
1408-1404	Arnuwanda III 4	
1404-1364	Suppiliuliuma II 40	
		{Hittites destroyed by Sea Peoples in 1364 BC.}

Clarity Mitanni Kings List

Except for Tushratta and Wasashatta, I've given these kings reigns of 25 years.

1685-1660	Kirta	
1660-1635	Parshatatar	
1635-1610	Shaushtatar	{sacked Ashur; contemporary of Idrimi of Alalakh}
1610-1585	Artatama I	{temp. Amenhotep II; treaty with Thutmose IV}
1585-1560	Shuttarna II (1578)	{sent daughter to wed Amenhotep III; EA #182-184}
1560-1542	Tushratta 18	{EA #17-29 (1552)}
1542-1517	Artatama II	{treaty with Suppiliuliuma I}
1517-1492	Shuttarna III	{contemporary with with Suppiliuliuma I}
1492-1467	Shattiwaza	{became vassal of Adad-nirari I of Assyria}
1467-1452	Wasashatta 15	

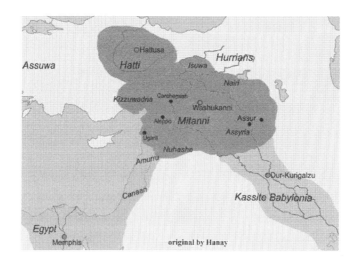

Clarity Alalakh Kings List

Yarim-Lim (Samsuiluna's brother, not Yarim-Lim I of Yamhad)
Amaitakum
Hammurapi (not Hammurapi of Yamhad)
Idrimi
Niqmepa (not Niqmepa of Yamhad)
Ilim-ilimma (not Ilim-ilimma of Yamhad)
Itur-addu

Mediterranean Civilizations

My dates for Egypt and other civilizations are not just considered to be 'high', but extremely 'high' by hundreds of years; yet they mesh much better with other chronologies. A period of Greek Bronze Age history is labeled Mycenaean for the city of Mycenae which was excavated. In archaeological terms, the mainland of ancient Greece is 'Helladic' to complement its Aegean island group, the Cyclades which was given the term Cycladic. Though LH refers to 'Late Helladic', LC usually refers to 'Late Cyprus', not 'Late Cycladic' unless so identified. Thankfully, those items produced on the island of Crete were referenced by their Minoan culture; so LM refers to 'Late Minoan'. Within the Cyclades is an island called Santorini which was known in ancient times as Thera. A major eruption of Thera destroyed eastern cities on Crete, disrupting Minoan trade, and is referred to as the Theran eruption or the Minoan eruption.

Crete (Minoan Island)

The primary culture on the island of Crete was Minoan derived from the name of king Minos of the Greek myth of the labyrinth and the minotaur. Like many cultures throughout the world, the Minoans began with high technology and skills which diminished over time. Their eras are roughly divided by their palace structures and subdivided into early, middle, and late; which were further divided by Roman numeral and letter designations: prepalatial (Early Minoan), protopalatial (Middle Minoan IB and MMII), neopalatial (MMIIIA to Late Minoan IB), and postpalatial (LMII to LMIIIC). The Theran eruption is the dividing point between LM IA and LM IB which I place at 1651 BC, ending Hatshepsut's reign.

Ancient Crete experienced several devastating earthquakes. There was a quake prior to the Minoan/Theran eruption during LMIA pottery. Ancient Greeks took advantage of the weakened state of the island and conquered or overwhelmed their population through immigration. Another larger quake halted production of LMII pottery. Then a more massive volcanic eruption completely annihilated the Minoan culture in 1310 BC, which was the 8th year of Rameses III when he fought the Sea Peoples seeking to immigrate.

Pharaohs of the Bible

Chronology of Canaan and the Levant

In 1848 archaeologists gave Europe and the fertile crescent a chronology based upon the tools found: stone, bronze, and iron. These ages were subdivided into early, middle, and late; which were further divided by Roman numeral and letter designations. Hence, MB IIB is "Middle Bronze two-b". But all these dates relied upon the 'stable' chronology of Egypt.

Due to "seal impressions of the early 13th Dyn. from an advanced but not late MB IIA (= MB I) context at Ashkelon (the moat between ph. 14/13, corresponding Tell el-Dabᶜa ph. G/4)" and "scarabs from the graves of the late MB IIA (= MB I) at Rishon Lezion dating to the 13th Dyn. Even the end of the MB IIC (= MB III) had to be pushed down into the 18th Dyn. to the beginning of or even early Thutmoside Period."[128] Dr. Maeir of Ber Ilan University dates MB IIA to 2000-1750 B.C.,[129] and is criticized for it being too high; whereas I date it from 1950-1850 BC but will be criticized for combining so many dynasties into my First Intermediate Period.

Though Crete, Cyprus, and Greece each have a Late III period, the Levant does not. I suggest the period from 1450 – 1300 BC should be the Late Bronze III period. This period is when the Israelites conquered Canaan and then were ruled by judges. The Israelites' enemies had iron chariots (Judges 1:19; 4:3), so it is also proper to label the period Iron IA. Even unto the time of king Saul in 1095 BC (I Samuel 13:19-22), the Israelites were still largely in the Late Bronze Age III; but they caught up under kings David and Solomon.

---

128 SCIEM2000 Project 11 Summary at http://www.oeaw.ac.at/sciem2000/Pr11main.html
129 Maeir, Aren M., "Jerusalem before King David: An Archaeological Survey from Pre-Historic Times to the end of the Iron Age," *The History of Jerusalem: The Biblical Period*, p. 40

Chronology Overview

Clarity Synchronization of Egypt, Mediterranean, and Levant

"Three different types of chronological designation are common and serve indiscriminately, side by side, in the relevant literature: dates expressed in years, dates given by Egyptian dynasties, and dates relating to archaeological periods. The result is confusion, because different scholars use different dates, according to their preference."[130]

My chart includes the years Before Christ, the Egyptian dynasty numbers, and the archaeological periods of the Levant as well as those of Crete, Cyprus, and Greece.

These are rough approximations based upon much conflicting data.

Date B.C.	Egypt Dynasty #	Crete	Cyprus	Greece	Levant (Israel)
2320-2200	1	EMI	ECI	EHI	EBIA-B
2200-2100	2	EMII	ECII	EHI	EBIIA-B
2100-2050	2	EMIII	ECIII	EHII	EBIII
2050-2000	3,7	MMIA	MCI	EHII	EBIV
2000-1950	4,5,7,9,12 [FIP]	MMIB	MCII	EHII-III	MBI
1950-1900	4,5,8,9,12,13	MMIIA	MCII	EHIII	MBIIA
1900-1850	4,5,8,9,10,12,13,14	MMIIB	MCII	MHI	MBIIA
1850-1800	6,9,10,11,12,13,14, pre-15,15,16 [SIP]	MMIIIA	MCIII	MHII	MBIIB
1800-1725	6,9,11-13,15,16,17	MMIIIB	LCIA1	MHIII	MBIII
1725-1650	17,18	LMIA	LCIA2	LHI	LBIA
1650-1575	18	LMIB	LCIB	LHI-II	LBIB
1575-1500	18	LMII	LCIIA-B	LHIIA	LBIIA
1500-1450	19	LMIIIA1	LCIIC	LHIIB	LBIIB
1450-1400	19	LMIIIA2	LCIIIA	LHIIIA	IronIA (LBIIIA)
1400-1350	19	LMIIIB	LCIIIB	LHIIIB	IronIA (LBIIIA)
1350-1300	Setnakht, Rameses III	LMIIIC	LCIIIB	LHIIIB	IronIA (LBIIIB)

Some extend LBII B to 1200 BC. Stone-age people groups are present throughout history.

---

130 Ben-Tor, Amnon, "Do the Execration Texts Reflect an Accurate Picture of the Contemporary Settlement Map of Palestine?" *Essays on Ancient Israel in its Eastern Context*, Eisenbrauns, 2006, p. 64

Date B.C.	Egypt's Pharaohs	Philistine	Israel	Israel's Leaders
1300-1200	Rameses III-XI	Iron IB	(LBIIIB)	Deborah - Jepthah
1200-1100	Herihor (Smendes I) – Menkheperre (Psusennes I)	Iron IC	(LBIIIC)	Izban - Samuel
1100-1000	Smendes II (Amenemope) – Osorkon I	Iron IIA	(LBIIIC) Iron I Iron IIA	King Saul King David King Solomon
1000-900	Osorkon I – Sheshonk III	Iron IIB	Iron IIB	King Solomon – Ahab/Jehoshaphat

Iron Age II lasts until 600 BC, and Iron Age III lasts until the birth of Jesus Christ.

Canaanite cities destroyed by Thutmose III were mostly LBI.
Canaanite cities destroyed by Joshua were mostly LBII with a few Iron IA.
Canaanite cities destroyed by Kings Saul and David were mostly Iron IC-IIA, and many new Israelite cities were established which were mostly Late Bronze IIB-IIIC with a few Iron I. After pushing the Philistines back to the coast, king Saul built a fortress[131] with a casemate wall in the Elah Valley to establish his western border (see page 279). David fortified Hebron, his first capital, and Jerusalem, his second capital. Otherwise, it was king Solomon who did the most fortress building with casemate walls and 6-chamber gates in Hazor, Megiddo, and Gezer. Kings Rehoboam and Jeroboam fortified towns for a few years before the attack of pharaoh Shishak in 970 BC.

So the Israelite cities destroyed by Shishak could have ranged from LBIIB-IIIC (newly created under Israel's monarchy) to Iron I (recently captured Canaanite cities by kings Saul and David and newly occupied by Israelites) to Iron IIB (newly constructed fortified cities of kings Solomon, Rehoboam, and Jeroboam).

"The ages have been classified as follows with some slight variation in dates by different archaeologists:
The Early Bronze Age, 3000 to 2000 B.C.
The Middle Bronze Age, 2000 to 1600 B.C.
The Late Bronze Age, 1600 to 1200 B.C.
The Early Iron I Age, 1200 to 900 B.C.
The Early Iron II Age, 900 to 600 B.C.
The Early Iron III Age, 600 to 300 B.C."[132]

---

131 Elah fortress is known as Khirbet Qeiyafa at http://en.wikipedia.org/wiki/Khirbet_Qeiyafa
132 Kyle, Melvin Grove, *Excavating Kirjath-Sepher's Ten Cities*, Eerdman's, 1977, p. 39

Shem's Pharaohs

"And the sons of Noah, that went forth of the ark, were Shem, and Ham, and Japheth: and Ham is the father of Canaan."
(Genesis 9:18)

Father of Empires: Hebrews, Arabians, Chaldeans, Assyrians, and Syrians

Shem's great-grandson, Eber became the namesake of the Hebrew people and their language. Eber's son Joktan and his sons settled in Arabia. Joktan's son Diklah settled in the plains just west and north of the Persian Gulf which became known as Chaldea and Chaldee by possibly transposing Di-klah to klah-Di. The city of Ur was built originally as a port on the Persian Gulf among the marshy estuaries of the Tigris and Euphrates rivers.

The land of Mesopotamia, 'land of two rivers', (Tigris and Euphrates) was populated by several other clans as well. Shem's son Asshur had established the Assyrian empire in the northern part of the rivers.[133] Further north in Syria, Peleg's grandson, Serug founded the city Sarugi west of (C)Harran.[134] Serug's son was Nahor, and Nahor's son was Terah, and they all lived in Syria. Terah moved to Ur. Terah's sons were Haran, Nahor, and Abram.

Eber's great-great-grandson, Terah, lived in Ur of the Chaldees, but he wanted to return to Syria. Terah's son Haran died in Ur. Terah took his son Abram, who had married Sarai, and Abram's nephew Lot with him as he travelled north along the two rivers of the fertile crescent to Harran[135] (in what is now Turkey). Terah died there; and Abram, Sarai, and Lot continued to Canaan and Egypt in 1921 BC. I will pursue important links between Shem and Abram and Isaac. Shem is the pivotal man who could have taken the Genesis (1:1-6:9) *toledoth* scrolls from Noah[136] and handed them to Abraham or Isaac.

Shem, himself, may have travelled widely among his extended family during his long life of 602 years, documenting genealogies. Shem was born in 2448 BC, 100 years before the flood, and he died in 1846 BC, 502 years after the flood began. Abram was born in 1996 BC; therefore Shem's life overlapped Abram's life by 150 years, but I don't think they ever met because Abraham did not sign his name to writing any of his history in Genesis. Isaac was born in 1896 BC; therefore Shem's life overlapped Isaac's life by 50 years. I will present facts and supposition about how their lives may have intersected.

---

133 Genesis 10:11-12, 22
134 Cooper, Bill, *After the Flood*, New Wine Press, 1995, p. 178
135 Genesis 11:31
136 Noah's father, Lamech, overlapped Adam's life by 56 years; thus their could have been a transfer made.

Shem's Descendants and Events

Birth year BC

2448	(Shem)	2348 (Noah's Flood)	
2346	Arphaxad	(Sumerian empire)	
2311	Salah	(Nimrod founded Babel)	
2281	Eber		**Ice Age**
2247	Peleg	(Earth divided into nations)	Snow-blitz
2217	Reu	2244? (Tower of Babel begun)	
2185	Serug	(Chaldean empire)	Glacial Max.
2155	Nahor	2174? (Babel tower destroyed)	
2126	Terah		
1996	Abram	By 1924 sea levels had risen from final ice melt.	End of Ice Age
1896	Isaac		
1836	Jacob		
1745	Joseph		

Shem lived 602y

*And Abram passed through the land to the place of Sichem, to the plain of Moreh. And the Canaanite was then in the land. And the LORD appeared to Abram, and said, To your seed will I give this land: and there built he an altar to the LORD, who appeared to him. And he removed from there to a mountain on the east of Bethel, . . . And Abram journeyed, going on still toward the south. And there was a **famine** in the land: and Abram went down into Egypt to sojourn there; for the famine was grievous in the land. (Genesis 12:4-10)*

When Abram was 75 years old (1921 BC) and was "*going on still toward the south*" in Canaan, a severe famine occurred. This is the first mention of famine after Noah's flood. I think God sent Shem ahead of time into Egypt to prepare for the famine Abram encountered, just as God later sent Joseph ahead of time to preserve Abraham's descendants from the third Biblical famine.

From Building Noah's Ark to Building Djoser's Pyramid

God gave Noah about 100 years to build the ark and prepare for the world-wide flood.[137] During a large portion of that time, Shem helped his father build the ark. Cages and stalls had to be built for the various animals in such a way that eight people could care for them for a year. According to Jewish scholar Ben-Uri, the ark was a 6,000 ton ship with a 15,000 ton cargo capacity.[138] The logistics to prepare and store a year's provisions for the family and the roughly 16,000[139] animals was a daunting task. About four million liters of water and 2,500 tons of food[140] had to be stored with a means for easy distribution.

Noah's family of eight people likely hired workmen, and Shem would have become accustomed to directing workmen on the enormous project. Shem had the mathematic and scientific knowhow and experience to build on a massive scale. He also knew how to safely store and distribute food on a massive scale, and to protect it from violent thieves. I think God told Shem to approach Djoser with a plan for a huge food distribution fortress which would include a large pyramid tomb for a monument to his forethought which would save the people. The monument would assure Djoser's name was not forgotten, but Shem's name just means "name", so maybe Djoser called him *Imhotep*, "one who comes in peace".

Djoser's step-pyramid was the first pyramid built in Egypt. Shem trained his engineers well, and many pyramids were built afterwards. He built south of the delta flood plains in high and dry Saqqara, which was close enough to the Nile to dig canals to supply the area.

---

137 Genesis 5:32-8:22
138 Freidler, Y., "What the Ark was really like" *Jerusalem Post*, October 10, 1967
139 Woodmorappe, John, *Noah's Ark: A Feasibility Study*, Institute for Creation Research, 1996
140 Woodmorappe, pp. 48-49

Pharaohs of the Bible

The complex sits on 37 acres surrounded by a 285 X 145 X 20 cubit high[141] protection wall with only one entrance. The wall protected grain silos in the southern and northern ends of the complex, and much of the wall and complex still stand after 4,000 years. Even more remarkable are the miles of tunnels dug beneath the complex at a depth of 27.5 feet deep.

Djoser's Food Distribution Fortress

The eleven southern bunker silos are 15 cubits (28.6 m; 93.8 feet) deep with 2 cubit (1 m) extensions above ground. Slanted shafts from the opening at the bottoms of each connect them to the one silo which has a staircase[142]; thus the older grain was used first. Grain was discovered at the bottom of each of them. Pictures of servants carrying grain sacks up stairs are found in Thebes and at the tomb of Iti.[143] More granaries and stored food were found beneath the north wall area. In the pyramid eleven air shafts (16 cubits deep) on the east side of the pyramid connect to tunnels and hundreds of rooms, called galleries. Burials were found in five northern galleries; but in six southern galleries, forty thousand stone storage jars of food were found. Some air shafts could be closed during the heat of the day to keep the food stuffs from spoiling; an ultimate food cellar. One tunnel connects the pyramid rooms underneath the grand courtyard to the southern "tombs" staircase, thus enabling stewards to bring food stuffs up to buyers waiting in the grand courtyard above.

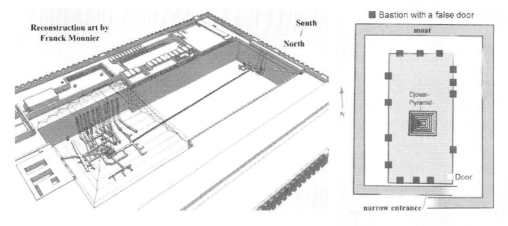

Canal and Moat: building, protection, and provision

There is a forty meter wide trench surrounding Djoser's complex; the quarried rock was used as wall masonry, encased by limestone. Saqqara was about five km from the Nile. The limestone quarry of Tura was about twelve km down the Nile. The most ancient canal was made at Aswan on the Upper Nile, but many others have been discovered. The current

---

141 (149 X 76 X 10.5 m; or 489 X 149 X 34.4 ft)
Reconstruction after Lauer of Djoser complex on http://www.narmer.pl/pir/dzeser_en.htm
142 Wyatt, Mary, *Joseph in Egypt*, http://www.wyattnewsletters.com/joseph/joseph07.htm accessed 2006
143 *Revealing God's Treasure* video based on Ron Wyatt's discoveries, http://www.youtube.com/watch?v=vaN2acVMGC8&feature=player_embedded# accessed 2/10/10

Maryoutiya canal could have been built upon an ancient one which led to Djoser's complex so as to float limestone directly to the site. The limestone from Tura was the finest and whitest of all the Egyptian quarries, so it was used for facing stones for the richest tombs. It was long since pillaged from Djoser's tomb, thus exposing its mud bricks to erosion.

The moat would also be useful for loading and unloading grain at the three southern bastions. Those using animals to carry the grain would be directed to one of the other bastions while the seller entered the only door to make arrangements with the merchants.

Merchant Transactions

When a buyer walked through the only entrance into Djoser's complex, he entered a narrow walkway bounded by forty beautiful columns. The entrance colonnade had 46 stalls, one for each nome; and later for merchants of various languages to make transactions. They haggled over the price for the quantity of grain or dried goods, and then the merchant handed the buyer a token or papyrus with the quantities of his purchase in exchange for his 'money', and was told which bastion it would be delivered to. The buyer sent his steward back out the door to get the pack animals or boat to the correct bastion while the buyer continued through the colonnade to the courtyard to hand his token/papyrus to those who would weigh out the amounts. Locals in the courtyard watched as their purchases were taken up to the wall platform to be delivered over the wall to their awaiting animal handlers or barge captains.

Djoser's entrance colonnade

Archers posted along the wall would assure purchases were received and not stolen. Underneath the west wall platform were the barracks for this fortress. At the northern end Lauer found the brick remains of what he called the 'house of the master builder'.[144]

Wealthy buyers might be accommodated in one of the large guest homes, otherwise smaller guest homes were available. Socket holes atop faux columns on the building's facade would receive the wooden handle of standards for nomes, and later, an occupant's homeland. (Note three sockets on top of the left picture of the stone guest house on the next page.) A few opulent guest houses were made with solid stone interiors as lasting memorials. Some archaeologists say the others were filled with rubble when they were constructed, and were never meant to be occupied.[145] I think they were functional for hundreds of years, and filled with debris much later to keep out vagrants.

---

144 Winston, Alan, *The Step Pyramid of Djoser at Saqqara in Egypt, Part V: The Mortuary Temple, Serdab, Northern Courtyard and the West Mounds*, http://www.touregypt.net/featurestories/dsteppyramid3.htm, accessed February 2010

145 Houses of North and South on ancient-egypt.org accessed February 8, 2010.

Pharaohs of the Bible

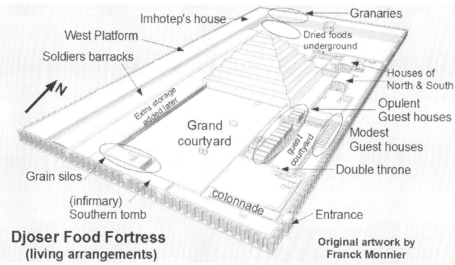

Djoser Food Fortress
(living arrangements)

Original artwork by
Franck Monnier

The "house of the north" and "house of the south" had limited interior access to wall niches with the rest solid stone. The "house of the south" had one concave-fluted column which resembled a dried giant hogweed (which grows to 5 meters, or 16.4 feet, and was used as a rigid building material) native to the hills and plains fed by the mountain streams near Lake Van south of Mount Ararat[146]; its capital was not found. Giant hogweed would have been a common building material to Shem after the flood. The "house of the north" had three concave-fluted columns (preceding the identical Greek Doric columns by 2,000 years) with papyrus capitals representing the Nile delta. When pharaoh visited, he might have stayed at the mortuary with its large walled courtyard furthest away from all the business, and with easy entrance to the pyramid. Should the pharaoh wish to meet his guests, there was a double throne dais at the southern end of the guest courtyard. The arched roofs of all these houses resemble the reed structures still made in ancient Sumeria (now Iraq). The reed "guest house" is *mudhif* in Arabic.

Oppulent Stone Guest House

Reed Guest House (*mudhif*)

---

146 Rohl, David, *Legend: The Genesis Of Civilisation*, Butler & Tanner, United Kingdom, 1998, p. 376

Imhotep, Architect and Builder of Djoser's Complex

On the base of a statue of Pharaoh Djoser, with his Horus name, Netjerikhet, is an inscription which reads, "Imhotep, Chancellor of the King of Lower Egypt, Chief under the King, Administrator of the Great Palace, Hereditary Lord, High Priest of Heliopolis, Imhotep the Builder, the Sculptor, the Maker of Stone Vases . . ." (Djoser also had construction projects in Heliopolis where Imhotep may have been a high priest. King of Upper Egypt at this time was Netjerikhat Netiqerty.) Djoser's complex is the first sculpted stone monument. The 10.5 meter high Tura limestone wall encloses 15 hectares; an area 2.5 times larger than the Old Kingdom town of Hierakonpolis.[147] In some of the recessed paneling decoration, the cut stones mimic the earlier mud-brick royal monuments in Egypt and Sumeria, by being the same dimensions. The stonework mimics other objects as well.

Upon entering the sole door to the complex, one proceeds through a small foyer to an open stone door that appears to be made of cedar which welcomes the visitor into the colonnade. The 13 cubit (6.8 m; 21.6 foot) high columns in the entrance colonnade are convex-fluted to resemble bundled reeds topped by leather, with smooth and rounded log beams resting on top of them. After exiting a double columned vestibule and walking straight through the grand courtyard, a visitor would see the grain silos, and looking up would see a row of giant hooded cobra heads warning of severe judgment to all thieves who could be imprisoned below in the "infirmary".

Imhotep, the Physician

I labelled the "southern tombs" of Djoser's Complex the "infirmary" because a wooden stretcher and "medicine" jars were discovered there[148], and because Imhotep was well-known as a physician. Manetho wrote of Imhotep's medical skill: he had "the reputation of Asclepius" (the Greek god of medicine). The main air shaft culminates in a granite space too small to bury a man. The walls of the galleries are lined with blue faience, which reminds me of a hospital's sterile tile walls. Faience is the first high technology ceramic, often glazed with crushed copper to yield a blue-green finish. Djoser was known to have mined copper and turquoise from Sinai. There is a large pink granite room which could be used as a morgue or tomb.

In a different section of the complex, a million mummified ibis in earthenware pots were discovered.[149] One of Imhotep's many titles was "The Great One of the Ibis;" it was known as his sacred bird. Long after his death (about 1580 BC), pilgrims bought ibis sacrifices to purchase their healing. They also bought baboon sacrifices to purchase wisdom and knowledge, as well as hawk sacrifices. "These galleries connected to a pit that extends down to a funerary chamber which contains an empty coffin. . . . this chamber belonged to a

---

147 Bard, Kathryn A., *An Introduction to the Archaeology of Ancient Egypt,* Oxford, Blackwell Publishing Ltd, 2008, pp. 128-33
148 South Chapel and Tomb on ancient-egypt.org accessed February 8, 2010.
149 Wilkinson, Raymond, *Search for Imhotep*, Aramco World Magazine, July/August 1971 pp. 32-36

Pharaohs of the Bible

very large mastaba tomb which contained a second chamber full of broken stone vessels, and in the tomb's storerooms were jars whose clay-stoppers had the seal impression of Djoser!"[150] Archaeologists still search for the remains of Imhotep. Shem died 502 years after the flood (outliving Abram), but there is no record of his burial.

Deities Maat and Thoth

Maat is the concept of truth and justice. Maat embraced the "balance" of the universe: heavenly movements and the cycle of the seasons; as well as fair and honest transactions with true weights ("balance"). From the 5th dynasty onwards, the vizier responsible for justice was called the "Priest of Maat"; and judges wore images of Maat later on.[151]

Maat was deified as a goddess with an ostrich feather in her headdress. Her consort is Thoth who stands upon a foundation of truth with a papyrus scroll. Thoth is *dhwty* in glyphs, and also means 'ibis'; though he is also depicted as a baboon. Thoth has the head of an ibis and its curved beak. Pharaohs are often depicted with Maat's feather of truth or standing upon the foundation platform of Maat to emphasize their role in upholding the laws of the Creator. Both Maat and Thoth hold an 'ankh' (the cross shape with a loop) which represents eternal life.

Thoth is credited with the invention of hieroglyphs and writing, as well as possessing all knowledge of science, religion, philosophy, and magic. During Moses' time, the power of words was considered magical, and the title "scribe-magician" (Heb. *khartome,* meaning to engrave, write, and astrology) came into favor.[152] Thoth was the "vizier who reveals Maat and reckons Maat; who loves Maat and gives Maat to the doer of Maat".[153] He weighed the heart of the deceased against Maat's feather of truth to see if eternal life was warranted.

Imhotep, the Scribe

The Egyptian language is a combination of Semitic and Hamitic languages[154] from Noah's sons Shem (Middle East) and Ham (Africa). From Egypt's beginning with Mizraim, hieroglyphic writing, "god's speech", was established, but it was very time intensive. During the 3rd dynasty, a ligatured script of quickly written clustered signs, known as

---

150 Wyatt, Mary, *Joseph in Egypt,* http://www.wyattnewsletters.com/joseph/joseph08.htm accessed 2006
151 Morenz, Siegfried, Egyptian Religion, translated by Ann Keep, Cornell Press, 1992, pp. 117-125
152 Exodus 7:11; Roccati, "Scribes," p. 65-66; Jan Quaegebeur, "On the Egyptian Equivalent of Biblical Hartummîm," *Pharaonic Egypt: The Bible and Christianity* (edited by Sarah Israelit-Groll; Jerusalem: Magnes Press, 1985)
153 Black, James Roger, *The Instruction of Amenemope: A Critical Edition and Commentary*, p. 131
154 Black, ibid., pp. 119-120

hieratic, was developed by Imhotep.[155] Several hieratic symbols are almost identical to the Hebrew letters of beth, gamlu, he, mem, and 'ayin.[156] Imhotep was also credited with improving scrolls, possibly with better preservation.

Various Imhotep statues as a scribe reading a scroll.

The statues of Imhotep depict him as a seated scribe reading a scroll. These statues all show Imhotep with a large head and a slight smile. Statues of Imhotep were made well into 300 BC; he was a much loved person. It is possible that Shem/Imhotep was reading to the Egyptians from the pre-flood *toledah* scrolls. They heard Shem read Creator *Elohim* (which is a plural form of deity) spoke light and sky into existence, and they attributed this to Thoth and other gods. This may be why Egyptian creation legends are similar to Genesis.

Egyptologist James Henry Breasted stated of Imhotep, "He was the patron spirit of the later scribes, to whom they regularly poured out a libation from the water-jug of their writing outfit before beginning their work." Each scribe's kit contained a small idol of Thoth as a baboon. Imhotep was later deified, and I think Thoth and Imhotep were based upon Shem. Shem, like Noah, was a *"preacher of righteousness"* (*maat*) and eternal life.[157] God may have given the Egyptians the ankh cross of eternal life through Shem/Imhotep as a prophetic symbol of *"the Seed"* (Messiah) who would defeat Satan and death by dying on a wooden cross for sins and rising from the dead three days later conquering sin and death;

---

155 Baines, *Literacy*, p. 577
156 Goedicke, Hans, "A Bamah at the First Cataract" in Time-lines *in honor of Bietak* Vol. 2, 2006, p. 119-127
157 II Peter 2:5

Imhotep, the Maker of Stone Vases

Among the other great accolades given to Imhotep, "maker of stone vases" doesn't seem as astounding until you know that these hard stone vases were hollowed out with machines and tools our current technology has yet to replicate. I suggest Shem retrieved vases, and the tools to make them, from the ark to use them again for food storage with their unique preserving properties.

Amazed by the craftsmanship of the 30,000+ diorite, basalt, quartz crystal, and schist stone vases found beneath Djoser's step pyramid, Graham Hancock wrote, ". . . many of the vessels were tall vases with long, thin, elegant necks and widely flared interiors, often incorporating fully hollowed-out shoulders. No instrument yet invented was capable of carving vases into shapes like these . . ."[159]

Djoser Stone Vase

Engineer and machinist, Christopher Dunn, diagrammed how he worked a similar 'vase' in the much easier medium of stainless steel for the aerospace industry by using several L-shaped tools assisted by a powerful light and a small mirror.[160]

After Sir William Flinders Petrie made careful measurements inside and outside of the *Pyramids and Temples of Gizeh* (1883), he ascertained, "The forms of tools were straight saws, circular saws, tubular drills, and lathes." Petrie continued, "That the Egyptians were acquainted with a cutting jewel far harder than quartz, and that they used this jewel as a sharp pointed graver, is put beyond doubt by the diorite bowls with inscriptions of the fourth dynasty, of which I found fragments at Gizeh . . ." Petrie especially noted, "The diorite bowls and vases of the Old Kingdom are frequently met with, and show great technical skill . . . this was certainly not a chance result of hand-work . . . and it is clear proof of the rigid mechanical method of striking curves." Petrie's photos show machine marks of pieces worked on lathes, as well as those with tubular drill cores still in place.[161]

Professor Peter Lu applies his knowledge of physics and engineering to ancient artifacts. In 2005, Lu reported evidence that the Chinese used diamonds to polish ceremonial stone burial axes as early as 2500 BC.[162] I think Noah and Shem taught the Chinese not only how to cut and polish stone, but how to make the machines to do it. A year prior, Lu presented evidence that ancient Chinese craftsmen used precision compound machines to craft spiral

---

158 Genesis 3:15 and I Corinthians 15:3-4 and John 3:14-17
159 Hancock, Graham, *Fingerprints of the Gods*, Three Rivers Press, 1996, p. 333
160 Dunn, Christopher, *Giza Power Plant: Technologies of Ancient Egypt,* 2010, pp. 170-171
161 Picture of Plate XIV at http://www.ronaldbirdsall.com/gizeh/petrie/photo/plate14.html
 Also see http://www.theglobaleducationproject.org/egypt/articles/hrdfact3.php
162 Lu, Peter J.; Yao, N.; So, J. F.; Harlow, G. E.; Lu, J. F.; Wang, G. F.; Chaikin, P. M., "The Earliest Use of Corundum and Diamond, in Prehistoric China," *Archaeometry* 47, 2005, pp. 1–12

grooves on Chinese jade burial rings around 800 – 400 BC.[163]

Shem's Pharaohs

Though Shem's long life (2446-1846 BC) encompassed the reigns of dozens of pharaohs, he mainly interacted with pharaohs of the third dynasty for the purpose of preserving Abraham during the first Biblical famine after Noah's flood.

2062-2043	Sanakhte (Nebka) [Thinis]	7th dynasty in Thinis
2043-2014	**Djoser**-It (Netjerykhet) [Memphis]	Netjerikare (Netiqerty)
2014-2007	**Sekhemkhet** (Djoser-Ti)	Menkare (Neferka)
2007-2001	Khaba	Neferkare II (Nefer)

Djoser

Djoser moved Egypt's capital from Thinis north to Memphis. Djoser's food fortress in Saqqara, south of Memphis, was completed and fully stocked with grain and dried fruit. Djoser died and was entombed there instead of in an earlier tomb started in Abydos, south of Thinis/Tunis. Abydos is near the modern towns of el-'Araba el Madfuna and al-Balyana.

Sekhemkhet

Imhotep's name is only found upon the pyramid complexes of Sekhemkhet and Djoser. A graffito with Imhotep's name is on the enclosure wall of Sekhemkhet's complex.[164] The walls, the underground tomb, and the pyramid's first step were completed when Sekhemkhet died after the seventh year of his reign. Sekhemkhet's pyramid is also known as the buried pyramid. Many other pharaohs built their memorial tombs near Djoser's.

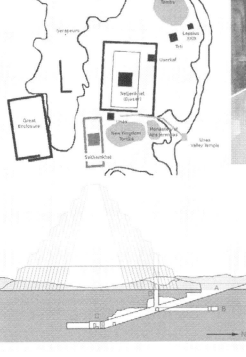

Imhotep, above, was the architect of step-pyramid complexes for pharaohs Djoser and Sekhemkhet. Sekhemkhet's underground structure, left, was much more simple than Djoser's, as it was only for burial.

---

163 Lu, Peter J., "Early Precision Compound Machine from Ancient China," *Science* 304 (5677), p. 1638, 2004
164 Malek, Jaromir 'The Old Kingdom' in *The Oxford History of Ancient Egypt* by Ian Shaw (ed.) Oxford

Khaba

No engravings or graffitos with Imhotep's name were discovered at Khaba's layer pyramid near Giza, but based upon its similarities, Imhotep may have also been the architect for it as well. If that is so, Imhotep would have been building pyramids in Egypt for 40 years, from 2043-2002 BC.

Noah and Shem in China

Imhotep's mummy has never been found, and I don't think it ever will be. I think Shem was summoned to China by his father. In Bishop Ussher's *Wall Chart of World History* he noted that Noah, Fohi/Yao, was the first emperor of China and that he invented a symbolic mode of writing. The Great Flood occurred during the life of Yao according to the Chinese.

> "At the time of the miracle is said to have happened that the sun during a span of ten days did not set, the forests were ignited, and a multitude of abominable vermin was brought forth. 'In the lifetime of **Yao [Yahou]** the sun did not set for full ten days and the entire land was flooded.'"[165]

The ancient Chinese language is incredibly complex with hundreds of pictograms, ideograms, and phonetic characters. The ancient Chinese characters for "boat" include the pictograms for 'vessel', 'eight', and 'mouth/person'. "Create" is comprised of 'dust/mud', "p'ieh"/life, and 'walking'.[166] "Devil" is composed of 'man/son', 'garden/field', and 'secret/private'; but "tempter" places the "devil" pictogram under 'cover' of two 'trees'. In the "*garden of Eden*" Elohim created Adam from the dust and breathed into him the breath of life. YHWH gave Adam the choice of eating from the tree of life or the tree of knowledge of good and evil which would bring death. The devil tempted Eve, and Eve and Adam ate of the tree which brought death into the world.[167] These correlations were first noted in 1950 by K.T. Khang in *Genesis and the Chinese*, and then improved by his grandson, C.H. Kang who is a minister of the gospel in Singapore.

University Press, Paperback 2002, p. 92
165 Velikovsky, Immanuel, *Worlds in Collision*, NY, Doubleday, 1950, p. 114
166 Kang, C.H., and Nelson, Ethel R., *The Discovery of Genesis: How the Truths of Genesis were found hidden in the Chinese Language*, Concordia Publishing House, 1979, pp. xii-xiii and 3-4
www.bibleetnombres.online.fr/genesis.pdf
167 Genesis 2 and 3

Though the Chinese did not build towers or pagodas until the Buddhist era[168], they have a unique word for "tower". "United" is a combination of 'mankind', 'one', 'mouth/speech'. When placing "grass" over "united", it becomes the verb "to undertake". "Tower" combines "to undertake" with clay/brick.[169] The combination of pictograms for 'thousand mouth/tongue' and 'right leg' equal the Chinese word for "rebellion/confusion".[170] The Chinese word for "migration" combines 'great', 'division', 'west', and 'walking'.[171] This indicates that thousands of people migrated to China after the Tower of Babel division of languages in 2174 BC. I think Noah obeyed God's division of the land at Peleg's birth (2247 BC) and went to China, and that God gave him the ability to create the written Chinese language after the Tower of Babel.

"Confucius, born in 551 B.C. . . . sifted through the records of remote antiquity and drew out those principles which he felt worthy of promotion. His models of virtue were Yao and Shun."[172]

Emperor Yao

Shun was also called Shennong/Shin-Nong ('divine farmer'), the second emperor of China. According to Ussher's *Wall Chart of World History*, Shin-Nong taught "animal husbandry, the method of making bread from wheat, wine from rice, etc. Perhaps Shem of the Bible." Shennong is also considered the father of Chinese medicine,[173] and he reformed their calendar.

In Ussher's chart Noah and Fohi/Yao died in 1998 BC. "The Tî said, 'Come, you Shun. I have consulted you on (all) affairs, and examined your words, and found that they can be carried into practice;--(now) <u>for three years</u>. Do you ascend the seat of the Tî.' Shun wished to decline in favour of some one more virtuous, and not to consent to be (Yâo's) successor. On the first day of the first month, (however), he received (Yâo's) retirement (from his duties) in the temple of the Accomplished Ancestor."[174]

Emperor Shun

---

168 Durant, Will, *The Story of Civilization: Our Oriental Heritage*, Simon and Schuster, 1942, p. 224-225
169 Kang and Nelson, p. 106
170 Kang and Nelson, *The Discovery of Genesis,* p. 107
171 Kang and Nelson, p. 109
172 Kang and Nelson, p. 13
173 http://en.wikipedia.org/wiki/Shennong and http://en.wikipedia.org/wiki/Great_Flood_(China)
174 Part two of the *Books of Yu*: Book 1, the Canon of Shun, p. 38. "Accomplished Ancestor" may be Adam. http://www.sacred-texts.com/cfu/sbe03/sbe03009.htm accessed on 6/9/11

If Shem left Egypt in 2002 BC, and arrived at his father's home in China in 2001 BC, three years later would be 1998 BC. Yao had divided China into nine provinces. Shun "instituted the division (of the land) into twelve provinces, raising altars upon twelve hills in them. He (also) deepened the rivers"[175] to avoid flooding (from glacial melt, I think).

"He exhibited (to the people) the statutory punishments, enacting banishment as a mitigation of the five (great) inflictions; with the whip to be employed in the magistrates' courts, the stick to be employed in schools, and money to be received for redeemable offences. Inadvertent offences and those which could be ascribed to misfortune were to be pardoned, but those who transgressed presumptuously and repeatedly were to be punished with death. 'Let me be reverent! Let me be reverent!' (he said to himself.) 'Let compassion rule in punishment!'"[176]

In Ussher's chart, the 146 year reign of Shun/Shin-Nong ended in 1852 BC and Shem died six years later in 1846. If Shem had brought copies of the *toledoth* genealogies with him, then the Chinese people had the first ten chapters of the book of Genesis 500 years before Moses compiled and completed it.

One of Japheth's clans made the trek in 2172 BC to what is now called the Kiangsi province of China, and are known as the Miatsu. Edgar Truax translated their oral history and discovered, ". . . they were in possession of surprisingly accurate recollections of the Creation and the Flood, and some of the close detail of their accounts coincides almost identically with the Genesis record."[177] The Miatsu recited their rich lineage at weddings and funerals through Jephthah, son of Noah, back to the first man called 'Dirt' because God made him from dirt.[178]

I suggest that Shun relinquished his throne in 1852 BC because Yahweh commanded him to take the *toledoth* scrolls to Isaac in Canaan. Shem was capable of engineering and navigating a sailing vessel for transport from China to the Gulf of Aqaba. [Khety of the 9th dynasty was overseeing trade on the Mediterranean Sea 100 years prior (from 1956-1886 BC).] Shem may have trained Isaac about what types of things to include in his toledoth by having Isaac write about his father Abraham in a new scroll. Or possibly Isaac showed Shem the unsigned scroll which Abraham wrote. Shem may have prophesied about the sons Isaac would have who would continue the awesome responsibility of recording the history of God's chosen people.

---

175 Part two of the *Books of Yu*: Book 1, the Canon of Shun, p. 40
176 Part two of the *Books of Yu*: Book 1, the Canon of Shun, pp. 40-41 footnote: "Those five great inflictions were-branding on the forehead; cutting off the nose; cutting off the feet; castration; and death, inflicted in various ways."
177 Cooper, Bill, *After the Flood*, New Wine Press, England, 1995, p. 243
178 Ibid., p. 244-5; and Genesis 2:7

Abraham's and Isaac's Pharaohs

*"And there was a famine in the land:
and Abram went down into Egypt to sojourn there;
for the famine was grievous in the land."*
(Genesis 12:10)

1996 Abram was born in Ur of Chaldea
1921 God's promise to Abram in Canaan; Abram continued on to Egypt due to famine
1919 Abram returned to Hebron in Canaan
1918 Abram and Lot separated due to abundance of flocks
1916 Lot dwelt in Sodom
1913 Abram rescued Lot and received blessing of Melchizedek
1910 Ishmael was born when Abram was 86 years old
1896 Isaac was born when Abraham was 100 years old; his new name given one year prior
1891 Ishmael mocked Isaac when Isaac was weaned, beginning 400 years of persecution
1821 Abraham died

Abram's Call to Canaan

Terah is eight generations from Shem. Abram's father, Terah, move the family from Ur back to (C)Harran. Terah died there; and Abram, Sarai, and Lot continued to Canaan.

*So Abram departed, as the LORD had spoken to him; and Lot went with him: and <u>Abram was seventy and five years old when he departed out of Harran</u>. . . . And Abram passed through the land to the place of **Sichem**, to the plain of Moreh. And the Canaanite was then in the land. <u>And the LORD appeared to Abram, and said, To your seed will I give this land</u>: and there built he an altar to the LORD, who appeared to him. And he removed from there to a mountain on the east of **Bethel**, . . . And Abram journeyed, going on still toward the south. And there was a **famine** in the land: <u>and Abram went down into Egypt to sojourn there</u>; for the famine was grievous in the land. (Genesis 12:4-10)*

Abram may have only stayed a month or so in each place in Canaan as he was "*going on still toward the south*" when the first severe famine hit. But God had prepared food storage in Egypt ahead of the famine, so Abram travelled across the Sinai Peninsula to the Nile delta. At one time all of North Africa was as fertile as the Nile delta. This was the first among many droughts and famines which slowly turned North Africa's lush grasslands into deserts. In Genesis 13:10 Lot compared the well-watered plain of Jordan to lower Egypt.

Amenemhat I (1954-1924 BC) of the 12th Dynasty

Amenemhat I was not born of royal parentage. He may have been stationed by Khety of the 9th dynasty at the junction of the Nile and its road to the fayyum. Khety called his capital in the east delta *Ḥaʔat-Wūrat 'Great House', later known as Avaris. Since other dynasties were forming at the beginning of the First Intermediate Period, Amenemhat I established his own dynasty, and named his capital city Amenemhat-Itjtawy, "Amenemhat, the seizer of two lands". To protect Khety's lucrative trade network from bedouin stealing goods from boats travelling to Avaris, Amenemhat I built the Wall (*shur* in Hebrew) of the Ruler, a north/south barrier from the Bitter Lakes to El-Ballah Lake. Djoser built forts at El-Ballah Lake and Wadi Tumilat to protect the shipping of his copper and turquoise mining operations. Wadi Tumilat connects the Nile to the Red Sea's Gulf of Suez and its other arm the Gulf of Aqaba, which ended at the port of EzionGeber at the time (the port for the Timna Valley copper mines).[179] Copper and turquoise also came from Egypt's mines in Serabit el-Khadim since at least the 3rd dynasty.[180] Amenemhat I sought to expand the vast Mediterranean trade into Nubia. He campaigned against Nubia in his 29th year (1925 BC), and subdued the people of Wawat, then built forts at Semna, Kerma, and Halfa in Nubia.

Prophecy of Neferty to Sneferu (1977-1953 BC):
"The river of Egypt is dry, the water is crossed on foot.
…The herds of foreign lands will drink
from the rivers of Egypt ...
Then a king will come from the South,
Ameny, the justified, by name
Son of a woman of Ta-Seti, child of Nekhen.
He will take the white crown,
He will wear the red crown ...
Asiatics will fall to his sword,
Libyans will fall to his flame,
Rebels to his wrath, traitors to his might,
As the serpent on his brow subdues the rebels for him. [note picture above]

Funerary relief of Amenemhat I

He will build the **Walls-of-the-Ruler**
To bar Asiatics from entering Egypt
if they request water in the proper manner, to let their flocks drink.
Right is returned to its place, and evil is expelled." [analyzed in its entirety on pages 392-394]

---

179 http://www.bibleplaces.com/timnavalley.htm Timna has inscriptions of pharaohs from Seti I to Ram. V.
180 There is a bas relief of Sekhemkhet. http://www.touregypt.net/featurestories/serabit.htm

Abram's Arrival in Egypt (1921 BC)

Abram and Sarai encountered forts and troops in the Sinai Peninsula and as they passed around El-Ballah Lake on their approach to the Nile delta. As they travelled down the Pelusiac to the Giza plateau, Djoser's pyramid was not the first one they saw. Their eyes beheld the largest building on earth: Khufu's great pyramid in Giza. It created the builder's desired effect; immediate fear. A pharaoh that powerful could do whatever he wanted. As they came closer, they also saw the largest stone monument on earth with a pharaoh's head and a lion's body. The sphinx was made by Khufu's son, Djedefre.[181]

Djedefre built the sphinx to guard Khufu's pyramid

*And there was a **famine** in the land: and Abram went down into Egypt to sojourn there; . . . when he was come near to enter into Egypt, that he said to Sarai his wife, Behold now, I know that you are a fair woman to look on: Therefore it shall come to pass, when the Egyptians shall see you, that they shall say, This is his wife: and they will kill me, but they will save you alive. Say, I pray you, you are my sister: that it may be well with me for your sake; and my soul shall live because of you. (Genesis 12:10-13)*

Sarai was Abram's half sister of the same father, but different mothers. Abram was seventy-five years old and Sarai was sixty-five years old.[182] Abram lived to be 175 and Sarai to 127, so 65 was closer to middle-age than old age. Even so, Sarah is equated with beauty in the New Testament as well (I Peter 3:3-6). I suggest Abram and Sarai went to the grain merchants at Djoser's Complex in Saqqara built by Imhotep, and then decided to stay.

---

181 According to Vassil Dobrev: http://www.independent.co.uk/news/media/answer-found-to-riddle-of-sphinx-6156137.html
182 Genesis 17:17 They are ten years apart in age.

Pharaohs of the Bible

Djedefre and Khafre, Khufu's Sons

Djedefre honored his father by placing ready made materials for at least two 143 foot long solar barges beneath the wall surrounding Khufu's great pyramid. Dr. Vassil Dobrev documented how Djedefre further honored Khufu by placing his face on the Great Sphinx. It was Djedefre who designed the first sphinx, using his chief queen as a model. Hetpheres II was beautiful and long-lived like Sarai. She was likely born during Sneferu's reign (1978-1954) and died during Shepseskaf's (1866-1862 BC).

Hetpheres II as a sphinx (possibly the first) Daughter of Khufu, and wife of Djedefre

And it came to pass, that, when Abram was come into Egypt, the Egyptians beheld the woman that she was very fair. The princes also of Pharaoh saw her, and commended her before Pharaoh: and the woman was taken into Pharaoh's house. And he entreated Abram well for her sake: and he had sheep, and oxen, and he asses, and menservants, and maidservants, and she asses, and camels. (Genesis 12:14-16)

Diorite statue of Khafre

Khufu's son Khafre came to the throne upon the death of his brother Djedefre in 1920 BC. Another year *"came to pass"*, when several of Khafre's sons told him of Sarai, and guards took her by force and pharaoh gave Abram an extravagant bride-price for her. In today's vernacular, some might say Abram 'pimped out' his wife, but God intervened with plagues. Notice the morality of this pharaoh in the next scripture. Could Imhotep's influence have made the Egyptians attentive to the Creator God as Shem told them how Elohim destroyed his wicked world by a flood?

And the LORD plagued Pharaoh and his house with great plagues because of Sarai Abram's wife. And Pharaoh called Abram and said, What is this that you have done to me? why did you not tell me that she was your wife? Why said you, She is my sister? so I might have taken her to me to wife: now therefore behold your wife, take her, and go your way. And Pharaoh commanded his men concerning him: and they sent him away, and his wife, and all that he had. (Genesis 12:17-20)

Abraham's and Isaac's Pharaohs

These are the first recorded plagues of God, and they happen to be in Egypt where more would come. They are not described, but Khafre immediately realized they were on account of Sarai. Unlike the pharaoh of the exodus, Khafre's heart is open and obedient to God. Khafre had not had sexual relations with Sarai, and did not require his gifts back, but sent them under armed escort back to Canaan in 1919 BC. The famine lasted one to two years.

Abram in Hebron; Lot in Sodom

Abram, Sarai, Lot, and their former servants and herds plus their newly acquired ones returned to the place between Bethel and Ai where they had camped two years prior. But the land could not support all their new livestock, so they separated. Lot chose the fertile plain of Jordan near Sodom, and Abram moved to the plain of Mamre in Hebron. God told Abram, *"Lift up now your eyes . . . For all the land which you see, to you will I give it, and to your seed for ever. And I will make your seed as the dust of the earth: so that if a man can number the dust of the earth, then shall your seed also be numbered."* (Gen. 13:14-16)

After two years (1916 BC), Lot took up residence in Sodom. Then in 1913 BC a war between nine kings occurred (Genesis 14); and Lot, his family, and all his possessions were taken away to Damascus as booty.

Warrior Abram's Victory Celebration at King's Dale, Salem

Abram took 318 of his own trained servants and men of the families of Mamre, Aner, and Eschol, and they pursued the victors north all the way to Hobab outside of Damascus and attack them at night and slaughtered them. Abram's band made a long 140 mile march back with all the people and goods. Kings from all around Canaan, who had been paying tribute to the northern kings for years, went out to greet the conquering heroes. They met them at a place called the plain of the valley (*shaveh*) which was also known as the *"king's dale"*; named after the *"king of Salem"*. According to Josephus, it was located "Two stadia from Jerusalem"[183] or about a quarter mile. Another author placed it at the bottom of the mount of Olives.[184] Both were correct, as it lies at the southern end of the Kidron Valley below Gihon Spring. The *"king's dale"* is referred to again when *Absalom* ('father of peace') placed a pillar there in II Samuel 18:18.

[Children throw rocks at this monument below the Temple Mount which is associated with Absalom.]

---

183 Flavius, Josephus, *Antiquities*, vii. 10, 3
184 Hotting, Edward, *Cippi Hebraici*, p. 26

Pharaohs of the Bible

Salem, the city of the Great King

The old aqueduct from the Gihon Spring dates back to 2,000 BC.[185] It emptied into the lower pool. The Gihon Tower and Warren's Shaft were dated from pottery shards to at least 1700 BC, and a similar tower guarded the upper pool.[186] Ian Stern noted the size of the foundation stones of these towers was not equalled again until the time of Herod.[187] Salem was a well-fortified city with water for weary travellers and their animals. Because it was a city of peace, it was a neutral spot for kings to assemble. Salem encompassed three peaks: Mount Zion and two on Mount Moriah with "*the place of the skull*" at the highest elevation and the altar rock below it, where Abraham would later return to offer up Isaac.

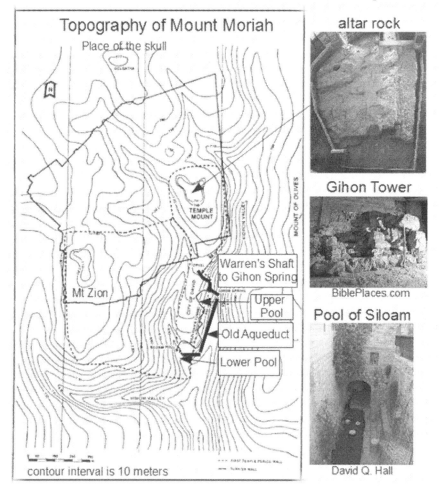

---

185 Geva, Hillel, "Jerusalem, Water Systems of Biblical Times" accessed from
   http://www.jewishvirtuallibrary.org/jsource/Archaeology/jerwater.html on 5/13/10
186 "Warren's Shaft" on Wikipedia accessed at http://en.wikipedia.org/wiki/Warren%27s_Shaft
187 Stern, Ian on "Warrior King" episode of Zola Levitt Presents viewed on 5/13/10

Abram Blessed by Melchizedek, King of Salem

*And Melchizedek king of Salem brought forth **bread** and **wine**: and he was the priest of the most high God [El Elyon]. And he blessed him, and said, Blessed be Abram of the most high God [El Elyon], possessor of heaven and earth: And blessed be the most high God [El Elyon], which has delivered your enemies into your hand. And he gave him tithes of all. (Genesis 14:18-20)*

Salem or *Shalem* means friendly, just, peaceable, quiet, perfected, and whole. This priest of El Elyon exemplified the kingdom of God in which is "*righteousness, peace, and joy*".[188] Melchizedek particularly blessed El Elyon, a new title for Elohim, for delivering enemies into Abram's hand. Abram rescued those who had been stolen by destroying those who had stolen them. In a similar manner, the Messiah will destroy kings attacking Israel when He returns in His wrath. In a messianic psalm, David wrote:

The LORD said to my Lord, Sit you at my right hand, until I make your enemies your footstool. The LORD shall send the rod of your strength out of Zion: rule you in the middle of your enemies. . . . The LORD has sworn, and will not repent, <u>You are a priest for ever after the order of Melchizedek</u>. The Lord at your right hand shall strike through kings in the day of his wrath. (Psalm 110:1-5)

That Melchizedek is a pre-incarnation of the Son of God is verified by Jesus Himself (Mat. 22:42) and Peter (Acts 2:32-36) and the author of the letter to the Hebrews.

For this Melchizedek, king of Salem, priest of the most high God, who met Abraham returning from the slaughter of the kings, and blessed him; To whom also Abraham gave a tenth part of all; first being by interpretation King of righteousness, and after that also King of Salem, which is, King of peace; Without father, without mother, without descent, having neither beginning of days, nor end of life; but made like to the Son of God; stays a priest continually. (Hebrews 7:1-3)

Shem had descendants; mysterious Melchizedek did not. So Abram's life is saved by the 'man of peace', Imhotep/Shem; and then he is blessed by the "*King of peace*", who is Jesus. This king of righteousness and peace also provided bread and wine to Abram, which Yeshua also offered to His disciples on Passover to receive Him as the Lamb of God.

And the king of Sodom said to Abram, Give me the persons, and take the goods to yourself. And Abram said to the king of Sodom, I have lift up my hand to the LORD, the most high God, the possessor of heaven and earth, That I will not take from a thread even to a shoelatchet, and that I will not take any thing that is yours, lest you should say, I have made Abram rich: Save only that which the young men have eaten, and the portion of the men which went with me, Aner, Eshcol, and Mamre; let them take their portion. (Genesis 14:21-24)

---

188 Romans 14:17

Ishmael and Isaac

Eight years passed since God told Abram to leave his country and that He would make him a great nation, yet Sarai remained barren. Abram talked to God about it, and God reconfirmed that Abram's seed would become as numerous as the stars.[189] After two more barren years, Sarai gave her Egyptian handmaid, Hagar, to Abram as a concubine to produce Abram an heir.[190] Abram agreed, and Hagar conceived and gave birth to Ishmael the following year (1910 BC) when Abram was 86.[191]

Thirteen years later (1897 BC), God commanded Abram to circumcise all the males in his household as a perpetual covenant.[192] God reconfirmed His promises to Abram again, and changed his name from 'father' to 'great father' (*Abraham*), and his wife's name to 'princess' (*Sarah*) because the son born through her would produce kings of nations.[193] Abram laughed at the thought of a son being born to a couple at 100 and 90 years old. Sarah later laughed as well[194] when God came again in physical form to confirm His promise yet again. When God's promised seed became reality, they named him 'laughter' (*Isaac*).[195]

Though Abraham pleaded with God not to destroy Sodom if He could find at least ten righteous men there,[196] Sodom and the wicked cities of the plain were destroyed with fire and brimstone (1898).[197] So Abraham moved south from Hebron and sojourned with his flocks and herds between Kadesh (near Seir's Petra) and Shur ('wall' in Nile delta), and also in Gerar (between Gaza and Beersheba). Abimelech, the king of Gerar, decided to take Abraham's "sister" into his household, but did not have relations with her. God immediately closed all the wombs of the women there and revealed to the king in a dream that He would kill him unless he restored Sarah to her husband, which he did along with a bride-price fit for a princess, and permission to settle peacefully in the land.[198] Then God visited Sarah and she conceived and gave birth to Isaac[199] in 1896 BC, during the reign of Khafre, who built the second largest pyramid next to Khufu's.

Abraham offers Isaac; Sarah dies; Isaac weds; Abraham weds again

While the 4th dynasty pharaoh Menkaure was busy constructing the third pyramid at Giza next to those of Khufu and Khafre, Abraham was settling well disputes with Abimelech

---

189 Genesis 15:1-6
190 Genesis 16:1-4
191 Genesis 16:15-16 In Gen. 16:7 Hagar was on the "way to Shur". *Shur* means 'wall', Amenemhat's wall.
192 Genesis 17:23-27
193 Genesis 17:15-17
194 Genesis 18:12
195 Genesis 21:3
196 Genesis 18:16-33
197 Genesis 19:1-29
198 Genesis 20:1-18
199 Genesis 21:1-5

and the Philistines at Beersheba.[200] In 1876 BC, when Isaac was twenty years old, Abraham prepard to offer him to God on Mount Moriah, but God provided a ram as a substitute.[201] Seventeen years later, Sarah died. Abraham bought the cave of Machpelah in Ephron's field in Hebron for a permanent burial place,[202] now known as Cave of the Patriarchs. Abraham then secured a wife for Isaac, so he would be comforted after the death of his mother.[203] And Abraham married Keturah, and she bore him six sons.[204]

Isaac and Rebekah

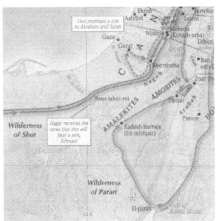

Sarah died in 1859 BC when Isaac was 37 years old. To comfort him, Abraham sought out a wife for Isaac by sending his servant to his kin in Padan-Aram (southeast Turkey). Isaac took his mother's tent and left the town of Beersheba for the wilderness of the Negeb ('south'). He dwelt at *Beer-laha-roi*, the well the "Living One sees" as Hagar called it, near the road to Shur.[205] Isaac went out to the field to meditate.[206] In 1856 BC when he was 40 years old, Isaac saw a caravan of camels approaching with his new bride.

And Isaac brought her into his mother Sarah's tent, and took Rebekah, and she became his wife; and he loved her: and Isaac was comforted after his mother's death. (Genesis 24:67)

Second Famine of the Bible (1856 BC)

<u>And there was a famine in the land, beside the first famine that was in the days of Abraham</u>. And Isaac went to Abimelech king of the Philistines to Gerar. And the LORD appeared to him, and said, <u>Go not down into Egypt</u>; dwell in the land which I shall tell you of: Sojourn in this land, and I will be with you, and will bless you; **for to you, and to your seed, I will give all these countries**, and I will perform the oath which I swore to Abraham your father . . . And Isaac dwelled in Gerar: And the men of the place asked him of his wife; and he said, She is my sister . . . And it came to pass, <u>when he had been there a long time</u>, that Abimelech king of the Philistines looked out at a window, and saw . . . Isaac was sporting with Rebekah . . . and said, Behold, of a surety she is your wife . . . What is this you have done to us? one of the

---

200 Genesis 21:22-34
201 Genesis 22:1-19
202 Genesis 23
203 Genesis 24
204 Genesis 25:1-2
205 Genesis 16:6-16 Wilderness of Shur ('wall') is in Sinai Peninsula and has a road back to Wall of the Ruler.
206 Genesis 24:62-63

people might lightly have lain with your wife, and you should have brought guiltiness on us. And Abimelech charged all his people, saying, He that touches this man or his wife shall surely be put to death. Then Isaac sowed in that land, and received in the same year an hundred times: and the LORD blessed him. (Genesis 26:1-13)

The first Biblical famine was connected to Abraham's chronology of going into Egypt in 1921 and returning to Canaan about 1919 BC, but this second famine does not provide a clear time-frame. Genesis 25 includes Abraham's death (1821 BC) listed prior to the birth of Isaac's twin sons in 1836 BC, so it is not in chronological order; neither is Genesis 26, parts of which must have occurred prior to 1836 since Isaac and Rebekah were still a childless couple in that chapter[207], able to use the ruse of brother and sister as his father and mother had.[208] This famine had to occur between 1856-1836, and I choose 1856 BC because Isaac was in the wilderness and had just married, and they carried on the ruse with Abimelech "*a long time*". Twenty years is the maximum amount of time possible. Since the first famine was two years or less, I suggest Isaac's famine lasted 3 years (1856-1853 BC). A "*long time*" after the famine began (twenty years), the truth of Isaac and Rebekah being man and wife was made known, and Isaac sowed a field and reaped greatly.[209]

Nomarchs of Egypt under Sneferu (1977-1953 BC)

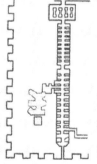

Djoser's complex

As the population of Egypt grew, the land was divided into districts known in Egyptian as *sepats* (akin to "satraps", but *nomes* in Greek);[210] as extra help was needed in governing Egypt. When Imhotep built Djoser's complex (3rd dynasty), he made a colonnade with a groups of 26 stalls and a group of 20 stalls which may have equalled the number of nomes at the time in upper and lower Egypt respectively. The delta still has twenty. Each *sepat*/nome had its own god and/or goddess. The governor of a nome, a 'nomarch', was given various responsibilities: lay and collect taxes, maintain canals and dams, organize expeditions, represent pharaoh in the local temples, administer justice, and secure the borders.

Huni was the last pharaoh of the 3rd dynasty. Sneferu married Huni's daughter, thus making a smooth transition from the 3rd to the 4th dynasty. In the "Hall of Domains" of Sneferu's Valley Temple next to his bent pyramid, the nomes of Upper Egypt are depicted on the west wall and the nomes of Lower Egypt are depicted on the east wall.[211]

---

207 Genesis 25:21
208 Genesis 20:2 Destruction of Sodom and Gomorrah was in 1898, then Abraham and Sarah sojourned in the Negev, then went to Gerar; which I place in 1896. *Abimelech* means "father of king" and could be a title; but it could be the same man encountered in 1856, who would be looking for a similar deception.
209 Genesis 26:8-12 They were infertile until 1836 "*a long time*" (v8) and so could keep up the ruse.
210 Daniel 6:1-7 Districts were called satraps in Babylon.
211 Leeman, Diane, *The Nomes of Ancient Egypt*, p. 1-3, accessed 5/12/113, http://content.yudu.com/Library/A1ikn5/TheNomesofAncientEgy/resources/40.htm

Metjen began as Huni's scribe, but became a wealthy nomarch under Sneferu. While the average Egyptian of his day had a 100 square meter living space, Metjen had a 10,000 square meter mansion as nomarch of the Nile delta. The tomb of Metjen contains the earliest surviving biography of a nomarch. A false door inscription in his elaborate tomb lists the names of the nomes he oversaw; six throughout the Nile delta, one of the east Fayyum, and one which contained the entrance road to the western oases (not pictured below). Nomes 4 and 5 were considered one nome which were later subdivided.[212]

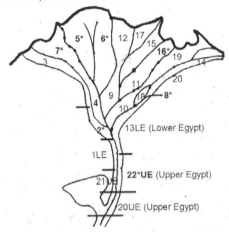

Metjen, nomarch of 2, 4-8, 16, and 22UE

"The provinces in Lower Egypt varied, growing over time as marshes were converted to cultivated land and as the river branches of the Nile Delta shifted over the centuries."[213]

I conjecture Metjen ruled over the Egyptian-controlled delta at the time, including nome #3 and lands and forts to the west; with most of the eastern delta inhabited by Canaanites who ran Egypt's import-export business, and Nubians who provided protection. To bring Metjen's considerable wealth back into the family, Sneferu placed his son Netjeraperef as overseer of nomes #4-7.[214] The balance between delegation of power to local entities with centralized government has always been tenuous. During the period of Great Pyramid Builders, nomarchs made elaborate tombs because Egypt was wealthy.

Hereditary Nomarchs of Asyut during 9th - 10th dynasties (1956-1776 BC)

Khety was the founder of the 9th dynasty from Siut/Asyut to Herakleopolis just south of the Fayyum and eventually onto Herakleopolis Parva on the Mediterranean (the "Northland" of the delta). A namesake nomarch, who had married King Khety's daughter, recalled the death of his nomarch father Khety, and how his mother, Sit, ruled as nomarch until he matured. King Khety mourned for nomarch Khety, whose son Khety, eventually ruled as nomarch. Same names is part of what makes Egypt's chronology so difficult.

"Saith [Kheti] .... born of Si[t] .... night watch .... in glorifying his name. .... [Then mourned] the king himself, all Middle Egypt and the Northland .... The king himself and the counts were gathered together [for the burial. He was interred in his tomb of the] highlands. The son of his daughter made his name to live and glorified [him]. .... [His daughter ruled in Si]ut, the worthy stock of her father [reigned in the city] .... beloved of

---

212 Leeman, Diane, *The Nomes of Ancient Egypt*, Australia, 2005, p. 4
213 Leeman, Diane, *The Nomes of Ancient Egypt*, Australia, 2005, p. 10
214 Smith, W. Stevenson, *The Old Kingdom of Egypt*, Cambridge Press, 1962, p. 21

> Upwawet, rejoicing in doing good to [her city] .... beloved of the king, his favorite. The city was satisfied with that which she said. .... [She acted as] lord, until her son became strong-armed ...."[215]

Sit's son, Khety, had the good sense to name his son, Tefibi. Tefibi was a nomarch of Asyut during the transition of the cFIP to the cSIP under the reign of 10th dynasty kings Wahkare Khety II (1870-1861 BC) and Khuy (1881-1856 BC). Tefibi recounted his battles against the southern nomes. Tefibi may have won, but Khuy defintely lost.

> "The first time that my soldiers fought with the southern nomes, which came together southward as far as Elephantine and northward as far as /////////, [they] smote them (?)] as far as the southern boundary."[216]

Tefibi named his son Khety, who succeeded him as nomarch of Asyut. Tefibi's son wrote how king Merikare (1861-1856 BC) of the 9th dynasty purposed to restore temples. Thus the 9th and 10th dynasties were intertwined.

> "Thy city-god loves thee, Tefibi's son, Kheti. He hath [presented (?)] thee, that he might look to the future in order to restore his temple, in order to raise the ancient walls, the original places of offering, to [///] the venerable ground, [/// /// ///] which Ptah built with his fingers, which Thoth founded, for Upwawet, lord of Siut, [by (?)] command of the king, the ruler (HqA) of the Two Lands, the king of Upper and Lower Egypt, Merikere, to make a monument for the souls of Anubis . . . that he might repeat Sed Jubilees . . ."[217]

Hereditary Nomarchs of 12th dynasty (1954-1772 BC)

Twelfth dynasty pharaoh Nubkhaure Amenemhat II is said to have overturned nomarch appointments for hereditary succession based upon text in the tomb of Djehutyhotep declaring himself the "**hereditary** prince".[218] The reality is that nomarchs and foreign vassals would voluntarily or involuntarily send their children to the palace school, Kap, to be trained to assume government positions, which also secured the loyalty of the nomarch or vassal.[219] So nomarchs were based upon heredity and appointment. Amenemhat II appointed Khnumhotep II as nomarch of Oryx in the 19th year of his reign (1871 BC). He was the son of the previous nomarch, but on the tomb of Khnumhotep II, he stated, "He **appointed** me, the Majesty of the Horus, . . . the king of Upper and Lower Egypt, Nubkhaure."[220] His service continued into the 6th year of Senusret II (1852 BC).

---

215 James Henry Breasted *Ancient Records of Egypt* ; Part One, §§ 407 ff
216 J. H. Breasted, *Ancient Records of Egypt*, Part One, § 393ff
217 J. H. Breasted, *Ancient Records of Egypt*, Part One, § 398ff
218 Breasted translation of Tomb of Djehutyhotep.
219 Ryholt, K.S.B., *Political Situation in Egypt during the SIP*, 1997, p. 93
220 Breasted translation of Tomb of Djehutyhotep.

Eight of the 39 tombs cut into the cliff at Beni Hasan are for "the Great Overlords of the Oryx Nome," and the tomb of Khnumhotep II was the last and most elaborate. The wall of Khnumhotep's II grand chapel shows a group of Asiatic men, women, and children in colorful clothing moving to Egypt.[221] The "hill country" could have been Edom, Canaan, or Amurru; or all three. So many Asiatic immigrants came to Egypt during the 2nd Biblical famine (1856-1853), this nomarch recorded their migration.

Asiatics moving from the "hill country"

Many of these Canaanites settled the area around Wadi Tumilat. A Wadi Tumilat "survey found that exactly half of the 42 survey sites contained MB II cultural material remains and that all these sites came into existence during the Early Second Intermediate Period, if not already at the end of the Twelfth Dynasty (several of the sites including MB IIa cooking pots) . . . These sites mark the first extensive settlement of the Wadi."[222]

> "It was the increasing power of the nomarchs that led to the disintegration of the Old Kingdom. The nomarchs used to be buried with the pharaohs, but closer to 2200, they were building their own elaborate tombs. While the pharaoh had a small bodyguard, the nomarchs commanded their own armies; priests made gifts of land to their friends and family, thus diminishing the pharaoh's resources. <u>The climate may also have changed during this period.</u>"[223] -C. Wright

> "Mira Bar-Matthews of the Geological Survey of Israel had found a unique record of past climates, locked in the stalactites and stalagmites of a cave near Tel Aviv. What they show is a sudden and dramatic drop in rainfall, by 20%. . . . And the date? 2,200 BC."[224]

The 2200 BC 'climate change' is my ice age date. Geologist Gerard Bond determined from ocean floor cores "one mini ice age occurred at 2,200 BC"[225] which decreased precipitation. I place glacial maximum of Bond's ice age at 2174 BC, but it had nothing to do with the nomarchs. The early nomarchs of Abram's time were content during the first Biblical famine (1921-1919 BC) during the reigns of Djedefre and Khafre. The next famine

---

221 Rohl, David, *Pharaohs and Kings: A Biblical Quest*, Crown Publishers Inc., New York, 1995, p. 359
    The text on the wall explained there were 37 people in all led by the chief of the hill country, Abishai.
222 Ryholt, K.S.B., *Political Situation in Egypt during the SIP*, 1997, p. 293, fn 1042
223 Wright, C., History of Ancient Egypt: a concise overview of Egyptian history,
    http://www.scinet.cc/articles/egypt/historyofegypt.html, accessed 5/12/11.
224 "Disaster that struck the ancients", *BBC NEWS*, Thursday, 26 July, 2001, 12:12 GMT 13:12 UK
225 "Disaster that struck the ancients", *BBC NEWS*, Thursday, 26 July, 2001, 12:12 GMT 13:12 UK

was caused from too much water inundating crops and grasslands, and brought about the nomarch war and the Ethiopic War; and Djoser's complex came into use once again.

On my time-line the second Biblical famine occurred at the end of the concurrent 4th and 5th dynasties of my cFIP in which there was a war between nomarchs. Nomarch Ankhtifi declared Edfu in nome #3 had become like a marsh. This famine inundated Upper Egypt with too much water. In Koptos, nome #5, during the cFIP there is a text that a man "stood in the doorway of his excellency the overseer of priests Djefy handing out grain to (the inhabitants of) this entire town to support it in the painful <u>years</u> of famine."[226]

Queen Khentkaus I of 4th dynasty (1861-1859 BC) and Seth II

Just prior to the second famine, the last pharaoh of the 4th dynasty ruled and died. Though Egyptologists give this queen a Roman numeral I, in my time-line she rules after queen Khentkaus II of the 5th dynasty who was married to Neferirkare Kaki. Both queens had elaborate pyramid complexes and mortuary cults. Since the pyramid complex of queen Khentkaus I of the 4th dynasty was built closely to that of Menkaure's, she was likely his daughter. In the mortuary temple of queen Khentkaus I, she was depicted as a pharaoh with a false beard, (nemes) striped head-cloth, and the (uraeus) cobra diadem.[227] She and Shepsekaf were brother and sister. Shepsekaf had a short reign, and so Khentkaus I assumed pharaonic titles and duties after he died.

Besides her title of "king's mother", queen Khentkaus I had a title which could be translated "mother of two dual kings". If her father had married her to Wahkare Khety II, who ruled the 13th nome of Anubis from Asyut, and she gave birth to twins Merikare and Neferkare VII; then Queen Khentkaus I would have been "mother of two dual kings". Khety, the father of Wahkare Khety II, wrote *Teaching for King Merykare* to his grandson. He wrote of trade to distant lands guaranteed by his statues, and of constant war in Egypt:

> "Dispatch your statues to a distant land of which they shall not render an inventory, for he who destroys the goods of an enemy will suffer.
> The enemy cannot be quiet (even) within Egypt, but troops shall subdue troops, in accordance with the prophecy of the ancestors about it, and men fight against Egypt (even) in the necropolis."[228] [analysis of full text on pages 381-385]

Sneferu had opened trade with Byblos for cedar. I suggest Khentkaus I requested that Byblos send her an overseer for the cedar trade, and that these foreigners became the pre-15th dynasty by default when the queen died. Egypt may have been trading grain from Djoser's food complex at Saqqara for the cedar, and so the pre-15th dynasty would be well

---

226 Seidlmayer, Stephan, 'The First Intermediate Period' in *The Oxford History of Ancient Egypt*, (ed. Ian Shaw), Oxford University Press, paperback 2002, p. 129
227 Thamphthis/Djedefptah, wikipedia, accessed 5/16/11 This 'Djedefptah' may have tried to usurp the throne, or it may be part of her throne name. Her name, Khentaus, in a cartouche has not been found.
228 Translation by R. O. Faulkner, William Kelly Simpson (ed.), *The Literature of Ancient Egypt*, New Haven and London, 1973, pp. 180-192. http://www.reshafim.org.il/ad/egypt/merikare_papyrus.htm

aware of that facility when the famine hit. Only the vowel 'I' remains of the first pre-15th 'king', but the second name was Seth [II]. It might be because of his actions to save the people with grain during the famine that later pharaohs adopted his name (like Seti).

Pharaohs and Nomarchs of Second Biblical Famine (1856-1853 BC)

During the reigns of Seth II, Unas, Amenemhat II, Khuy, Intef I, Intef II, Merikare, Neferkare VII, and Sheshi there was a severe famine in Egypt which brought about war. Theban kings Intef I (1878-1856 BC) and Intef II (1866-1817 BC) defeated nomarch Ankhtifi's attack at Thebes, and acquired his southern nomes #2-3. Ankhtifi, of Hierakleonpolis (ancient Nekhen), had already taken the city of Edfu (nome #2) from its governor. Ankhtifi allied himself with Neferkare Terure VII and the prince of Elephantine (at the first cataract under Nubian rule) to attack Thebes. Intef I waited until the attacking soldiers were hungry and thirsty, and then his army killed their armies, though the leaders escaped.

Pharaohs and Nomarchs of Second Biblical Famine (1856-1853 BC)

14th & pre-15th Dyn. in Nile Delta	4th & 6th Dynasty in Memphis	12th Dynasty in Itjtawy	9th and 10th Dynasties in Herakleopolis Magna	11th Dynasty in Thebes 13th dynasty various cities	Other Nomes
1860-1856 I... (1st king of pre-15th)	1861-1859 (4th) Khentkaus I	1890-1852 Amenemhat II	1886-1856 (5th) Wenis/Unas	1878-1856 Intef I (11th) 1866-1817 Intef II	Ankhtifi of Mo'alla nome 3 - Hierakonpolis
1874-1821 Sheshi (14th)	1856-1854 Seth II (pre-15th)	1858-1839 Senusret II	1861-1856 Merikare (9th) 1861-1856 Khuy (10th)	(Nedjemibre) (13th) (Sewesekhataway)	Djehy, priest in nome 5 of Koptos
1854-1850 Sunu... (pre-15th)	1856-1844 Teti (6th)		1856-1845 Neferkare VII (9th)	11y Neferhotep I, Sihathor 9y Sobekhotep IV, 5y Hori	Djehutyhotep, nome 15 of Hermopolis

King Unas (1886-1856 BC), last pharaoh of 5th dynasty in Nen-Nesu

King Unas, sometimes called Wenis, had two wives and seven daughters, but no sons. Unas built his pyramid complex next to Djoser's complex. I conjecture this was because Unas had to use Djoser's food complex to feed starving people depicted along his causeway (pictured below). Carved into Unas' pyramid walls were incantations and directions to overcome evil forces of the underworld and to reanimate his body in the hereafter; these became known as "pyramid texts". Some of these spells were written by magicians from Byblos to ward off poisonous snakes. Moshe Bar-Asher of Hebrew University said, "Most all the words found [in these texts] are also found in the Bible."[229] Yeshiva University's Steiner added, "A lot of the characteristics of Hebrew that we know from the Bible are already present in these texts."[230] Thus the written Hebrew language was well established by at least 1900 BC. [See Appendix B, page 395 for early Hebrew text during the reign of Amenemhat III. For the chart on Nile water levels at Semna, see page 397.]

---

229 Milstein, Mati, "Ancient Semitic Snake Spells Deciphered in Egyptian Pyramid," *National Geographic News*, February 5, 2007

230 Ibid.

Pharaohs of the Bible

Emaciated Egyptians on relief in the pyramid of Unas. Left, is Unas' funerary chamber. Below, Unas built his complex next to Djoser's complex wall.

Kagemni: nomarch of Unas, vizier to Teti

It is assumed Unas named Teti as his successor before his death. A man named Kagemni served Unas as a judge and nomarch after beginning his career during the reign of his predecessor, Djedkere Isesi. Kagemni became overseer of judges and vizier to Teti and married his daughter, Nebty-nebu-khet. Kagemni built a lavish mastaba of eight rooms with raised reliefs including his biographical information. The outer walls were cased in expensive white Tura limestone.[231] Besides milking a cow, another scene shows hyenas being force-fed in a manner similar to that in the tomb of Mereruka.[232]

Cow milked in Kagemni's mastaba

Teti (1856-1844 BC), first pharaoh of 6th dynasty in Memphis

Teti reigned during the famine, the battle against Thebes, and the Ethiopic War in the delta. When Sheshi of the 14th dynasty restored order to Egypt's economy, Teti's kingdom also flourished. Teti had at least four wives, one of whom was named Khent or Khentkaus (III), which would have been his sister. Teti's favorite wife was Seshseshet,[233] and they had nine daughters named after her.

---

231 Benderitter, Thierry, "Kagemni" at http://www.osirisnet.net/mastabas/kagemni/e_kagemni_01.htm
232 Lauer, Jean Phillipe, *Saqqara: The Royal Cemetery of Memphis - Excavations and Discoveries since 1850*, Charles Scribner's Sons, 1976
233 In the Ebers Papyrus written hundreds of years later, Teti's mother is named Sesheshet within a remedy for baldness. But it is more likely that queen Sesheshet was one of Teti's wives. "Sesheshet", wikipedia

Mereruka, Teti's vizier

Statue of Mereruka in his mastaba

Teti's vizier, Mereruka, married a daughter of one of Teti's other wives. Mereruka was so wealthy that he built the largest known tomb of any Egyptian official. His mastaba had 33 rooms full of elaborately painted reliefs of hunting, fishing, and jewelry making. Most of Mereruka's wealth could have been inherited prior to the famine, or like Isaac, he could have become very wealthy afterwards. Tombs of Teti's nobles surround his pyramid complex in Saqqara.

Merikare, third pharaoh of the 9th dynasty

As stated above, Merikare was the son of queen Khentkaus I and Wahkare Khety II. Merikare's parents established his "kingdom" between their two kingdoms of Memphis and Asyut in *Hwt-Nen*-Nesu, 'house of royal child'. King Wenis/Unas failed to produce heirs, so he may have agreed to train Merikare as a co-regent until he died. The city was renamed Herakleopolis Magna to help acceptance of the transition to a new dynasty. Unas may have been ill at the time of the agreement, but then recovered and lived to see the awful results of the famine upon the people. Khuy in Asyut was defeated by Ankhtifi, but his (probable) son or grandson Wankhare Khety III ruled Asyut after Neferkare Terure VII and others ruled Herakleopolis Magna; and so the 9th and 10th dynasties continued to coexist.

Khety of the 9th destroyed tombs in Thinis and Akhmim to receive tribute from the "Southland", but repented for doing so in *Teaching for King Merykare*.[234] Merikare took the instruction to heart and lived peacefully, but his brother Neferkare VII had other ideas.

Khuy (1861-1856 BC), next to last pharaoh of the 10th dynasty in Asyut

Khuy built a large pyramid at Dara located 30 km north of Asyut in Middle Egypt. It had a 130 meter square base with unique rounded corners. Some think it was not finished. His mud-brick mortuary temple had a length of 35 meters.[235] Khuy's home was in Edfu in nome #2. Ankhtifi usurped Khuy's home nome (#2) when it was overcome by a Nile flood.

Ankhtifi, nomarch of nome #3 in El-Mo'alla

Ankhtifi's biography in his tomb in El-Mo'alla provides his view of how he "rescued" people from famine and war. In the following passage ancient Armant was renamed Hermonthis by the Greeks, and is 12 miles southeast of Thebes.

---

234 Translation by Wim van den Dungen at http://www.sofiatopia.org/maat/merikare.htm
235 Mounir, Moata, Khui of "First Intermediate Period" accessed 6/12/11 at
   http://thenilepharaoh.blogspot.com/2007/11/first-intermediate-period-7th-and-8th.html#links

"I found the House of Khuy inundated like a marsh, abandoned by him who belonged to it, in the grip of the rebel, under the control of a wretch. … The general of Armant said to me: 'Come, oh honest man. Sail with the current down to the fortress of Armant!' I then went down to the country to the west of Armant and I found that the forces of Thebes and Koptos had attacked the fortress of Armant ... I reached the west bank of the Theban province ... Then my courageous crack troops, yes my bold crack troops, ventured to the west and the east of the Theban nome, looking for an open battle. But no one dared to come out from Thebes because they were afraid of my troops."[236]

Ankhtifi was emboldened to attack because he had allied himself with the "prince of Elephantine" who marshalled Nubian "crack troops" who were prepared to fight. Intef I was wise to keep Thebe's gates closed.

Neferkare VII, 4th pharaoh of the 9th dynasty

Neferkare Terure VII may be the (twin) brother of Merikare. Merikare's reign ended, and Neferkare's started as the famine began in 1856 BC, and he continued to rule until 1845 BC. Neferkare Terure was ambitious and used the crisis to attempt to expand his borders to Thebes by plotting attacks with nomarchs Hotep, north of Thebes, and Ankhtifi, just south of Thebes. This "Hotep" was Djehutyhotep of the Hare nome (#15). According to Ankhtifi's biography, Neferkare first directed Ankhtifi to take over Khuy's home nome in Edfu which was loyal to Thebes. Ankhtifi accomplished this by giving the people food, and stating that Khuy had abandoned them.[237]

Intef I (1878-1856 BC), second pharaoh of 11th dynasty in Thebes

Intef I was the son of Montuhotep (also Mentuhotep) who was nomarch of Thebes (#4) as listed by Thutmose III in his hall of ancestors in Karnak.[238] Intef I ruled Thebes when Ankhtifi attacked. Intef waited until they retreated. Then he allied himself with nome #5 of Koptos and attacked them and gained nome #3. He also gained Denderah, south of Qena.

---

236 Grimal, Nicolas, *A History of Ancient Egypt*, Blackwell Books: 1992, p.142, from Vandier's *Inscriptions*
237 "Ankhtifi," wikipedia
238 "Mentuhotep I," wikipedia

Intef II (1866-1817 BC), third pharaoh of 11th dynasty in Thebes

Intef II continued expanding his kingdom all the way south to the first cataract at Aswan; ousting Ankhtifi and gaining nomes #1 and #2. Then Intef II pushed northwards, and found Abydos (in #8) a difficult city to control; but fought his way north, and gained all the nomes up to nome #13 about 1854 BC. Intef II had a long reign which stabilized Egypt. A statue of Intef II in a sed robe in Elephantine (nome #1) supports his control of those lands into his 30th year.[239]

The "prince of Elephantine"

In 1856 BC, the "prince of Elephantine" joined Ankhtifi to attack Thebes, but Intef I held out in Thebes and the Nubians fell back. Intef II eventually drove them all the way back to Elephantine. Famine forced this prince to gather any willing Kushite tribes to join him and travel to the delta where other Kushite tribes of the 14th dynasty lived in safety and prosperity. So while Intef II was busy expanding his territory, ships of black Nubians and Kushites slipped downstream on the high Nile, northward to the Nile delta.

Ethiopic War (1854 BC) and Sheshi of the Kushite 14th dynasty

In the midst of Isaac's famine, the Kushites/Ethiopians between the third and fourth cataracts, allied themselves with the prince of Elephantine, ruling between the first and third cataracts, and travelled all the way to the Nile delta to obtain new pasture lands by force. Kushite pharaoh Sheshi had good rapport and trade with the prince of Elephantine. Sheshi's scarab seals were found in nine different cities from the first to the third cataract, and another in Kerma in Kushite territory.[240] Just as Egyptian nomes warred against each other, black tribes in the south also warred against each other, but would unite against a common foe, which happened to be those in the eastern Nile delta. The Medjay tribe of Nubia is famous for its warriors, but so are the Kushite tribes of the Upper Nile.

I deduce from the mass pit graves between levels G and F at Tell el-Dabᶜa that when the Ethiopian fleet arrived, a battle ensued with Sheshi at Avaris in which many were killed; and that Sheshi allowed the Nubians and Kushites to take the lands of the native Egyptians named Casluhim and Caphtorim (which was more dominant) who were then living in the eastern delta. They almost annihilated all who dwelt along the Pelusiac branch, and they destroyed their main city[241] (Herakleopolis Parva, now Port Said). Some native Egyptians fled on foot to Gaza to join the Philistines,[242] and others fled by sea to Crete becoming Keftiu. This was the result of the Ethiopic War. The city of Avaris is now called Tell el-Dabᶜa in which vast archaeological discoveries have been made by Manfred Bietak.

---

239 Grimal, Nicolas, *A History of Ancient Egypt*, Blackwell Books: 1992, p. 145

240 Ryholt, K.S.B., *The Political Situation in Egypt during the Second Intermediate Period*, 1997, pp. 107 and 369

241 Josephus, *Jewish Antiquities* I, vi. The Greeks called the city Pelusium; the Hebrews called it Sin.

242 Deuteronomy 2:23 and Amos 9:7. Casluhim was a son of Mizraim (Gen. 10:14)

Avaris/Tell el-Dabᶜa

Tell el-Dabᶜa ". . . was more substantially settled during the 13th Dynasty (stratum G) and was afterwards partly abandoned, perhaps as the result of an <u>epidemic</u>, signs of which may be discerned in some of the excavated remains (see below)."[243] [emaciated because they had been starving during the famine]

Strata of Tell el-Dabᶜa AREA A (H-D/3) from oldest to youngest strata (level)

Date BC	Canaan	Level	(Avaris) Tell el-Dabᶜa objects	Kerma, Kush
1890	MB II A	H	Egyptian enclosure walls	
			ASH LAYER	
1870	MB II A3	G	Polished Syro-Palestinian jug; major Egyptian limestone monument	
1854			<u>Mass pit graves</u> (of Ethiopic War)	
1850	MB II B1	F	Tomb of deputy treasurer 'Amu (foreigner) Amorite temple; Golden lion amulet; foreign and local pottery.	
1830		E/3	Scarab of Sobekhotep IV; Long narrow building like palace of Tell el-Ajjul	alabaster jar with Sobeknakht I or II
1810	MB II B2	E/2	Infant burials in large two-handled amphorae – a Canaanite practice. Mortuary temples and huge settlement.	Statuette of Sobeknakht II (El-Kab nomarch)
1790	MB II B3	E/1	Type VI scarabs with d5 sides.	
1770		D/3	Three warriors: golden diadems, knife, dagger, battle axe, alabaster ointment jar, scarabs on their fingers and on necklaces.	

"Concerning str. H = d/2 (late Twelfth Dynasty – early Fourteenth Dynasty, it is reported that 'Despite intensive plundering, 50 percent of the male burials yielded weapons, which indicates that warriors played an important part in the society. Egyptian types such as a dagger with ivory pommel are an exception. Nearly all the bronzes are of MB IIA types'."[244]

---

243 Bietak, Manfred, *Avaris and Piramesse: Archaeological Exploration in the Eastern Nile Delta,* Oxford University Press, 1979-1986, p. 7
244 Ryholt, p. 295 including quote from Bietak, *BASOR*, 281, p. 33

Bietak noted the archaeological link between Kush and the 14th dynasty at Avaris.

> "Servants were interred in front of the tomb chambers of some tombs in stratum F. <u>It is interesting that the practice of servant burials appears at the same time more than 2000 km to the south in the kingdom of Kush.</u>"[245] - Bietak

> "While the centre of the settlement at F/I continued to be inhabited, in the eastern part of the settlement, in area A/II . . . , occupation came to a temporary halt after stratum G. <u>Settlement areas were converted into cemeteries</u>, which soon spread to surround a large, newly constructed temple (III) of Middle Bronze Age type (stratum F)."[246]

William Ward, wrote that according to Bietak at Tell el-Dabᶜa, "The Middle Kingdom houses of Level G were destroyed by burning and the succeeding Level F yielded non-Egyptian burials typical of the MB II period in Syria-Palestine."[247] Ward alluded to donkey burials which have also been found in Egypt at Inshas, Tell el-Farasha, and Tell el-Maskhuta.[248] According to the royal scarab seals and two blocks of Nehesy originally at strata F found by Bietak at Tell el-Dabᶜa (Avaris), Sheshi was the father of Nehesy.[249] Strata F is also where Bietak uncovered two warriors each buried with a bronze dagger and battle axe,[250] and donkey burials at the tomb door.[251] A Middle Kingdom donkey burial was recently discovered in Abydos.[252] Middle Kingdom is 11th - 14th dynasties. Avaris stratum G was burned, and areas converted into cemeteries to accommodate the great loss of life which Bietak ascribed to an epidemic, but I, to the Ethiopic War during Sheshi's reign.

In response to the Ethiopic War (1854 BC) and to avoid another similar attack, Senusret III had the following stelae placed in Semna (ancient Heh) and southward in his 8th year (1839 BC):

> "Southern boundary, made in the year 8, under the majesty of the King of Upper and Lower Egypt, Khekuer, who is given life forever and ever; in order to prevent that any Negro should cross it, by water or by land, with a ship, (or) any herds of the Negroes; except a Negro who shall come to do trading in Iken, or

---

245 Bietak, Manfred, *Avaris:The Capital of the Hyksos: Recent Excavations at Tell el Dabᶜa,* British Museum Press, London, 1996, p. 45
246 Bietak, Manfred, *Avaris and Piramesse: Archaeological Exploration in the Eastern Nile Delta,* Oxford University Press, 1979-1986, p. 36
247 Ward, William, *Egypt And The East Mediterranean World 2200-1900 B.C.: Studies in Egyptian Foreign Relations during the First Intermediate Period,* American University of Beirut, Lebanon,1971, p. 39 fn153
248 Bietak, Manfred, *Avaris and Piramesse: Archaeological Exploration in the Eastern Nile Delta,* p. 246
249 Ryholt, K.S.B., *The Political Situation in Egypt during the Second Intermediate Period,* Museum Tusculanum Press, 1997, pp. 46-49
250 Bietak, Manfred, *Avaris and Piramesse: Archaeological Exploration in the Eastern Nile Delta,* plate X
251 Ibid, pp. 244-246
252 Abydos Reveals Some of its Secrets, May, 2005, accessed 5/16/11, http://www.guardians.net/hawass/press_release_Abydos_05-05.htm,

Pharaohs of the Bible

with a commission. Every good thing shall be done with them, but without allowing a ship of the Negroes to pass Heh, going downstream, forever."

It took nineteen years for the Egyptians to fully recover authority over Nubia again.

Nubians and Kushites in Nile delta

In stratum F was the Tomb of deputy treasurer 'Amu. *ʿ3mw* means 'foreigner', not necessarily Asiatic. The first chieftains of the 14th dynasty were 'Ammu, Yakbim, Y'ammu, and Qareh; so it is not strange the treasurer was also *ʿ3mw*. Sheshi married queen Tati of Kush, and their son, *Nehesy*, means Kushite and black. Nubian and Kushite forces remained in the delta through the 18th dynasty. In Hatshepsut's relief, the Nubian warriors hold bows, arrow, and duck-billed axes. Burials of men and a duck-billed axe was found at Avaris in level H.[253] A mold for a duck-billed axe was also found at Tell el-Dabʿa in strata immediately after 18th dynasty pharaoh Ahmose's conquest of Avaris.[254] Bietak also found numerous Nubian arrowheads and Kushite pottery called Kerma ware.

18th dynasty depiction of Nubian warriors

"Some of the skeletons show negroid physical features and are most likely to be identifiable as southern Nubians. Such a conclusion can be corroborated by finds of Kerma beakers and cooking pots, as well as missiles of Kerma type within the next stratum (ph. C/3 = str. d) of the first half of the 18th Dynasty, following ph. D/1.1, showing that Kerma people were engaged as archers in the Egyptian army."[255]

Sphinx of Amenemhat II

So Nubian and Kushite soldiers were present at Avaris from the 14th dynasty of level H to the 18th dynasty; a period of at least 200 years. Back to the second famine in Egypt.

Amenemhat II, third pharaoh of the 12th dynasty

Amenemhat I seized the two nomes of the Fayyum and founded his capital Itjtawy (which was buried by Nile silt upon which the town of Lisht sits). With only 20 miles between Itjtawy and Saqqara, Amenemhat II was able to secure food during the famine. Though most dynasties raided the Nubians for slaves, gold, and cattle; the 12th dynasty established forts there. An annual stone

---

253 at stratum d/2 in F/I; Schiestl, Robert, "The Cemeteries of F/I in the Strata d/2 (H) and d/1 (G/4), late 12th Dynasty and early 13th Dynasty,"Avaris website http://www.auaris.at/html/stratum_f1_en.html
254 Ibid., p. 19
255 Bietak, Manfred; Marinatos, Nanno; Palivou, Clairy, *Taureador Scenes in Tell el-Dabʿa (Avaris) and Knossos,* Austrian Academy of Sciences Press, 2007, p. 18

found in Memphis of Amenemhat II's earlier regnal years described him destroying two cities in Canaan and receiving tribute from Nubians.[256] There is only one record of an inspection of a fortress in Nubia in the 35th and final year of Amenemhat's II reign. Earlier his explorations were in the Sinai and Punt: in his 24th year (1866 BC) he opened a turquoise mine in the Sinai, and a nobleman led an expedition to Punt in his 28th year. Amenemhat II built the white pyramid in Dashur.

Djehutyhotep of Hare Nome

Though Djehutyhotep's tomb is in El-Beresh, hieratic graffiti at the quarries in Hatnub state the nomarchs of the Hare nome allied with the king of Herakleopolis Magna (Neferkare VII) against the forces of an unnamed king from the south, most likely Intef II.[257] Djehutyhotep made himself a lavish tomb covered in reliefs with soldiers which demonstrate that building projects continued during times of war.[258]

Colossus on sled being pulled with armies marching above it in Djehutyhotep's tomb

Building projects were carried out by Egyptians during the season of inundation (Akhet, August – November) when the fields were flooded. There is no taskmaster with a whip. Pharaohs wisely provided work for decent pay during this season. With the Nile at its

---

256 "Amenemhat II", wikipedia
257 Faulkner, R.O., "The Rebellion of the Hare Nome", *Journal of Egyptian Archaeology*, Vol. 30 (Dec., 1944), pp. 61-63, http://www.jstor.org/pss/3855182
258 Relief art from Lespius' *Alphabet*, vol. 2, band 4, block 134; http://edoc3.bibliothek.uni-halle.de/lepsius/page/abt2/band4/image/02041340.jpg

highest level, supplies and large stones could be transported right to the building sites by barge. Many of the pyramid complexes have a dock for such purposes. But sometimes, the materials would have to be pulled on a sled over sand which was dampened (note the man at the foot of the colossus pouring oil before the sled).[259] The colossus is either Amenemhat II or Senusret II whom Djehutyhotep served.

Second Famine and Ethiopic War Review

To recap, the second famine in the Bible had to occur between 1856 when Isaac and Rebekah married and 1836 when Esau and Jacob were born to them. I suggest 1856 BC because Isaac and Rebekah's ruse of being brother and sister before Abimelech lasted "*a long time*" before she gave birth to twins.

In Egypt, king Neferkare Terure VII in nome #20 took advantage of the famine crisis by allying himself with nomarchs Djehutyhotep of nome #15 and Ankhtifi of nome #3 to attack king Intefs I and II of Thebes in nome #4. On Neferkare's orders, Ankhtifi first subdued Khuy's home nome #2, and allied himself with the "prince of Elephantine" of nome #1. Together they attempted to attack Thebes. Intef I allied himself with nome #5 which helped him obtain the city of Denderah, and together they regained nome #3. Long-lived Intef II continued fighting until nomes #1-13 were subjected to him. Meanwhile, the prince of Elephantine and many Kushites moved to the Nile delta and attacked the Kushite 14th dynasty already there as well as decimating the Casluhim and Caphtorim. Sheshi's 14th dynasty resumed policing food shipments for Amenemhat II, and other Nubians and Kushites remained in Egypt's service in the delta through to the 18th dynasty.

Isaac and Rebekah have Twins and Move (1836 BC)

And the man waxed great, and went forward, and grew until he became very great: For he had possession of flocks, and possession of herds, and great store of servants: and the Philistines envied him. For all the wells which his father's servants had dig in the days of Abraham his father, the Philistines had stopped them, and filled them with earth. And Abimelech said to Isaac, Go from us; for you are much mightier than we. And Isaac departed there, and pitched his tent in the valley of Gerar, and dwelled there. And Isaac dig again the wells of water, which they had dig in the days of Abraham his father; for the <u>Philistines had stopped them after the death of Abraham</u>: and he called their names after the names by which his father had called them. (Genesis 26:13-18)

If the famine occurred in 1856 BC and Abraham died in 1821 BC, Isaac and Rebekah were in Gerar becoming wealthy for 35 years before they buried Abraham.

. . . the years of Abraham's life which he lived, an hundred three score and fifteen years. And his sons Isaac and Ishmael buried him in the cave of Machpelah, in the

---

259 Brier, Bob and Hobbs, Hoyt, *Daily Life of the Ancient Egyptians*, Greenwood Press, 2008, p. 214

field of Ephron the son of Zohar <u>the Hittite</u>, which is before Mamre; The field which Abraham purchased of the <u>sons of Heth</u>: there was Abraham buried, and Sarah his wife. And it came to pass after the death of Abraham, that God blessed his son Isaac; and Isaac dwelled by the well Lahairoi. (Genesis 25:7-11) [These "sons of Heth" are Canaanite Hittites, not Anatolian Hittites.]

Philistines

The Philistines were first mentioned in a business encounter with Abraham when he purchased a well for seven sheep from Abimelech. Beersheba means 'well of seven', and it is 30 miles inland, but the strength of Philistine land was along the Mediterranean coast which became mixed with the Casluhim and Caphtorim of Egypt (some of whom went to Crete and became known as Keftiu).

Thus they made a covenant at Beersheba: then Abimelech rose up, and Phichol the chief captain of his host, and they returned into the land of the Philistines. And Abraham planted a grove in Beersheba, and called there on the name of the LORD, the everlasting God. And Abraham sojourned in the Philistines' land many days. (Genesis 21:32-34)

"Philistine = 'immigrants' 1) an inhabitant of Philistia; descendants of Mizraim who immigrated from Caphtor (Crete?) to the western seacoast of Canaan."[260]

Semites and Hebrews

With distinguishing between Canaanite Hittites and Anatolian (Turkey) Hittites, we also need to distinguish between who were Semites and Hebrews, and which group of Semitic Hebrews were enslaved in Egypt. Semites came from Shem; Hebrews came from Eber. Abram was descended from Shem and Eber. Abraham's first son through Sarah's Egyptian maidservant Hagar was Ishmael. Ishmael was therefore half Hebrew and half Egyptian (Ham's lineage). Many of Ishmael's descendants inhabited the Arabian Peninsula and are thus called Arabs. Sarah was Abraham's half sister, a Hebrew. Their child, Isaac, was fully Hebrew. Isaac married Rebekah, who was the grand-daughter of Abraham's brother Nahor;[261] and their twin sons Esau and Jacob were fully Hebrew. YHWH renamed Jacob as Israel, thus the children of Israel are fully Hebrew. Jews are fully Semitic; whereas Arabs and some ethnic groups from Mesopotamia only retain a distant link to Shem. Isaac and his children are not in the following map so as to make a distinction between the Semitic Hebrews who dwelt in Egypt for 215 years (1706 - 1491), and the Semitic Habiru.

Abram married a woman named Keturah, of unknown lineage, and had six sons with her but they did not share in Isaac's inheritance.[262]

---

260 Brown-Driver-Briggs' Hebrew definitions
261 Genesis 24:15
262 Genesis 25:1-6

* notes the cities of Ur and Harran

Who were the Habiru/Apiru?

Except for the underlined descendants of Shem and their families, all the rest are descendants from Eber, and were ethnically Hebrews even if they spoke different languages.[263] Abraham was of Eber's lineage and did speak Hebrew. It was through Abraham's son Isaac that a nation of Hebrews dwelt in Egypt and became enslaved; these were not the Habiru. The other Hebraic descendants living in the fertile crescent and the Arabian Peninsula were the Habiru/Apiru of the Armana letters and other texts.

---

263 Cooper, Bill, *After the Flood*, New Wine Press, England, 1995; and from Genesis 10 and 25. A version of his book is available at http://www.ldolphin.org/cooper/

Hebrews through Isaac, the Promise

The promised "seed", Isaac, and his descendants would be afflicted 400 years, and would return to Egypt in the fourth generation in accordance to God's prophetic word.

> *And he said to Abram, Know of a surety that your seed shall be a stranger in a land that is not their's, and shall serve them; and <u>they shall afflict them four hundred years</u>; And also that nation, whom they shall serve, will I judge: and afterward shall they come out with great substance. And you shall go to your fathers in peace; you shall be buried in a good old age. But in the fourth generation they shall come here again: for the iniquity of the Amorites is not yet full. . . . In the same day the LORD made a covenant with Abram, saying, To your seed have I given this land, from the river of Egypt to the great river, the river Euphrates: (Genesis 15:13-18)*

> ". . . the '*River of Egypt*,' the eastern Pelusiac arm of the Nile River which was well known as the border of Egypt through the ages . . ."[264]

```
1996   Abram born
1921   Promise to Abram; he goes to Egypt due to famine  ⎫
1896   Isaac (seed) born 1st generation                  |
1891   Isaac weaned at 5; Ishmael "mocked" him          ⎫|
1836   Jacob born   2nd gen.                             ||
1745   Joseph born  3rd gen.                             ||
1715   Joseph second to Ahmose I          400 years   430 years
1707   Two sons born to Joseph 4th gen.                  ||
1706   Seventy of Jacob's clan move to Egypt             ||
1571   Moses born                                        ||
1491   Exodus from Egypt                                ⎭⎭
```

The word "afflict" can also mean "disdain". When Isaac was weaned at five (1891 BC), Sarah saw his half-Egyptian teen-age brother "*mocking*" Isaac (Genesis 21:9). Isaac was the first generation of promise, then Jacob (2nd), then his twelve sons including Joseph (3rd); and after Joseph had two sons (4th), Jacob and all his progeny went to dwell in Egypt. 1896 – 1707 = 189 years. So the fourth generation from Abram entered into Egypt; this is the subgroup of Eber's descendants we call the Hebrews which left Egypt four generations later (1707 – 1491 = 216 years). Four hundred years after the initial mocking, the exodus of the Hebrews from Egypt occurred the night of Passover on Nisan 14, 1491 BC. Exodus 12:41 and Galatians 3:16-17 reference the exodus as being 430 years from the Genesis 15 promise which was given to Abram on Nisan 14, 1921 BC. But the actual 400 years is from when Ishmael mocked Isaac when he was weaned in 1891 BC.

---

[264] Rainey, Anson and Notley, R. Steven, *The Sacred Bridge: Carta's Atlas of the Biblical World*, CARTA Jerusalem, 2006, p. 30

Pharaohs of the Bible

Pharaoh Djedefre, his pyramid, and his wife Hetepheres II (1st sphinx)

Abram's Pharaohs: the Dynasty of the Pyramid Builders

  1996 Huni ruled Egypt when Abram was born in Ur
  1921 **Djedefre** ruled the delta when Abram travelled to Canaan and onto Egypt
  1919 Khafre sent Abram and Sarai back to Canaan where they settled in Hebron
  1918 Abram and Lot separated
  1913 Abram rescued Lot and was blessed by Melchizedek in king's dale
  1910 Khafre ruled the delta; Ishmael was born
  1897 Abraham told king Abimelech of Gerar that his wife was his sister
  1896 Isaac[265] was born; Baka ruled from Memphis 1895-1893; Menkaure 1893-1865
  1876 Qareh ruled the delta; Isaac offered on Mount Moriah above the king's dale
  1859 Sarah died, Abraham bought burial cave and field in Hebron; Isaac wed Rebekah
    ?   Abraham married Keturah[266]
  1856 Isaac and Rebekah go to king Abimelech in Gerar because of famine; *deja vu*
  1836 Sheshi ruled the delta; Abraham witnessed birth of his grandsons, Esau and Jacob
  1821 Nehesy ruled the delta; Abraham died and was buried in Hebron

---

265 Isaac lived 1896-1716, through the last half of the pyramid builders and all of the Hyksos dynasty.
266 Genesis 25:2 "And she bore him Zimran, and Jokshan, and Medan, and Midian, and Ishbak, and Shuah."

Nehesy (1821-1820 BC), the second pharaoh of 14th dynasty in Avaris

Panehsy means "the black one"; *Nehsy* can also be translated Kushite. Because Sheshi ruled so long prince Nehsy/Nehesy only lived to rule as king about one year by himself before he died and his son, Djehuti/Djehuty, became king. Salitis of the 15th dynasty attacked Avaris; so Djehuty fled south to start the 16th dynasty.

Djehuty, Nehesy's son, first pharaoh of 16th dynasty south of Thebes

Djehuty ruled part of one year in the Delta, and then he ruled south of Thebes for three years according to the Turin Kings List. "King Djehuty was married to a granddaughter of the Vizier Ibiaw who is attested during the reign of King Ibiaw of the Thirteenth Dynasty . . ."[267] She became queen Monthhotep/Montuhotep. "Lilyquist dates most of the burial equipment of Queen Monthhotep, the spouse of Djehuty, to the Late SIP."[268]

From Drought to Floods

The first Biblical famine was caused by drought, but the second Biblical famine was caused by the overabundant flooding of the Nile. At the island of Elephantine is the first cataract of the Nile which makes it a good place to take readings of the Nile's flood level above its normal flow level. During the reign of Senusret I (1934-1889 BC), a 'good flood' was considered 21.5 cubits (11 meters; 37 feet).

At the second cataract between Semna and Kumma, where Senusret III built forts, Nile levels were recorded on the cliffs. The average flood level during the reigns of 12th dynasty pharaohs Sobekneferu (1914-1910 BC) to the beginning of Amenemhat III (1827 BC) was 19 meters at the second cataract, which would have fully irrigated farm lands along the Nile. But between the 20th and 32nd years of the reign of Amenemhat III (1807 and 1795), the Nile flood levels spiked close to 21 meters four times out of his six remaining records.[269] [See Appendix B for chart on page 397.] Sobekhotep VIII of the 13th dynasty recorded the flooding of the Karnak temples, and Rahotep of the 17th dynasty restored their walls.[270]

Tomb of the Patriarchs

> . . . *the years of Abraham's life which he lived, an hundred three score and fifteen years. . . . And his sons Isaac and Ishmael buried him in the cave of Machpelah, in the field of Ephron . . . The field which Abraham purchased of the sons of Heth: there was Abraham buried, and Sarah his wife. (Genesis 25:7-10)*

---

267 Ryholt, p. 152
268 Ryholt, p. 152 footnote 552 Lilyquist (*Egyptian Stone Vessels*, 59-61)
269 Rohl, David, *Pharaohs and Kings: A Biblical Quest*, 1995, pp. 335-340
270 Ryholt, p. 145, fn525 Rahotep's stela referred to restoration of Koptos temple; a contemporary priest's stela from Abydos described rebuilding of enclosure walls. Antef VII rebuilt a series of chapels at Koptos. Sobkemsaf II restored structures at Madamud.

Pharaohs of the Bible

Later Isaac and Rebekkah and Jacob and Leah were also buried with Abraham and Sarah. Thus the three patriarchs of Judaism: Abraham, Isaac, and Jacob were buried in the cave of Machpelah in Hebron. It is the second most holy site to the Jews. The cave and their most holy site, the Temple Mount, are under control of the Muslim Waqf.

When Herod made expansions to the Temple Mount, he also enclosed the cave and its shrine by a six-foot thick wall which still stands due to the amazing stonecutters of that day. The wall enclosing the tomb and the "wailing wall" are difficult to tell apart. Several buildings by Jews, Christians, and Muslims have stood over the cave at different times. The Jews enter the shrine from the southwest, and Muslims enter from the northeast.

Herodian walls and Muslim roof atop the Cave of the Patriarchs

Dore's Burial of Sarah

Abram/Abraham

Ur		Charran	Egypt	Canaan
1996-1923		1922	1921-1919	1919-1859

Egyptian Pharaohs in Memphis

Huni (3rd)	Sneferu (4th)	Khufu (4th)	Djedefre (4th)	Khafre (4th)	Baka – Khentkaus I
2001-1977	1977-1953	1953-1930	1930-1919	1919-1895	1895-1859 (4th)

Abram/Abraham

Canaan
1859-1821

Egyptian Pharaohs in Memphis

I . . . (p15)	Teti (6th)	Pepi I (6th)
1860-1856	1856-1844	1842-1817

Jacob's Pharaohs

"Your name shall be called no more Jacob, but Israel: for as a prince have you power with God and with men, and have prevailed." (Genesis 32:28)

Jacob had twelve sons

And Isaac called Jacob, and blessed him, ... Arise, go to Padanaram, to the house of Bethuel your mother's father; and take you a wife from there of the daughters of Laban your mother's brother. And God Almighty bless you, and make you fruitful, and multiply you, that you may be a multitude of people; And give you the blessing of Abraham, to you, and to your seed with you; that you may inherit the land wherein you are a stranger, which God gave to Abraham. (Genesis 28:1-4)

Jacob went to Harran and worked as a shepherd for his uncle Laban to purchase his wives Leah and Rachel, who each had a handmaid (made concubines) Bilhah and Zilpah. Through these four women, twelve sons were born to Jacob: Reuben, Simeon, Levi, Judah, Issachar, and Zebulun; Dan and Naphtali; Gad and Asher; and Joseph and Benjamin.[271] When Jacob returned to Canaan in 1742 BC, God renamed him Israel.[272] The next year Rachel died birthing Benjamin. Thus we have the twelve sons of Jacob who become the twelve tribes of Israel (but Joseph later becomes two tribes, and Levi is set apart). Jacob lived from 1836-1689 BC. Jacob was born as the period of the great pyramid builders ended and trade in the Nile delta flourished under Sheshi (14th). Jacob moved to Egypt during the reign of Ahmose I (18th dynasty) in the second year of the third Biblical famine (1706 BC).

Nubian Medjay and Kushite/Kerman Warriors of Amenemhat I

Archaeological evidence places Nubian soldiers at Avaris from the 13th to the 18th dynasties,[273] but I suggest they were established by Amenemhat I of the 12th dynasty in 1954 BC. The *Prophecy of Neferty* was copied by Sneferu and stated that Ameny/Amenemhat had a dark-skinned, likely Nubian, mother from the #1 nome of Ta-Seti (Land of the Bow) from Elephantine (downstream of the first cataract) to just south of Edfu. Petrie noted, "The 12th dynasty was due to the emergence of a ruling family from Nubia."[274] Ameny's father was likely a Theban priest named Senusret. Amenemhat I led an army north and 'seized the two lands', *Itjtawy*, the name of his capital which was across from the fayyum. I propose his army had Nubian archers from Medja, and Kushite warriors with links to the Masai.

---

271 Genesis 35:23-26
272 Genesis 32:28
273 Booth, Charlotte, *The Hyksos Period in Egypt*, Shire Publications Ltd, UK, 2005, p. 28 from level H/1
274 Petrie, *The Making of Egypt*, 1939, p. 176

Pharaohs of the Bible

"Amenemhat's Ta-Seti army and conscripts came to be known as Ta-Itj-tawy. In modern languages this is pronounced Bigawy, Bedjawi or Bejawi."[275]

Beja Warriors early 1900's

The Beja warriors carry round shields with no decoration. The 14th dynasty was Kushite based on their scarab designs.

Kushite/Kerman 14th Dynasty in Nile Delta

Masai shields

Kenyan flag

Kushite 14th Dynasty Seals

Ahotepre **'Ammu**   Sekhaenre **Yakbimu**   Nubwoserre **Y'ammu**

Khawserre **Qareh**   Maaibre **Sheshi**   Prince **Nehesy**

Dr. Daphna Ben-Tor has graciously allowed me to copy and rearrange her seal drawings from *Scarabs, Chronology, and Interconnections* included in this graphic and on pages 122-124 in this chapter.

---

275 "Beja People" wikipedia

The Nubian district of Medja (*md3y*) was between the first and second cataracts of the Nile in Nubia, and the Medjay archers were employed by my cFIP and cSIP pharaohs to protect Avaris and its shipments. From the 18th to 20th dynasties the Medjay became the elite police force throughout Egypt. But the fiercest fighters were *nhsyw* (Nehesiu, 'black ones') from Kush. I suggest Amenemhat I set a Kushite warrior over the Nile delta's imports and exports at Avaris. The first four Kushite chiefs of the 14th dynasty were Ammu, Yakbimu, Y'ammu, and Qareh; but Sheshi's long reign encouraged him to become a king, and to bestow the kingship upon his son, Nehesy. Jacob was born (1836 BC) when Sheshi was king. Sheshi married a Kushite princess named Tati,[276] and named their son 'black one' likely because Sheshi was also Kushite. Ryholt wrote "Returning to the evidence provided by the seals, it is conspicuous that the Fourteenth Dynasty apparently had closer relations with Kerma, the royal residence of Kush, than with the Thirteenth Dynasty."[277] Like the Nubian Medjay, the Masai tribe (now much further south in today's Kenya) is also known as a warrior tribe. Kenya borders Lake Victoria, from which the White Nile flows through Uganda and Sudan. I suggest such Masai shields were used in Kush at the time of the 12th dynasty's rule during my cFIP and cSIP.

Jacob is transliterated from Hebrew as "Ya-aq-ob" and pronounced /yah-ak-obe'/. Jacob lived in the Nile delta during the reign of Ahmose I of the 18th dynasty, and was given scarab-seal signet rings engraved with the name Yaqub-har. Some Egyptologists place Yaqub-har's scarab-seals in the 14th dynasty, but none of his seals include the curved side panels of the Masai warrior shields. No other dynasty has curved side panels. The first Kushite warrior overseeing the import/export business at Avaris was called a foreigner, *'Ammu*. Based on 2 scarabs of *yakbmw* in Tel Kabri and 3 scarabs as a prince,[278] I propose Ammu's son was called Yaqub'ammu or Yakbimu (as glyphs on his seals are inconsistent); and that Yakbimu's son was called Y'ammu. A kinsman named Qareh also ruled.

Two Seals of Ya-k-ʿ-r-b attributed to Yakbimu, not Jacob

Petrie published a crudely cut scarab of Yaqub-R which can be read Yaqub-El.
"Inasmuch as in Egyptian 'r' takes the place of 'l' of the Semitic languages, while 'h' does not count at all, this name is equivalent to Yaqub-el, our familiar Hebrew Jacob, written in full, with the divine determinative of el, God, at the end. . ."[279]

El is short for Elohim. The name Jacob-El was common among Aramaens, people with

---

276 Ryholt, p. 299, pp. 253-4, and p. 180 for description of *md3y* and *nhsyw*
277 Ryholt, p. 114
278 Ryholt, K. S. B., *The Political Situation in Egypt during the Second Intermediate Period*, p. 251
  Yakbim uses an owl for the 'k' sound, whereas Yakbimu uses the basket glyph; so Ryholt declares them to be two separate individuals. Yosef Mizrachy considers the seals to belong to the same man in *Tel Kabri: The 1986-1993 Excavation Seasons,* chapter 9 on seals, 2002, p. 331
279 Peters, John P., "Archaeology History of Hither Asia including Egypt," *The Universal Anthology*, Volume 32, 1899, p. 325

whom Jacob spent forty years, but was not known among Canaanites or Phoenicians[280] as a person's name; though a city of Jacob-El (Tell Malhata) flourished in southern Canaan. Another seal with this name was later found, and Ryholt contended both are skillfully cut; and added ". . . all seals of Ya'qub-Har and his successors have decorated bases, unlike the two seals . . . reading y-k-b-ʿ-l . . ."[281] According to Ryholt, the two seals of Ya-k-ʿ-r-b are very similar to those of an unpublished seal of Yakbim. It is possible that Yakbimu had the y-k-b-ʿ-l seals made in order to do business with the prosperous city of Jacob-El.

14th Dynasty Seals

Yakbimu had a long reign with 122 seals with his name (7 in Canaan, 4 in the Nile delta, 1 in Upper Egypt, 2 in Nubia, and 108 from unknown provenances), while only 26 have been found with Y'ammu's name.[282] Thirty scarab-seals have been found for Qareh, and 62 for 'Ammu (6 in Canaan, 1 in the Nile delta, 1 in Upper Egypt, 1 in Nubia, and 53 from unknown provenances);[283] 'Ammu and Yakbimu did their import/export jobs well. One seal from 'Ammu, Yakbimu, and Qareh were found in Abydos, so the short Abydos dynasty[284] may have ruled concurrently during their rule and the beginning of Sheshi's.[285] Eight of Sheshi's 399 seals were found in Abydos, nine were found in cities throughout Nubia, and one in Kerma of Kush. Seals of a couple 13th dynasty rulers were also found at the Nubian forts and in the delta. Ryholt noted 14th dynasty officials stationed in 13th dynasty forts in Nubia, and 13th dynasty officials stationed in the 14th dynasty fort of Avaris; concluding ". . . the two states could only station officials within each other's territory by mutual consent."[286]

Though Nehesy did great trade, his son, Djehuty, was attacked and burned out by Salitis; so Djehuty fled south and married into the 16th dynasty; and ruled nomes #1 and #2 of southern Egypt. There are over forty names in columns VIII and IX of the Turin King List after Nehesy which I think were Kushite warrior chiefs who averaged terms of two years stationed throughout Egypt's trading posts with the authority of one of Sheshi's scarab-seals to distribute food and goods. The fifth, seventh, and tenth names in column IX are based on "provisions of food"[287] possibly for soldiers manning trading posts.

Uronarti, Nubia Evidence for my Condensed cSIP

Amenemhat I travelled at least 750 miles via the Nile to campaign against hostile Nubian tribes, and he built a fort at Semna in his 29th year (1925 BC) to hold his border.

---

280 Zobel, 1990, p. 189
281 Ryholt, K. S. B., *The Political Situation in Egypt during the Second Intermediate Period*, p. 102 fn 340
282 Ryholt, K. S. B., *The Political Situation in Egypt during the Second Intermediate Period*, pp. 359-363
283 Ibid., pp. 363-366
284 Ryholt, K. S. B., *The Political Situation in Egypt during the Second Intermediate Period*, pp. 163-166
285 Ibid., p. 61 "Aamu can be dated to the reign of Sheshi or shortly thereafter. This date is corroborated by the stratigraphical position of the tomb (str. b/3 = str. F of Area A) in the mid/late Fourteenth Dynasty."
   Treasurer Aamu is not to be confused with king 'Ammu, though both their names mean 'foreigner'.
286 Ibid., p. 111
287 Ryholt, K. S. B., *The Political Situation in Egypt during the Second Intermediate Period*, p. 300

Semna is between the Nile's second and third cataracts, and Uronarti is three miles north of Semna. Among the 4000 seal-impressions (sealings) found at the Nubian fortress in Uronarti, most belonged to two 13th dynasty kings known by their Horus names: Khabaw and Djedkheperew. In granary room 157, a sealing of Maaibre (Sheshi) was found among them.[288] Based upon Stuart Smith's estimation that these seals were deposited within the course of one year,[289] Ryholt wrote ". . . Sheshi, was contemporary with Djedkheperew of the early Thirteenth Dynasty."[290] "A single seal of a third king, Meritawy, was found within one of the barracks."[291] Pepi I of the 6th dynasty was named Meritawy before he was renamed Merire. In my chronology Pepi I ruled Memphis from 1842 to 1817 BC concurrent with Sheshi's reign. The Nubian sealings support co-rule of the 6th, 13th, and 14th dynasties.

According to Papyrus Reisner I, Senusret I had provided grain rations for a large building project which may have been the Nubian forts. Senusret III built the Uronarti fortress in his 16th year to repel the Iwentiu.[292] In Papyrus Reisner II during the 33rd year of Amenemhat III, grain rations were specified for soldiers and bowmen. Wooden ration tallies in shapes of loaves were found in Uronarti building A.[293]

Pre-15th Dynasty in Memphis and Seth II in Avaris

The last part of column X of the Turin Kings List contains the names of the six kings of the 15th dynasty, so I ascribe the first eleven names in the column to the pre-15th dynasty. I suggest the first name, 'I[. . .]', was sent from Byblos to aid queen Khentkaus I at Memphis in the import/export business from Avaris and Heracleopolis Parva and other ports. In the first year of the second Biblical famine 'I[. . .]' was succeeded by Seth II.[294] I conjecture that when the famine hit, Seth II used the stored grain at Saqqara to meet people's needs, and he was venerated as a savior with a colossal statue and small pyramid tomb in Avaris. The tomb was situated in the palace garden. The battered remains of the twice life-size statue is of an Asiatic pharaoh with skin painted yellow and mushroom-shaped hair painted red. He has the throwstick of a pharaoh over his right shoulder.[295] In the Byblos Montet Jar was an ivory label to "treasurer of the king Horus-Seth".[296] (The 18th dynasty built a temple to Seth in Avaris. Since Seti I was born with red hair, he may have been named after Seth II.) I suggest the Byblite pre-15th dynasty in Memphis worked with the Kushite 14th dynasty at

---

288 Ryholt, pp. 42, 321-322
289 Smith, Stuart T., "Administration at the Middle Kingdom Frontier: Sealings from Uronarti and Askut," pp. 207-209
290 Ryholt, pp. 321 and 75
291 Ryholt, p. 321
292 Janssen, J.M.A., "The Stela (Khartoum Museum No 3) from Uronarti," *Journal of Near Eastern Studies* 12(1953), pp. 51-55
293 Smith, Stuart T., "Administration at the Middle Kingdom Frontier: Sealings from Uronarti and Askut," pp. 203-204
294 Meribre Seth I was a pharaoh of the 13th dynasty located in the 23rd position of column VI of Turin List
295 Bietak, Manfred, *Avaris: the Capital of the Hyksos*, British Museum Press, 1996, plate 4
296 Ward, William and Dever, William, *Studies on Scarab Seals volume 3*, Van Siclen Books, 1994, p. 92, fn 8

Avaris to implement the trade mandates of the 4th, 6th, and 12th dynasty. There was no conflict among these trade dignitaries who were given pharaonic authority to execute trade.

Hyksos 15th Dynasty in Nile Delta

. . . that is until Salitis decided to be a king instead of a mere trade dignitary. Seth II is the second name of column X in the Turin King List, and Salitis is the fifteenth. I conjecture Salitis attacked Djehuty at Avaris, and the refugees of the 14th dynasty returned to Kush or remained with Djehuty south of Thebes. Salitis established the reign of Phoenician *Hyksos*, 'foreign rulers/chiefs' in the Nile delta. Manetho described the transition:

> "Tutimaeus. In his reign . . . there came, unexpectedly, men of ignoble birth from the east, and they were bold enough to make an expedition into our country, and easily subdued it by force, because we did not even hazard a battle with them. So when they had overpowered our rulers, they afterwards **burnt** down our cities, and demolished the temples of the gods, and treated all the inhabitants in the most barbarous manner. Some of them they slew, and led their children and their wives into slavery. At length they made one of themselves king, whose name was Salitis; he also lived at Memphis, and he made both the upper and lower regions pay tribute, and left garrisons in places that were the most suitable for them. . . . He found in the Sethroite nome a city very suitable for this purpose, on the east side of the Bubastic channel of the river, which for theological reasons was called Avaris. He rebuilt it, and made it very strong by the **walls** he built around it, and put in a very large **garrison** of two hundred and forty thousand armed men, to guard it. Salitis came there in summer time, partly to gather his corn, and pay his soldiers their wages, and partly to exercise his armed men, and thereby to intimidate foreigners. . . . *Hyksos*: but some say that these people were Arabians."[297] -
> - Manetho via Josephus via Eusebius

The "Sethroite nome" is the east delta with Avaris as its capital. It may be that Seth-Peribsen of the 2nd Dynasty was the first authority in this part of the eastern delta, or it could refer to Seth II. Salitis, Beon, Sakir-Har, and Khyan continued to serve the 6th dynasty pharaohs of Memphis while building their own kingdom in Avaris. I suggest Salitis came to power near the end of the reign of Pepi I. Then it was Apepi (the sixth Hyksos' king of the 15th dynasty) who conquered Memphis, not Salitis. Apepi conquered Memphis in 1754 BC while Dudimose I ('Tutimaeus') reigned at Edfu. After Apepi, Khamudi held Avaris and Memphis until Ahmose I of the 18th dynasty grew up and conquered him.

Jacob moved to Goshen during the reign of Amenhotep I (1712-1688 BC)

The 6th, 9th, 11th, second half of the 12th, second half of the 13th, end of the 14th, the 15th, 16th and 17th dynasties were concurrent during Jacob's life in Canaan. The pharaoh prior to Amenhotep I was Ahmose I who raised up Jacob's son, Joseph, to be vizier of all Egypt. When Ahmose died, Ahmose-Nefertari ruled while Amenhotep was a child with Joseph being "*a father to pharaoh*". In the second year of the third Biblical famine (1706 BC),

---
[297] Eusebius, Chronicle 2, pp. 153-154 at http://www.attalus.org/translate/eusebius1.html

Joseph sent wagons to bring all of Jacob's clan, all 66 relatives, and all their flocks and herds to Goshen.[298] Like Ishmael, Joseph's two sons were half Egyptian; thus bringing the total of Jacob's clan to 70. Goshen referred to grazing lands occupied by shepherds during the reign of the Phoenician Hyksos whose capital in the Nile delta was Avaris.

Seals of Yaqub-Har are seals of Jacob for Egyptian import/export

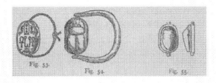

Above are 1908 examples of beetle-like scarab-seals with top and side view (Fig. 55): one with twine (Fig. 53) and one enclosed by a metal frame (Fig. 54), both of which could be worn as rings; hence, signet rings. The other two scarab-seals were included in Flinders Petrie's 1917 work, *Scarabs and Cylinders* which covered over 5,000 seals from the 1st through the 31st dynasties; the majority of which were scarab-shaped seals. Yes, the seal misspelled Yaqeb-hor as Yaqeb-orh, as was common with seals made by Canaanites; that's the problem with outsourcing to people unfamiliar with your language. It uniquely also contains the prenomen Merwoserre. Petrie listed 9 scarab-seals of Yaqub-Har at that time.

Petrie placed Yaqub-Har after Khayan in the 15th dynasty. The stylistic similarity between the scarabs of seals of Khayan and Yaqub-har have been noted by several Egyptologists.[299] Khayan (**1805**-<u>1765</u> BC) was the third to last pharaoh of the 15th dynasty. Jacob moved to Egypt in 1706 BC, and likely supervised Egypt's import and export business from Avaris the next year (1705 BC). **1805** – 1705 = 100 years between Khayan's seals and Yaqub-Har's seals, or <u>1765</u> – 1705 = 60 years.

Dr. Bietak found nine royal sealings at Avaris in a scribe's niche in 18th dynasty palace G with the name Merwoserre ('strong is Re's love').[300] Yaqub-Har means 'Jacob-mountain'. "Canaanite *harru*, 'mountain', figures in several Semitic names of Middle Kingdom and Second Intermediate Period date as a divine element;"[301] like chancellor Har of the 15th. Jacob's divine mountain must have been Mount Moriah (later called the Temple Mount of Jerusalem) where Abraham prepared to sacrifice Jacob's father, Isaac, when an angel stopped Abraham and provided a ram substitute. Ryholt lists 19 seals of Yaqub-Har from unknown provenance, plus three from Canaan (Pella, Shikmona, and unknown), 2 from Tell el-Yahudiyeh in Lower Egypt, one from Hu in Upper Egypt, one said to be from Saqqara;

---

298 Genesis 45:6, 21 and 46:26-27
299 Ben-Tor, Daphna, *Scarabs, Chronology, and Interconnections*, Academic Press Fribourg, 2007, p. 106
300 Bietak, Manfred, "Seal Impressions from the Middle till the New Kingdom", *Scarabs of the Second Millennium BC from Egypt, Nubia, Crete and the Levant*, Vienna, Austria, 2004, p. 48-49
301 Ryholt, K. S. B., *The Political Situation in Egypt during the Second Intermediate Period*, 1997, p. 100
    'Anat-Har, a Canaanite chieftain during the 12th dynasty; and Sakir-Har, a Hyksos king of the 15th dynasty.

Pharaohs of the Bible

and one sealing from Kerma, Nubia.[302]

Several of Yaqub-Har's seals have paired triple scroll borders. The triple scroll borders were also common on 12th (Amenemhat II and III)[303], 13th, and especially the 14th dynasty scarabs of Sheshi and Nehsy, and may represent continuity of trade in the Nile Delta.

Khayan Seals #1-8; Yaqubhar Seals #9-18

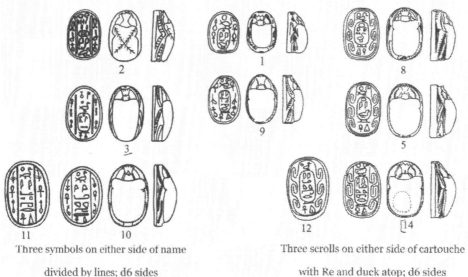

Three symbols on either side of name divided by lines; d6 sides

Three scrolls on either side of cartouche with Re and duck atop; d6 sides

The duck and sun glyphs mean "son of Re". The ankh and triangular ben-ben at the bottom mean "given life" or "forever". Yaqub-Har's seal (below) was found in Shikmona, Israel "in an archaeological context which reflects the transition MB II/a-b . . ."[304]

---

302 Ryholt, K. S. B., *The Political Situation in Egypt during the Second Intermediate Period*, p. 382
303 Ben-Tor, Daphna, "Two Royal-Name Scarabs of King Amenemhat II", Metropolitan Museum Journal, 2004. The seal drawings on this page are courtesy of Dr. Daphna Ben-Tor.
304 Ryholt, K. S. B., *The Political Situation in Egypt during the Second Intermediate Period*, p. 42

Jacob's Pharaohs

> "In 1969 a scarab containing the hieroglyphic name Y'qb-HR was found in a Middle Bronze II tomb at Shikmona, a suburb of Haifa, Israel. . . . Even after all the finds in the tomb, including the pottery, were carefully analyzed, it was clear that this scarab had to be dated to about 1730 B.C.."[305]

Regarding "the archaeological context of the Yaqub-har scarab from Shikmona," Daphna Ben-Tor noted, "the complete absence of any royal-name scarab . . . in an earlier or even contemporary context."[306] This would signify Jacob was the first and last Egyptian dignitary to do business with this community near Haifa.

Without supporting evidence, Nicolas Grimal stated Yaqub-Har reigned for 18 years.[307] 1706 - 1689 = 17 years, or 18 inclusive, of Jacob's life in Egypt. The following chapter will explain how Joseph settled his father in Avaris and gave him royal signet rings to continue business with the Minoans as the Phoenician Hyksos had done, and to seek food from around the Mediterranean for Egypt during the continuing famine.

> "The scarab distributions of Sheshy and Yaakob-har run from Nubia in the south to Palestine in the north. Items of Khayan betray the maintenance of, at the very least, extensive trade networks as far as Anatolia, Crete and Mesopotamia, if not diplomatic contacts as well. More recently, many scholars have contributed to a rapidly expanding knowledge of the character and extent of Hyksos trade relations throughout the ancient world. Holladay gives evidence of Egyptian trade routes in the Hyksos period proceeding from economically important sites such as Tell el Daba, Tell el-Maskhuta and Tell el-Yahudiya, and running the entire length of the Transjordan, east into Babylonia, north into Hittite territory and northeast into Cyprus, Anatolia and Greece. There is also evidence for trade with the far East, southern Arabia and inner Africa, which led Holladay to characterize the Asiatic settlements in the Delta as 'a major port-of-trade probably unequaled in the Eastern Mediterranean.'"[308]

12th Dynasty Scarab Evidence for my Condensed cSIP

In a 1994 excavation of the pyramid complex of Senusret III (1845-1815 BC), a stash of his wife's jewelery was discovered. Her name meant 'united with the white crown", and she is known as queen Weret II. Among her jewelry of thousands of beads were two amethyst scarab-seals of Amenemhat II[309] (1890-1852 BC), who was likely her father. Because Senusret III

---

305 Kempinski, Aharon, "Jacob in History," *Biblical Archaeology Review* 14:01, Jan/Feb 1988. Very close.
306 Ben-Tor, Daphna, *Scarabs, Chronology, and Interconnections*, Academic Press Fribourg, 2007, p. 109
307 Grimal, Nicholas, *The History of Ancient Egypt*, 1994, Blackwell Publishing, p. 187
308 Chimko, Corey J., "Foreign Pharaohs: Self-legitimization and Indigenous Reaction in Art and Lit.", p. 17
309 Ben-Tor, Daphna, "Two Royal-Name Scarabs of King Amenemhat II from Dahshur", *Metropolitan*

all the sutures of her skull were completely fused, it was estimated she died in her 70's.[310] If queen Weret II was twenty at the beginning of her husband's reign, she would have died about 1795 BC during the reign of Amenemhat III. The paired triple-scroll motif used in the 12th, 13th, 14th, and 15th dynasties may have been particular to international trade.

throne name   birth name
Amenemhat II

The two scarabs of Amenemhat II showed signs of wear on the gold bezels which attached to a metal ring,[311] proving it had been worn as a signet-ring, and was not recently made as a burial heirloom. Amenemhat II has two sphinxes in Qatna, Syria; a northern border of his kingdom, and there was Egyptian influence on Syrian seals during his reign.[312] These two scarabs for the 'perfect god' (the glyphs which look like a spoon and flag on top) have caused problems for traditional chronology which spans over 300 years between the 12th and 15th dynasties, but are contemporary in mine.

Daphna Ben-Tor commented regarding the groups of scarabs found in archaeological deposits that ". . . the evidence is usually insufficient to distinguish between late 12th and 13th Dynasty deposits, and frequently between late Middle Kingdom and early Second Intermediate Period deposits in most relevant sites."[313] Middle Kingdom is the 11th → 14th dynasties, and I propose the deposits can't be distinguished because they were all contemporary, ruling at different locations in Egypt.

A time compression based on archaeological contexts of scarabs was championed by William Ward.[314] Ward upheld a contemporary context of a scarab inscribed with mid-12th dynasty pharaoh Senusret II found in level XI at Beth-Shean, Israel[315] which spans Early Bronze Age IV to Middle Bronze Age I fitting in general phase G at Tell el-Dabᶜa (dated 1710-1690 BC by Bietak, and 1875-1825 BC by Dever)[316] for Senusret II (dated 1858-1839 BC by me). Though Ward's assumption that large to small scarab sizes indicated a chronological progression[317] was incorrect; statistically, small ring-sized scarabs are predominantly royal.[318] Ward's co-writer for *Studies on Scarab Seals volume 3*, William

---

Museum Journal, 2004, p. 17. The seal drawings on pages 121-122 are courtesy of Dr. Daphna Ben-Tor.

310 Brier, Bob and Zimmerman, Michael, "The Remains of Queen Weret II", *Chungara, Revista de Antropología Chilena Volumen 32*, No. 1, 2000, p. 23-26 at http://www.scielo.cl/scielo.php?pid=S0717-73562000000100005&script=sci_arttext

311 Ben-Tor, Daphna, "Two Royal-Name Scarabs of King Amenemhat II from Dahshur", p. 17

312 Teissier, Beatrice, *Egyptian Iconography on Syro-Palestinian Cylinder Seals of the Middle Bronze Age*, University Press, Switzerland, 1996, p. 13

313 Ben-Tor, Daphna, *Scarabs, Chronology, and Interconnections*, Academic Press Fribourg, 2007, p. 5

314 Ward, William, "Scarab Typology and Archaeological Context," *Jstor American Journal of Archaeology*, Vol. 91, No. 4 (Oct., 1987), pp. 507-532. And in Ward and Dever's *Studies on Scarab Seals volume 3*

315 Ben-Tor, Daphna, "Two Royal-Name Scarabs of King Amenemhat II from Dahshur", p. 22

316 Dever, William G., "Tell el-Dabᶜa and Levantine Middle Bronze Age Chronology: A Rejoinder to Manfred Bietak," *BASOR #281*, Egypt and Canaan in the Bronze Age, February 1991, p. 74, chart.

317 Tufnell, *Studies on Scarab Seals Volume 2*, Aris and Phillips, 1984, p. 158

318 Guthmann, Sarah, "Using Statistics to Analyze the Ancient Egyptian Scarab," *Nebraska Anthropologist*, 1996, paper 95, p. 41, at http://digitalcommons.unl.edu/nebanthro/95

Dever, wrote regarding the chronology of Tell el-Dabᶜa:
> "The material culture of the early, 'Asiatic' level in Strata G-F has significant correlations with Palestinian MB II A. Bietak's 'ultra-low' chronology, however, is 50 to 125 years too low."[319]

The use of cylinder seals throughout my condensed cFIP and cSIP also solves the problem of their use ending and then reappearing throughout a more linear chronology.

Tell el-Dabᶜa is Ancient Avaris

The following chart is based upon Walter Kutschera's preliminary carbon 14 dates filtered by Bayesian sequencing from seeds and other once living objects taken from strata at Tell el-Dabᶜa.[320] Levels H, I, K, and L were not given Carbon 14 dates.

Clarity dates align with most Carbon 14 dates for Tell el-Dabᶜa strata

Clarity BC yr	Bietak's General phase	Carbon 14 date ranges BC by W. Kutschera	Clarity Pharaohs (Dynasty #)
1480	B/2		Seti I – Rameses I (19th)
1510	B/3		Horemheb – Ay (18th)
1530	C/1		Tutankhamun – Nefertiti
1550	hiatus		Akhenaten – Thutmose IV
1590	C/2	1680-1530 aligned	Amenhotep II – Thutmose III
1620	C/3	1780-1620 aligned	Thutmose III – Hatshepsut
1670	D/1.1	1730-1640 aligned	Thutmose II – Amenhotep I
1720	D/1.2	1730-1640 aligned	Ahmose I (18th)
1740	D/2	1740-1650 aligned	Khamudi – Apepi (15th)
1760	D/3	1850-1780	Apepi
1780	E/1	1780-1700 aligned	Khyan
1800	E/2	1780-1700	Salitis (15th)
1820	E/3	1840-1750 aligned	Nehsy – Sheshi (14th)
1840	F	1870-1770 aligned	Sheshi
1854	famine		Sheshi (14th)
1860	G	1880-1790 aligned	Sheshi & Amenemhat II

319 Dever, Ibid., pp. 73-79
320 Wiener, Malcolm H., *Egypt and the Levant* Vol. 16, 2006, pp. 325–339, C14 chart on page 332

Pharaohs of the Bible

1870	G/4	1950-1810 aligned	Qareh & Amenemhat II
1880	H		Ya'ammu & Amenemhat II (12th)
1890	H		Yakbimu & Harnedjheritef (13th)
1900	I, no J		Yakbimu & Neferusobek (12th)
1910	K		Yakbimu & Senusret I
1920	L		Yakbimu & Senusret I
1930	M	2140-2000	'Ammu & Amenemhat I
1940	N/1	2150-2040	'Ammu (14th) & Amenemhat I
1950	N/2-3	2150-2040	Amenemhat I (12th) & Khety
1960	O		Khety (9th)

The evidence in the strata at Tell el-Dab‘a begins with the 9th-10th dynasty followed by the 12th dynasty which included one ruler of the 13th dynasty, the Kushite chieftains of the 14th dynasty, trade with Byblos in the pre-15th and 15th dynasties, followed by Ahmose of the 18th dynasty who conquered the final pharaoh of the 15th dynasty. Since Nubian warriors fought with Ahmose I against the 15th dynasty, it is reasonable that Uronarti, Nubia contained sealings of 13th, 14th, and 18th dynasties, but not any from the 15th dynasty.

Before the second Biblical famine, my dates for general phases span ten years (older strata being more compressed); and after the famine my dates for general phases span twenty years. Most of Bietak's general phases span thirty years. My dates for Tell el-Dab‘a's general phases E/2, M, N/1, N/2-3 are slightly outside the Carbon 14 dates; whereas almost all of Bietak's dates are 50 to 125 years off.

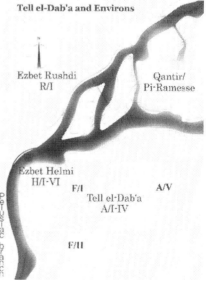

Tell el-Dab'a covered an enormous 250 hectares at a time when other large port cities averaged 75 hectares. General phases of the grand Tell el-Dab‘a complex are divided into the town during the Middle Kingdom called Ezbet Rushdi, the Middle Bronze Age former town center (A/I-IV), the east side (A/V), Qantir/Pi-Ramesse, and the citadel of Ezbet Helmi. The MBA ended when Ahmose I took control of Avaris; " . . . the demise of Avaris is perhaps a justifiable benchmark for determining the end of the Middle Bronze Age."[321] The following charts contain my dates and pharaohs.

---

321 Ilan, David, "The Middle Bronze Age," *The Archaeology of Society in the Holy Land*, 1995, p. 315

Clarity's Compilation of Bietak's Excavations at Tell el-Dabᶜa and vicinity

Year BC	Gen. phase	**F**	**A**	**H**	**P**	Features	Pharaoh
	A/1						
	A/2					Rectangular pool	
	B/1						(19th)
1480	B/2			*b/1*	*b/1*	Pi-Ramesse enclosure walls	Seti-Ramses I
1510	B/3			*b/2*		Big fortress; temple of Seth renewed	Horemheb-Ay
1530	C/1			*b/3*		Fortification walls at lake	Tut-Nefertiti
1550	hiatus	→	→	*b/c*		Pasture lands	Akhenaten-Thutmose IV
1590	C/2	-	-	*c*		Palaces; workshops w/ pumice	Amen2-Thut3
1620	C/3	-	-	*d*		Palaces F + G with Minoan fresco paintings	Thutmose III-Hatshepsut
1670	D/1.1	-	-	*e/1.1*		Military camp; Nubian soldier burials (Jacob)	Thutmose II – Yaqub-Har
1720	D/1.2	-	-	*e/1.2*		Small palace C with 30 ten-cubit temporary silos (Joseph)	Amenhotep I - Ahmose I 18
1740	D/2	-	*D/2*	*e/2-f*		Hyksos palace; long fortification wall; chancellor Har scarab	Khamudi - Apepi
1760	D/3	-	*D/3*	*g-h*		Apepi scarab; 3 warriors w/ scarabs; Neferhotep I plates	Apepi
1780	E/1	*a/2*	*E/1*			Hyksos temple; Senusret I scarab	Khyan
1800	E/2	*b/1*	*E/2*			Nubian scarabs; Sobekhotep seal	-Salitis (15th)
1820	E/3	*b/2*	*E/3*			Limestone column bases; oak trees; scarab of Sobekhotep IV	Nehsy-Sheshi
1840	F	*b/3*	*F*			Blue temple with Nehsy door jambs; deputy treasurer 'Amu	Sheshi & Senusret II
1854	famine					Mass graves between F and G	Sheshi (14th)

General phases encompass the whole area, and are in normal type.
Locations bold: **F**=Former town, **A**=Tell el-Dabᶜa, **H**=Ezbet Helmi, **P**=Pi-Ramesse
Specific strata to each location in italics. Phase B/2 from 1510-1480 BC.

Clarity's Compilation of Bietak's Excavations at Tell el-Dabᶜa and vicinity

Year BC	Gen. phase	R	F	A	Features	Pharaoh
1860	G	-	c	G/1-3	Syrian storm-god cylinder seal	Amenemhat II
1870	G/4	-	d/1	G/4	Brick barracks; 3 Neferusobek statues	Amenemhat II
1880	H	-	d/2a	H	Tents & tombs; seal of Amenemhat I	Amenemhat II
1890	H	b/1	d/2b		Levantine Painted Ware (12th)	Senusret I
1900	I, no J	b/2	-		(13th)	Harnedjheritef
1910	K	c/1-2	-		Memorial temple for Amenemhat I	Neferusobek
1920	L	d	-		one Minoan potsherd	Senusret I
1930	M	e/1-4				Amenemhat I
1940	N/1	?	e/1		(12th)	Amenemhat I
1950	N/2-3	?	e/2-3		Temple/palace built by Amenemhat I	AmenI - Khety
1960	O	?			Foundation of Khety of Herakleopolis	Khety (9th)

General phases encompass the whole area, and are in normal type.
Locations bold: **R**=Ezbet Rushdi, **F**=Former town, **A**=Tell el-Dabᶜa,
Specific strata to each location in italics. Phase O from 1970-1960 BC

Minoan Frescoes in 18th Dynasty Palaces at Ezbet Helmi

> "Not a single sherd of Minoan pottery has been found in the Late SIP strata at Tell el-Dabᶜa, and accordingly it seems clear that there was no regular trade between the Fifteenth Dynasty and Crete. The same situation is found at Alalakh and Tell Kabri where Minoan style frescoes have also been found in MB II palaces and again without any trace of Minoan pottery."[322]

Though no Minoan sherds were found in strata of the traditional SIP, one was found during the 12th dynasty in my cFIP. Ezbet Helmi lies roughly 1250m from Tell el-Dabᶜa proper. Hundreds of painted fresco sherds were found in Ezbet Helmi (indicated by H, whose areas were subdivided) in H/I-III. Area H/III is located some 150m to the southeast of Area H/I[323] and just to the north of Area H/II. Area H/III contains two levels dating to the

---

[322] Ryholt, p. 142

[323] Ryholt, p. 142 fn 512 "Most recently the excavators have come to believe that the platform construction in H/I in fact dates to the very beginning of the Eighteenth Dynasty, and Bietak – Marinatos (*Egypt & Levant*, p 62) cautiously suggests that this might place the frescoes, at least from this area, within the same period . . ."

late Hyksos and early 18th Dynasty periods. According to archaeologists Bietak and Marinatos, Area H/III had an 18th Dynasty enclosure wall with "Minoan wall paintings on both sides of the wall and concentrating around a portal [and] since these frescoes were found *in situ*, an early 18th Dynasty date is clear."[324] Below this 18th Dynasty enclosure wall was a Hyksos building with the lower-most part of the facade which still had lime plaster typical of Minoan wall paintings, similar to that found in Area H/I. They concluded, "this evidence supports the stratigraphical analysis . . . that Minoan wall paintings existed in Avaris both during the late Hyksos period and the early 18th Dynasty."[325]

15th dynasty of Hyksos abused their power in the Delta and were destroyed.

[14th] & 15th Dynasty (Hyksos) in Delta	6th Dynasty in Memphis *(pre-15)*	12th Dynasty in Itjtawy/Lisht	9th & 10th Dynasties in Herakleopolis Magna	11th Dynasty in Thebes 13th Dynasty various cities	16th Dynasty in El-Kab & Edfu
[1874-1821 Sheshi]	1856-1844 Teti ▲		1861-1856 Merikare▲	1878-1856 Intef I (11th)	[Ankhtifi of Mo'alla]
[Sheshi to Nehesy; Nehesy to Djehuty]	*Hor . . .* 3 lost	1858-1839 Senusret II ▲	1861-56 Khuy▲ 1856-1845 Neferkare VII ▲	1866-1817 Intef II (11th)▲	1850-1840 Zeket . . . 1840-1830 Ar . . .
[1821-1820 Nehesy; [Djehuty fled south]	1844-1842 Userkare, usurper	1847-1808 Senusret III ▲	1845-1825 Shed...+ H... 1845-1830 Neferkahor	11y Neferhotep I, Sihathor 9y Sobekhotep IV, 5y Hori	1830-1820 ...nia... 1820-1817 Djehuty
	1842-1817 Pepi I ▲	1827-1779 ▲ Amenemhat III	1830-1825 (Neferkare) Pepiseneb VIII (9th)	Montuhotep V, Dedumose 10y Sobekhoteps III, V-VII	1817-'01 Sobekhotep VIII 1801-1800 Neferhotep III
1820-1815 Salitis15th 1815-1810 Beon	*Nib . . . Mer?en*		1825-1815 (Wankhare) Khety III	Nebnun, Renseneb, Neferhotep II, Nedjemibre	1800-1799 Montuhotepi 1799-1773 Nebiriau I
1810-1805 Sakir-Har	*Penensetsepet*		1825-'15 Neferkamin II	Seb,Kay, 3y Amenemhat VII	-Sobeknakht II El-Kab
1805-1765 Khyan	*Shepesu (Kheretheb) (Khut . . . hemet) lost*		1815-1801 (Nebkaura) Khety IV (10th)	2y Imyremashaw, 3y Ined, 11y Wahibre Ibiau; Ibi	1773-1772 Nebiretawe 1772-1771 Nebiriau II
	1817-1804 Nemtyemsaf I ▲		1815-1805 Kaukara 1805-1795 Neferkaure 2	3y Sewadjtu; Senebmiu, Sankhptahi {13th ends 1780}	1771-1759 BebiAnkh 1759-1758 Shedwaset
1765-1731 Apepi	1804-1760 Pepi II ▲	1781-1772 /▲\ Amenemhat IV	1795-1790 (9th) Neferkauhor Khu Hepu	1817-1815 Intef III (11th) 1y (Sehotepkare) Intef V	Montemsaf at Edfu Dudimose I + II Edfu
	1760-1759 Nemtyemsaf II	[1772-1764 Montuhotep IV]	1790-1785 Neferirkare II	1815-1772 Montuhotep II (Upper Egypt only) (11th)	Senusret IV 17th Dyn. N. of Thebes
(Apepi conquered Memphis in 1754.)	1759-1754 (Netjerikare) Siptah	(1772-1761 by 11th dynasty)	(1785-1761 by 11th dynasty)	1772-1764 Montuhotep II Middle and Upper Egypt	1761-1757 Rahotep 5y Nub Intef VI ▲
				> Montuhotep IV at Lisht 1764-1761 Montuhotep III	1757-1754 Sobekemsaf I 2y wep Intef V
1731-1720 Khamudi	(1754-1720 15th dyn)	(17th dynasty)	(then 17th dynasty)	(then 17th dynasty)	> Intefs VII + VIII

17th Dynasty continued
1754-1747 Sobekemsaf II
1747-1746 Ahmose [formerly Tao I]
1746-1742 Tao [formerly Tao II]
1742-1738 Kamose

Ahmose I (1738-1712) of the 18th dynasty defeated Khamudi of the Hyksos in 1720 BC.

---

324 Bietak and Marinatos 1995, p. 49
325 Ibid.

Nebkherure Montuhotep II (1815 – 1764 BC) of the 11th Dynasty

History prior to the Ahmose's victory is vital. The 11th dynasty in Thebes became very powerful toward the end of the cSIP as the other dynasties came to an end. While Hyksos' Beon, Sakir-Har, and Khyan were ruling in the delta, Montuhotep II was ruling Upper Egypt from Thebes. In 1785 BC when Neferirkare II of the 9th dynasty died, Montuhotep took over Herakleopolis Magna which was close to Lisht. So 12th dynasty king Amenemhat IV, without male heirs, could see a bitter future as Montuhotep II was expanding his realm to include Middle Egypt. When Amenemhat IV died in 1772 BC, Montuhotep II took over. I propose he placed his (grand)son Nebtawyre Montuhotep IV as king in the former 12th dynasty palace at Lisht, so it's understandable that he had a vizier named Amenemhat.

Montuhotep II had his heb-sed festival in 1785 BC, and every three years thereafter. In 1770 BC, in his 45th year and his sixth festival he gave himself the new nebty name of 'he who unifies the two lands'. He had made a tiny statue of himself seated on his throne dressed in the white heb-sed tunic wearing the red crown of Lower Egypt (which he hoped to gain); his skin was painted black in honor of Osiris. The statue was found beneath his mortuary temple which was the first to be built in Deir el-Bahari in western Thebes, over the hills from the Valley of the Kings.

Reliefs and Statue

Montuhotep II's mortuary temple

After Montuhotep II died in 1764 BC, his son Sankhka-re/ptah Montuhotep III ruled in his place for three years, then Rahotep of the 17th dynasty gradually added all the lands of the 11th dynasty to his own. {Sewedjare Montuhotep V ruled during the 13th dynasty; and Montuhotep I (1889-1878 BC) began the 11th dynasty at the end of the cFIP.}

17th Dynasty

1761-1757 (Sekhenre Wahkhaw) Rahotep
1757-1754 (Sekhemre Shedtawy) Sobekemsaf I
        2y during father's reign (Sekhemre Wepmaat) Intef V
        5y began in father's reign (Nubkheperre) Intef VI
        1y (Sekhemre Herhermaat) Intef VII [co-reign]
1754-1747 (Sekhemre Wadjkhaw) Sobekemsaf II
1747-1746 (Senakhtenre) Ahmose [formerly Tao I]
1746-1742 (Seqenenre) Tao [formerly Tao II]
1742-1738 (Wadjkheperre) Kamose

Sobekemsaf II and Khonsu at Madamud

    The 17th dynasty began to extend their rule from Theban nome #4 to nome #20 of the fayyum. All the other dynasties, except the 15th, had ended; but the 17th pharaohs lacked the longevity to solidify an empire. According to his Koptos stela, Rahotep restored the enclosure wall of the ruined temple,[326] I think, from the damage of extensive flooding during the reign of Amenemhat III. Rahotep only likely controlled nomes #4-8. Sobekemsaf I was the father of at least two sons named Antef/Intef who ruled during his reign. Sobekemsaf I began a necropolis at Dra' Abu el-Naga' near Deir el-Bahari. His son Intef VI may have asked Intef VII to co-reign with him.[327]

Sobekemsaf II (1754-1747 BC)

    Through marriage Sobekemsaf I also made alliances with Nubia and Kush. Sobekemsaf II married a Kushite woman named Nubemhet. "A Statuette of the Senior Queen Nubemhet was found at the temple of Kawa . . ."[328] between the third and fourth cataracts. Sobekemsaf II has a dual statue in Elephantine and a grafitto in Wadi el-Shatt el-Rigal roughly 10 miles north of Kom Ombo and Aswan. A mining expedition left a series of rock inscriptions with Sobekemsaf II's name along Wadi Hammamat, and one was dated to his seventh year.[329] Having the longest reign in this short dynasty, he was able to do some building. At Madamud 7km NE of Luxor, Sobekemsaf II completed a columned hall begun by Sobekhotep III, and completed decorations of a gateway of Senusret III.[330]

(Senakhtenre) Ahmose [formerly Tao I] (1747-1746 BC)

    A limestone door of SenakhtenRe at the Temple of Karnak was recently discovered.[331]

---

326 Stewart, H.M., *Egyptian Stelae, Reliefs and Paintings from the Petrie Collection. Part Two: Archaic to Second Intermediate Period*, Warminster 1979, pp. 17-18, no. 78; an image of the stele with translation at http://www.digitalegypt.ucl.ac.uk/koptos/uc14327.html
327 Ryholt, K. S. B., *The Political Situation in Egypt during the Second Intermediate Period*, p. 276
328 Ibid., p. 272, fn 983
329 Ibid., p. 174
330 Ibid., p. 309
331 "All hail the new king: New ancient Egyptian Pharaoh discovered," Fox News, March 8, 2012,

In March 2012, French Egyptologists published the inscriptions for the pharaoh commonly known as Tao I. Senakhtenre's true titulary on the door is "*Hr mry-mAa.t nswt bjty snxt-n-ra sA ra jaH-ms*" which translates as "The Horus Merymaat, the king of Upper and Lower Egypt Senakhtenre, the Son of Re Ahmose,"[332] or Iahmose (moon's son). He will now likely be named Ahmose, the elder. The inscription also noted that the door and other limestone blocks had been transported from Hyksos' controlled Tura (across the Nile from Saqqara and Memphis). In 1754 BC Apepi had captured Memphis.

King Ahmose, the elder, married Tetisheri who gave birth to Seqenenre Tao, Ahhotep (f), and Kamose.[333] Their daughter Ahhotep I married her brother Seqenenre Tao and birthed a son named Ahmose (I); and Ahmose-Nefertari, and three other Ahmose-[ ] daughters.

Tao [formerly Tao II] (1746-1742 BC)

Sobekemsaf II had good relations with Nubia and Kush, and Tao needed a place to train them to work as one army. Tao built a mud-brick palace and military post where king Djehuty had placed his at Deir el-Ballas[334] (between Edfu and Thebes). Kerma ware was prevalent at the site.[335] *The Quarrel of Apophis and Seqenenre* is a strange rendition of king Apepi's arrogance toward Tao as a mere nomarch who should keep the hippopatami of Thebes quiet. But I think it was a ruse for his messenger to ascertain Tao's military strength. By this time Tao

Head of Tao with several axe wounds

may have ruled over nomes #1-14, and Apepi still hadn't made as much progress beyond Memphis. Thebes controlled access to the gold and ivory of Nubia and Kush. Apepi controlled access to the hardwoods of Amurru (Syria and Lebanon of Phoenicia) and the luxury items of the Mediterranean Sea. The *Quarrel* stated that the people of Avaris were in misery under Apepi's taxation and religious policy.[336] Tao began skirmishing with Apepi of the Hyksos. Between 1745-1742 BC, the skirmishes between Tao and Apepi became full battles, and Tao died of axe wounds to the head.[337] Examinations determined he was initially attacked from below (thus he was likely in a chariot), and the fatal wounds were inflicted by an Asiatic axe.[338] Jacob's beloved Rachel gave birth in 1745 BC to Joseph.

---

http://scitech.foxnews.mobi/quickPage.html?page=23952&content=67878171&pageNum=1
332 Biston-Moulin, S., "Le roi Sénakht-en-Rê Ahmès de la XVIIe dynastie", *ENIM* (Egypte Nilotiques et Mediterraneen) 5, mars 2012, pp. 61 - 72
333 Ryholt, K., *The Political Situation in Egypt during the Second Intermediate Period*, 1997, p. 280
334 Ibid., p. 174, footnote 625
335 Shaw, Ian, *The Oxford History of Ancient Egypt*, Oxford University Press, 2000, p. 199
336 *The Quarrel of Apophis and Seqenenre* is at http://www.reshafim.org.il/ad/egypt/texts/apophis.htm
337 Tao II article, mummy head wound, from http://en.wikipedia.org/wiki/Seqenenre_Tao_II on 6/2/10
338 Bietak and Strouhal, *Annalen des Naturhistorischen Museums in Wien* 78, pp. 29-52

Kamose (1742-1738 BC), last pharaoh of the 17th dynasty

Kamose controlled nomes #1 (Kom Ombo as capital) to #14 (Cusae as capital) according to his first stela: "We are calm in our part of Egypt. Elephantine is strong and the interior is with us as far as Cusae. . . . He (i.e. Apepi) holds the land of the Asiatics, and we hold Egypt. . . ." After almost 100 years, the south had almost acquiesced ownership of the delta to Phoenician foreigners. His stela continued, "None can pass through it as far as Memphis (although it is) Egyptian water! See he (even) has Hermopolis!"[339]

Kamose found his holdings being squeezed from the north and the south between two "pharaohs" which he referred to as "chieftains". (Commanders at Buhen, Nubia placed their names and 'ruler of Kush' in cartouches.)[340] Kamose wrote on a tablet:

> "I should like to know what serves this strength of mine, when a chieftain in Avaris, and another in Cush, and I sit united with an Asiatic and a Nubian, each in possession of his slice of Egypt, and I cannot pass by him as far as Memphis. . . . No man can settle down, when despoiled by the taxes of the Asiatics. I will grapple with him, that I may rip open his belly! My wish is to save Egypt and to smite the Asiatic!"[341]

But Kamose first had to subdue the encroaching *nhsyw* of Kush at the second cataract[342] who were of different tribes than his Medjay-Nubian archers stationed at the Deir el-Ballas fort. Prior to his third year he conquered the Wawat-Nubians from the first cataract (near Aswan) to the second cataract (near Semna), and retook the fort at Buhen and placed his stela there noting an intercepted letter from Apophis seeking military aid from the Nubians. The Kushites and Nubians overran the Buhen fort, marred the name of Kamose on his stela, and set the fort on fire.[343] Kamose would later return to put an end to the Nubian rebellion, but he marched towards the delta in his third year to break the embargo and gain tax relief.

The Second Stela of Kamose goes on to state the Cynolpolite nome (#17) and the Bahariyah Oasis are in his possession in his third regnal year, and that he pushed back "that Syrian prince" Apophis/Apepi up to Atfih in nome #21, which is roughly 30 miles south of Memphis. Kamose plundered all south-going ships and reclaimed territories previously controlled by Apepi, but Kamose did not make it to Avaris itself. Kamose captured Apepi's messenger on the way to Kush to seek military aid, and recorded on his stela how Apepi blamed Kamose and former Egyptians for the war and sad state of affairs. First Kamose listed the horses and luxury goods he'd taken from Apepi's ships . . .

---

339 Translation at http://www.reshafim.org.il/ad/egypt/kamose_inscription.htm
340 Smith, H., *The fortress of Buhen: The inscriptions*, Londres 1976, pp. 55-56 and Plate 72
341 Pritchard, James B., *Ancient Near Eastern Texts*. Princeton, 1969, pp. 232-233, Carnarvon Tablet I
342 Ryholt, p. 179
343 Ryholt, p. 91 fn 293 ". . . the evidence of fire and destruction at Buhen has been interpreted as a raid on this fortress by the Kermans and seen as a sign of conflict between the Kushites and Egypt during the Thirteenth Dynasty. However, recent reexaminations of this evidence by Bourriau and Smith strongly suggests that the raid dates to the Late SIP and it remains unclear who attacked whom."

Pharaohs of the Bible

" . . . all the fine products of Retenu - I have confiscated all of it! I haven't left a thing to Avaris to her (own) destitution: the Asiatic has perished! <u>Does **your** heart fail, O **you vile Asiatic**, **you** who used to say: 'I am lord without equal from Hermopolis to Pi-Hathor upon the Rekhty water. (As for) Avaris on the Two Rivers, I laid it waste without inhabitants; I destroyed their towns and burned their homes to reddened ruin-heaps forever, because of the destruction they had wrought in the midst of Egypt: they who had allowed themselves to hearken to the call of the Asiatics, had forsaken Egypt, their mistress!'"</u> [attributed to **Apepi**]

Kamose is not taking credit for destroying Avaris, Apepi is taking credit for how Salitis destroyed Avaris long ago and blaming it on the former Egyptians forsaking their gods.

After Kamose boxed Apepi back into the delta, Kamose returned to Thebes to appoint a successor before his second campaign into Nubia. At Toshka and Arminna between the first and second cataracts there are rock inscriptions with the names of Kamose and his nephew Ahmose I together[344] verifying their coregency in the 4th year of Kamose. Kamose returned to Buhen to reestablish his authority there, and he was likely killed in battle. Thus Ahmose I began his reign as a prepubescent boy (1738 BC) with his mother Ahhotep I as regent. Though Kamose won many battles, it would be his his wife, Ahhotep II, who would continue to fight in his place as general until her nephew Ahmose was old enough to fight.

Queen Ahhotep II ("moon is satisfied"), wife/widow of Kamose

Queen Ahhotep II was given a king's royal burial in Dra' Abu el-Naga', the necropolis of 17th dynasty kings, whereas Ahhotep I was buried in Deir el Bahari. Buried with Ahhotep II were the griffin axehead and other items of Ahmose I, three gold flies for bravery in battle, silver jewelry, and a couple items of Kamose[345] including a barque usually attributed to him. The stylized Ah/Iah moon glyph was used on her sarcophagus; similarly on relief below.

Sacred barque, gold jewlery, weapons and military honors in queen Ahhotep II's burial

stylized "Ah/Iah" moon

Ahmuch, Ahhotep, Ahhotet?; and son of UE, Ahmose

---

344 Ryholt, K., *The Political Situation in Egypt during the Second Intermediate Period*, 1997, p. 182
345 Tyldesley, Joyce, *Chronicles of the Queens of Egypt*, Thames & Hudson, London, 2006

Ahhotep II realized the Hyksos forts were supplied by Mediterranean traders. Kamose's widow pursued winning the war through a marriage alliance in order to gain their support against the Hyksos who had blocked trade with Thebes, so she married an island king and became 'Mistress of the shores of Haunebut'.[346]   I propose she married the king of Thera. Thera, now Santorini, is about 200 km (120 miles) southeast from Greece's mainland.

> Several Egyptian pharaohs claimed ownership over "Haunebut", which means "Behind the Islands." The Greek portion of the Rosetta Stone text clearly translates the phrase Haunebu – meaning "the people of Haunebut" – as Greek or Hellene. And Greece does lie "behind the islands" of the Aegean Sea, when viewed from Egypt. Thutmosis III boasted that he had "trussed... the Haunebut" and struck those that lived "in the midst of the Great Green Sea" (the Mediterranean Sea). In a single year, he claimed to have collected 36,692 deben of gold from his conquered subjects – the equivalent of three metric tons – of which 27,000 kilos is specifically said to have come from the Asian provinces and the Isles in the Midst of the Great Green Sea (the Greek islands).
>
> In 1946, Spyridon Marinatos, best known for his work on **Thera** (Akrotiri), had found a series of **grain silos** in Boiotia. Marinatos also believed that the Mycenaeans helped the Egyptians to expel the Hyksos and were rewarded with the gold that has been found in the so-called shaft tombs in Mycenae. These tombs date from the first 80 years after the expulsion of the Hyksos. Some tombs show Egyptian influences, although the Mycenaeans were much more careless with their dead than the Egyptians. On the topic of the grain silos, Marinatos stated that they greatly resembled Egyptian silos. Of course, his colleagues were unable to accept such a comparison.
>
> One of these silos measured 30 metres high and 100 metres wide. The entire grain production of Argolid could be stored in this complex; only an organised state could and would resort to such a mechanism. But Greece did not have an organised state when the silos were built and used. The logical conclusion [was] that the Greek land was used as a supply of grain that was exported to Egypt.[347] - Philip Coppens

Queen Ahhotep II had Thera prepare for Joseph's famine. Griffins are associated with queens. Referring to the griffin found at Tell el-Dab^ca, Bietak mused, "Just as a heraldic pair of griffins decorate the throne room at Knossos, so our large griffin could equally be from a queen's throne room, if it is not – as at Thera – part of a divine representation."[348]

---

346 Bietak, Manfred, *Avaris, The Capital of the Hyksos: Recent Excavations at Tell el-Dab^ca*, British Museum Press, London, 1996, p. 80, footnote #141: Gauthier 1927, 12; Gardiner 1947, 206f. The German historian Eduard Meyer (1928, 54, 7), translating this toponym as Crete, took the title of Queen Ahhotep to mean that during a regency for her sons Kamose and Ahmose she had formed special ties with the Minoans, with whose help the Hyksos were finally overthrown. He explained the title as arising from a marriage of the widowed Egyptian queen to the Minoan king. This is stretching the evidence too far, of course, but it is interesting to note this suggestion of a dynastic link made already many decades before the discovery of Minoan frescoes at Avaris.

347 Coppens, by Philip, "Egypt: origin of the Greek culture: For centuries, scholars have identified the Greek culture as the source of the western civilisation. But what if the Greek culture itself was a legacy – a colony – of the ancient Egyptians?" *Frontier Magazine* 5.3, May-June 1999

348 Bietak, Manfred, *Avaris, The Capital of the Hyksos: Recent Excavations at Tell el Daba*, British Museum

Pharaohs of the Bible

Egypt is known for its papyrus, Greece is not. Could the griffin on the river represent Ahhotep II on the Nile? At the Walters Art Museum there is a Phoenician scarab of a king facing a winged goddess. A griffin with spirals was found in a 'treasury' room in stratum VIIA at Megiddo. The throne room at Knossos, Crete has griffins, with a seat for a woman:

Frescoes beneath Thera's ash

Griffin on a river

Lady with papyri

Could it be Ahhotep II?

Papyrus plants

> "A room reserved for the epiphany of a goddess, who would have sat in the throne, either in effigy, or in the person of a priestess, or in imagination only. In that case the griffins would have been purely a symbol of divinity rather than a heraldic motif. It is also speculated that the throne was made specifically for a female individual, since the indent seems to be shaped for a woman's buttocks, as well as the extensive use of curved edges and the **crescent moon** carved at its base, both symbolic of femininity." - Wikipedia

(note spirals)

Griffin detail of queen's throne room in Knossos

I propose the moon was carved on the Minoan throne for queen Ahhotep II, whose

---

Press, London, 1996, p. 80

name means the "moon is satisfied". Dr. Bietak wrote, "The connections with the Minoan world would fit well in the time of King Ahmose, whose ceremonial weapons display distinctly Aegean, if not Minoan, motifs, such as the Aegean griffin."[349] There are fragments of griffin depictions from Tell el-Dab'a comparable to the griffins from the queen's throne room at Knossos.[350] I suggest the throne room at Tell el-Dab'a was made for Hatshepsut.

Though Ahmose I would be given the credit for winning the final battles against the Hyksos and reuniting Egypt, even he recognized it was only because of his aunt Ahhotep II. Ahmose I wrote of queen Ahhotep II on a stela:

> "She is the one who has accomplished the rites and taken care of Egypt...
> She has looked after her soldiers, she has guarded her, she has brought back her fugitives and collected together her deserters, she has pacified Upper Egypt and expelled her rebels."[351]

Ahhotep II **Knossos elite woman** **Theran fresco**

The Knossos woman in the frieze fragment has a sacral knot at the back of her neck which signified she was a goddess. I posit that Ahhotep II renewed offerings to the gods and remained in Egypt as general for 3-7 years, and then married the Theran king and moved to the island where she continued her efforts through international trade embargoes against the Hyksos. Ahhotep II was Egypt's Joan of Arc. Knossos honored her with a throne room. Minoan art and patterns began to be included in ports of trade; possibly at the request of such a woman. Ahhotep II likely corresponded with Ahmose I as to when the embargoes would be at greatest effect to launch a campaign against the delta.

---

349 Bietak, Manfred, "Minoan Paintings in Avaris," Sept. 4, 1997,
http://www.therafoundation.org/articles/art/minoanpaintingsinavarisegypt, accessed 5/2/11
350 Ibid., (Bietak 1999, pl. IX)
351 Ahhotep I, http://en.wikipedia.org/wiki/Ahhotep_I, accessed 5/2/11

In the tenth year of Ahmose I (1728 BC), Jacob's sons came to their father with Joseph's multicolored coat smeared with blood. Jacob rent his clothes and mourned the "death" of his son for many days; but Reuben had stopped the other brothers from killing Joseph, and Judah suggested selling him to the slave traders, who then sold him to Potiphar in Egypt.[352]

Joseph sold to Potiphar

Campaigns of Ahmose I

Ahmose learned Avaris was resupplied with grain, wine, and soldiers from two forts: one at Heliopolis, and another to the northeast called Tjaru/Siles on the Mediterranean. Tjaru would no longer be resupplied by Minoan ships due to the influence of Ahhotep II; and Aegean troops would support him. According to the Rhind Papyrus, Ahmose ("he of the south") fought against both of these cities before proceeding to Avaris: in July of Ahmose's 11th year (1727 BC) he attacked Heliopolis, and he conquered Tjaru (Tell Hebua) in October.[353] Ahmose led three attacks against Avaris, went to quell an uprising in a town south of Avaris; then returned and conquered and plundered Avaris in 1723 BC and drove the Hyksos east to Sharuhen. Ahmose besieged Sharuhen for three years and drove the Hyksos out (1720 BC). Ahmose then spent the next two years defeating Nubian archers. In his 22nd year (1716 BC) Ahmose's Levant campaign reached Kedem, near Byblos;[354] and on his return he acquired Canaanite cattle.[355] Mud-brick enclosures for cattle breeding were unearthed at Ezbet Helmi's area H/V at the time Ahmose conquered Avaris.[356] So for eleven years, Ahmose fought to restore and to extend Egypt's borders; as did his aunt. Ahhotep II may have given Ahmose an axe inscribed with his name which had a griffin, and a dagger with Minoan motifs of a lion chasing a calf;[357] which he later placed in her tomb.

The military exploits of Ahmose I were recorded in the tomb of one of his marines, Ahmose of Nekheb, who also fought under Amenhotep I and Thutmose I. Soldiers would cut off the hand of a slain enemy for confirmation. Ahmose I rewarded his brave soldiers, like Ahhotep II, with gold and spoils.

"Now when I had established a household, I was taken to the ship "Northern", because I was brave. I followed the sovereign on foot when he rode about on his chariot. When

---

352 Genesis 37:22-36
353 Al-Ayedi, Abdul Rahman, "Tharu: The staring point on the 'Ways of Horus'", 2000, p. 49; and wikipedia
354 Weinstein, James M. *The Egyptian Empire in Palestine, A Reassessment*, p. 6. Bulletin of the American Schools of Oriental Research, #241. Winter 1981. Ahmose wanted to hit the 15th dynasty's home port.

355 Redford's *History and Chronology of the 18th Dynasty* notes, "a graffito in the quarry at Tura whereby 'oxen from Canaan' were used at the opening of the quarry in Ahmose's regnal year 22." pp. 195-197
356 Bietak, Manfred, Tell el-Dab'a website, http://www.auaris.at/html/helmi_en.html, at general phase D/2 which is dated by pottery to be the end of the 15th dynasty and beginning of 18th dynasty.
357 Ibid., footnote #139: The weapons were found together with other precious objects of kings Ahmose and Kamose in the coffin of Queen Ahhotep I, perhaps the wife of King Senachtenre of the 17th Dynasty.

the town of <u>Avaris was besieged</u>, I fought bravely on foot in his majesty's presence. Thereupon I was appointed to the ship "Rising in Memphis". Then there was fighting on the water in Padjeku <u>(Pelusiac) of Avaris</u>. I made a seizure and carried off a hand. When it was reported to the royal herald the gold of valour was given to me. Then <u>they fought again in this place</u>; I again made a seizure there and carried off a hand. Then I was given the gold of valour once again.
<u>Then there was fighting in Egypt to the south of this town</u>. and I carried off a man as a living captive. I went down into the water - for he was captured on the city side - and crossed the water carrying him. When it was reported to the royal herald I was rewarded with gold once more.
<u>Then Avaris was despoiled</u>, and I brought spoil from there: one man, three women; total, four persons. His majesty gave them to me as slaves.
<u>Then Sharuhen was besieged for three years</u>. His majesty despoiled it and I brought spoil from it: two women and a hand. Then the gold of valour was given me, and my captives were given to me as slaves.
Now when his majesty had slain the nomads of Asia, he sailed south to Khent-hen-nefer, to <u>destroy the Nubian Bowmen</u>. His majesty made a great slaughter among them, and I brought spoil from there: two living men and three hands. Then I was rewarded with gold once again, and two female slaves were given to me. His majesty journeyed north, his heart rejoicing in valour and victory. He had conquered southerners, northerners." - Ahmose of Nekheb

Tell el-Ajjul (Sharuhen) [Royal Scarabs] and Volcanic Eruptions

The majority of Middle Kingdom scarabs were recovered from Tell el-Ajjul in Canaan. Recently, Peter Fischer has been the director of excavations at Tell el-Ajjul.

> "Keel (1997: 106-512) has listed 1,244 scarabs/scaraboids and other objects with iconographic decorations from Tell el-'Ajjul. The site also produced numerous objects of excellent jewellery. A large quantity of objects came from Egypt, Cyprus, Crete, Greece, Syria and other Levantine sites. These finds demonstrate the cosmopolitan nature of the societies of Tell el-'Ajjul."[358]

Tell el-Ajjul was a wealthy Mediterranean trading post. A 'fosse', ditch or moat, and rampart were built around it during the late Middle Bronze Age IIA according to Fischer,[359] which would be the beginning of the 13th dynasty according to Tell el-Dabᶜa levels in Egypt. This was a Hyksos fortress of a Hyksos-controlled city which Kempinski and Bietak have determined to be Sharuhen.[360] Sharuhen is a city which Ahmose I would capture[361] and

---

358 Fischer, Peter, director of excavations, from his "Scientific Objectives: Previous Research" at Tell el-Ajjul, http://www.fischer.praktikertjanst.se/
359 Ibid.
360 Kempinski, A.,"Tell el-Ajjul: Beth-Aglayim or Sharuhen?," *IEJ*, 1974, pp. 145-152; and Bietak, M., 1994, p. 58
361 Fischer, Peter, *et al.*, "Tell El-Ajjul 2000 Second Season Preliminary Report," "It is tempting to ascribe

Pharaohs of the Bible

would later be taken by Joshua.[362] Tell el-Ajjul provides facts about the eruption of Thera.

Fischer found several pieces of Theran pumice at Tell el-Ajjul. Fischer listed his excavation levels by Horizon numbers H1-H8, youngest to oldest. I'm adding my pharaohs.

Horizon	# of Theran pumice pieces in Horizon	Clarity Pharaohs
Coluvial	1-Bo	
Old excavation	2-Bo	
H1 (late 18th dyn.)	2-Bo	Ay to Horemheb
H2 (mid 18th dyn.)	4-Bo, 2-Bm/u	Amenhotep IV to Tutankhamun
H3-4 (first half 18th dyn.)	12-Bo	Thutmose III to Amenhotep III
H5 (early 18th dyn.)	23-Bo	Ahmose I to Hatshepsut

In Clarity chronology, the 18th dynasty spans 1738-1493 BC. Tell el-Ajjul is 600 miles away from Thera, and some pumice can float on the sea for at least a year. Fischer did not find any pumice in the Middle Bronze Age H6-H8, and concluded "Thera erupted at the end of H6 or transitional H6/5 or at the beginning of H5;"[363] whereas I suggest Thera erupted at the end of H5 during the reign of Hatshepsut.

Vulcanologists provide the following chronology of Thera's eruptions.[364]

6,000 – 3,000 BC	Minoan eruption (Bo 1-4)
21,000 BC	Cape Riva eruption (CR)
40,000 BC	Upper Scoriae 2 eruption
60-40,000 BC	Upper Scoriae 1 eruption
60-50,000 BC	Vourvoulos eruption
60,000 BC	Middle Pumice eruption (Bm I-II)
70-60,000 BC	Cape Thera eruption (CT 1-3)
180,000 BC	Lower Pumice 2 eruption (Bu 2)
203,000 BC	Lower Pumice 1 eruption (Bu 1)

Since I believe Elohim terraformed the Earth in 4004 BC and said it was "*good*", that means it was not scarred or broken apart with tectonic plates ringed by volcanoes until Noah's flood in 2348 BC when the abyss was broken apart. So I place Thera's oldest eruptions at the time of Noah's flood, and the rest subsequent to it with the Minoan eruption (Bo 1-4) during Hatshepsut's reign. Scientists stated " . . . the Akrotiri, Thera, volcanic

---

    the evidence of destruction to the forays of Ahmose into southern Palestine after the defeat of the Hyksos at Avaris judging from the locally produced Middle/Late Bronze Age 'transitional' pottery types." p. 20

362 Joshua 19:6

363 Fischer, Peter M., "The Preliminary Chronology of Tell el-Ajjul: Results of the Renewed Excavations in 1999 and 2000," *The Synchronisation of Civilisations in the Eastern Mediterranean in the Second Millennium B.C. II,* Osterreichische Akademie der Wissenschaften Wien, 2003, p. 290

364 Data from http://www.decadevolcano.net/santorini/santorini_volcanism.htm

destruction level and using the new IntCal04 radiocarbon calibration curve, we get an overall 95.4% confidence range for the destruction level (and the very soon following eruption) of c.1684-1615 BC. These date ranges (in approximate terms a 'mid-to-later 17th century BC date') are thus the appropriate 'high' chronology date ranges now."[365] I propose 1651 BC for the Minoan eruption which ended Hatshepsut's reign for lack of protecting her people from natural disasters (lack of maat).

"On present estimates, Thera was an extraordinary, 1 in 300 years, estimated Volcanic Explosivity Index 6.9, volcanic event."[366] There have been dozens of Aegean volcanic eruptions since Hatshepsut's time. 1651 – 300 = 1351 Another large eruption occurred during the 8th year of Rameses III, which is 1310 BC in my chronology; and fits the time-frame for another major eruption fairly well. The eruption during the reign of Rameses III was likely from a different volcano of the Southern Aegean arc. [See page 238 for map.]

Occupation of Tell el-Ajjul (Sharuhen)

Petrie, Albright, Kempinski, Fischer, and others have excavated at Tell el-Ajjul and have their opinions as to the occupation levels and times. I am using *Kempinski's dynasty attributions*.[367] Though Sharuhen's history is older, I'm beginning with its first palace. This is my synopses for the city and its main palace/fortress from oldest to youngest. City level IIA which Kempinski attributed to the 15th dynasty contained scarabs from the 13th, 14th, and 16th dynasties; thus supporting my cSIP.

City Level	Palace/Fortress	Canaanite Age	*Dyn.* Important Object
III	I	MB II C (III)	*14th*, 6 meter deep fosse
IIA	I	Chariot horses in tomb	*15th*, Sheshi scarab (14th) and Neferhotep I (13th) and 16th dynasty scarabs
II	II	LB (Bronze) I	*15th*, Apophis scarab
I	III	LB I	*early 18th*
	IV	LB II A	jar of Hatshepsut & Thutmose III
	V	I (Iron) A	Rameses II

The Way of Horus connected Avaris to Sharuhen. Amenemhat I had built a north/south barrier called the Wall of the Ruler from the Bitter Lakes to Tjaru at El-Ballah Lake at which the Way of Horus began.[368] I suggest that as Mentuhotep II attempted to expand his borders, he sent his general Intef to cut off supplies to the 15th dynasty of Apophis/Apepi around 1765-1764 BC by attacking palace/fortress II during city level II, and Intef recorded the event on the wall of his tomb.[369] It may have been effective, because Apepi did not conquer Memphis until 1754 BC; and then he carved his name into two sphinxes of Amenemhat II.

---

365 Manning *et al.*, update to *A Test of Time*, 2006. The original dates were 1687-1638BC on page 256.
366 Manning, Sturt, *A Test of Time*, Oxbow Books, 1999, p. 451 based upon Decker 1990:451
367 Manning, Sturt, *A Test of Time*, Oxbow Books, 1999, p. 184; see appendix B
368 Rawlinson, George, *History of Ancient Egypt*, Dodd. Mead & Company, New York, 1882, p. 148
369 Grajetzki, Wolfram, *Court Officials of the Egyptian Middle Kingdom*, Duckworth, 2009, p. 102, fig. 44

Pharaohs of the Bible

In 1715 BC, Ahmose I had troubling dreams, and his cupbearer explained how Joseph had interpreted his dream and that of the baker correctly. Ahmose I summoned Joseph from prison, Joseph interpreted the dream wisely, and Ahmose I made Joseph his vizier. Then seven years of plenty were followed by seven years of famine. In the midst of the first seven years, Ahmose I died in 1712 BC, and his young son Amenhotep I began his reign under the guidance of his mother, Ahmose-Nefertari.

Young Amenhotep I

In the second year of the famine (1706 BC) Joseph sent wagons to retrieve Jacob and the entire clan of 66 people. Amenhotep I met Jacob and asked, *"How old are you?"*

Jacob and Joseph before young Amenhotep I

And Jacob said to Pharaoh, The days of the years of my pilgrimage are an hundred and thirty years: few and evil have the days of the years of my life been, and have not attained to the days of the years of the life of my fathers in the days of their pilgrimage. And Jacob blessed Pharaoh, and went out from before Pharaoh.[370]

And with young Amenhotep's blessing, Joseph set his father and brothers in the best of the land of Rameses.[371] I propose Joseph established Jacob as governor of international trade with signet rings bearing the name Yaqub-Har (Jacob-mountain). Some of Joseph's brothers and their families may have helped in the business while others took care of the Canaanite cattle of Ahmose I. I suggest when Joseph spent time in Heliopolis (On) that some of his family took the flocks south to be near him. I propose Jacob worked in imports/exports with queen Ahhotep II who was in the Aegean.

> "The spread of urban trading networks, and their extension along the Persian Gulf and eastern Mediterranean, created a complex molecular structure of regional foci so that as well as the zonation of core and periphery (originally created around Mesopotamia) there was a series of interacting civilizations: Mesopotamia, Egypt, the Indus Valley; then also Syria, central Anatolia (Hittites) and the Aegean (Minoans and Mycenaeans). Beyond this was a margin which included not only temperate areas such as Europe, but the dry steppe corridor of central Asia. This was truly a world system, even though it occupied only a restricted portion of the western Old World. Whilst each civilization emphasized its ideological autonomy, all were identifiably part of a common world of interacting components."[372] - Robert Allen Denemark

---

370 Genesis 47:8-10 1836 – 1706 = 130 years
371 Genesis 47:11
372 Denemark, Robert A., *World System History*, 2000, p. 124

Recall God changed Jacob's name to Israel; from "supplanter" to "prince of El," short for Elohim who would lated declare Himself on Mount Sinai as Yahweh.

*And **Israel** dwelled in the land of Egypt, in the country of Goshen; and they had possessions therein, and grew, and multiplied exceedingly. <u>And Jacob lived in the land of Egypt seventeen years: so the whole age of Jacob was an hundred forty and seven years</u>. And the time drew near that Israel must die: and he called his son Joseph, and said to him, If now I have found grace in your sight, put, I pray you, your hand under my thigh, and deal kindly and truly with me; bury me not, I pray you, in Egypt: But I will lie with my fathers, and you shall carry me out of Egypt, and bury me in their burial plot. And he said, I will do as you have said. And he said, Swear to me. And he swore to him.* (Genesis 47:27-31)[373]

In 1689 BC Joseph, Amenhotep's vizier, presented his two Egyptian-born sons, Manasseh and Ephraim, to his father to receive his blessing. This was when the twelve sons/tribes of Israel were changed into thirteen. Jacob told Joseph he had given him an extra portion of land, and now claimed Ephraim and Manasseh as his own sons who would each have a land inheritance in Canaan.[374] Jacob then crossed his hands and blessed the youngest son, Ephraim, before the eldest son, Manasseh. Joseph protested, but Israel assured him that it must be so.[375] And Jacob/Israel prophesied of the exodus yet to come, *"Behold, I die: but God shall be with you, and bring you again to the land of your fathers."*[376]

Death of Queen Ahhotep II

Ahmose I's aunt queen Ahhotep II physically fought and directed the Minoan trade business to Egypt's favor, but I think her body was returned to Egypt for a royal burial. Ahhotep II's chief steward left a limestone stela in the necropolis of Dra' Abu el-Naga' in her honor which was dated to the tenth year of Amenhotep I[377] (1692 BC), which I propose was the year of her death. The representation of the hieroglyph for "ah/iah" (moon) changed between years 18 and 22 (1716 BC) of Ahmose I.[378] Since Ahhotep II's name is inscribed on her sarcophagus using the earlier stylized form of the glyph, some suppose she must have died before the glyph change; but her coffin may have been prepared prior to her death, or the craftsman preferred to write her name in the style she used in life. If Ahhotep II died in 1692 BC, it would only have been three years prior to the death of Jacob in 1689 BC.

My question would be, did Ahmose I change the style of the glyph in 1715 BC because the God of Jacob, named Yahweh, gave him a dream and told him not to worship Iah, the moon god anymore because the short form of His name "Yah" sounded similar?

---

373 1706 – 1689 = 17 years more until Jacob died
374 Genesis 48:5, 22 thus giving Joseph's two land portions to Ephraim and Manasseh
375 Genesis 48:5-20
376 Genesis 48:21
377 Kares stela (CG 34003)
378 Roth, Ann Macy, "The Ahhotep Coffins," *Gold of Praise: Studies of Ancient Egypt in honor of Edward F. Wente*, 1999

Jacob's Blessings and Astronomical Signs which became Ensigns

Jacob called for his twelve sons to come to him to receive their blessings, and he prophesied over them as recorded in Genesis 49. Based on the descriptions in that chapter, the 12 constellations of the zodiac were matched with the 12 sons of Israel;[379] and were depicted on their banners during the exodus, when YHWH brought out His *"armies"*.[380]

1. REUBEN was "*Unstable* (pouring out) *as waters*" likened to AQUARIUS, represented as a man pouring waters from an urn.
2. SIMEON and LEVI were brothers told "*be not you united*" because together, they killed a man; likened to GEMINI, the Twins.
3. JUDAH "*is a lion's whelp*" likened to LEO, the lion.
4. ZEBULUN "*shall be for an haven of ships*" likened to CANCER, the crab. The Latin and Greek words for Cancer mean 'to hold' or 'to encircle'. The territory of Zebulun stretched from the Sea of Galilee to the Mediterranean Sea.[381]
5. ISSACHAR "*is a strong ass*" or *ox*, both used in husbandry, likened to TAURUS, the Bull.
6. and 7. DAN "*shall be a serpent by the way, an adder in the path, that bites the horse heels.*" The space occupied by SCORPIO and LIBRA, has the constellation Ophiochus, the snake holder, towering above them. The snake is named Serpens. In ancient zodiacs, Ophiochus is the 13th constellation. Libra, the scales of justice, is better linked to "*Dan shall judge his people.*" Dan, the serpent, is not listed as a tribe of the 144,000 in Revelation 7, neither is Ephraim because God held these two tribes responsible for leading the 10 tribes into idolatry (1 Kings 12:26-33; Jer. 7:15). Dan's initial territory was on the coast south of Benjamin, but they moved up north.
8. GAD was "*A troop*". *Gad* reversed is *dag*, a fish, the sign PISCES. Pisces is two fish bound together, representing the Jews and Gentiles bound together by Messiah.
9. ASHER: "*His bread shall be fat*" likened to VIRGO, who is generally represented as holding wheat in the star Spica.
10. NAPHTALI "*is a hind let loose*"; a mountain gazelle. Israel's national animal is the mountain gazelle. *Naphtali* means struggle, but the end of the name by itself, *taleh*, means a lamb likened to ARIES. According to the rabbis, Aries, known as the ram, is the sign for the Jewish people as a whole.
11. JOSEPH, "*his bow stayed in strength*" likened to SAGITTARIUS, the *archer* or *bowman*; commonly represented with his bow bent in full strength with the arrow drawn up to the head.
12. BENJAMIN "*shall shred as a wolf*". CAPRICORN on the Egyptian sphere was represented by a goat led by Pan holding a wolf's head.

---
379 Ferguson, Clyde, *The Stars and the Bible*, Exposition Press, 1978, pp. 13-15
380 Exodus 12:51 see banners at http://banahtorah.blogspot.com/2006/07/12-tribes-of-israel-banners.html
381 Joshua 17:10-16 and Deuteronomy 33:18-19

Jacob's Death (1689 BC), Mummification, and Burial in Canaan

And he charged them . . . bury me with my fathers . . . In the cave that is in the field of Machpelah, which is before Mamre, in the land of Canaan, which Abraham bought with the field of Ephron the Hittite for a possession of a burial plot. There they buried Abraham and Sarah his wife; there they buried Isaac and Rebekah his wife; and there I buried Leah. . . . And when Jacob had made an end of commanding his sons, he gathered up his feet into the bed, and yielded up the ghost, and was gathered to his people. And Joseph fell on his father's face, and wept on him, and kissed him. (Genesis 49:29-50:1)

Upon Jacob's death, Joseph had the physicians embalm him, which was a forty day process followed by thirty more days to completely dry out organs with natron. Thus the Egyptians mourned Jacob for a total of seventy days.[382]

And Joseph went up to bury his father: and with him went up <u>all the servants of Pharaoh</u>, the <u>elders</u> of his house, and <u>all the elders of the land of Egypt</u>, And <u>all the house of Joseph</u>, and his brothers, and his father's house: only their little ones, and their flocks, and their herds, they left in the land of Goshen. And there went up with him <u>both chariots and horsemen: and it was a very great company</u>. (Genesis 50:7-9)

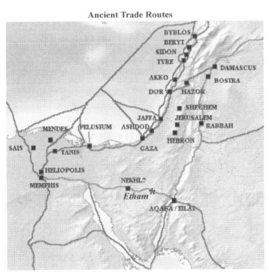

That must total at least two hundred people. Since it might appear to the Canaanites that an Egyptian war host was coming up the coastal road (the traditional quick route for war), they chose to take the longer trek from Joseph's home in Heliopolis, across the Way of the Wilderness to Eilat, then up the king's highway and the Arabah to the Dead Sea. The Egyptians didn't even enter Canaan, but remained on the eastern side of the Jordan River at Atad for seven days while the twelve sons of Jacob/Israel took the mummified body of their father to his resting place beside Abraham and Sarah, and Jacob's wife Leah in Hebron. And then they all returned using the same roads back to Egypt together.[383]

It's fitting Jacob/Yaqub-Har was taken by trade routes to his final resting place after 17-18 years directing trade.

---

382 Genesis 50:3
383 Genesis 50:10-14

Pharaohs of the Bible

Canals linked Avaris to the Mediterranean Sea and the Red Sea. The El-Ballah Lakes no longer exist at present. Tell el-Yehudiyeh is where a particular type of pottery was made.

Jacob's Chronology

1836	Esau and Jacob were born.
1782	Jacob travelled to Harran and began 7 years of service as a bride-price.
1775	Jacob, at age 61, married Leah and Rachel
1774	Reuben born of Leah
1773	Simeon born of Leah
1772	Levi born of Leah
1771	Judah born of Leah
1770	Dan born of Bilhah
1768	Naphtali born of Bilhah
1766	Gad born of Zilpah
1764	Asher born of Zilpah
1757	Issachar born of Leah
1755	Zebulun born of Leah
1754	Dinah born of Leah
1748	Jacob began service for cattle.
1745	Joseph born of Rachel
1742	Jacob's family left Laban for Canaan.
1742	El Elyon renames Jacob, Israel; and they dwelt in Shalem, five miles east of Shechem.
1741	Rachel died giving birth to Benjamin in Bethlehem.
1728	Joseph, at age 17, was taken to Egypt.
1716	Isaac died, aged 180.
1715	Joseph, at thirty, governor of Egypt
1706	Benjamin, by age 35, had ten sons.
1706	Jacob and 65 kin moved to Egypt.
1689	Jacob died in Egypt but was buried in Canaan.

Clarity East Nile Delta Map

Jacob/Israel

Canaan	(C)Harran	Canaan	Goshen, Egypt
1836-1782	1782-1742	1742-1706	1706-1689

Egyptian Pharaohs in the Nile delta

Sheshi (14th) 1874-1821	Salitis (15th) 1820-1815	Beon (15th) 1815-1810	Sakir -Har 1810-1805	Khyan (15th) 1805-1765	Apepi (15th) 1765-1731	Khamudi (15th) 1731-1720	Ahmose I (18th) 1720-1712	Ahmen-hotep I + Nefertari 1712-1702	Ahmen-hotep I (18th) 1702-1688

Joseph's Pharaohs

"Joseph was brought down to Egypt"
(Genesis 39:1)

The spoiled child

When Jacob went to Harran he fell in love with Rachel, Laban's younger daughter, and gladly worked seven years to pay her bride price. But Laban gave him Leah instead, and had him work seven more years for Rachel.[384] Joseph was Rachel's first born son.

Now Israel loved Joseph more than all his children, because he was the son of his old age: and he made him a coat of many colors. And when his brothers saw that their father loved him more than all his brothers, they hated him, and could not speak peaceably to him. (Genesis 37:3-4)

Joseph further compounded his father's favoritism by tattling on his brothers and then telling them his dreams of exaltation over them.[385] Then Israel sent Joseph to see how his brothers and the flocks were fairing, and his brothers plotted against him.

Come now therefore, and let us slay him, and cast him into some pit, and we will say, Some evil beast has devoured him: and we shall see what will become of his dreams. (Genesis 37:20)

Reuben kept them from shedding innocent blood. They stripped off Joseph's coat and placed him into a dry pit. Judah noticed a caravan of Ishmaelites from Midian, and suggested making a profit while getting rid of their bratty brother. Then, without Reuben's knowledge, they sold Joseph for twenty pieces of silver to the spice merchants who were heading to Egypt. The brothers then dipped Joseph's coat in goat's blood and showed it to their father who assumed Joseph had been eaten by a wild animal. The spice merchants then sold Joseph to Potiphar, who was pharaoh's captain of the guard.[386]

Joseph was born in 1745 BC during the reign of Tao (17th dyn.). Joseph was 17 when he was sold into slavery (1728 BC) which was during the reign of Ahmose I (18th dyn.).

---

384 Genesis 29:15-30
385 Genesis 37:2, 5-11
386 Genesis 37:22-36

Ahmose I, first pharaoh of the 18th Dynasty

The Hyksos period of 'foreign rulers' of the 15th dynasty was coming to a close as the 17th dynasty rulers Tao and his brother Kamose attacked them. Before kings went to war, they appointed their successors as co-regents to avoid questions of ascension should they die in battle. Kamose and Ahhotep II had no sons, so Kamose made his nephew, Tao's son Ahmose, his co-regent. Ahmose I is also referred to as Ahmosis and Amenes. '*Iah/Jah/Yah*' was their moon god; '*mose*' means 'son'. *Ahmose* was the "moon's son".

Ahmose I lost his father and uncle in their battles against the Hyksos, and began his reign about the age of ten with his mother guiding him. Ahmose I must have hated the Hyksos shepherds for killing his father and uncle, and desecrating Memphis monuments. Eleven years later he took up the war against the Hyksos and eventually drove them out and reconquered Canaan. Thus Ahmose I reunited Egypt and began its New Kingdom Era.

Ahmose I drives out Hyksos and reunites kingdom of Egypt

1727-1720 he fights the Hyksos
1720-1718 he fights the Nubians
1718-1716 he fights into Syria (oxen)
1716-1713 he builds quarries and mines

Axehead of Ahmose I striking enemy (Minoan griffin) buried with Ahhotep II

Ahmose I fighting Hyksos from chariot (first time pictured)

The painting is the first depiction of Egyptians using horses and a war chariot.[387] The war chariot was so effective that Ahmose I pushed the Anatolian Hittites back up through Canaan and Syria and reclaimed the Levant as part of the Egyptian kingdom. He attacked Kedem near Byblos to keep the Phoenicians subjugated to him. With such fierce fighting along the main roads, I doubt caravans were using them, so I propose Joseph arrived in Egypt the year prior to the beginning of Ahmose's victorious campaign; and then he later interpreted his dream about the cows and corn and served as his grand vizier at the end of his reign during his short rebuilding phase.

---

387 First use of the Egyptian word 'chariot' – *wrrt* was in the tomb biography of Ahmose of Nekheb, a marine.

Joseph as Slave and Prisoner

And the LORD was with Joseph, and he was a prosperous man; and he was in the house of his master the Egyptian. And his master saw that the LORD was with him, and that the LORD made all that he did to prosper in his hand. And Joseph found grace in his sight, and he served him: and he made him overseer over his house, and all that he had he put into his hand. (Genesis 39:2-4)

After about ten years of faithful service, Potiphar's wife schemed to seduce Joseph. Joseph rebuffed her advances, so she falsely accused him of trying to rape her. Potiphar placed Joseph in the prison under his jurisdiction which was on his property.[388]

But the LORD was with Joseph, and showed him mercy, and gave him favor in the sight of the keeper of the prison. And the keeper of the prison committed to Joseph's hand all the prisoners that were in the prison; and whatever they did there, he was the doer of it. The keeper of the prison looked not to any thing that was under his hand; because the LORD was with him, and that which he did, the LORD made it to prosper. (Genesis 39:21-23)

After Joseph's first year in prison, Ahmose I became angry with his butler and baker and threw them into prison. Joseph took care of them. One day they were especially downcast, and Joseph inquired as to why.[389]

And they said to him, We have dreamed a dream, and there is no interpreter of it. And Joseph said to them, Do not interpretations belong to God? tell me them, I pray you. (Genesis 40:8)

Joseph correctly interpreted their dreams, and requested that the butler ask pharaoh to get him out of prison. Within three days the baker was hanged, and the butler was reinstated to his position.[390] But the butler forgot to talk to pharaoh about Joseph, until two years later[391] (1715 BC) when Ahmose I had troubling dreams which no one could interpret.

Joseph as Grand Vizier

Then Pharaoh sent and called Joseph, and they brought him hastily out of the dungeon: and he shaved himself, and changed his raiment, and came in to Pharaoh. And Pharaoh said to Joseph, I have dreamed a dream, and there is none that can interpret it: and I have heard say of you, that you can understand a dream to interpret it. And Joseph answered Pharaoh, saying, It is not in me: God shall give Pharaoh an answer of peace. (Genesis 41:14-16)

---

388 Genesis 39:5-20 and 40:3
389 Genesis 40:1-7 and 41:1, 9-12
390 Genesis 40:9-23
391 Barnes' Bible Commentary

Ahmose I told Joseph his dreams, and Joseph explained to him that God had shown him what would shortly come to pass regarding seven years of plenty followed by seven years of famine. Joseph then also offered a solution: that a wise and discreet man should be appointed over Egypt to appoint officers to collect one-fifth of the food during the productive years to be stored in the cities under pharaoh's control.

And Pharaoh said to his servants, Can we find such a one as this is, a man in whom the Spirit of God is? And Pharaoh said to Joseph, For as much as God has showed you all this, there is none so discreet and wise as you are: You shall be over my house, and according to your word shall all my people be ruled: only in the throne will I be greater than you. And Pharaoh said to Joseph, See, I have set you over all the land of Egypt. And Pharaoh took off his ring from his hand, and put it on Joseph's hand, and arrayed him in clothing of fine linen, and put a gold chain about his neck; <u>And he made him to ride in the second chariot which he had; and they cried before him, Bow the knee: and he made him ruler over all the land of Egypt.</u> And Pharaoh said to Joseph, I am Pharaoh, and without you shall no man lift up his hand or foot in all

the land of Egypt. And Pharaoh called Joseph's name Zaphnathpaaneah; and he gave him to wife Asenath the daughter of Potipherah priest of On. And Joseph went out over all the land of Egypt. And Joseph was thirty years old when he stood before Pharaoh king of Egypt. And Joseph went out from the presence of Pharaoh, and went throughout all the land of Egypt. (Genesis 41:38-46)

Joseph became thirty years old in 1715 BC during the rebuilding phase of Ahmose. When Ahmose made Joseph grand vizier by giving him his signet ring of authority, he also made certain all the people knew of Joseph's authority over them, and sent him throughout the land in his second best chariot. Ahmose I also gave Joseph a new name and a wife. Some translations of the new name are 'bread man', 'bread of life', 'bread of salvation', 'life saver', and 'savior of the world'. The city of On was Heliopolis (still known as "the place of bread"), where Joseph settled next to his new in-laws. It was the capital of nome #13 of *Heqat*, the "prospering sceptre". His new wife later bore him two sons. Joseph went throughout Egypt to establish grain silo centers in each major city for the people of that city. This was a great incentive for Egyptians to prepare for seven years for the seven year famine that was to come. But a small portion of Egypt's overall bounty would also need to be saved for the refugees from other countries who would eventually seek their aid.

Joseph as Food Tsar (*sar* means ruler in Hebrew)

Hunger can drive people to violence, so the silos were attached to administrative halls and/or some form of military presence in order to keep operations peaceful and secure.

photo by N. Moeller, Tell Edfu Project

**Columned administration hall
and silos in Edfu, Egypt
excavated in 2008**

photo by G. Marouard, Tell Edfu Project

According to the University of Chicago, the largest silo at Edfu had a diameter of 21 feet. According to Werner Keller in *The Bible as History*, Egyptian granaries were "about twenty-five feet in diameter" and "were not uncommon on the Nile". Archaeologists conjecture that all Egyptian cities had grain storage silos of some sort. And Egyptologists have concluded that Djoser's complex was primarily used for storage; I say, food storage.

Djoser's Food Fortress Expanded

Sadly, Isaac died the year prior to Joseph's installation as second to pharaoh. But it is reasonable that Isaac previously relayed the story of Abram's sojourn into Egypt to his sons, Jacob and Esau, as well as to his grandson Joseph. The details may have been sketchy, and many pyramids had been built since the first famine; but after a bit of inquiry, Joseph located Djoser's Food Fortress in Saqqara and decided to use it.

Even with the eleven large bunker silos and the amazing amount of storage rooms, Joseph concluded it wouldn't be enough for seven years with the increased population after 200 years as well as foreigners seeking assistance. With the vast labyrinth of underground tunnels, he could not dig more bunker silos within the protective walls; but Joseph could

Pharaohs of the Bible

build shafts to connect to them and use the safety of the tunnels beneath the pyramid by connecting to them from just outside the eastern wall. Joseph could also build onto the western wall platform inside the complex.

Expansion of West Walled Platform (West Masiff)

The original platform which Imhotep built along the west wall was 400 meters long by 25 meters wide by 5 meters high (roughly 1312 X 82 X 16 feet). The northernmost part contained his brick home; whereas the rest could have been used as soldier's barracks, but Joseph needed it for storage. According to Jean-Phillipe Lauer, who spent his life excavating Djoser's complex, the two inner platforms were much later constructions, with the lowest one actually leaning upon the pyramid. They had five shafts with staircases connecting them to the substructure beneath the pyramid. The storage rooms contained fragments of broken stone vessels, barley, wheat, and dried fruit.[392]

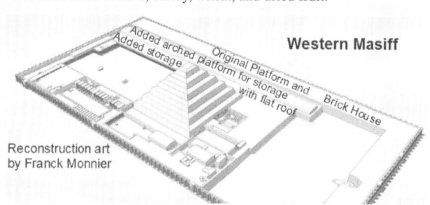

Expansion of Eastern Silos and Tunnels

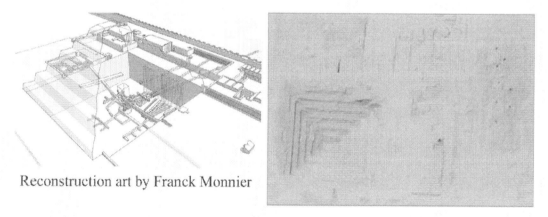

Two tunnels from pyramid shafts to beyond the east wall to more silos

---

392 Alan, Winston, http://www.touregypt.net/featurestories/dsteppyramid3.htm, accessed 2/10/10

Eight silos are visible beyond the east wall in the GoogleEarth picture;[393] there may be more still buried under the sand. The two tunnels leading from them to two of the eleven shafts on the eastern side of the pyramid were discovered by a Latvian team in 2007.[394] These outer silos may have been where the grain from the seven plentiful years was deposited and then stored beneath the Djoser complex for later. Any grain left in those silos would be sold at the beginning of the famine since they were not well protected.

Fresh Water Supply: Bahr Yussef

Famine is usually preceded by drought. There is an ancient canal connecting the Nile to Lake Moeris in the Fayyum in order to be a reservoir for Nile flood waters. The canal is called *Bahr Yussef*, "the waterway of Joseph". Twelfth dynasty pharaohs enlarged the canal to 15 m wide and 5 m deep. Joseph likely had it dredged and repaired during the seven plentiful years of rain. Part of Bahr Yussef still functions today.[395]

Amenhotep I, young pharaoh of seven year famine

The rebuilding phase of Ahmose I only lasted three years before he died. His eldest son had died before him, thus leaving the throne to a much younger son named Amenhotep. So the young child Amenhotep I began his reign under his mother Ahmose-Nefertari as regent. Ahmose-Nefetari trained Amenhotep to govern, and her bitterness against the Hyksos shepherds was duly transferred as well.

Ahmose-Nefertari and Amenhotep I

The governmental responsibilities to prepare the land for the four remaining plentiful years and the seven years of famine were solely shouldered by Joseph. When people came to Amenhotep for food during the famine, he directed them to do whatever Joseph said; and Joseph opened up all the storehouses he made in each city to sell food to the Egyptians.[396] Over the years, the Egyptians sold their livestock, their land, and lastly themselves as slaves to pharaoh. Joseph would later state that God "*has made me a **father** to Pharaoh, and lord of all his house, and a ruler throughout all the land of Egypt.*"[397] This is reasonable with Joseph being over thirty and Amenhotep just a young child.

---

393 *Grain Silos at Step Pyramid Complex*, http://josephandisraelinegypt.wordpress.com/ accessed, 2/10/10
394 Video "The Secrets of the Pyramid of Djoser" accessed February 10, 2010
   http://www.youtube.com/watch?v=os0Z6JgpjT0
395 "Bahr Yussef" from wikipedia, http://en.wikipedia.org/wiki/Bahr_Yussef, accessed 5/14/11
396 Genesis 41:55-56
397 Genesis 45:8

Amenhotep I

1712 -1702 under mom   Ahmose-Nefetari   1702 -1688
1715-1708 = 7 years plenty   as an adult
1707-1700 = 7 years famine

Joseph Tests His Brothers

Though Joseph's primary residence was in On, during the fourteen years as overseer of Pharaoh's granaries, he likely took up residence in the "house of the master builder" at Djoser's step pyramid in Saqqara. He personally sold grain to many of the foreigner buyers.

> *And Joseph was the governor over the land, and he it was that sold to all the people of the land: and Joseph's brothers came, and bowed down themselves before him with their faces to the earth. (Genesis 42:6)*

Joseph recalled his dream of eleven sheaves of grain bowing to his sheaf, but now only ten were present since Israel wouldn't allow Benjamin to go with them. It had been 21 years, and they didn't recognize him; so he spoke harshly to them and questioned them to test their character. He got them to admit there was another brother yet at home with his father in Canaan. So Joseph accused them of being spies and placed them into prison (the southern tombs) for three days. Afterward he told them, through an interpreter, that he would only keep one of the brothers in prison while the rest could take food back to Canaan and could bring the youngest brother back to prove they were not spies. Joseph listened carefully as they bemoaned the fact that they were now being punished for the crime they committed against Joseph, and Joseph quickly turned aside and wept; but composed himself to determine which, if any, were not repentant for what they had done to him. Joseph then selected Simeon to remain in prison while he sent his brothers back with their money in their grain sacks. They returned to Canaan and told their father what that had transpired, and that they could not return to Egypt unless they took Benjamin with them.[398]

---

398 Genesis 42:7-38

Joseph's Pharaohs

When the rations of grain were depleted, Israel relented and sent Benjamin back with them to buy more grain, taking double the money as well as a gift of local produce. When Joseph saw his brothers had returned, he had his steward prepare a lavish meal for them. The steward assured the brothers he had received full payment the last time they were there and brought Simeon out to them. When Joseph arrived home, they presented the gift and bowed before him, all eleven. Upon seeing Benjamin, Joseph turned aside and wept, then sat apart from them as they ate. He had them seated in their birth order, and gave Benjamin five times as much food.[399]

Joseph had their money returned to their grain sacks again, but he also placed his silver cup in Benjamin's sack. He had his servants overtake his brothers to discover who had 'stolen' his cup. Judah declared, "*God has found out the iniquity of your servants*," and he offered to take Benjamin's place in prison.[400] Judah had passed the test. Joseph then revealed himself to his brothers with so much weeping and wailing, that the "*house of pharaoh*" heard it. Joseph told them:

> *Now therefore be not grieved, nor angry with yourselves, that you sold me here: for God did send me before you to preserve life. For these two years has the famine been in the land: and yet there are five years, in the which there shall neither be ripening nor harvest. And God sent me before you to preserve you a posterity in the earth, and to save your lives by a great deliverance. So now it was not you that sent me here, but God: and he has made me a father to Pharaoh, and lord of all his house, and a ruler throughout all the land of Egypt. Haste you, and go up to my father, and say to him, Thus said your son Joseph, God has made me lord of all Egypt: come down to me, tarry not: And <u>you shall dwell in the land of Goshen, and you shall be near to me</u>, you, and your children, and your children's children, and your flocks, and your herds, and all that you have: And there will I nourish you; for yet there are five years of famine; lest you, and your household, and all that you have, come to poverty. (Genesis 45:5-11)* [Goshen's lands were near Heliopolis.]

Joseph revealed to his brothers

---
399 Genesis 43:11-34
400 Genesis 44

Pharaohs of the Bible

Joseph, Overseer of Pharaoh's Granaries by Sir Lawrence Alma-Tadema 1874

The year was 1706 BC, the second year of the famine. Joseph said God made him lord of all Egypt, and Joseph issued the command, without asking pharaoh, to retrieve his family from Canaan so they could dwell near his nome #13. Egypt's nomes were along the Nile for farming; Goshen was land used for grazing animals west of nomes #13 and #20, and north and south of Wadi Tumilat's nome #8. Amenhotep was delighted when he heard the news, and commanded that wagons and provisions be sent along with Joseph's brothers to transport their wives and children.[401]

When Amenhotep I met Joseph's father, he asked his age with child-like wonder. Jacob replied that he was 130 years old, but not yet as old as the ages his ancestors attained, and he blessed pharaoh.[402] Before Joseph presented five of his brothers to pharaoh, Joseph warned them not to tell pharaoh they were shepherds, because the Egyptians despised shepherds due to the Phoenician Hyksos. But his brothers refused to lie, and told Amenhotep they were shepherds. Surprisingly, Amenhotep told Joseph:

The land of Egypt is before you; in the <u>best of the land</u> make your father and brothers to dwell; in <u>the land of Goshen</u> let them dwell: and if you know any men of activity among them, then make them rulers [sar] over my cattle. (Genesis 47:6)

Recall that Ahmose I, Amenhotep's father, had warred against Canaan and had acquired oxen from that area. Amenhotep saw Joseph's brothers could be useful to him, assuming they would know the feeding habits of the cattle, being from the same vicinity; and made them his cattle tsars. "A graffito in the quarry at Tura whereby 'oxen from Canaan' were

---

[401] Genesis 45:17-21
[402] Genesis 47:7-10

used at the opening of the quarry in Ahmose's regnal year 22."[403]

'*Rameses*' is the name for grazing lands

A pharaoh named Rameses won't arrive until the next dynasty, but the land was already called Rameses. The grazing lands of Rameses was in the nome of Goshen.

*And Joseph placed his father and his brothers, and gave them a possession in the land of Egypt, in the <u>best of the land</u>, in the **land of Rameses**, as Pharaoh had commanded. (Genesis 47:11)*

Dr. Shaw stated '*remsosch*' meant 'shepherds' in the Egyptian language. Basically, Amenhotep was giving them the pasture lands of the Hyksos shepherds whom his father conquered.[404] The "*land of Goshen*" and "*land of Rameses*" were synonymous. Saqqara, in nome #1, was about 38 km away from On. Avaris, was located in nome #20 on the Pelusiac branch of the Nile Delta at a site now called Tell el Dabᶜa.[405]

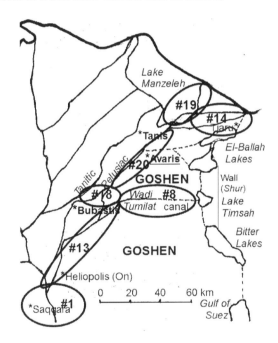

---

[403] Redford, Donald B., *History and Chronology of the 18th Dynasty of Egypt*, University of Toronto Press, 1967, pp. 195-197
[404] In John Gill's Bible commentary, taken from *Travels*, second edition, p. 307
[405] Tell el Dabᶜa, http://www.bibleorigins.net/RamesesMapAvaris.html accessed 2009

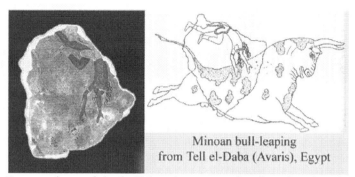

Fresco piece of the bull-leaping taureador found at Avaris

When pharaoh Amenhotep told Joseph to give his father and brothers the "*best of the land*", I assume he included the Hyksos capital, Avaris, recently conquered. Manfred Bietak has been excavating ancient Avaris (Tell el Dabᶜa) for decades. In his *Taureador Scenes*, under the heading, "The Beginning of the New Kingdom, ph. D/1" is the following quote:

"Between the citadel of the Hyksos period and the palace district of the Tuthmoside Period remains of at least two strata were found which should be examined in terms of relative and absolute chronology. Both date right back to the very early 18th Dynasty. The first of the two intermediary strata (ph. D/1 = str. E/1) was found in area H/III and in H/VI south. In the northern section of our excavations the platform (C) of the late Hyksos period had been taken down and a **storage compound** was set on top of it. It consisted of at least 30 round **grain silos** and probably more (Fig. 7). Each silo was about 5.25 m (10 cubits) in diameter. The construction was flimsy and looks as if it was meant to be short-lived. This amenity was used to store enormous quantities of grain (more than c. 5000 cubic meters) and probably other foodstuff for a considerable number of people. . . . Many more silo complexes were found to the south in area H/VI within a palatial compound enclosed by an enormous mudbrick wall [spring 2002 excavations] In that area the silos had been renewed up to four times – an indication as it is, that it is not right to assign only a short time span to this stratum. The palatial building had a big reception (?) room with a brick paved floor. No wall paintings at all have been found in this context. Proof positive that we are dealing with a phase as early as the time of the 18th Dynasty – and after the conquest of Avaris . . . by Ahmose – was provided by ceramic examination."[406] [of UE Marl A vessels]

---

406 Bietak, Manfred; Marinatos, Nanno; Palivou, Clairy, *Taureador Scenes in Tell el-Dabᶜa (Avaris) and Knossos,* Austrian Academy of Sciences Press, 2007, p. 18

After Ahmose I conquered Avaris and had the dreams, Joseph quickly began establishing silos there and throughout Egypt. It's interesting that these huge silos were "meant to be short-lived" - possibly 7 years? And that other silos were built inside the mudbrick wall of the Ahmose's palace complex. Joseph had promised his family:

And <u>there will I nourish you; for yet there are five years of famine</u>; lest you, and your household, and all that you have, come to poverty. (Genesis 45:11)

Bietak discovered remains of ancient Minoan frescoes of bull-leaping in Avaris, which were thought to be reserved for the Minoan palace in Crete. From the fine details on the leaper's hair-braids and arm-bands, Bietak concluded the artist was Minoan. Bietak wrote, "Besides human hunters we also have representations of lions and leopards chasing fallow deer and mountain goats."[407] Prior to Joseph's 7-year famine, the delta was verdant with all kinds of game animals.

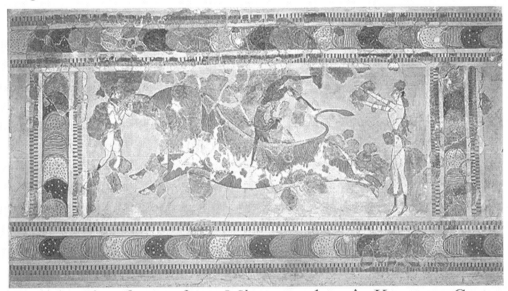

Bull-leaping fresco from Minoan palace in Knossos, Crete

Knossos, Crete is roughly 500 miles away across the Mediterranean Sea. There is much evidence of the Minoans and the Hyksos being trading partners with each other and with other cultures around the Mediterranean, but queen Ahhotep II halted it to win the war.

About 75 miles north of Knossos is the island of Thera, now called Santorini, on which a Minoan mural about a foot wide ringed the tops of an ancient room. It connects via several boats the great palace of Knossos with a city surrounded by canals to represent Avaris. Above the city of Avaris in the upper left of the picture is a lion chasing deer in the hills.

---

[407] Bietak, Manfred, "Minoan Paintings in Avaris," Sept. 4, 1997, http://www.therafoundation.org/articles/art/minoanpaintingsinavarisegypt, accessed 5/2/11

Miniature Ships Fresco in Akrotiri, Thera (Santorini), Greece from National Archaeological Museum, Athens

Santorini lies in the Aegean Sea to the west of Turkey (which was ancient Anatolia). The mural celebrates the reunion of seamen from both areas at sea.

The split of the Pelusiac branch of the Nile above Tell el-Dab‘a is the same as the split above the city of Avaris in the Minoan mural. Between the split is the city of Qantir to which Apepi had moved his stolen monuments to prepare them to be shipped and sold abroad.

Avaris (Tell el-Dab'a)

Minoan Pottery

Top left shows a wave motif of the island people.
Bottom left is Impressed Ware in which mollusk shells were impressed into the wet clay to make designs, here along the top.
Below is Marine Ware with fish, seaweed, and an octopus.

Dr. Bietak found nine royal sealings with the name Yaqub-Har at Avaris. Jacob was involved in international trade since in Canaan "three Jacob-Her scarabs were found in Israel: two at Kabri, near Nahariya, and one at Shikmona, near Haifa";[408] also one scarab in Nubia, one sealing in Kerma along with one scarab at Saqqara and two scarabs in Tell el-Yahudiyeh in the southern Nile delta.[409] Since none of Jacob's scarabs have been found in the Mediterranean islands, I assume that queen Ahhotep II ran that end of the business. Queen Ahhotep II continued trade with Egypt from Crete while Jacob opened up new partners like Shikmona in Canaan from Egypt. Jacob was the head of the family with a mind for business, and Joseph may have given him such royal seals and authority during the 17 years he lived at Avaris.

Jacob's/Israel's Death (1689 BC)

After the seventh year of famine passed, and the land became fertile again. The people gave pharaoh 1/5 of their produce as they had promised. Amenhotep I owned all the land and people of Egypt, except for the land of the priests and the land of Goshen which was given to Jacob's/Israel's descendants.[410] The children of Israel owned the land of Goshen between the lakes north of the Gulf of Suez and the eastern nomes. Twelve years after the famine ended, Jacob blessed and prophesied over his sons and Joseph's sons before he died.[411] The physicians embalmed him; and the Egyptians mourned Jacob for 70 days.[412]

Pharaohs of Joseph's elderly years

Thutmose I (1688-1674 BC)

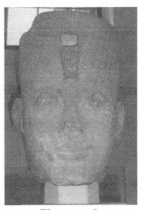
Thutmose I

Amenhotep I died shortly after their return to Egypt, and Aakheperkare Thutmose I succeeded him. Kush immediately rebelled upon his coronation, so Thutmose personally led his army and killed the king of Kush. Then he had a former canal at the first cataract of the Nile dredged to foster better control of the area. The next year Thutmose extended his control to the third cataract and set up a stele, and eventually extended rule to the fourth. His next campaign went further north than any previous pharaoh, all the way to Carchemish on the Euphrates river (*Nhrn* or "Naharin" on tomb biography) which the soldiers called "inverted water" since it flowed from north to south which is opposite of the Nile. He paved the way for Thutmose III to establish forts there.

---

408 Bietak, Manfred, "The Center of Hyksos Rule: Avaris (Tell el Dabᶜa)" in *The Hyksos: New Historical and Archaeological Perspectives*, 1997, p. 115
409 Ryholt, K., *The Political Situation in Egypt during the Second Intermediate Period*, 1997, p. 382
410 Genesis 47:22-27
411 Geneses 48 and 49
412 Genesis 50:2-3

"The glory of king Aakheperkare, the blessed, he has brought these elephant tusks, from his victories [in the southern and northern countries. His majesty hunted x] elephants [in the land of Naharin, being on a] horse carriage after his majesty had set out in order to subdue Upper [Reten]u on [his x-th victorious campaign. His majesty reached the land] Ny [and found there these elephants.]"[413]

Extent of Egypt after Thutmose III

Though Ahmose I had a pyramid, pyramid building ceased under Thutmose I who initiated being buried in the Valley of the Kings. Joseph was 57 years old when Thutmose I began his reign in 1688 BC, and I propose the new pharaoh wanted an Egyptian man to take the place of the revered, but foreign, vizier. For the last 20 or so years as vizier, I suggest Joseph was grooming such a man to take over his position as superintendent of the granaries, treasury, and workmen. His name was Ineni (or Anena), and he was also the architect under Amenhotep I. Ineni carved out Thutmose's tomb, and he built the hypostyle hall at Karnak along with several pylons, statues, and a barque shrine.

Thutmose I and queen Ahmose had a daughter named Hatshepsut. Thutmose later had another wife named Mutnofret who gave birth to Thutmose II, who married Iset and had Thutmose III.

Thutmose II and Hatshepsut (1674-1672 BC)

Drawing of mummy of Thutmose II

Thutmose II immediately declared young Thutmose III as his successor, when he was crowned as pharaoh, to establish his lineage. For political power, Thutmose II married his older sister, Hatshepsut; and they had a daughter named Neferure. Hatshepsut's steward, Senemut, became Neferure's steward as well. During his two year reign, Thutmose II went to hunt elephants in Ny. His general saved his life cutting off the trunk of an elephant which charged him.[414]

---

413 "After Sethe", *Urk. IV*, p.104 [uncertain text in brackets]
414 Shillinger, Shimone, producer of documentary "Egypt's Lost Rival," in which Peter Pfelzner and his archaeological team discovered ancient elephant bones in a NW room in Qatna. Ny (Nii, or Niya) is 45

Queen Hatshepsut (1672-1651 BC)

After the death of Thutmose II, Hatshepsut elevated herself to pharaoh. Ineni produced several statues of her, and wrote kindly about her on the walls of his tomb. Hatshepsut had Senemut build her a lavish mortuary temple, 97 ft. tall, under Ineni's supervision before he died. She dredged the Tumilat canal to connect the Nile to the Red Sea[415] and had five new 70 ft. long ships built on the Red Sea to facilitate greater trade. Hatshepsut sought myrrh from Punt. (See map on prior page.) But there is evidence queen Hatshepsut travelled even more widely, and may have held court at Knossos, Crete; possibly as Ahmose's aunt, queen Ahhotep II had done before her.

Hatshepsut with fake beard

The short-seated, short-backed throne upon which pharaoh Hatshepsut is seated (below) is very similar to the throne pictured at Knossos. The throne room of palace F at Ezbet Helmi, west of Tell el-Dabᶜa, is almost an exact copy of the one for Ahhotep II at Knossos.[416]

"The Minoan goddess associated with the palm, rosette and griffin is a solar goddess of kingship. It is she who is worshipped on the Tell el-Dabᶜa Bull Frieze. . . . Thus, applying a Syro-Anatolian and Levantine lens to Minoan art has yielded results. We may conclude that the bull games are dedicated and constitute an offering to the Minoan solar goddess."[417] [who was Hatshepsut]

---

miles south of Qatna, Syria, and 45 miles west of Baalbek, Lebanon. The elephant charge was recorded in the general Amenemhab's tomb in Egypt.

415 Dollinger, Andre', "Canals", http://www.reshafim.org.il/ad/egypt/timelines/topics/canals.htm

416 Manfred Bietak, Nanno Marinatos, and Clairy Palivou; *Taureador Scenes in Tell el-Dabᶜa (Avaris) and Knossos*, Austrian Academy of Sciences Press, 2007, p. 40

417 Manfred Bietak, Nanno Marinatos, and Clairy Palivou; *Taureador Scenes in Tell el-Dabᶜa (Avaris) and Knossos*, Austrian Academy of Sciences Press, 2007, p. 148

Pharaohs of the Bible

At Knossos are fresco fragments of a procession with two women that have groups of 3 stripes on their dresses wearing white stockings or shoes; one is royal and is being presented gifts from kilted Keftiu servants bearing various vessels. Another Knossos frieze has ladies with white stockings wearing red, white, and blue skirts with seagull or modified 'v'-shape 3-stripe patterns. Near palace G at Ezbet Helmi similar fresco fragments were found of a woman wearing a white skirt with a v-hem of alternating blue and red stripes, and blue anklets over her white stockings.[418]

Knossos: fragments and drawing of procession

In his 1996 *Avaris*, Bietak stated, "Returning to the discovery of Minoan wall-paintings in the 18th Dynasty palatial complex, we are confronted with the problem of how to explain them. Minoan wall-paintings have also been found in other centres of the Levant, in contexts of the late Middle Bronze Age culture, such as at Alalakh, Tell Kabri and probably Qatna. The excavators of Kabri have suggested that the employment of Minoan artists (who may perhaps have been sent by the king of Knossos as a show of favour to friendly kings and princes in the Levant) indicates the high esteem in which Minoan art was held. Niemeier sees support for this view in the mythological poetry of Ugarit, which refers to the bringing of the god of handicrafts and art Kothar wa-Khasis from his throne in Kptr (Kaphtor) to build a palace for the god Baal."[419] The Kaphtor Keftiu also worshipped Hathor, the goddess of turquoise, as they worked the mines in the Sinai. When Canaanites joined them, they called Hathor, Baalat.

I conjecture Kaphtor/Caphtor was the eastern Nile delta, and that the Ethiopic War drove most of the Caphtorim/Keftiu into the isles of the sea and into the Sinai, but they were welcomed back to Egypt by Hatshepsut. The Keftiu in Sinai joined Philistines who drew griffins on their pottery. Kathryn Eriksson stated, ". . . it is in the reign of Hatshepsut . . . that we get the numerous representations in some tombs of foreigners bearing so-called tribute. There was nothing like this before. New Kingdom Egypt's recognition of the outside world reached its peak of sophistication at this time."[420]

Philistine griffin and flying fish

---

418 Ibid., p. 42

419 Manfred Bietak, *Avaris, The Capital of the Hyksos: Recent Excavations at Tell el Dabᶜa,* British Museum Press, London, 1996, pp. 78-79

420 Eriksson, Kathryn, "A Preliminary Synthesis of Recent Chronological Observations on the Relations Between Cyprus and Other Eastern Mediterranean Societies During the Late Middle Bronze – Late Bronze II Periods," *The Synchronisation of Civilisations in the Eastern Mediterranean in the Second Millennium B.C. II,* Osterreichische Akademie der Wissenschaften Wien, 2003, p. 421

Pharaoh Hatshepsut not only opened trade with Punt, but she bolstered Egypt's trade throughout the Mediterranean after the Keftiu and Minoans welcomed her as their solar goddess queen. Like queen Ahhotep II, Hatshepsut sent Minoan artists to beautify the trade buildings throughout the area: Santorini of the Aegean Sea; Alalakh, Turkey; Ugarit and Qatna, Syria; and Tel Kabri, Israel.

"Hatshepsut's reign was characterized by great devotion. She restored and founded temples both in Egypt and abroad; a good example of the latter is the Hathor temple for the miners at Serabit el Khadim in the Sinai. This could be one reason why she was the first Egyptian monarch that the Keftiu approached for 'the breath of life', an Egyptian expression for vassalage – the acceptance of the Egyptian king as overlord. These Keftiu, portrayed with long wavy hair and sporting the loincloth and codpiece well-known from representations of themselves in Crete, first appeared bearing gifts in Hatshepsut's chief steward Senenmut's tomb started two years after her accession."[421]

Hatshepsut's mortuary temple built by Senemut

Myrrh tree in basket

Hatshepsut and Thutmose III (1672-1651 BC)

Hatshepsut had her mortuary temple built next to the one of Montuhotep II at Deir el-Bahari. Hatshepsut brought back 31 myrrh trees and had them transplanted to her mortuary temple which has a relief depicting the voyage and the trees. Besides her mortuary temple, Senemut also built a temple of Pekhet (lioness war deities), and the famous Red Chapel upon which she leads Thutmose III. Hatshepsut sent Senemut to retrieve two great obelisks quarried in Aswan to place at Karnak, but one broke while being positioned.

---

421 J. Alexander MacGillivray, Jan Heinemeier & Walter L. Friedrich, "Time's Up! Dating the Minoan eruption of Santorini", *Monographs of the Danish Institute at Athens, Volume 10*, November 2007, p. 164

Pharaohs of the Bible

The 30th anniversary of the beginning of her father's reign occurred in 1658 BC.[422] She had dyad statues of Neferhotep I of the 13th dynasty (possibly her father's distant relative) buried at Karnak beneath one of the 96 ft. obelisks of pink granite.[423] Hieroglyphs on the north face state, "she celebrates <u>for him</u> the first time of the Sed Festival." Thutmose I did not make it to his 30th year, but his daughter held a magnificent Sed festival for him anyway. She and her teen-age step-son and nephew, Thutmose III, celebrated in grand style. Hatshepsut wore the male, royal ceremonial attire for the occasion, but she had statues and reliefs of herself in typical feminine attire as well. Hatshepsut made a statue of Thutmose II wearing a Sed-robe seated on a throne engraved with "for my brother" (half-brother/husband). It was a family reunion of sorts. No references to Senemut exist after the Sed festival, though he lived several years longer.

Thutmose III & Hatshepsut on Red Chapel

Senemut's ceiling waves

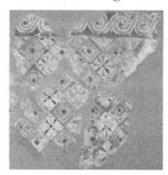

Minoan rosettes and wave and hill patterns in Knossos plaza

Senemut photos by Keith Shengili-Roberts

Part of rosette between Senemut's spirals

Senemut's profile sherd

Some suggest that he and Hatshepsut were lovers, and that he was sent away. His tomb (TT353) was influenced by Minoan art, and also has conjunctions of planets in the southern sky which may represent an important date.

> "The real meaning of 'the irrational orientation of the southern panel' and the 'reversed position of **Orion**' appears to be this: the southern panel shows the sky of Egypt as it was before the celestial sphere interchanged north and south, east and west. The northern panel shows the sky of Egypt as it was on some night of the year in the time of **Senemut**."[424] - Immanuel Velikovsky

---

422 Scholars argue whether the Sed-festival was held in Hatshepsut's 15th or 16th year. I've chosen her 16th.
423 Roberta, "More Secrets from Karnak", 2005 at http://archaeologynews.multiply.com/journal/item/161
424 Velikovsky, Immanuel, *Worlds in Collision*, MacMillan Publishers, 1950, p. 120

Senemut's depiction of chaos on the southern panel may allude to the chaos which ensued after a volcanic eruption in 1651 BC, ending Hatshepsut's reign. The disruption in the trade and prosperity which Hatshepsut brought might have been blamed on her lack of divine status as a woman. Though the physical fallout produced beneficial pumice, the spiritual fallout based upon acceptance of a female as pharaoh may have brought about the defacement of Hatshepsut's depictions throughout Egypt. Queen Ahhotep II never claimed to be pharaoh.

Thera/Santorini Eruptions of 1651 BC

The authors of "Time's Up! Dating the Minoan eruption of Santorini" placed the eruption of Santorini during Hatshepsut's reign,[425] right where it started before all the ice core and tree-ring testing. They noted David Sewall's wind tests at Thera which determined the eruption most likely occurred during the early summer before insect eggs had hatched. They also remarked on the wetter climate which followed the Theran eruption enabling the *Tilia* lime tree to grow in the area again.[426] The authors also provided an overview of the Santorini/Thera eruption.

    1. Major earthquake possibly linked to the seismic destruction of the Knossos palace

    2. Soon after the earthquake, a tephra plume carried by south-southeast winds deposited about 0.08 m of ash on Thera's south side, including Akrotiri, without pause.

    3. Thera's first eruption lasted about 8 hours, depositing 7 meters of tephra on Akrotiri.

    4. Thera's second eruption ejected huge lava boulders into the upper stories of Akrotiri's abandoned buildings, and deposited about two cubic kilometres of pumice on Thera.

    5. The third eruption included pyroclastic flows which may have produced a landslip type of tsunami represented on the coast at Palaikastro, Crete. This tsunami devastated harbors and coastal settlements throughout the Eastern Mediterranean, and reached the Nile delta only one hour after it began.

    6. "Deposits attributable to the eruption's fourth major phase show that activity continued without pause from the previous phase. Great mudflows deposited the last of the tephra over much of Thera, and could well have caused further tsunami. There is general agreement that, apart from the possibility of short intervals between the earthquake, precursor eruption, and the first major, Plinian, phase, the major eruption was a single event lasting approximately four days."[427]

A chart of tree ring growth for Ireland, England, and Germany has a major spike at 1650 and 1628 BC[428] which could be indicative of volcanic eruptions because they are then followed by sharp rises of tree-ring growth (due to cooler weather and reflected sunlight

---

425 J. Alexander MacGillivray, Jan Heinemeier & Walter L. Friedrich, "Time's Up! Dating the Minoan eruption of Santorini", *Monographs of the Danish Institute at Athens, Volume 10*, November 2007, p. 164
426 Ibid., pp. 158-159
427 Ibid., pp. 157-158
428 The 1628 drop is twice that of the 1650 drop, and may be due to a volcanic eruption on Iceland which would have effected Europe moreso than the Mediterranean.

Pharaohs of the Bible

brought on by aeresols).[429] This supports Thera erupting in 1651 BC, and putting an end to Hatshepsut's reign and causing some to eradicate her likeness because she ended maat.

Thera's Eruption and its Effects on the Minoans

The Minoan culture, largely based in Crete, was advanced in metallurgy, architecture (with indoor plumbing), and arts which it disseminated throughout the eastern Mediterranean. Its coastal trading posts at Avaris, Egypt; Tel Kabri (near Nahariya), Israel; Ugarit (near Latakia), Syria; and Alalakh (near Antakya), Turkey displayed unique Minoan wall paintings. Minoan frescoes at Akrotiri, Thera were found under volcanic ash, so it was assumed that the entire Minoan culture had been destroyed. Volcanic Ash has a chemical fingerprint which links it to the volcano from which it came, and can even distinguish between eruptions. Thera eruptions are linked to the demise of the Minoan culture during the reign of Hatshepsut and Thutmose III according to the pottery and pumice found at sites.

> "There is Theran pumice from New Kingdom levels at Tell Hebwa in northern Sinai. Theran pumice was also found in larger quantities at level H 5 at Tell el-'Ajjûl together with the first appearance of WS I, BR I, RLWM, in combination with Egyptian Marl B pottery approximately of the time of Hatshepsut and Tuthmosis III. In the same time-range Theran pumice also appears at Tell el-Dabᶜa."[430] [Pottery: WS I = White Slip I ; BR I = Base Ring I; RLWM = Red Lustre, Wheel-Made]

> "Both WS I and BR I wares make their appearance at Tell el Dabᶜa not earlier than during phase C/3, well into the XVIII dynasty (most likely during the reigns of Hatshepsut and Thutmosis III; Bietak and Hein 2001; Bietak 2000; 2003b; 2004)."[431]

Akrotiri River with griffin top left, animal in flying gallop below, and chase scene right.

---

429 Manning, Sturt, *A Test of Time: The Volcano of Thera and the chronology and history of the Aegean and east Mediterranean in the mid second millennium B.C.*, Oxbow Books, 1999, p. 265

430 Bietak, Manfred, Review of Sturt Manning's *A Test of Time* in *Bibliotheca Orientalis* LXI #1-2, January-April 2004, based upon research from P. Fischer & M. Sadeq, *E&L* 12 (2002), pp. 125-129, 138-141

431 Fantuzzi, Tiziano, "The Debate on Aegean High and Low Chronologies: an overview through Egypt", p.5

Akrotiri was the capital of Thera. Santorini/Thera Bo is often called the Minoan eruption, but it did not destroy the Minoan culture at that time. That Minoans who lived on Santorini left prior to its huge eruption is verified by the absence of skeletons beneath the 100 feet of ash. Prior to eruption, the outgassing of noxious fumes drove the people away with their amazing crafts and pottery to destinations of fellow sea-farers like the Philistines.

> "Digging on the island of Mochlos last summer, two archaeologists discovered what they called the first direct and conclusive evidence that the volcanic eruption 70 miles away on Thera, the present-day island of Santorini, did not destroy the Minoan civilization of ancient Crete, as had been widely assumed. They uncovered architectural and ceramic remains indicating instead that the civilization continued to flourish for some **150 years** after the eruption in about 1600 B.C. The archaeologists found in the ruins of a Minoan settlement a layer of volcanic ash from the time of the Theran eruption. The ash covered a pavement of stone slabs and distinctive pottery from the late Minoan period. Above the ash, more significantly, a house had been substantially rebuilt in the Minoan style and contained remnants of Minoan pottery."[432] 1600 − **150** = 1450

I date the Minoan eruption of Thera/Santorini at the end of Hatshepsut's reign in 1651 BC, and a different volcanic eruption during the 8th year of Rameses III to 1310 BC which made the "Sea Peoples" swarm the mainlands as refugees. Other volcanoes with similar chemical fingerprints to Thera in the southern Aegean volcano arc are Kos, Gyali, Nisyros, and Milos. Thera's "Minoan" Bo (it's last big) eruption curtailed Minoan pottery production for a season during the reigns of Hatshepsut and Thutmose III, but Minoan culture ended after a different Aegean eruption, possibly Methana's, during the 8th year of Rameses III 240 years later (quite a bit more than 150 years).

Thera's Eruption and its Effects on Trade

The Thera Bo eruption at the end of Hatshepsut's reign changed Egypt's trading partners during the second half of the 18th dynasty from primarily Minoan Crete (LM for Late Minoan) to Mycenae, Hellene (LH for Late Hellene of the early Greeks) and Cyprus (LC for Late Cyprus). The Mycenaeans and Cypriots sold their wares while Crete recovered.

> "Theran pumice suddenly appears in large quantities at the 18th Dynasty levels from stratum C/2 onwards, to be dated to the Thutmoside period. At the Hyksos and early 18th Dynasty levels pumice is very rare and does not originate from Thera, but from older eruptions such as those at Kos, Gyali, or Nisyros. . . . Time of Hatshepsut and Thutmose III is when Theran pumice appears in Tell el-Dabᶜa, Tell el Ajjul, and Tell Hebwa. The pumice prior to this was not from Thera.

---

[432] Wilford, John Noble, "Minoan Culture Survived Ancient Volcano, Evidence Shows," *New York Times*, November 28, 1989

Robert Merrillees – who identified the Theran WS I bowl late in its series argues, 'the beginning of LC IA should date to at least 50 years and probably 75 years before the volcanic eruption.' This would mean that LC IA started around <u>1700 BC at least</u> and this would push back also the beginning of LM IA to a similar date as the major part of LM IA has happened before the eruption (high chronology now 1645 plus or minus 7 years BC)."[433]

In *A Test of Time*, Sturt Manning compared MBA ear-rings and crocus garlands in Akrotiri paintings to Tell el-Ajjul hoards, claiming they were also MBA. Bietak rhetorically asked, "Should we date now with the same authority as Manning the Akrotiri paintings to the time of Tuthmosis III? It would match the razor study of Kathryn Eriksson from LM IA-B contexts perfectly."[434] But then Bietak concluded, "The only alternative left must also be to raise the beginning of the New Kingdom by between 100 to 150 years." 200 years works.

Thutmose III (1651-1618 BC)

Thutmose III was a warrior king. He conducted 17 campaigns. When Hatshepsut died, Syria rebelled against subjugation and travelled 300 miles from Kadesh to trap Egypt's army at Megiddo. There are two passes around the Mount Carmel ridge, and they divided the troops in half to cover both, but Thutmose III took the Aruna pass through the mountains and took the Syrian army by surprise (1650 BC).

Thutmose III

The Syrians retreated to Megiddo while the Egyptians looted instead of pursuing them, so then they had to lay siege to the city for seven months before capturing it (1649 BC). Megiddo was the hub of trade between north and south, and Thutmose III exclaimed, "The capturing of Megiddo is the capturing of a thousand towns."

The Annals of Thutmose III describe his first through sixth campaigns during his 22nd - 30th regnal years. In his first campaign, he passed the east delta border fort at Tjaru, which was the first fort beginning the Way of Horus. A New Kingdom fort and temple were discovered at Tell Hebua.[435] The temple has engravings from reigns of Thutmose II through to Rameses II.[436] An inscription with the name Tjaru was found in Hebua I on a votive

---

433 Bietak, Manfred, "Science Versus Archaeology: Problems and Consequences of High Aegean Chronology," p. 28
434 Ibid., p.29, fn Eriksson, Kathryn, "A Close Shave: The New Evidence for Chronology of Egyptian New Kingdom Mechak Razors found in Late Cypriot I Tombs in Northwestern Cyprus" in *Contributions to the Archaeology and History of the Bronze and Iron Ages in the Eastern Mediterranean. Studies in Honour of Paul Astrom*. Osterreichisches Archaologisches Institut Sonderschriften 39, Viena, 2001, p. 188
435 Tell Hebua is about 4 miles east of the Suez Canal and four miles north of Tell Ahmer (also called Tell Abu-Sefeh, ancient Tjaru/Siles).
436 "New Kingdom Temple Discovered in the Sinai", http://www.drhawass.com/blog/press-release-new-

statue.[437] Fortress Tjaru was 500 meters by 250 meters with massive mud-brick walls 13 meters thick, and surrounded by a moat.[438] The Annals state that after his victory, the troops of Tjaru moved to Sharuhen, south of Gaza (which was later given to the tribe of Simeon).[439] Thutmose III continued trade of myrrh from Punt and wood from Lebanon.

Thutmose III suppressed those that did not pay tribute in Canaan (Djahy) all the way to Tunip on the Euphrates in his 29th regnal year. In regnal year 30, Thutmose III collected tribute from Syria (Retenu) and hunted elephants in Ny, like Thutmose I had done. Thutmose III fought the Shashu in his 39th year. In his 47th regnal year, Thutmose III first went south to slaughter bedouin tribesmen near Aswan (Ta-Seti); then he travelled north passed Carchemish, and "the numerous armies of Mitanni were overthrown in the space of an hour."[440] He sailed down the Euphrates, and destroyed cities and burned villages while confiscating all their grain and cattle.

Thutmose III engraved a list of cities he conquered and collected tribute from in the Temple of Amun at Karnak. In alphabetical order they are Achshaph, Acre, Adummim, Alashiya, Aleppo, Anaharath, Aruna, Arzawa, Ashtaroth, Beeroth, Beth-anath, Beth-Shan, Carchemish, Chinneroth, Damascus, Dibon, Dothan, Edrei, Emeq, Geba, Geba-Shumen, Gezer, Ham, Hamath, Hazor, Ibleam, Iteren, Iursa, Jacob-El, Joppa, Joseph-El, Kadesh, Karmaim, Khashabu, Kishion, Laish, Lydda, Makkeday, Megiddo, Merom, Migdol, Mishal, Negeb, Ny, Ono, Pahel, Rabbah, Rebi, Rehob, Rosh-Kadesh, Shamash-Edom, Sharon, Shunem, Socho, Taanach, Tjerekh, Tunip, Ullaza, Unqi, and Yehem. [See Appendix A for how some of these cities' strata verify being conquered by Thutmose III.]

Thutmose III co-reign with Amenhotep II (1622-1618 BC)

Thutmose III led one final campaign into Nubia in his 50th year (1622 BC), and so he made his son Amenhotep II co-regent before he left for war. He died four years later near the end of his 54th regnal year, but only 28 of those years were sole rule.

Joseph's elderly years

Over the years Joseph saw his great grand-children through Manasseh, and his great, great grand-children through Ephraim. While Thutmose III was ruling, Joseph gave explicit directions to his brothers regarding his death.

And Joseph said to his brothers, I die: and God will surely visit you, and bring you out of this land to the land which he swore to Abraham, to Isaac, and to Jacob. And Joseph took an oath of the children of Israel, saying, <u>God will surely visit you, and</u>

---

kingdom-temple-discovered-sinai accessed 4/12/11

437 Hoffmeier, James and Millard, Alan, editors, *The Future of Biblical Archaeology*, Eerdman's Pub., Michigan, 2004, p. 112

438 Morrison, Dan, "Egypt's Largest Pharaoh-Era Fortress Discovered", http://news.nationalgeographic.com/news/2007/07/070727-egypt-fort.html, accessed 4/19/11

439 Joshua 19:6

440 Hoffmeier, James, translation of Gebel Barkal Stela of Thutmose III

*you shall carry up my bones from hence. So Joseph died, being an hundred and ten years old: and they embalmed him, and he was put in a **coffin** in Egypt. (Genesis 50:14-16)*

I disagree with David Rohl's conclusion that the empty grave and cult statue at Avaris were Joseph's;[441] I think they belonged to Seth II. Joseph's tomb was more likely in ancient On. Joseph's descendants knew the location of his coffin, likely containing precious scrolls. Joshua was born 99 years after Joseph, and Joshua also died at 110 years old.

Joseph's Tomb in Shechem, Israel

Exodus 13:19 states, "*Moses took the bones of Joseph with him*" when they left Egypt.

And the bones of Joseph, which the children of Israel brought up out of Egypt, buried they in Shechem, in a parcel of ground which Jacob bought of the sons of Hamor the father of Shechem for an hundred pieces of silver: and it became the inheritance of the children of Joseph. (Joshua 24:32)

After current Israel turned Nablus (Shechem) over to the Palestinians, Muslims began to desecrate Joseph's tomb in 1999 with hammers, then they painted its dome green (for Islam); they eventually destroyed it by fire in 2001, hoping to erect a mosque in its place.

But now they break down the carved work thereof at once with axes and hammers. They have cast fire into your sanctuary, they have defiled by casting down the dwelling place of your name to the ground. (Psalm 74:6-7)

And Joseph died, and all his brothers, and all that generation. And the children of Israel were fruitful, and increased abundantly, and multiplied, and waxed exceeding mighty; and the land was filled with them. Now there arose up a new king over Egypt, which knew not Joseph. (Exodus 1:6-8)

A generation, forty years, after Joseph's death would be during the reign of Thutmose IV. Amenhotep III was the next pharaoh to reign, and he did so without knowledge of Joseph, and Amenhotep III enslaved the Hebrews and killed their male babies. During Joseph's entire life, the children of Israel were not enslaved in Egypt but were free to pursue business and their own dreams. That does not mean the Hebrews were not "mocked" during Joseph's life and thereafter. The "Asiatic" Hebrews who primarily lived in the "*lands of Goshen*" east of the eastern delta may have often been lumped together with the dreaded Hyksos shepherds from Phoenicia who made Avaris their capital in the eastern delta. Phoenicia encompassed the city-states of Byblos, Tyre, Sidon, Zemar, Arvad/Arpad, and Berytus (Beirut) which appear in the Amarna letters, and also appear in the Bible (except Beirut).

---

441 Rohl, David M., *Pharaohs and Kings: A Biblical Quest*, Crown Publishers, New York, 1995

Joseph's Pharaohs

1745 Joseph was born in Canaan during the reign of Tao (II) in Egypt
1728 Joseph entered Egypt as a slave during the reign of Ahmose I
1715 Joseph was made grand vizier by Ahmose I; the first of seven years of plenty began
1712 Amenhotep I (under his mom, Ahmose-Nefetari) began to reign Egypt
1688 Amenhotep I died soon after Joseph returned from burying his father Jacob
1688-1674 Thutmose I
1674-1672 Thutmose II and Hatshepsut
1672-1651 Hatshepsut with Thutmose III

1651-1618 Thutmose III

1635 Joseph died during the reign of Thutmose III

1622-1596 Amenhotep II (4 year co-reign)
1596-1588 Thutmose IV
1588-1550 Amenhotep III
 ("*knew not Joseph*")

Amurru/Phoenicia

Joseph

Canaan	Egypt
1745-1728	1728-1635

Egyptian Pharaohs in the Nile delta

Apepi I (15th) 1765-1731	Khamudi (15th) 1731-1720	Ahmose I (18th) 1720-1712	Amenhotep I (18th) 1712-1688	Thutmose I (18th) 1688-1674	Thutmose II 1764-1762	Hatshepsut (18th) 1762-1651	Thutmose III (18th) 1651-1618

Pharaohs of the Bible

Amenhotep II (1622-1596 BC, first four years co-reign)

Thutmose III married a non-royal woman named Merytre-Hatshepsut who gave birth to Amenhotep II. He was raised at the palace complex at Ezbet Helmi which was called Peru-nefer ('good port', 500 meters west of Tell el-Dab^ca), excavated by Manfred Bietak.

Amenhotep II

Thutmose IV

"The palatial precinct which covered an area of 5.5 hectar (13 Feddan) was surrounded by an enclosure wall with an entrance pylon in the north. Together with the town in the south and the bay at the river in the north it can most probably be identified with Peru-nefer, the major Egyptian naval and military stronghold. The palace which dates precisely from Tuthmosis III and Amenophis II, the time when Peru-nefer was active, the presence of Nubian soldiers as evidenced by Kerma pottery and Kerma arrow tips as well as workshops producing arrows and slingshots proves the presence of military units."[442]
[palaces and workshops evident in Tell el-Dab^ca's general phase C/2]

As prince, Amenhotep II oversaw shipments at the docks; and he was made high priest of Lower Egypt.[443]

According to an inscription on his great Sphinx stela, Amenhotep II began his sole rule when he was 18 years old:

"Now his Majesty appeared as king as a fine youth after he had become 'well developed', and had completed eighteen years in his strength and bravery."[444]

---
442 Bietak, Manfred at http://www.auaris.at/html/history_en.html
443 Gardiner, Alan, *Egypt of the Pharaohs*, Oxford University Press, 1964, p. 198
444 Urk. IV. 1279, pp. 8-10

Amenhotep II campaigned against the Mitanni in the Levant in his 3rd, 7th, and 9th years, concluding when the princes of Mitanni came to Egypt to seek peace.[445] A column at Karnak between the fourth and fifth pylons commemorated his receiving tribute from the Mitanni. He also completed a temple his father had started at Amada in Nubia.

The mortuary temple of Amenhotep II was destroyed in antiquity, but his KV35 tomb survived with his mummy undisturbed in his sarcophagus. The X-ray of his mummy showed he was about 40 when he died.[446] 18 + 26 year reign = 44 years at death

Thutmose IV (1596-1588 BC)

Amenhotep II's queen Tiaa gave birth to Thutmose IV. After Thutmose IV wrote several letters to the king of Mitanni to seal their peace through marriage, he acquiesced and sent him his daughter.[447] In the first regnal year, Thutmose IV had a Dream Stele carved and placed between the paws of the Great Sphinx to proclaim the gods had designated him to be pharaoh. He also completed Thutmose III's eastern obelisk, and had the 105 foot 'unique obelisk'[448] erected at Karnak where he also built a small alabaster temple for commoners. Of his monuments, the latest was dated to his eighth regnal year.[449]

Detail of Dream Stele of Thutmose IV

---

445 Redford, Donald B, *Egypt, Canaan, and Israel in Ancient Times*, Princeton University Press, Princeton NJ, 1992, p. 164; as noted on the walls at Karnak

446 Der Manuelian, Peter, *Studies in the Reign of Amenophis II*, Hildesheimer Ägyptologische Beiträge 26, Gerstenbeg Verlag, Hildesheim, 1987, p. 44
 26 - 4 = 22 years of sole reign which began at 18. 22 + 18 = 40

447 As recorded by his grandson in El Amarna letter #29 (EA 29)

448 Clayton, Peter, *Chronicle of the Pharaohs*, Thames & Hudson Ltd, 1994, p. 114

449 Bryan, Betsy, *The Reign of Thutmose IV*, The Johns Hopkins University Press, Baltimore, 1991, p. 6

Moses' Pharaohs

". . . she called his name Moses: and she said, Because I drew him out of the water." (Exodus 2:10b)

Amenhotep III

Early in his reign, Amenhotep III opened new limestone quarries in Tura and embarked on extensive monument building in Nubia and a new religious complex in Thebes. Some consider Egypt to have reached its apex of artistic splendor during his reign. He only fought one battle against Kush (Sudan) to secure supplies of gold. Egypt was powerful and at peace with its neighbors, and he was determined to keep it that way.

When the Anatolian capital, Hattusa, of Tudhaliya II was burned down, Amenhotep III wrote to Tarhundaradu, the king of Arzawa, to make an alliance to take advantage of their mutual enemy, the Anatolian Hittites.[450]

> "Amenhotep III initiated contacts with almost all the countries surrounding the Hittites, and a pattern is evident in which he was seeking both new alliances and a means to take advantage of, and to constrain, the Hittites when they were (temporarily) weak. . . . Tudhaliya II mounted a campaign of reconquest, and returned the Hittites to their dominant regional positions."[451]

The literal descendants of Jacob/Israel had become a population of well over a million in the Nile delta; a possible threat. Egypt's vassals in Canaan and Syria cried out for more supplies and soldiers to maintain control. To solve both problems, he enslaved the Israelites and had them build treasure cities with which to keep the vassals supplied.

*And he said to his people, Behold, the people of the children of Israel are more and mightier than we: Come on, let us deal wisely with them; lest they multiply, and it come to pass, that, when there falls out any war, <u>they join also to our enemies, and fight against us</u>, and so get them up out of the land. Therefore they did set over them taskmasters to afflict them with their burdens. And they built for Pharaoh treasure cities, Pithom and **Raamses**. But the more they afflicted them, the more they multiplied and grew. And they were grieved because of the children of Israel. (Exodus 1:9-12)*

Amenhotep III feared that the Israelites would ally with enemies against him just as he had done to the Hittites. The Israelites did not build pyramids, they built treasure cities and palaces for Amenhotep III and his family. The city of Raamses (now Qantir) was built just north of Avaris, and Pithom was built along Wadi Tumilat near the canal.

---

450 El-Amarna letter #31
451 Manning, Sturt, *A Test of Time*, Oxbow Books, 1999, p. 229 based on Clinc (1998:248-249)

Pharaohs of the Bible

Ahmenhotep III   **He, queen Tiye, & Henuttaneb**

After the Hebrew slaves had completed building the brick treasure cities of Pithom and Raamses,[452] Amenhotep III had them build his brick palaces at Malkata (southwest of Thebes) and Akhmim (north of Thinis) in his 11th regnal year (1577 BC). He also may have used them to build his harem and royal school (*kap*) west of El-Lahun (Fayyum).[453] Thus if there were no Hebrew families there, they were transported to those various places.

> ". . . the reign of Amenhotep III correlates with the beginning of (or early part of) the LHIIIA2 period, and the beginning of the established (palatial) dominance of Mycenaean Greece. A ceiling of Amenhotep III's palace at **Malkata** is decorated in Aegean style (Barber 1991:348-350), and LHIIIA2 pottery is found in Egypt from his reign."

The Mycenaean Greek period was roughly from 1900-1100 BC, or from the beginning of my cSIP to the beginning of my cTIP. Malkata's ceiling depicts red, white and blue eagles with outspread wings extended to each wall. (A similar ceiling remains at Hathor's temple in Denderah.) Other walls still standing have the stripes, spirals and rosettes typical in other Minoan wall paintings. After Thera's eruption which destroyed cities of eastern Crete, the Minoan culture declined and the Mycenaeans ascended in power and influence.

Malkata palace ruins near Thebes

---

452 Hoffmeier, James K., *Israel in Egypt: the evidence for the authenticity of the Exodus tradition*, 1996, pp. 117-119. Archaeology supports Qantir as Pi-Ramesses, and Tell el-Retaba on Wadi Tumilat to Pi-thom.

453 Parcak, Sarah, "Egypt-What Lies Beneath" Science Channel, 2011. Small head of queen Tiye (far left in picture below) was discovered west of El-Lahun in area of harem and Kap discovered using infrared.

Baby-killing and baby saving

The harsh labor plan had the opposite effect; the more the Hebrews were afflicted, the more they multiplied. So Amenhotep III called in the Hebrew midwives and commanded them to kill the male babies. They disobeyed, and God blessed the midwives. Then Amenhotep III commanded all of his people to throw Hebrew baby boys into the Nile.[454]

Jochebed was one of those multiplying women who added another life into the world. She managed to keep him a secret for three months, before deciding to put him into a waterproof basket on the Nile with his sister Miriam watching out for him. Moses was eighty years old at the exodus (1491 BC); thus he was born in 1571 BC during the reign of Amenhotep III. I suspect his oldest daughter, Sitamun, found Moses at Akhmim.

And the daughter of Pharaoh came down to wash herself at the river; and her maidens walked along by the river's side; and when she saw the ark among the flags, she sent her maid to fetch it. And when she had opened it, she saw the child: and, behold, the babe wept. And she had compassion on him, and said, This is one of the Hebrews' children. Then said his sister to Pharaoh's daughter, Shall I go and call to you a nurse of the Hebrew women, that she may nurse the child for you? And Pharaoh's daughter said to her, Go. And the maid went and called the child's mother. And Pharaoh's daughter said to her, Take this child away, and nurse it for me, and I will give you your wages. And the women took the child, and nursed it. And the child grew, and she brought him to Pharaoh's daughter, and he became her son. And she called his name Moses: and she said, Because I drew him out of the water. (Exodus 2:5-10)

Amenhotep III had at least six children; two sons and four daughters. Thutmose, the eldest, was trained to be pharaoh; and Amenhotep IV, was trained by his uncle Anen to be a priest. Three of four daughters are represented on Cairo's colossal statue of the family of Amenhotep III: Henuttaneb in the center, Nebetah on the right, and one whose name was destroyed on the left (Sitamun), likely because she had compassion toward the Hebrews and rescued one who floated into her life. Miriam arranged for her brother to be nursed by their mother. As noted with Ishmael, babies were nursed until about age five. So Moses was raised in the safety of his parent's home during those years and instilled with their faith and values. "Give me a child until he is five, and he is mine forever," has been attributed to many, because those formative years shape the personality of the child for life. Moses knew he was a Hebrew who worshipped the Creator of the universe who made a covenant with Abraham, Isaac, and Jacob. I imagine Amram and Jochebed especially told him all about Joseph in order to prepare him for a lifetime in the palace. Moses could have lived in the palace at Malkata built out of mud bricks like the treasure cities, but I suggest he began living at queen Tiye's palace near Akhmim, and then accompanied her to her east-delta fortress made of fired bricks called the "Lion's Lair".

---

454 Exodus 1:12-22

Pharaohs of the Bible

Amenhotep's III palace at Malkata, the "Palace of the Dazzling Aten", had a canal cut from the Nile emptying into its harbor for ease of travel. The Malkata palace was a self-contained city with a private lake. Queen Tiye's palace at Akhmim was near her parents, and it also had a man-made lake. At both palaces, Sitamun had private quarters. I propose Sitamun rescued Moses at Akhmim visiting her mother while her father was at Malkata. So that would mean Moses' family lived in UE nome #9 and helped build the palace at Akhmim in 1577 BC. When Amenhotep III married Tiye he gave her a fort as a wedding present.

Fortress Tjaru (Tell Hebua) existed in the time of Thutmose III and protected Egypt's eastern delta border. A description of Seti's 1st year campaign on a lower east wall at Karnak shows the following in order: Canal A, Tjaru fort, Canal B, Lion fort with rectangular pool, tower with horseshoe enclosed pool, Udjo fort, and the district Imy well.[455] I suggest Amenhotep III had the smaller (120 X 80 meters) Lion fort built for his new lioness.[456] The "Lion's Lair" or "Mansion of the Lion" was discovered four miles east of Fort Tjaru at Tell el-Borg.[457] According to Dr. James Hoffmeier, it was built of fired bricks to protect the building from the moat surrounding it. At Lion Fort, red wine jar handles were stamped with cartouches of Tiye, Akhenaten, Nefertiti, Smenkhkare and Tutankhamun. Remains of horses and pieces of gold were discovered there.[458] Roughly 250 soldiers and charioteers were stationed at Lion Fort. It may be Queen Tiye was the official in charge of the delta treasure cities, Ramses and Pithom, and used the Lion Fort as a base to receive goods from vassals and to send goods to kings. Another small fort (Tell el-Ebedah), the Udjo fort, was discovered seven miles from the Lion fort.

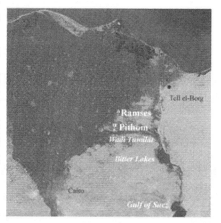

The store city of Ramses was built near Avaris (Tell el-Dabᶜa) at Qantir. If Ramses had been named for a god or pharaoh it would have had the prefix of 'Pi', like Pi-Tum "house of Atum (the setting sun)," called Pithom, on Wadi Tumilat west of current Ismalia. *Ramsosh* means pasture in Egyptian, and described the fields. Archaeologists discovered ancient canals from Tell el-Borg to Tjaru and to the Pelusiac tributary leading to Ramses, in accordance to stelae transported by boat.[459]

---

455 Hallo, William, editor, *Context of Scripture, Volume 2 Monumental Inscriptions from the Biblical World*, Brill Publishers, Boston 2003, p. 24
456 Stanek, Steven, "Giant Statue of Ancient Queen Found", *National Geographic News*, 2008 Statue of queen Tiye was discovered along with ten statues of Sekhmet, the **lion** goddess of war and healing.
457 Morrison, Dan, "Egypt's Largest Pharaoh-Era Fortress Discovered", http://news.nationalgeographic.com/news/2007/07/070727-egypt-fort.html, accessed 4/19/11
458 Jarus, Owen, "Tell El Borg: Peace Fortress of the Amarna Kings", http://heritage-key.com/egypt/tell-el-borg-peace-fortress-amarna-kings, accessed 4/19/11
459 Hoffmeier, James K., *Ancient Israel in Sinai: the evidence for the authenticity of the wilderness tradition*, Oxford Press University Press, New York, p. 101. Papyrus Anastasi V #24

Queen Tiye

I suggest princess Sitamun was an adult when she rescued baby Moses, and after he was weaned, she raised him as her own son.[460] She and Moses travelled with her mother from Akhmim to the mansion of the lion in the delta. Moses may have even gone on the boats bringing or taking treasure to the treasure cities of Pithom and Ramses. It's possible that during Moses' time at Lion Fort he visited relatives in the delta. There, Moses reached the age of 20 (1551 BC); while in Thebes, Amenhotep III made his son Amenhotep IV his successor the year before he died. Queen Tiye survived her husband twelve years, and continued in her foreign correspondence with kings.

King Tushratta of Mitanni had sent his daughter to marry Amenhotep III in his 36th year (1552 BC) in return for a bride price which included solid gold statues of himself and his daughter. Amenhotep III had them made, but died (1550 BC) before he could send them. Then Tadu-Heba became the wife of Amenhotep IV, and he sent gold-plated statues to his father-in-law instead. King Tushratta sent a letter (EA27) requesting the original agreement be honored, but he did not respond. So the king sent a letter (EA26) to Tiye:

"To Tiye, Lady of Egypt. Thus speaks Tushratta, King of Mitanni

Everything is well with me. May everything be well with you. . . .
You should continue sending joyful embassies, one after another.
Do not suppress them.

I shall not forget the friendship with Mimmuriya, your husband. At this moment and more than ever, I have ten times more friendship for your son, Napkhuria.

You are the one who knows the words of Mimmuriya, your husband, but you have not sent me yet the gift of homage which Mimmuriya, your husband, has ordered to be sent to me. I have asked Mimmuriya, your husband, for massive gold statues ... But your son has gold-plated statues of wood. As the gold is like dust in the country of your son, why have they been the reason for such pain, that your son should not have given them to me? ...

To Napkhuria, king of Egypt, my brother, my son-in-law, . . .
Tadu-Heba, my daughter, your wife, your other wives, your sons, . . .
may they all enjoy excellent health."

---

460 Acts 7:21

Pharaohs of the Bible

Queen Tiye   Queen Tiye from Hathor's Temple in Sinai

She wore the *Shwti* (two feathers), one *shw* was for Maat. Though Queen Hatshepsut did the most building at Hathor's Temple in Sinai, Queen Tiye was also represented there. According to Petrie, early mining parties camped up high on the hills to protect themselves from wild animals, and "One valley in Sinai has been named from the lioness (*labwa*);"[461] possibly after queen Tiye came from her Mansion of the Lion to worship at Hathor's temple. Amenhotep III and queen Tiye had several children including Amenhotep IV.

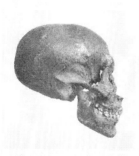

Amenhotep IV/Akhenaten   Tutankhaten/Tutankhamun
father of Tutankhaten

Amenhotep IV

Mummy 61075 from KV55 was identified by Zahi Hawass and his team as Amenhotep IV in 2007.[462] It had an elongated skull and a cleft palate. He and his son Tutankhamun[463] were both depicted with long arms and exceptionally wide hips. Tutankhamun's loin cloths found in his tomb proved he had very wide hips. These anomalies made them appear more

---

461 Petrie, Flinders W.M., *Researches in Sinai*, E. P. Dutton & Company, New York, 1906, p. 40
462 Ahkenaten, Wikipedia, accessed 4/9/10
463 Verified by DNA tests in 2010 http://news.nationalgeographic.com/news/2010/02/100216-king-tut-malaria-bones-inbred-tutankhamun/, accessed 4/9/10

effeminate. The cleft palate may have also impeded Amenhotep's speech and accounted for his odd facial expressions in artwork. It was common for the pharaohs of the 18th dynasty to marry their sisters and/or daughters which passed on genetic weaknesses. Amenhotep III remarked the Hebrews were *"mightier"* which can mean "to crunch the bones". The Hebrews were likely a physically stronger people than the Egyptians.

Amenhotep IV was prepared by Ay, the high priest of the rising sun, to be a religious leader. Possibly, as Amenhotep IV discussed faith with monotheistic Moses, the thought of elevating one god above the Egyptian pantheon came into his mind. It might be a solution for their country which was inundated with many gods and all their temples which constantly needed repair, and priests who were often in a power struggle with the pharaoh.

Amenhotep IV becomes Akhenaten

Amun was one of several sun gods, and was the local god of Thebes. Amun was a major deity in Egypt during this 18th dynasty, sometimes causing a power struggle between the priests of Amun and the pharaoh. During the first year of his reign, Amenhotep IV erected a pylon in Karnak (eastern Thebes) to Aten. In earlier dynasties the Aten was the sun disc which empowered sun gods, but Amenhotep IV was declaring it to be a god in its own right. In his third year, he had a lavish temple built to Aten in Karnak, but there was still too much competition with the other temples and gods there.

In his fifth regnal year, Amenhotep IV, like his father, decided to use the Hebrew slaves to build a city for his newly envisioned god Aten with sandstone "bricks" called *talatat*. He chose virgin land with a split in the cliffs which could represent the sun coming over the horizon, and extended the "rays" of that "sun" as a grid upon which the city of *Akhenaten* (horizon of Aten) was built and later named el-Amarna. He moved his family from the Malkata palace and lived in a big tent while it was under construction. It was during this time that Amenhotep IV changed his name to Akhenaten.

Amarna boundary stele and locations

On stelae boundary stones Akhenaten IV had the following engraved regarding his new city, "It is the Aten, my [father], who advised me concerning it, (saying) "Behold, [fill] Akhet-Aten with provisions -- a storehouse for everything!" while my father, Hor-Aten, proclaimed to me, "It is to belong to my Person, to be Akhet-Aten continually forever.""" (Translation from Murnane, 1995)[464] Could it be that Moses told Akhenaten IV about Joseph and the storage of food for famine?

In the ninth year of his reign Akhenaten IV declared the sun disc to now be the creator god, supreme to all others, and himself as Aten's only prophet and intermediary, conveniently undermining the authority of all other gods and their priests.[465] He confiscated the land and wealth of the priests of Amun in a death blow to the priestly power of Thebes. He had the name of Amun and references to "gods" scratched out of the temples. He alone would hold spiritual and governmental power. At first this might have seemed to be a good idea to Akhenaten's vizier, Ay, and his general, PaAtenemheb; but they found it hard to control the people who rebelled against the new scheme. They didn't need trouble within their borders when they also had troubles beyond their borders.

Amarna Letters (1588 - 1520)

The Nile was the base of power for the Egyptian Empire, but it maintained vassal states in Libya, Nubia, the Sinai, and Canaan (Retenu). Egypt's main enemies were the Hittites to the north, with Syria and Canaan as the battlefields. Mitanni was Egypt's ally. Assyria was a buffer for Babylon.

Correspondence between all these areas was found in Akhenaten's new city. Three hundred eighty two of their cuneiform clay letters (like the one pictured here) were discovered in el-Amarna, and designated with "EA" in museums.

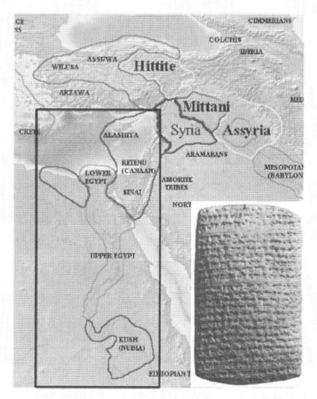

---

464 Magaera, Lorenz, "Neferkheperure Waenre Akhenaten" http://www.heptune.com/akhen.html - 4/9/10
465 Ancient Egypt Online, http://www.ancientegyptonline.co.uk/akhenaten.html - 4/9/10

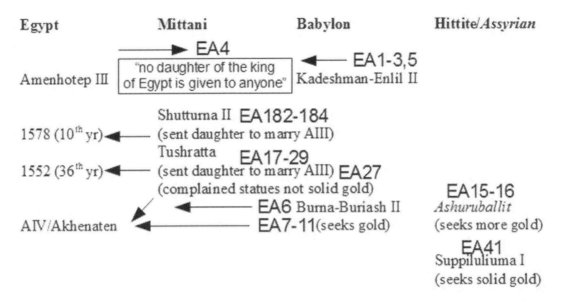

Amarna Letter Headaches

When Akhenaten IV moved his capital, he took his father's royal correspondence; and the foreign kings began addressing their letters to him as Neffeure (EA7) instead of prenomen Neferkheperure. Akhenaten inherited his father's foreign wives and the obligation of sending "gifts" of gold to the lands from which they came. Ashuruballit defeated Shutturna II, freeing the Assyrians from being a Mitanni vassal state. Ashuruballit came to Akhenaten's palace for a visit (EA256) to secure Egypt's help in case of attack; this was an affront to Burna-Buriash II who considered Assyria as their vassal. But when Burna-Buriash II died, Ashuruballit made Babylon their vassal state instead. Besides correspondence with foreign powers, many of the Amarna letters are from "kings", who are more like governors or mayors of city-states in Canaan and Syria.

Vassals in Canaan and Syria under fire

The Amarna letters provide names of other contemporary rulers: like the first two kings of Ugarit, Ammittamru I and Niqmaddu II; and the first two kings of Amurru, Abdi-Ashirta and Azira. Though there are routine orders for glass from Yursa (EA235+314) and Acco (EA235) and Ashkelon (EA323), most of the letters plead with Egypt to send military aid because their cities are under attack and they name traitors to the crown. From Beirut, one mayor wrote to pharaoh, but another wrote to Yanhamu, Egypt's commissioner, accusing him of neglecting Egypt's protectorates so that the cities from Byblos to Ugarit had aligned themselves with Egypt's enemy Aziru. Rib-Hadda of Byblos wrote Akhenaten 68 letters requesting military aid, 16 of which mention Yanhamu. Rib-Hadda wrote that the Amurru had hired Habiru mercenaries (EA74+81), that the Hittites were burning cities in Syria

Pharaohs of the Bible

(EA126) and that Suppiluliuma and Abdi-Ashirta had conquered the Mitanni (EA75). Others also wrote of the Habiru and the Hittites and traitors:

Etakkama of Kadesh – EA 189
Biryawaza of Damascus – EA 197
Abi-Milku of Tyre – EA 151
Ayyab of Ashtaroth – EA 256, 364
Sawardata of Atlit (Qiltu) – EA 280, 283
Biridiya of Megiddo – EA 244-5
Labaya of Shechem – EA 252-254
Mutbaal, Labaya's son of Pella – EA 245
Milkilu of Gezer – EA 267-271
Tagi, Milkulu's father-in-law,
  of Jamnta – EA 264-6
Abdi-Hiba of Jerusalem – EA 285-290
Zimretta of Lachish – EA 329

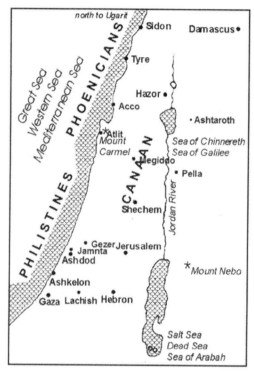

Traitorous Vassals

Biryawaza informed Akhenaten that chariots from Ashtaroth were given to Apiru who were aligned with the Hittites to whom he was losing land. He also fought against Labaya and his sons, but they captured Megiddo. Biridiya informed Akhenaten that Labaya was captured by Zurata of Acco, but that he released him for a bribe. Labaya invaded Gezer and turned Milkilu to his side. They and Yidya of Ashkelon gave food and quarter to Apiru who then attacked Jerusalem. Etakkama informed Akhenaten that Biryawaza had joined the Hittites. Biryawaza wrote him that Labaya was killed by the men of Jenin.

Sawardata informed Akhenaten that thirty cities were attacking him, but that Surata of Acco and Endaruta of Achshaph (northeast of Acco) came to his aid. Then he accused Abdi-Hiba of being another Labaya. Abdi-Hiba responded to Akhenaten, "Why do you love the Habiru, and hate the regents? Because I say, 'The lands of the king, my lord, are lost,' therefore am I slandered to the king, my lord."[466]

Akhenaten's Response

Amenhotep II boasted of capturing 3600 Apiru on stelae at Memphis and Karnak.[467] The Amarna letters confirm why Amenhotep III worried about the Hebrew slaves possibly aligning themselves with their enemies the Hittites, because their cousins the Habiru/Apiru were doing just that by the end of his reign and throughout that of Akhenaten's. Rarely, did

---

466 EA 286 from http://www.specialtyinterests.net/eae.html#286, accessed 4/19/10
467 http://en.wikipedia.org/wiki/Apiru, accessed 4/19/10

Akhenaten send military aid when requested (EA367). More often he sent a commissioner to placate his vassals. I speculate commissioner Yanhamu was young Horemheb. Milkilu accused Yanhamu of using extortion (EA270).

Akhenaten's Family

Akhenaten and Nefertiti had six daughters; the oldest being Meritaten. One of their other daughters died prematurely. A picture of her death also showed a wet nurse holding a baby boy,[468] who was most likely Tutankhamun. Akhenaten was Tut's father, but Nefertiti was not his biological mother.[469] After six girls, he needed a wife to produce a male heir.

Akhenaten, Nefertiti, and their daughters

Akhenaten died in the seventeenth year of his reign (1534 BC). Crown prince Tut was only ten, so Smenkhkare reigned with his queen Meritaten for three years, followed by the brief reign of Nefertiti. These three years were later usurped by king Tut who was first attested in his fourth year. Smenkhkare's throne name was Ankhkheprure, and three years of olive oil from Amarna were stamped with his throne name.[470] Following the 17th year of Akhenaten's wine jar labels, were labels for years one and two for Ankhkheprure. Then there was a year one wine label with a different title for the vintner, which was likely for Nefertiri.

---

468 http://www.ancientegyptonline.co.uk/tutankhamun.html
469 http://en.wikipedia.org/wiki/Tutankhamun
470 Hornung, *Untersuchungen*, pp. 88-89

Pharaohs of the Bible

Smenkhkare (1534-1531 BC)

Ahkenaten's daughter, Meritaten, married a man named Smenkhkare, possibly her uncle. In Amarna letters she is referred to as queen Mayati.[471] The high priest of Aten, MeryRa, had an unfinished relief of Smenkhkare and Meritaten in his tomb which artist Lena Wennburg Sweden Orust has reconstructed borrowing heavily from Akhenaten's features and sculptures of Meritaten. Smenkhkare's body on the relief has the same odd proportions as Ahkenaten's and Tutankhamun's: thin waist and arms, and very wide hips.

Smenkhkare and Meritaten

Queen Nefertiti

When her husband Amenhotep IV changed his name to AkhenAten, Nefertiti changed her name to Neferneferu Aten-Nefertiti,[472] with the first one becoming her throne name later. She gave birth to six daughters. One relief shows the family mourning the death of their teen-age daughter Meketaten. Nefertiti means "the beauty has come", but she also had power. On a limestone relief Nefertiti is shown smiting a female captive on a barge.[473] By the twelfth year of Akhenaten's reign, she may have been elevated to the status of co-regent. The coregency stela has her name chiselled out with Ankhkheprure's name written over it.[474] Succession is rarely smooth. Nefertiti's sole rule was about one year.

Nefertiti Bust

But then Tutankhaten took the throne. From Akhenaten's reign and throughout all these changes (1551-1533 BC), Ay continued as vizier. Ay was an in-law to the royal family, possibly as Nefertiti's father. PaAtenemheb's son, Horemheb, became Tutankhaten's general. Horemheb had no blood or marriage link to the royal family.

---

471 EA 10 and EA 11 and possibly EA 155
472 http://en.wikipedia.org/wiki/Neferneferuaten
473 http://en.wikipedia.org/wiki/File:NefertitiRelief_SmitingSceneOnBoat-CloseUp.png
474 Reeves, Nicholas, *Akhenaten: Egypt's False Prophet*, Thames & Hudson, 2005, p. 172

Vizier Ay   General Horemheb

King Tut

Through the influence of Ay and Horemheb, in the third year of his reign, Tutankhaten changed his name to Tutankhamun, and restored the worship of Amun. He moved back to Malkata palace near Thebes, and rebuilt the power-base there. On the restoration stele at Karnak, the young pharaoh had the situation inscribed.

> "The temples of the gods and goddesses ... were in ruins. Their shrines were deserted and overgrown. Their sanctuaries were as non-existent and their courts were used as roads ... the gods turned their backs upon this land."[475]

This may reference the devastating pandemic toward the end of Akhenaten's reign.[476] To regain the favor of the gods and the people, King Tut began extensive rebuilding projects throughout Egypt. He sent general Horemheb out on campaigns to Nubia (south) and Syria (north) to shore up Egypt's political power in areas Akhenaten had neglected.

King Tut married, but his wife bore two stillborn daughters. To assure continuance of the kingdom, Tut made general Horemheb his heir apparent.

> "Hereditary Prince, Fan-bearer on the Right Side of the King, and Chief Commander of the Army . . . attendant of the King in his footsteps in the foreign countries of the south and the north" (Horemheb's tomb)[477]

King Tut restored normalcy to Egypt, and the people adored him for it. So when he died just a few years later, both natives and foreigners offered many gifts to accompany him into the afterlife, filling his tomb with vast treasures. His tomb also contained many walking sticks from when he broke his leg; likely, in a chariot accident.

---

475 Hart, George (1990) *Egyptian Myths,* University of Texas Press, p. 47
476 Akhenaten, http://www.ancientegyptonline.co.uk/akhenaten.html, accessed 4/10/10
477 John A. Wilson "Texts from the Tomb of General Hor-em-heb" in Ancient Near Eastern Texts (ANET) relating to the Old Testament, Princeton Univ. Press, 2nd edition, 1955, pp. 250-251

Pharaohs of the Bible

1551-1534	Amenhotep IV/Akhenaten
1534-1531	Smenkhkare and queen Meritaten/Mayati
1531-1530	Nefertiti/Neferneferuaten
1534-1524	Tutankhamun
1524-1520	Ay
1520-1493	Horemheb

Tut using walking stick

Moses at 40

Queen Tiye may have asked Moses to keep his Hebrew identity a secret while Amenhotep III was alive. After their deaths, Moses may have sought ways to relieve the burdens of his people without letting the Hebrew community know. As an 'Asiatic', Moses was unlikely to be considered to rule in Egypt, though "technically" he was a prince.

Moses had witnessed the religious upheaval of Egyptian society under Akhenaten's rule. Then he witnessed the political upheaval after Akhenaten's death with two different pharaohs in three years. Moses turned forty in 1531 BC during the change of reign between Smenkhkare and Nefertiti. Even if the young pharaoh didn't pin the blame on Moses' monotheistic beliefs, Ay or Horemheb might have. Nefertiti had most likely died by this time, and his adoptive mother, Meritaten, might be the only reason Ay and Horemheb tolerated Moses at all. Moses might have believed he could help stabilize the situation by appealing to his Hebrew brethren in the north while the royal court moved south.

> *And it came to pass in those days, when Moses was grown, that he went out to his brothers, and looked on their burdens: and he spied an Egyptian smiting an Hebrew, one of his brothers. And he looked this way and that way, and when he saw that there was no man, he slew the Egyptian, and hid him in the sand. And when he went out the second day, behold, two men of the Hebrews strove together: and he said to him that did the wrong, Why smite you your fellow? And he said, <u>Who made you a prince and a judge over us? intend you to kill me, as you killed the Egyptian?</u> And Moses feared, and said, Surely this thing is known. Now when Pharaoh heard this thing, he sought to slay Moses. But Moses fled from the face of Pharaoh, and dwelled in the land of Midian: (Exodus 2:11-15)*

Were Nefertiti and Smenkhkare slain by Ay or Horemheb? Did Moses think violence was the only remedy? Was he going to pick off the taskmasters one at a time? Why didn't he just order the taskmaster off or distract him? Was Moses' life already in danger? Did he think killing Egyptians would beholden him to his own people? Moses took the time to look around, and *"saw there was no man"*. He was calculating whether or not he could get away with murder. It was a very costly decision.

Moses' Pharaohs

Moses slaying the Egyptian
by Sir Edward Poynter

The Hebrew slave who observed the murderous act had been subjected to a woman, a man, and a boy as new pharaohs over him; and probably surmised it was Ay who "placed" Tutankhamun as pharaoh. Horemheb or Ay or Tutankhamun could have given Moses charge over the Hebrews, so the slave's question could have been an honest one, followed by true fear for his life if Moses had been given such authority. Gods from Aten to Amun and capitals from Amarna to Thebes . . . maybe a Hebrew now ruled?

But Moses had acted without authority, and knew it imperiled his own life. So he fled from Egypt, and travelled across the Sinai Peninsula (named for the god Sin) and around the Gulf of Aqaba to arrive in Midian (northwestern Saudi Arabia). He was received by distant Hebrew relatives (through Abraham's wife Keturah, see page 110) known as some of the Habiru/Apiru in the Amarna letters. Moses came to the aid of Jethro's daughters, and Jethro gave one of his daughters, Zipporah, to be Moses' wife;[478] and she bore him two sons.[479]

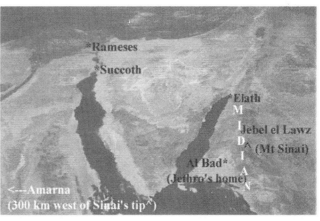

---

478 Exodus 2:16-22
479 Exodus 18:3-4

Moses at 79

Moses, a former prince of Egypt, lived a simple shepherd's life in the ancient land of Midian. He learned more about the Creator from Jethro, who was a priest[480] who lived in Al Bad. And then Moses personally encountered the LORD, upon seeing a fire which did not consume a bush (<u>seneh</u>). Mount <u>Sinai</u> was a specific peak in the *Horeb* (desolate) mountain range of NW Arabia[481] which Moses named for the fiery bush (*seneh*).

God called to him out of the middle of the bush, . . . I am the God of your father, the God of Abraham, the God of Isaac, and the God of Jacob. And Moses hid his face; for he was afraid to look on God. And the LORD [YHWH][482] said, I have surely seen the affliction of my people which are in Egypt, and have heard their cry by reason of their taskmasters; for I know their sorrows; And I am come down to deliver them out of the hand of the Egyptians, and to bring them up out of that land to a good land and a large, to a land flowing with milk and honey; to the place of the Canaanites . . . I will send you to Pharaoh, that you may bring forth my people the children of Israel out of Egypt. . . . When you have brought forth the people out of Egypt, you shall serve God on this mountain. And Moses said to God, Behold, when I come to the children of Israel, and shall say to them, The God of your fathers has sent me to you; and they shall say to me, What is his name? what shall I say to them? And God said to Moses, I AM THAT I AM [Eheyeh asher Eheyeh]: and he said, Thus shall you say to the children of Israel, I AM [AHWH - Eheyeh] has sent me to you. And God said moreover to Moses, Thus shall you say to the children of Israel, the LORD [YWHW] God of your fathers, the God of Abraham, the God of Isaac, and the God of Jacob, has sent me to you: this is my name for ever, and this is my memorial to all generations. . . . I have surely visited you, and seen that which is done to you in Egypt: And I have said, I will bring you up out of the affliction of Egypt. (Exodus 3:4-17)

The LORD was going to fulfill His promise to Abraham (Gen. 15:7-14), and return his seed to the land of Canaan; He would deliver them Himself, using Moses as his emissary.

And the LORD said to Moses in Midian, Go, return into Egypt: for <u>all the men are dead</u> which sought your life. (Exodus 4:19)

This text does not reflect only one pharaoh ruling during Moses' 39 years in Midian. Pharaohs Tut, Ay and Horemheb had all died, and then Rameses I began his reign.

---

480 Exodus 18
481 Galatians 4:25 ". . . Mount Sinai in Arabia . . ." Josephus wrote, "Mount Sinai is the highest of mountains in the region of the city of Madian."
482 'LORD' represents four Hebrew letters (YHWH = yod, heh, vav, heh) of Creator God's personal Name, which is sometimes pronounced Yahweh or Jehovah. Adam, Abraham, Isaac, and Jacob knew this Name (Gen. 4:1; 12:8; 26:22; 28:13-16), but Joseph called Him *Elohim* (Gen. 50), so His Name may have gone out of use. God also gave Moses the meaning of His Name: I AM (AHWH = aleph, heh, vav, heh).

Rameses I (1493-1491 BC)

Originally named Pa-ra-ma-su, Rameses took his name from the land of his birth, Rameses. His father, Seti, was commander of the army of Egypt[483]; and Rameses' uncle had married into the family who were viceroys of Kush. This was a family of power and political influence. In his youth, Rameses likely accompanied his military father, Seti, to the fortifications across the Sinai Peninsula along the road from the delta to Gaza (Way of Horus). These forts were probably constructed by Ahmose I after ousting the Hyksos from Egypt.[484] The most impressive of these fortresses was at Tjaru/Tharu, the gateway to the Nile.[485] Egypt's vassals in Syria and Canaan had continued to deteriorate since the reign of Akhenaten, making these old fortresses of utmost importance. Suppiluliuma had united the cities of Syria and was beginning to draw many of the Canaanite cities to himself as well.

Rameses I was well aware of the large population of Israelite slaves under his father's control. After general Seti's death, pharaoh Horemheb appointed Rameses to succeed his father as commander of the army of Egypt, expecting him to keep the slaves docile and to quell the unrest among the vassals.

Libya was content to maintain peace with Egypt through intermarriage in exchange for large dowries. Rameses married a red-headed Berber or European, likely from Libya, because his son and grandson (who would be pharaohs Seti I and Rameses II) had red hair and associated themselves with the god Seth, or Seth II, who had red hair.[486]

Horemheb realized Egypt needed the stabilization of a dynasty of male heirs, but he had none, so he designated Rameses to succeed him because he already had sons and a grandson and was an able vizier and military commander. He was also a high priest of Amun, thus he already had the respect of the people and was a well known authority. Pharaoh Rameses I moved the capital of Egypt to the city of Rameses (Qantir). His reign began late in 1493 BC and lasted at least 17 months, with his last year <u>1491 BC, the year of the exodus</u>.

Rameses I 1493-1491

Seti I 1491-1480

Rameses II 1480-1414

---

483 EA 234 and 288 mayors of Acco and Jerusalem mention Suta as the king's emissary.

484 Tanis stela recounting victory over Hyksos as 400 years prior, but it's about 300 years prior by my chronology, http://www.specialtyinterests.net/inscr400.html accessed 8/17/10

485 Sharp, Alastair, "Sinai fort may hold clues to ancient Egypt defenses", May 7, 2009; "Egyptians used seashells to strengthen the mud brick used to build the garrison, with a 15 meter thick and 12 meter high wall to discourage attack." http://www.reuters.com/article/idUSTRE5465N120090507 accessed 8/17/10

486 Earlson, Karl, "Redheaded Pharaoh Rameses II", http://www.white-history.com/earlson/rameses.htm accessed 8/18/10

Control of the Sinai Peninsula meant access to its mineral deposits in the mountains of the south: turquoise, manganese, iron, and copper.

> "A beautiful piece of work remains in the lower part of a limestone tablet of Ramessu I. The portion which is preserved of the figure is carefully wrought, and in the dress resembles the work of Akhenaten; it shows that what we know as the distinctively coarse Ramesside work did not begin till the second Ramessu. The inscription gives for the first time the complete names of the king; the vulture and uraeus name, and the Horus on *nubti* name, were only imperfectly known before. Another curious survival of Akhenaten's time is that the king is said to be 'prince of every circuit of the Aten.' To find the Aten mentioned thus after the ruthless Amenism of Horemheb is remarkable. Hitherto the latest mention of it was under King Ay. Ramessu is said to restore monuments to glorify the name of his mother Hathor, 'mistress of turquoise'. Another tablet in sandstone, representing the king offering to Hathor, was also found here. It is rare to meet with any inscriptions of this king, as he only reigned for two years."[487]

Petrie also had a collection of scarabs and sealings of Rameses I, the first pharaoh of the 19th dynasty. A seal impression of Ramesses I with Seth was found 50 km from Tell Hebua at the large fortified temple which has inscriptions from Thutmose II to Ramesses II.[488]

From Ten Plagues to Ten Commandments

DeMille's movie "The Ten Commandments" deviates from the Biblical script a few times and introduces new characters and scenarios, but contains the basics of the story. DreamWorks' "The Prince of Egypt" is a more scholarly attempt. The emphasis in both is Creator God had chosen Israel's descendants to be His special people upon the earth, and He demanded *"Let My people go!"* But it was more intimate and important than that.[489]

And thou shalt say unto Pharaoh, Thus saith Jehovah, Israel is my son, my first-born: and I have said unto thee, Let my son go, that he may serve me; and thou hast refused to let him go: behold, I will slay thy son, thy first-born. (Exodus 4:22-23)

---

487 Petrie, Flinders W.M., *Researches in Sinai*, E. P. Dutton & Company, New York, 1906, pp. 127-8
488 Press release at http://www.drhawass.com/blog/press-release-new-kingdom-temple-discovered-sinai
489 Exodus 13:2, 11-16

Pharaoh Rameses I was reluctant to release his slave force to an unknown God, so YWHW proved Himself to be Almighty by deposing the gods of Egypt through ten plagues[490]. Moses turned 40[491] on the 7th of Adar before the plagues began, and the last plague was on the 14th of Abib/Nisan; thus the Ten Plagues (Exodus 7-12) lasted 5 weeks.

Plagues on Egypt and Goshen	Plagues on Egypt, not Goshen
1st Nile and water to blood	4th Swarms of flies/mosquitos
2nd Frogs - burned in piles	5th Plague which killed cattle
(Magicians could copy first two plagues.)	6th Boils on men and beasts
	7th Hail smote trees & grain
3rd Lice	8th Locust ate what was left
(Magicians couldn't copy, and they began to fear.)	9th Thick darkness 3 days
	10th Death of firstborn

Egyptians worshipped the Nile and several gods were associated with it.[492] Nun was the snake god of swampy water chaos from which life emanated. Khnum was the guardian of the Nile, and supposed to have created man from its mud. Sobek was a creator god with the body of a man and the head of a crocodile whose job was to protect the pharaoh. Tauret was the hippopotamus goddess of the Nile. Ammut was depicted with the head of a crocodile and the rear of a hippo. The Nile was considered the "bloodstream" of Osiris, god of death and the underworld, and so it was fitting to turn the river to blood.

Heket was the wife of the creator of the world and the goddess of birth. Heket was always shown with the head and body of a frog. Hapi was the god of the Nile who was fed by crocodiles and frogs. Though the magicians could also produce frogs, they could not remove them, so Rameses I pleaded with Moses to ask God to remove them.[493]

God made lice from the "*dust of the earth*".[494] Geb was god of the land of Egypt, so this made him look bad. The magicians could not produce lice, and finally feared the real God.

Ahti was a goddess of chaos and evil with the head of a wasp and body of a hippopotamus. The stinging swarms were unleashed upon the Egyptians only, with God making a distinction between them and the children of Israel in Exodus 8:22-23.

---

490 Exodus 12:12-13
491 Exodus 7:7-8 "And Moses was fourscore years old, and Aaron fourscore and three years old, when they spoke to Pharaoh. . . . Take your rod, and cast it before Pharaoh, and it shall become a serpent."
492 Padfield, David, "Against all the gods of Egypt", http://www.padfield.com/2002/egypt_1.html
493 Exodus 8:1-15
494 Exodus 8:16-19

The god Apis was represented as a bull, and the Apis bull was the living image of the god Ptah. Ptah was a creator God who spoke things into existence. There were also Buchis bulls and calves which were worshipped. Hathor was the goddess of the desert and its mines; she was depicted as a cow or a woman with cow's ears. Though YHWH demonstrated He was more powerful than these bull gods, there were many who still clung to the bull gods,[495] or to the "*ashes*" (Ex. 9:10) of Isis for healing, among the Hebrews.

Egyptians considered themselves to be very advanced in medicine which healed both man and beast. Though Imhotep was a man, he was worshipped as a god of healing. Heka was the god of magic and miracles sometimes represented by two entwined snakes. Thoth was considered the god of science and medicine and astronomy. None of them kept the horses, camels, cattle, and sheep from dying in the fields from the plague or gave the cattle and people relief from the boils.[496]

Nut and Horus were sky gods, and Isis and Seth were supposed to protect the crops. The mother/daughter goddess team of Ernutet and Nepri guarded the grain. The fiery hail killed man and beast which remained outside and destroyed the flax and barley.[497] The locusts came and ate all the greenery that was left. Even more miraculous was that when Moses prayed for God to remove them, not one locust was left within Egypt's boundaries.[498]

After all the misery one would expect the Egyptians to hate the Hebrews. God fulfilled His promise to Abraham to bring his descendants out with riches by causing the Egyptians to favorably give gold and jewels and clothing to all the Hebrews who asked.[499]

Then YWHW-Jehovah struck at Egypt's most revered gods of the sun (Ra, Aten, Atum), moon (Aah, Khons, Isis), and stars (Thoth, Nut, Seshat), by surrounding the Egyptians for three days with a tangible darkness[500] which even snuffed out attempts to make fire.

As God brought the Hebrews out of Egypt, He corrected their calendar, clarifying Nisan as the first month.[501] God commanded them to take an unblemished lamb into their homes on the 10th of Nisan, and to kill their lambs at dusk on the 14th of Nisan.[502]

"And thus shall ye eat it: with your loins girded, your shoes on your feet, and your staff in your hand; and ye shall eat it in haste: it is Jehovah's passover. For I will go through the land of Egypt in that night, and will smite all the first-born in the land of Egypt, both man and beast; and against all the gods of Egypt I will execute judgments: I am Jehovah. And the blood shall be to you for a token upon the houses where ye are: and when I see the blood, I will pass over you, and there shall no plague be upon you to destroy you, when I smite the land of Egypt." (Ex. 12:11-13)

---

495 Exodus 32 The people demanded Aaron to make them a god, and he fashioned a calf of gold.
496 Exodus 9:1-12
497 Exodus 9:19-20, 31
498 Exodus 10:15-19
499 Genesis 15:13-14; Exodus 11:2-3; 12:35-36
500 Exodus 10:21-23
501 Exodus 12:2
502 Exodus 12:3-6

The last plague was also the first feast the Israelites would celebrate on the first full moon of their new religious year. It's called Passover, because the angel of death "*passed over*" the homes which had lamb's blood on the door frame. They ate the lamb and unleavened bread, and then left their homes and travelled to Succoth as the Egyptians cried in mourning that night.[503] Besides women, children, flocks and herds, God brought out 600,000 fighting men, His armies,[504] and they camped in orderly fashion. But God did not consider them ready for battle: "*God led them not through the way of the land of the Philistines, although that was near; for God said, Lest peradventure the people repent when they see war, and they return to Egypt.*"[505]

They travelled day and night for seven days, stopping to pitch tents during the heat of day to rest and eat unleavened bread. They crossed the Red Sea on the 8th day, then had several adventures for the next six weeks until they heard the Ten Commandments from the fire of God atop Mount Sinai on the 50th day, later called Pentecost.

Burnt Jebel el Lawz (Mount Sinai)

The history of the exodus of Jacob/Israel's descendants from Egypt is celebrated in five of the seven feasts God commanded Israel to celebrate: Passover, Unleavened Bread, First Fruits, Weeks (Pentecost), and Tabernacles/Booths (*succoth*). Though Tabernacles is celebrated in the fall, it is clearly done as a remembrance of the exodus, and the giving of the Ten Commandments at the Feast of Weeks.[506]

*The fifteenth day of this seventh month shall be the feast of **tabernacles** for seven days to the LORD. . . . on the eighth day shall be an holy convocation to you; . . .* <u>*You shall dwell in **booths** seven days*</u>*; all that are Israelites born shall dwell in booths:* <u>*That your generations may know that I made the children of Israel to dwell in booths, when I brought them out of the land of Egypt*</u>*: I am the LORD your God. (Lev. 23:33-44)*

The eighth day was special because that was the day they crossed the Red Sea to freedom and saw the Egyptian army destroyed. This victory was also celebrated during Nisan as the feast of First Fruits. Then there were six more weeks until feast of Weeks was celebrated to commemorate God speaking His ten commandments.

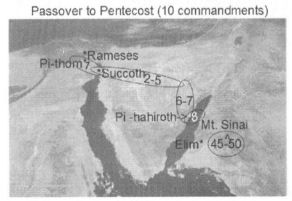
Passover to Pentecost (10 commandments)
7 days of unleavened bread prior to crossing

---

503 Exodus 12:29-30 ". . . there was not a house where there was not one dead." Exodus 12:37-38
504 Exodus 6:26; 7:4; 12:17, 41, 51 and Numbers 1:3
505 Exodus 13:17
506 Deuteronomy 31:10-11

King Solomon later erected two engraved pillars at both beaches of the Red Sea (Gulf of Aqaba) crossing site. The Pi-Hahiroth (Nuweiba beach) column was discovered by Ron Wyatt in 1978.[507] Ron Wyatt and his two sons crossed into Saudi Arabia in 1984, and discovered the other column on the Saudi side (*Baal-zephon*).[508] The next year he returned with a Saudi royal to discover Mount Sinai with much Biblical evidence on and around it: boundary wells (Ex. 19:12), the v-shaped altar to God at the base (Ex. 20:24), the altar to the golden calf further off (Ex. 32:19) with many petroglyph bulls of Hathor, a menorah petroglyph, white column pieces to the twelve columns (Ex. 24:4), "the cleft of the rock" (Ex. 33:22), and Elijah's cave (I Kings 19:8).[509] That's not a shadow on Mount Sinai; the rocks are burnt black for 200 feet on top; it's where the fire of God descended (Ex. 19:18).

And God spoke all these words, saying, I am the LORD your God, which have brought you out of the land of Egypt, out of the house of bondage. You shall have no other gods before me. You shall not make to you any graven image, or any likeness of any thing that is in heaven above, or that is in the earth beneath, or that is in the water under the earth. You shall not bow down yourself to them, nor serve them: for I the LORD your God am a jealous God, visiting the iniquity of the fathers on the children to the third and fourth generation of them that hate me; And showing mercy to thousands of them that love me, and keep my commandments. You shall not take the name of the LORD your God in vain; for the LORD will not hold him guiltless that takes his name in vain. Remember the sabbath day, to keep it holy. Six days shall you labor, and do all your work: But the seventh day is the sabbath of the LORD your God: in it you shall not do any work, you, nor your son, nor your daughter, your manservant, nor your maidservant, nor your cattle, nor your stranger that is within your gates: For in six days the LORD made heaven and earth, the sea, and all that in them is, and rested the seventh day: why the LORD blessed the sabbath day, and hallowed it. Honor your father and your mother: that your days may be long on the land which the LORD your God gives you. You shall not kill. You shall not commit adultery. You shall not steal. You shall not bear false witness against your neighbor. You shall not covet your neighbor's house, you shall not covet your neighbor's wife, nor his manservant, nor his maidservant, nor his ox, nor his ass, nor any thing that is your neighbor's. (Exodus 20:1-17)

Not only were these words spoken by God and heard by the descendants of Israel, they were inscribed by God on stone tablets. When Joshua entered the land promised to Abraham, Isaac, and Jacob/Israel and had conquered Jericho and Ai, he obeyed Moses' instructions to write these words on large plastered stones at the base of Mount Ebal north of Shechem.[510] Whereas the stelae boundary stones of the city of Akhenaten claimed "it" belonged to Aten. God claims the "*people*" are His because He delivered them from bondage, and they are to worship only Him in the way He prescribed, or be proscribed (condemned and exiled).

---

507 Wyatt, Ron, "Red Sea Crossing", http://wyattmuseum.com/red-sea-crossing-03.htm accessed since 2000
508 Wyatt, Ron, "Mount Sinai", http://wyattmuseum.com/mount-sinai-02.htm accessed since 2000
509 Wyatt, Ron, "Mount Sinai", http://wyattmuseum.com/mount-sinai-03.htm accessed since 2000
510 Deuteronomy 27:1-8 and Joshua 8:30-35

God's Destruction of Rameses I Army in Red Sea

When Moses and Aaron first approached Rameses I, it was with the request to let the Hebrews go three days journey into the desert to make sacrifices to the LORD. But after three days journey into the Sinai Peninsula, the Hebrews did not stop to sacrifice, but kept on travelling toward Etham (Al Thamad today). Scouts returned to the palace to inform Rameses *"the people fled"*.[511] If not already, Rameses would have made Seti his co-regent.

And he made ready his chariot, and took his people with him: And he took six hundred chosen chariots, and <u>all the chariots of Egypt</u>, and captains over every one of them. (Exodus 14:6-7)

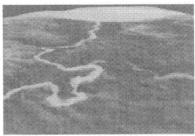

As Egypt's army was in pursuit, another scout met them and told them that instead of turning north to go around the gulf of Aqaba, the Hebrews had turned south and were now *"entangled"* and *"shut in"* on Wadi Watir. It is a serpentine wadi through a rugged mountain canyon which ends at *"Pi-Hahiroth"* ("mouth of the hole" in Ex. 14:2) and a huge beach named by the Arabs *Nuwaybi al Muzayyinah* ("Waters of Moses Opening").

Wadi Watir to Nuweiba Beach

There is a 7 to 10 mile wide land bridge in shallow water connecting Nuweiba Beach to the beach on the Arabian side eight miles away. All night of Nisan 21, God's angel and column of fire/cloud positioned at *Pi-Hahiroth* kept the Egyptians at bay;[512] and God's wind blew the sea floor dry so Hebrews could walk across it at dawn and be safely across by dusk. In "*the morning watch*"[513] on Nisan 22, from dusk to midnight, the Egyptians pursued them with all of pharaoh's horses and chariots and army;[514] but God removed their chariot wheels and closed the Red Sea over them so that not one of them was left alive.[515] That first Passover began on a Sabbath, with the "*morrow after the sabbath*"[516] (First Fruits), eight days later on a Sunday.

"All the Chariots of Egypt"

The first pharaoh depicted riding in a chariot was Ahmose, but by the time of Thutmose III, Egypt had hundreds of chariots. Those used by royalty were gilded or plated with gold. From Thutmose III's battle of Megiddo inscribed on the walls at Karnak behind pylon VI is

---

511 Exodus 14:5
512 Exodus 14:19-20
513 Exodus 14:24 better translated "the beginning of watches" or at the end of Nisan 22ⁿᵈ at dusk, God removed their chariot wheels and collapsed the waters upon them, destroying the Egyptian army.
514 Exodus 14:9, 17-18
515 Exodus 14:24-31
516 Leviticus 23:10-11 Feast of First Fruits

the following quote:

> "His majesty set out on a chariot of fine gold, decked in his shining armour like strong-armed Horus, . . . [List of the booty which his majesty's army brought from the town of] Megiddo. Living prisoners: 3,400. Hands: 83. Horses: 2,041. Foals: 191. Stallions: 6. Colts: --. One chariot of that foe worked in gold, with a [pole] of gold. One fine chariot of the prince of [Megiddo], worked in gold. [Chariots of allied princes: 30]. Chariots of his wretched army: 892. Total: 924."[517]

Divers along the Red Sea crossing from Nuweiba beach have found chariot boxes, and chariot wheels with four, six and eight spokes. On one of the dives, Ronnie Wyatt tried to bring up a gold painted chariot wheel, but it was too deteriorated. Egypt must have had hundreds of chariots. Seti I would need to retrieve them, especially the ones made of gold.[518]

Chariot wheels with axle at bottom of crossing

The last update Seti had was that the Hebrews did not stop to sacrifice after the third day[519] (near Nekhl), but proceeded to Etham. Since they were travelling on the "king's highway"[520] Seti expected them to turn north up the Arabah passed the east side of the Dead Sea and then cross the Jordan River into Canaan, which is where the Hebrews had their burial cave in Hebron.

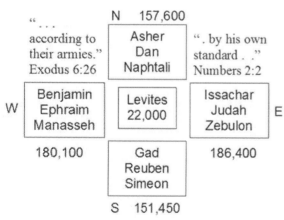

The Way of Horus had eleven forts full of soldiers so that they could easily be gathered to attack the north. Tjaru/Tharu could hold 50,000 soldiers;[521] times 11 forts would be 550,000. But the fighting men of the children of Israel totaled 697,550 according to Numbers 2. God directed the camping arrangements for 3 million people according to their tribes, gathered around banners or "*standards*". Numbers 2:2

"*. . . shall pitch by his own standard, with the ensign of their father's house*"

---

517 "Annals of Thutmose III" translated by J.A. Wilson, pp. 85-95

518 Rameses I was an old man when he became pharaoh. He came from a large family of five sisters and three brothers, and I think he had a large family with several sons and grandsons which assured Horemheb of a dynasty that would last. No Egyptian history would admit the God of slaves whupped them.

519 Exodus 3:18, 5:3, 8:27 A three day journey would get them beyond populated areas into wilderness.

520 Numbers 20:17-21

521 Alastair, Sharp, "Sinai fort may hold clues to ancient Egypt's defenses", May 7, 2009 http://www.reuters.com/article/idUSTRE5465N120090507, accessed 8/17/10

Campaigns of Seti I's First Year

Days passed without any word from the army. There were no chariots left in Egypt, and few horses left in pharaoh's stables. Seti had a new chariot quickly made for him. A group of Arabs who saw the slaves leave and the Egyptian army in pursuit, seized the opportunity and attacked the city of Zal near Heliopolis.[522] Seti and his palace guardsmen first squashed that uprising, and then killed others along the Way of Horus, adding soldiers of the forts to their army as they went. Of Seti's first year, an inscription reads: "He attacked the hostile Shashu, who inhabit the town of Pithom, even to the land of Kanana."[523] Another interpretation states Seti attacked "the fortress of Khetam in the land of Zalu to the land of Kan'aan".[524] The Shashu were Bedouin, desert dwelling Arabs, and six groups of them are listed on the column bases at the temple in Soleb.[525] Seti sought to intercept the Hebrews when they attempted to cross the Jordan River from "the king's highway". The Beth Shean stele describes how Seti's forces split at Beth Shean with one division going south along the Jordan river, conquering the cities of Rehob and Hamath; one division crossing the Jordan and taking Pahel (Pella), and one division going north and conquering Yanoam, Hazor, and Beth Anath.[526]

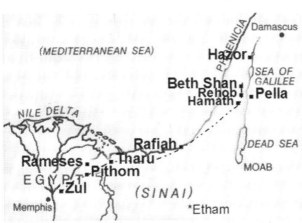

Seti I captured cities along the Jordan River

Seti's forces had secured the Jordan River and were waiting to pounce upon the Hebrew slaves, but they didn't arrive. I speculate Seti received a report from a traveller that corpses and war debris were washing up on the shores of the Gulf of Aqaba, so he sent a division who brought back his father's body with the sad news not one man survived. Seti may have assumed that whatever tidal wave wiped out the Egyptian army also swept the Hebrews out to sea. Seti returned disappointed through Rafiah (near Gaza). Thus the Hebrews were safe, and Seti had subdued the cities along the Jordan, so that it was prepared for the Hebrews to enter later from the king's highway.

---

522 Cooper, William Ricketts, *An Archaic Dictionary: biographical, historical, and archaeological from the Egyptian, Assyrian, Etruscan, monuments and papyri*, http://books.google.com/ accessed 8/23/10

523 http://www.archive.org/stream/nilejordanbeinga00kniguoft/nilejordanbeinga00kniguoft_djvu.txt "Nile and Jordan" accessed 2009

524 Brusch-Bey, Henry from German translation, *A History of Egypt Under the Pharaohs: derived entirely from the monuments*, 1879, http://www.massciana.org/brugsch2.htm, accessed 8/30/10

525 Discovery Media, http://www.servinghistory.com/topics/Shashu, accessed 8/23/10

526 Dollinger, Andre', "Campaign of Seti I in Northern Palestine," http://www.reshafim.org.il/ad/egypt/seticampaign.htm , accessed 9/20/09

Now that Seti had reestablished Egyptian dominance in Canaan, the Hittites would be less likely to attack. The Hittites were skilled charioteers, and Seti needed a way of transporting the valuable war chariots from the Gulf of Aqaba back to Egypt to protect his empire. Pithom was situated on Wadi Tumilat with Lake Timsah to the east. He needed workers to dredge the Bitter Lake canals to the Gulf of Suez so he could retrieve the chariots by ship,[527] but he no longer had a slave force.

Seti's Canal Project to the Red Sea

The Sallier and Anastasi papyri contain scribal letters of the early 19th dynasty "about the time of the Exodus".[528] The name of the master scribe was Ameneman, who was also the chief librarian, treasurer, and architect in Seti's court. Ameneman wrote the following letter regarding the life of the Egyptian peasant farmer.

> ". . . Even before it is ripe, insects destroy part of his harvest. . . . Multitudes of rats are in the fields; next come invasions of locusts, cattle ravage his harvest, sparrows alight in flocks on his sheaves. If he delays to get in his harvest, robbers come to carry it off from him; his horse dies of fatigue in drawing the plough; the tax collector arrives in the district, and has with him men armed with sticks, negroes with palm branches. All say, 'Give us of your corn' and he has no means of escaping their exactions. <u>Next the unfortunate wretch is seized, bound, and carried off by force to work on the canals</u>; his wife is bound, his children are stripped. And at the same time his neighbors have each of them his own trouble."[529]

If the Hebrews were still enslaved at this time, why were Egyptian peasants captured and forced to work on the canals? Though negro slaves were mentioned, Seti later ordered several expeditions into Nubia to secure more slaves. Seti I would eventually move his capital south of the delta to Memphis, and Ameneman built a temple there using Erythrean slaves with red skin.[530] But for Seti's first few regnal years, Pi-Rameses was abuzz.

Seti's Chariot Workshop at Qantir (Avaris/Pi-Rameses)

The Hittites would hear the news of the calamity which destroyed much of the Egyptian army. Seti's recent Canaan campaign might make them question just how weak they were. Seti had to rebuild Egypt's military strength by making chariots and shields and weapons.

During his excavations at Qantir, E. B. Pusch uncovered a "large-scale metalworking industry adjacent to a series of workshops," which included melting channels and furnaces.

---

527 Dollinger, Andre', "Canals", http://www.reshafim.org.il/ad/egypt/timelines/topics/canals.htm
528 Mahaffy, Sir John P., *Prolegmena to ancient history . . . containing A Survey of Egyptian Literature*, 1871, pp. 324-5
529 Lenormant, Francois, *A manual of the ancient history of the East to the commencement of the Median wars*, Lippincott, 1871, p. 258
530 Brusch-Bey, Henry, p. 91; Stated as Rameses II temple, but he co-opted many which weren't his.

Moses' Pharaohs

On the floor were found hundreds of chariot pieces including yoke knobs and decorative glass discs. The workshops included those for working in wood, leather, and stone.[531] Wood and stone were needed for javelins and bows and arrows, and wood and leather were used in making chariots. Leather harnesses were needed for the horses. The stables excavated by Bietak could hold 460 horses.[532]

Seti I Captured Qadesh on the Orontes River in his Second Year

As soon as the canals were dredged, the reclamation project of chariots from the Gulf of Aqaba began. After Seti had sufficiently restored the equipment for his forces, he addressed the Hittite threat. In his second year, Seti placed a victory stela in Qadesh (also Kadesh).[533]

Seti conquered cities along the coast as he returned to Egypt. A portion of his victory stela at Tyre was found, and there are scenes of chiefs of Lebanon cutting down trees for him on a relief in Karnak.[534] He quashed any rebellions southward, and took Syrian, Aramaean, and other prisoners back to Egypt as much needed slaves, and quartered them near Heliopolis; thus replacing the Shashu which were killed at Zul.

(left) Seti I rides to an easy victory over Beth Shan in his first year campaign.

(below) Seti's second year victory over the larger and better equipped Hittites.

[drawings from Seti's tomb]

Israel in the Wilderness

Most Biblical wildernesses are named for a mountain within or nearby (Sinai, Paran, and Zin), but the wilderness of Sin (in Akkadian) is named after the moon-god worshipped there.[535] Israel camped in the Wilderness of Sin in the second month.[536] In the third month they camped in the Sinai Wilderness where they received "*a fiery law*".[537] Jethro, Moses' father-in-law lived in the wilderness of Sin, but Jethro was a priest of YHWH. He came to

---

531 Brand, Peter James, *The monuments of Seti I: epigraphic, historical, and art historical analysis,* 2000, pp. 129-130
532 Edgar, Monroe, "Qantir, Ancient Pi-Ramesse", http://www.touregypt.net/featurestories/qantir.htm,
533 "Campaign of Seti I in Northern Palestine", http://www.reshafim.org.il/ad/egypt/seticampaign.htm
534 Brand, Peter James, *The monuments of Seti I,* p. 122
535 Mark Hall, *A Study of the Sumerian Moon-god, Sin,* PhD., 1985, University of Pennsylvania; Nanna and Suen and Asimbabbar were popular Sumerian names for the moon-god.
536 Exodus 16 and 17
537 Deuteronomy 33:2

Moses at Mount Sinai with Moses' wives and sons.[538]

Moses Sent Spies into Canaan

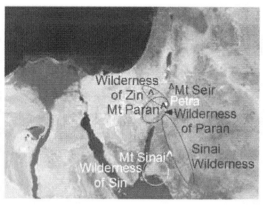

Two years and two months after their exodus from Egypt, God moved the Hebrews from their camp in the wilderness of Mt Sinai in Midian to the wilderness of Paran and Mount Paran[539] about fifty miles north of Aqaba near Petra, which they called *Kadeshbarnea* (set apart place wandering).[540] It took at least five weeks to get there since they had to bury people in "the graves of lust" (*Kibroth-hattaavah*)[541], making it late July. During July and August the first grapes ripened in Canaan.[542] The wilderness of Zin was north of and adjacent to, the wilderness of Paran. Moses told the spies,

> *And be you of good courage, and bring of the fruit of the land. Now the time was the time of the first ripe grapes. So they went up, and searched the land from the wilderness of Zin to Rehob, as men come to Hamath. And they ascended by the south, and came to Hebron; where Ahiman, Sheshai, and Talmai, the children of Anak, were. (Now Hebron was built seven years before Zoan in Egypt.) (Numbers 13:20b-22)*

Rehob and Hamath were the two cities south of Beth Shean which Seti subdued a year prior to the arrival of the spies. Hebron was also known as *Kirjath-arba* which means "the city of the four" referring to the four giants noted above.[543] These giants built their city seven years before Zoan was built in Egypt. Hebron existed long before Abram got there. Canaan and Mizraim (Egypt) were both sons of Ham who founded their namesake lands about the same time. It is reasonable that only a few years difference existed between the establishment of their ancient cities. But Egyptians boasted that Zoan (Tanis) was the most ancient of cities, and so Moses clarified the issue. The spies reported,

> *We saw the children of Anak there. The Amalekites dwell in the land of the south: and the Hittites, and the Jebusites, and the Amorites, dwell in the mountains: and the Canaanites dwell by the sea, and by the coast of Jordan. (Numbers 13:28-29)* [These are Canaanite Hittites.]

---

538 Exodus 18 Jethro gave him the advice to delegate his judging to others, then returned home.
539 Numbers 10:11-12 See http://www.flickr.com/photos/crystaleagle/165171256/
540 Numbers 32:8
541 Numbers 11 They were sick of manna and wanted meat, so God sent quail and then sent a plague.
542 *Barnes' Commentary* on Numbers 13:20
543 *Adam Clarke's Commentary on the Bible*

Seti had already subdued the Anatolian Hittites of the north and the Canaanites of the sea and along the Jordan, so the promised land was ready for them to take. But ten of the spies promoted how insignificant they felt in view of the giants and their well-fortified cities which caused the people to fear and to doubt God.

Say to them, As truly as I live, said the LORD, as you have spoken in my ears, so will I do to you: Your carcasses shall fall in this wilderness; and all that were numbered of you, . . . from twenty years old and upward which have murmured against me. Doubtless you shall not come into the land, concerning which I swore to make you dwell therein, save Caleb the son of Jephunneh, and Joshua the son of Nun. But your little ones, which you said should be a prey, them will I bring in, and they shall know the land which you have despised. . . . And your children shall wander in the wilderness forty years[544] *. . . After the number of the days in which you searched the land, even forty days, each day for a year. . . and you shall know my breach of promise. (Numbers 14:28-34)*

Some of the Hebrews decided they could avert God's punishment by changing their minds and attacking. They approached from the south and went up into the hill country, and were beaten back south to Hormah; and then they returned to Kadesh dejected.[545] Moses used the opportunity to encourage them to offer sacrifices for their sins and to add blue to the fringe of their garments to remember to faithfully obey all the commandments.[546]

Sennedjem designed Tombs for Seti I and Rameses II

Above are scenes of plowing and harvesting from Sennedjem's beautiful tomb. About a kilometer from the Valley of the Kings lay the ruins of *Set Maat* ("place of truth", now Deir el-Medina). It was the city for the laborers and artisans who worked on the tombs of the pharaohs. On their days off they could work on their own personal tombs, one of which belonged to Sennedjem, Servant in the Place of Truth, and architect of the tombs for Seti and Rameses II. Seti's tomb (KV17) is the longest in the Valley of the Kings at 446 feet, and

---

544 The forty years was inclusive of the first year and a half from the exodus which began when Moses was eighty and concluded when he died at 120 years old.
545 Numbers 14:44-45 and Deuteronomy 1:41-46
546 Numbers 15

Pharaohs of the Bible

still retains most of its brilliant, colorful decoration. Rameses' II tomb (KV7) has lost most of its decoration, but the tomb for his sons (KV5) is the largest with over 100 rooms. Of Rameses' many wives, Nefertari was his favorite, and he spared no expense on her tomb. Sennedjem did an impressive job.

photo by Jean-Pierre Dalbera

(above) Tomb ceiling of Seti I
depicting the sky
(right) Tomb of Queen Nefertari

Rameses II

Seti I acknowledged his eldest teen-aged son as the heir apparent. In Seti's eighth year he battled against encroaching Libyan tribes (Tjehenu, Libu, and Meshwesh), and prince Rameses accompanied him.[547] Seti's eleventh year was his last, but he left a strong empire for his son.

Seti's battles against the Libyans left quite an impression, for in Rameses' first two years he established at least three forts east and two forts west of Alexandria to defend Egypt from the Libyans.[548] Also in his second year, Rameses II came up with a brilliant strategy to defeat the Mediterranean Sea pirates. He set a trap of soldiers and ships along the delta's coast and captured them when they attacked; and he then inducted many into his own bodyguard.[549] Their round shields and long swords are among his ranks in several reliefs of his famous battle of Qadesh. Possibly due to the military needs of the delta, Rameses II moved his capital back to Pi-Rameses where Seti had made weapons factories.

Also in Rameses II's early regnal years (possibly his third), he quelled revolts in Ethiopia and Nubia. The Hittites began stirring up revolts in Syria, Phoenicia, and Canaan,

---

547 Brand, Peter James, *The monuments of Seti I,* pp. 312-321, evidence against co-regency
548 Tell Abqa'in, http://www.militaryarchitecture.com/conservation/49-ancient/588-tell-abqain-egypt.html, accessed 9/17/10 and Fox, Troy, "Ramesses II: Anatomy of the Pharaoh, a military leader", http://www.touregypt.net/featurestories/ramessesiimilitary.htm , accessed 9/17/10
549 Fox, Troy, "Ramesses II: Anatomy of the Pharaoh, a military leader"

so in his fourth year, Rameses II removed troublemakers from Canaan to Nubia, and moved troublesome Nubians into Canaan.[550] He hoped this relocation would eliminate the revolts, but it wasn't enough.

Drawing of relief of Rameses II striking a Nubian chief.
Relief of Rameses II at Battle of Kadesh.

Battle of Qadesh on the Orontes River and Treaty with the Hittites

In Rameses II's fifth year he "led" his army into battle, but his mercenary troops did not follow; and he found himself surrounded by Hittite chariots, and courageously fought his way out. Though in Egypt Rameses engraved it as a victory, Muwatalli II, the Hittite king, stated he chastened Rameses. Their truce lasted two years. Muwatalli took over Syria and continued to press southward, forcing Rameses again to shore up his strength in Canaan.

In Rameses II's eighth year he besieged the Canaanite cities of Debir, Beth Amuth, and Kunon; as well as Salem, the city of the Jebusites. In his ninth year he erected a stele at Beth Shean, and the next year erected one in Beirut, and somehow secured the Beka Valley as well. But by his eleventh year Egypt had lost most of Canaan and barely hung onto Ashkelon.[551] It was time for a revolutionary way to establish boundaries: a peace treaty.

In Rameses II's 21st year (1459 BC by my account) at the signing of the treaty with the Hittites, the Hittites gave him the fortress of Coele-Syria which lies at the southern end of the Beka Valley in Lebanon as Egypt's northernmost boundary. Rameses II then made a temple to the Hittite god Sutekh in Tanis. No Egyptian god temples were made in the land of the Hittites by king Hatusilli III. Rameses II also married Hatusilli's daughter as part of the peace process. Rameses II then left Canaan alone and focused on building Egypt. Yahweh again used Egypt to prepare Canaan for Israel's occupation.

---

550 Lenormant, Francis and Chevallier, E., A manual of ancient history of the East to the commencement of the Median wars, published by Lippencott in Philadelphia in 1921, p. 249
551 Lenormant, Francis, p. 254

Moses and Aaron and Water from the Rock (Petra)

In the first month of the Hebrews' third year after the exodus (around April, 1489 BC), Miriam died at Kadesh-barnea which is between Mt Hor and Mt Halak.[552] The people complained for lack of water, and Moses and Aaron got angry and struck the rock to bring forth water after God told them to just speak to it, and so they lost the privilege of taking the people into the promised land.[553] Petra (*Sela*) is just north of Mt Halak. Of the dozen springs in Petra, Moses' spring (*ain Musa*) is the most productive, and Wadi Musa runs along the main road toward Elath.[554] The 2-4 million children of Israel remained in Kadesh-barnea and its environs for the next 36 years.[555] Some secretly returned to the worship of the heavenly bodies.[556] Aaron died in the fortieth year in the fifth month at Mount Hor, renamed Mt Aaron (*Jebel Harun*).[557] Moses sent a request to the Edomites to let them travel north safely along the king's highway, but the Edomites threatened to attack if they did. Instead, God told them to buy food from them and go around both Edom and Moab.[558]

Israel avoids fighting other Hebrews

Israel travelled northwest and stayed along Edom's western border. As they neared Oboth (now Ir Ovot), the king of Arad in Canaan kidnapped some of their people[559], and the children of Israel asked God to help them *"utterly destroy"* (*hormah*) them, and the fighting men under Joshua destroyed their cities. But they could not continue to conquer Canaan because their forty years weren't quite over. They complained to Moses, weary of their continued journey through the wilderness.[560] They camped in Oboth, then went northeast to Edom's northern border at the Dead Sea and Moab's southern border on Zered river (now just a wadi). Then they camped in the valley of Zered before turning north. God would not let them fight the Ammonites or Moabites[561], but had them go between their borders via the Amorite city of Heshbon. They conquered all the cities up to the Yarmuk river.

Israel's Victories East of Jordan

This day will I begin to put the dread of you and the fear of you on the nations that are under the whole heaven, who shall hear report of you, and shall tremble, and be in anguish because of you. (Deuteronomy 2:25)

---

552 Rudd, Steve, "Kadesh-Barnea", http://www.bible.ca/archeology/bible-archeology-exodus-kadesh-barnea-petra.htm, accessed 9/19/10 Numbers 20:1
553 Numbers 20:2-12
554 Rudd, Steve, "Petra, Jordan (Kadesh-Barnea)", same website as above, but different page 9/19/10
555 Deuteronomy 2:1,14 "compassed" means on the border of the Seir mountain range
556 Amos 5:25-26
557 Numbers 33:38 http://wikimapia.org/4808031/Jebel-Harun contains shrine to Aaron
558 Deuteronomy 2:2-9
559 Numbers 21:1-3
560 Numbers 21:4-9 God sent serpents, but if they looked at Moses' brass serpent they were healed.
561 Moab was Lot's son through his eldest daughter, and Ammon was Lot's son through his youngest.

In order to prepare the people and the land for conquest, the battles for the land on the east side of the Jordan river took place. Moses sent a messenger to king Sihon of Heshbon to request free passage through their land to the Jordan river. Sihon refused and attacked the Israelites who defeated him and took all his cities.[562] Then Og, king of Bashan, attacked them, and the Israelites killed all their people and took their cities as well.[563] From Moab's perspective . . . *"there is a people come out from Egypt: behold, they cover the face of the earth, and they abide over against me."*[564] But while the Israelites camped at Shittim, the Moabites invited them to sacrifice to Baal-Peor who was considered a lord of heaven and earth and a god of storms; afterwhich the real LORD of heaven and earth killed 24,000 of the Hebrews with a plague.[565] Yet the Hebrews were still able to muster an army of 601,730 men over age twenty.[566] Except for Moses, and Joshua and Caleb (the two spies who returned with a good report and faith in God), all the other adult men who initially refused to fight the Canaanites thirty eight years prior had died in the wilderness.[567]

Moses Commissions Joshua

Moses wrote down all the laws and history and gave the books (Genesis, Exodus, Leviticus, Numbers, and Deuteronomy) to the priests to be put into the ark of the covenant.[568] Though Joshua had been leading Israel's army from the beginning of their wanderings, he would now also become their spiritual leader. With Eleazar the high priest presiding in the midst of the assembly, Moses commissioned Joshua to be the judge of Israel. Joshua was 85 years old.

Moses Sees the Promised Land, and Dies

And the LORD said to Moses, Get you up into this mount Abarim, and see the land which I have given to the children of Israel. And when you have seen it, you also shall be gathered to your people, as Aaron your brother was gathered. For you rebelled against my commandment in the desert of Zin, in the strife of the congregation, to sanctify me at the water before their eyes: that is the water of Meribah in Kadesh in the wilderness of Zin. (Numbers 27:12-14)

---

562 Numbers 21:21-32 and Deuteronomy 2:24-37
563 Numbers 21:33-35 and Deuteronomy 3:1-10
564 Numbers 22:5b
565 Numbers 25:1-9
566 Numbers 26:51
567 Numbers 26:63-65
568 Deuteronomy 31:9

Mount Nebo is in the Abarim mountain range, and Nebo's top peak is called Pisgah. From this point today you could see the northern end of the Dead Sea, and the thin ribbon of the Jordan river, and a few miles of the land beyond it. But God supernaturally enabled Moses to see all of the promised land.

> *And Moses went up from the plains of Moab to the mountain of Nebo, to the top of Pisgah, that is over against Jericho. And the LORD showed him all the land of Gilead, to Dan, And all Naphtali, and the land of Ephraim, and Manasseh, and all the land of Judah, to the utmost sea, And the south, and the plain of the valley of Jericho, the city of palm trees, to Zoar. And the LORD said to him, <u>This is the land which I swore to Abraham, to Isaac, and to Jacob, saying, I will give it to your seed: I have caused you to see it with your eyes</u>, but you shall not go over thither. So Moses the servant of the LORD died there in the land of Moab, according to the word of the LORD. (Deuteronomy 34:1-5)*

On the 7th of last month of the fortieth year, Moses died at 120 years old on his birthday.[569] The people mourned for thirty days. I speculate that Joshua, his faithful attendant for forty years, was with Moses on Mount Nebo so that he could finish writing the book of Deuteronomy, in which he stated, *"And he buried him in a valley in the land of Moab, over against Bethpeor: but no man knows of his sepulcher to this day."*[570] Beth can mean house or any form of shelter. *Peor* means cleft; so a cave is likely. The following is from II Maccabees:

> "It is also found in the records, that Jeremy the prophet . . . being warned of God, commanded the tabernacle and the ark to go with him, as he went forth <u>into the mountain, where Moses climbed up, and saw the heritage of God. And when Jeremy came thither, he found an hollow cave, wherein he laid the tabernacle, and the ark, and the altar of incense, and so stopped the door</u>. And some of those that followed him came to mark the way, but they could not find it. Which when Jeremy perceived, he blamed them, saying, As for that place, it shall be unknown until the time that God gather his people again together, and receive them unto mercy."[571] [Jeremy being Jeremiah]

Forty Years and 360 Day Calendar

> *And the LORD's anger was kindled against Israel, and he made them wander in the wilderness <u>forty years, until all the generation</u>, that had done evil in the sight of the LORD, was consumed. (Numbers 32:13)*

---

569 Deuteronomy 31:2; 34:1-8 The 7th of last month of year, plus thirty days, plus 3 days for people to prepare food (Joshua 1:11) while spies reconnoitered (Joshua 2:22-24) brings to 10th of Nisan when Israel crossed the Jordan (Joshua 4:19); thus was the day of Moses' birth and death determined.
570 Deuteronomy 34:6
571 II Maccabees 2:1-7 from the Apocrypha

The Israelites had a combined lunar-solar calendar which maintained the patterns of the seven-day week with a sabbath, and the forty-year generation. A 13th month of thirty days every six years until reaching the 36th year when the extra month was added to the 40th year. Thus it is likely Moses died in the thirteenth month of a leap year. Every forty years this ancient Hebrew 360-day calendar was in sync with the modern 365.25-day calendar.[572]

From Mt. Sinai God Made Way for His People to Enter Canaan

God came from Teman, and the Holy One from mount Paran. Selah. His glory covered the heavens, . . . Before him went the pestilence, and burning coals went forth at his feet. He stood, and measured the earth: he beheld, and drove asunder the nations; and the everlasting mountains were scattered, the perpetual hills did bow: his ways are everlasting. I saw the tents of Cushan in affliction: and the curtains of the land of Midian did tremble. . . . Your bow was made quite naked, according to the oaths of the tribes, even your word. Selah. You did split the earth with rivers. . . . You did march through the land in indignation, you did thresh the heathen in anger. You went forth for the salvation of your people, even for salvation with your anointed . . . (Habakkuk 3:3-13a)

"*Mountains*" are related to empires throughout the Bible, and thus, "*hills*" would be smaller kingdoms; both of which were established by God beforehand. Teman is in Edom, and Cushan and Midian are both in northern Arabia. "*Salvation*" is *yesha* in Hebrew and "*anointed*" is *mashiyach*, from which we get *messiah*. The pre-incarnate Christ as the "*angel of the LORD*"[573] led Israel in the desert for 40 years, and brought them to the promised land. The name Joshua is *yehoshua* in Hebrew and means "Yah saves" as does Yeshua (Jesus). Joshua is a prototype of the messiah who would save the world.

Reports spread that the God of the Hebrews destroyed the Egyptian army. Though the children of Israel were too fearful to enter earlier; the nations remained in fear of them for forty years as Rahab testified.[574]

Moses' Pharaohs[575]

1588-1550	Amenhotep III	"*daughter . . . called his name Moses*"
1551-1534	Amenhotep IV/Akhenaten	influenced by Hebrew monotheism
1534-1531	Smenkhkare	
1531-1530	Nefertiti/Neferneferuaten	
1534-1524	Tutankhamun	"*Moses fled from the face of Pharaoh*"
1524-1520	Ay	
1520-1493	Horemheb	

---

572 www.360calendar.com
573 Exodus 3:2; 13:21-22, 14:24-25; 33:14-16 and Numbers 22:22-35 and Judges 2:1
574 Joshua 2:10-11
575 Schengili-Roberts, Keith took photos of Nefertiti, Rameses I, and Seti I available on wikimedia.com

Pharaohs of the Bible

1493-1491   Rameses I   pharaoh of ten plagues and exodus[576]
1491-1480   Seti I
1480-1414   Rameses II   Moses died in 1451 on Mt. Nebo

Moses' Pharaohs

Amenhotep III — Akhenaten — Nefertiti — Smenkhkare
Tutankhamun — Rameses I — Seti I — Rameses II

(Ay and Horemheb not pictured here)

Moses

Egypt 1571-1531	Midian 1531-1491 In 1491 Moses returned to Egypt to lead the exodus.	Camps 1491	Kadesh-barnea 1490-1449	Camps '49-'51

Egypt's Pharaohs

Amenhotep III (18th) 1588-1550	Amenhotep IV Akhenaten 1551-1534	Smen-khkare 1534-1531	Nefer-titi 1531-1530	Tut-ankh-amun 1534-1524	Ay 1524-1520	Horemheb 1520-1493	Ram-eses I 1493-1491 (19th)	Seti I 1491-1480	Rameses II 1480-1414

---

576 Osman, Ahmed, "The Exodus in Egyptian Sources", http://www.dwij.org/forum/amarna/1_exodus.html, accessed 9/14/10. He states Rameses I is Pharaoh of the exodus.

Joshua's Pharaohs

"And the LORD said to Joshua, This day have I rolled away the reproach of Egypt from off you." (Joshua 5:9)

The verse above was spoken at Gilgal (*gal* means 'roll') after the men were circumcised. Rameses II still reigned in Egypt when in 1451 BC the Israelites began their conquest of Canaan. After Rameses II treaty with the Hittites in 1471 BC, he never again attacked north during his reign which ended with his death in 1414 BC. This gave the Israelites plenty of time to eradicate all idol worshipers living in Canaan, but they fell short of all.[577]

Wilderness Wanderings are Over

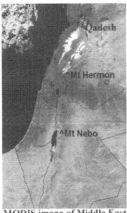

MODIS image of Middle East

Every place that the sole of your foot shall tread on, that have I given to you, as I said to Moses. From the wilderness and this Lebanon even to the great river, the river Euphrates, <u>all the land of the Hittites</u>, and to the great sea toward the going down of the sun, shall be your coast. (Joshua 1:3-4)

The Israelites were currently in the wilderness between Mt Nebo and the Dead Sea. Seventy miles north was the snowy peak of Mount Hermon (*Lebanon* means white mountain), and about 200 miles northeast from Mount Hermon (of the anti-Lebanon range) is the Euphrates river. God was promising anew to Joshua what He told Moses,[578] but here God specifically cited the Hittites who possessed the strongest army in the north, extending to Kadesh/Qadesh.

Joshua sent two spies ten miles from camp to Jericho. They returned with the words of one of their citizens named Rahab.

And she said to the men, <u>I know that the LORD has given you the land, and that your terror is fallen on us, and that all the inhabitants of the land faint because of you.</u> For we have heard how the LORD dried up the water of the Red sea for you, when you came out of Egypt; and what you did to the two kings of the Amorites, that were on the other side Jordan, Sihon and Og, whom you utterly destroyed. And as soon as we had heard these things, our hearts did melt, neither did there remain any more courage in any man, because of you: for the LORD your God, he is God in heaven above, and in earth beneath. (Joshua 2:9-11)

---

577 Joshua 13:1-6
578 Deuteronomy 11:24

God Spiritually Prepares a New Generation

Just as God had miraculously brought their parents through the Red Sea on dry ground, now God would bring them across the Jordan River on dry ground. This was during the first month of spring in which the Jordan overflowed its banks.[579] When the feet of the priests carrying the ark of the covenant touched the river, its waters heaped up roughly twenty miles north, and soon the priests stood in the middle on dry ground. A leader from each tribe took a river rock and placed it as a memorial on the other side at their camp, Gilgal.[580]

Their parents had not obeyed God's command to circumcise their sons on the eighth day during their wilderness years.[581] So God *"rolled away"* the disgrace of Egyptian idol worship by having all the men enter a blood covenant with Him alone by being circumcised. The day they crossed the Jordan river and were circumcised was the tenth day of the first month; the day they were to select a lamb for the Passover to be eaten on the fourteenth, a full moon. Miraculously all of the men were healed by then (as it usually takes a week to heal), and none of their enemies came upon them for fear of God.[582]

Then the captain of the LORD's army appeared to Joshua and gave him explicit instructions to take Jericho: his soldiers should march around the city once for six days silently while the ark and the priests blow trumpets in the middle of the army, and then on the seventh day march around seven times in the same manner and then give a shout.[583]

These instructions parallel the legend of king Keret found in Ugarit in which the king, referred to as the son of god, needs an heir to the throne. He sends the men of war, the rest of the people, and the trumpeters on a six day march in which they are to remain silent until the seventh day. A woman would save two messengers and become the mother of a king. The enthronement ritual of Tyre is similar and occurs on New Year's Day, the morning after the spring full moon.[584]

From Babylonian influence, many Canaanite cities worshipped the moon. Jericho was named after the male moon god, *yerech*,[585] and was its spiritual stronghold. Just as God miraculously defeated the gods of Egypt before their parents eyes, He would now defeat the main Canaanite god of this new generation.

[Seated man has an inverted crescent moon necklace.]

Hazor devoted to the moon

---

579 Joshua 3:15
580 Joshua 3 and 4
581 Joshua 5:1-9 and Leviticus 12:1-3
582 Joshua 5:1, 8-10 The next day God's provision of manna ceased (Joshua 5:12)
583 Joshua 5:13 to 6:5
584 Livingstone, Dr. David, "The Fall of the Moon-City", http://www.ancientdays.net/mooncity.htm, accessed 11/10/10
585 There was no /j/ sound in the local Canaanite or Hebrew language.

Tell es-Sultan
Jordan crossing, Gilgal, and
Jericho in bronze by Ghiberti

The East Doors of the Florence Baptistry portray Old Testament stories.[586] In the panel above Ghiberti depicts the priests with the ark standing on the dry river bottom of the Jordan with a couple men hoisting rocks from it for the memorial to this miracle. Behind the priests, Joshua rides a chariot. The middle scene portrays the camp of Gilgal with men and women waiting during the Feast of Unleavened Bread. The top scene portrays the seventh day shout with trumpets which crack Jericho's walls, tipping over one of its towers as it all begins to fall. Jericho's walls fell on the Feast of First Fruits, forty years to the day of the crossing of the Red Sea when YHWH destroyed Israel's slave-owners, the Egyptian army.

Destruction of Jericho

Kathleen Kenyon's description of the walls of Jericho (Tell es-Sultan) are as follows:

- "The walls were of a type, which made direct assault practically impossible. An approaching enemy first encountered a stone abutment 11 feet high, back and up from which sloped a 35° plastered scarp reaching to the main wall some 35 vertical feet above.

- The steep, smooth slope prohibited battering the wall by any effective device or building fires to break it.

- An army trying to storm the wall found difficulty in climbing the slope, and ladders to scale it could find no satisfactory footing."[587]

---

586 Daniel Ventura took photo.
587 Biblical Archaeology, "Conquest of Canaan in Biblical Archeology",
   http://www.truthnet.org/biblicalarcheology/6/conquestcanaan.htm, accessed 9/20/09

Scarabs in the cemetery outside the walled city of Jericho have inscriptions of Thutmose III, Hatshepsut, and Amenhotep III.[588] One Carbon-14 sample of charcoal[589] found in the final Bronze Age city was dated by the British Museum to 1410 BC, plus or minus 40 years,[590] but was then later recalibrated to support Kenyon's 1550 BC date.

On the seventh day of marching, which was Feast of First Fruits (since every 40 years the Hebrew calendar realigns), the people gave a great shout and the red mud-brick walls fell down (and are still at the base of Jericho's mound, or 'tell') and provided a ramp for the men to *"go straight up"* over the stone revetment walls. Joshua set fire to the city, and large jars of burnt grain were also found in the three feet of ash in this destruction layer.[591]

*When you be come into the land which I give to you, and shall reap the harvest thereof, then you shall bring a sheaf of the **first fruits** of your harvest to the priest:... . And you shall offer that day when you wave the sheaf an he lamb without blemish of the first year for a **burnt offering** to the LORD. And the meat offering thereof shall be two tenth deals of fine flour mingled with oil, an offering made by fire to the LORD ... (Leviticus 23:10-13)*

Joshua's instructions were to utterly destroy every living thing human and beast in Jericho, but to consecrate all of its gold, silver, brass, and iron into the LORD's treasury; otherwise a curse would be upon them.[592] One man hid some of the silver and gold in his tent.[593] Joshua sent only three thousand men to attack the little city of Ai, but they were routed and 36 were killed.[594] Joshua sought God as to why, and eventually Achan confessed to his sin, and the whole community stoned Achan and his family with all their possessions, including what he had hidden, and burned it at the valley of Achor ('trouble').[595]

Destruction of Ai and Bethel

Joshua set up an ambush of 30,000 soldiers to the west near Bethel and 3,000 to the north of Ai. Then he with the rest of the army attacked Ai, and retreated to draw them out of Ai and Bethel. Then those lying in wait set Ai on fire and began to attack them from behind, and Joshua and his troops turned and attacked, and they slew all 12,000 inhabitants, and hung the king's body on a tree. This time God told them to keep the cattle and precious metals as spoil. Based upon Biblical descriptions, Khirbet Nisya ("forgotten ruins") is the

---

588 Wood, Dr. Bryant G., "Did the Israelites Conquer Jericho? A New Look at the Archaeological Evidence", http://www.biblearchaeology.org/post/2008/05/01/Did-the-Israelites-Conquer-Jericho-A-New-Look-at-the-Archaeological-Evidence.aspx, 2008, accessed 9/20/09

589 Joshua 5:24 "And they burnt the city with fire, and all that was therein ..."

590 Kenyon, Kathleen M., Jericho 5, p. 763, sample BM-1790

591 Wood, Bryant Dr., http://www.biblearchaeology.org/post/2008/06/The-Walls-of-Jericho.aspx#Article

592 Joshua 6:18-21

593 Joshua 7:20-21

594 Joshua 7:3-5

595 Joshua 7:6-26

most likely site of Ai, with el-Bireh to its west as the site of Bethel.[596]

Then Joshua and all the people travelled (from where Abram built his second altar to the LORD between Bethel and Ai) about twenty miles north to Shechem (where Abram built his first altar to God after receiving the promise of the land of Canaan to his descendants).[597] Shechem lies in the valley between Mount Ebal on the north and Mount Gerizim on the south. There Joshua wrote the Ten Commandments on large plastered stones, and he read the entire law to the people to reestablish God's covenant with them.[598] After Canaan was subdued, Joshua would later erect God's tabernacle at Shiloh, midway between Abram's altars at Mt. Moriah (Jerusalem) and Shechem.[599]

Destruction of Amorite Cities (1451 BC)

Joshua's Southern Campaign

The Amorites lived along the Lebanon mountain ranges in the land of Amurru, but expanded south to Gaza and east across the Jordan. The Hivites lived in the cities of Gibeon, Chephirah, Beeroth, and Kirjathjearim. Through a ruse to avoid being slaughtered, the Gibeonites became slaves to the Israelites.[600] The kings of Jerusalem, Hebron, Jarmuth, Lachish, and Eglon united against the large city of Gibeon for making a treaty with the Israelites. Joshua came to Gibeon's aid and defeated their attackers with supernatural help (hailstones and lengthened daylight).[601] And then he went on to defeat Makkedah (where the five kings were hiding), Libnah, Lachish, Eglon, Hebron, and Debir.[602]

So Joshua smote all the country of the hills, and of the south, and of the vale, and of the springs, and all their kings: he left none remaining, but utterly destroyed all that breathed, as the LORD God of Israel commanded. And Joshua smote them from Kadeshbarnea even to Gaza, and <u>all the country of Goshen</u>, even to Gibeon. And all these kings and their land did Joshua take at one time, because the LORD God of Israel fought for Israel. (Joshua 10:40-42)

---

596 Stichting, "Was Ai a Ruin at the time of the Conquest?"; Dutch Bible, History, and Archaeology, 1999, http://www.bga.nl/en/articles/ai.html, accessed 9/29/10. Excellent research on Biblical Ai and Bethel
597 Genesis 12:6-8
598 Joshua 8:30-35
599 Joshua 18:1 Altars at Shechem (Genesis 12:6-7) and Mt. Moriah (Genesis 22:9)
600 Joshua 9:3-27
601 Joshua 10:10-14 See appendix B for notes.
602 Joshua 10:1-43

Pharaohs of the Bible

Joshua began his southern campaign from the 'place of wandering' (*Kadeshbarnea*).[603] A line can be drawn from there northwest to Gaza, and another line from southwest to northeast from the "*country*" (*eh-rets* is land) or 'land' of Goshen[604] to Gibeon encompassing Israel's southern border, the border of the tribe of Judah. Within Judah was the tribe of Simeon which lived in cities along the Wadi Shellaleh and its tributaries. Joshua took the land of Goshen back from Rameses II, the great loser, who built monuments to his 'greatness' in the south, because he had lost the north. Rameses II lost Retenu (Syria) to the Hittites in 1471 BC, and he lost the land east of the Pelusiac to the children of Israel who had escaped the grip of his grandfather, Rameses I, and returned and reclaimed their land.

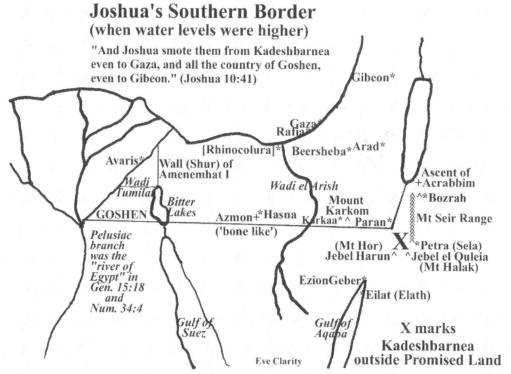

*This then was the lot of the tribe of the children of Judah by their families; even to the border of Edom the wilderness of Zin southward was the uttermost part of the south coast. And their south border was from the shore of the salt sea, from the bay that looks southward: And it went out to the south side to Maalehacrabbim, and passed along to Zin, and ascended up on the south side to Kadeshbarnea, and passed along to Hezron, and went up to Adar, and fetched a compass to **Karkaa**: From there it passed toward **Azmon**, and <u>went out to the river of Egypt</u>; and the*

---

603 My thanks to Steve Rudd and his research on places in the Bible at http://www.bible.ca/archeology/bible-archeology-exodus-kadesh-barnea-southern-border-judah-territory.htm
604 There was also a city of Goshen in Judah near Debir (Joshua 15:1, 49-51).

goings out of that coast were at the sea: this shall be your south coast. (Joshua 15:1-4)

Rhinocolura is in brackets because it didn't come into existence until Hellenistic times. Because it is the last city of Egypt before the red note "border of Egypt and Palestine" on the Madaba Map made 2000 years after Joshua took the land, some Bible commentaries state that Wadi el Arish was Israel's western border. Though the Wadi el Arish did become Israel's western border later through a deal between king Solomon and Osorkon I, the Pelusiac branch of the Nile was the border from Joshua's time up until king Saul's reign.

Some have tried to correlate Joshua's campaign with the Amarna letters (1588-1520). Abdi-Hiba was king of Jerusalem in the Amarna letters, but Adoni-zedek was king when Joshua attacked. Zimretta was king of Lachish in the Amarna letters, but Japhia was king when Joshua attacked.[605]

Destruction of Northern Kings

Hazor was the crossroads city of the north, and its king often led the neighboring cities.[606] Jabin sent word to over a dozen kings near him, including those of the Hittites and Jebusites, to come attack the Israelites at Merom, southwest of Hazor. Thousands came with horses and chariots. Joshua attacked them by surprise and took all their lands from Dor to Sidon on the coast, eastward to the Valley of Mizpeh (now called Beka Valley in Lebanon), and to the Jordan River.[607] He burned Hazor.[608] Though the initial battle at Merom was brief, the whole process of defeating the individual cities took several years.[609]

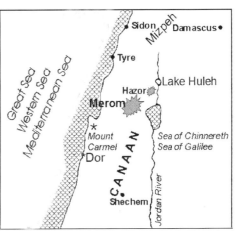

Joshua's Northern Campaign

And the LORD said to Joshua, Be not afraid because of them: for to morrow about this time will I deliver them up all slain before Israel: you shall hamstring their horses, and burn their chariots with fire. . . . they smote them, until they left them none remaining. And Joshua did to them as the LORD bade him: he hamstrung their horses, and burnt their chariots with fire. (Joshua 11:6-9)

These Canaanite cities were already in Iron Age I with many chariots, while the Israelites had been a nomadic people typical of the Late Bronze Age. Yahweh did not want

---

605 Joshua 10:3
606 Joshua 11:10
607 Joshua 11:1-20
608 Yudkin, Gila, http://www.itsgila.com/highlightshazor.htm, accessed 10/11/10 At Hazor "Ben Tor found over three feet of charcoal and ash, evidence of a raging fire of 1300 degrees centigrade."
609 Joshua 14:7-11 Caleb was 40 in 1489 when he spied out the land, and 85 when it was conquered = 1444.

Israel to depend upon chariots and horses to conquer their enemies,[610] but to depend upon Him. Joshua obeyed the LORD in this, whereas king Solomon did not.

Joshua Conquered Canaan in Iron Age IA (1451-1444 BC)

Though some cities like Dan and Beth-Shemesh had iron workshops, oppressors kept other cities from working metal sporadically for 400 years until the time of king David. According to I Samuel 13:19-22, the Philistines did not allow smithing in Israelite cities, and only Saul and Jonathan had a metal sword and spear in their army. Periods of Philistine persecution disrupting metal-working were 1350 - 1340, 1224-1206, and 1195-1155 BC.

> "Archaeologically, the Iron Age in Israel/Palestine is roughly divided into 2 segments, based mainly on the occupational sequence in the Central Hill country: 'Iron I,' in which the highlands were apparently settled by egalitarian rural societies; and 'Iron II,' which displays in this region phenomena customarily equated with a state system (settlement hierarchy, fortified administrative centers, and the like). . . . it was only natural to associate 'Iron I' with the tribal society described in **Joshua**-Judges, and to start 'Iron II' with the United Monarchy of David and Solomon. . . . <u>the 'Iron I | Iron II' transition is customarily placed at 980 BCE . . . based upon the **assumption** that the destructions typifying late Iron I sites were caused by [David] . . . and concluded well before the end of his 40-yr reign</u> (about 970 BCE) . . ."[611]

[Note that their end of David's reign is 45 years off.] Many of the Iron I sites in Israel were captured or destroyed by David: some while he was king Saul's captain (1063-1060 BC)[612], and others during his own reign (1055-1015 BC) by himself or his general, Joab. Thus there was a 75-year difference between the Biblical transition date (1055 BC) and the archaeologically accepted date (980 BC), which has broadened to a 125-yr difference based upon certain carbon 14 dates only four years after this article was printed.[613] Because their Egyptian and Biblical chronologies are wrong, archaeologists are looking for Joshua's conquest of Canaan 250 years too late: in 1200 instead of 1450 BC.

Canaanite cities destroyed by Joshua from 1451-1444 BC were mostly LBII in the hills, "egalitarian rural societies", and Iron IA trading forts at major crossroads and ports. Canaanite cities destroyed by kings Saul and David from 1663-1015 BC were mostly Iron IC-IIA. The LORD delivered several massive stone fortresses into Joshua's hands; Jericho and Hazor were the only ones specifically burned. So Israelites occupied Iron IA fortresses.

---

610 Deuteronomy 17:16 ". . . shall not multiply horses to himself, nor cause the people to return to Egypt . ."
611 Sharon, Ilan, "Report on the First Stage of the Iron Age Dating Project in Israel: Supporting a Low Chronology," RadioCarbon, Vol. 49, No. 1, 2007, p. 2
612 I Samuel 18:5-13 beginning after David slew Goliath
613 Transition at Tel Rehov placed at 830 BC. Finkelstein, Israel and Piasetzky, Eli, "The Iron Age Chronology Debate: Is the Gap Narrowing?" *Near Eastern Archaeology*, 74:1, 2011, p. 50

Destruction of Giants

Except for the cities of Gath, Gaza, and Ashdod; Joshua slew all the other giants (Anakim) from BaalGad below Mt Hermon to Israel's new southern border of Judah.[614] Several stones of the temples in Baalbek weigh around 1,000 tons.[615] One of the foundation stones of Jebus (later named Jerusalem) weighs over 500 tons.[616] There are still giants in modern times, like Andre the giant, and those listed in *Ripley's Believe it or Not*.

Allotment of Land to Tribes

Moses assigned the alloted portions to Reuben, Gad, and half of the tribe of Manasseh east of the Jordan River from the Arnon River north to Mount Hermon before Joshua's campaign west of the Jordan.[617] Moses also promised the land Caleb trod as a spy would be his,[618] so Joshua gave Caleb the hill country of giants, Kiriath-Arba, named Hebron as a portion within the allotment to Judah.[619] The sons of Judah did not drive out the Jebusites from Jerusalem.[620]

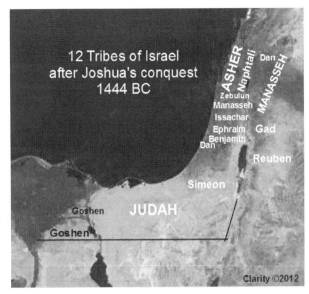

Then Joshua gave the sons of Joseph, Ephraim and Manasseh, their allotments. Ephraim was given territory which included Gilgal, Bethel, and Shiloh. The other half of the massive tribe of Manasseh was given a very large portion above Ephraim's which included Shechem and Megiddo from the Jordan River to the Great Sea, but complained it was not enough because so much of the land was forested.[621] Dan could not drive the people out of their allotment, so they moved up north to Laish.

To refocus attention on what God wanted, Joshua had all the people move from Gilgal to Shiloh to erect YHWH's tabernacle there. Joshua sent scouts from the remaining seven tribes who reported back their boundaries.[622] Then Joshua cast lots for each tribe's

---

614 Joshua 11:21-22
615 "Baalbek", http://en.wikipedia.org/wiki/Baalbek, Baalbek -50 miles north of BaalGad, accessed 9/20/09
616 "Western Stone", http://en.wikipedia.org/wiki/Western_Stone, accessed 9/30/10
617 Numbers 32:1-42; Deuteronomy 3:13-17; Joshua 13:8-33
618 Deuteronomy 1:36
619 Joshua 14:6-15 recounted in Judges 1:8-16 and 20
620 Joshua 15:63
621 Joshua 17:1-17
622 Joshua 18:1-10

allotment, and the people gave Joshua a city within Ephraim.[623] The LORD was the inheritance of the Levites, so they just received 48 cities.[624] Since Joseph's tribe became two tribes, there are actually thirteen tribes of Israel, but Jacob had twelve sons, so Israel is often referred to as having twelve tribes since only twelve had territories.

Joshua reestablished Covenant, then Died

Joshua ended his military conquest of Canaan in 1444 BC (first sabbath year), but the individual tribes continued to drive out Canaanites from their allotments.[625] Like Moses, Joshua established judges and military officers; and each tribe had elders and heads of clans. These he called together when he was 110 years old (1426 BC) and encouraged them to continue trusting in the LORD who had fought for them and given them the land He promised.[626] Then Joshua summoned all the tribes to Shechem to recommit themselves to serve the LORD at a sanctuary built there. Joshua died[627] and they buried him in Timnath-serah in Ephraim.[628] This was during the reign of Rameses II which ended in 1414 BC.

Joshua's Tomb

Timnath means 'portion'; *sereh* could be related to *sarah* which means prince/princess, or it's close to *sered*, which was a scribe's awl. The city was later named *Timnath-heres*[629], and *heres* means to scrape or itch. The village is now Kefl Hares and is under Palestinian control. The tombs of Joshua's father, Nun; and Caleb, his fellow spy who brought a good report, are nearby.

Joshua's Tomb in Kifl Hares

For the next eight years (1426-1418 BC), the elders ruled over Israel. There first order of business was to ask God how to drive out the rest of the idol worshippers in Canaan.

After Joshua died, Israel stopped celebrating all the LORD's Feasts

And all the congregation of them that were come again out of the captivity made booths, and sat under the booths: for since the days of Jeshua the son of Nun to that day had not the children of Israel done so. And there was very great gladness. (Nehemiah 8:17)

---

623 Joshua 18:11-19:51
624 Joshua 20:1-42
625 Joshua 14-15 Caleb took Hebron, but the tribe of Judah did not drive out the Jebusites from Jerusalem.
626 Joshua 23:1-16
627 Joshua died on the 26th of Nisan (twelve days after Passover) according to Hebrew tradition.
628 Joshua 24:1-30
629 Judges 2:9 -Photo of Joshua's Tomb by Shuki

Elders of Israel

Now after the death of Joshua it came to pass, that the children of Israel asked the LORD, saying, Who shall go up for us against the Canaanites first, to fight against them? And the LORD said, Judah shall go up: behold, I have delivered the land into his hand. (Judges 1:-2)

Judah asked the tribe of Simeon to help them, and together they slew 10,000 men in Bezek. The lord of Bezek (*AdoniBezek*) escaped, but they caught him and brought him to Jerusalem where he died.[630] Under Caleb in 1451, Jerusalem had been taken and set on fire, but the Jebusites had reoccupied it, and the tribe of Benjamin could not now drive them out.[631] The tribes of Judah and Simeon did destroy the Canaanites from Zapheth[632] and the coastal cities of Gaza and Ashkelon, and more inland Ekron; but they could not drive them out of the valleys because the Canaanites had iron chariots[633] as a protectorate of Egypt. Judges 1:27-35 list other cities and peoples which were not completely destroyed, and the LORD's angel came and rebuked them for not destroying them and their idolatrous altars.[634]

During this time (1426-1425 BC), old Rameses II, age 54, still ruled Egypt. His last war was against the Nubians when he was 22 (1458 BC). He likely received word that Egypt's Canaanite defense, to keep the Hittites (Khatti) from attacking, had been conquered along the coast by a nomadic people called Israel. The children of Israel had caused his father, Seti I, enough problems; and Rameses II chose to leave them alone and trust the Hittites would continue to honor the treaty he signed with them over thirty years prior.

With Elders Dead, People Rebel

Israel served the LORD all the years of Joshua and the elders,[635] until 1418 BC when Caleb, the last eye-witness of the parting of the Red Sea, died. Without a leader of faith, the Israelites quickly turned away to other gods of those they neglected to drive out.

And the children of Israel dwelled among the Canaanites, Hittites, and Amorites, and Perizzites, and Hivites, and Jebusites: And they took their daughters to be their wives, and gave their daughters to their sons, and served their gods. And the children of Israel did evil in the sight of the LORD, and forgot the LORD their God, and served Baalim and the groves. Therefore the anger of the LORD was hot against Israel, and he sold them into the hand of Chushanrishathaim king of Mesopotamia: and the children of Israel served Chushanrishathaim eight years. (Judges 3:5-8)

---

630 Judges 1:4-7 They marked AdoniBezek as a coward by cutting off his thumbs and big toes.
631 Judges 1:8 and 21
632 *Zapheth* means 'watchtower', and was likely in the wilderness of Tekoa. There was also a watchtower at Deir al-Balah, about ten miles SW of Gaza. It would give the larger Canaanite coastal cities early warning of Egyptian movement. Even the Templars chose it for a stronghold during the crusades.
633 Judges 1:17-19
634 Judges 2:1-5
635 Judges 2:7

Pharaohs of the Bible

The words translated "*Mesopotamia*" are *aram naharayim* mean "Aram two rivers" and refer to the Aramaens of the upper Tigris and Euphrates who were later called Syrians. Shem's son Aram had a son Uz who founded Damascus.[636] "*Chushanrishathaim*" means "Cushan, doubly wicked". Israel was subjected to the Aramaens for eight years, paying them tribute.[637] Even the Babylonian cuneiform of the Amarna letters was influenced by an early Aramaic.[638] It may be at this point that Aramaic became the trade language in Israel.

Merenptah (1414-1394 BC) of the 19th Dynasty

Merenptah (also spelled Merneptah) was likely the fourth child of the second wife of Rameses II. Because his father had lived so long, Merenptah was probably in his forties[639] when he ascended the throne. Like his father, he had to fight to keep the Libyans, aided by Aegean "sea people", out of Egypt. Unlike his father, he decided to put Canaan under Egyptian authority again.

In his fifth year (1409 BC) as pharaoh, he reused a stele of Amenhotep III, and had it inscribed with his conquest of Libya and this final paragraph:

> "The princes are prostrate saying: "Shalom!" Not one of the Nine Bows lifts his head: Tjehenu is vanquished, Khatti at peace, <u>Canaan is captive with all woe</u>. Ashkelon is conquered, Gezer seized, Yanoam made nonexistent; **Israel is wasted, bare of seed**, Khor is become a widow for Egypt. All who roamed have been subdued. By the King of Upper and Lower Egypt, Banere-meramun, Son of Re, Merneptah, Content with Maat, Given life like Re every day."[640]

Merenptah's stele contains the first non-Biblical mention of Israel as a country. Other defeated Egyptian enemies listed besides Israel; Ashkelon, Gezer and Yanoam,[641] were given determinatives for a city-state ("a throw stick plus three mountains designating a foreign country") But the hieroglyphs for Israel use the determinative for *foreign peoples,*

---

636 Genesis 10:22-23 Clarke's Commentary The land of Aram was called "Padanaram" in Genesis 25:20.
637 Jacob served Laban the Aramaen in Harran for 20 years. Genesis 25:20; 27:30; 31:41
638 El Amarna Tablets, http://www.searchgodsword.org/enc/isb/view.cgi?number=T8649, accessed 11/9/10
639 Rameses II became prince regent at 14 and had two wives and kids before he became pharaoh at age 20.
640 "The Israel Stela (Merneptah Stele)", http://www.bible-history.com/archaeology/egypt/2-israel-stela-bb.html, accessed 9/25/10. Tjehenu lived west of the Nile Delta. Khatti (Hittites) lived in Turkey.
641 *Yanoam* means 'built by people'. I think it may be the same city as Jabneel ('built by God') in Joshua 15:11, later called Jabneh in 2 Chronicles 26:6; and is current day Yavne, which is 20 miles north of Ashkelon, on the road to Tel Miqne (Gath).

typically used for nomadic tribes without a fixed city-state,[642] which well described Israel under the rule of the elders. Judah had recently conquered and inhabited Gaza, Ashkelon, and Ekron; but they placed no kings in these cities; instead they had elders and officers and heads of families. Gezer, 20 miles east of Ashkelon, was occupied by Israelites who had conquered it in 1451 BC. The key sentence is also translated, "Israel is laid waste; its seed is no more," which could refer to the practice of burning an enemy's grain supply to keep them from being a threat. Merenptah killed some Israelites, but he did not wipe them out or burn all of Canaan. His egotistical coloring of history is much like his father's (battle of Qadesh). Merenptah's stele is on display at the Cairo Museum.

"Israel is laid waste; its seed is no more."

Merenptah 1414 – 1394 BC

Merenptah was the last pharaoh to bother Israel for the next three hundred years.[643]

And also all that generation were gathered to their fathers: and there arose another generation after them, which knew not the LORD, nor yet the works which he had done for Israel. And the children of Israel did evil in the sight of the LORD, and served Baalim: . . . they forsook the LORD, and served Baal and Ashtaroth. And the anger of the LORD was hot against Israel, and he delivered them into the hands of spoilers that spoiled them, and he sold them into the hands of their enemies round about, so that they could not any longer stand before their enemies. . . . Nevertheless <u>the LORD raised up judges</u>, which delivered them out of the hand of those that spoiled them. And yet they would not listen to their judges, but they went a

---

642 "Merneptah Stele", http://en.wikipedia.org/wiki/Merneptah_Stele, accessed 9/12/09
643 Yurco, Frank, Merenptah's victory reliefs at http://www.jewishhistory.com/pdf/3200_year_old.pdf

whoring after other gods, and bowed themselves to them:... And when the LORD raised them up judges, then the LORD was with the judge, and delivered them out of the hand of their enemies all the days of the judge:... And it came to pass, when the judge was dead, that they returned, and corrupted themselves more than their fathers, in following other gods ... And the anger of the LORD was hot against Israel; and he said, Because that this people has transgressed my covenant which I commanded their fathers, and have not listened to my voice; I also will not from now on drive out any from before them of the nations which Joshua left when he died: That through them I may prove Israel, whether they will keep the way of the LORD to walk therein, as their fathers did keep it, or not. (Judges 2:10-22)

Hence, some of the Canaanites, Hittites, Amorites, Perizzites, Hivites, and Jebusites remained in Israel until kings Saul and David defeated them. Canaanites also retook several of the cities Joshua had conquered. It may be during the time of the judges that the Jebusites built their retaining wall (millo) and castle at Jebus.

Joshua

Egypt 1536-1491	Camps 1491	Kadesh-barnea 1490-1449	Camps 1449-1451	Canaan battles 1451-1444	Tribal Israel 1444-1426

Egypt's Pharaohs

Akhenaten 1551-1534 (18th)	Smenkhkare 1534-1531	Nefertiti 1531-1530	Tutankhamun 1534-1524	Ay 1524-1520	Horemheb 1520-1493	Rameses I 1493-1491 (19th)	Seti I 1491-1480	Rameses II 1480-1414

Pharaohs of Israel's Judges

*"For the LORD is our judge, the LORD is our lawgiver,
the LORD is our king; he will save us."*
(Isaiah 33:22)

Judges of Israel

After the elders died, God established judges to rule over Israel.

1409	Othniel	1206	Jepthah
1369	Ehud (overlap with Shamgar)	1200	Ibzan
1366	Shamgar	1193	Elon
1339	Deborah	1183	Abdon
1291	Gideon	1175	Samson
1251	Tola	1155	Eli
1228	Jair	1115	Samuel

Throughout the period of the judges of Israel, pharaohs are not mentioned in the Bible; Egypt is strangely silent. I surmise that after Merenptah's reign, Egyptian pharaohs of the second half of the 19th dynasty were focused largely upon their own borders, trying to keep Upper and Lower Egypt united without legal heirs; much like the end of the 18th dynasty. The 20th dynasty of infighting among the sons of Rameses III (Rameses IV, V, VI, and VIII), and the Nile droughts eventually shifted the power of Egypt to the temple priests in Thebes (dynasty 21A) bringing about the turbulent Third Intermediate Period.

Othniel (1409-1369 BC) judges Israel from Merenptah to Tausret's reign

And he [Caleb] went up there to the inhabitants of Debir: and the name of Debir before was Kirjathsepher. And Caleb said, He that smites Kirjathsepher, and takes it, to him will I give Achsah my daughter to wife. And Othniel the son of Kenaz, the brother of Caleb, took it: and he gave him Achsah his daughter to wife. (Joshua 15:15-17)[644]

Othniel was Caleb's nephew who made himself Caleb's son-in-law by capturing Debir in 1451 BC. Debir is Tel Beit Mirsim, and its strata E of Late Bronze Age I of the 15th century BC had a destroyed east gate tower prior to its being 'abandoned' (the people having been slaughtered). Ten miles NNW lies Tell ed-Duweir (Lachish) which shows violent destruction by fire with a thick ash layer in which a scarab of Rameses II (1480-1414) was discovered,[645] and a clay bowl with an Egyptian inscription of the fourth year of a pharaoh.

---

644 This history is repeated in Judges 1:11-13.
645 Quartz Hill School of Theology, "The Conquest of Canaan," http://www.theology.edu/conquest.htm, accessed 9/20/09; so they dated the destruction to about 1230 BC during Rameses' II conventional reign.

Tel Beit Mirsim (Debir) and Tell el-Hesi also had a layer of ash which archaeologists attributed to Merenptah's conquest in Canaan,[646] though these cities are not listed on Merenptah's Stele. But Lachish and Debir were conquered by Joshua (Joshua 10:32-38).

> . . . the children of Israel served Chushanrishathaim eight years. And when the children of Israel cried to the LORD, the LORD raised up a deliverer to the children of Israel, who delivered them, even Othniel the son of Kenaz, Caleb's younger brother. And the Spirit of the LORD came on him, and <u>he judged Israel, and went out to war</u>: and the LORD delivered Chushanrishathaim king of Mesopotamia into his hand . . . And the land had rest forty years. And Othniel the son of Kenaz died. (Judges 3:8-11)

The Aramaens subjected Israel from 1417-1409 BC when God delivered them by Othniel after Merenptah's campaign into Israel. Then the land had rest under Othniel's judgeship for 40 years (1409-1369 BC). Merenptah's son and heir was Seti II. When Merenptah died, a rival began ruling in Upper Egypt, named Amenmesse (1394-1391 BC); but eventually, Seti II secured all of Egypt under his authority before his death. Born of a Canaanite concubine[647], Merenptah Siptah assumed the throne as a child, with his royal stepmother, Tausret (also spelled Twosret) as regent,[648] who was made queen after young Siptah's death. Tausret's and Siptah's names are linked to the turquoise mines at Serabit el Khadim and Timna in the Sinai.[649]

Seti II (1394-1388 BC)

Seti II had three queens: Tausret, Takhat and Tiaa. Tausret was his chief queen. In 1908, a small tomb (KV56) for a royal infant was discovered in the Valley of the Kings which contained gold earrings with Seti II's name.[650] The tomb of Seti II was KV15, and KV14 was for queen Tausret. Seti II built a barge dock and small temple for himself at the Karnak complex for Amun, Mut, and Khonsu. Seti II is credited with building the temple of Hathor at Timna, and expanding copper production and trade. Hathor is the patron goddess of miners. Tomb KV13 was built for chancellor Bay, but an ostracon in the tomb noted Bay was executed by Merenptah Siptah.

Seti II

Amenmesse (1394-1390 BC)

Amenmesse ruled in Nubia, and his third and fourth years are attested in Thebes.

---

646 Cornfeld, Gaalyah, *Archaeology of the Bible: book by book*, Harper and Row, 1976, p. 72
647 "Siptah", http://en.wikipedia.org/wiki/Siptah, accessed 10/9/10
648 Statue of Siptah seated on Tausret's lap. Callender, Vivienne G., "Queen Tausret and the End of Dynasty 19," *Studien zur Altägyptischen Kultur*, Bd. 32, 2004, pp. 81-104
649 Singer, Itamar, "Merenptah's Campaign to Canaan," *Bulletin of the American Schools of Oriental Research*, No. 269 (Feb., 1988), pp. 1-10
650 http://en.wikipedia.org/wiki/KV56

Pharaohs of Israel's Judges

Merenptah Siptah (1388-1381 BC)

Merenptah Siptah

Bay boasted of his abilities in placing Siptah on the throne on a stela found in Aswan, but Siptah executed him as a traitor in his fifth year.[651] KV47 was Siptah's tomb, but his mummy was discovered in a cache in KV35. He had curly red-brown hair and died as a teenager with a crippled left foot. Siptah was building a 60 X 45 meter temple at Karnak. Script on one of the blocks noted, "year seven of the king".[652] Queen Tausret acted as his regent, and assumed his regnal years and his large temple upon his death.

Tausret (1388-1381 as regent; 1381-1378 BC sole rule)

Tausret in Nubia

"In the course of the season's work another inscription was discovered on one of the massive foundation blocks (FB2) in Trench TB8 (Fig. 4). The inscription was examined by our expedition Heiraticist, Dr. Robert Demerée of Leiden University, who stressed that the first line reads clearly: "Year 8, 2nd month of shemu, day 29". This has particular significance, for it provides confirmation for the text we discovered in 2006 on an adjacent foundation block (FB1) which was dated also to the eighth year of the queen's reign. Although Tausert's reign (including her regency for Siptah) has been understood commonly as being seven years (as stated by Manetho in his History), or eight at the most, the inscriptions on the foundation blocks show otherwise. Because they were made when the temple was begun, and we now have archaeological evidence that the temple was completed or nearly so (it must have taken a couple of years), these texts indicate clearly that <u>Tausert must have reigned nine, or perhaps, even ten years</u>."[653]

Year 7 at the temple was the last attributed to Siptah, and foundation blocks of part of the temple were attributed to queen Tausret beginning in year 8. So I give king Siptah seven years and queen Tausret ten years which include the seven she was regent, so she only ruled three years on her own. During her ten years plus her time as queen of Seti II, her name travelled on objects throughout Egypt and Canaan.[654] A vase with Tausret's cartouche was found at Deir Allah in Jordan. Tausret's tomb portrayed she and Seti II, but it was later usurped by Setnakhte and extended. The 19th dynasty ended at the death of queen Tausret.

---

651 http://en.wikipedia.org/wiki/Siptah
652 Wilkinson, Richard, "The Tausret Temple Project," *The Ostracon*, vol. 18, #1, summer 2007, p. 8, fig. 9
653 Wilkinson, Richard, "The Tausret Temple Project," *The Ostracon*, vol. 22, fall 2011, p. 8
654 http://en.wikipedia.org/wiki/Twosret

Pharaohs of the Bible

Egypt's Civil War and Anarchy after Tausret's Death

There were no heirs and no men of valor who could keep the empire together, so it fell into anarchy (1378-1323 BC).[655] Setnakhte who later stood up to take control had no affiliations with previous lines of pharaohs.[656]

The Great Harris Papyrus informs us about the transition between the 19th and 20th dynasties.

> "The land of Egypt was overthrown from without, and every man was thrown out of his right; they had no "chief mouth" for many years formerly until other times. The land of Egypt was in the hands of chiefs and of rulers of towns; one slew his neighbour, great and small. Other times having come after it, with empty years, Irsu, ('a self-made man'), a certain Syrian (Kharu) was with them as chief (wr). He set plundering their (i.e.: the people's) possessions. They made gods like men, and no offerings were presented in the temples."

Setnakhte's year 4 stela

I calculate 55 years as the "many years" without a pharaoh. In his second year Setnakhte erected a stela in Elephantine which described how he saved Egypt from Asiatic mercenaries hired by nomarchs.

> "The [crim]inals before him, fear of him seized their hearts, and they fled - (as) tits and sparrows with a falcon after them - having abandoned the gold, silver and [bronze] of Egypt which they gave to these Asiatics to bring about a quick victory for them; for the [chiefs] of Egypt were disastrous conspirators and ineffectual plotters(?)."

---

655 If other pharaohs or greater regnal lengths are discovered, years can be taken from this period of anarchy.
656 "Setnakht", http://en.wikipedia.org/wiki/Setnakhte, accessed 10/16/10

Othniel's Pharaohs[657]

Othniel's Pharaohs

The elders ruled Israel from Joshua's death in 1426 BC until the invasion of Merenptah in 1409 BC. Since Merenptah's stela does not refer to Othniel or one judge ruling over Israel, I assume Othniel began judging Israel after Merenptah's campaign.

The judges of Israel were often military leaders who delivered them from an oppressor. They made decisions between tribes and for the nation as a whole in the role of a governor. A few were also spiritual leaders.

And the children of Israel did evil again in the sight of the LORD: and the LORD strengthened Eglon the king of Moab against Israel, because they had done evil in the sight of the LORD. And he gathered to him the children of Ammon and Amalek, and went and smote Israel, and possessed the city of palm trees. So the children of Israel served Eglon the king of Moab eighteen years. (Judges 3:12-14)

---

657 Photo of Amenmesse by Keith Schengili-Roberts. Photo of Siptah by John D. Croft.
Note the square faces of Merenptah and Seti II, father and son.

Ehud and Shamgar judge Israel during Egypt's anarchy

After Othniel died the Israelites immediately turned to other gods, and the LORD put them under subjection to Eglon of Moab for 18 years (1369-1351 BC), who had the Ammonites and remaining giants of Amalek join him in his initial attack.[658] Ehud became the emissary to deliver tribute to Eglon of Moab, possibly the entire 18 years, since he gained Eglon's confidence to meet with him privately. Moab's king had built a new palace a couple miles <u>west</u> of the Jordan river near Beth-Hoglah (Almog) or Beth Arabah (Beit HaArava) within site of Reubenite Bohan's carved boundary stone.[659] Ehud stealthily assassinated Eglon and escaped backed into Israel's thickly wooded hills of Ephraim where he blew a shofar and called upon the people to join him in routing the Moabites. That day they slew 10,000.[660]

> . . . and took the fords of Jordan toward Moab, and suffered not a man to pass over. . . . So Moab was subdued that day under the hand of Israel. And the land had rest fourscore years. (Judges 3:28c and 30)

The particular land which had rest for eighty years (1351-1271 BC) was that of the fords of the Jordan which had been in contention. Israel changed Eglon's palace into a fort and kept the Moabites to their borders <u>east</u> of the Dead Sea. Ehud served twenty years (1369-1349) up north while Shamgar (1366-1340) the son of Anath slew six hundred Philistine men with an ox goad to deliver Israel.[661] Barne's Bible Commentary's definition of ox goad:

> "An instrument of wood about eight feet long, armed with an iron spike or point at one end, with which to spur the ox at plow, and with an iron scraper at the other end with which to detach the earth from the plowshare when it became encumbered with it."

Shamgar was in good shape to wield such a weapon, and thus reinforce Israel's southwest border. It is unclear how long the Philistines were attacking the southern tribes. Shamgar was contemporary with Ehud in the north, and then judged Israel after Ehud's death for several years. Then Shamgar died, and Israel was without a leader for a year. Possibly the rebellious spirit of anarchy in Egypt spread to Israel. Overlapping Israel's problems with the Moabites on the east, they also experienced twenty years of oppression by king Jabin ruling from Hazor in the north which ended at the beginning of Deborah's judgeship when a woman named Jael killed Sisera, Jabin's captain.[662]

---

658 Judges 3:12-13 Eglon possessed the city of palm trees, which may have been where the Jordan empties into the Dead Sea (the new Kadeshbarnea of Joshua 10:41) on the eastern shore of the Jordan.
659 "Stone of Bohan" from Joshua 15:6. *Peseel* was translated "*quarries*" in Judges 3:26, but can also mean carved stone or idol. See Joshua 15:6; 18:17 which describes Benjamin's borders.
660 Judges 3:14-30 Verse 19 suggests the king was at this city which overlooked Gilgal on the west side of the Jordan.
661 Judges 3:31
662 Judges 4:1-24

Pharaohs of Israel's Judges

Deborah and Barak defeated king Jabin of Hazor

Deborah judged disputes among Israelites at mount Ephraim from 1339-1299 BC. Jabin, king of Canaan in Hazor, oppressed Israelites into harsh servitude 1358-1338 BC. Joshua had fought another Jabin[663] of Hazor during his northern conquest (1451 BC and following) and had burned Hazor to the ground. After a generation or two had passed, Hazor was rebuilt and fortified with its occupants itching for revenge.

And the LORD sold them into the hand of Jabin king of Canaan, that reigned in Hazor; the captain of whose host was Sisera, which dwelled in Harosheth of the Gentiles. And the children of Israel cried to the LORD: for he had nine hundred chariots of iron; and twenty years he mightily oppressed the children of Israel. (Judges 4:2-3)

Harosheth (El Harathiyeh) was located at the base of Mount Carmel a few miles north of Yokneam, which is ten miles northwest of Megiddo (the best crossing place for chariots). The meaning of *Harosheth* is cutting and carving, and might have been the base camp for preparing lumber for shipping to Sidon. Mount Tabor is ten miles west of the southern tip of the Sea of Galilee. The mountains of Israel were densely wooded at this time, and captain Sisera would have known about the taskmasters of the woodcutters on Mount Tabor. But those who hew wood with axes certainly have the strength to wield axes against those who oppressed them.

And I will draw to you to the river Kishon Sisera, the captain of Jabin's army, with his chariots and his multitude; and I will deliver him into your hand. (Judges 4:7)

The kings came and fought, then fought the kings of Canaan in Taanach by the waters of Megiddo; they took no gain of money. . . . the stars in their courses fought against Sisera. The <u>river of Kishon swept them away</u> . . . (Judges 5:19-21)

Sisera and his 900 iron chariots were not locked up in the hills of Hazor, but were ready to win a battle on the plains of Jezreel suited for chariots. Mount Tabor is 19 miles northeast of Megiddo, with the Kishon river flowing between them. Barak requested Deborah to be with him to give the word to advance, and she did, and the two armies met at the Kishon river (X on map) which was dire for the chariots and men of Sisera, who were all killed. Deborah, the only female judge of Israel, served forty years and the land had rest.[664]

Battle of Deborah and Barak against Sisera

---

663 Jabin means "intelligent" and might be a title for their leader, and not a given name.
664 Judges 4-5 Sisera's death would be 1338 BC.

Pharaohs of the Bible

Deborah judged Israel (1339-1299 BC) during Setnakhte and Rameses III

*LORD, when you went out of Seir, when you marched out of the field of Edom, the <u>earth trembled</u>, and the <u>heavens dropped</u>, the clouds also dropped water. The <u>mountains melted</u> from before the LORD, even that Sinai from before the LORD God of Israel. <u>In the days of Shamgar</u> the son of Anath, in the days of Jael, the <u>highways were unoccupied</u>, and the travelers walked through byways. The inhabitants of the <u>villages ceased, they ceased in Israel, until that I Deborah arose</u>, that I arose a mother in Israel. They chose new gods; then was **war** in the gates: <u>was there a shield or spear seen among forty thousand in Israel</u>? . . . They that are delivered from the noise of archers in the places of drawing water, there shall they rehearse the righteous acts of the LORD (Judges 5:4-11b)*

Disheartened people turned to war and theft, and there was fear of bandits along highways and watering holes from the days of Shamgar, to the day Jael killed Sisera.[665] *"The inhabitants of"* is not in the Hebrew, but reads, *"perazon chadol*, or "villages ceased". *Perazon* means magistrates or chieftains, from a root meaning leader or warrior. Most warriors were killed protecting their homes from Sea Peoples, so God elevated a woman.

In Deborah's song she recounted several portions of recent history. Though her praise of YHWH from Sinai and Seir likely refers back to the giving of the Law at Sinai and marching passed Seir on the way to Canaan,[666] it's odd description could also note geologic catastrophes involving earthquakes and volcanic eruptions through which she lived.

The Dead Sea Fault is from the Gulf of Aqaba through Mount Seir to the Dead Sea and continues into the Jordan Rift. The mountain range of Sinai is parallel to the gulf of Aqaba.[667] A volcanic eruption may have caused mountain ranges from Sinai to Seir to have earthquakes and mudslides (*"mountains melted"*) due to the unusually high rainfall it brought to that dry area. The word "rain" is not used, but *"dropped"* which means "ooze," possibly because of ash particulate, called aerosols, in the air.

Specific volcanic eruptions occurred from 1313-1310 BC during the reign of Rameses III and during Deborah's rule. It could have been from one volcano or a combination of volcanoes on the west Arabian Peninsula, and/or in the South Aegean Arc: Aegina, Methana, Milos, Kos, Nisyros, or Yali. Abutting the Red Sea is the Arabian Shield with lava flows, *harrat*, as large as the state of Missouri.

> "By counting the number of vents and eruptions that have occurred on northern Harrat Rahat, vulcanologists estimate that, during the past 4500 years, there have been 13 major eruptions—one every 346 years, on average."[668]

---

665 Judges 4:17-24 Sisera fled battle and took refuge in Jael's tent, but she hammered a peg thru his skull.
666 Deut. 33:2
667 Klinger, et.al., "Seismic Behavior of the Dead Sea Fault along the Arabah Valley", *Geophys. J. Int.*, 2000, 142, p. 769. Earthquakes occur along the Dead Sea Fault about every 200 years. The one in 1995 had a 7.6 magnitude.
668 Harrigan, Peter, "It Started with Tremors," *Saudi Aramco World,* March/April 2006, pp. 2-13

Setnakhte (1322-1318 BC), first pharaoh of the 20th Dynasty

"But when the gods inclined themselves to peace, to set the land in its rights according to its accustomed manner, they established their son, who came forth from their limbs, to be ruler, LPH, of every land, upon their great throne, Userkhaure-setepenre-meryamun, LPH, the son of Re, **Setnakhte-merire-meryamun**, LPH. He was Khepri-Set, when he is enraged; he set in order the entire land which had been rebellious; he slew the rebels who were in the land of Egypt; he cleansed the great throne of Egypt; he was ruler of the Two Lands, on the throne of Atum. He gave ready faces to those who had been turned away. Every man knew his brother who had been walled in. He established the temples in possession of divine offerings, to offer to the gods according to their customary stipulations."[669] [LPH = Life, Prosperity, Health]

Setnakhte's origins are unknown; he did not claim any royal descendants, but he is acclaimed for restoring order after anarchy. This may be the period when *The Admonitions of Ipuwer* was written [see Appendix B, pages 427-433]; in which, like Deborah, he noted the roads were barren. Were Arabian volcanoes spewing fire, lava bombs, and ash?

". . . the roads are watched; men sit in the bushes until the benighted traveler comes in order to plunder his burden, . . . Seed goes forth into mortal women, but <u>none are found on the road</u>. . . . If three men travel on the road, they are found to be only two, for <u>the many kill the few</u>. . . . he goes on the road until he sees the **flood**; the road is washed out and he stands worried. . . . Behold, the <u>fire has gone up on high</u>, and its burning goes forth against the enemies of the land. . . . <u>the Residence is thrown down in a moment</u>"[670]

"Squalor is throughout the land, and there are none indeed whose clothes are white in these times." (because of sewage or ash?)

"Indeed, [hearts] are violent, pestilence is throughout the land, blood is everywhere, death is not lacking, and the mummy-cloth speaks even before one comes near it. Indeed, many dead are buried in the river; the stream is a sepulcher . . ."

Trade with Byblos and Keftiu (of Crete) ceased, and "foreign bowmen" took advantage of their dire situation. People's hair fell out because of "years of noise" ("of tumult"). Some attribute Ipuwer's woes to the plagues of the exodus, but due to its emphasis on how "the Residence" is brought down, it may best be placed during the anarchy (see Appendix B). This dire period was followed by a worse period of volcanic activity from the Aegean.

---

669 Breasted, James, H., *Ancient Records of Egypt, Vol No.4*, 1906
670 The Leyden Papyrus 334 translation, 5, 7, and 12, http://www.reshafim.org.il/ad/egypt/texts/ipuwer.htm

Rameses III (1318-1286 BC) and the Sea Peoples

Memorial temple of Rameses III

Setnakhte named his son Rameses. Rameses III built a memorial temple in Thebes, now near Medinet Habu, which still has 7,000 square meters of decorated surfaces. Its walls contain depictions of victories over foreigners collectively called "Sea Peoples"[671] in his 5th and 8th years (1313 and 1310 BC respectively), which was no small undertaking considering the devastation they had caused elsewhere as inscribed on the wall:

"The foreign countries (ie. Sea Peoples) made a conspiracy in their islands,
All at once the lands were removed and scattered in the fray. No land could stand before their arms: from Hatti, Qode, Carchemish, Arzawa and Alashiya on, being destroyed at one time. A camp was set up in Amurru. They desolated its people, and its land was like that which has never come into being. They were coming forward toward Egypt, while the flame was prepared before them. Their confederation was the Peleset, Tjekker, Shekelesh, Denyen, and Weshesh, lands united. They laid their hands upon the land as far as the circuit of the earth, their hearts confident and trusting: 'Our plans will succeed!'"[672]

Labu,   Shasu,   Canaanite, Asiatic prisoner and a Denyen

---

671 From wikipedia's "Sea Peoples", the Karnak inscription of Merneptah's victory against the Sea Peoples lists Ekwesh, Teresh, Lukka, Sherden, and Shekelesh.

672 Medinet Habu inscription of Ramesses III's 8th year, lines 16-17, trans. by John A. Wilson in Pritchard, J.B. (ed.) Ancient Near Eastern Texts relating to the Old Testament, 3rd edition, Princeton 1969, p. 262. Amurru (Amorites) held the land between Byblos and Ugarit on the Mediterranean to the Orontes River.

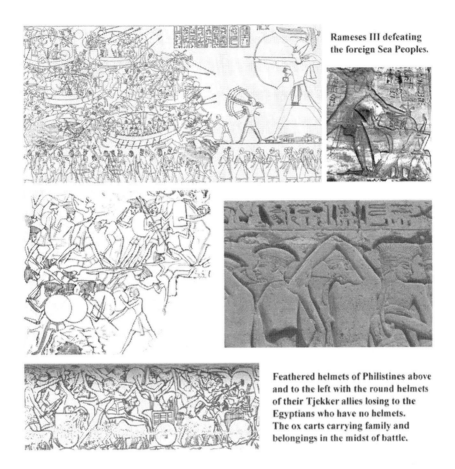

Rameses III defeating the foreign Sea Peoples.

Feathered helmets of Philistines above and to the left with the round helmets of their Tjekker allies losing to the Egyptians who have no helmets. The ox carts carrying family and belongings in the midst of battle.

The first attack was by both land and sea, but Rameses' III fleet was waiting in the delta,[673] and easily defeated their "sails only" ships by rowing out, affixing grappling irons and capsizing them. Rameses' III soldiers killed the land force comprised of Tjekker (Thekel) and Peleset (Philistine) accompanied by women and children in ox carts.[674] The Sherden, or Shardana, warriors are in the top right boat of the top picture with their horned helmets. They were likely from the island of Sardinia west of Italy. The Labu (Libyans) allied themselves with the Sea Peoples in attacking Egypt.

Sherden warrior between Sardinia figurines

---

673 Just as Rameses II waited for the Sherden, Shardana, Lukka, and Shekelesh (Sea Peoples), "Rameses II", http://en.wikipedia.org/wiki/Ramesses_II#Battle_against_Sherden_sea_pirates, accessed 9/20/2009

674 T.R. Bryce, "The Lukka Problem - And a Possible Solution," *Journal of Near Eastern Studies*, Vol. 33 # 4, October 1974, p. 371

Pharaohs of the Bible

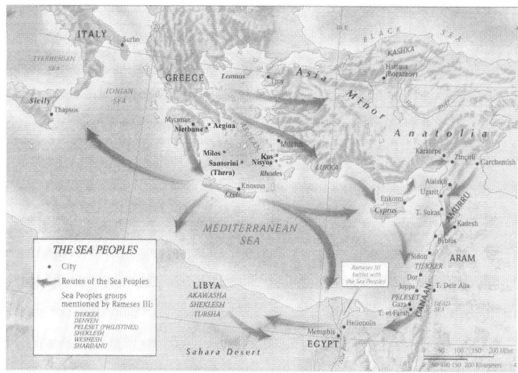

"almost every city between Troy and Gaza was violently destroyed"[675] (by tsunamis)

If Aegina and/or the 32 volcanoes on the Methana peninsula began spewing volcanic debris in 1313 BC accompanied by earthquakes,[676] it explains the first attack. If major eruptions occurred three years later (1310 BC), it explains why these Sea Peoples were fighting along with their families looking for a new place to live, and would not give up. Rameses III took troops up the coast of Canaan to their camp at Amurru, and killed thousands. Then he returned to the Nile delta where archers waited to shower arrows upon their ships, but instead of killing all of them, he settled some along the Mediterranean coastline as tax-paying subjects, since the military expenses had drained Egypt's treasury.

> "I extended all the boundaries of Egypt; I overthrew those who invaded them
> from their lands. I slew the Denyen in their isles; the Thekel and the Peleset
> were made ashes. The Sherden and the Weshesh of the sea, they were made as
> those that exist not, taken captive at one time, brought as captives to Egypt, like
> the sand of the shore. I settled them in strongholds, bound in my name.
> Numerous were their classes like hundred-thousands. I taxed them all, in
> clothing and grain from the storehouses and granaries each year." [677]

---

675 "Bronze Age Collapse" dated to 12th century BC, on wikipedia.com, accessed 11/4/10
676 "Methana Volcano" on wikipedia.com, accessed 12/13/11
677 Sec. 403 of "Great Papyrus Harris" from the California Institute of Ancient Studies,

Philistine Pottery

Fanciful flying animals

Bichrome Ware bowls

Philistines

The Peleset (Philistines) were originally descended from Egypt's (*Mizraim's*) son Casluhim,[678] from the coast of Caphtor[679], which means "crown" and is likely related to the encircling shape of natural or man-made harbors along Egypt's Mediterranean coastline like Abu Qir Bay and Lake Idku, or Lake Burullus and Lake Manzala, or possibly an ancient Lake Tanis. During the Ethiopic War (1854 BC), the Casluhim and Caphtorim of the eastern Nile delta were destroyed as a distinct people and survivors were displaced along with groups travelling by sea to homestead islands (and became known as Keftiu) while others travelled up the coast to Canaan and joined their Philistine kinsmen.

> *And the Avims which dwelled in Hazerim* [villages]*, even to Azzah* [Gaza]*, the Caphtorims, which came forth out of Caphtor, destroyed them, and dwelled in their stead. (Deuteronomy 2:23)*

Some groups of Sea Peoples were displaced Egyptians. The Peleset/Philistines were attempting to return to their native homeland. After understanding their plight, Rameses III allowed the refugees to rebuild and settle around the forts of the Sinai Peninsula on the Mediterranean and in the pentapolis of the Philistines: Gaza, Ashkelon, Ashdod, Gath, and Ekron, which the Israelites had conquered soon after Joshua's campaigns.[680]

Upon the burnt ashes of Judah's conquests, the Israelites had built new cities with 4-room houses and made a monochrome pottery similar to Mycenaean IIIC. But they were displaced by the Sea People Philistines who made bichrome pottery.

The Philistines were more advanced in ceramic, iron-work, and architecture than the Israelites as were many of the other Sea Peoples. From the base camp in Amurru, Sea Peoples either conquered or made an alliance with Hazor and began making iron chariots.

---

http://www.specialtyinterests.net/harris.html, accessed 11/3/2010
678 Genesis 10:13-14 "*Mizraim begat . . . Casluhim, out of whom came Philistim and Caphtorim.*"
679 Amos 9:7 and Jeremiah 47:4 ". . . the Philistines, the remnant of the country of Caphtor."
680 Judges 3:3 and 1:17-19 Judah and Simeon drove out Philistines from Gaza, Ashkelon, and Ekron (1426).

Pharaohs Rameses III – IX Overview

Rameses III was the last great New Kingdom pharaoh, but his end was a rocky one. A harem conspiracy failed to end his life. Twenty years after the major eruption (1290 BC), Egypt could not feed its elite tomb workers at Deir el Medina who went on strike and wrote a letter to the vizier declaring they would not work until their wheat rations were met.[681]

Conditions for the artisans improved under Rameses IV to the point he doubled their workforce to 120.[682] In his third year he sent Ramessesnahkt, the high priest of Amun, to lead over 9,000 men to quarry at Wadi Hammamat, a 200 km waterway connecting the Red Sea to the bend of the Nile north of Thebes.[683] During the first year of Rameses' V reign, the artisans stopped working for fear of "the enemy" attacking them.[684] Libyan raiders were threatening Thebes, and Ramessesnakht assumed more power. Ramessesnakht acquired gold for Rameses' VII and IX.

Egypt's power continued to decline under Rameses VI and VII. Rameses VI reduced the artisans back to 60, and was the last king of the New Kingdom whose name was attested in the Sinai.[685] Rameses VIII was one of the last sons of Rameses III, and made way for his grandson, Rameses IX, to become pharaoh. During Rameses' IX 16th year, investigations were made into tomb robberies in the Valley of the Kings.[686] People no longer considered the pharaohs as gods, and hunger drove them to loot their tombs.

The Amalekites

Amalek was the grandson of Esau who dwelt in the Negev of Canaan.[687] They were the first nation to attack Israel during the first years of their exodus.[688]

Then came Amalek, and fought with Israel in Rephidim. . . . And the LORD said to Moses, Write this for a memorial in a book, and rehearse it in the ears of Joshua: for I will utterly put out the remembrance of Amalek from under heaven. . . . the LORD will have war with Amalek from generation to generation. (Exodus 17:8, 14-16)[689]

After Othniel died and Israel rejected God, Elohim sent Amalekites against Israel and made Israel subject to Moab.[690] A generation doesn't go by without war with Amalek. Amalek joined the Midianites to oppress Israel for seven years prior to Gideon's judgeship.

---

681 "Deir el Medina", http://en.wikipedia.org/wiki/Deir_el_Medina#Strike, accessed 11/5/10
682 Papyrus Turin 1891 recto attributed to the second year of Rameses IV.
683 "Turin Papyrus Map", http://en.wikipedia.org/wiki/Turin_papyrus, accessed 11/5/10. The expedition is recorded on the first geological map with the source of the Nile (south) at the top.
684 "Rameses V", http://en.wikipedia.org/wiki/Ramesses_V, Turin Papyrus Cat. 2044, accessed 11/5/10
685 Grimal, Nicolas, *A History of Ancient Egypt*, Blackwell Books, 1992, p. 288
686 "Abbot Papyrus", http://en.wikipedia.org/wiki/Abbott_Papyrus, accessed 11/5/10
687 Genesis 36:8-12 and Numbers 13:29
688 Numbers 14:25-45 When Israelites disobediently attacked Canaan from the south after rejecting report.
689 Deuteronomy 25:16-19 Moses reminds them again to wipe out Amalek.
690 Judges 3:13-14

The Midianites

The Midianites were descendants of Abraham through his wife Keturah[691] who settled east of the Gulf of Aqaba in what is now northwestern Saudi Arabia. Moses fled to the land of Midian where he met YHWH on Mount Sinai.[692] The Israelites travelled through the land of Midian during their exodus, and the tribe of Jethro, Moses' father-in-law, known as the Kenites joined them.[693] Other Midianites did not welcome 3 million Israelites tromping through their land and camping on it. These elders of Midian made an alliance with Moab to hire the prophet Balaam, son of Beor, to curse the Israelites, but instead, Balaam blessed them and cursed the Amalekites and Kenites.

> *Out of Jacob shall come he that shall have dominion, and shall destroy him that remains of the city. And when he looked on Amalek, he took up his parable, and said, Amalek was the first of the nations; but his latter end shall be that he perish for ever. And he looked on the Kenites, and took up his parable, and said, Strong is your dwelling place, and you put your nest in a rock. Nevertheless the Kenite shall be wasted, until Assur shall carry you away captive. (Numbers 24:19-22)*

Balaam told the king of Moab how to conquer his enemies by corrupting them.[694] The Israelites brought a curse and a plague upon themselves by worshipping Baalpeor, and committing fornication with Midianite women. This betrayal and corruption was answered by God's command to smite the Midianites.[695]

> *And the LORD spoke to Moses, saying, Avenge the children of Israel of the Midianites: . . . Of every tribe a thousand, throughout all the tribes of Israel, shall you send to the war. . . . and they slew all the [adult] males. And they slew the kings of Midian . . . Balaam also the son of Beor they slew with the sword. And the children of Israel took all the women of Midian captives, and their little ones, and took the spoil of all their cattle, and all their flocks, and all their goods. And <u>they burnt all their cities wherein they dwelled, and all their goodly **castles**, with fire</u>. (Numbers 31:1-10)*

This war occurred at the end of 1452 BC, and archaeologists should find burnt strata of "*castles*" (fortresses or palaces). The "*little ones*" grew up and had children of their own until they once again became a strong people by 1298 BC; strong enough to now oppress those who had killed their great grand-parents. Amalekites of the south and others from the east joined them to overrun and destroy Israel, forcing the Israelites into hiding.[696]

---

691 Genesis 25:4
692 Exodus 2:15; 3:1-6
693 Numbers 10:29 Moses invited brother-in-law to join him. Judges 1:16 They lived in Judah near Arad.
694 Numbers 31:16
695 Numbers 25:1-17
696 Judges 6:2-5

Pharaohs of the Bible

Gideon (1291-1251 BC) judged Israel during reigns of Rameses III - IX

*And the children of Israel did evil in the sight of the LORD: and the LORD delivered them into the hand of Midian seven years.[1298-1291] . . . and because of the Midianites the children of Israel made them the dens which are in the mountains, and caves, and strong holds. . . . And it came to pass, when the children of Israel cried to the LORD because of the Midianites, That the LORD sent a prophet to the children of Israel, which said to them, Thus said the LORD God of Israel, I brought you up from Egypt, and brought you forth out of the house of bondage; . . . And I said to you, I am the LORD your God; fear not the gods of the Amorites, in whose land you dwell: but you have not obeyed my voice. . . . <u>Gideon threshed wheat by the wine press, to hide it from the Midianites</u>. And the angel of the LORD appeared to him, and said to him, The LORD is with you, you mighty man of valor. . . . Go in this your might, and you shall save Israel from the hand of the Midianites: have not I sent you? . . . Then Gideon built an altar there to the LORD, and called it Jehovahshalom: to this day it is yet in **Ophrah** of the Abiezrites. (Judges 6:1-24)*

This Ophrah may have been Ephron in east Manasseh, about 15 miles east of Beth Shean.

Then all the Midianites and the Amalekites and the children of the east were gathered together, and went over, and pitched in the valley of Jezreel. But the Spirit of the LORD came on Gideon, and he blew a trumpet; and Abiezer was gathered after him. And he sent messengers throughout all Manasseh; who also was gathered after him: and he sent messengers to Asher, and to Zebulun, and to Naphtali; and they came up to meet them. (Judges 6:33-35)

The Jezreel valley is where the army of Sisera was destroyed by Barak's army and the Kishon river, and then Sisera fled only to be killed by a Kenite woman. Now different enemies established themselves upon the same battlefield. The local tribes responded to Gideon's summons, and he set up camp south of the enemy. Then God had Gideon sent thousands of his troops home until only 300 were left, so that they would not claim a victory in their own strength. God caused confusion in the enemy's camp, and routed them before Gideon. Gideon asked Ephraim to stop the enemy's retreat, and they killed two of Midian's princes along with others.[697]

As they continued to pursue the enemy, Gideon sought bread for his men from the towns of Succoth and Penuel, which both refused (because of a recent famine which sent Naomi to Moab). After catching the enemy, Gideon punished the elders of Succoth with thorns and briers, and slew the men of Penuel.[698] Upon interrogating the kings of Midian, Gideon

---

697 Judges 7
698 Judges 8:4-17 120,000 of the enemy died initially, and Gideon's men pursued the remaining 15,000.

discovered they killed his brothers, so he killed them and took the ornaments from their necks and their camels. They worshipped the moon god and wore gold crescents or whole moons, as well as gold earrings. Gideon requested all the earrings as his booty and made an ephod out of it.[699]

Gideon refused to become king or establish a dynasty, but promoted the LORD as King. Gideon judged Israel in peace for forty years (1291-1251 BC), during which time he acquired many wives and had 71 sons. He also had a son, Abimelech (means father-king), through a concubine in Shechem. Abimelech did want to be king, and he killed 70 brothers to establish himself as such among the people of Shechem. After ruling Shechem for three years, he sought to broaden his domain, but the people turned against him and ran to the fortress temple of Berith for protection. Abimelech set the place on fire and killed them and hoped to do the same in Thebez where he was killed.[700]

Ancient Shechem is Tell Balata in a mountain pass between Mt Gerizim and Mt Ebal. Archaeologists uncovered the large city gate with three sets of piers and two chambers,[701] and a large fortress temple with walls 17 feet thick[702] – the one Abimelech burned.

Tola & Jair judged Israel in reigns of Rameses IX - XI

And after Abimelech there arose to defend Israel Tola the son of Puah, the son of Dodo, a man of Issachar; and he dwelled in Shamir in mount Ephraim. And he judged Israel twenty and three years, and died, and was buried in Shamir. And after him arose Jair, a Gileadite, and judged Israel twenty and two years. (Jdgs. 10:1-3)

This period of 45 years appears to have been a peaceful one in Israel. Tola judged Israel from 1251-1228 BC during the reigns of pharaoh Rameses IX - XI. Jair judged Israel from 1228-1206 BC during the reign of Rameses XI.

Jair was descended from the Jair who settled the sixty cities of Argob after the Israelites slew all the inhabitants of Bashan and renamed them Bashan-Havothjair.[703] To distinguish him from his ancestor, he was surnamed Bedan,[704] but in like fashion he conquered thirty cities and named them Havothjair.[705] Four years into Jair's judgeship, the children of Israel forsook YHWH and turned back to foreign gods, so Yahweh sent Ammonites to attack them and placed His people in subjection to the Philistines for 18 years (1224-1206 BC).[706]

---

699 Judges 8:18-27
700 Judges 8:22-31; 9:1-57 Jotham, Gideon's youngest son, escaped to Beer.
701 Judges 9:35 "The entering of the gate of the city" implies it was more than a simple gate.
702 "The Period of Judges", http://www.truthnet.org/Biblicalarcheology/7/Judges-Bible-Archeology.htm, accessed 9/15/10 also Murphy-O'Connor, Jerome, *The Holy Land: an Oxford archaeological guide from earliest times to 1700*, p.496 for a schematic.
703 Numbers 32:41 and Deut. 3:4+14
704 1 Samuel 12:11 and 1 Chronicles 7:17
705 Judges 10:4 *Havoth* means villages.
706 Judges 10:6-9

Rameses IX and the Tomb Robbers

Rameses IX
Keith Shengili-Roberts

Ramessesnakht, high priest of Amun-Re at Karnak, began gaining power through his extended family which included the mayor of Karnak, Paser III. (Karnak is eastern Thebes; the tombs called Valley of the Kings are in western Thebes.) In Rameses' 9th year, royal tombs were robbed by temple workers. Vizier Khamwese investigated: the robbers were caught and punished, and a delegation was sent to reseal the tomb of Rameses VI.[707] In the tenth year of Rameses IX, Ramessesnakht's son, Amenhotep, took over his dead father's posts as high priest and vizier. Nibmare-nacht became vizier in his 14th year, so Rameses IX had several viziers. Rameses IX established his son, Nebmaatre, as high priest of Re in Heliopolis, and built several monuments there.[708]

About the same time the tomb workers of Deir el-Medina requested safety from continual nomadic raids, and their grain rations from the storerooms of the temple. The Abbott Papyrus stated in Rameses' 16th year, his own tomb and that of his son, Mentuherkhepeshef, were robbed and investigations made by Paser and vizier Khaemwese.

Paser implied his subordinate mayor of western Thebes, Paweraa, was either complicit or negligent. The Abbott Papyrus also recorded "year 1 . . . corresponding to year 19" twice, separated by a month and two weeks in "the first season" which alluded to the brief period of regnal overlap when Rameses IX died in his 19th year and Rameses X began his rule.[709] The Mayer A Papyrus begins: "Year 1, of *whm-mswt*, fourth month of the third season, day 13. On this day occurred the examination of the thieves of the tomb . . ."[710] and records the prosecution of the thieves listed on the Abbott Papyrus. *Whm-mswt* means "rebirths", as the gods are considered reborn in the new pharaoh.

Paweraa cleared his name before Paser stating that only one tomb had been raided and those robbers imprisoned, while the seals on the other tombs were intact (but the tombs had been broken into from the rear). The next year Paser and Amenhotep recovered tomb artifacts from the tomb workers in a house to house search.[711] The hungry artisans knew the locations and points of access to the tombs.

When Rameses IX died in 1237 BC, only half of his tomb decorations were completed, and the later half were done with less care. His tomb lies opposite the tomb of Rameses II.

---

707 Grimal, Nicholas, *A History of Ancient Egypt*, Blackwell Publishing, 1988, p. 289; also Abbott Papyrus
708 Wiki articles on Rameses IX, Ramssesnahkt, Amenhotep, and Nebmaatre
709 Terry E., letter on "The Renaissance Era" at http://disc.yourwebapps.com/discussion.cgi?disc=177754;article=9635; accessed 11/16/10
710 Mayer Papyri at http://www.reshafim.org.il/ad/egypt/texts/mayer_papyri.htm, accessed 11/16/10
711 "Tomb Robbery and the 20th Dynasty Trials", http://egyptian-mysteries.com/?q=node/49, accessed 11/11/10. Based upon the Abbot papyrus, the Amherst papyrus, and the Mayer papyri.

High Priests of Amun-Re in Thebes

High priests coronated new pharaohs. The pharaoh's wife or daughter became Amun's wife, able to produce a god-king. The high priest was appointed by pharaoh and acted as his political advisor. High priests married, had children, and passed their appointment to their male heir. His primary service was to the gods. He appointed as many priests/priestesses as were needed to serve in the various temples. They began as wab priests, and then were elevated to prophets of varying levels with the first prophet being the high priest of Amun (HPA).

High priest Amenhotep and Rameses IX at Karnak

Usually a high priest was depicted kneeling before pharaoh, or a smaller size than pharaoh, but an equal-sized Amenhotep is shown just one step below Rameses IX.

The high priests of Amun owned most of the ships and shipping. They owned slaves and land (15% - 80%). They rented out land to people who repaid them in grain and livestock. The high priest was usually the overseer of granaries which included grain taxation, rationing and protection (especially of precious metals).

Thutmose III before the gods in Amada, Nubia

As high priest, Ramessesnakht wrote a letter addressed to three princes of Nubia: Anytun, Senut, and Terbadydy. He recounted how Nubian bowmen joined with bowmen from the Nubian temple to Amun-re in Amada under Ramessesnakht's command to defeat the gold-seeking bedouin from Syria. Members of this Nubian temple police force were called Medjay.[712] He encouraged them to be diligent and to deliver the gold safely to pharaoh.[713] The Egyptian army was too weak on its own to repel the raiders; and needed the temple guard, accustomed to acquiring taxes by force and protecting payments, and other Nubian warriors to do so.

---

712 Medja, in northern Sudan, was known for its warriors who became a police force in Egypt called Medjay.
713 Dollinger, Andre', "Letter by Ramses-nakht concerning supplies for the troops protecting gold miners in Nubia", http://www.reshafim.org.il/ad/egypt/texts/ramses-nakht.htm, accessed 11/11/10

King's Son of Kush (KSOK)

After Ramessesnakht died, Wentawuat became Rameses' IX viceroy to Nubia to protect gold deliveries. Wentawuat would have lead the Medjay to rout the bedouin. In addition to "king's son of Kush" (KSOK), charioteer, and steward; Wentawuat was also given the title of high priest of Amun and Khnum at Thebes, and first prophet of Amun since he was leading temple guards. But most importantly, he was "overseer of the gold lands of Amen-Re".[714] After Wentawuat died in the 18th year of Rameses IX, Piankh took over his positions.

Panehsy, the black prince of the south

In Egyptian, *panehsi* means "the black". [Nubia and Kush were both lands of Negroes south of Elephantine (Aswan) which are now Sudan and Ethiopia.] Panehsy was a black prince who worked with Egypt's KSOK from the 11th year of Rameses IX to the 29th year of Rameses XI. When Rameses IX discovered Amenhotep had a relief of himself chiselled at the same scale as himself, Amenhotep "was suppressed" for nine months. Between the sixth and ninth month, barbarians seized the Temple at Medinet Habu and a "portable chest" of valuables was misappropriated and set on fire. Rameses IX sent Panehsy with his Nubian/Kushite warriors to quell the attack. Panehsy pursued the thieves 250 miles north to Hartai (now Al Qeis) and killed them but destroyed Hartai in the process; it was a slaughter which earned Panehsy an evil glyph affixed to his name. Amenhotep either fled or died during the siege.[715] According to the P. Turin 1986, Panehsy became KSOK after Piankh died and served the 12th - 17th years of Rameses XI.

Late Ramesside Letters

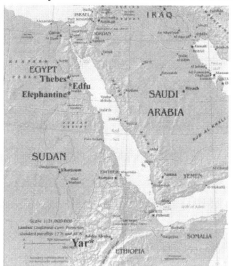

The Late Ramesside Letters (LRL) are a group of roughly fifty official documents spanning the reigns of Rameses IX, X, and XI.[716] Only two of them give a year but not the name of the pharaoh: #37 in which chantress Hennutawi wrote in "year 2" (of Rameses IX) of strict grain measurement, grain in a sealed chest, and grain which she provided for offerings, and #9 in which scribe Dhutmose wrote in "year 10" (of Rameses XI) of being abandoned in Yar. The "Mayor of west Ne, Paweraa," is mentioned in #33. In #4 Dhutmose noted his superior, general Piankh (#13, 28, 40), "will go up to meet Panehsy".

---

714 Reisner, George A., "The Viceroys of Ethiopia (II)" in The Journal of Egyptian Archaeology, Vol. 6, No. 1. (Jan., 1920)

715 Wente, Edward, "The Suppression of High Priest Amenhotep", Journal of Near East Studies, Vol. 25, 1966, http://www.jstor.org/pss/543967, accessed 11/31/10

716 Wente, Edmund, translation of "Late Ramesside Letters", University of Chicago, 1967.
   One letter, #41, was written during King Herihor's reign. (see appendix C for the Late Ramesside Letters)

Theban Necropolis scribe Dhutmose placed Wenamun and other young wab-priests under the supervision of scribe Butehamon (#12), Dhutmose's younger brother or son. Dhutmose, nick-named Tjaroy, was sent to "Yar of Namekhay" (#1), a "far-off land" (#9). 1,100 miles south of Aswan (Elephantine) is the city Nekemte, Ethiopia; and 25 miles further south in the "hills" is the town of Arjo. The area is known for its gold and platinum. I suggest Dhutmose was sent to oversee the gold mines in Yar (Arjo, Ethiopia). When HPA Amenhotep was suppressed (years 17-18 of Rameses IX), Dhutmose was recalled to Thebes, and 2nd prophets Hekanufe and Penhershefi took his place.[717]

The island of Elephantine and its fort stood at the border between Egypt and Nubia, just before the first cataract of the Nile. It was an excellent defensive site for a city and its location made it a natural cargo transfer point for river trade. In LRL #2 Dhutmose stated, he left his superior, Piankh, in Elephantine in the company of Herere, his wife. Elephantine was likely the home of Piankh and Herere. Year 19 of Rameses' IX death was year one of *whm-mswt* of Rameses X.[718]

Rameses X (1237-1228 BC)

Rameses X inherited the tomb trials and the foreign incursions into Upper Egypt. In the third year of Rameses X, the artisans did not work on the tombs for several days because of the Libyan marauders known as Meshwesh. Libyans also expanded into the western Nile delta. Problems delivering grain rations to workmen also continued. Panehsy ordered Dhutmose to collect grain from royal domains and temple estates and entrust it to Paweraa and Henuttawi to meet the needs of the workmen.[719]

A Karnak oracle mentioning Piankh is dated to Year 7 of the *whm-mswt*[720] of Rameses X. In LRL #28, general Piankh[721] is also given the titles "high priest of Amun, Viceroy of Kush, overseer of the southern foreign lands, overseer of granaries of Pharaoh's granaries, and leader of Pharaoh's troops."[722]

Piankh ordered chief necropolis scribes, Butehamon and Tjaroy (Dhutmose's nickname), to remove debris from a tomb entrance and to have an inspector ready upon his return from the south. Dhutmose and Butehamon's names are visible graffitos throughout the Valley of the Kings as they performed their duties to locate and loot tombs,[723] and rebury the mummies in more secretive caches. Rameses X died in his ninth year. Papyrus Turin 2034 stated year 1 of *whm-mswt* corresponded to year 9 to indicate the gods reborn in Rameses XI.[724]

---

717 LRL #23 and 24. See appendix for further explanations and chronological order of all these letters.
718 Dollinger, Andre, Mayer Papyri at http://www.reshafim.org.il/ad/egypt/texts/mayer_papyri.htm
719 Papyrus Turin 1895
720 Nims, C.F., JNES 7 (1948), pp. 157-162
721 Piankh by name in #13, and simply as General in #18-21 and 34-35.
722 Wente, Edmund, "Late Ramesside Letters", University of Chicago, 1967, p. 59
723 Mertz, Barbara, *Temples, Tombs and Hieroglyphs*, 1964, p.267. from Late Ramesside Letters (papyri)
724 E., Terry, http://disc.yourwebapps.com/discussion.cgi?disc=177754;article=9635, accessed 11/12/10

Pharaohs of the Bible

Clarity Chronology Detail-A of the end of 20th Dynasty

Thebes

Pharaoh	Rameses IX up to 9th year	Rameses IX 10th year	Rameses IX 11th 12th years	RamesesIX 14th - 16th years	RamesesIX 17th - 18th years	Rameses IX 19th year, and he died	Rameses X 1st year (Mayer Papyri)
Vizier	Khamwese	Khamwese	Khamwese	Nibmare-nacht 14-16	Khamwese (went to Byblos?)	Nibmare-nacht 19th year	
HPA High Priest of Amun	Ramesses-nakht, who dies	Amenhotep (rewarded for Karnak)	Amenhotep	Amenhotep	Amenhotep suppressed 9 months	Nesuamon	Nesuamon
2nd prophet	Amenhotep	Nesuamon	Hekanufe	Penhershefi	Nesuamon	Hekanufe	
KSOK Viceroy to Kush/Nubia	Wentawuat	Wentawuat	Wentawuat	Wentawuat	Wentawuat	Piankh	Piankh
Chief scribes of Necropolis	Esamon & Dhutmose	Esamon & Dhutmose	Efnamon & Dhutmose	Khaemhedj &Dhutmos	Dhutmos& Butehamon	Dhutmose & Butehamon	Dhutmose & Butehamon
Mayor of Thebes east	Paser	Paser	Paser				
Mayor of Thebes west	Paweraa	Paweraa	Paweraa	Paweraa		Psmennakht	
Nubian			Panehsy	Panehsy	Panehsy	Panehsy	Panehsy

Clarity Chronology Detail-B of end of 20th Dynasty

Thebes

Pharaoh	Rameses X up to 2nd year	RamesesX 9th year, dies	Rameses XI 1st year	Rameses XI 7th year	Rameses XI 11th year	Rameses XI 12th year	Rameses XI 19th year	Rameses XI 29th year, dies
Vizier	Nibmare-nacht				Piankh		Herihor	Herihor
HPA High Priest of Amun	Nesuamon	Nesuamon	Piankh	Piankh 7th	Piankh	Herihor, Piankh's son-in-law	Herihor	Herihor
General	Piankh	Piankh	Piankh	Piankh	Piankh	Herihor	Herihor	Herihor
KSOK Viceroy to Kush/Nubia	Piankh	Piankh	Piankh	Piankh 7th-11th y	Piankh 11th y Piankh dies	Panhesy 12th - 17th y (Turin P.)	Herihor	Herihor
Chief scribes of Necropolis	Dhutmose & Bute-hamon	Dhutmose & Bute-hamon	Khaemhedj & Butehamon	Khaem-hedj & Buteham	Dhutmose & Bute-hamon	Dhutmose & Bute-hamon	Dhutmose & Bute-hamon	Dhutmose & Butehamon
Nubian	Panehsy	Panehsy	Panehsy	Panehsy	Panehsy		Panehsy	Panehsy

". . . by year 7 of the repetition of births, the high priest named in an item of correspondence is Piankh."
(*The Third Intermediate Period in Egypt* by Nick Thom, April 2008, p. 4)

Rameses XI (1228-1199 BC)

Ramesses' XI lineage is uncertain. He married Tentamun who bore daughters Tentamun and Henuttawi. Smendes, an official in Lower Egypt, later married young Tentamun.

Piankh died in Rameses' 11th year, and Panehsy became viceroy of Kush in the 12th year. Rameses' XI plan to "protect" the mummies from desecration while replenishing Egypt's treasury with their tomb furnishings continued, and he used his own tomb as a workshop.[725] King's Valley tomb #35 (KV35) was the tomb of Amenhotep II and his son, but it was used as a mummy cache for Thutmose IV, Amenhotep III and Queen Tiye, Merenptah, Seti II, Siptah, Rameses' IV-VI, and a few others yet to be identified.[726]

Rameses XI sent Panehsy an order in his 17th year to cooperate with the king's butler,[727] and to relinquish taxation and granary duties in Thebes back to the high priest who was now general Herihor, Piankh's son-in-law.[728] They worked out the logistics by Rameses' XI 18th year (1210 BC), in a way which allowed Panehsy to retain the honor of his people and pharaoh. Herihor was then given the titles which Piankh once held, thus fully combining military and sacred power again. Rameses' XI 27th year is inscribed on an Abydos stela.

Dhutmose died, and Butehamon served "Years 10, 11, 12, 13 of an unspecified ruler, but in company with Pinudjem I as high priest, in a series of Theban graffiti."[729] Butehamon served as chief necropolis scribe with Ankhefenamun. The 'unspecified ruler' was Herihor.

Herihor, HPA then king

King Herihor

Herihor began as vizier to Rameses XI, and after the death of Piankh he became HPA at Thebes. After his arrangement with Panhesy, he also served Rameses XI as KSOK. After the death of Rameses XI, he served as king. On walls at Karnak's Khonsu temple, high priest Herihor presents offerings in his own name, not that of pharaoh Rameses XI. Next, Herihor in the high priest's robe with the pharaoh's double crown and royal uraeus (cobra - pictured) had his high priest title and name in a royal cartouches.[730]

At the ruins of the temple of Mut (*Mut el-Krarab*) in the Dakhla Oasis, 140 miles west of Thebes, is a block of an HPA with the broad collar and double shebyu collar (in picture) wearing a short Nubian wig. The block ends at the eye.[731] In Karnak, Herihor is depicted once wearing a short Nubian wig.[732]

---

725 "Twentieth Dynasty", http://www.touregypt.net/hdyn20b.htm, accessed 11/12/10
726 Sitek, Dariusz, *KV35*, http://www.narmer.pl/kv/kv35en.htm, accessed 11/12/10. Sealed with blocks dated with year 13.
727 Turin Papyrus 1896
728 In LRL #35, general Piankh wrote to Nuteme, which could be his nick name for his daughter Nodjmet. Nodjmet later married Herihor.
729 Kitchen, K. A., *The Third Intermediate Period*, 1973, p. 38, also see Spiegelberg footnote
730 Gardiner, Allen, *Egypt of the Pharaohs*, 1961, p. 304
731 Kaper, Olaf, *Epigraphic Evidence from the Dakhleh Oasis in the Libyan Period*, The Libyan Period in Egypt, 2009, pp. 154-5
732 Kaper, Olaf, ibid., footnote #27, *Scenes of King Herihor in the Court*, 1979, plate 33

Nodjmet Papyrus of she and Herihor

Like Rameses II and III, Herihor has a wall devoted to his family of 19 sons and 19 daughters, and his wife queen Nodjmet. The names of his sons begin with typical Egyptian names of Ankhefenmut and Ankhefenamun; but his 7th and 17th sons are Masaharta and Osorkon which are Libyan names. Later in his reign Herihor may have made a marriage alliance with Libya to keep his western boundary secure. Although the HPA normally passed the position to his son, I think Panehsy may have made a condition that one of Piankh's sons would become HPA after Rameses XI died. So when Herihor declared himself king in his sixth year, Pinedjem became HPA. Smendes remained a trusted official and treasurer in Tanis. When Herihor died, both Smendes and Pinedjem I declared themselves kings.

Because of *whm-mswt* debates, many Egyptologists do not accept that high priest Herihor became king Herihor. They point to the fact that all "administrative documents" are in Herihor's name with titles of High Priest, King's Son of Kush, or Vizier[733], but not King; never reasoning that as king, he would have appointed others to take over his administrative duties – like elevating Smendes to vizier. Other kings are accepted with little or no physical evidence, whereas Herihor has his name in cartouches on several walls and columns as "king of upper and lower Egypt". Sheshonk I didn't call himself pharaoh until his fifth year, and I suspect Herihor called himself pharaoh soon after his fifth year because of the Wenamun fiasco in trying to purchase lumber without the title.

Not born of royalty, Herihor did not call himself pharaoh, but had the oracle at Khonsu proclaim his right to rule engraved on a stela there.[734] Herihor has a coronation scene and images of fulfilling his royal duty by offering Maat. He is even shown celebrating the Heb Sed Festival,[735] which celebrates a pharaoh's thirtieth regnal year. Th heb-sed festival was a jubilee year of no taxation; thus all people prayed their pharaoh would have a long life.[736] To be prepared for his departure to the next life, he needed a sacred barque (wooden ship) to transport him. This ship was also central to the annual Festival of Opet and the Sed Festival. Securing wood from Byblos was the purpose of the *Report of Wenamun*.

Report of Wenamun (same as Wenamon)

On the official papyri of the Late Ramesside Letters, Wenamun is listed among 9 young wab-priests in the early years of Rameses IX to be placed under Butehamon's supervision, and as a watchman with doorkeeper Dhutmose.[737] *The Report of Wenamun* and *The Letter*

---

733 Until Rameses III, it was common for pharaoh to have one vizier in the north and another in the south.
734 Blyth, Elizabeth, *Karnak: Evolution of a Temple*, 2006, p. 182
735 Blyth, Elizabeth, *Karnak: Evolution of a Temple*, 2006, p. 183
736 If Rameses XI had reigned 30 years or more, there would have been some memorial of it.
737 Wente, Edmund, "Late Ramesside Letters", University of Chicago, 1967; #12 and #47 respectively

of Wermai were discovered together.[738] The first describes how in "year five" Wenamun was given money and a purchase order for Lebanese cedar wood by Herihor, the high priest of Amun, to "the organizer of the country" Nesbanebded (Smendes) and Tentamun in Tanis who secured a ship and sent him on his way. When Wenamun's shipped docked in the "Tjekker-town" of Dor, his money was stolen. He told prince Beder "Search for my money, for indeed the money belongs to Amen-Re', King of the Gods, the lord of the lands, it belongs to Nesbanebded, it belongs to Herihor my lord and to the other great ones of Egypt."[739] Wenamun eventually arrived in Byblos broke, and tried to convince prince Tjikarbaal to fulfill the order in exchange for long-life from Amun, but he scoffed and waited for more funds to arrive from Smendes and Tentamun before providing the timber. While Wenamun waited several months, Tjikarbaal reminded him about the envoys Khamweset (part of Rameses' IX name, and name of his vizier) sent who were delayed there 17 years until they died and were buried. Tjikarbaal and his cupbearer derisively used the word 'pharaoh'. Wenamun neither used the term 'pharaoh' nor 'king' except for Amun as king of the gods, and himself as Amun's messenger.

It is apparent throughout Wenamun's account that there is no one called 'pharaoh' in Egypt at this time. Even Tjikarbaal's cupbearer seemed to know this, and made a deprecating joke about it. Wenamun referred to Herihor as "my lord" and "high priest of Amun". The names of Smendes and Tentamun appear in Wenamun's report.[740] He doesn't refer to Smendes singularly, but always in connection with Tentamun. Tentamun was the daughter of Rameses XI, so Smendes married into the royal line, and together they administered northern Egypt.

I suggest Wenamun's "year five" belonged to Herihor. Herihor tried to reign as high priest, but after the purchasing problems it caused Wenamun abroad, he took on the title of pharaoh. Herihor may have resorted to building a barge from pine since the cedar was taking over a year to procure. "Herihor's inscriptions in the Khonsu temple actually stating that he made a new barge/barque of pine used in the Feast of Opet"[741] solidifies Wenamun's story.[742]

Barque at Ramesseum

The Letter of Wermai was written by an old man who had been accused of crimes and expelled from home. This could possibly be Wenamun changing his name after false accusations, or maybe he wrote on behalf of his father or another relative.

---

738 "Story of Wenamun" wikipedia.com, accessed 11/5/10. Second papyrus is also titled "Tale of Woe".
Ritner, Robert. K., *The Libyan Anarchy: Inscriptions from Egypt's third Intermediate Period*, 2009, p. 87
"The format of the papyrus itself conforms to that of official documents," regarding story of Wenamun.
739 "Story of Wenamun", http://realhistoryww.com/world_history/ancient/Misc/Egypt/s_Wenamen.htm
740 Ritner, Robert. K., *The Libyan Anarchy: Inscriptions from Egypt's third Intermediate Period*, 2009, p. 88
741 Wente, Edward, "The Oriental Institute of the University of Chicago Studies in ancient oriental civilization #33," 1967, p. 4 footnote. Pharaoh was often coronated again at the Feast of Opet.
742 Wenamun may be the apprentice scribe "Wenemdiamun" who received instructions on letter writing detailing the loading of barges with timber in the Papyrus Lansing.

Jepthah judged Israel during reigns of Rameses XI and Herihor

After being in subjection to the Philistines for 18 years (1224-1206 BC) and suffering attacks from the Ammonites, the Israelites finally confessed their sins of following other gods, and pleaded with YHWH to deliver them again.[743] Jepthah was a bastard who was driven from his home in Gilead eastward to the land of Tob, but he was also a mighty warrior who knew Israel's basic history. The elders of Gilead sought him out to be their captain against the Ammonites. Distrustful of those who had formerly banished him, he made them take an oath at Mizpeh before the LORD that they would indeed establish him as their leader.[744] That was in 1206 BC.

Jepthah sent an inquiry to the people of Ammon as to why they were instigating this war with Israel, and they replied because Israel took the lands of the Amorites where they dwelt when they came into Canaan and they demanded the lands be returned. Jepthah sent a message correctly reciting the history of how the children of Israel requested to pass through the lands of the Amorites peacefully but were refused by king Sihon, so YHWH delivered their people and lands into Israelite hands.[745] Gilead refers to the lands on the east of the Jordon possessed by Gad, Reuben, and half of Manasseh; but formerly half belonged to Sihon and half to king Og.[746] Though 1451 – 1206 = 245 years, Jepthah rounded it up to to 300 to rub it in their faces:

> *While Israel dwelled in Heshbon and her towns, and in Aroer and her towns, and in all the cities that be along by the coasts of Arnon, three hundred years? why therefore did you not recover them within that time? Why I have not sinned against you, but you do me wrong to war against me: the LORD the Judge be judge this day between the children of Israel and the children of Ammon. (Judges 11:26-27)*

Sadly, Jepthah learned the Canaanite rituals of human sacrifice in Tob, and vowed he would make a burnt sacrifice of whomever greeted him from his victory against the Ammonites, and paid his vow with his daughter.[747] This example led the Israelites back into pagan worship, and so God subjected them to the Philistines for 40 more years (1195-1155 BC). The Ephramites on the west of the Jordan did not help the men of Gilead quell the Ammonites, and yet feigned as if they would have, in order to pick a fight with Jepthah; so Jepthah's army killed 42,000 of them. Jepthah only served as Israel's judge for six years (1206-1200 BC).[748]

---

743 Judges 10:15-18
744 Judges 11:1-11
745 Judges 11:12-25
746 I Kings 4:19
747 Judges 11:26-40
748 Judges 12:1-7

Pharaohs of Israel's Judges

Ibzan, Elon, and Abdon judged Israel during the reign of Herihor

And after him Ibzan of Bethlehem judged Israel. And he had thirty sons, and thirty daughters, whom he sent abroad, and took in thirty daughters from abroad for his sons. And he judged Israel seven years. . . . And after him Elon, a Zebulonite, judged Israel; and he judged Israel ten years. . . . And after him Abdon the son of Hillel, a Pirathonite, judged Israel. And he had forty sons and thirty nephews, that rode on three score and ten ass colts: and he judged Israel eight years. (Judges 12:8-14)

Izban judged Israel from 1200-1193 BC, Elon from 1193-1183 BC, and Abdon from 1183 to 1175 BC; all during Herihor's reign. Pharaoh Herihor reigned from 1199-1169 BC as the first pharaoh of my dynasty 21A of Theban high priests.

Samson judged Israel during reigns of Pinedjem I and Smendes I

In Zorah, a man named Manoah had a barren wife to whom the angel of the LORD appeared and said, "*. . . you shall conceive, and bear a son; and no razor shall come on his head: for the child shall be a Nazarite to God from the womb: and he shall begin to deliver Israel out of the hand of the Philistines.*"[749] Manoah prayed the angel would return to give instructions how to raise such a son, and when He did, Manoah offered a burnt sacrifice unto YHWH on an altar.[750] The altar of Tel Tzora is not far from the tomb with gravestones of Manoah and Samson, and the northeast path ends at the lookout over the valley of Sorek.[751] Samson judged Israel for twenty years[752] (1175-1155 BC).

Samson's final act

Samson had several fights with Philistines; his most renown being that of slaying a thousand men with the jawbone of an ass.[753] During his judgeship he fell in love with a Philistine woman named Delilah who lived in the valley of Sorek. He told her his strength came from obedience to the command not to shave his head, and Delilah betrayed him for money.[754] The Philistines "*put out his eyes*" and bound him to a millstone in Gaza.[755] In time, Samson's hair grew back, and he was taken to the temple of Dagon to be mocked; but instead he asked God to give him vengeance on his enemies, and he pushed the main pillars out of place and brought down the roof, killing 3,000.[756]

---

749 Judges 13:5
750 Judges 13:8-23 The angel was a pre-incarnation of Yeshua, the "secret name"; for they had seen God.
751 "The Philistines are upon you, Samson," ynet travel; also see Judges 16:31.
752 Judges 15:20
753 Judges 15:14-19
754 Judges 16:1-20
755 Judges 16:21
756 Judges 16:22-30

Pharaohs of the Bible

Archaeologists found two Philistine temples: one at Tel Qasile (near Tel Aviv), and one in Tel Miqne (Gath, 21 miles south of Tel Aviv). Both temples contain two central stone bases six feet apart upon which wooden pillars supported the roof.[757] Tel Miqne's large public building was destroyed violently in stratum IVA in the 12th century BC of Samson.

The Unified Families of Dynasties 21 and 21A

Smendes I

After the 20th dynasty ended, Egypt was peacefully divided into two with the high priests of Amun reigning as kings in Thebes (21A dynasty) and descendants of Rameses XI reigning from Tanis in the eastern delta (21st dynasty).[758] The 21A dynasty began when Herihor coronated himself as pharaoh. He placed Piankh's son Pinedjem as high priest of Amun; and they both served for thirty years together at Thebes. Smendes and Tentamun began their reign as treasurers for Herihor as described in Wenamun's report.[759] Smendes wife was the daughter of Rameses XI, so they had a legal claim to royalty which they asserted after Herihor's death. Smendes I took the prenomen of Hedjkheperre Setepenre which would become popular in the next dynasty.

Pinedjem I became pharaoh when Herihor died. He had just as much claim to royalty because he married the devotee of Hathor, Duathathor-Henuttawy, also a daughter of Rameses XI. Her name is in a cartouche as queen on a door lintel and on a relief in the Khonsu temple in Karnak.[760] Pinedjem's sons Masaharta, Djedkhonsuefankh, and Menkheperre served as general and high priest of Amun at Thebes one after the other (the first two during Pinedjem's reign). After Pinedjem's death, Menkheperre also took on the role of pharaoh. Pinedjem and Henuttawy's son Psusennes I became pharaoh in Tanis after Amenemnisu, the son of Smendes and Tentamun,[761] who ruled after Smendes' death.

Menkheperre married his sister [ ]hetepi, and seven generations later a daughter named Mehetemweskhet was born. She married a Meshwesh chief named Sheshonk A and was the grandmother of Sheshonk I. Mehetemweskhet also married another man through whom 21st dynasty pharaoh Osorkon, the elder, was born.

The daughter of Psusennes I also married Menkheperre. Menkheperre's son, Smendes B, had a son who became pharaoh Pinedjem II. Pinedjem II married a daughter of Menkheperre, and their son, Psusennes II, became pharaoh. The daughter of Psusennes II married the son of Sheshonk I, Osorkon I. Thus dynasty 22 married into dynasty 21.

In addition to the genealogies there is an abundance of regnal year evidence from the

---

757 "The period of the Judges in Biblical Archeology" on Biblical Archaeology at www.truthnet.org
758 See appendix A for genealogy trees.
759 Ritner, Robert. K., *The Libyan Anarchy: Inscriptions from Egypt's' third Intermediate Period*, 2009, p. 88, 1/4 and 1/7
760 Dodson, Aidan & Hilton, Dyan, *The Complete Royal Families of Ancient Egypt*, Thames & Hudson, 2004, p. 206
761 Ibid., pp. 196-209

linen wrappings and tags (red leather mummy braces also called 'stola')[762] which included the name of the pharaoh in Tanis and the HPA in Thebes at the time of burial.[763] Andrzej Niwinski compiled an enormous amount of regnal data based upon the typology of yellow coffins of the high priests of Amun of dynasty 21A. During the 21st dynasty ornate tombs, which were being robbed, were abandoned for more ornate coffins placed into protected rock caches. [For a summary of Niwinski's regnal data, see pages 435-437, and for regnal and genealogy charts see pages 438-440 in Appendix B.]

Istemkheb

Tomb art applied to the coffins of the 21st dynasty

Duat-Hathor
Queen Henuttawy

Niwinski noted the richly ornate identical coffins of Duathathor-Henuttawy and Nodjmet, and a similarly gilded coffin of Pinudjem I who was husband and brother respectively.[764] They were gilded with gold and had red, green, and blue paste inlays. As the 21st dynasty progressed, wood and gold became very scarce.

Pharaoh and HPA Pinedjem I (dynasty 21A)

When pharaoh Herihor died, Smendes declared himself pharaoh, and Pinedjem I quickly had his son Masaharta replace him as HPA so that he could also proclaim himself pharaoh as his brother-in-law had done. Pinedjem's reliefs at the temple of Khonsu immediately follow those of pharaoh Herihor.

---

762 Taylor, John H., "Coffins as Evidence for a 'North-South Divide'," *The Libyan Period in Egypt*, Nederlands Institute, 2009, p. 389
763 Niwinski, Andrzej, *21st Dynasty Coffins from Thebes: Chronological Typology Studies*, 1988, p. 29
764 Niwinski, Andrzej, *21st Dynasty Coffins from Thebes: Chronological Typology Studies*, 1988, pp. 40, 49

Pharaohs of the Bible

Courtesy of Russian Academy of Sciences, Centre for Egyptological Studies
Coffin of Pinedjem I with gold adzed off

Ushabti box of Pinedjem I

A ushabti was a funerary figurine representing a slave to assist in the after-life. Ushabtis became numerous and common in the 21st dynasty. Groups of 4 ushabti can be seen on top of either side of Pinedjem's ushabti box.

Pinedjem I boasted of making more silver and gold monuments to Amun at Karnak than any other king.[765] Sadly, he acquired the silver and gold from tombs of kings from earlier dynasties in order to 'protect' them from tomb robbers. He also recycled their ornate coffins for his own deceased family and friends. In his eighth year Pinedjem I issued decrees to give "Osiris status" to Ahmose I and his son Siamun. In his sixteenth year he issued a dispatch to "renew the burial" of another, soon to be, poorer soul.[766] This was his method of official looting.

Later, someone else did to Pinedjem's coffin as he had done to others, by stripping off its gold gilding.

Pharaoh and HPA Menkheperre (dynasty 21A)

Besides King's Daughter, King's Wife, and King's Mother, Queen Duathathor-Henuttawy also held the title Mother of Generalissimo[767] which referred to Menkheperre. After Pinedjem's death, Menkheperre began his reign as both king and high priest of Amun. Menkheperre's long reign enabled him to undertake many construction projects for which he used the quarry at Wadi Hammamat, and left his royal inscriptions on the rocks there. He built a fortress at el-Hibeh (roughly forty miles south of Faiyum) and stamped bricks with his royal name, and on bricks at a fort in Gebelein he even included his queen's name.[768] On bricks at Karnak, Menkheperre used "First Prophet of Amun" as his prenomen like Herihor did.[769] In his 48th year, Menkheperre purchased land from dozens of people and built an encasement wall to protect the Karnak temple precinct from urban sprawl.[770] The authority of HPA/king Menkheperre stretched from Elephantine to el-Hibeh, and controlled 2/3 of Egypt's Nile, while Tanite kings only controlled 1/3.

---

765 Ritner, Robert. K., *The Libyan Anarchy: Inscriptions from Egypt's' third Intermediate Period*, 2009, p.112
766 Ibid., p. 116 Egyptologists try to ascribe these to a Tanite king's regnal years.
767 Dodson, Aidan & Hilton, Dyan, *The Complete Royal Families of Ancient Egypt*, Thames & Hudson, 2004, pp. 205-206
768 Goff, Beatrice, *Symbols of Ancient Egypt in the Late Period*, Mouton Publishers, 1979, p. 68
769 Ritner, Robert. K., *The Libyan Anarchy: Inscriptions from Egypt's' third Intermediate Period*, 2009, p. 135
770 Ibid., pp. 130-137 Land purchase noted on Khonsu column 1; and wall noted on Karnak stela in year 48.

El-Hibeh Temple of Amun
enclosed by mudbrick walls

The Banishment Stela[771]

A black stela (1.3 x 0.8 meters) was discovered in Karnak's environs by Maunier in 1860. It does not mention any Tanite kings, neither Smendes nor Amenemnisu, though it is often incorrectly attributed to their reigns. King Smendes did have one stela in a quarry 40 km south of Thebes to procure stone to rebuild the flood damage to a canal wall abutting a temple king Menkheperre built.[772] The boundary between north and south at that time was the city of El-Hibeh. There, the bricks of Pinedjem I are below the bricks of Menkheperre of the large boundary wall,[773] and both of their names are engraved on the banishment stela. As general, Menkheperre was heading south, likely from the fortress he built in El-Hibeh,[774] and he received acclamations upon his arrival in Thebes according to the stela.

The banishment stela covered a one year period from the end of June in regnal year 25 to the five intercalary days after July of the next year. During those days a New Year festival was held with a procession of the appearance of the god.[775] Since Menkheperre was called "High Priest of Amun-Re, King of the Gods, the great general, Menkheperre, the justified, son of king Pinedjem"[776] prior to the first procession when the titles were reiterated by Amun, it had nothing to do with Menkheperre becoming high priest or king or general; and so I suggest the 25th regnal year belongs to Menkheperre. It was called the banishment stela because Menkheperre made a request of the gods to restore to Thebes the "quarrelsome servants" and their families from their banishment to the oasis, and to protect them from those who would slay them; with the stela acting as the gods' decree to end their banishment.

---

771 Text at http://www.specialtyinterests.net/maunier.html
772 Goff, Beatrice, *Symbols of Ancient Egypt in the Late Period*, Mouton Publishers, 1979, p. 56; and see Kitchen, K.A., *The Third Intermediate Period in Egypt (1100-650 BC)*, Aris & Phillips, 1996. p. 256
  Since 'Menkheperre' was a name used by Thutmose III, the temple wall was incorrectly attributed to him. This undated stela is the only known artifact made by Smendes.
773 Ibid., p. 61
774 Ritner, Robert. K., *The Libyan Anarchy: Inscriptions from Egypt's' third Intermediate Period*, 2009, pp. 122-123; an earlier letter from El-Hibeh regarded general and HPA Masaharta's illness.
775 Finnestad, Ragnhild, *Image of the World and Symbol of the Creator*, Germany, 1985, pp. 101-103
776 Ritner, Robert. K., *The Libyan Anarchy: Inscriptions from Egypt's' third Intermediate Period*, 2009, p.126

Pharaohs of the Bible

Pharaohs Amenemnisu and Psusennes I (dynasty 21)

After pharaoh Smendes I died, cousins Psusennes I and Neferkare Amenemnisu began their co-reign in Tanis. Their co-reign is substantiated by "the juxtaposed cartouches of the two kings on a set of bow finials found in the Tanite tomb of Psusennes I."[777] Manetho gave 'Nepherkheres' a four year reign and Psusennes I a 46 year reign. There are no dated monuments or documents for Psusennes I, but he accomplished large building projects and has several artifacts with his name. I accept Psusennes' I 46 year reign with a 4 year co-reign, so he had a sole reign of 42 years afterward Amenemnisu died. The tomb of Psusennes I was found intact with his mummy inside a silver coffin (left) with a gold funerary mask (center and right). Psusennes' tomb also contained bracelets given by HPA Smendes II. The tomb was found beneath houses near the Tanis temple area. The wooden coffin and granite sarcophagi were both usurped from others.

Psusennes I Silver coffin & gold mask

Theban dominance of early dynasty 21A over dynasty 21 is noted by Psusennes I using "first prophet of Amun" with his cartouche, and by his building the Great Temple at Tanis dedicated to the Theban triad of Amun, Mut and Khonsu;[778] a mini Karnak north. Hence, the HPA title was no longer limited to Thebes. The temple of Amun measured 300 x 750 feet, and the temple of Khonsu measured 75 x 150 feet. Psusennes I reused limestone and granite from former dynasty buildings and added about a million bricks stamped with his name to make an immense enclosure wall (700 x 1000 ft) which Petrie estimated "originally measured 45 feet high, 70 feet thick, and 3400 feet in length." I agree with Karl Jansen-Winkeln that Theban kings dated documents by their own regnal years which have been incorrectly attributed to pharaohs of dynasty 21, and that the dominance of Theban 21A began to shift north to dynasty 21 during pharaoh Amenemope's reign.

---

777 Wente, Edward, "On the Chronology of the Twenty-First Dynasty," *Journal of Near Eastern Studies,* The University of Chicago Press, 1967, p. 155
778 Nicolas Grimal, *A History of Ancient Egypt*, Blackwell Books, 1992, pp. 315-317 He reused materials.

Israel's Judges: Eli (1155-1115 BC) and Samuel (1115-1095 BC)

Shiloh was where the Tent of Meeting was established and the Levitical priests served Yahweh. Eli was both judge and high priest, and his two sons Hophni and Phinehas also served as priests. Three times a year all the men were commanded to worship where the LORD placed His NAME,[779] but at Passover the whole family often came to offer and partake of a sacrificed lamb.[780] Such was the case of Elkanah and his two wives, Peninnah, a mother who teased Hannah; and Hannah, who was barren. They had travelled 30 miles from Ramah, which was only four miles north of what would later become Jerusalem.

Hannah asked the LORD for a child beneath her breath, and Eli thought she was drunk as he watched her lips move without hearing words, but he eventually blessed her to receive what she had asked of Yahweh. And Hannah conceived and gave birth to a son, and named him Samuel, because [781] *Shemuel* means "asked of El". Like Samson, Samuel would be a Nazarite who's hair was not cut. Abraham's son Ishmael was weaned at age 5 roughly 800 years prior, so I imagine the age for weaning had likely dropped to about age 3. When he was weaned, Samuel's parents entrusted Eli to apprentice their son, but Eli hadn't raised his own sons to honor Yahweh.[782] Hannah made a coat and brought it to Samuel each year at passover, and God blessed her with five more children.[783] As a young man Samuel heard Yahweh calling him, and thought it was Eli; but Eli told him to respond, "Speak, LORD; for your servant hears."[784] There was quite a contrast.

And Samuel grew, and the LORD was with him, and did let none of his words fall to the ground. And all Israel from Dan even to Beersheba knew that Samuel was established to be a prophet of the LORD. And the LORD appeared again in Shiloh: for the LORD revealed himself to Samuel in Shiloh by the word of the LORD. (I Samuel 3:19-21)

Now Eli was very old, and heard all that his sons did to all Israel; and how they lay with the women that assembled at the door of the tabernacle of the congregation. And he said to them, Why do you such things? for I hear of your evil dealings by all this people. . . . you make the LORD's people to transgress. If one man sin against another, the judge shall judge him: but if a man sin against the LORD, who shall entreat for him? Notwithstanding they listened not to the voice of their father, because the LORD would slay them. (I Samuel 2:22-25)

---

779 Deuteronomy 16:16
780 Deuteronomy 16:1-7
781 I Samuel 1:1-28
782 I Samuel 2:12-17
783 I Samuel 2:19-21
784 I Samuel 3:1-9 "child" in v1 is *na'ar* which is also translated "young man" in Gen. 18:7

Though Eli may have acted as a judge for the nation of Israel, there were still local judges in each city who gave judgments. As high priest, Eli should have known that he and his sons were responsible to entreat the LORD's pardon of the people's sins; so Eli was neither a good father nor priest. Yahweh sent a prophet to Eli and foretold that his two sons would be killed in one day;[785] which came to pass by the hand of the Philistines when they took the ark of the covenant; on hearing it, Eli, age 90 (1115 BC), fell over and died also.[786]

Samuel as priest, prophet and judge

The presence of the ark brought plagues to the Philistine cities of Ashdod, Gath, and Ekron, so after 7 months they sent it back to Israel.[787] Twenty years after the Philistines returned the ark of the covenant (1095 BC), Samuel's preaching for the people to repent of their idolatry so that Yahweh could deliver them from the Philistines was finally acted upon with prayer and fasting at Mizpeh.[788] When the Philistines heard of it, they attacked Israel.

And as Samuel was offering up the burnt offering, the Philistines drew near to battle against Israel: but the LORD thundered with a great thunder on that day on the Philistines, and discomfited them; and they were smitten before Israel. And the men of Israel went out of Mizpeh, and pursued the Philistines, and smote them, until they came under Bethcar. Then Samuel took a stone, and set it between Mizpeh and Shen, and called the name of it Ebenezer, saying, Till now has the LORD helped us. So the Philistines were subdued, and they came no more into the coast of Israel: and the <u>hand of the LORD was against the Philistines all the days of Samuel. And the cities which the Philistines had taken from Israel were restored to Israel, from Ekron even to Gath; and the coasts thereof did Israel deliver out of the hands of the Philistines.</u> And there was peace between Israel and the Amorites. And Samuel judged Israel all the days of his life. And he went from year to year in circuit to Bethel, and Gilgal, and Mizpeh, and judged Israel in all those places. And his return was to Ramah; for there was his house; and there he judged Israel; and there he built an altar to the LORD. (I Samuel 7:10-17)

Ramah is now the Jerusalem neighborhood of Ramot in which the tomb of Samuel sits atop a steep hill in an 18th century church which was converted into a mosque.[789] When Samuel became old he appointed his sons as judges, but they took bribes and perverted justice; so the elders requested a warrior king like all the other nations.[790]

Samuel at Mizpeh

---

785 I Samuel 2:27-36
786 I Samuel 4:11-18 Phineas' wife gave birth at the news and named him Ichabod, "the glory has departed".
787 I Samuel 4:1 – 5:1
788 I Samuel 6:1 and 7:1-6
789 I Samuel 28:3 "Tomb of Samuel" http://en.wikipedia.org/wiki/Neby_Samwil
790 I Samuel 8:1-5

Samuel as anointer of kings

Samuel made it clear to the people that a king would take a tenth of all they had and make their children serve him. Since they had rejected YHWH as their King, Yahweh gave them a king.[791] The LORD selected a shy, tall, handsome man from the tribe of Benjamin named Saul and sent him on a journey to encounter Samuel.[792] Then Samuel anointed him and prophesied over him.

Then Samuel took a vial of oil, and poured it on his head, and kissed him, and said, Is it not because the LORD has anointed you to be captain over his inheritance? . . . you shall meet a company of prophets coming down from the high place with a psaltery, and a tabret, and a pipe, and a harp, before them; and they shall prophesy: And <u>the Spirit of the LORD will come on you, and you shall prophesy with them, and shall be turned into another man</u>. (I Samuel 10:1, 5b-6)

Samuel continued as priest, prophet, and judge throughout the reign of Saul; and died only a year or so before king Saul did.[793] But Saul was not devoted wholeheartedly to YHWH, so Yahweh had Samuel secretly anoint a king to replace Saul, named David.[794]

And Samuel said to Jesse, Are here all your children? And he said, There remains yet the <u>youngest</u>, and, behold, he <u>keeps the sheep</u>. And Samuel said to Jesse, Send and fetch him: . . . Now he was <u>ruddy, and with of a beautiful countenance, and goodly to look to</u>. And the LORD said, Arise, anoint him: for this is he. Then Samuel took the horn of oil, and anointed him in the middle of his brothers: and <u>the Spirit of the LORD came on David from that day forward</u>. So Samuel rose up, and went to Ramah. But the Spirit of the LORD departed from Saul, and an evil spirit from the LORD troubled him. And Saul's servants said to him, Behold now, an evil spirit from God troubles you. Let our lord now command your servants, which are before you, to seek out a man, who is a cunning player on an harp: and it shall come to pass, when the evil spirit from God is on you, that he shall play with his hand, and you shall be well. . . . Behold, I have seen a son of Jesse the Bethlehemite, that is <u>cunning in playing, and a mighty valiant man, and a man of war, and prudent in matters</u>, and a comely person, and the LORD is with him. Why Saul sent messengers to Jesse, and said, Send me David your son, which is with the sheep. . . . And David came to Saul, and stood before him: and he loved him greatly; and he became his <u>armor bearer</u>. (I Samuel 16:11-22)

David was 22 or 23 years old when he became king Saul's armor bearer.

---

791 I Samuel 8:6-22
792 I Samuel 9:1-27
793 I Samuel 25:1, and chapters 28 and 31
794 I Samuel 15:10-25

Israel's Periods of Oppression during rule of Judges

Dates B.C.	Oppressor(s)	Reference
1417-1409	by Cusham-rishathaim of Mesopotamia (Aram = Syria)	Judges 3:8
1369-1351	by Eglon of Moab and Ammonites and giants in east	Judges 3:14
1350?-1340	by Philistines (during Shamgar's judgeship) in west	Jg. 3:31 and 5:6
1358-1338	by Jabin, king of Canaan at Hazor, and Sisera in north	Judges 4:3
1298-1291	by Midianites and Amalekites	Judges 6:1-3
1224-1206	by Philistines and Ammonites	Judges 10:8
1195-1155	by Philistines (Samson born 1195; judged 1175-1155 BC)	Judges 13:1
1115-1095	by Philistines (during Samuel's judgeship)	I Samuel 7:1-13

Then Samuel took a flask of oil and poured it on his head, and kissed him and said: 'Is it not because the LORD has anointed you commander over His inheritance?'... And Samuel called the people together to the LORD to Mizpeh; And said to the children of Israel, <u>Thus said the LORD God of Israel, I brought up Israel out of Egypt</u>, and <u>delivered you out of the hand of the Egyptians</u>, and <u>out of the hand of all kingdoms, and of them that oppressed you</u>: <u>And you have this day rejected your God</u>, who himself saved you out of all your adversities and your tribulations; and you have said to him, No, but set a king over us. (1 Samuel 10:1, 17-19)

During the life of Samuel there was a transition in Israel from having judges to having kings. When king Saul proved to be disobedient, the LORD maneuvered his replacement to be at his side to learn the ways of kingship, both good and bad. Eventually king Saul understood that David, and not his own son Jonathan, would become king of Israel; and so Saul drove David away and sought to kill him. Though pharaohs are not mentioned during the reigns of king Saul and king David, Egypt and Egyptians are mentioned.

Israel's Judges Beginning Time-line

Israel

Elders 1426-1409	Othniel 1409-1369		Ehud 1369-1349		Deborah 1339-1299
			Shamgar 1366-1340	Barak and Jael 1338	
	40 years land rests (Judges 3:11)		(Judges 3:30 and 5:31)	40 years land rests	
				1351-1271 fords of Jordan 80y of rest	

Oppressor

Aramaens 1417-1409		Jabin of Hazor 1358-1338	
		Eglon of Moab 1369-1351	Philistines 1350? - 1340

Egypt

Rameses II 1480-1414	Marenptah 1414-1394	Seti II 1394-1388	Merenptah Siptah 1388-1381	Tausret 1381-1378	anarchy 1378-1323	Setnakht 1322-1318	Rameses III 1318-1286
			Amenmesse 1394-1390				

In 1313 and 1310 BC major volcanic eruptions in the Aegean Sea caused "Sea Peoples" to seek new homelands.

Without a judge after Deborah, the children of Israel "*did evil*" and were oppressed by the Midianites for seven years (1298-1291 BC).

Pharaohs of the Bible

Israel's Judges Ending Time-line

Israel

Gideon 1291-1251	Tola 1251-1228	Jair 1228-1206	Jepthah 1206-1200	Ibzan 1200-1193	Elon 1193-1183	Abdon 1183-1175	Samson 1175-1155	Eli 1155-1115
40y land rests (Jg.8:28)								
	Abimelech ruled Shechem for 3y							

Oppressor

Midianites 1298-1291		Philistines 1224-1206		Philistines 1195-1155	
Amalekites		Ammonites			

Egypt

Rameses III 1318-1286	Ram. IV 1286-1279	Ram. V 1279-1275	Ram. VI 1275-1266	Ram. VII 1266-1258	Ram. VIII 1258-1256	Ram. IX 1256-1237	Ram. X 1237-1228	Rameses XI 1228-1199	Herihor 1199-1169	Pinedjem I 1169-1148

Samuel preached during Philistine oppression from 1115 to 1095 BC when God routed Israel's enemies. Then Samuel anointed Saul king, but Samuel continued to judge in Israel until a few years before king Saul died.

Clarity Chronology of High Priests (21A) and 21st Dynasty during Israel's Judges

Pharaoh Tanis	Smendes, as treasurer	Smendes I 1169-1146	Psusennes I 1146-1100 Amenemnisut 1146-1142	Amenemope 1100-1091
HP-king Thebes	Herihor 1199-1169	Pinedjem I 1169-1148	Menkheperre 1148-1099	Smendes II 1099-1097

Israel Judge	Ibzan 1200-1193	Elon 1193-1183	Abdon 1183-1175	Samson 1175-1155	Eli 1155-1115	Samuel 1115-1095

Assyria	Ashur-nirari III 1203-1197	Enlil-kudurri-usur 1197-1192	Ninurta-apal-Ekur 1192-1179	Ashur-Dan I 1179-1133	2 kings 1133	Ashur-resh-ishi I 1133-1115	Tiglath-Pileser I 1115-1076

Saul and David's Pharaohs

"Saul has slain his thousands, and David his ten thousands."
(1 Samuel 18:7b)

1095		Samuel anointed Saul, and Samuel continued to judge Israel
1095		Saul defeated Nahash, the Ammonite, at Jabesh-Gilead (I Samuel 11)
1094		Saul and Jonathan won the battle at Michmash (I Samuel 13)
1085		David was born to Jesse
1068-7?		Saul fought Amalekites at Shur ('Wall' of the Ruler) during Siamun's reign
1063		Samuel anointed David
1062/1		David slew Philistine Goliath of Gath
1057		David fled to Philistine king Achish of Gath
1055		David slaughtered Amalekites at Shur ('Wall') during Sheshonk I's reign
1055		Saul and his sons were killed on Mount Gilboa; David reigned 40 years
1050		David conquered the Philistines
1045		David conquered Ammon, Moab, and Edom (Hadad fled to Egypt) [with prince Hadad, age 6-10]
1040		David conquered Syrian Hadadezer of Aram-Zobah up to the Euphrates
1035?		Prince Hadad married the sister of Sheshonk I's queen Tahpenes
1023		Prince Absalom rebelled
1115		Solomon was coronated king in Spring and again in Fall
1010?		Prince Hadad returned to rule Edom as its king

Saul

Saul lived in *Gibeah* (Hebrew, "hill") just north of Jerusalem in the small tribe of Benjamin. When Samuel planned to present Saul to the people at Mizpeh, he was hiding among the baggage, and had to be brought out before the people.[795]

> ... *when he stood among the people, he was higher than any of the people from his shoulders and upward. ... And all the people shouted, and said, God save the king.*
> *(I Samuel 10:23b-24b)*

He may have shied away from public speaking, but Saul was a mighty military leader. First to test his mettle was Nahash, the Ammonite, who camped against Jabesh-Gilead. The evidence at Tell Abu Kharaz suggests this city was located one and a half miles east of the Jordan River, and nine miles southeast of Beth-shan.[796] Jabesh was 45 miles NE of Gibeah.

---

795 I Samuel 10:22-23a
796 "Jabesh-Gilead," *Walking in their sandals* at http://www.ancientsandals.com/overviews/jabesh-gilead.htm

KING SAUL'S MILITARY BATTLES

BATTLE	Israel #	Foe #	VICTOR	SUMMARY	REF.
Jabesh-gilead	330,000	?	Israel over the Ammonites	Saul delivered the people of Jabesh.	I Samuel 11:1-11
Geba	1,000	garrison	Israel led by Jonathan	Jonathan defeated the Philistines.	I Samuel 13:3-4
Cliffs above Michmash	2	Michmash garrison	Prince Jonathan and his armor bearer	They killed 20 men	I Samuel 14:1-15
Michmash	600 soldiers & ? citizens	30,000 chariots 6,000 cavalry	Undecided, the "Philistines went to their own place."	"they smote the Philistines that day from Michmash to Aijalon"	I Samuel 13:5; 14:1-31, 46
Amalek cities to <u>Wall</u> of the Ruler	210,000	?	Israel, but Saul disobeyed the LORD's instructions	"Saul smote the Amalekites from Havilah until you come to <u>Shur</u>"	I Samuel 15:2-9
Valley of Elah	?	?	Israel: Philistines fell at Shaaraim, to Gath and Ekron	David slew Goliath and Israel routed Philistines back to the coastlands.	I Samuel 17:1-58
Mount Gilboa	?	?	Philistia: Israel was defeated.	Saul and his sons were killed.	I Samuel 31:1-13

A Roman garrison contained 300 to 1,000 soldiers. Except for Saul's battle against the Ammonites and the Amalekites (which he did not totally defeat according to I Samuel 28:16-19), Saul was fighting against Philistines in the battles above. *Shur* means 'wall' in Hebrew, and refers to the defensive wall Amenemhat I built from the Bitter Lakes north to El-Ballah Lake. It was known as the Wall of the Ruler, and *Shur* for short.

Jabesh-Gilead

> *. . . Saul put the people in three companies; and they came into the middle of the host in the morning watch, and slew the Ammonites until the heat of the day: and it came to pass, that they which remained were scattered, so that two of them were not left together. . . . Then said Samuel to the people, Come, and let us go to Gilgal, and renew the kingdom there. And all the people went to Gilgal; and there they made Saul king before the LORD in Gilgal . . . (I Samuel 11:11-15a)*

Michmash

> *Now <u>there was no smith found throughout all the land of Israel</u>: for the Philistines said, Lest the Hebrews make them swords or spears: But all the Israelites went down to the Philistines, to sharpen every man his share, and his coulter, and his ax, and his mattock. . . . in the day of battle, that there was neither sword nor spear found in the hand of any of the people that were with Saul and Jonathan: but with Saul and with Jonathan his son was there found. (I Samuel 13:19-22)*

The Philistines assured their control of Israel through metallurgical dominance and weapon control. After Jonathon's foray into the enemy's lookout post, the LORD sent an earthquake and *"saved Israel that day"*.[797] King Saul made a rash vow which jeopardized Jonathon's life.[798]

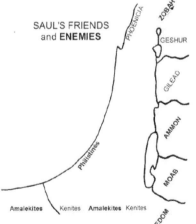

> *So Saul took the kingdom over Israel, and fought against all his enemies on every side, against **Moab**, and against the children of **Ammon**, and against **Edom**, and against the kings of **Zobah**, and against the **Philistines**: and wherever he turned himself, he vexed them. And he gathered an host, and smote the **Amalekites**, and delivered Israel out of the hands of them that spoiled them. . . . And <u>there was sore war against the Philistines all the days of Saul</u>: and when Saul saw any strong man, or any valiant man, he took him to him. (I Samuel 14:47-48, 52)*

Vengeance on Amalekites, grace on Kenites, for actions during the Exodus

> *Thus said the LORD of hosts, I remember that which Amalek did to Israel, how he laid wait for him in the way, when he came up from Egypt. Now go and smite Amalek, and utterly destroy all that they have, and spare them not; but slay both*

---

[797] I Samuel 14:15, 23
[798] I Samuel 14:24-45

man and woman, infant and suckling, ox and sheep, camel and ass. . . . And Saul said to the Kenites, Go, depart, get you down from among the Amalekites, lest I destroy you with them: for you showed kindness to all the children of Israel, when they came up out of Egypt. So the Kenites departed from among the Amalekites. And Saul smote the Amalekites from Havilah until you come to Shur [wall], *that is over against Egypt (I Samuel 15:2-7)*

The Semitic Havilah dwelt on the western coast of Arabia, and Josephus called them Euilat;[799] thus Saul is referring to Eilat on the tip of the Gulf of Aqaba. This had been the accepted border with Egypt since the time of Joshua, but it had been settled by Amalekites. This battle likely took place while Siamun was pharaoh. But king Saul disobeyed YHWH's commandment and kept the best sheep and oxen to "sacrifice"; hence Yahweh's reply, "*To obey is better than sacrifice.*" (I Samuel 15:22)

And Samuel said to him, The LORD has rent the kingdom of Israel from you this day, and has given it to a neighbor of yours, that is better than you. (I Samuel 15:28)

And then Samuel anointed David to be king, and king Saul sent for David to play music for him and to be his bodyguard.[800] David was age 23 or 24 when he slew the giant of Gath, named Goliath,[801] in the power of the Name of Yahweh.[802] Afterwards, Jonathan made a covenant with David, surrendering his right to the throne and recognizing David as the next king.[803] King Saul was jealous of David and planned to get him killed by requesting a bride-price of 100 Philistine foreskins for his daughter Michal, but David was victorious.[804]

King Saul ruled Israel during the second half of Dynasties 21 and 21A

In the 21st dynasty of Lower Egypt, Amenemope, Osorkon, Siamun, and Psusennes II ruled during king Saul's forty years; and the following pharaohs ruled Upper Egypt's dynasty 21A: Smendes II, Pinedjem II, and Psusennes III.

Amenemope was a son of Psusennes I. King Amenemope's name was found on a door jamb and bas-relief at the temple of Isis in Giza, and on a block at the temple of Ptah near Memphis; and on a statue of Horus Amenemope's name is accompanied by both titles of king and HPA.[805] King Amenemope's name appears on several Theban burial objects: twice alone, once with HPA Smendes B, and the others with HPA Pinedjem II, but otherwise he is not attested outside the Nile delta. Manetho gave him a nine year reign.

Smendes II was a son of Menkheperre and Isetemkheb, the daughter of Psusennes I.

---

799 Cooper, Bill, *After the Flood*, New Wine Press, 1995, p. 177
800 I Samuel 16
801 Goliath's name at http://archaeology.about.com/b/2007/01/22/archaeology-dig-2007-tell-es-safigath.htm
802 I Samuel 17:45-47
803 I Samuel 18:1-4
804 I Samuel 18:25-29
805 Goff, Beatrice, *Symbols of Ancient Egypt in the Late Period*, Mouton Publishers, 1979, p. 75

Smendes II was a king as well as HPA; though some refer to him only as Smendes B, as HPA. Smendes II's name is inscribed at Karnak. He only reigned two years, and is not even mentioned by Manetho.

Pinedjem II was a son of Menkheperre and Isetemkheb, and a brother of Smendes II. Pinedjem II married his sister Istemkheb D and Nesikhons, the daughter of Smendes II. Pinedjem II included the reign of Smendes II on mummy tags. Nesikhons was a prophetess of shrines from nome #3 to #14 and used titles of "officer of the countries of the South" and "Viceroy of Cush" which were previously used only by men.[806] She died young while pregnant or during childbirth, and Pinedjem II wrote a funerary decree so that she would do him only good in the afterlife.[807]

Pinedjem II offers to Osiris

HPA Pinedjem II ruled in Thebes while Amenemope, Osorkon, and Siamun ruled in Tanis. Osorkon, the elder, ruled for six years according to Manetho. Osorkon was an uncle of Sheshonk I.

In the fourth month of winter in Siamun's tenth year (1075), the mummies of Seti I and Rameses I and II were moved from Seti's tomb (KV 17) to the high crag-tomb of Inhapi; and then three days later they were moved to the newly constructed tomb of Pinedjem II (DB 320) who had been buried that same day.[808] A transaction of silver was inscribed on a stela in Siamun's 16th year.[809] A fragment from Karnak of the *Annals of the High Priests of Amun* is inscribed with 'pharaoh' Siamun's 17th year;[810] the first time 'pharaoh' was used as a title.

Bronze double axe - Crete

In Tanis, where the majority of Siamun artifacts were found, a calcite bas-relief depicts Siamun in the traditional pose smiting an enemy holding a double axe, or labrys, with narrow "unevenly sized blades"[811] by its head with the handle toward the ground. Avaris had been a port of commerce for Minoans; and Keftiu and other Sea Peoples who used such axes had returned to live in the Nile delta in 1310 BC. I maintain that Joshua retook the "*country of Goshen*" in 1451-1444 BC, and that the weak pharaohs of the 19th, 20th, and early 21st dynasties did nothing about it. I conjecture that Siamun drove the Judahites and Sea Peoples out of Goshen and reestablished Egypt's border at the Wall (*Shur*) of the Ruler. I further propose that Siamun also held his Wall border when "*Saul smote the Amalekites from Havilah until you come to Shur, that is over against Egypt.*" (I Samuel 15:7)

---

806 Ibid., p. 80
807 Ritner, Robert. K., *The Libyan Anarchy*, 2009, pp. 145-157
808 According to coffin texts and wall dockets, see http://anubis4_2000.tripod.com/mummypages1/21A.htm and http://anubis4_2000.tripod.com/mummypages2/19A.htm which has pics and translations
809 Ritner, Robert. K., *The Libyan Anarchy*, 2009, pp. 161-162
810 Goff, Beatrice, *Symbols of Ancient Egypt in the Late Period,* Mouton Publishers, 1979, p. 80
811 Ash, Paul S., *David, Solomon, and Egypt: a Reassessment*, Sheffield Academic Press, England, 1999, pp. 39-40

Psusennes II/III

After the death of his father, Pinedjem II, in 1075 BC in the 10th year of Siamun, Psusennes took over as king/HPA;[812] and after the death of Siamun in 1066 BC, Psusennes took over as pharaoh in the delta as well. Egyptologists refer to the reign of HPA Psusennes III and LE pharaoh Psusennes II, but most accept he is the same man.

On the north face of the seventh pylon at Karnak, a text is inscribed securing the property rights of Psusennes II's daughter, Maatkare B, ending with a death threat to anyone who contested her purchased land rights.[813]

Necropolis and Marriage transfer of power to 22nd Dynasty

Sheshonk (who would become Sheshonk I) served Psusennes II as advisor and general of Egypt's army. After the marriage of general Sheshonk's son, Osorkon, to Maatkare B, Psusennes II granted Sheshonk the privilege to establish a necropolis in Abydos for his relatives, and Sheshonk buried his father, chief Nimlot/Namlot, there. Sheshonk's father, Nimlot A, was one of a long list of the great chiefs of the Meshwesh (often shortened to Ma). A red granite stela in Abydos recorded this formal contract for Nimlot's funerary endowment.[814] In the text, general Sheshonk asked, "Will you cause that he (Sheshonk) be favored with the festivals of his majesty (Psusennes II) in receiving victory, joined as a co-partner (united as a single act)?"[815] To which a rhetorical "yes" was assumed. I suggest the last three years of the reign of Psusennes II was in a lesser type of co-regency with Sheshonk I, with Psusennes II dying during Sheshonk's third or fourth year.

Sheshonk I (1055-1022 BC)

Hedjkheperre Sheshonk only referred to himself as the "great chief of Ma" in the delta as he waited for the elderly pharaoh Psusennes II to die. Possibly in Sheshonk's third year, he positioned his son Iuput to take over as HPA as soon as Psusennes died. By Sheshonk's fifth year he began to use full pharonic titles.[816] Sheshonk I quickly installed loyal family members and friends into positions of authority throughout Egypt.

Sheshonk I appointed his second son, Iuput A, as high priest of Amun in Thebes and generalissimo and governor of Upper Egypt. Third and fourth prophets of Amun also had close ties to the new Libyan pharaoh. In Memphis, Sheshonk's brother-in-law, Shedsunefertem, became the new high priest of Ptah. Sheshonk's third son by his wife Patareshnes, Nimlot B, was established "leader of the entire army" at Herakleopolis. Sheshonk I sent Wayheset, son of another chief of Ma, to Dakhla to restore order.[817]

---

812 A grafitto at Abydos refers to Psusennes II as king and HPA. See Jansen-Winkeln in Hornung, Krauss & Warburton, *Ancient Egyptian Chronology* (Handbook of Oriental Studies), Brill, 2006, p. 222
813 Ritner, Robert. K., *The Libyan Anarchy*, Society of Biblical Literature, 2009, pp. 163-166
814 Ibid., pp. 166-172
815 Ibid., p. 168 with footnote 2 translation
816 Gardiner, Allen, JEA 19, 1933, 23; "Kar." no. 3; LdR III, p. 307
817 Kitchen, Kenneth A., *The Third Intermediate Period in Egypt*, 1973, pp. 289-291

Sheshonk I's Military Victories

I suggest in his first year Sheshonk I aided general David in killing "*the Amalekites . . . as you go to Shur*" (I Samuel 27:8) north of the Bitter Lakes. Sheshonk's stela at Karnak recorded victory over the Sinai bedouin: "His majesty made a great slaughter of them . . . on the bank of the shore of the Bitter Lakes."[818] The Dakhla stela dated to pharaoh Sheshonk's 5th year described "a state of war and turmoil" in Libya (Meshwesh).[819]

There are also out-of-place blocks at Karnak with inscriptions of Sheshonk I. Block A-b mentions his victory over the Shashu (bedouin).[820] Block D, line 5 states: "Oh Amun, what I have done to the land of Nubia . . ." Block E, line 8 states: " . . . all things which come to thee from the land of Nubia . . ." with the next three lines listing Nubian products and animals continued onto the next four lines of block F.[821]

The Shashu bedouin which Sheshonk I encountered at the wall (*shur*) of the Bitter Lakes were the Amalekites who were being pursued by David and his men in 1055 BC. Siamun and Saul fought the Amalekite bedouin at the Wall of the Ruler about 1067 BC, but David set out to obey God's commands to annihilate the Amalekites. Saul and David enabled both pharaohs to claim they protected their northeastern border, when neither Saul nor David (at that time) intended to cross it. Sheshonk I had to keep Avaris secure as he began to reestablish Egypt's borders and trade routes by conquering cities in Phoenicia and Aram.

In Sheshonk's 21st year he began a massive building project called 'the Mansion of Hedjkheperre Setepenre in Thebes'. The inscription begins with classical exultation of the king, and line 2 states "thou hast trodden down the natives of Nubia,"[822] later followed by Amun's blessing on his building plans" (lines 12-17). Next to this great wall is the 'Bubastite Gate' which features three masterfully engraved scenes of Sheshonk and his son, HPA and general Iuput, accompanied by their illustrious titles.

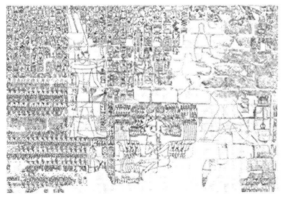

Sheshonk completed the court and gate and seven engraved scenes of himself and Iuput.[823] The triumphal scene appears full and even cramped, though Kitchen wrote it wasn't "completely finished"[824]. This scene was planned to exhibit Iuput's and Sheshonk's victories over the Meshwesh of the west, the bedouin at Bitter Lakes in the

---

818 Wilson, Kevin, *The Campaign of pharaoh Sheshonk I in Palestine*, p. 68, lines 7-8
819 Gardiner, Allen, *Egypt of the Pharaohs*, 1961, p. 327, line 4 of stela
820 Muller, Whilhelm, *Egyptological Researches*, 1910, p. 146
821 Muller, Whilhelm, *Egyptological Researches*, 1910, pp. 150-1
822 Kitchen, K.A., *The Third Intermediate Period in Egypt*, 1973, p. 293, footnote #284
823 Ritner, Robert. K., *The Libyan Anarchy*, Society of Biblical Literature, 2009, pp. 193-207
824 Kitchen, K.A., *The Third Intermediate Period in Egypt*, 1973, p. 72

Pharaohs of the Bible

north, and the Nubians of the south. The captives in the center were to become mercenaries[825] led by Iuput. Amun is the left figure with shuti blessing Sheshonk who is wearing the white crown with a mace over his head.[826] The shuti is a double crown of two falcon feathers engraved flat whereas the human figure is in bas relief.

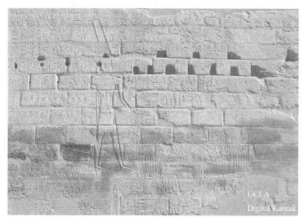

Victory relief of Hedjkheperre Sheshonk

Sheshonk I as sphinx

Sheshonk's Trade Agreements

Byblite kings inscribed their names upon statues given to them from pharaohs with whom they traded. Sheshonk I gave Abi-Baal, king of Byblos, a seated statue of himself[827] in recognition of their continued trade agreements. Sheshonk's son, Osorkon I, gave Elibaal a statue of himself.[828] Sheshonk I had several statues of himself as a sphinx made.

Near the *Annals of Thutmose III* in the Temple of Amun at Karnak, Sheshonk I recorded his dues "when I made it as thy tribute (i.e. Amun's) of the land of Canaan (Khuru) which had turned away from thee."[829] Aside from this obscure inscription, "no direct record survives" of Sheshonk's temple gifts from a Canaanite campaign.[830] I suggest that Sheshonk's stela in Megiddo[831] re-established that city alone in Canaan as a vassal of Egypt in order to do trade with Egypt. Sheshonk's delta residence was Pi-Ese (estate of Isis) in the central delta at Sebennytos (now Samannud),[832] not Bubastis (near Zagazig) thirty miles SE.

---

825 Ritner, Robert. K., *The Libyan Anarchy*, Society of Biblical Literature, 2009, p. 206
826 Ibid., p. 204. The large human image on the right is now hard to see. Digital Egypt has high resolution photos at http://dlib.etc.ucla.edu/projects/Karnak/archive/query?feature=BubastitePortal
827 Kitchen, K.A., *The Third Intermediate Period in Egypt*, 1973, p. 292
828 James, Peter, http://www.centuries.co.uk/faq.htm#q5 class=, accessed 3/8/11. Shipitbaal (son of Elibaal)
829 Barguet, *Temple d'Amon-re a Karnak*, 1962, pp.122-3; block D, a, line 6 (Muller, Egyptol, Researches, II, 147, fig. 52 top)
830 Kitchen, K.A., *The Third Intermediate Period in Egypt*, 1973, p. 300
831 Ritner, Robert. K., *The Libyan Anarchy*, Society of Biblical Literature, 2009, pp. 218-219
832 Ibid., p. 191 on the Gebel es-Silia stela in his 21st regnal year; see also http://egyptsites.wordpress.com/2009/03/03/behbeit-el-hagar/

David as a Fugitive

After jealous king Saul hurled a javelin at David the third time,[833] David spent several years (1060-58) in the wilderness and gathered an army[834] and struck down Israel's enemies while Saul searched for him.[835] At En-gedi, Saul ventured into a cave where David and his men were hiding, and David cut off a piece of Saul's robe, though David's men encouraged him to kill Saul. After Saul left the cave, David came out and shouted to him . . .

David with part of Saul's robe in hand

Behold, this day your eyes have seen how that the LORD had delivered you to day into my hand in the cave: and some bade me kill you: but my eye spared you; . . . see the skirt of your robe in my hand: for in that I cut off the skirt of your robe, and killed you not, know you and see that there is neither evil nor transgression in my hand, and I have not sinned against you; yet you hunt my soul to take it. The LORD judge between me and you, and the LORD avenge me of you: but my hand shall not be on you. . . The LORD therefore be judge . . . and plead my cause, and deliver me out of your hand.. . . And Saul lifted up his voice, and wept. And he said to David, You are more righteous than I: for you have rewarded me good, whereas I have rewarded you evil. . . . I know well that you shall surely be king, and that the kingdom of Israel shall be established in your hand. Swear now therefore to me by the LORD, that you will not cut off my seed after me, and that you will not destroy my name out of my father's house. And David swore to Saul. (I Samuel 24:10-22a)

A woman named Abigail stopped David from avenging himself on her fool of a husband, Nabal. After Nabal died, Abigail became David's wife.[836] In the wilderness of Ziph, David was given another opportunity to kill Saul, but David said, *"As the LORD lives, the LORD shall smite him; or his day shall come to die; or he shall descend into battle, and perish."*[837] David and his 600 men fled to *"Achish, the son of Maoch, king of Gath"*[838] who gave David and his men the town of Ziklag in which they dwelt one year and four months.[839] I suggest Ziklag is Tell Sera' midway between Gaza and Beersheba.

---

833 I Samuel 18:8-11; 19:9-10
834 I Samuel 22:1-2 a ragtag group of distressed, indebted men
835 I Samuel 23:19-29
836 I Samuel 25:1-44
837 I Samuel 26:10
838 I Samuel 27:2
839 I Samuel 27:6-7

David at Egypt's Wall (*Shur*) of the Ruler

And David and his men went up, and invaded the Geshurites, and the Gezrites, and the Amalekites: for those nations were of old the inhabitants of the land, as you go to Shur [wall], even to the land of Egypt. (I Samuel 27:8)

The Geshurites lived northeast of the Sea of Galilee. Strabo mentioned the land of the Gezrites lying between Rhinocolura and Pelusium in the desert area of the northern Sinai Peninsula.[840] Amalekites lived in the Negev ("south"). Neither Saul nor David mention engaging Egyptian troops at their wall border. David left no humans alive, finishing what Saul failed to complete. Or so he thought. There were still pockets of Amalekites living in the Sinai who heard what David had done to their kinsmen. So when David's band gathered with the Philistines at Aphek,[841] other Amalekites carried off their families and belongings and set Ziklag on fire. After returning from a 54 mile three day march, the men were exhausted and ready to stone David.[842] David left 200 men behind with their baggage at Nahal Besor, and pursued the Sinai Amalekites. David's men encountered an Egyptian slave who had been left behind three days prior, after his Amalekite masters had invaded the coastlands of Judah and burned Ziklag.[843] David convinced the slave to lead him to the Amalekite camp, and David's men slew all of them "*save four hundred young men, which rode on camels, and fled.*"[844] And David and his men recovered all their own people and stuff as well as the other spoils the Amalekites had taken. Some of his men did not want to share the other spoils with the 200 men left behind, but David instituted a new law that men who guarded the camp would share in spoils with men who fought.[845] David sent gifts of spoil to prominent men throughout Judah and the Negev.[846]

Zayit Stone

The burning of Ziklag (Tell Sera') likely occurred within days of king Saul's death. A stone with Hebrew letters was discovered in 2005 at Tell Zayit, 4 miles west of Tell Sera'.
> "Its locus was a stratum caused by a fire dated by the excavators to the 10th century BCE, meaning that the inscription dates from before that century. It preserves writing – simple graffiti – plus an ordered list of letters . . . Its placement in a wall, and the context of its inscriptions ("help/warrior" and "bowl/throne") may indicate a belief that the letters possessed magical/apotropaic power to ward off evil spirits."[847]

---

840 Strabo, *Geographia XVI*, 2, pp. 31-32
841 I Samuel 29:1
842 I Samuel 30:1-6
843 I Samuel 30:9-14
844 I Samuel 30:17c
845 I Samuel 30:20-25
846 I Samuel 30:26-31
847 "Zayit Stone" *Wikipedia*

Zayit Stone with 11th century Hebrew writing

King Saul's Death

The Philistines were encamped in Shunem (now Sulem) in the Jezreel valley, then moved to an "enclosure/fortress".[848] About 7 miles west of Beth Shean lies the 500 meter high Gilboa range where the Israelites were camped, about 5 miles south of Shunem.

*Now the Philistines fought against Israel: and the men of Israel fled from before the Philistines, and fell down slain in mount **Gilboa**. . . . and the Philistines slew Jonathan, and Abinadab, and Melchishua, Saul's sons. And the battle went sore against Saul, and the archers hit him . . . Then said Saul to his armor bearer, Draw your sword, and thrust me through therewith; lest these uncircumcised come . . . and abuse me. But his armor bearer would not . . . Therefore Saul took a sword, and fell on it. . . . <u>So Saul died, and his three sons, and his armor bearer, and all his men, that same day together.</u> And when the men of Israel . . . saw that the men of Israel fled, and that Saul and his sons were dead, they forsook the cities, and fled; and the Philistines came and dwelled in them. . . . when the Philistines came to strip the slain, that they found Saul and his three sons fallen in mount Gilboa. And they cut off his head, and stripped off his armor, and sent into the land of the Philistines round about, to publish it in the house of their idols, and among the people. And they put his armor in the house of Ashtaroth: and they fastened his body to the wall of Bethshan. And when the inhabitants of Jabeshgilead heard of that which the Philistines had done to Saul; All the valiant men arose, and went all night, and took the body of Saul and the bodies of his sons from the wall of **Bethshan**, and came to Jabesh, and burnt them there. And they took their bones, and buried them under a tree at **Jabesh**, and fasted seven days. (I Samuel 31:1-13)*

Saul had delivered the people of Jabesh, and they repaid their debt to him and his sons. Israelites deserted the cities of the Jezreel valley and the Philistines moved in. David's band was fighting in the Sinai Peninsula about the same time as this battle at Mount Gilboa in which Saul and his sons died.[849] An Amalekite killed Saul and took his crown and bracelet and delivered them to David, thinking he would be rewarded; but David had him killed.[850] Saul's general, Abner, survived and took action to save Saul's kingdom.

---

848 I Samuel 28:4 and I Samuel 29:1 Enclosure or fortress is the meaning of *Aphek.*
849 II Samuel 1:1-2
850 II Samuel 1:1-17

Pharaohs of the Bible

Ishbosheth, Saul's son

But Abner the son of Ner, commander of Saul's army, took Ishbosheth the son of Saul and brought him over to Mahanaim; and he made him king over Gilead, over the Ashurites, over Jezreel, over Ephraim, over Benjamin, and over all Israel. Ishbosheth, Saul's son, was forty years old when he began to reign over Israel, and he reigned two years. Only the house of Judah followed David. (II Samuel 2:8-10)

Then a battle ensued between general Abner and David's general Joab at Gibeon (now Jib, just north of Jerusalem) in which 360 of Abner's men and 20 of Joab's men died.[851] Skirmishes continued until Ishbosheth chided Abner for having sex with one of Saul's concubines, and so Abner went to Hebron to help king David and brought David his wife Michal, and David agreed to let Abner leave in peace. But Joab sought revenge for his brother's death, and slew Abner. David cursed Joab for doing so, and fasted during Abner's burial.[852] When Ishbosheth heard the news, he and his household knew their days were numbered, and so a servant escaped with Jonathon's son, Mephibosheth, before two assassins came and killed Ishbosheth. David hung the assassins and gave Ishbosheth a proper burial.[853] Ishbosheth reigned as king of Israel while David reigned as king of Judah.

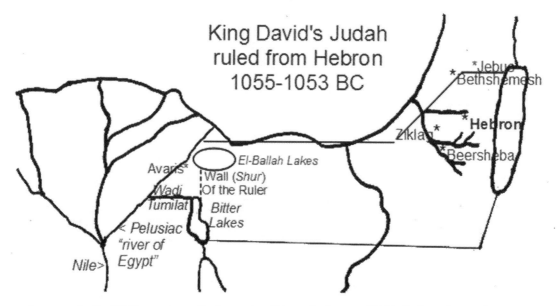

Amenemhat's Wall went north from the Bitter Lakes to El-Ballah Lake. The northern Sinai had been neglected by Egypt since Rameses III sent Keftiu to live with their Philistine brothers in 1310 BC. After David cleared it of Amalekites, Israelites could have moved in.

---

851 II Samuel 2:12-32
852 II Samuel 3:1-39
853 II Samuel 4:1-12

The LORD's Commands for Israel's Kings

As YHWH through Moses prepared the children of Israel to go into their promised land, He gave them the following commands.

When you are come to the land which the LORD your God gives you, and shall possess it, and shall dwell therein, and shall say, I will set a king over me, like as all the nations that are about me; You shall in any wise set him king over you, whom the LORD your God shall choose: one from among your brothers . . .
*- But he shall not multiply **horses** to himself, <u>nor cause the people to return to Egypt, to the end that he should multiply horses</u>: for as much as the LORD has said to you, You shall from now on return no more that way.*
*- Neither shall he multiply **wives** to himself, that his heart turn not away:*
*- neither shall he greatly multiply to himself **silver and gold**.*
- And it shall be, when he sits on the throne of his kingdom, that <u>he shall write him a copy of this law in a book</u> out of that which is before the priests the Levites: And it shall be with him, <u>and he shall read therein all the days of his life</u>: that he may learn to fear the LORD his God, to keep all the words of this law and these statutes, to do them: That his heart be not lifted up above his brothers, and that he turn not aside from the commandment, to the right hand, or to the left: to the end that he may prolong his days in his kingdom, he, and his children, in the middle of Israel."
(Deuteronomy 17:14-20, hyphens and emphasis added)

As a priest, Samuel likely conveyed to David what YHWH expected of him as king.

King David

For a third time, David was anointed king over Israel. David's first anointing was by a prophet (I Samuel 16:13), his second by warriors (I Chron. 12:23-40 in 1055), and his third by elders (II Sm. 5:1-3 and I Chron. 11:1-3 in 1053) after king Ishbosheth was assassinated.

David was thirty years old when he began to reign, and he reigned forty years. In Hebron he reigned over Judah seven years and six months: and in Jerusalem he reigned thirty and three years over all Israel and Judah. (II Samuel 5:4-5)

I propose the first *"six months"* was counted from Nisan,[854] when he was coronated in Hebron by his fellow warriors, to Tishri when he was coronated by the elders.

And the king and his men went to Jerusalem to the Jebusites, the inhabitants of the land: which spoke to David, saying, Except you take away the blind and the lame, you shall not come in here: thinking, David cannot come in here. Nevertheless David took the strong hold of Zion: the same is the city of David. And David said on that day, Whoever gets up to the <u>gutter</u>, and smites the Jebusites, and the lame and the blind that are hated of David's soul, he shall be chief and captain. Why they said,

---

[854] I disagree with Ussher in *Annals*, paragraph 460, who places the beginning of David's reign in Fall.

*The blind and the lame shall not come into the house. So David dwelled in the **fort**, and called it the city of David. And David built round about from **Millo** and inward. (II Samuel 5:6-9)*

The city of Salem had been taken over by Jebusites. *Jebus* means "trodden down". Salem was trodden down of the Canaanite gentiles until David restored it, and called it "holy peace" (Greek: *hierosalem*). The "*gutter*" is now known as Warren's Shaft (pg. 90), a mostly natural connection of the waters of the Gihon Spring to the Spring Tower and Pool Tower and reservoir which enabled the Jebusites to access fresh water safely from within the city. Joab was the one who climbed up the "*gutter*" and then opened the city gate. Joab also repaired the battle damage done to the city.[855] So he redeemed himself in David's eyes. The "*fort*" and "*Millo*" and two towers were all fortified stone structures acquired by David, but not built by him. Jebus, being on a hill (pg. 90), needed extensive retaining walls (millos) to produce a firm, level area for a foundation for a stone palace. David built additional millos beginning at the original one.[856] A tenth century millo in the city of David was discovered with large palatial foundation stones which had been above it, now fallen to its base.[857]

Jebusite millo with David's additions

And Hiram king of Tyre sent messengers to David, and cedar trees, and carpenters, and masons: and they built David an house. . . . The Philistines also came and spread themselves in the valley of Rephaim. (II Samuel 5:11+18)

The valley of *Rephaim* (giants) was to the west of Jerusalem, separated from Jerusalem's valley of ben-Hinnom by just a narrow ridge.[858] David asked the LORD if he should attack the Philistines; God said 'yes' and broke the enemies ranks, and David's men were victorious and burned the Philistine's idols.[859] The Philistines inhabited the area again, and this time YHWH told David to circle behind them and await His signal to attack;[860] and David's army "*smote the Philistines from Geba until you come to Gezer.*"[861]

David acquired and built other forts and castles throughout his realm, and placed Jehonathan as their overseer.[862] And David placed tsars over the land's produce and livestock.

---

855 I Chronicles 11:5-8 "castle"; http://www.sciencedaily.com/releases/2010/02/100222094757.htm
856 II Samuel 5:9 ". . . David built round about from Millo and inward."
857 Mazar, Eilat, "Did I find King David's Palace?" *Biblical Archaeology Review*, http://www.bib-arch.org/e-features/king-davids-palace.asp#location1 and http://en.wikipedia.org/wiki/Large_Stone_Structure discovered by Eilat Mazar
858 Joshua 15:8
859 II Samuel 5:17-21
860 II Samuel 5:22-25a
861 II Samuel 5:25b
862 I Chronicles 27:24-25

West Gate of David's Fortress in Elah Valley

Saul built a fort where the Philistines had encamped between Azekah and Socoh, now called Khirbet Qeiyafa[863] and Khirbet Daoud (David's ruins). David built it into Israel's boundary fortress with the Philistines. It is located in the valley of Elah 5 km south of Shaaraim (Khirbet esh-Sharia) which lies along the road to Gath.[864] Tel Adullam is 7 km SE and Tel Yarmut is 4 km NE of this fortress in accordance with Joshua 15:35. A 'tenth' century piece of pottery (ostracon) with the earliest alphabetic script was found there:[865]

"1 you shall not do [it], but worship (the god) [El]
2 Judge the sla[ve] and the wid[ow] / Judge the orph[an]
3 [and] the stranger. [Pl]ead for the infant / plead for the [po]or and
4 the widow. Rehabilitate [the poor] at the hands of the king
5 Protect the po[or and] the slave / [supp]ort the stranger."[866]

Israel from Nile to Orontes River

*And let us bring again the ark of our God to us: for we inquired not at it in the days of Saul. And all the congregation said that they would do so . . . So David gathered all Israel together, from <u>Shihor of Egypt</u> even to the entering of **Hemath**, to bring the ark of God from Kirjathjearim. (I Chron. 13:3-5)*

David's early kingdom from Shihor river to Hamath
(not including Phoenician or Philistine coastal cities)

Instead of referring to the "wall" of Egypt, David now refers to the dark, turbid river (*shichor* comes from root meaning 'black') which was the Nile;[867] with its Pelusiac branch ending near Port Said. Once again Israel's lands

---
863 http://en.wikipedia.org/wiki/Khirbet_Qeiyafa Stratigraphy of the tell in appendix A
864 Shaaraim is in the Nahal Timna valley on the way to Gath (Tel Miqne). See I Samuel 17:19-52
865 Video at http://zomobo.net/play.php?id=f46e7v160yU
866 Galil, Gershon, "Most ancient Hebrew biblical inscription deciphered," Haifa, January 10, 2010
867 Also Is. 23:3 and Jer. 2:18. When Pelusiac dried up, Wadi El-Arish was assumed. See "Rhinocorura"

included the *"country of Goshen"*[868] where they had been enslaved. This loss of territory occurred while Sheshonk I was pharaoh, possibly while he was in the south. Ancient Hemath/Hamath is now Hamah, Syria on the Orontes River. Hamah is roughly 100 miles north of Damascus. David had fought to include the Sinai Peninsula and Lebanon within Israel's borders. *Kirjathjearim* means "city of forests" and is now Kiryat Ye'arim about nine miles west of Jerusalem.

King David and the Ark of the Covenant

After residing seventy years at Kirjathjearim (1115 to 1045 BC), David had the ark of the covenant placed onto a cart to take it to Jerusalem; but Uzzah was killed by God when he touched it in order to steady it.[869] Instead the ark was placed into the house of Obededom. King David was supposed to have written for himself a copy of the Torah (Genesis to Deuteronomy). After taking three months to do so, he understood the ark had to be carried by the Levitical priests and so instructed them.[870] David wrote a psalm and organized priests, musicians, elders and warriors to bring up the ark in style; and he sacrificed animals to YHWH every six paces.[871]

And David danced before the LORD with all his might; and David was girded with a linen ephod. So David and all the house of Israel brought up the ark of the LORD with shouting, and with the sound of the trumpet. (II Samuel 6:14-15)

They placed the ark in a tent in Jerusalem and had a great celebration. As king David sat in his opulent palace,[872] he desired to build a house for the ark. The LORD responded to him through Nathan the prophet that since He had driven out their enemies and given the people of Israel a secure land that He would give David a *"house"*; a prophetic eternal kingdom from his seed as well as a son after him who would build His house/temple.[873]

---

868 Genesis 47:27 and Joshua 10:41; 11:16
869 I Chronicles 13:1-12
870 I Chron. 15:2, 11-14 based on Numbers 4:1-20 includes the warning not to touch the ark or death results
871 I Chron. 16:7 (possibly Psalm 68 or 132; see Numbers 10:35 and II Chron. 6:41), and II Samuel 6:13
872 See discovery of David's palace at http://www.bib-arch.org/e-features/king-davids-palace.asp
873 II Samuel 7:7-17

KING DAVID'S MILITARY BATTLES from Jerusalem

BATTLE	SLAIN #	VICTOR	SUMMARY	REF.
Valley of Rephaim		Israel defeated Philistines two times		II Sam. 5:17-25
Gath to Giah near Ashkelon		Israel took the plains of provision	David isolated Philistines to coast	I Chron. 18:1
Moab		Israel killed 2/3 of Moabites		II Sam. 8:2
Zobah, a city between Hamath and Damascus		Israel attacked Hadadezer, king of Zobah (but king of Hamath was Toi who sent gifts to David)	*"David took from him a 1,000 chariots, 700 horsemen, and 20,000 footmen"*	II Sam. 8:3-4, 9-11
Aram and Syria all the way to the Euphrates River	22,000 Syrians	Israel subjugated the Syrians who came to aid Hadadezer. Cities Tibhath and Chun gave David brass.	*"David put garrisons in Syria of Damascus: and the Syrians became servants to David"*	II Sam. 8:5-6 and I Chron. 18:3-10
Valley of salt	18,000 Edomites	Israel (Abishai) slew Edomites		I Chron. 18:12
Edom		Israel took six months to kill all the males in Edom *And Edom shall be a possession . . .* (prophesy in Numbers 24:18)	*"And he put garrisons in Edom; and all they of Edom became David's servants."*	II Sam. 8:14 and I Kings 11:15-16
Madaba, Jordan is 38 miles east of Jerusalem	700 chariot men 40,000 cavalry	Israel routed the Syrians (Aramaeans) hired by Hadarezer (Rezon), king of Ammon; subjugating Ammon	Ammon *"hired 32,000 chariots, from king of Maachah; pitched before Medeba."*	II Sam. 10:18 and I Chron. 19:1-19
Gezer to Gath		Israel slew giants of the Philistines	4 separate battles with 4 different heroes	I Chron. 20:3-8

David's Battles Abroad and at Home

Siege of Rabbah

David retook the plains from Gath[874] to Giah (now Ge'a, about a mile inland from greater Ashkelon),[875] and built up a fortification overlooking the Elah valley.[876] David's armies killed two-thirds of the Moabites east of the Dead Sea.[877] David continued to push the Philistines back to their coastal cities. David did not forget his promise to Saul to care for his descendants, so David took Mephibosheth into his palace.[878] After the battle at Medeba, king David remained in Jerusalem and sent general Joab to attack the fortress city of Rabbah[879] in Gilead;[880] and David had sex with Uriah's wife, Bathsheba, and then had Uriah killed.[881] Nathan exposed David's sin and prophesied that their love child would die, which he did.[882] The child of David and Bathsheba's marriage was Solomon; and Nathan declared Solomon to be Jedidiah which means 'beloved of the LORD'.[883] Meanwhile Joab's siege of Rabbah had cut off their water supply, and he sent a messenger to tell David to come and take it if he wanted the credit for it, which he did.[884] So king David increased his empire to include lands east and south of the Dead Sea: the Ammonites, Moabites, and Edomites.

David's first-born son Amnon raped his half-sister Tamar, whose brother was Absalom. David got angry, but didn't deal with the situation. So two years later at a feast for the princes, Absalom had his brother Amnon murdered, and Absalom fled to the king of Geshur, his grandfather.[885] Absalom's mom was a *"daughter of Talmai king of Geshur"*.[886] In fact, David had at least six wives while he ruled at Hebron.[887] Absalom spent three years in Geshur, then Joab tricked David into returning him to Jerusalem, but they did not see each other for two more years.[888] Then *"Absalom stole the hearts of the men of Israel,"*[889] moved to Hebron and planned to take his father's kingdom. David fled Jerusalem, and Absalom came in and had sex with David's ten concubine's on the roof for all to see.[890] Then the civil war took 20,000 lives before David reclaimed his throne (II Samuel 17-20).

874 Tel Miqne was the "royal city" of Gath. It's 18km east of Ashdod and 7km west of Tel Batash (Timnah).
875 II Samuel 8:1 based on II Samuel 2:24 and I Chronicles 18:1
876 David's ruins at http://en.wikipedia.org/wiki/Khirbet_Qeiyafa_pottery_sherd
877 II Samuel 8:2
878 II Samuel 9:1-13
879 Rabbah info #2 at http://www.jewishvirtuallibrary.org/jsource/judaica/ejud_0002_0017_0_16246.html
880 Gilead was originally territory of Sihon and Og, east of Jordan. see http://en.wikipedia.org/wiki/Gilead
881 II Samuel 11:1-27
882 II Samuel 12:1-23
883 II Samuel 12:24-25
884 II Samuel 12:26-31
885 II Samuel 13:1-39
886 II Samuel 3:3 Geshur was a district of east Manasseh between the Yarmuk River and Jabesh.
887 II Samuel 3:2-5
888 II Samuel 14:1-43
889 II Samuel 15:6
890 II Samuel 15 and 16

Prince Hadad escaped to Sheshonk I, married, and returned to Edom

A main god of Syria was Hadad/Adad, the storm god. When a man became king, he often took on a form of his name. Both *Hadad-ezer* and *Hadar-ezer* means 'Hadad helps'.

As David conquered the land promised to Abraham, Isaac, and Jacob; Hadad, the child prince of Edom, was carried off to Egypt by servants, and later returned to rule Edom as an adult. The history is given below.

*And the LORD stirred up an adversary to Solomon, Hadad the Edomite: he was of the king's seed in Edom. For it came to pass, when David was in Edom, and Joab the captain of the host was gone up to bury the slain, after he had smitten every male in Edom; (For six months did Joab remain there with all Israel, until he had cut off every male in Edom:) That Hadad fled, he and certain Edomites of his father's servants with him, to go into Egypt; Hadad being yet a little child. And they arose out of Midian, and came to Paran: and they took men with them out of Paran, and <u>they came to Egypt, to Pharaoh king of Egypt; which gave him an house, and appointed him victuals, and gave him land. And Hadad found great favor in the sight of Pharaoh, so that he gave him to wife the sister of his own wife, the sister of Tahpenes the queen</u>. And the sister of **Tahpenes** bore him Genubath his son, whom Tahpenes weaned in Pharaoh's house: and Genubath was in Pharaoh's household among the sons of Pharaoh. And when Hadad heard in Egypt that David slept with his fathers, and that Joab the captain of the host was dead, Hadad said to Pharaoh, Let me depart, that I may go to my own country. Then Pharaoh said to him, But what have you lacked with me, that, behold, you seek to go to your own country? And he answered, Nothing: however, let me go in any wise. (I Kings 11:14-22)*

I suggest that prince Hadad and company came under the protection of Sheshonk I, who had at least three sons, and his wife Patareshnes (a similar name to Tahpenes).[891] Her father was Nemareth, the "Great Chief of the Foreigners," and more likely open to a marriage arrangement with a foreigner. The sister of Patareshnes, Hadad's bride, is not named; but their son was named Genubath. I suggest this wedding took place about 1035 BC during the latter years of Sheshonk I.

Sekhmet statue of Sheshonk I in Karnak

Like Amenhotep III who built queen Tiye the Mansion of the Lion near Avaris, Sheshonk I may have associated his wife Patareshnes with the lioness god Sekhmet, and made this statue and built her a city near Avaris. On the El-Hibeh temple reliefs, Sheshonk I offers oil jars to Sekhmet.

King David died in fall of 1015 BC, which was during the reign of Osorkon I when Hadad likely asked to return to Edom and was given leave. By 1010 BC Hadad became a warring opponent to Solomon.

---

891 This queen has a city named after herself spelled Tahpanhes in Jer. 43:7-9; 46:14, Tahapanes in Jer. 2:16, and Tehaphnehes in Ezekiel 30:18. It is now Tel Dafneh 18 miles SE of Tanis near Lake Ballah.

3-Year Famine: 1023-1020 BC

Because king Saul had ordered Doeg to slay the priests and people of Nob[892] (which lies north of Jerusalem in the former lands of the Gibeonites), the LORD sent a famine upon the land.[893] For reparations, the Gibeonites asked to slay children of Saul, and David sent them seven but not Mephibosheth.[894] This was the fifth Biblical famine, and it was localized to Israel. There is no record of a famine during Sheshonk I's reign.

In his last battle, elderly David fainted and would have been killed by the giant Ishbibenob, if Abishai had not intervened.[895] With the LORD's help, king David by 1021 BC had conquered all the land promised to Abram in 1921 BC.

David took a Census which brought a Plague and a place for the Temple

Maybe David had ceased reading the Torah's rules about such things, but he chose to take a census of the number of military-aged men in Israel without requiring the half shekel to make atonement for their souls and stave off a plague.[896] David would not relent even after Joab pleaded with him not to do it. Joab began taking the census in 1017 BC, and it took nine and a half months to complete.[897] Joab did not count the men of Benjamin or Levi, but Judah had 461,000 military-aged men and Israel had 1,100,000 men.[898]

Through the prophet Gad, the LORD gave king David a choice of three punishments for his sin: three more years of famine,[899] three months being destroyed by his enemies, or three days of a plague from YHWH; and David chose plague.[900] David repented and Yahweh stopped the death angel at the threshing floor of Ornan/Araunah after 70,000 men had been killed, and He told David to set up an altar there.[901] David bought Ornan's oxen and wooden threshing instruments, and offered burnt offerings to YHWH. David exclaimed, *"This is the house of the LORD God, and this is the altar of the burnt offering for Israel."*[902]

Transfer of Purpose, Power, and Plans

David began preparations for the house of God: wood, marble, stone, precious stone common metals and precious metals.[903] He also may have placed the double triangle hexagonal 'shield of David' (*magen david*) upon cut ashlar stones prepared for construction.

---

[892] I Samuel 22:9-23
[893] II Samuel 21:1
[894] II Samuel 21:2-14
[895] II Samuel 21:15-17
[896] I Chronicles 21:1-4 and Exodus 30:11-16 Military age was over 20.
[897] Date from Ussher's *Annals*, and timing from II Samuel 24:8
[898] I Chronicles 21:5-6
[899] To reconcile II Samuel 24:13 (7 years) and I Chron. 21:12 (3 years), I include the sabbatical Tishri year 1024-1023 BC as the first year of no sowing prior to the counting of first three years of famine to total 4.
[900] I Chronicles 21:10-13
[901] I Chronicles 21:14-19
[902] I Chronicles 22:1; see http://en.wikipedia.org/wiki/Foundation_Stone
[903] I Chronicles 22:1-5, 11; 29:2 100,000 talents of gold, 1,000,000 talents of silver, abundant brass and iron

The faint lines of this symbol, also known as Solomon's seal, were found on an ashlar in stratum IV at Megiddo.[904] David prophesied over Solomon. David commanded all the princes to help Solomon build the Temple and other buildings on Mount Moriah.[905]

> *My son, as for me, it was in my mind to build an house to the name of the LORD my God: But the word of the LORD came to me, saying, You have shed blood abundantly, and have made great wars: you shall not build an house to my name, because you have shed much blood on the earth in my sight. Behold, a son shall be born to you, who shall be a man of rest; and I will give him rest from all his enemies round about: for his name shall be Solomon, and I will give peace and quietness to Israel in his days. He shall build an house for my name . . . (I Chron. 22:7-10a)*

Since Amnon and Absalom had both been killed, that left Adonijah as David's eldest living son. Adonijah was Absalom's brother, and like him, he had chariots and 50 men run before him.[906] Prince Adonijah saw his father planning for Solomon to become king after him, and he wasn't inclined to help his half-brother with the Temple. Adonijah, with the help of general Joab and Abiathar, the high priest, made himself king east of Jerusalem.[907] When Bathsheba and Nathan told David of this, David ordered Solomon to be anointed king in Gihon west of Jerusalem by Zadok the priest and Nathan the prophet.[908] When Adonijah heard this, he fled to the sanctuary and took hold of the horns of the altar; and was pardoned by the grace of king Solomon and set free upon his vow of submission.[909]

David then established clear civil and religious structure, and set the "*courses*" or yearly schedule for the priests' service in the tabernacle/temple.[910] King David handed Solomon all of the floor-plans for the houses, porches, treasuries around the Temple, and the ark of the covenant and items in the Temple as Yahweh had communicated them to him.[911]

David's Floorplans

> <u>*All this, said David, the LORD made me understand in writing by his hand on me, even all the works of this pattern*</u>. *And David said to Solomon his son, Be strong and of good courage, and do it: fear not, nor be dismayed: for the LORD God, even my God, will be with you; he will not fail you, nor forsake you, until you have finished all the work for the service of the house of the LORD. (I Chronicles 28:19-20)*

---

904 Guy, P.L.O., "New Light from Armageddon: Second Provisional Report (1927-1929)," University of Chicago Press, 1931, p. 37 picture and report at http://oi.uchicago.edu/research/pubs/catalog/oic/oic9.html
905 I Chronicles 22:17
906 II Samuel 15:1 and I Kings 1:5
907 I Kings 1:7-11 Enrogel is east of Jerusalem, see Joshua 15:7-8
908 I Kings 1:12-40 Gihon was a pool west of Jerusalem, see II Chronicles 32:30
909 I Kings 1:41-53
910 I Chronicles 23-27; 28:21
911 I Chronicles 28:11-18

The tabernacle of Moses remained at Gibeon until Solomon finished the temple.[912] Many sacrifices were made to the LORD at Gibeon during Solomon's second coronation most likely on the first day of Tishri. Just as when Moses allowed the people to contribute materials to build the tabernacle, the Israelites added greatly to David's provisions for the Temple with willing hearts.[913]

> *And did eat and drink before the LORD on that day with great gladness. And they made Solomon the son of David king **second time**, and anointed him to the LORD to be the chief governor, and Zadok to be priest. (I Chronicles 29:22)*

> *Now the acts of David the king, first and last, behold, they are written in the book of Samuel the seer, and in the book of Nathan the prophet, and in the book of Gad the seer. (I Chronicles 29:29)*

The two books of Samuel survived, whereas the books of Nathan and Gad did not.

Final Instructions

> *Now the days of David drew near that he should die; and he charged Solomon his son, saying, . . . keep the charge of the LORD your God, to walk in his ways, to keep his statutes, and his commandments, and his judgments, and his testimonies, as it is written in the law of Moses, that you may prosper in all that you do, and wherever you turn yourself . . . David slept with his fathers, and was buried in the city of David. . . . Then sat Solomon on the throne of David his father; and his kingdom was established greatly. (I Kings 2:1-12)*

David's instructions to Solomon

King David left a list of people for Solomon to kill, whom Solomon executed in short order.[914] Adonijah made one final attempt to take the kingdom through marriage to a young concubine of his father, so Solomon killed him.[915]

According to Josephus, Solomon placed great treasure in David's tomb, and 3,000 talents of it were given to Antiochus Epiphanes to lift his siege of Jerusalem. During Jesus ministry on earth, David's stone sepulcher was still well known,[916] and may have been one of the "*houses*" for which the LORD gave him a plan to build. Cave tombs for other family members were discovered.[917] David left a large, secure kingdom to Solomon so he could focus on building. David also left a legacy of psalms to Yahweh; with psalm 23 beginning "*The LORD is my shepherd*," his most famous.

---

912 I Chron. 6:32,48-49; 16:39-40; 21:29 and II Chron. 1:3-6 and I Kings 3:2-4
913 Exodus 25:1-9 and I Chronicles 29:5-9, 21
914 I Kings 2:5-9, 25-46
915 I Kings 2:13-24
916 Acts 2:29
917 Under the Muycha home http://www.cityofdavid.org.il/vtour_eng.asp?id=24

Osorkon I (1022-988 BC) of 22nd dynasty

Osorkon I

Osorkon I was the first-born son of Sheshonk I and Karomat A. He succeeded his father after his death. His three wives were Maatkare B, Tashedkhonsu, and Shepensopdet A. Their children were Shoshenq C, Iuwelot, Smendes III, and Takelot I.

Devastating Theban Flood in 3rd year (1019 BC)

On the Karnak quay an inscription of a flood of more than two feet (62 cm) above the Luxor temple pavement was recorded. This corresponds to a graffito of 51 lines written by priest Nakhtefmut[918] which has incorrectly been attributed to the third year of Osorkon II or III, though it refers to Osorkon I in line 46: "King of Upper and Lower Egypt Osorkon and his brother [Iuput . . .]."[919] Neither Osorkon II nor III had a brother named Iuput, but HPA Iuput A was the brother of Osorkon I with Sheshonk I as their father. Priest Nakhtefmut died about seven years later, and was reburied in the 33rd year of Osorkon I with a tag bearing his name in a cartouche.[920] Though half of Luxor was inundated (line 33), that also meant devastation at upstream forts as well. Osorkon I and HPA/general Sheshonk C took advantage of the situation by raiding the land of Kush.

Raid of Kushite Wealth in 4th year (1018 BC)

The Bubastite portal derives its name primarily from the buildings of Osorkon at Bubastis: a monumental granite gateway, a hypostyle hall, and a smaller temple of Atum.[921] A red granite pillar in the small temple contained the record between years one and four of Osorkon's vast donations of gold, silver, lapis lazuli and "black copper".[922] The list includes offering stands, braziers, bowls, and censers which some have attributed to Shishak's loot from Jerusalem's temple, but also listed are "2 divine apes" and "6 altars"[923] of fine gold which would not have come from the Temple. I suggest Osorkon I had a successful Kushite raid. The mountains of southern Sudan and Ethiopia are still being mined for gold. The Grivet monkey is native to Nubia and was worshipped at Hermopolis.[924] Central Africa's Zambia and Congo contain a copper belt which is rich in azurite.[925] Azurite is often mislabeled as lapis lazuli, and with heat "azurite turns to black copper oxide."[926]

---

918 Ritner, Robert. K., *The Libyan Anarchy*, Society of Biblical Literature, 2009, pp. 415-421
919 Ibid., p. 419 The letters of "Iuput" were not as clear as the rest of the script.
920 See notes on 22nd dynasty in the appendix.
921 Ritner, Robert. K., *The Libyan Anarchy*, Society of Biblical Literature, 2009, p. 237
922 Ibid., pp. 249-258
923 Ibid., p. 253
924 Shaw, John Farquhar, "Sketches of Scripture Zoology," *The Youth's Magazine*, London, Reed and Pardon, 1857, p. 253
925 "Copperbelt" http://en.wikipedia.org/wiki/Copperbelt
926 "Azurite," at http://en.wikipedia.org/wiki/Azurite

Other Projects

Osorkon I added to the temple of Isis at Atfih, and built a new military stronghold ('Estate of Osorkon I') near the entry to the Fayyum. Part of a large alabaster vase with Osorkon's names inscribed on it, and the capacity of 81 hin, was discovered at the royal palace site in Samaria, Israel,[927] so there was trade between Egypt and Israel. Like Sheshonk I, Osorkon I also sent Alibaal of Byblos a seated statue of himself.[928] But unlike Sheshonk's reliefs at Karnak which always have HPA Iuput in them, an HPA is never pictured in the three scenes of Osorkon I at the Bubastite portal.[929] At the El-Hibeh temple to Amun "Great of Roarings (War-shouts)",[930] Osorkon I added five scenes to complete the decoration started by his father.[931] In one of the scenes he offers libations to the hawk-headed deity Khonsu juxtaposed to Sheshonk I offering incense to Khonsu;[932] so, like Karnak, the temple was dedicated to Amun, Khonsu, and Mut.

HPA's at El-Hibeh and Thebes

The moon-god Khonsu was the child of the sun-god Amun and Mut (world-mother, lady of heaven). Mut was the creator god whose name began with the vulture glyph like the word mother, and she was sometimes depicted with vulture wings. The great temple at Karnak is dedicated to Amun, Khonsu, and Mut. During the 22nd dynasty there were also high priests of Amun at the temple built by Sheshonk I in el-Hibeh. Like HPA's in Thebes, they were also generals who kept order throughout their jurisdiction in Middle Egypt. The first HPA at el-Hibeh was Nimlot B under Sheshonk I, who was followed by Shedsunefertem under Osorkon I.

Osorkon I married the daughter of Psusennes II, known as Maatkare B. Their eldest son was Sheshonk C. Sheshonk C succeeded Iuput A (Sheshonk I's son) as high priest of Amun at Thebes. I have Sheshonk C dying six years prior to his father. Osorkon I's sons Iuwelot and Smendes C followed Sheshonk C as HPA at Thebes in order. HPA Iuwelot is attested by Karnak Nile Level Text (KNLT) #16, 20-21 which were slightly above normal flows. HPA Smendes C is attested by KNLT #17-19 which were below normal flows. These HPA's recorded the levels according to their own years, not those of a king in the north. This lineage of HPA's at Thebes began with Iuput A of the 23rd dynasty. Some of them, like Smendes C, also took on the title of king; thus becoming Smendes III. The 22nd - 26th dynasties are called the Third Intermediate Period, as Egypt divided into smaller factions again. In Clarity chronology, the Tanite/Bubastite 22nd and Theban 23rd dynasties were concurrent and then followed by the Saite 24th and 26th dynasties which were concurrent with the Kushite 25th dynasty takeover of Thebes.

---

927 *The Cambridge Ancient History III Part 1*, 2003, p. 558
928 Ritner, Robert. K., *The Libyan Anarchy*, Society of Biblical Literature, 2009, p. 233
929 Ritner, Robert. K., *The Libyan Anarchy*, Society of Biblical Literature, 2009, p. 229
930 Interactive temple pictures at http://nes.berkeley.edu/hibeh/explore_temple/840.htm
931 Ritner, Robert. K., *The Libyan Anarchy*, Society of Biblical Literature, 2009, p. 235
932 Ritner, Robert. K., *The Libyan Anarchy*, Society of Biblical Literature, 2009, pp. 223 and 236

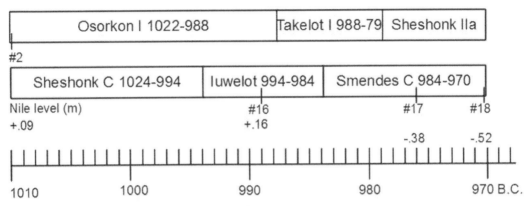

Karnak Nile Level Texts #2, 16-18

Sheshonk C (1024-994 BC) of 23rd dynasty

Osorkon I appointed his son, Sheshonk C, leader of the army and high priest of Amun in Thebes. Sheshonk C dedicated a 7 foot tall statue of the Nile-god, Hapi to Amon-Re.[933] The translation of its back pillar reads:

> "Made by the First Prophet of Amon-Re, King of the Gods, Sheshonk, beloved of Amon, for his lord Amon-Re, Lord of the Thrones of the Two Lands, Foremost of Karnak, in order to beseech life, prosperity, health, a long lifetime, advanced and goodly old age, valor, and victory against every land and every foreign land [in a single] feat of [strength,] and all valiant might. What his land brings to the Lord of Upper and Lower Egypt, the leader Sheshonk, beloved of Amon, who is at the head of all the great armies of Egypt, royal son of the Lord of the Two Lands, Lord of ritual performance, **Osorkon**, beloved of Amon, whose mother is Maatkare, princess of the Lord of the Two Lands, Hor Pseusennes (II), beloved of Amon, given life, stability, and dominion like Re forever."[934]

Sheshonk C was referring to 'his' mother Maatkare who was the wife of Osorkon I. HPA Sheshonk C became the father of Harsiese. The Durham Bes Statue refers to pharaoh Osorkon I as the father of first prophet Sheshonk (C), and Harsiese as just a prophet. Harsiese A became a prophet of Amun under his father who was HPA and general.[935] When Harsiese A became high priest, he did not refer to his father as pharaoh or king. None of Sheshonk C's three wives referred to themselves as wife of a king.

---

933 Ibid., p.111 Dodson labels him Sheshonk Q, and attributes it to "Maakheperre".
934 Ritner, Robert K., *The Libyan Anarchy: Inscriptions from Egypt's Third Intermediate Period*, Society of Biblical Literature, 2009, p. 266
935 Ibid., "Durham Bes Statue", p. 269

Iuwelot (994-984 BC) of 23rd dynasty

On the Appanage[936] Stela of Iuwelot, HPA Iuwelot is dressed in the traditional priestly garment of a panther skin while offering maat to Amun and Mut.[937] Iuwelot granted the fields in nome #13 near the "good mound" where he began his service to his father Osorkon I in his tenth regnal year[938] to Khaemwese, a nomarch and prophet of Amun, and to his sons in perpetuity.[939]

On the Solar Hymn stela of Iuwelot, he and his wife are kneeling before a solar barque. Iuwelot praises Re as the self-created one without form, and requests spiritual cleansing.[940] Their son, Wasakawasa, became HPA briefly, as attested by a pectoral.[941]

King David ruled 40 years and 6 months

King David's forty years and six months were from Spring 1055 to Fall 1015. This is why God let us know David reigned seven years and six months in Hebron,[942] because he ruled six months prior to Tishri 1st and the beginning of his first official regnal year. David died before January, 1014 BC. David and Solomon shared 1015 BC as a regnal year.

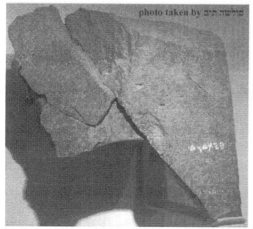

"House of David" on Tel Dan Stele in Israel Museum

Tel Dan Stele

The first fragment was discovered in 1993, and the other two followed the next year. It was the first time the name of king "David" had been found in an archaeological context. The Aramaic text contains the Syrian viewpoint of II Kings 8-9 and translates as follows:

"[...]...[...] and cut [...] [...] my father went up [against him when] he fought at[....] And my father lay down, he went to his [fathers]. And the king of I[s-]rael entered previously in my father's land. [And] Hadad made me king. And Hadad went in front of me, [and] I departed from [the] seven[.....] of my kingdom, and I slew [seve]nty kin[gs], who harnessed thou[sands of cha-]riots and thousands of horsemen (or: horses). [I killed Jeho]ram son of [Ahab] king of Israel, and I killed [Ahaz]iahu son of [Jehoram kin]g of the House of **David**. And I set [their towns into ruins and turned] their land into [desolation...] other ...[... and Jehu ru-] led over Is[rael...and I laid] siege upon [...]"[943]

---

936 An appanage is the grant of an estate or other things of value to the younger male children of an authority. It can also describe funds given by the state to certain royal families.
937 Ritner, Robert. K., *The Libyan Anarchy*, Society of Biblical Literature, 2009, p. 272
938 Ibid., pp. 273-4, lines 1-3
939 Ibid., p. 277, lines 23-26
940 Ibid., pp. 279-280
941 Ibid., pp. 280-291
942 II Samuel 5:5
943 http://en.wikipedia.org/wiki/Tel_Dan_Stele

After the genealogies of the sons of David in I Chronicles 3 is the following:

*And the sons of Ezra were, Jether, and Mered, and Epher, and Jalon:*and **she** bore Miriam, and Shammai, and Ishbah the father of Eshtemoa. And his wife Jehudijah bore Jered the father of Gedor, and Heber the father of Socho, and Jekuthiel the father of Zanoah. And these are the sons of **Bithiah** the daughter of Pharaoh, which Mered took. And the sons of his wife Hodiah the sister of Naham, the father of Keilah the Garmite, and Eshtemoa the Maachathite. (I Chronicles 4:17-19; underlined sentence should be placed at the asterisk)*

This is one of the rare copyist errors in the Bible. Mered had two wives who bore him sons; one was a Jewess who worshipped Jah/Yah (*Jehudijah*) and one was an Egyptian (*Bithiah*) who worshipped Iah/Yah. *Bithiah* means 'daughter of Iah'; so these 'names' might only describe his wives. Bithiah may have been part of the "mixed multitude" which left Egypt with the Hebrews. Since Rameses I had sons and at least one grandson when he took the throne, its reasonable to assume he also had daughters. A daughter who lived through the ten plagues, and saw her oldest brother die because her father refused to let the Hebrews leave may have decided to join the victors.

In EA 4, Amenhotep III wrote, "From time immemorial, no daughter of the king of Egypt is given to anyone." Though queen Ahhotep II was not a princess, after she married the king of Thera, the island erupted. It may be that a pharaoh deliberately married his daughter to king Solomon in the hope that the mighty nation of Israel would be destroyed; and it was, very soon after Solomon died.

Clarity Chronology of High Priests and 21st Dynasty during the Kingdom of Israel

LE=Lower Egypt (Delta); ME=Middle Egypt; UE=Upper Egypt (Thebes)

LE king	Osorkon 1091-85	Siamun 1085-66	Psusennes II 1066-1052	Sheshonk I 1055-1022	Osorkon I 1022-988		Takelot I 988-979	Sheshonk IIa 979-970
ME				Nimlot B, general	Shedsunefertem			
UE king	Pinedjem II 1097-1075	Psusennes III (II) 1075-1052						
HPA Thebes	Pinedjem II 1097-1075	Psusennes III (II) 1075-1052		Iuput A 1052-1024	Sheshonk C 1024-994		Iuwelot 994-984	Smendes C 984-970

Israel	Saul 1095-1055		David 1055-1015		Solomon 1015-975
			Ishbosheth 1055-1053		

Syria (Damascus)						Hezion	Tabrimon	
Assyria	Tiglath-Pileser I 1115-1076	Asharidapal-Ekur 1076-1074	Ashur-bel-kala 1074-1056	Eriba Adad II 1056-1054	Shamshi Adad IV 1054-1050	Ashur-nasir-pal I 1050-1031	Shalmaneser II 1031-1019	Ashur-nirari IV 1019-1013	Ashur-rabi II 1013-972

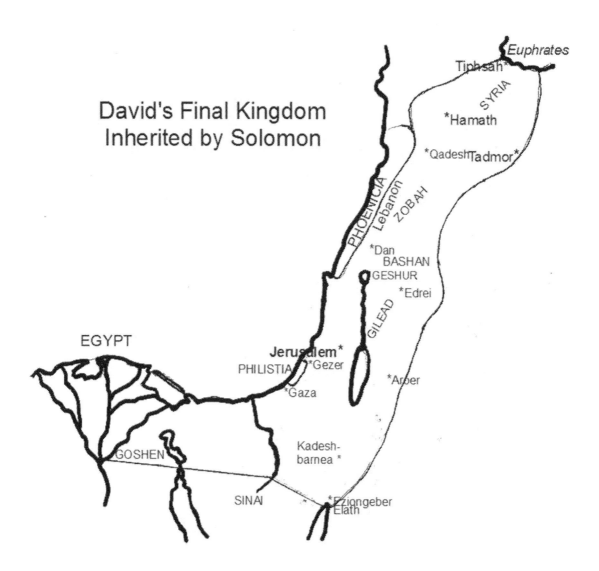

I place the Amalekites being slaughtered at the Bitter Lakes and Wall (*Shur*) between Sheshonk from the west and David from the east during Sheshonk's first year (1055 BC). The introduction and regnal year regarding it is missing from Sheshonk's Karnak stela. Then sometime during the next fifteen years, David retook the land of Goshen so that his eastern boundary was the "*Shihor of Egypt*", the Nile.[944]

---

944 Based upon I Samuel 27:8 and I Chronicles 13:5. I place Siamun's encounter with Saul at the Wall (*Shur*) in the latter years of Siamun's reign in 1068 or 1067 BC.

Solomon & Rehoboam's Pharaohs

". . . in the four hundred and eightieth year after the children of Israel were come out of the land of Egypt, in the fourth year of Solomon's reign over Israel, in the month Zif, which is the second month, that he began to build the house of the LORD."
$\underline{1491} - 480 = \textbf{1011}$ *(1 Kings 6:1)*

Israel's Regnal System

And let Zadok the priest and Nathan the prophet anoint him there king over Israel: and blow you with the trumpet, and say, God save king Solomon. (1 Kings 1:34)

The blowing of the trumpet (*shofar*) is associated with the inauguration of a king. The first day of the seventh month of the Hebrew calendar, Tishri, begins the civil New Year (*Rosh Hashanah* – head of the year), also known as the Feast of Trumpets. Israel's kings were attributed regnal years based upon how many New Year's days they reigned.[945] If a king only reigned a month before and after Rosh Hashanah, he would be attributed a whole year. If a king reigned for eleven months not including Rosh Hashanah, he would be attributed eleven months. Both a vice-regent[946] and a viceroy would number their regnal years from the time so appointed.

David's son Adonijah attempted to make himself king without his father's knowledge, but Nathan and Bathsheba alerted David, and David had his son Solomon anointed as king in Spring of 1015 BC. The Tishri to Tishri regnal year of 1016-1015 was attributed to both David and Solomon. So that fall, Solomon was attributed one year of ruling: fall of 1014 – 2 years, fall of 1013 – 3 years, fall of 1012 – 4 years. It was in the spring of his 4th regnal year in 1011 BC that the Temple's foundation was laid in the second month, and it was completed in seven and a half years. Solomon's 4th regnal year was from Tishri 1, 1012 to Tishri 1, **1011**. But Israel's religious calendar is counted from the first month of the year in spring which is Nisan; religious years are calculated from Nisan to Nisan. The exodus occurred in Nisan ($\underline{1491}$) BC as did Israel's entrance into Canaan 40 years later. In accordance to I Kings 6:1, 480 years after the exodus in the first month of Nisan, Solomon began to build the Temple in the second month of Zif. $\underline{1491} - 480 = \textbf{1011}$ BC

---

[945] Edwin Thiele, in *The Mysterious Numbers of the Hebrew Kings*, states the following: "a Tishri-to-Tishri year was used in the reckoning of Solomon's reign" (p. 51), and "that Judah almost at the close of its history was still counting its regnal years from Tishri-to-Tishri is indicated by 2 Kings 22:3 and 23:23" (p. 52). But Thiele thought Israel's kings used Nisan to Nisan years. Sigmund Mowinckel taught both kingdoms counted reigns from Tishri 1 since forty Psalms describe this Feast of Trumpets at the new moon (Psalms 47, 81, 98) to enthrone the LORD as King over the earth (Psalm 24, 45, 68, and 95-99).

[946] Vice-regent is a co-king. Viceroy is part of a king duo. Jehoram was the only vice-regent, beginning in Jehoshaphat's 16th year, and then made viceroy in Jehoshaphat's 22nd year. II Kings 8:16-17

Pharaohs of the Bible

Though Adonijah forced David to anoint Solomon as king in Spring at the Gihon spring, a proper coronation was held at the beginning of Fall in Gibeon at the tabernacle with great ceremony and feasting; after which, David relinquished the throne.

And they sacrificed sacrifices unto the LORD, and offered burnt offerings unto the LORD, on the morrow after that day, even a thousand bullocks, a thousand rams, and a thousand lambs, with their drink offerings, and sacrifices in abundance for all Israel: And did eat and drink before the LORD on that day with great gladness. And they made Solomon the son of David king the second time, and anointed him unto the LORD to be the chief governor, and Zadok to be priest. <u>Then Solomon sat on the throne of the LORD as king instead of David his father</u>, and prospered; and all Israel obeyed him. And all the princes, and the mighty men, and all the sons likewise of king David, submitted themselves unto Solomon the king. And the LORD magnified Solomon exceedingly in the sight of all Israel, and bestowed upon him such royal majesty as had not been on any king before him in Israel. (I Chronicles 29:21-25)

Solomon's Time-line

1015	Solomon became king of Israel in Spring and ruled for 40 years
1012	Spring - 479 years after Exodus; Fall - Solomon's 4th year began
1011	480 years after Exodus completed, Temple foundation was laid in 2nd month
1010?	Prince Hadad returned from Egypt and ruled Edom as king Hadad
1007?	Pharaoh conquered Gezer as a dowry for his daughter to marry Solomon
1004	Temple completed in the eighth month; furnishings (I Kings 7:40-50)
1003	Temple dedicated in the seventh month during Feast of Tabernacles[947]
1002	Ninth Jubilee began in the fall
998	Solomon's Palace and House of the Lebanon Forest completed (1 Kings 7:1)
991	The *"king's house"* (1 Kings 9:10) and Temple complex were completed
991	Solomon recaptured Hamath and built store cities and a navy (1 Kings 9:10)
987?	Solomon completed his Millo and the wall of Jerusalem (I Kings 3:1; 9:24)
984	Solomon built cities (II Chron. 8); Queen of Sheba (1 Kings 10)
980?	Solomon lost Edom to Hadad, and lost Damascus to Rezon
979?	Solomon's foreman Jeroboam fled to Shishak in Egypt (I Kings 11:40)
975	Solomon likely died in January, and his son Rehoboam reigned
975	Jeroboam began ruling Israel likely in March; Rehoboam ruled Judah
970	Shishak attacked Israel and plundered Jerusalem's Temple and king's palace

---

[947] Jesus was born 1000 years later on Tishri 1, 3 BC. Christ "tabernacled with us" (John 1:14), and referred to His body as a temple (John 2:19). Solomon's Temple construction began and ended in a Sabbath year.

Solomon married daughter of Osorkon I

Part of the bride's dowry was Osorkon's destruction of Gezer. Though there is no record of Osorkon I attacking Gezer, neither is it in Karnak's list of cities which Shishak campaigned against. Normally a princess would be accompanied by a dowry of gold and jewels, so Osorkon I must have been too poor or cheap at the time, and could only muster an army to destroy one city; though in his fourth year (1018 BC) ". . . Osorkon I enumerated gifts totaling 383 tons of gold and silver (over 10,000 talents) that he provided for the various gods and goddesses of Egypt . . ."[948] Solomon may have given the western Sinai peninsula up to Wadi el-Arish to Osorkon I as a bride-price for his daughter. This marriage alliance had to occur prior to the Temple's completion in 1004 BC. Maybe it was 1007 BC because the house for pharaoh's daughter was squeezed into the Temple Complex. Osorkon I had two wives and one recognized consort, and one of their daughters became Solomon's wife early in his reign. She was housed outside of the building complex until her house was finished; then she moved into her Egyptian styled home adjoining Solomon's palace.

And Solomon made affinity with Pharaoh king of Egypt, and took Pharaoh's daughter, and brought her into the city of David, until he had made an end of building his own house, and the house of the LORD, and the wall of Jerusalem round about. Only the people sacrificed in high places, because there was no house built to the name of the LORD, until those days. (I Kings 3:1-2)

But Pharaoh's daughter came up out of the city of David to her house which Solomon had built for her: then did he build Millo. (I Kings 9:24)

In addition to the millo upon which David built his palace upon Ophel,[949] Mount Moriah needed much 'landfill' (*millo*) to make a level area for the complex and wall. Millo can also be translated 'retaining wall'. After Solomon's Temple and palace were completed, Solomon hired Jeroboam to oversee the Ephramites' work on another Millo to which the latter verse alludes.[950] Part of this millo retaining wall is now the east gate cemetery with part of Solomon's wall still supporting the Temple Mount.[951] Eilat Mazar recently excavated part of Solomon's city wall.

> "The tenth-century B.C. wall is 230 feet (70 meters) long and about 6 meters (20 feet) tall. It stands along what was then the edge of Jerusalem—between the Temple Mount . . . and the ancient City of David."[952]

---

948 Longman III, Tremper, and Garland, David E., editors, *The Expositor's Bible Commentary* Revised Edition, volume 4, Zonervan, 2010, p. 175

949 II Samuel 5:9 and II Kings 12:21

950 I Kings 11:26-27

951 Laperrousaz, Ernest-Marie, "King Solomon's Wall Still Supports the Temple Mount," *Biblical Archaeology Society*, 13:03 (May/June 1987)

952 Milstein, Mati, "King Solomon's Wall Found—Proof of Bible Tale?" *National Geographic News*, February 26, 2010 at http://news.nationalgeographic.com/news/2010/02/100226-king-solomon-wall-jerusalem-bible/

Pharaohs of the Bible

Solomon's Temple and Palace Complex

And it came to pass at the end of twenty years, when Solomon had built the two houses, the house of the LORD, and the king's house . . . And this is the reason of the levy which king Solomon raised; for to build the house of the LORD, and his own house, and Millo, and the wall of Jerusalem, and Hazor, and Megiddo, and Gezer. . . . And this is the reason of the levy which king Solomon raised; for to build the house of the LORD, and his own house, and Millo, and the wall of Jerusalem, and Hazor, and Megiddo, and Gezer. For Pharaoh king of Egypt had gone up, and taken <u>Gezer, and burnt it with fire</u>, and slain the Canaanites that dwelled in the city, and given it for a present to his daughter, Solomon's wife. (I Kings 9:10,15-16)

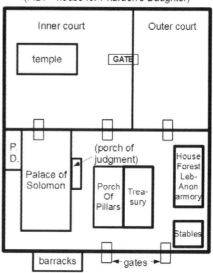

Simplified plan of Solomon's Complex
(P.D. = house for Pharaoh's Daughter)

Solomon had taxed the people heavily for his building programs. It took twenty years to build this complex, Jerusalem's wall, and three store cities. Three of the five gates in this complex have six compartments (three on each side), just like the gates discovered at Hazor, Megiddo, Gezer, and Lachish[953]; and so they are called Solomonic gates.

Solomon's 6-chambered Gates

Megiddo gate

Hazor gate

". . .levy which king Solomon raised; for to build the house of the LORD, and his own house, and Millo, and the wall of Jerusalem, and Hazor, and Megiddo, and Gezer."
(I Kings 9:15)

Gezer gate reconstruction with barracks above

The gate at Gezer is built on top of melted lime. Very hot fires melt limestone into lime (Osorkon I burned it). The 6-chambered gates were preceded by two watchtowers. The chambers could have been used to collect city taxes and to provide business permits while scrutinizing visitors.

Next, king Solomon hired Hiram of Tyre to build him a navy and equip him with seamen on the Red Sea (I Kings 9:26-27) and the Mediterranean Sea (I Kings 10:22) to facilitate trade.

---

953 Magnusson, Magus, *Archaeology of the Bible*, 1977, p. 189

Queen of Sheba

The ancient state of Sheba (*Saba* in Arabic) only had queens as sovereigns, and was known for its frankincense and myrrh.[954] Hatshepsut acquired apes from the land of Punt (possibly Somalia) and then purchased myrrh trees from Saba (about 1660 BC). Seti I dredged the canals to reopen access to the Red Sea (about 1490 BC), but it is not clear if he also reopened trade with these lands.

According to Keller's, *The Bible as History*, Sheba was one of the spice kingdoms of the southern Arabia Peninsula which had its capital at Marib, Yemen.[955] Prior to Solomon building a navy and port at Ezion-Geber next to Eloth (Eilat),[956] camels had to travel 1250 miles of desert to get to Eilat from Marib. The queen travelled to Jerusalem to make negotiations with the king of Israel who had so masterfully opened shipping lanes on the Gulf of Aqabah.

And she came to Jerusalem with a very great train, with camels that bore spices, and very much gold, and precious stones: and when she was come to Solomon, she communed with him of all that was in her heart. (1 Kings 10:2)

Besides these gifts, she also left seeds from which balsam bushes were cultivated in the plain of Jericho.[957] Solomon and the queen would have discussed the 'cut' the "*king's merchants*" would receive along with any import/export taxes.[958]

Solomon's Building Campaign Continued

*And Solomon went to Hamathzobah, and prevailed against it. And he built **Tadmor** in the wilderness, and all the store cities, which he built in **Hamath**. Also he built Bethhoron the upper, and Bethhoron the nether, fenced cities, with walls, gates, and bars; And Baalath, and <u>all the store cities that Solomon had</u>, and all the <u>chariot cities</u>, and the <u>cities of the horsemen</u>, and all that Solomon desired to build in Jerusalem, and in Lebanon, and throughout all the land of his dominion. (II Chronicles 8:3-6)*

At Tel Megiddo between 1927 and 1934 AD two stable complexes were excavated from Stratum IVA. The buildings were about 21 X 11 meters wide. Stone mangers were between stone tie poles. Both stable complexes could hold from 450-480 horses combined,[959] but they were built by Ahab. Stratum VA-IVB contained Solomon's stables which were destroyed by Shishak.

Stables at Megiddo

---

954 Virgil and Pliny according to Clarke.
955 Keller, Werner, *The Bible as History*, 1956, 206-210 and 215. About three miles from Marib is a temple to the moon-god Almaqah, though it may have been built around 700 BC.
956 1 Kings 9:26
957 Josephus, also see Ezekiel 27:17
958 1 Kings 10:28 and II Chronicles 1:16

In an archaeologist's vernacular, the stables were called 'tripartite pillared buildings', or TPB's. Professor Jeff Blakely studied Solomon's TPB's and found they were strategically placed at major crossroads around Solomon's kingdom.

> "10th-century TPBs are built at sites on trade routes as they enter/leave a polity that is defined by a circle of sites. Starting with Tel Hadar and moving clockwise, they are built at Tel Hadar where the trade routes from Damascus and Mesopotamia enter Israel, at Tel Masos (and its successor Tel Malhata if it is later 10th century B.C.E.) where the incense route from South Arabia enters Judah, at Tell el-Hesi where the road from Gaza enters Judah, at Tell Beth Shemesh where the Sorek Valley Road enters Judah from Philisitia leading to Jerusalem, at Tel Qasile where the Via Maris enters Israel from the south, and Tell Abu Hawam where the Via Maris enters Israel from the north if one follows the coast, at Megiddo where the Via Maris entered Israel from the north if one crossed the Megiddo pass, and probably at Ta'anach where a secondary road crosses the Carmel range as one enters Israel from the north."[960]

Blakely mapped these tells and cities and noticed that they matched Solomon's twelve districts in I Kings 4 very well. There were scores of defensive fortresses as well.

*And Solomon had twelve officers over all Israel, which provided victuals for the king and his household: each man his month in a year made provision. . . . mount Ephraim . . . Bethshemesh, . . . Sochoh, . . . Dor; . . . Taanach and Megiddo, and all Bethshean, . . . Jokneam . . . Ramothgilead . . . Gilead . . . region of Argob, which is in Bashan, <u>three score great cities with walls and brazen bars</u> . . . Mahanaim . . . Naphtali . . . Asher . . . Issachar . . . Benjamin . . . <u>And Solomon reigned over all kingdoms from the river to the land of the Philistines, and to the border of Egypt</u>: they brought presents, and served Solomon all the days of his life. And Solomon's provision for one day was thirty measures of fine flour, and three score measures of meal, Ten fat oxen, and twenty oxen out of the pastures, and an hundred sheep, beside harts, and roebucks, and fallow deer, and fatted fowl. For he had dominion over all the region on this side the river, from **Tiphsah** even to **Azzah**, over all the kings on this side the river [Euphrates]: and he had peace on all sides round about him. . . . And Solomon had forty thousand stalls of horses for his chariots, and twelve thousand horsemen. And those officers provided victual for king Solomon, and for all that came to king Solomon's table, every man in his month: they lacked nothing. Barley also and straw for the horses and dromedaries brought they to the place where the officers were, every man according to his charge. (I Kings 4:7-28)*

Solomon's northern border was "Tipshah" (Thapsacus), a large town on the west bank of

---

959 "Tel Megiddo" Wikipedia
960 Blakely, Jeff, ""Davidic and Solomonic Bazaars, Barracks, Stables, Warehouses, Toll Stations, Tripartite Pillared Buildings, or Entrepôts ...Whatever: Beyond the Structures Themselves"

the Euphrates River.[961] Solomon's southwestern border from the Euphrates was Gaza.

Jeff Blakely concluded:
> "It is easy to see them as stables located at border sites, protecting the roads and ensuring that proper tolls are paid. It is easy to see them as the toll stations themselves, placed at Israelite/Judahite border sites along major roads where, if possible, topographic features constrict movement, facilitating the collection of tolls and limiting toll evaders."[962]

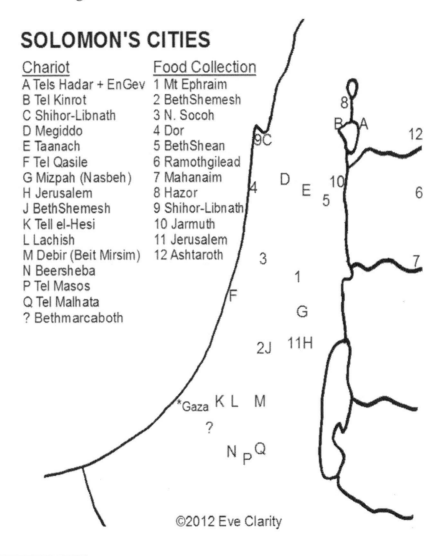

---

961 For possible locations see http://en.wikipedia.org/wiki/Thapsacus
962 http://www.bibleinterp.com/articles/Davidic_and_Solomonic.shtml

And Solomon had four thousand stalls for horses and chariots, and twelve thousand horsemen; whom he bestowed in the chariot cities, and with the king at Jerusalem. And he reigned over all the kings from the [Euphrates] river even to the land of the Philistines, and to the <u>border of Egypt</u>. And the king made silver in Jerusalem as stones, and cedar trees made he as the sycamore trees that are in the low plains in abundance. <u>And they brought to Solomon horses out of Egypt,</u> and out of all lands. (II Chronicles 9: 25-28, disobeying Deut. 17:16)

At this point King Solomon retained the borders of Israel from the Euphrates river to the Pentapolis of the Philistines, but no longer to the Pelusiac of Egypt, but "*to the border of Egypt*"; hence the likelihood he had transferred the Sinai passed Wadi el-Arish to Egypt for Osorkon's daughter. Solomon was on good terms with pharaoh Takelot I, and did vast business with him in direct opposition to Yahweh's commands not to return to Egypt to buy and multiply horses. Yahweh fought Israel's battles, and did not want them to trust in chariots and horses,[963] especially not by making alliances with Egypt to procure them. Solomon did celebrate the three required festivals for men to attend in Jerusalem.[964]

As Solomon aged he disobediently acquired more horses and 1,000 women, and he built his foreign wives shrines and temples to sacrifice to their gods.[965] So the LORD sent enemies against Solomon in order to get him to repent. Osorkon I had allowed Hadad to leave Egypt, and king Solomon was pestered by Hadad of Edom throughout his reign. Solomon lost Damascus and Syria to Rezon,[966] and would lose his kingdom to Jeroboam.

Jeroboam escaped to Shishak (Sheshonk IIa)

To oversee workers building a millo, Solomon had selected Jeroboam, and placed him in charge of laborers from Ephraim and Manasseh.

And Jeroboam the son of Nebat, an Ephrathite of Zereda, Solomon's servant, whose mother's name was Zeruah, a widow woman, even he lifted up his hand against the king. <u>And this was the cause that he lifted up his hand against the king: Solomon built Millo, and repaired the breaches of the city of David his father.</u> And the man Jeroboam was a mighty man of valor: and Solomon seeing the young man that he was industrious, he made him ruler over all the charge of the house of Joseph. (I Kings 11:26-28)

Some scholars write "*the cause*" was the way Solomon built this millo and wall which blocked northern entrances into Jerusalem that David had left open, while others say it was the heavy taxation Jeroboam was required to exact from the two tribes of Joseph in order to build the millo. The taxation is later at issue, but both may have been reasons at the time. Jerusalem is actually located in the southern area of the tribe of Benjamin, just north of

---

963 Psalm 20:7
964 II Chronicles 8:12-13
965 I Kings 11:3-8
966 I Kings 11:9-25

Judah's land, and Ephraim's land is north of Benjamin. Solomon's wall did have access on the north side of Jerusalem through the Ephraim Gate.[967]

> *And it came to pass at that time when Jeroboam went out of Jerusalem, that the prophet Ahijah the Shilonite found him in the way; and he had clad himself with a new garment; and they two were alone in the field: And Ahijah caught the new garment that was on him, and rent it in twelve pieces: And he said to Jeroboam, Take you ten pieces: for thus said the LORD, the God of Israel, Behold, I will rend the kingdom out of the hand of Solomon, and will give ten tribes to you: (But he shall have one tribe for my servant David's sake, and for Jerusalem's sake, the city which I have chosen out of all the tribes of Israel:) Because that they have forsaken me, and have worshipped Ashtoreth the goddess of the Zidonians, Chemosh the god of the Moabites, and Milcom the god of the children of Ammon, and have not walked in my ways, to do that which is right in my eyes, and to keep my statutes and my judgments, as did David his father. . . . Solomon sought therefore to kill Jeroboam. And <u>Jeroboam arose, and fled into Egypt, to Shishak king of Egypt</u>, and was in Egypt until the death of Solomon. (I Kings 11:29-40)*

Ahijah and Jeroboam

An unspecified amount of time passed between Jeroboam's work on the millo and his encounter with the prophet from Shiloh. Ahijah prophesied that Jeroboam would be given ten tribes to rule, while Solomon's lineage would continue to rule only the large tribe of Judah and the small tribe of Benjamin which was noted for containing Jerusalem; hence the southern kingdom was often referred to only as Judah. This was a private prophesy between the two men; so it is likely Jeroboam blabbed about becoming king, and then had to run for his life.

I Kings 11:40 is the first time a king of Egypt is named in the Holy Bible. Jeroboam fled to "*Shishak*" between 979-976 BC and remained in Egypt until Solomon's death in 975 BC.

Takelot I (988-979 BC) of the 22nd dynasty

Takelot I was a son of Osorkon I and Tashedkhons, and succeeded his father. Takelot I married Kapes and had Osorkon II.[968] Osorkon II built a tomb in the Amun temple complex at Tanis, and there he buried his father with the following dedication inscription:

> ". . . King Takelot, beloved of Amun, in this Mansion that is in the Residence of Aten, to cause that he rest in this Mansion in the vicinity of Him-whose-name-is-hidden (Amun) according to the making by a son of benefactions for his father . . ."[969]

---

967 II Kings 14:13
968 Pasenhor's Serapeum Stela
969 Ritner, Robert K., *The Libyan Anarchy: Inscriptions from Egypt's' third Intermediate Period*, 2009, p. 283

Amenhotep III initiated Aten worship and must have built a temple to Aten in Tanis which still stood at this time. Now only Psusennes I's Temple complex to Amun, Khonsu, and Mut remains in Tanis (which contained a nilometer on the since silted Tanitic branch of the Nile).⁹⁷⁰ The 22ⁿᵈ dynasty tombs are low lying mastabas made of recycled stone. Takelot I was buried in a reused sarcophagus.⁹⁷¹ The early wealth of Osorkon I vanished rapidly and did not trickle down to his progeny.

After Sheshonk I and Osorkon I, Manetho wrote that three other kings served a total of 25 years, and then he gave Takelot 13 years (a total of 38 years, but my total is 28 years). Physical evidence only attests a regnal year nine for Takelot I. Manetho's three other kings may well be Sheshonks II a, b, and c.

Sheshonks II of the 22ⁿᵈ dynasty

Sheshonk IIa (Heqakheperre)
Sheshonk IIb (Tutkheperre)
Sheshonk IIc (Maatkheperre)

Heqakheperre Sheshonk IIa, Tutkheperre Sheshonk IIb, and Maakheperre Sheshonk IIc followed Takelot I.⁹⁷² A minimal amount of evidence has surfaced on these three Sheshonks with nothing regarding the lengths of their reigns. To add more confusion, there is also a high priest referred to as Sheshonk C who died just a few years prior to their reigns. Some state that Sheshonk IIa is the same as Sheshonk C, but there is no mention of Thebes or high priest on the coffin of Sheshonk IIa.

Gold mask of Heqakheperre Sheshonk

Heqakheperre Sheshonk IIa (979-970 BC)

This pharaoh's hawk-headed (Khonsu) silver coffin was reburied in the tomb of Psusennes I in Tanis, possibly because of water damage. The original burial site may have been closer to the base of the Delta, and the king's residence and capital, before it was moved north. The "rough handling" of the trip may be the cause of the coffin's "broken trough" noted Dodson.⁹⁷³ An inscription on the coffin reads, "King Sheshonk, beloved of Amun, Heqakheperre-setepenre Sheshonk". Another reads, "Osiris King Sheshonk, beloved of Amon, take for yourself bread in Memphis, cool water and offerings in Heliopolis."⁹⁷⁴ Upon the mummy of Heqakheperre Sheshonk's face was a gold funerary mask, much

---

970 Great pictures at http://www.phouka.com/tr/egypt/photos/tanis/templeAmun-01.html
971 Ritner, Robert K., *The Libyan Anarchy: Inscriptions from Egypt's' third Intermediate Period*, 2009, p. 282
972 David Aston gives them a total of 5 years (p.22) and Broekman gives the last two a total of six years (p.92), but both have them following Takelot I; *The Libyan Period in Egypt*, 2009. Manetho in appendix.
973 Aidan M. Dodson, *The Canopic Equipment of the Kings of Egypt*, Kegan Paul Intl: London, 1994, p. 92
974 Ritner, Robert K., *The Libyan Anarchy: Inscriptions from Egypt's Third Intermediate Period*, Society of Biblical Literature, 2009, p. 270

smaller and in a different style than that of Psusennes I. Also on his mummy was a jeweled pectoral inscribed with "Sheshonk, Great Chief of the Ma" which belonged to his father Sheshonk I before he was king, as well as two bracelets (one with a wedjat eye) bearing the regnal name of Sheshonk I, and gold sandals. It was common for a child to be buried with heirlooms of their parents.

Burial goods of Shoshenk IIa

Dr. Douglas Derry examined Sheshonk IIa's mummy and determined that the king died of a massive septic infection from a head wound at about the age of fifty.[975] A head wound is often associated with warfare. Thus I suggest Sheshonk IIa is the biblical Shishak who returned victorious from his campaign in Israel and ordered the names of captured cities to be engraved on the wall of the stunning figure of Sheshonk I, his namesake; but that he shortly succumbed to the infected head wound and died. Because he had obtained the treasures of Jerusalem's Temple, his hawk-headed coffin was overlaid with silver, and he had four miniature silver coffins for his organs instead of pottery canopic jars. Silver was considered to be more valuable than gold in Egypt, so his burial was extravagantly wealthy.

Tutkheperre Sheshonk IIb (970-965 BC) of the 22nd dynasty

Tutkheperre Sheshonk was written in black ink on a piece of pottery, an ostraca, near the temple of Osiris in Abydos, and inscribed on a limestone lintel in the temple of Bubastis; thus Sheshonk IIb was recognized in both Upper and Lower Egypt.[976] Tutkheperre was the prenomen for Psusennes II. The five year reign is a guess for both Sheshonks IIb and IIc.

Maakheperre Sheshonk IIc (965-960 BC) of the 22nd dynasty

This pharaoh is also written as Maatkheperre Sheshonk. Maakheperre Sheshonk was written over a Cairo statue (CG42192) made for Thutmose III.[977] I think Sheshonk IV eliminated all other references to Maakheperre Sheshonk.

---

975 Sheshonk II, www.thefullwike.org/Sheshonk_II
976 "Tutkheperre Sheshonk", http://en.wikipedia.org/wiki/Tutkheperre_Sheshonk, assessed 3/7/11
977 Dodson, Aidan, *The Transition Between the 21st and 22nd Dynasties Revisited*, The Libyan Period in Egypt, 2009, p. 110

HPA Smendes C (984-970 BC), then Smendes III of the 23rd dynasty

Of his three Nile Level Texts, HPA Smendes' C highest regnal date was his 14th year. For the first ten years of his reign as Smendes III (970-950 BC), he was both king and HPA; then for the last ten years he was simply king and appointed Harsiese (A) as his HPA.

King Solomon's Legacy

King Solomon was considered the wisest man in the world at one point in his life, even excelling the wisdom of Mesopotamia and Egypt.

And Judah and Israel dwelled safely, every man under his vine and under his fig tree, from Dan even to Beersheba, all the days of Solomon. . . . And God gave Solomon wisdom and understanding exceeding much, and largeness of heart, even as the sand that is on the sea shore. And Solomon's wisdom excelled the wisdom of all the children of the east country, and all the wisdom of Egypt. . . . And he spoke three thousand proverbs: and his songs were a thousand and five. And he spoke of trees, from the cedar tree that is in Lebanon even to the hyssop that springs out of the wall: he spoke also of beasts, and of fowl, and of creeping things, and of fishes. And there came of all people to hear the wisdom of Solomon, from all kings of the earth, which had heard of his wisdom. (I Kings 4:25-34)

Besides Song of Solomon and much of Proverbs, Solomon also wrote the book of Ecclesiastes, a treatise on wisdom, in the Bible. Sadly, his great wisdom did not keep him from committing idolatry later in life. The glorious kingdom of Israel would be broken in two after his death. Greatness without Yahweh doesn't last long. The great Temple plans which he executed so well, would become ruins at the hands of Nebuchadnezzar II. Solomon's tomb is unknown. It could be that his tomb was dismantled because of the disgrace he brought to Israel, or in order to pay tribute to other kings later.

. . . You shall not give your daughters to their sons, nor take their daughters to your sons, or for yourselves. Did not Solomon king of Israel sin by these things? yet among many nations was there no king like him, who was beloved of his God, and God made him king over all Israel: nevertheless even him did outlandish women cause to sin. Shall we then listen to you to do all this great evil, to transgress against our God in marrying strange wives? (Nehemiah 13:25-27)

Sketch of Solomon's Temple Complex

Rehoboam, southern kingdom of Judah (975-958 BC)

Rehoboam was born to Solomon and Naaman, an Ammonite woman. Rehoboam was 41 years old when he began his reign, and so was born to Solomon a year before he started his reign in Spring (possibly March) of 1015 BC.[978] Solomon died after Tishri 1 in his 40th Tishri regnal year of 976-975 BC in early winter (like our January); thus Solomon reigned 6 months prior to Tishri 1 of 1015, and 6 months after Tishri 1 of 976, giving a total of 40 regnal years. After the funeral, Rehoboam was coronated at Shechem and reigned for 17 years.[979] Rehoboam's first Tishri regnal year was 976-975 BC, though he began in 975. Shishak attacked Israel in Rehoboam's fifth Tishri regnal year of 971-970 BC,[980] and since most wars were waged in Spring, it would have been Spring of 970 BC.

Jeroboam, northern kingdom of Israel (975-953 BC)

Jeroboam likely assumed that Solomon told his son Rehoboam about Ahijah's prophecy, and so Jeroboam made plans before he returned to Israel. Jeroboam may have made an alliance with Shishak/Sheshonk IIa to attack Judah after he became king of Israel, and promised Shishak the treasures in Jerusalem. After Rehoboam was crowned, a group sent word to Jeroboam to join them to petition the king against harsh taxation.[981]

Jeroboam and a group of Israel's leaders came to Rehoboam at Shechem and asked if he was going to levy heavy taxes on them as his father had. Rehoboam unwisely responded he would be more harsh than his father had been. The group then made Jeroboam their king and stoned Rehoboam's tax-collector. Rehoboam fled back to Jerusalem retaining only the tribes of Judah and Benjamin.[982]

> *And it came to pass, when all Israel heard that Jeroboam was come again, that they sent and called him to the congregation, and made him king over all Israel: there was none that followed the house of David, but the tribe of Judah only. (I Kings 12:20)*

Jeroboam most likely became king in early March of 975 BC, and in the next weeks he observed the men of Israel travelling to Jerusalem to keep the Passover in the first month of Nisan. Men were required to travel to Jerusalem for three feasts each year (in Nisan, Sivan, and Tishri), and he would not allow that.[983] So on the 23rd of Sivan, which is remembered with fasting by the Jews, Jeroboam erected a golden calf in Bethel (southern border) and one in Dan (northern border) for the people of Israel to worship, saying, "*It is too much for you to go up to Jerusalem: behold your gods, O Israel, which brought you up out of the land of*

---

978 1 Kings 14:21 and 1 Chronicles 12:13
979 I Kings 12:1 and II Chronicles 12:13
980 I Kings 14:25
981 I Kings 12:3-4
982 I Kings 12:1-20
983 I Kings 12:27

Egypt."[984] Jeroboam replaced YHWH, with Egypt's Apis bull representation of Ptah to which many Israelites had turned after the death of unbeliever's first-born sons during the first Passover while waiting at Mount Sinai for God's Laws. God told Jeroboam his first-born son would die and be mourned unlike the rest of his sons who would be killed.[985]

On the 25th dynasty Shabaka Stone, Ptah is the center of existence who called forth creation.[986] Ptah was also the god of regeneration. Ptah 'manifested' as an Apis bull, and the Apis bull was a manifestation of pharaoh. "Strong bull of Hathor" was a common pharaonic title. People came to the Apis bull to be 'blessed' with virility and fertility. The Apis bull was selected by markings and provided a harem and a grand funeral at death, entombed at the Serapeum.

"... the Apis bull had to have a certain set of markings suitable to its role. It was required to have a white triangle upon its forehead, a white vulture wing outline on its back, a scarab mark under its tongue, a white crescent moon shape on its right flank, and double hairs on its tail."[987]

Jeroboam's worship of Ptah instead of YHWH

Jeroboam proceeded to another corrupting sin which brought about Israel's destruction as a nation.[988] Jeroboam altered the fall feasts of the LORD from God's ordained celebrations in the seventh month to the eighth month;[989] he had created a counterfeit, but parallel, religion to Judaism with its own set of priests and rituals claiming to be worshipping the one, true Creator of the universe. The LORD immediately sent a prophet to curse his altar to the golden calf in Bethel, and prophesied a redeemer named Josiah would overthrow Jeroboam's religious system.[990] Thus Jeroboam perpetuated the sin which began at Mount Sinai; turning the house of Israel away from YHWH to worship a creator god of Egypt, for which the northern tribes of Israel would be sent into exile 390 years later.

God told King Rehoboam not to attack his brethren to the north. Instead, Rehoboam spent the next three years preparing for Egyptian attacks and sieges by fortifying cities along all the western river valley approaches and southern hill approaches to Jerusalem.

---

984 I Kings 12:28 see I Kings 14:15-16 for God's promise of punishment
985 I Kings 14:9-18 and 15:28-30 In the 3rd year of Asa, Baasha killed all of Jeroboam's descendants.
986 http://en.wikipedia.org/wiki/Shabaka_Stone
987 http://en.wikipedia.org/wiki/Apis_(Egyptian_mythology)
988 I Kings 14:15-16 and Ezekiel 4:1-6 – Jerusalem would be under siege 390 days; Israel would last 390 yr
989 I Kings 12:32-33
990 Fulfilled 340 years later in Josiah's 18th year (II Kings 23:15-20)

*And Rehoboam dwelt in Jerusalem, and built cities for defense in Judah. He built Beth-lehem, and Etam, and Tekoa, And Beth-zur, and Soco, and Adullam, and Gath, and Mareshah, and Ziph, and Adoraim, and Lachish, and Azekah, and Zorah, and Aijalon, and Hebron, which are in Judah and in Benjamin, fortified cities. And he fortified the strongholds, and put captains in them, and stores of victuals, and oil and wine. And in every city he put shields and spears, and made them exceeding strong. . . . So they strengthened the kingdom of Judah, and made Rehoboam the son of Solomon strong, three years; for they walked three years in the way of David and Solomon.
(II Chron. 11:5-12, 17)*

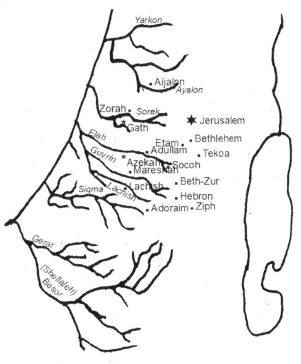

Rehoboam's Fortresses to Withstand Shishak

Jeroboam could have sent communications to Sheshonk IIa regarding the fortress cities and requested his help. I conjecture that Sheshonk IIa feigned commitment to help Jeroboam while privately making plans to attack Jeroboam's cities in Israel as well. I place Gath at Tel Miqne. Of Rehoboam's forts, most agree that Shishak attacked Aijalon, but I think Shishak also attacked Hebron (#40) and Lachish (#42), and lesser cities around them.

Shishak's attack was Yahweh's Punishment for Idolatry and Sodomy

In Rehoboam's fourth year, Judah also turned to worship other gods, so in his fifth year, Yahweh sent Shishak/Sheshonk IIa to punish both Israel and Judah.

*And Judah did evil in the sight of the LORD, and they provoked him to jealousy with their sins which they had committed, above all that their fathers had done. For they also built them high places, and images, and groves, on every high hill, and under every green tree. And there were also sodomites in the land: and they did according to all the abominations of the nations which the LORD cast out before the children of Israel. And it came to pass in the fifth year of king Rehoboam, that **Shishak** king of Egypt came up against Jerusalem: And he took away the treasures of the house of the LORD, and the treasures of the king's house; he even took away all: and he took* *away all the shields of gold which Solomon had made. . . . Now the rest of the acts of Rehoboam, and all that he did, are they not written in the book of the chronicles of the kings of Judah? And there was war between Rehoboam and Jeroboam all their days. And Rehoboam slept with his fathers, and was buried with his fathers in the city of David. (1 Kings 14:22-31a)*

*And it came to pass, that in the fifth year of king Rehoboam **Shishak** king of Egypt came up against Jerusalem, because they had transgressed against the LORD, <u>With twelve hundred chariots, and three score thousand horsemen: and the people were without number that came with him out of Egypt; the Lubims, the **Sukkiims**, and the Ethiopians. And he took the fenced cities which pertained to Judah, and came to Jerusalem.</u> Then came Shemaiah the prophet to Rehoboam, and to the princes of Judah, that were gathered together to Jerusalem because of **Shishak**, and said to them, Thus said the LORD, You have forsaken me, and therefore have I also left you in the hand of Shishak. Whereupon the*

Shishak loots the Temple

*princes of Israel and the king humbled themselves; and they said, The LORD is righteous. And when the LORD saw that they humbled themselves, the word of the LORD came to Shemaiah, saying, They have humbled themselves; therefore I will not destroy them, but I will grant them some deliverance; and my wrath shall not be poured out on Jerusalem by the hand of **Shishak**. Nevertheless they shall be his servants; that they may know my service, and the service of the kingdoms of the countries. So **Shishak** king of Egypt came up against Jerusalem, and took away the treasures of the house of the LORD, and the treasures of the king's house; he took all: he carried away also the shields of gold which Solomon had made. (II Chronicles 12:2-9)*

Sheshonk IIa attacked with 1200 chariots, 60,000 cavalry, and mercenaries from Libya, Tunisia(?), and Cush. *Sukkiim* comes from *sachah* meaning 'covering' and is often associated with tents and booths, but *Clarke's Commentary* suggested these people covered themselves with dirt in caves as troglodytes who possibly lived on the coast of the Red Sea. In 1913 AD pictures were taken from a blimp of cave dwellers in Matmata, Tunisia and cliff dwellers in Medenine, Tunisia.[991] Since Tunisia shares the northwestern border of Libya, it is reasonable to be Egypt's ally. Shishak had a lot to haul away, as David had dedicated all the gold and silver from the cities and nations he conquered to the house of the LORD:[992] at least 8,000 talents of gold, 17,000 talents of silver, and 18,000 talents of brass.[993] A Hebrew

---

991 "Airship Startles Primitive African Cave Dwellers," *The New York Times*, 1913
992 II Samuel 8:10-11; I Chronicles 18:6-11, 28:12-17; II Chronicles 5:1
993 I Chronicles 29:2-8

talent weighed approximately 75 pounds. That would be 300 tons of gold, 637.5 tons of silver, and 675 tons of brass; but some portion had been used upon the Temple itself, and some items like the ark would have been hidden, and would be subtracted from the total. A silver coffin and gold mask for a pharaoh of such a campaign would be expected.

Karnak Victory Relief of Sheshonks I and IIa

In 1828 AD when Champollion saw the famous relief of Hedjkheperre Sheshonk I and the cities of conquest in Karnak, he assumed Sheshonk I must have been the Biblical Shishak, because he was the first of a few Sheshonks known at that time; now there are a dozen. There is no year attributed to the conquest on the relief. [Analysis of Sheshonk I's stela dated to his regnal year 21 in the quarries of Gebel es Silsila to quarry and construct a court and gateway at the temple in Karnak[994] is provided in Appendix B, pages 447-448.]

Some captured cities

Based upon the list of conquered cities, after conquering Sharuhen, Shishak/Sheshonk IIa divided his forces and sent troops south to the Negev (who then continued east of the Dead Sea and Jordan), while others took the central route toward Jerusalem and destroyed the fortress cities of king David (#29-30, #101-109). Sheshonk IIa attacked cities (#23-28) along the Aijalon-Gibeon road on the way to Jerusalem, and then captured Rekem's Field (#96-97) and Beit Hanani (#98-99) before camping his troops in the Valley of Hinnom (#94-95) at Jerusalem's doorstep. Rehoboam submitted to be pharaoh's vassal and gave him Jerusalem's treasures. Since Jerusalem was not conquered, but only looted, it's no surprise its name does not appear in the list. Sheshonk IIa marched north to Jeroboam's home in Zeredah (#150) and his capital (#20) and palace (#111-112) at Shechem, then he went through Tirzah (#59) to the Jezreel valley (#11-18). With his annals lost, city names were possibly gathered from unit commanders. Of the 155 remaining names listed, thirty are known to be within Jeroboam's territory, though #141-149 might be located in northern Israel as well.

I propose that the original victory relief of Sheshonk I had a figure of Iuput A (like all the other reliefs) facing forward; but that artisans of Sheshonk IIa carved over Iuput's head in the center and reworked the original group of soldiers, and squeezed in the captured cities portion of Sheshonk IIa's campaign into the lower left of Sheshonk I's victory relief. In Iuput's right hand appears to be a miniature double curved bow held closely to his chest; in his left hand is a feather of maat. Only his torso remains. There is also a feather of maat underneath the lowest sets of men's elbows. It's not the first time one pharaoh had usurped an earlier pharaoh's monument for himself. [For more incongruities on Shishak's victory wall, see pages 449-451.]

---

994 Rohl, David, *Pharaohs and Kings: A Biblical Quest*, Crown Publishers, 1995, p. 414, footnote #2

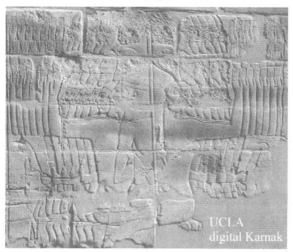

Victory relief of Sheshonk I has been reworked.

Center of Sheshonk I victory relief   Center detail

Most of the original list of captured cities were contained in 10 rows on the left side: the first 5 rows had 13 name rings each, and the last 5 rows had 17 name rings each for a total of 150 names. Only five name rings remain of a row on the bottom right side.

"The list is rapidly perishing; four names in the seventh row (Nos. 105-8) long ago fell out and are in Berlin; No. 27, Megiddo, has either fallen out or been removed; many names once legible are no longer so."[995]

The name rings were ordered right to left (because #65-66 make one name). The list appears to subdivide into twenty-two groupings. Name rings #1-9 are called the "nine bows"[996] followed by the heading: "copy of foreigners" in #10 of what had been written in campaign annals now lost. The following groups were likely conquered by several divisions of Heqakheperre Sheshonk's army: #11-18 in the Jezreel valley, #19-20 at Arumah and Shechem, #21-22 northern Jabbok River, #23-31 near Gibeon and Makkedah, #32-35 south of Mt. Carmel, #36-44 near Hebron, #45-52 in Moab, #53-56 south of the Jabbok River, #57-64 near Zemaraim in Benjamin's territory, #65-67 near Jericho, #68-70 east of the Jordan river opposite Jericho, #71-76 at the southern end of the Dead Sea, #77-89 SW of Hebron, #90-93 in the Negev, #94-99 near Jerusalem, #100-109 between Ziklag (Tell Sera') and Gath (Tell Miqne), #109-112 could be translated "great fugitive house of Jero(b)oam"[997] as a single reference to Shechem, #113-115 lost, #116-117 NE of BethShan, #118-133 near Gibeon, Gaza, or Hebron, and #134-156 most of which are unknown.

---

995 Breasted, James, *Ancient Records of Egypt, volume 4*, University of Chicago, p. 348 footnote 'a'
996 Wilson, Kevin, *The Campaign of Pharaoh Shoshenq I into Palestine*, Germany, 2005, p. 102
997 *Pharaoh* is a modified phonation of the Egyptian phrase "great house," and pharaoh Sheshonk IIa may have given the same title to Jeroboam (even with the 'b' dropped in his name).

Pharaohs of Solomon and Rehoboam

Karnak Victory Relief Campaign List

#	Name	Clarity suggestion	Location
1	*T3smcw*	Upper Egypt	
2	*T3mhw*	Lower Egypt	
3	Wawat of	Upper Nubia	between 1st and 2nd cataracts
4	[*Thnw*]	Libyans	
5	S[hetiam]	western oases	
6	*Mn[tywnwstt]*	Bedouin	
7	Bow[men of feather]		
8	*S3t* (Seti)	Lower Nubia	nome #1 between Edfu and Elephantine
9	*H3wnbwt*	Haunebut	Aegean islands
10	*mitt c3mw*	copy of *Amu* (foreigners)	
11	*G3[d(t?)]*[998]	Jezreel?	between Mountains Gilboa and Carmel
12	*M[q]3[d]*	Megiddo	about 10 miles west of Jezreel
13	*Rbyt*	Ramoth? (Kokab el-Hawa)	15 miles east of Jezreel; 10 m N of Rehob
14	*T3nki3*	Taanach	about 8 miles W of Jezreel below Carmel range
15	*S3nmci3*	Shunem	about 5 miles NE of Jezreel
16	*B3ts3nri3*	Beth-shean	about 8 miles SE of Jezreel
17	*Rwh3bi3*	Rehob/Rehov	10 m SE of Jezreel; 5 miles SE of Beth-shean
18	*H3pwrwmi3*	Hapharaim	between Jezreel + Shunem and Shihon[999]
19	*'Idrm3*	Arumah ('high')	about 5 miles south of Shechem (Nablus)
20	[ ]	[Shechem?]	
21	*S3w3dy*	(Kirbet ash Shawahid)	in Jordan near Jabbok river
22	Mahanaim[1000]	"two camps"	on Jabbok river across from Penuel
23	*Qbc3n3*	Gibeon	now Jib, about 40 miles SW of Nablus
24	*B3thw3rwni3*	Beth-horon	5 miles NW of Gibeon; 40 m NW of Jerusalem
25	*Q3dtm*	Adithaim	5 miles SW of Beth-horon
26	*'Iywrwn*	Aijalon	foot of Beth-horon pass, 5 m SW of Adithaim
27	*Mckdiw*	Makkedah	12 miles south of Aijalon
28	*'Idyrw*[1001]	Gederah	5 miles west of Aijalon
29	YadhaMelek	"king's hand/power"	David's fortress[1002] just south of Beth-Shemesh
30	[*Hb*]*rt(?)*	?Aderet	near David's fortress in Elah valley
31	*H3i3nm*	(valley of) Hinnom[1003]	or town of Enam, 3 miles SE of Yarmut
32	*'3r3n3*	Aruna	SE of Dor

---

998 This is not Gaza. Shishak did not attack Philistine cities. Jezreel makes much better geographic sense.
999 Joshua 19:18-19
1000 Genesis 32:1-3
1001 Most translate in Adar. It might be Jarmuth/Yarmut, near Beth-Shemesh
1002 http://en.wikipedia.org/wiki/Khirbet_Qeiyafa near Beth-Shemesh, 20 miles west of Jerusalem
1003 Joshua 15:8 "valley of Hinnom" (*hin nome'* which means lamentation) south of Jerusalem

33	*B3rwm3*	Ibleam[1004]	10 miles east of Aruna
34	*D3dptrw*	?Dothan[1005]	3 miles SW of Ibleam
35	*Y[w]h3m3*	Yehem	5 miles SW of Aruna
36	*B3tᶜ3rwm3m*	Bethlehem {N}	8 miles north of Jokneam
37	*K3q3rwy*[1006]	?Kurkar	for Tel Qasile ancient port of Tel Aviv
38	*S3iwk3*	Socoh	(Tel Zeror) 15 miles NE of Joppa
39	Bethtappuah[1007]	"house of apple"[1008]	2 miles north of Hebron or just NW of Shiloh
40	*'Ib3rw*	?Hebron	
41	[ ]*htp*	?(Tel Zayit)	
42-44	[ ]	[Lachish, and Halhul[1009]?]	
45	*B3tdbi[ ]*	Beth-diblathaim[1010]	near Dibon in Moab, east of the Dead Sea
46	*kk[ ]*	?	
47-50	[ ]	?[other cities in Moab]	
51	*ssd[ ]*	?	
52	[ ]	?	
53	*[P]nwi3rw*	Penuel[1011]	20 miles east of Jordan on Jabbok River
54	*H3dsst*	Hadasah	'myrtle', between Penuel and Succoth?
55	*P3-ktt*	'little one'	between Succoth and Adam?
56	*'Idmi3*	Adam[1012]	at the bend of the Jordan and Jabbok rivers
57	*d3[m]rwm3*	Zemaraim[1013]	'2 fleeces' 20 miles W of Jordan; 6 m N of Michmash
58	*[Mg]drw*	Migdol	a 'tower', Mizpah ('watchtower') 5 m W of Michmash
59	*[T?]rwdi3*	Tirzah	north of Shechem
60	*[ ]n3rw*	?Janoa or Arumah, both south of Shechem	
61-63	[ ]	[Michmash, Baal-Hazor (Tel Azur), Shiloh or Jeshanah?]	
64	*H3[ ]3pn*	?Ephron	5 miles NE of Zemaraim[1014]
65-66	pa-Emeq-ezemi	The "'valley' Keziz (abrupt)"[1015]	7 miles southeast of Jericho
67	*'In3rwi*	?Naara(h/n)[1016]	in western Jordan plain, near Jericho

---

1004 Joshua 17:11
1005 II Kings 6:13
1006 Tel Qasile is made of "kurkar" stone. Or possibly it's Karka (Mount Karkom) in the Negev.
1007 Joshua 15:53
1008 Ritner, Robert K., *The Libyan Anarchy*, Society of Biblical Literature, Atlanta, 2009, p. 212 fn 31
1009 Joshua 15:58   Halhul is 5 miles north of Hebron on highest peak in area.
1010 Jeremiah 48:22 OR Beth-zur, 2 miles north of Halhul in Joshua 15:58
1011 I Kings 12:25 Jeroboam built Shechem and Penuel
1012 Now Damiya. Joshua 3:16 near Zerathan http://en.wikipedia.org/wiki/City_of_Adam
1013 Joshua 18:22
1014 Joshua 15:9 or Chepharhaammonai in Joshua 18:24 which is 3 miles west of Zemaraim; or Heleph
1015 Joshua 18:21
1016 Joshua 16:7

68-	*P3-h3qrwi3*	The Field/Fort (of)	
69	*Ftyws3i3*	?(Khirbet Futeis, Hagar-Pattish) Photis east of Gaza[1017]	
70	*'Ir3hrwrw*	Elealeh[1018]	2 miles NE of Heshbon, east side of Jordan river
71-	*P3-h3qrwi3*	The Field/Fort (of)	
72	*Iwb3r3m*	Abarim[1019]	hills on east side of Jordan river, south end Dead Sea
73-	Shibboleth	'stream'/'brook' (wadi)	
74	*Ngb-3rwy*	?Negev-Zered	east-west Wadi Zered at south end of Dead Sea
75-	Shibboleth	'stream'/'brook' (wadi)	
76	*W3r3kyt*	Ar and Kir,[1020]	forts on the wadi east of Dead Sea
77-	*P3-h3qrwi3*	The Field/Fort (of)	
78	*n^c3d3yt*	?Nazib ('garrison')[1021]	5 miles NW of Hebron near Telem
79	*Dd[ ]i3*	?Debir[1022]	near Anab[1023] about 12 miles SW of Hebron[1024]
80	*D3p3qi3*	Dophkah[1025]	possibly a Midian namesake site near Debir
81	*M[ ]i3*	?Maon	7 miles South of Hebron near Carmel and Ziph[1026]
82	*T3p[w . . .]*	Tappuah	(Tapuah) 3 miles west of Hebron[1027]
83	*G3n3it*	?Anim	(Khirbet **G**hwein et-Tahta)18 miles south of Hebron[1028]
84-	*P3-n3gbw*	The Negev, 'south country' (of)	
85	*^cd3nst*	Dannah[1029]	8 miles NW of Hebron, or Astinah 8 m W of Hebron
86	*T3sdn3w*	?Eshtemoa[1030]	14 miles SE of Hebron
87-	*P3-h3qrwi3*	The Field/Fort (of)	
88	*S3n3i3*	?Shamir[1031]	between Debir (12 miles SW of Hebron) and Anim
89	*H3q3*	?(Ap)Heqah[1032]	3 miles SE of Hebron, near Janim and Tappuah?
90-	The Negev	'south country' (of)	
91	*W3htrww3k[ ]*	?Oboth[1033]	(Ir Ovot), in Arabah 20 miles SE of Dimona

---

[1017] http://198.62.75.1/www1/ofm/mad/discussion/110discuss.html
[1018] Numbers 32:3
[1019] Numbers 33:47-48 "mountains of Abarim" hills across or opposite the lower Jordan river
[1020] http://en.wikipedia.org/wiki/Kir_of_Moab
[1021] Joshua 15:43 Beit Nasib
[1022] http://bibleatlas.org/debir_2.htm
[1023] Joshua 15:49-50 also Judges 1 :10-15
[1024] http://www.ancientsandals.com/overviews/debir.htm
[1025] Numbers 33:12-13 They camped at Dophkah after crossing Red Sea into Midian.
[1026] Joshua 15:55
[1027] Northern Tappuah is 2 miles NW of Shiloh.
[1028] Better than word association of Gad ayd. *Ayd* is 'witness heap', near Jordan and Gilead in Josh. 22:9-34
[1029] Joshua 15:49 http://bibleatlas.org/dannah.htm
[1030] Joshua 15:50 http://bibleatlas.org/eshtemoa.htm
[1031] Joshua 15:48
[1032] Joshua 15:53
[1033] OR Rehoboth SW of Beersheba OR possibly Hazar-shaul in Joshua 15:28 near Beersheba

Pharaohs of the Bible

92-93	*Is3h3tit*	'south country' (of) ?Hittites	who dwelt in Judah's mountains[1034]
94-95	*P3-h3qrwi3* *H3n3nyy*	The Field/Fort (of) Hanani	near Jerusalem
96-97	*P3-h3qrwi3* *Irwq3d*	The Field/Fort (of) ?Rekem[1035]	between Gibeon and Jerusalem
98-99	*Iwd3mt* *H3n3nyy*	Land (of) (Beit) Hanani	4 miles north of Jerusalem
100	*Iwdr3i3*	Ether[1036]	near Tel Burna, 24 miles SW of Jerusalem
101-102	*Iwd3mt* *Trww3n*	Land (of) ?Terebinth (*Elah*=oak)	"valley of Elah"[1037] 20m SW of Jerusalem
103-104	*H3ydbi3* *S3rwnrwim*	Highlands (of) (wadi) Shellaleh	now Nahal Besor[1038], Tell el-Far'ah South
105-106	*H3ydbi3* *Dyw3ty*	Highlands (of) David[1039]	Khirbet Qeiyafa near Azekah
107-108	*P3-h3qrwi3* *ʿ3rwdi3t*	The Field/Fort (of) *Aradet* ('fugitive')	where David fled to the king of Gath[1040]
109	*Rwb3t*	Rabba(t)h[1041] ('great')	12 miles NE of Gath; 6 miles NE of Beit Jibrin
110	*ʿ3rwdi3y*	Arad (Tel Arad)[1042]	20 miles SE of Hebron, near Dead Sea
111-112	*n B3tt* *Ywr3hm*	House of Jeroham[1043]	near Mt Ephraim, where Jero(bo)am lived
113-115	[ ]	?	
116	*Iwdy3[r?]*	?Aduru	south of Lake Huleh or Adar[1044] near Mt Halak
117	*Iwdr[ ]*	?Edrei	32 miles east of Jordan on the Yarmuk River
118	*[ ]b3yi3*	?Gibeah	between Jerusalem and Gibeon
119	*[ ]hgi3*	?Bethhoglah[1045]	near Jericho between Benjamin and Judah

---

1034 Numbers 13:28-29
1035 Rekem near Gibeon; Joshua 18:25-27 http://bibleatlas.org/rekem.htm
1036 Joshua 15:42
1037 I Samuel 17:2 OR ElTolad in Joshua 15:30; 19:4 near Hormah OR Telem, near Edom in Joshua 15:24
1038 I Samuel 30:10 Some of David's men were to tired to cross "brook Besor" outside of Ziklag
1039 Kitchen, Kenneth, *Biblical Archaeological Research*, Jan/Feb 1999, p. 34
1040 Modern Aderet is 7 miles NE of Beit Guvrin/Jibrin; 1 Samuel 27:1-3, 8 miles SW of Ether. OR Harada(t)h ('fear'), 50 miles north of Eilat in Numbers 33:24-25 http://bibleatlas.org/haradah.htm
1041 Joshua 12:60 http://en.wikipedia.org/wiki/Rabbah There is another Rabbath in Jordan. http://en.wikipedia.org/wiki/Rahat. The current city of Rahat is 20 miles SE of Gaza. The area of Ein Yahav is rich in copper and a vital place for water and trade routes.
1042 *Arad* means 'fugitive' or 'sequester' in Hebrew, but in Chaldee it means 'wild ass'. http://en.wikipedia.org/wiki/Tel_Arad
1043 I Samuel 1:1 Jeroham was Samuel's grandfather; Samuel's father lived near Mount Ephraim. "Jeroboam built Shechem in mount Ephraim . . ." (I Kings 12:25) OR It's possibly modern Yeruham in the Negev.
1044 Joshua 15:3 and I Chronicles 8:3
1045 Joshua 15:6

120	*[ ]3rywk*	?BeneBerak[1046]	just east of Tel Aviv
121	*Fr3tmʿi3*	?Pharah[1047]	now Ofra (Ophrah), 10 miles N of Jerusalem
122	*Iwb3r3*	?Abel	just west of Dan in the north
123	*B3irwr3d3*	Beer Luz[1048]	'well of the almond' in southern Judah
124	*B3t-ʿnt*	BethAnoth[1049]	3 miles NE of Hebron, near Halhul
125	*S3r3h3n3*	Sharuhen[1050]	(Tell el-Ajjul) mouth of Ghazzah wadi, south of Gaza
126	*'Irm ʿtn*	?Rammah-Gittaim[1051]	'high double wine press' in Benjamin
127	*Grwn3i*	Gallim[1052]	(Khirbet Kakul) near Gibeah of Saul
128	*Iwd3m*	?Adummim[1053]	halfway between Jerusalem and Jericho
129	*[ ]rh3t*	?Beeroth[1054]	near Gibeon, north of Ramah
130	*H3[ ]r3i*	?Hazor (S)	near Gibeon
131	*Mʿrw[ ]*	Maarath[1055]	5 miles north of Hebron
132	*'Irwr[m?]*	?Aro'er	(Tell Esdar) SE of Beersheba
133	*Ywrd3*	Yursa/Yurza	(Tell Jemmeh) 8 miles south of Gaza
134-138	[ ]		
139	*Ywrhm*	?Joram, Jehoram[1056]	possibly near modern Yeruham or Mt. Yeruham
140	*'Iwnyny*	?Ithnan[1057]	between southern Hazor and Ziph
141	[ ]	[Hazor?]	
142	*3[ ]g[ ]*		
143-144	[ ]		
145	*MʿK[t?]*	Maacha(th)[1058]	Macaah between Geshur and Aram-Zobah
146	*'I[ ]dy[ ]*		
147-148	[ ]	[Dan?]	
149	*[ ]3*		
150	*Ywrwdn*	Zereda(n)[1059]	on Jordan between Adam and Bethshan

The bottom right cities:
1a is Sludd/Sharudad. 2a is Raphia. 3a is Labuna (Libnah). 4a is en Gluna. 5a is Ham.

1046 Joshua 19:45 BeneBerak means children of Berak.
1047 Joshua 18:21-23 cited along with Bethhoglah OR Peleth in I Chron. 2:33
1048 Judges 1:26 in the land of the southern Hittites
1049 Joshua 15:58-59 http://bibleatlas.org/beth-anoth.htm
1050 Breasted, James, *Ancient Records of Egypt, volume 4*, University of Chicago, p. 354 and Joshua 19:6
1051 Nehemiah 11:33 listed as two separate cities, but may have been one name to differentiate it from others
1052 I Samuel 25:44
1053 Joshua 15:7 http://en.wikipedia.org/wiki/Adummim
1054 Joshua 18:27
1055 http://bibleatlas.org/maarath.htm
1056 II Chronicles 22:7 Jehoram means 'Yaweh raised'.
1057 Joshua 15:23 http://bibleatlas.org/ithnan.htm
1058 Joshua 12:5 ". . . all Bashan, to the border of the Geshurites and the Maachathites, and half Gilead . . ."
1059 I Kings 11:26 also known as Zerothan

Pharaohs of the Bible

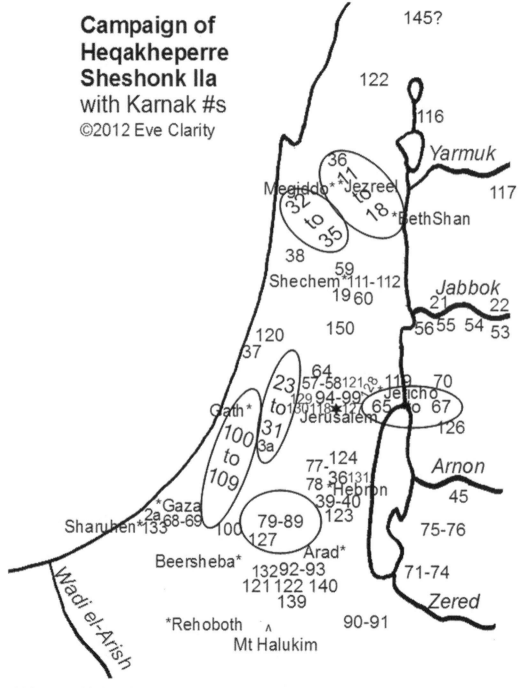

Shishak avoided Rehoboam's forts south of Jerusalem, and attacked all the northern cities around it instead. Several units likely brought back their lists of conquered cities.

Noticeably absent from the Karnak list is the southern fortress of Beersheba.

> "The earliest fortification was probably built by Solomon and consisted of a solid mud-brick wall approximately thirteen feet thick and a gateway. It was surrounded by a glacis (a plastered slope) and a moat. The city was destroyed by fire perhaps in the late tenth century and rebuilt using the original brick wall and gateway. The destruction may have occurred when Shishak, king of Egypt, invaded Judah."[1060]

Cities Destroyed by Shishak/Sheshonk IIa

The Israelite cities destroyed by Shishak could have ranged from LBIIB/IIIC to Iron IA-IC (under king Saul) to Iron IIA (recently captured Canaanite cities by David and newly occupied by Israelites) to Iron IIB (newly constructed fortified cities of kings Solomon, Rehoboam, and Jeroboam). Jeroboam had built Shechem and Penuel in his first regnal year,[1061] only to have Shishak destroy them four years later. Shishak's destruction levels are often designated as IronIIA or IronIIB or the transition thereof in the early 10th century.

Megiddo was one of king Solomon's chariot cities built with his new 6-chambered gate, and a destruction layer is evident after that structure was built. Secular archaeologists disagree. Amihai Mazar is a Biblical archaeologist who has directed excavations at Tel Rehov, Beth Shean, and Tel Batash (Timnah). In reply to a secular archaeologist, Mazar stated regarding Megiddo's controversial "stables", palaces 6000 and 1723, and gate:

> "I see no difficulty in retaining the 'Solomonic' date of the monumental Ashlar buildings 6000 and 1723 and the six-chamber gate at Megiddo as well as the six-chamber gates at Hazor and Gezer."[1062]

I applaud Mazar for holding onto higher dates for this strata. Secular archaeologists continue to lower dates of other cultures to get them to correspond with their incorrect low dates for Egypt. Dating strata by pottery types is a subjective science under constant revision, but there is an abundance of data supporting Shishak's campaign in the 10th century BC. When archaeologists accept Shishak is Sheshonk IIa instead of Sheshonk I, it will greatly ease their chronology battles. But because there is disagreement with the dating of strata there is also disagreement as to which destruction layer of a city is attributable to Shishak.[1063] Some of the cities in Canaan had been inhabited since soon after the flood of Noah in the 24th century BC, and had several layers of destruction. After aligning cities' strata with my higher chronology dates and high Egyptian chronology, it became clear who destroyed which city when. [See my notes in appendix A.] Summarized charts follow.

1060 DeVries, LaMoine F., *Cities of the Biblical World*, Hendrickson Publishers, 1997, p. 153
1061 I Kings 12:25
1062 Mazar, A., "Iron Age Chronology: A Reply to I. Finkelstein," *Levant* XXIX, 1997, pp. 157-167
1063 Junkaala, Eero, *Three Conquests of Canaan: A Comparative Study of Two Egyptian Military Campaigns and Joshua 10-12 in Light of Recent Archaeological Evidence*, 2006, Abo Akademi University Press

Pharaohs of the Bible

Strata of Northern Cities in Israel

12-Megiddo	17-Rehob	16-BethShean	14-Taanach	38-Socoh(Zeror)	?-Achshaph	141?-Hazor
XVIII-XVII EBI	H EBI-II	XVIII-XVII EBIA				XXI EBII
XVI-XV EBII-III	(then abandoned)	XVI EBIB				XX EBIII
XIV EBIV		XV-XII EBII-IV				XIX EBIV
XIII MBI		XI MBI		MBI		XVIII MBIIA
XII MBII		(XI MBI)		MBIIA		XVI-XVII MBIIB
XI-X MBIIC		Xa-b MBII		MBIIB-C		Post-XVI MB *
IX LBI *T	D11 MB/LBI *^T	IX-R2 LBI		LBI *T	13 LBI *T	XV LBI *T
VIII LBIIA	D10 LBI-IIA	IX-R1b		LBIIA		(rebuilt)
VIIb LBIIB *J	D9 LBIIB <Seti 1	IX-R1a *Seti 1	IA LBII *J	LBIIB <J		XIV LBIIA *^J
VIIa LBIIB *R	D8 LBIIB	VIII-S5 LBIIB		IronIA-C		XIII LBIIB
VIb IronI	D7-6 IronIA	LVI-S3 IronIA			12 IronIA	XII IronIA
VIa IronI *^Q	D5-4 IronIB *B	UVI-S2 IronIB			12 *Sea People	XI IronIB
Vb IronI <D	D3/VII IronIB	LV-S1 IronIB *D	IB IronI *D		11 IronC	X IronIIA
Va IronIIA	D2/VI IronIIA *	UV IronIIA	IIA IronII	IronIIA	10 IronIIA	IXb
IVb IronIIA *^S	D1b/V IronIIA *S	IV IronIIA *^S	IIB IronII *S	IronIIB *S	9 IronIIB *S	IXa IronIIA *S
IVa IronIIB	D1a/IV IronIIA *			(IronIIC)	8 IronIIC	VIII VII *^?
IVb IronIIB	A-3 IronIB			(IronIIC)	7 IronIIC	VI IronIIB *Q
III IronIII *TP	A-2 IronIII <TP	III IronIII *TP		IronIIC *TP	6 IronIIC	V IronIIB *^TP
II IronIII				Babylonian		IV IronIIB
I Persian				Perisan		III IronIIB

< = conquered; * = destroyed; ^ = fire; T = Thutmose III; R = Rameses III; J = Joshua; B = Barak; D = David; S = Shishak; TP = Tiglath-Pileser III; Q = quake

318

Strata of Middle Cities of Israel

20?-Shechem	?BethShemesh	103-4 Shellaleh	129?-Beeroth	41?-Tel Zayit	42?-Lachish	?-Gezer
XXII EBI		EBI			EBI	XXVI-XXV EBI
XXI EBII		EBII			EBII	XXIV-XXIII EBII
(then abandoned)		EBIII *?			EBIII	XXII EBIII-MBI
XIX MBI-IIA		EBIV			EBIV	XXI MBIIA
XVIII MBIIB *^Senusret III		MBI			MBI MBIIA-B	XX MBIIB XIX MBIIC
XVII MBIIC		MBII	MBIIC	MBIIC	MBIIC	XVIII MBIIC
XVI LBIA	VII LBI	MBIII *T	LBIA <T	LBI	LBI	XVII LBIA *^T
XV LBIB		LBI; LBIIA *^?	LBIIA	LBIIA		XVI LBIB *Q
XIV LBIIA *J	VI LBII	LBIIB *^J	LBIIB *J	LBIIB *^J	VII LBIIB	XV LBIIB *^M
XIIIb IronIA *^Abimilech	V IronIA *^Seti I	X IronIA	IronIA *SP	IronIA	VI IronIA *^Joshua	XIV IronIA XIII IronIA *SP
XIIIa IronIB	IVa IronIA *^R	W IronIB	IronB *Q?	IronIB-C	V IronIA	XII IronIB *^Q?
XI IronIC *Q	IVb IronIB	V IronIC	IronIC			XI IronIB *?
X IronIIA	[IIIa] IronIC	U IronIIA	IronIIA			X IronIC
IXb IronIIA *Q	IIIb IronIIA					IX IronIIA *O
IXa IronIIA *S	IIa IronIIB *^S	T IronIIB *^S	IronIIB *S	IronIIA *^S	IV IronIIA *S	VIII IronIIA *S
VIII IronIIB	IIb IronIIB			IronIIB *^?	IronIIB	VII IronIIB
VII IronIIB *TP	IIc IronIIC *TP	S IronIIC	IronIIC			VI Iron IIC *TP
VIb IronIII *Sb	Ia IronIIC *Sb	R IronIII	IronIII	IronIIIC *Sb		
VIa IronIII *N			IronIII *N		I IronIIB *Bab.	V Iron IIC *N
V Babylonian						
	Ib Roman-Byz.	Roman		Roman		IV Persian

< = conquered; * = destroyed; ^ = fire; T = Thutmose III; M = Marenptah; R = Rameses III; J = Joshua; D = David; S = Shishak; N = Nebuchadnezzar II; SP = Sea Peoples; Bab. = Babylonians; A = Assyrians; TP = Tiglath-Pileser III; Sb = Sennacherib; Q = quake

Pharaohs of the Bible

Strata of Southern Cities of Israel

?9-Debir(Mirsim)	?-En-Rimmon	110-Arad	?-Beersheba	Tel Masos?	Tel Ira?	Tell Malhata?
	XIX EBIA	L-VI EBIA		EBI		1A EBIB
	XVII-XVI EBIB	L-V EBIB *?				1B EBI
J EBIII *^?	XV EBII *^?	L-IV EBIIA *^?			IX EBIII	
	XIV-III EBIII	L-III EBIIB	MBI	MBI *Hyksos?	(then abandoned)	2A MBI
I MBIIA *^?	XII EBIV	L-II mid-late B		MBII		2B MBIIA
H MBIIB	XI LBIA	L-I mixed				2C MBIIB-C *^T
G MBIII *^T	X LBIB *T			LBI		(then abandoned)
F LBI	IX LBIIA					
E LBII *^ Othniel	VIII LBIIB			IIIb IronIA		
D IronIA	VII IronI	U-XII IronIA	IX IronIA	IIIa IronIA		
C1 IronIB *^?			VIII IronIB	IIb IronIB		
C2 IronIC *?			VII IronIC	IIa IronIC *Q?		
B1 IronIIA		U-XIb	VI IronIIA	Ib IronIIA	VIII IronIIA	3A IronIIA
B2 IronIIA						
B3 IronIIB *S	VIC IronIIA *^S	U-XIa *^S	V IronIIB *^S	Ia IronIIB *S	VII IronIIB *S	(3A) IronIIB *^S
A1 IronIIB	VIB IronIIB	U-X IronIB	IV IronIIB *Q		VI IronIIBC	3B IronIIB
A2 IronIIC	(VIB) IronIIC	U-IX IronIIC	III IronIIB		(VI) IronIIC	
A3 IronIIC	(VIB) IronIIC	U-VIII IronIII	(III) IronIII		(VI) IronIII	
	(VIB) IronIII *Sb	U-VII IronIII *Sb	(III) IronIII ^*Sb		(VI) IronIII	
A4 IronIII *N	VIA IronIII *^N	U-VI *N	II-I N(exile)	Pre-I IronIIC *N	(VI) *N	3C IronIII *N

< = conquered; * = destroyed; ^ = fire; T = Thutmose III; M = Merenptah; R = Rameses III; J = Joshua; D = David, S = Shishak; N = Nebuchadnezzar II; SP = Sea Peoples, Bab. = Babylonians; A = Assyrians; TP = Tiglath-Pileser III; Sb = Sennacherib; Q = quake

Pharaohs of Solomon and Rehoboam

Strata of Mediterranean Coastal Cities of Israel

Tell Abu Hawam ?-Shihor-Libnath	Tel Shiqmona	?-Dor	Tel Mevorakh	Tel Qasile 37?-("Kurkar"?)	?-Ashkelon	133-Yurza (Tell Jemmeh)
	Lost #?		?		A EBI	
					B EBII *?	EB
			MBIA			
			MBIB	MBI	C MB	MB
		MBIIC	MBIIC			
		LBIA *^T	LBIA *T			K LBIA <T
VA LBIIA			LBIB			J LBIB
VB LBIIA *Seti I		(LBIIA)	LBIIA-B		D LBIIB *Israel	H LBIIA
VC LBIIB *R		LBIIB *^Tjeker		XIIa IronIA		G LBIIB
IVA IronIB		IronIA-C	IronIA *?	XIIB IronIB	Vc IronIA *^M	(G)
		(IronIA-C)		XI IronIB *^Q?	Vb IronIB *^SP	(G)
IVB IronIC *^D		9 IronIIA <D		X IronIIA <D	Va IronIIA *^D	(G)
IIIA IronIIA		(9 IronIIA)	VIII IronIIA	IX-2 IronIIA		F IronIIA
IIIB IronIIB *S	IronII *S	8b IronIIB <S	VII IronIIB *^S	(IX-2) *^S	VIb IronIIB *^S	E IronIIB <S
IIA IronIIC	IronIIC *TP	8a IronIIC <A	VI IronIIC *?	IX-1 IronIIA	VIa IronIII <A	D IronIIC
IIB IronIIC	IronIIC *Sb	(IronIIC) <TP	V IronIII *?	VII IronIIB *TP		C IronIIC
	Iron III *N		IV IronIII	(then abandoned)	VIIb IronIII *N	B IronIII <N
	Babylonian		III Bab.		VIIa Greek	A IronIII
I Persian-Byz.	PB Persian *Ax	Persian	II-I	VI Persian	VIIIc Roman	Persian-Greek

< = conquered; * = destroyed; ^ = fire; T = Thutmose III; M = Merenptah; R = Rameses III; J = Joshua; D = David; S = Shishak; N = Nebuchadnezzar II; SP = Sea Peoples; Bab. = Babylonians; A = Assyrians; TP = Tiglath-Pileser III; Sb = Sennacherib; Q = quake

Pharaoh Heqakheperre Sheshonk IIa returned to Egypt with great spoils of war. After he succumbed to the infection in his head wound, he was succeeded by Tutkheperre Sheshonk IIb who was followed by Maakheperre Sheshonk IIc to whom I give five regnal years each; and they ruled during the reigns of Rehoboam and Jeroboam. The three Sheshonks II were followed by Osorkon II, the son of Takelot I. The first few regnal years of Osorkon II overlapped the last few years of Rehoboam and Jeroboam.

HPA HarSiEse A, then Harsiese I (960-928 BC) of the 23rd dynasty

Harsiese I sarcophagus

Harsiese ('Har, son of Isis') was the son of HPA Sheshonk C. HPA Hariese A served Smendes III for ten years (960-650 BC) at the beginning of Osorkon's II reign. When Smendes III died, pharaoh Harsiese I appointed his own son [. . . dju . . .] to be HPA (950-935 BC). Because Nimlot C, high priest at Heracleopolis, had become very powerful in Middle Egypt; he was able to place his son, Takelot F (935-930 BC), as the next HPA in Thebes. When Nimlot C died, his son ruled in his place as king Takelot II (930-910 BC). The 22nd and 23rd dynasties were intermarried and cooperated with each other. At the entrance to Bab el-Gasus in Deir el-Bahri, George Daressy discovered a cache of 153 sarcophagi and 200 statues of HPA's from after the 21st dynasty.[1064]

Osorkon II (960-928 BC) of the 22nd dynasty

Osorkon II was the son of pharaoh Takelot I and queen Kapes. Pharaoh Osorkon II married Mutemhat, Isetemkheb, Djedmutesakh IV (who gave birth to Nimlot C), and Karomama. Queen Karomama was the mother of sons Shoshenq D and Hornakht, and daughters Tashakheper, Karomama Meritmut C, and [Ta?]iirmer.

A gray granite statue[1065] of Osorkon II once kneeled[1066] with votive offerings at the temple of Amun in Tanis with several lines of petition.[1067] Osorkon requested the gods help him establish his sons in their offices (line 11), and he placed his son Hornakht as HPA at Tanis and his son Nimlot C as

Osorkon II from Tanis statue

1064 Grimal, Nicholas, *A History of Ancient Egypt*, 1988, p. 291. See my notes in appendix B.
1065 Usurped from Khyan and Rameses II, see *The Cambridge Ancient History: Plates to Volume III*, Cambridge University Press, 1984, 1999, p. 128
1066 Kneeling on the right knee with the left leg stretched back, and arms outstretched with offerings was first depicted by Seti I. Blyth, Elizabeth, *Karnak: Evolution of a Temple*, Routledge, New York, 2006-2007, pp. 153-154
1067 Ritner, Robert K., *The Libyan Anarchy*, 2009, pp. 283-288

HPA in Heracleopolis.[1068] Osorkon II placed his eldest son, Sheshonk D, as high priest of Ptah in Memphis. Thus his three sons covered the north and the fayyum as his generals.[1069] Osorkon II had good reason to be concerned about the hostile *Pyt*-Libyans (line 16), or Libyans descended from Phut, who continued to be mercenaries for centuries.[1070] And Osorkon II did eventually overthrow the Libyans.[1071]

Osorkon II continued trade with Byblos, as one of his seated statues was found there.[1072] A block fragment at Karnak contained Osorkon's decree to provide for the Theban temple priests, and make an "exemption".[1073] This tax exemption decree in his 22nd year was also carved on a wall of his jubilee festival hall at the great temple of Amun in Bubastis,[1074] explaining that he exempted all of the female servants of Amun from Amun's "two cities" (Thebes and Tanis) from paying taxes in return for Amun's promise of a first jubilee. That Tanis was regarded as the Thebes of the north was noted in a dirge at the tomb of Osorkon II in Tanis.[1075] In his Bubastis 'Appearance in the Temple' relief, Osorkon II is pictured wearing the white crown[1076] since he acted on behalf of the people of Thebes.

> "Regnal year 22, month 4 of Inundation. Appearance in the temple of Amon that is in the Mansion of the Jubilee; sitting upon the litter; initiating the protection of the Two Lands by the king. **Exempting** the harem of the estate of Amon together with **all the women of his two cities** who had been servants since the time of his forefathers, being servants in any estate, **who were taxed** concerning their labor annually. Now, as His Majesty was seeking a great deed of benefit for his father Amon-Re, since he (Amon-Re) had announced a first jubilee for his son who sits upon his throne, and he (Amon-Re) had announced for him very many in Thebes, the Lady of the Nine Bows, the king thus said in the presence of his father Amon: 'I have exempted Thebes in her length and her breadth, while she is clear from legal claim and granted to her lord, with no interference against her by agents of the royal palace, so that her people might be exempted to the ends of time by the great name of the Good God.'"[1077]

Just as Sheshonk I had his festival hall stones quarried in his 21st year, Osorkon II sought a promise from Amon-Re before making plans to build his festival hall for his jubilee (heb-

---

1068 Nimlot C was not HPA at Thebes, but at (Harsaphes) Heracleopolis, as carved on the donation stela of Djedptahiuefankh and found in its vicinity. See *The Libyan Anarchy*, pp. 344-347
1069 Smendes III was ruling Thebes at the time.
1070 Genesis 10:6 and Ezekiel 27:10
1071 Ritner, Robert K., *The Libyan Anarchy*, 2009, p. 299
1072 Ritner, Robert K., *The Libyan Anarchy*, 2009, p. 288
1073 Ibid., pp. 287-290
1074 Ibid., pp. 306 and 324 Naville's west inner wall, letter I, register 9.
1075 Ibid., pp. 347-8 which referred to Tanis as "Thebes-the-divine-district"
1076 Ibid., p. 325
1077 Ibid., pp. 326-327 with line numbers removed and my emphasis.

sed); but unlike Sheshonk I, Osorkon II reworked stone already cut.[1078] In the festival hall of Osorkon II the glyphs for "heb-sed" are carved 69 times. Osorkon II is pictured several times wearing his red crown of Lower Egypt[1079] and his heb-sed robe.[1080] Ritner wrote that the "Osorkon reliefs provide the most detailed evidence for this pivotal ritual of divine kingship . . ."[1081] Some think Osorkon II died prior to his 30th year, or that he celebrated his jubilee in his 22nd year because of the copy of his decree in that year, but certainly the extensive preparations would have been stopped before carving so many reliefs and text if that were the case; yet all the walls are finished and provide the most complete description of the heb-sed festival. Others think Osorkon II reigned closer to 40 years, but since no artifacts of a second jubilee in his 33rd year have surfaced, I give Osorkon II a 32 year reign.

Conventional Egyptian chronology places Osorkon II at the Battle of Qarqar in 853 BC, which would be 100 years after his reign in my chronology. Though the Jubilee court of Osorkon II stated that upper and lower Retenu (Canaan) and ". . . all remote foreign countries are at the feet of this good god,"[1082] it does not mention any battles there.

In addition to the massive Jubilee court at the great temple of Bastet in Bubastis, Osorkon II, "son of Bastet," also built a smaller temple sixty miles north of it called the Mahes temple.[1083] There he placed a colossal red limestone statue which he had usurped.[1084] Osorkon II also built monuments at Tanis, Memphis, and Leontopolis.

When Nimlot C's son Takelot F was HPA in Thebes (935-930 BC), Osorkon II built two small chapels to Osiris at Karnak: Osiris Khenem Maat and Osiris Wep-Ished.[1085] The first chapel portrayed queen Karomama as "god's wife of Amun" with their grandson HPA Takelot F. The Osiris Wep-Ished chapel was dedicated to Isis and had seven Hathors as well as Osorkon II and HPA Takelot F, and is now commonly called "Temple J".[1086]

Sheshonk I, David, Solomon, and Phoenicia

The main cities of Phoenicia were Byblos (ancient Gebal), Sidon, and Tyre. Referring to these three cities, Sanford Holst wrote the following:

> "Though the cities are seen throughout history as working together on almost every enterprise (i.e., Solomon contracted with Tyre, knowing this would bring him Sidon's woodcutters) they broadcast a public image of being separate cities. For this reason, ancient writers would refer to one of these three cities, even though they often were including the others. For example, the Egyptians first came in contact with Byblos, so even when Tyre became the dominant city they

---

1078 Ritner, Robert K., *The Libyan Anarchy*, 2009, p. 291
1079 Ibid., pp. 328, 330 Naville's walls E/F scenes 1 and 2
1080 Ibid., pp. 332, 334 Naville's wall F, register 5
1081 Ibid., p. 291
1082 Ritner, Robert K., *The Libyan Anarchy*, 2009, p. 326
1083 Ibid., p. 341
1084 Ibid., p. 343
1085 *The Cambridge Ancient History III Part I*, University of Cambridge, 1982-2003, UK, p. 556
1086 Blyth, Elizabeth, *Karnak: Evolution of a Temple*, Routledge, New York, 2006-2007, p. 191

still referred to their Phoenician trade as being with Byblos, and they called the ships from Tyre the 'Byblos ships.' The Hebrew scribes did exactly the opposite, referring to Phoenicians as 'Sidonians'."[1087]

Sheshonk I sent a statue of himself to Abi-Baal of Byblos. Meander of Ephesus wrote "When Abi-baal was dead, his son Hiram received the kingdom from him, who, when he had lived fifty-three years, reigned thirty-four," and that the construction of Solomon's Temple began in the twelfth year of Hiram's reign,[1088] which I place at 1011 BC. If so, Hiram reigned from 1023 to 989 BC. I suggest Abi-Baal willed his son Hiram to rule over Tyre, and willed Eli-Baal (to whom Osorkon I gave a statue) to succeed his father in Byblos. Hiram traded with kings David and Solomon.

And Hiram king of Tyre sent messengers to David, and cedar trees, and carpenters, and masons: and they built David an house. (II Samuel 5:11)

So Hiram gave Solomon cedar trees and fir trees according to all his desire. And Solomon gave Hiram twenty thousand measures of wheat for food to his household, and twenty measures of pure oil: thus gave Solomon to Hiram year by year. And the LORD gave Solomon wisdom, as he promised him: and there was peace between Hiram and Solomon; and they two made a league together. (I Kings 5:10-12)

A sarcophagus of a "son of Ahiram, king of Byblos"[1089] was discovered in Byblos in 1923 thus verifying the royal name of Hiram. The sarcophagus has winged sphinxes carved into it, which also verifies Phoenician trade with Egypt. Hiram's sarcophagus may be at Qabr Hiram southeast of Tyre.[1090]

The pharaonic statues of Sheshonk I and Osorkon I sent to different Phoenician kings provide another verification that Sheshonk I could not have been the Biblical Shishak. The Biblical Shishak was Heqakheperre Sheshonk IIa.

1087 Holst, Sanford, "Byblos, Sidon, and Tyre" at http://www.phoenician.org/byblos_sidon_tyre.htm
1088 Josephus, *Antiquities* 8:144-460
1089 http://en.wikipedia.org/wiki/Ahiram
1090 http://en.wikipedia.org/wiki/Hiram_I

Clarity Chronology of Divided Kingdom's Beginning, Egypt, Syria and Assyria

King of Israel	Jeroboam I 975-954		Nadab 954-953	Baasha 953-930	Elah 930-929	Omri 929-918	Ahab 918-897 Ahaziah 898-896		Joram 896-884	
King of Judah	Rehoboam 975-958		Abijah 958-955	Asa 955-914			Jehoshaphat 914-889		Jehoram 889-885	Ahaziah 885-884

LE king	Sheshonk IIa 979-970	Sheshonk IIb 970-965	Sheshonk IIc 965-960	Osorkon II 960-928		Sheshonk III 928-889			Sheshonk IV 889-874	
ME	HPA's in north also			Nimlot C		Takelot II (935) 930-910		Thutmhat	Os B	Nimlot III	Djehutiemhat
UE king	Smendes III 970-950			HarSiEse I 950-928		Pedubast I SiEse 928-905	Iuput I (co-reign) 914-901			
HPA	Smendes C 970-960		HarSiEse A 960-950	..dju.. 950-935	Takelot F 935-930	HarSiEse B 930-901			Takelot B 901-890	Osorkon B 890-871 *Sheshonk VIa* 886-881

Syria	Hadad 980-916				Ben-Hadad I 916-885	
Assyria	Ashurreshishi II 972-967	Tiglath-Pileser II 967-935	Ashur-Dan II 935-912	Adad-nirari II 912-891	Tukulti-Ninurta II 891-884	

Appendix A

Clarity's Incomplete Tell List of Israel's Ancient Cities (modern name)

Khirbet means 'ruins of'. A 'tell' is a mound of ancient debris.[1091]

Abdon (Khirbet Abda): Tel Abdon
Abel-Beth-Maacah (Abil el-Qamh): Tel Avel Bet Maakha
Acco: Tel Akko/Tell el-Fukhkhar
Adam (Damiya)
Adoraim (Dura)
Ai (Khirbet Nisya) 2 km SE of al-Bireh
Aijalon (Yalo)
Achshaph (Yasir, 6.8 miles NE of Acre): possibly Tell Harbaj/Tel Regev
Achzib/Akzib (Ez-Zib): Tel Akhzib
Adullam (Hurvat Adulam), about 4 km south of the Valley of Elah, and about 20 miles west of Bethlehem. It has a hill about 140 m high with many caverns, some large enough to hold 300 men.
Anatoth (Anata)
Anim (Khirbet Ghwein et Tahta)
Aphek {N}: Tel Afek/Tel Ras el-'Ain
Aphek {mid}
Aphek {S}
Arad: Tel Arad; 17 miles SE of Hebron, 18.5 miles NE of Beersheba; main road to Edom + Elath
Aroer (Khirbet Ara ir): Tel Eseber
Aruboth (Khirbet el-Hamam) which had a 10th century BC fort and citadel
Ashdod: Tel Ashdod
Ashnah (Idhnah)
Azekah/Azekha (Azeqa): Tel Azekah/Tell Zakariya/Zakariyeh, a round hill about 800 feet high, on the north side of Wady es Sunt.
Azor (Yazur)
Baalath: Tel el-Mughar, between Jabneel and Shikkeron
Beeroth (al-Bireh)
Beersheba: Tell es-Seba
Bene-Berak (al-Khayriyya/Kheiriyeh = Ibn Ibraq), 6 miles east of Joppa between Azor and Ono
Beth-Anath (Safed el-Battikh)
Beth Arabah (Beit HaArava)
Beth-Dagon {N} (Khirbet deJun/Beit Jan): Tell Herashim[1092]
Beth-Emek: Tel Emeq/Tell Mimas
Beth-Hoglah (Almog)
(lower) Beth-Horon (Beit Ur Et-Tahta)
(upper) Beth-Horon (Beit Ur el-Foqa)

[1091] Excellent research and pictures on Israel's less known tells at http://www.biblewalks.com/Info/Tell.html
[1092] http://www.biblewalks.com/Sites/BeitJan.html

Pharaohs of the Bible

Bethsaida: Tell Bethsaida, 3 miles north of Sea of Galilee
Bethel (Beitin)
Beth Tappuah (now Tuffuh)
Beth-Zur is not Khirbet et-Tubeiqah since no fortifications of Rehoboam were found
BethShan/BethShean (Beisan): Tell el-Husn
BethShemesh {N} (Khirbet Tell er-Ruweisi), midway between Hazor and Achzib
BethShemesh (Khirbet Sheik esh-Shamsawi), south of the Sea of Galilee
BethShemesh {S}: Tell er-Rumeileh
Bozrah (Busaira)
Byblos (Jubayl) [Gebal – Josh. 13:5, Ezek. 27:9]
Cabul (Kabul), 9 miles SE of Acco
Carmel {south} (Karmil)
Chinnereth: Tel Kinrot, 10 km north of modern Tiberias
Dan: Tel Dan
Debir (Kirjath-sannah) {N}: Thour-ed-Dabar, on road from Jericho to Jerusalem
Debir (Kiriath-sepher) {S}: Tell Beit Mirsim
Dor (Khirbet el-Burj)
Dothan: Tel Dothan
Edrei, 32 miles west of Jordan on the Yarmuk river
Eglon ('calf-like'): Tel Nagila
(Solomon's) Elath: Tell el-Kheleifeh, now 500 meters (1/3 of a mile) from Gulf of Aqaba
Jezirat Fara'un (island south of Eilat) means 'island of the pharaohs' in Arabic
Ekron: Tell el-Hesi
En-Rimmon: Tell Halif and Khirbet um-Rammamim 1 km south of Tell Halif;
    it guards the approach to the hill-country from the Via Maris
Etam (Khirbet el-Khokh)
Gath: Tel Miqne
Gath-Hepher (Khirbet ez-Zurra): Tel Gat Hefer beside Mashed
Gaza: Tell es-Sakan or Tell Harrube
Gederah (Khirbet Ğudrayathe)
Gerar: Tell Haror/Abu Hureireh on Nahal Gerar
Gezer: Tell Jezer
Geshur capital: Tel Hadar
Gibeah: Tell el-Ful
Gibeon (now Jib): El-Jib
Gilgal (Khirbet el-Mofjir) – settled in Iron Age
Harosheth (El Harathiyeh)
Hazor: Tell el-Qedah
Hepher: Tell el-Muhaffer
Heshbon: Tell Hesban
Hebron: Tell Rumeida
Hormah in Arabah near Seir (Num 14:45; Deut. 1:44)
Hormah, formerly Zephath
Jabesh-Gilead: Tell Abu al-Kharaz or Tell al-Maqlub

Appendix A

Jarmuth/Yarmuth: Tell Jarmuth (Khirbet el-Yarmuk)
Jattir (Khirbet Attir): Horvat Yattir
Jericho: Ain es-Sultan
Jeroham: Tel Rahna
Jezreel: Tel Jezreel
Kadeh-Barnea {N}: Tell el-Qudeirat
Kadeh-Barnea {S}: in Arabah next to Petra
Kadesh {near Hazor}: Tell Qedes
Kadesh (between Megiddo and Tanaach): Tell Abu Kudeis
Kadesh {near Sea of Galilee}: (Qedish) Khirbet el Kidish
Kedesh/Qadesh on the Orontes River: Tell Nebi Mend
Kinah: Tell Uza on Wadi el-Qena
Kiriath-sepher [Debir]: Tell Beit Mirsim
Lachish: Tell el-Duwier
Libnah: Tel es-Safi
Makkedah: Tell Maresha/Beit Guvrin has extensive cave networks for 5 kings to hide in
Maon: Tell Main
Mareshah: Tell Sandahanna
Megiddo: Tell el-Mutesellim
Merom: Tell el-Kribeh
Tel Michal (Khirbet Makmish) 4 miles north of Yarkon river on Med. Coast
Misheal/Mashal: Tell Keisan/Kison
Mizpah: Tell en-Nasbeh
Moresheth-gath: Tell el-Judeidah/ Tel Goded
Oboth (Ir Ovot)
Ophrah (now Afula)
Penuel: Tell der Alla
Rabbah {Judean}: Rubba ruins
Rehob {N}: Rachaiya, inland between Tyre and Acco
Rehob {NW}: Tel Kabri, near Nahariya
Rehob {NE}: Tell Rehov, near Beth-Shean
Rehoboth (well on wadi Ruheibeh)
Samaria: Sebastiyeh
Sharuhen: Tell el-Ajjul
Shechem (Nablus): Tell Balatah – massive gate 4-guard rooms, 2 towers, stone paved square, paved processional, and 4-horned altar
Shihor-Libnath ['dark'-'white']: Tel Abu Hawam
Shiloh (Khirbet Seilum/Beit El) – Iron Age house destroyed by fire "1050 BC"; palace, then a fort
Shiqmona: Tel Malha
Shunem (Sulam)
Socoh {N}: Tel Zeror
Socoh {mid}: Tel Sokho, Khirbet Abbad and Khirbet Shuwaikah in the Valley of Elah
Socoh {S}: 22 miles south of Hebron and 5 miles SE of Eshtemoa
Succoth: Tell Deir Alla

329

Taanach: Tell Tinich
Tamar: En Haseva
Tappuah: Tell Sheikh Abu Zarad
Tekoa (Khirbet Teku)
Timna Valley {copper} in Arabah
Timnah: Tel Batash, near Gath (Tel Miqne)
Tirzah: Tell el-Farah North
Valley of Elah (Wadi es-Sunt)
Yursa: Tell Jemmeh/es-Jemmah
Zaphon: Tell es-Sa'idiyeh
Zerada/Zerothan: Tell es-Sa'idiyeh
Ziklag: Tell Sera'/Khirbet esh-Shariah
Ziph: Tell Zif
Tel 'Eton/Tell 'Aitun, 7 miles ESE of Lachish, and 2 miles north of Beit Mirsim
Tel Ira (Khirbet Ghara) could be Jagur (Johsua 15:21), YeKabzeel (Neh. 11:25), Zephath (Judges 1:17), or Ramat Negev (Johsua 19:8)
Tell Zayit (Zeitah)[1093] 4 miles north of Lachish
Mount Seir Range along eastern side of the Arabah includes Jebel Shara

Rehoboam's Fortified Cities

In II Chronicles 11:5, "*cities*" means 'watched or guarded' and "*defense*" means enclosed against siege. None of these cities were to guard against Jeroboam's Israel. Rehoboam was preparing for Egyptian troops to place Judah under siege. In verse 11, Rehoboam placed captains, food, oil, and wine in the "*strongholds [metsurah]*" (same word translated "*fenced*" in verse 10) which means 'hemming in, mound, rampart, and general fortification'.

Bethlehem ('house of bread') is 5 miles south of Jerusalem.
Etam ('hawk ground') is 6 miles south of Jerusalem.
Tekoa, now Tuqu, ('trumpet blast' or 'stockade') is 8 miles SE of Bethlehem.
>Beth-Zur ('house of rock') is likely north of Hebron.
Socoh ('bushy') is likely Khirbet Abbad in the Elah Valley.
Adullum ('justice of the people') is Hurvat Adulam, 2.5 miles south of the Valley of Elah, and about 12 miles SW of Bethlehem.
>Gath is Tel Miqne.
>Mareshah ('summit') is Tell Sandahanna, 2 miles from Beit Guvrin.
Ziph ('flowing' or 'battlement') is Tell Zif on a 100 foot high mound, 4 miles south of Hebron.
Adoraim ('double mound/wide/glory') is now Dura, 6 miles SW of Hebron.
Lachish ('invincible') is Tel Lachish.
Azekah ('tilled' or 'high hill') is Tel Azekah/Tell Zakariya/Zakariyeh, 16 miles NW of Hebron.
Zorah ('shout'), now Sar'a overlooking Valley of Sorek, is 14 miles west of Jerusalem.
Aijalon ('field of deer'), now Yalo, is 14 miles NW of Jerusalem.
Hebron means 'association'.
[> for city locations which differ from those currently accepted]

1093 Tell Zayit is only 8 hectares. An abecediary was discovered at Tell Zayit.

Appendix A

Clarity's Canaan/Israel City Strata

"Interpretation of archaeological information, even when it includes many laboratory reports and the most careful and objective recording, is still a subjective affair."[1094]

Some cities have been excavated only once but have not published the city's strata in an easily accessible form. Some cities have been excavated several times using different strata numbering or different dating methods. The following is an incomplete compilation of my notes with my high chronology centuries and my understanding of who was responsible for a destruction level. The century BC is a general time marker. [* = destroyed; ^ by fire, TPB = Tripartite Pillared Building (stables), < = conquered/captured, + = and, w/ = with; *lmlk* is for *la melek* meaning "to the king"] A "massebah" is a stone placed upright; a standing stone. A "menhir" is a very tall (average 4 meters) massebah. A "residency" is an Egyptian governor's business house in a Canaanite vassal city.

Cities Conquered by Shishak (Sheshonk IIa)

#11 Jezreel ('El sows'): Tel Jezreel - using Franklin's phases

Strata	Age	Cent.	Description	Unique
I	Iron IA		rock-cut cisterns	
II	Iron IB			
III	Iron IIA	11th	Solomonic 6-chamber gate (like Megiddo Va & Samaria II) casemate wall, ashlars, towers	
(IV?)	IronIIB	10th	[has not yet been verified, or the site is not Jezreel]	

#12 Megiddo ('place of crowds'): Tell el-Mutesellim (hill of the ruler) {Yadin}

Strata	Age	Cent.	Description	Unique
XVIII	EBIA	24th	settlements	bone and flint tools
XVII	EBIB	23rd	massive walls and gate rock-cut storage pits	* ?
XVI	EBII	22nd	gate and walls rebuilt	olive presses
XV	EBIII	21st	3 temples with a round high place, paved courtyard	
XIV	EBIV	20th	mud-brick wall 25 feet thick and 16 feet high	
XIII	MBI	19th	glacis	Thuthotep statue
XII	MBII	19th	<captured by Hittites	Hittite influence
XI	MBII	18th	Hyksos forticifcation: stone wall, glacis, and moat	
X	MBII	18th	Palaces and temples	
IX	LBI	17th	big multi-chamber gate *destroyed by Thutmose III	
VIII	LBIIA	16th	palace w/ sea-shell courtyard	Egyptian influence ivory art
VIIb	LBIIB	15th	*destroyed by Joshua	Rameses II scarab
VIIa	LBII	14th	palace w/ griffin, TPB's; gate *by Ram. III;	Rameses III ivory pen case
VIb	Iron I	13th	Philistine mugs+loomweights; ivory	{"just preceding King David"}
VIa	Iron I	12th	area AA and K-4 *^destroyed by earthquake and fire	
Vb	Iron I	11th	poor walls in area K-2	<captured by David
Va	Iron I	11th	Solomonic 6-chamber gate	large TPB stables – chariot city

---

1094 Rainey, Anson and Notley, R. Steven, *The Sacred Bridge: Carta's Atlas of the Biblical World*, CARTA Jerusalem, 2006, p. 24

Pharaohs of the Bible

IVb	Iron II	10th	large buildings, ashlars	*destroyed by Shishak
IVa	Iron II	10th	major rebuilding w/ ashlars (by Jeroboam)	
IVb	Iron II	9th	rock-cut water system, Omri and Ahab's stables	
IVa	Iron III	9-8th	stables and silos	
III	Iron III	8th	big palaces built	*destroyed by Tiglath-Pileser III
II	Iron III	7th	2 large Assyrian style bldgs.	
I	Persian			

According to a 2003 abstract, ". . . there is no convincing EB II presence anywhere on the mound of Megiddo."[1095]

P.L.O. Guy was the main excavator of Stratum VI in 1934. He uncovered pillared houses typical of the early Israelites.[1096] Guy wrote,
"There had obviously been a disaster of some sort in VI, of which the fire was the culmination, and that disaster may have been either a battle or an earthquake. . . . Some skeletons were found crushed under walls in postitions of obvious agony, but a number of others had been buried . . . It looked as if survivors had come back after the catastrophe and had left where they were those bodies which had been hidden by fallen walls but had hastily buried those who were visible. . . . The disaster, whatever it was, had been pretty sudden, for most of the rooms contained very large quantities of pottery *in situ* . . ."[1097]

Skeletons crushed under fallen walls from a sudden disaster sounds like an earthquake which 'culminated' in a fire. Neither was there evidence the site was quickly inhabited and rebuilt by a 'victor'; instead stratum Vb had walls of poor quality. The stela fragment of Sheshonk I was found in a "dump adjacent to a trench excavated by the German engineer Gottlieb Schumacher earlier in the century."[1098] "Guy's description of its discovery, however, makes clear that Schumacher's excavations in this area had not reached the destroyed remains of the preceding Stratum VI . . ."[1099] Therefore, Sheshonk I placed his stela at Megiddo during the 11th century of Stratum V or earlier.

Since king David attacked Syrian cities north of Megiddo, like Zobah, I assume Megiddo was already under his control or too impoverished to worth mentioning. Saul also made no mention of Megiddo, but Solomon did extensive building there.

Yadin includes a stratum Va-IVb for Solomon's structures which he defines as a casemate wall portion of #325, a 6-chamber gate with 2 towers, 2 palaces (including #6000), but no stables.[1100] Yadin attributes the current structures labelled as Solomon's stables to Ahab. Greek Geometric Pottery sherds were found in stratum Va-IVb.[1101]

1095 "What happened to Megiddo in the early bronze age II?" Eres Israel, 2003, vol. 27, pp. 66-72, 285
1096 Harrison, Timothy P., "The Battleground: Who Destroyed Megiddo? Was it David or Shishak?," *Biblical Archaeology Review*, Nov/Dec 2003, Vol. 29, p. 60
1097 Ibid.
1098 Ibid., p. 62
1099 Ibid.
1100 Yadin, Yigael, *Hazor: The Rediscovery of a Great Citadel of the Bible*, Weidenfeld and Nicolson, 1975
1101 Fantalkin, Alexander, "Low Chronology and Greek Proto geometric and Geometric Pottery in the Southern Levant," *LEVANT* 33, 2001, p. 119

Appendix A

A seal of Jeroboam II was found at Megiddo. It has a roaring lion with the inscription, "Shema servant of Jeroboam."[1102]

#14 Taanach ('sandy') [EA#248]: Tell Tinich, between Megiddo and Jenin

Strata	Age	Cent.	Description	Unique
	EBII	22nd	city wall with rectangular towers	pottery
	EBIII	21st	new wall, terraced millo, plastered glacis	
	EBIV	20th	funerary chambers like the 3rd dynasty	
	MBIIA	19th	city	
	MBIII	18th	residency (west bldg.)	
pre-1	LBI	17th	houses with casemate wall * by Thutmose III	
1b	LBIIA	16th	village during Amarna period (EA248); Akkadian cuneiform tablets cache	
1a	LBIIB	15th	subturranian structures *destroyed, king killed by Joshua (12:21-25)	
			gap	
2b	IronI	14th-12th	east fortress * by David	Canaanite cuneiform tablet
2a	IronIIAB	11th-10th	public buildings, palace, TPB stables,[1103] cult basins + altar * by Shishak	
3b	IronIIC	9th-8th	tower	
3a	IronIIC	7th-6th	Greek influence	
4b	Persian	5th	two rooms and pits	
4a	Arab	10th-11th AD	fortress and palace	

#16 BethShean/BethShan ('house of ease'): Tell el-Husn

Strata	Age	Cent.	Description	Unique
XVIII-XVII	EBIA	24th	scanty	
XVI	EBIB	23rd	large mudbrick bldg w/ 14 pillar bases; Esdraelon ware	
XV	EBIIA	22nd	*^destroyed by fire; rebuilt, resettled, then abandoned	
XIV	EBIIB	21st	unoccupied	
XIII	EBIII	20th	resettled	Khirbet Karek Ware
XII	EBIV	20th	rock-cut tombs in cemetery	
XI	EBIV-MBI	19th	shepherds, duckbill axhead	Senusret II scarab
Xb	MBIIA	19th	Lg. Square houses built around courtyard	
Xa	MBIIB-C	18th	Canaanite town with well-planned streets and dwellings	
IX-R2	LBI	17th	18th dynasty large temple, then abandoned	
IX-R1b		16th	19th dynasty inscriptions of Seti I and Rameses II	
IX-R1a		15th	*^destroyed by fire by Seti I who left a stela	
VIII-S5		14th	basalt column bases	anthropoid clay coffins
VII-S4	LBIIB	13th	inner fortress + tower, temple, 3-room houses, silos	
lowerVI-S3	Iron IA	12th	commander's quarters, cylinder seal, scarabs, Antit	
upperVI-S2	Iron IB	11th	[stelae of Seti I, Rameses II, statue of Rameses III]	
lowerV-S1	Iron IB	11th	Philistine control, temples to Resheph and Antit; *by David	
upperV	Iron IIA	10th	cylindrical and house-shaped offering stands	
IV	Iron IIA	10th	Solomon's admin. buildings, basalt stones *^ by Shishak	

1102 Cornfeld, Gaalyah, *Archaeology of the Bible: book by book*, Harper and Row, 1976, p. 115
1103 Sellin 1904: 18, 104; Guy, 1931: 44 and fig. 32; Currid 1992: 56, 61 n.11

Pharaohs of the Bible

III		8th	4-room houses, massive brick walls, then *^by Assyrians	
II	Greek/Roman	4th-1st	town (Nysa/Scythopolis) built below tell, temple on top	
I	Byzantine	4th-6th AD	mound settled w/ circular church; *quake of 749 AD	

In stratum VII there was a fortified tower and inner fortress and public granary. Seti's victory stela was found in stratum VII out of context. A cartouche of Amenhotep III was under the floor of stratum VII temple out of context.

In stratum VI a lintel with the name of Rameses III was found out of context. The objects in the foundational deposits of stratum VI had objects with the names of Rameses I and II.

In stratum V two Philistine temples were dedicated to Anat and Dagon with attached storehouses, and many cylinder seals with serpent motifs were found.

BethShean ". . . has a 30-degree slope on all sides. It can be approached only on the northwest . . . the only gateway found was excavated here."[1104]

#17 Rehob ('broad place'): Tell Rehov near BethShean {excavation director A. Mazar}

Strata	Age	Cent.	Description	Unique
H	EBI	23rd	sherds	
H	EBII	22nd	fortified city with glacis	
D-11	MB/LBI	17th	*^destroyed by Thutmose III	
D-10	LBI-IIA	16th		pond
D-9b	LBIIB	15th	buildings	clay figurine lion's head
D-9a	LBIIB	15th	cobble floor	
D-8	LBIIB	14th	plaster floor	
D-7	Iron IA	14th	bldg, a few Egyptian sherds	
D-6	Iron IA	13th	flimsy walls	{Mazar's dates}
D-5	Iron IB	12th	bldgs *destroyed by Barak?	{ca. 1130 BC}
D-4	Iron IB	12th	bldgs rebuilt, then *destroyed	
D-3 (VII)	Iron IB	11th	Philistine sherds	{until 980 BC}
D-2 (VI)	Iron IIA	11th	sanctuary * by David	{grain pits}
D-1 (V)	Iron IIA	10th	sanctuary *^ by Shishak	pottery= Megiddo IVb
A-4 (IV)	Iron IIA	9th	*destroyed and abandoned	{until 840 BC}
A-3 (III)	Iron IIB	8th		{until 732 BC}
A-2 (II)	Iron IIB-C	8th	then abandoned	

D-2 and D-1b were 50 years apart (1020-970 = 50). D-1 and D-2 had a sanctuary.
C-2 (VI) showed signs of an earthquake.
C-1b (V) had burnt grain and B-5 (V) was destroyed by fire.
C-1a (IV) was rebuilt and B-4 (IV) had casemate walls and a massive tower.
Strata V and IV had imported pottery.

[1104] *Encyclopedia of Archaeological Excavations in the Holy Land, Volume I*, Exploration Society of Jerusalem and Prentice Hall, 1975, p. 209

Appendix A

"The best parallels to the strata VI–IV assemblage are to be found at Megiddo strata VB and VA–IVB, Taanach periods IIA and IIB, Horvat Rosh Zayit strata 3–2, Tel `Amal, Tell el-Hammah and Jezreel. . . . It is tempting to relate the destruction of stratum V to the invasion of Shishak and that of stratum IV to the Aramean wars, following the end of the Omride Dynasty . . ."[1105] - Amihai Mazar

#20? Shechem ('shoulder' or 'ridge'): Tell Balata(h)

Strata	Age	Cent.	Description
[XXII]	EBI	23rd	pit hut town
[XXI]	EBII	22nd	village
[XX]	EBIII-IV	21st	outer wall 968; fill prep. for building constr. with square bricks
[XIX]	MBI-IIA	20th	wall 939, 20' high glacis, brick/stone wall, courtyard-temple enclosed by walls D+900
[XVIII]	MBIIB	19th	wall 902, casemate-courtyard temple; glacis between walls C+D *^Senusret III
[XVII]	MBIIC	18th	wall 901, pillar-courtyard temple, wall 900 rebuilt
[XVI]	LBIA	18th	walls 909-910, enlarged temple-fort, silos built into glacis
[XV]	LBIB	17th	cyclopean wall, multi-chamber gate, 17' thick fortress walls with rectangular bricks, fortress-temple 1-a
[XIV]	LBIIA	15th	wall B, east gate, fortress-temple 1-b with 2 small entrance massebahs * Joshua
[XIII]	LBIIB-IronIA	15th-14th	fortress-temple 2-a with one 1.45m square smooth massebah in stone socket (see Joshua 24 below),
XII	IronIB	13th	town, fortress-temple 2-b w/ 3 massebahs *^by Abimilech (1247) (vacant 50 years)
XI	IronIC	12th	fortified city; small shrine *quake?
X	IronIIA	11th	hasty reconstruction
IXb	IronIIA	11th-10th	better construction w/ casemate wall *quake?
IXa	IronIIA	10th	towers and gate built up by Jeroboam I as his capital *by Shishak
VIII	IronIIB	10th-9th	rebuilt; large plastered granary atop temple ruins
VII	IronIIB	8th	more Israelite 4-room houses *by TPIII
VIb	IronIII	7th	rebuilt *by Sennacherib?
VIa	IronIII	7th	rebuilt *by Neb.?
V	Babylonian	6th-5th	rebuilt city with wall
IV	Greek	4th	*by Alexander, then repaired
III	Greek	3rd	Garrison
II-I	Selucid	2nd - 1st	houses, but no wall *by John Hyrcanus, then abandoned

I could not find pre-Iron Age strata numbers for Tell Balata, so just continued from strata XII. Shechem's temple was 108 X 92 feet with walls 18 feet thick with a huge standing stone.[1106]

1105 Mazar, A. Based on article submitted to the *Encyclopedia of Archaeological Excavations in the Holy Land, Supplementary Volume* (edited by E.Stern) at http://www.rehov.org/Rehov/Results.htm

1106 Cornfeld, Gaalyah, Archaeology of the Bible: Book by Book, Harper & Row, 1976, p. 78

So Joshua made a <u>covenant</u> [berith] with the people that day, and set them a statute and an ordinance in Shechem. (Joshua 24:25)

And it came to pass, as soon as Gideon was dead, that the children of Israel turned again, and went a whoring after Baalim, and made Baal<u>berith</u> their god. (Judges 8:33)

*And when all the men of the tower of Shechem heard that, they entered into an hold of the house of the god <u>Berith</u>. And it was told **Abimelech**, that all the men of the tower of **Shechem** were gathered together. . . . Abimelech took an ax in his hand, and cut down a bough from the trees, . . . And all the people likewise cut down every man his bough, and followed <u>Abimelech, and put them to the hold, and set the hold on fire on them</u>; so that all the men of the <u>tower of Shechem</u> died also, about a thousand men and women. (Jg 9:46-49)*

Instead of recognizing Yahweh as the LORD of the covenant, they turned to many foreign gods (*baalim*) to be their covenant gods instead, and they received just judgment. Abimelech's fiery destruction was noted in stratum XII.

#23 Gibeon ('hill city'): El-Jib, 5 miles north of Jerusalem {excavated by J. Pritchard}

Age	Cent.	Description	Unique
EB	21st	sherds; 24 warrior tombs with weapons	
MBIIA	20th	tomb #58	
MBIIB	19th-18th	24 tombs; Tomb 15 scarab #18 of Kheperre has triple-scrolls	
		Mycenaean and Cypriot pottery	
LBIA	17th-16th	no houses found, but one double Tomb 10 w/ scarabs;	
IronI	15th-12th	16 acre city with huge pool (80' deep; 37' dia.) with 79 steps in circular staircase to the bottom; 5' thick masonry walls and tower (quarried hills), tunnel to spring; 63 wine cellars at 65 degrees^{1107}	[peace w/ Joshua]
IronII	12th-10th	56 jar handles inscribed with *gb'n*	*destroyed by Shishak
IronIIC	9th-7th	two fortresses; 10' thick masonry walls; 'horse' figurines	* by Neb.

#37? "Kurkar" for Tel Qasile, in Tel Aviv on Yarkon river, made of kurkar stone

Strata	Age	Cent.	Description	Unique
		MBI	sherds	
XIIa	14th	IronIA	Canaanite temple w/ plastered brick benches and lime floor	
XIIb	13th	IronIB	Philistine city, mud-brick bldgs	loom weights + whorls
XI	12th	IronIB	shrine (to Dagon?), enlarged temple, mud-brick wall on stone foundation	
			*^ by quake?	smelted copper
X	IronIIA	11th	Aegean-style temple #captured by David	
IX-2	IronIIA	11th	Solomon admin. complex, 4-room homes, silos,	TPB-stables *^ Shishak
IX-1	IronIIA	10th	partially rebuilt, smaller and poorer	stone-lined silos
VIII	IronIIB	9th	casemate wall, public bldg.	2 scarabs, 1 scaraboid seal
VII	IronIIB	8th	Hebrew ostracon, * by TPIII	Samarian Ware
VI	Persian 5th-4th		large public building, Hebrew seal	Attic Ware

---

1107 Magnusson, Magnus, *Archaeology of the Bible*, Simon and Schuster, 1977, p. 130

Appendix A

V	Greek	3rd - 2nd		
IV	Herodian 1st		large public building w/ one course of ashlars	
III	Romans 3rd-4th AD		large building, pottery kiln	
II	Byzantine 4th-6th		public bathhouse w/ plastered pool	* by ?
I	Islamic 7th		sherds	

#40 Hebron ('association'): Tell er-Rumeida/Tel Hebron

Strata	Age	Cent.	Description	Unique
	EBIII	21st	Hittite city	Abraham bought a cave
	EBIV	21st	fortified city	*^ ?
	MBI	20th	rebuilt as a Canaanite city	
	MBIIA	20th	Hyksos fortified city with huge cyclopeon wall	
	MBIIB-C	19th	4-room houses	
	LBIA-B	18th-17th	50 burials	* by Thutmose III
	LBIIA-B	16th-15th	stone wall collapsed and burnt	*^ by Joshua
	IronIA-B	14th-13th	Israelite pottery	
	IronIC	12th	Calebite town	
VIII	IronIB	11th	King David's capital for 7.5 years	
	IronIIA	10th-7th	forced exile by Nebuchadnezzar II	

"Hammond had indeed found evidence of Late Bronze occupation in six different areas of Tel Hebron! . . . During a new expedition in 1998, Israeli archaeologist Yuval Peleg found more than 50 burials with grave goods dating to the Late Bronze Age. Concerning Early Iron Age evidence of occupation, a great amount of pottery has recently been found, much of it in the conventional Israelite collared-rim style, typical of the Early Iron Age. The architecture and plastering techniques of the strata containing the collared-rim pottery was conventional Early Iron Age construction."[1108]

one of #42-44? Lachish ('invincible'): Tell el-Duweir/ Lachish, between Hebron & Gath

Level	Age	Cent.	Description	Unique
	EBI	24th	cave-dwellers	
	EBII	23rd	potter's clay lumps	Nubian diorite with part of a serekh
	EBIII	22nd	caves used as graves	Kirbet Karek sherds
	EBIV	21st	abandoned	
	MBI	21st	120 tombs of newcomers	
	MBIIA	20th	Hyksos fortress with lime-plastered glacis and moat ('fosse')	
	MBIIB	19th	phase 1 fosse temple	White Wash Ware
	MBIIC	18th		dagger w/ Canaanite inscription
	LBI	17th	phase 2 fosse temple	scarab of Thutmose III
VII	LBIIB	16th	phase 3 fosse temple	scarab of Amenhotep III
VI	IronIA	15th	*^ by Joshua; abandoned	ring and scarabs of Rameses II

1108 Reznick, Rabbi Leibel, "Did Hebron Disappear?" at http://www.aish.com/ci/sam/48964966.html

V	IronIIA 11th	fortified, palace A (royal city according to Holladay)
IV	IronIIA 10th	Solomon large 6-chamber gate + stables, glacis, and palace B
		Rehoboam's fortifications *partial destruction by Shishak
III	IronIIB 9th	Palace C, rock-cut water shaft Edomite pottery; *lmlk* jar sealings
IIA	IronIIB 8th	*^destroyed by Sennacherib ostraca to "my lord Yaush" "in 9th year"
I	IronIIB 7th	new city; last to be *destroyed by Babylonians (Jeremiah 34:7)

During Nebuchadnezzar's campaigns in Judah, 21 letters were exchanged by two military officers. Letter four described the watchman could see the signal fire from Lachish, but that the signal fire at Azekah had ceased, indicating Azekah had been conquered, and Lachish was last.[1109]

"The characteristic pottery vessels of the strata belonging to the destruction level at Lachish II are familiar from other sites in Judah, among them the City of David (particularly Stratum 10 of Area E and Strata 10C and 10B of Area G); Stratum 6 at Tel 'Ira; and Stratum 5 at En-Gedi (Tel Goren)."[1110]

"In the gateway, eight feet of burnt debris separated the floor of Level III from that of Level II . . . Two thousand skeletons with some of the bones calcined were found in a tomb outside the city."[1111]

Senacherib also totally destroyed "Lachish, Eglon, Beth-shemesh, Gibeah, Ramat Rahel, Beth-zur, En-gedi, and Arad."[1112]

"Hardly a trace of Philistine Bichrome pottery has been found at Lachish;"[1113] possibly because it was not inhabited by them, but by the Israelites.

#58 Mizpah ('watchtower' - *migdol*): Tell en-Nasbeh,[1114] 8 miles NW of Jerusalem

Strata	Age	Cent.	Description	Unique
	EBIB	23rd	small village	
5	EBII	22nd	pottery in tombs	rock-cut silo
	abandoned			
4	Iron I	12th	4-chamber inner east gate, wine and olive presses	Philistine pottery
3C	Iron II	11th	casemate-like wall, 4-room houses	
3B	Iron II	10th	2-chamber outer NE gate, 2 main towers (west tower built of ashlars) [captured by Shishak]	
3A	Iron III	9th	11 more towers on the city wall, glacis and fosse	
2	Iron III	8th - 6th	4-room houses, palace, and stables; *destroyed by Nebuchadnezzar II	
1	Greek and Roman			

1109 Devries, LaMoine, Cities of the Biblical World, Hendrickson Publishers, 1997, p. 213
1110 Lipschits, Oded, *The Fall and Rise of Jerusalem*, Eisenbrauns, 2005, pp. 192-193
1111 Cornfeld, Gaalyah, *Archaeology of the Bible: book by book*, Harper and Row, 1976, p. 174
1112 Ibid.
1113 Stager, Lawrence, "The Impact of the Sea Peoples in Canaan," *The Archaeology of Society of the Holy Land*, 1995, p. 342
1114 Archaeological map of the site at http://www.arts.cornell.edu/jrz3/siteplan.htm

Appendix A

Regarding Stratum 3, Jeffrey Zorn wrote, "It is important to note that for a period of at least four hundred years, the town was never destroyed." Also in reference to Stratum 3 Zorn wrote, "The prize . . . was the seal of Jaazaniah, which is possibly to be attributed to the officer of the same name who reported to Gedaliah at Mizpah (II Kings 25:23). This seal contains the image of a cock in a fighting stance; this is one of the earliest representations of this bird ever recovered."[1115]

#59 Tirzah ('favorable'): Tell el-Farah North, 7 miles NE of Shechem

Phase/Strata	Age	Cent.	Description	Unique
	EBIA	24th	hearths + limestone floors; flint + basalt tools, pit huts, pottery	
1	EBIB	23rd	rect. bldgs on stone foundations w/ stone bases for wooden pillars; wall (3 courses of stone topped with mud-brick) + towers, fortified gates, temple, 2 pottery workshops with kilns	
2		late 23rd	northern wall destroyed * by (quake?)	
3	EBII	22nd	solid stone wall built further southward with a rampart	
4	EBIII	21st	glacis	
5	EBIV	late 21st	western wall collapsed (quake?) and rebuilt; city abandoned	
6	MBII	19th	new wall + gate + glacis, and a citadel and Canaanite temple	
7a/ IV	LB	17th	new temple, silvered bronze goddess figurine; Cypriot + Mycenaen	
7b/ III	Ir IA	10th	Israelite 4-room houses w/ courtyards; fosse * by Shishak	
7c/	Ir IB	9th	new foundations laid	
7d/ II	Ir II	8th	conical seals, pottery model of temple, wealthy homes citadel (Omri's palace?), new gate with bench * by Assyrians	
I	Ir II	7th	Assyrian bowls; abandoned (exiled by Nebuchadnezzar II)	

#63? Shiloh ('tranquil')

Strata	Age	Cent.	Description	Unique
	MBIIA	20th	Room B, pottery	
VIII	MBIIB	19th	village	cooking pots rope decoration, erect rim
VII	MBIIC	18th	fortified city	whole mouth cooking pots
VI	LBI	17th	cultic place	
V	IronIA	15th	walled Israelite town, house A (tabernacle)	partial *by quake
IV	IronIIB	14th	continued	
		10th	*destroyed by Shishak	
	IronIIC	8th	forced abandonment by Tiglath-Pileser III	
III	Greek		large village, pottery + coins	some Persian pottery
II	Roman		village	
I	Byzantine		town, 2 churches	mosaic floor

1115 Zorn, Jeffrey R., "Tell en-Nasbeh: Biblical Mizpah in Benjamin" at http://www.arts.cornell.edu/jrz3/frames2.htm

#79? Debir (Kerjath-sepher, 'scribe city'): Tel Beit Mirsim, 13 miles SW of Hebron

Strata	Age	Cent.	Description	Unique
J	EBIII	20th	town	*^destroyed by fire
I	MBIA	19th	town	*^destroyed by fire
H	MBIIB	18th	rampart	
G	MBIII	17th	Canaanite fort, wall, + glacis	*^destroyed by Thutmose III
F	LBI	16th	town	
E	LBI	15th	east gate tower abandoned	*^partial destruction by Othniel
D	Iron IA	14th	rebuilt	
C1	Iron IB	13th	Israeli fort, grain pits	scarab of Thutmose I *^destroyed
C2	Iron IC	12th	town, stone lion	scarab of Amenhotep III *destroyed
B1	Iron IIA	11th	town	
B2	Iron IIA	11th	Israelite fort with Jerusalem-type gate (built by David?)	
B3	Iron IIB	10th	royal city with TPB stables	*destroyed by Shishak
A1	Iron IIB	9th	resevoir and aqueduct, rebuilding of west tower and gate	
A2	Iron IIC	8th	Israeli 2-storey pillared houses, rebuilding of west tower and gate	
A3	Iron III	7th	rebuilding of west tower and gate	
A4	Iron III	6th	rebuilding of west tower and gate	*^destroyed by Neb.
	Greek		pottery	
	Roman		fortress	
	Byzantine		bathhouse	
	Muslim		medieval occupation	

Tell Beit Mirsim has upper and lower wells (Joshua 15:15-19). The upper well is 1.5 miles north of the tell, and the lower well is 1 mile south of the tell. "Six successive well curbs are at the top of each of these wells,"[1116] demonstrating their long ages of use. In debris of level C were found a scarab of Thutmose I and a scarab of Amenhotep III.[1117]

*And from there he went against the inhabitants of **Debir**: and the name of Debir before was Kirjathsepher: . . . Caleb gave her the upper springs and the nether springs. (Jg. 1:11-15)*

#90-91 The Negev of Oboth ('waterskins')

Strata	Age	Cent.	Description	
	IronIIA	11th	fortress, Negevite ware	*by Shishak
	IronIIB	10th-9th	fortress w/ casemate wall, 4-gate, a moat, 3 storerooms, 2 granaries; site 4X's larger than other Negev fortress cities at 10,000 square meters	
	IronIIC	8th-7th	fortress w/ two towers set 46 ft apart, 74 cultic vessels of Edomite shrine like at Horvat Qitmit about 28 miles to the northwest. *by Neb?	
	Roman	1st-4th AD	fortress with towers	*by quake

1116 Kyle, Melvin Grove, *Excavating Kirjath-Sepher's Ten Cities*, Eerdman's, 1977, p. 34
1117 *Encyclopedia of Archaeological Excavations in the Holy Land, Volume I*, Exploration Society of Jerusalem and Prentice Hall, 1975, p. 176

Appendix A

#103-4 Highlands of Shellaleh (Nahal Besor/Wadi Shellaleh): Tell el-Far'ah South[1118]

Strata	Age	Cent.	Description	Unique
	EBI	24th	unwalled town	
	EBII	23rd	fort and wall-paintings	
	EBIII	22nd		*destroyed by Amorites?
	EBIV	21st		
	MBI	20th	copper and pottery and trade	
	MBII	19th	Hyksos fortified: fosse, wall atop glacis, towers + gate	
	MBIII	18th-17th		*destroyed by Thutmose III
	LBI	17th	Mycenaean and Cypriot pottery	
	LBIIA	16th-15th	Egyptian vassal with Residency, ovens	*^ by Rameses II (1473 BC)?
	LBIIB	15th	Residency stone foundation, storeroom; jar cartouche of Seti I	*^Joshua
X	Iron IA	14th-13th	under (Sea People) Philistine control; fortified with new lg. bldg.	
V-W	Iron IC	12th	Israelite 4-pillar houses, paved courtyards, ovens	
T-U	IronIIA	11th-10th	2m + 5m thick brick walls on stone foundation	*^ by Shishak
R-S	IronIIB	9th-7th	long building	
	Roman	1st AD	barracks and storehouses	

Scarabs of Merneptah, Seti I and II, and Rameses I, II, II, IV, and VI were all found here.

#105-6 Highlands of David: Khirbet Qeiyafa (David's ruins), just east of Azekah

It's plural because it includes the 35 square meter watchtower at Khirbet Quleidiya (Horvat Qolad), a few hundred meters east of Khirbet Qeiyafa (which I do not equate with Sharaim).

Age	Cent.	Description	Unique
EBII-III	22nd-21st	sherds and flint tools	
MB	20th-18th	fortified settlement, many sherds	bowls
IronI	15th-12th	collared-rim jars, cooking pots	
IronIIA-B	11th-10th	fort, 4-chambered gate, casemate wall	2-wing *lmlk* jar handle
		1-3m high upper and lower walls, terraces;	Qeiyafa ostracon

Sanctuary with 2 portable shrine models, 2 basalt altars, 2 pottery libation vessels, and 5 menhir
　　　　　　　　　　　　　　　　　　　　　　　　　　　　　　　　　　　　　　　* by Shishak

IronIIC	9th	wall repaired, wine and olive presses
Persian	5th-4th	isolated sherds
Greek	3rd-2nd	many sherds
Rom. - Arab	1st-8th AD	isolated sherds

Emile Peuch read the Qeiyafa ostracon as the concluding text of an administrative circular:
1. Do not oppress, and serve God . . . despoiled him/her
2. The judge and the widow wept; he had the power
3. over the resident alien and the child, he eliminated them together.
4. The men and the chiefs/officers have established a king.

1118　14 miles SE of Gaza, 18.5 miles west of Beersheba; tell covers (37 hectares) 4 million sq. ft. on the west bank of Nahal Besor which is the largest wadi in the northern Negev with G(e)rar and Beersheba as its largest tributaries. This was not a "town" but a well fortified city under Philistine control in Iron Age I.

5. He marked 60(?) servants among the communities/habitations/generations.[1119]

Peuch sees the ostracon recording the establishment of king Saul after a period of corrupt judges (including Samuel's sons).[1120] Because it mentions two separate groups of "men" (Mizpeh) and "officers" (Gilgal),[1121] I concur. If it had been referring to David's kingship, it would have mentioned "officers/warriors" and "elders".[1122]

#110 Arad ('sequester'), known as 'the Citadel': Tel Arad west of Dead Sea

Strata	Age	Cent.	Description	Unique
{Lower City}				
VI	EBIA	24th	unwalled well-planned town, water-supply system,	
V	EBIB	23rd	2.3m thick wall + strong towers, temple, public + private bldgs.	* ?
IV	EBIIA	22nd	Tammuz twin temples (remodel), bema	Egyptian jars *^ ?
III	EBIIB	21st	Egyptian trade	Narmer serekh
II	Bronze		Canaanite settlement	Egyptian pottery
I	mixed			
{Upper Mound}				
XII	IronIA	15th	Israelite enclosed farmland	(royal city according Holladay)
XIB	IronIIA	11th	Israelite citadel: casemate wall, gate + two towers, and temple	
XIA	IronIIB	10th	*^ by Shishak	bronze lion-shaped weight
X	IronIIB	10th	fortress, wall and temple rebuilt	Edomite ostraca
IX	IronIIC	9th	metal casting + perfume industires	
VIII	IronIII	8th		ostraca with "house of Yahweh"
VII	IronIII	7th	*destroyed by Sennacherib	bullae, 2 *lmlk* sealings
VI	Bab.	6th	*destroyed by Nebuchadnezzar II	Hebrew ostraca
V	Persian	5th - 4th	settlement with small fort	
IV	Greek	3rd - 2nd	settlement with tower	
III	Roman	1st AD	citadel and fort	
II	Muslim	7th +	inn	Kufic ostraca
I	Arab	10th-16th	graves	

Five other *lmlk* sealings were found elsewhere in the dig. The Israelite temple had the same layout as the Tabernacle.

#118? Gibeah ('hill') of Saul: Tell el-Ful, 3 miles north of Jerusalem

Strata	Age	Cent.	Description	Unique
pre-I	LB	13th	no bldg remains, potsherds, mace-head	claimed by Benjaminites
I	IronI	12th	pre-fortress	*^by Israelites
II	IronI	11th	Fortress I casemate walls w/ 4 towers	Saul's capital
IIA	IronII	10th	Fortress II with reinforcements	[captured by Shishak]

1119 Leval, Gerard, "Ancient Inscription Refers to Birth of Israelite Monarchy," *Biblical Archaeology Review*, vol. 38 #3, May/June 2012, p. 42
1120 Ibid., p. 43
1121 I Samuel 10 and 11 respectively
1122 warriors (I Chron. 12:23-40 in 1055 BC) and elders (II Sm. 5:1-3 and I Chron. 11:1-3 in 1053 BC)

Appendix A

Strata	Age	Cent.	Description	
IIIA	IronII	9th - 8th	Fortress IIIA *lmlk* sealings	*^by TPIII
IIIB	IronII	7th	Fortress IIIB with tower revetment	*^by Neb; exiled
IVA	Persian	6th - 5th	Fortress IVA	
IVB	Greek	3rd - 2nd	Fortress IVB	Ptolemy coins
V	Roman	1st - 1st		

#129 Beeroth ('wells): al-Bireh, 7 miles NW of Jerusalem

Strata	Age	Cent.	Description	
	MBIIC	18th	shards	
	LBI	17th	< by Thutmose III	
	LBIIA	16th		
	LBIIB	15th	fortified city	* by Joshua
	IronIA	14th		* by Sea Peoples?
	IronIB	13th		* by quake?
	IronIC	12th		
	IronIIA	11th	poor settlement	
	IronIIB	10th		* by Shishak
	IronIIC	9th	prosperous under Joash	
	IronIII	8th - 7th		* by Nebuchadnezzar II

#132 Aroer ('earthiness') in Negev: Tell Esdar, 13 miles SE of Beersheba

Strata	Age	Cent.	Description
IVb	EBI	23rd	silos, floors, painted pottery, flint axes, agate pendant
IVa	EBII	22nd	large fan scrapers, jar rims
III	IrIIAB	11th-10th	Israelite homes built in a circle, jars, chalices, lamps * by Shishak
II	IronIII	9th-8th	farm house and silos; (Hezekiah's) ashlar fortress, wall, and glacis
I	Roman		Israeli fort * by Romans in 70 AD

#133 Yursa/Yurza ('earthiness'): Tell Jemmeh, 8 miles south of Gaza on Nahal Besor

Strata	Age	Cent.	Description	Unique
8' (ft.)	EBA	23rd	Chalcholitic sherds	
8'	MBA	20th	traces of a settlement	
7' JK	LBI	17th	3 buildings, Philistine pottery	Thutmose III scarab <Thutmose III
6' GH	LBII	15th -12th	Israelite 4-room houses, smelting oven; human and animal figurines	
3' EF	IronII	11th - 10th	3 ovens; vault bricks w/ mud plaster, "long parallel rooms" TPB-stables <S
5' CD	Iron	9th - 7th	mud-brick barrel vaults pitch-brick technique; lots of Assyrian Palace Ware
9' AB	Bab.	6Th - 5th	2 lg bldgs around central court	Fikellura bowl + Ionian cup <N
	Persian-Greek	4th - 2nd	7 lg mud-brick granaries	imported Greek black-slip ware

There were ". . . stratigraphic mix-up in the excavations . . .".[1123]
"Examination of the EB III map of southern Israel and the results from unpublished surveys of the area indicate that settlement in this period spread to the northern Negev

---

1123 *Encyclopedia of Archaeological Excavations in the Holy Land, Volume II*, Exploration Society of Jerusalem and Prentice Hall, 1975, p. 546

as far as Tel 'Ira, but no further south . . . The large sites known to have existed in the southern Judaean Shephelah and in the coastal plain are Tel Erani, Lachish, Tel el-Hesi and Tel Ira of which the last-mentioned is most southerly. . . . It is interesting that settlement during the EB II extended over the entire Negev highlands, the Aravah, and southern Sinai, while during the EB III it was notably reduced, concentrating mainly in the south Hebron highlands, the Judaean Shephelah and the north western Negev . ."[1124]

#141? Hazor ('castle'): Tell el-Qedah/ Tel Hazor [excavated by Garstang] and {Yadin}

Strata	Age	Cent.	Description	Unique
XXI	EBII	24th	village	
XX	EBIII	23rd	city	Khirbet Karek Ware
XIX	EBIV	22nd	city	
XVIII	MBIIA	21st	huts	
pre-XVII	MBIIA	20th	burial caves	
XVII	MBIIB	19th	Hyksos scarab	
XVI	MBIIB	18th	city, glacis, citadel	clay drainage pipes
post-XVI	MBIIC	17th	*massive destruction layer by Thutmose III	
XV	LBI	16th	rebuilt, double temple	No Mycenaen pottery
XIV	LBIIA	15th	*^ destroyed by fire ["by Joshua about 1450 BC"]	
XIII	LBIIB	14th	temple; little Egyptian pottery found	
XII	Iron IA	13th	little of anything found but storage pits	
XI	Iron IB	12th	village and small temple with standing stones	
Xb	Iron IC	late 12th	Black on Red pottery first appears – Phoenician trade	
Xa	Iron IIA	11th	city, palaces, casemate wall, 6-chamber wall {Solomon}	
IXb	Iron IIA	late 11th	city, high places, {between Solomon and Ahab}	
IXa	Iron IIA	10th	*destroyed by Shishak	
VIII	Iron IIA	late 10th	fortified city double size of Xa with water system; TPB-stables and citadel with ashlars {Ahab}	
VII	Iron IIA	9th	Aramaean city *^destroyed by fire; torpedo jars	
VI	Iron IIB	late 9th	Israelite city *destroyed by quake {760 BC}	
Vb	Iron IIB	8th	Assyrian Palace Ware (APW) first appears	
Va	Iron IIB	late 8th	*^destroyed by fire {"by Tiglath-Pileser III in 732 BC"}	
IV	Iron IIB	7th	Israelite unfortified, poor town, but APW	
III	Iron IIB	late 7th	Assyrian citadel and fortress	
II		4th	Persian	
I		2nd	Greek; Maccabees	

Regarding Stratum VII, Yadin attested ". . . four fragmentary Hebrew inscriptions on jars . . ."[1125] Yadin wrote, "There was no reason to doubt that these were remains of the city destroyed by the Assyrian king Tiglath-pileser III in 732 BC as recorded in the Bible . . . stratum V . . ."[1126] Stratum

---
1124 Beit-Arieh, *Tel Ira: A Stronghold in the Biblical Negev*, Graphit Press, Israel, 1999, p. 175
1125 Yadin, Yigael, *Hazor: The Rediscovery of a Great Citadel of the Bible*, Weidenfeld and Nicolson, 1975, p. 158
1126 Ibid., pp. 147-148

Appendix A

Va had a jar with *lpqh*, 'belonging to Pekah', and Pekah reigned 759-740 BC.

Possibly #147 or 148 Dan ('judge'): Tel Dan/Tell el-Qadi, at foot of Mt. Hermon

Strata	Age	Cent.	Description	Unique
	EBI	23rd	settlement	Neolithic pottery
	EBII	22nd	city of 10,000 people	
	EBIII	21st	stone wall, (dismantled later for rampart), then abandoned	
	MBIIA	19th	massive ramparts w/ clay plaster, 2 towers, and mud-brick arched gateway	
	MBIIB-C	19th-18th	large 4-horned altar, house w/ cooking vessels	
	LBIA	17th	large wealthy tomb w/ Mycenaen and Cypriote pottery	* by Thutmose III
VIIb	LBIB	16th	coppger slag, furnaces, metal work	
VIIa	LBII	15th	silos, then a layer of ash	*^ by Danites (1410?)
VIb	Iron I	14th	many vessels	
VIa	Iron I	13th	3.6m thick city wall w/ 2 towers, limestone santuary w/ bench	
V	Iron I	12th	fine masonry acropolis	
IV	Iron II	11th	major city gate, basalt bema for statue (of Jeroboam I)	
III	Iron II	10th	gate and wall destroyed, 3 feet of burnt mud-brick	*^ by Shishak
II	IronIII	9th-8th	lg bldg w/ 300 juglets (1 *l'ms*)	
I	IronIII	7th - 6th	Phoenician inscription "belonging to Baal-Pelet"	* by Sennacherib

BenHadad attacked Dan during the reign of king Asa (956-915 BC) in I Kings 15:20. A victory stela referring to the "house of David" was found at Tell Dan.

#150 Zerada/Zerothan ('fortress'): Tel es-Saidiyeh

Strata	Age	Cent.	Description
XI	IronII	10th	*destroyed by Shishak
X		10th	rebuilt
IX		9th	
VIII		8th	
VIIB		7th	stone-paved streets with water channels
VIIA		7th	houses with beaten earth floors, plastered pit, then silt of gap
VI		6th	houses
V		6th	Israelite 4-room houses of 40 sq. meters *destroyed by Babylonians
IV		5th	rebuilt, then possible gap
III		4th	large square temple-fort with courtyard
II	Roman		
I	Byzantine		

#3a Libnah ('white'): Tel es-Safi/Zafit ('bright'), on the south bank of the Elah Valley

Strata	Age	Cent.	Description	Unique
1	EB-LB	21st - 16th	stone and brick bldgs.	Egyptian beads and part of stela
2	Ir. I-II	11th-10th	bldg. w/ 3 stone pillars; 4-room homes	Mycenaen sherds; no Philistine
			[no finds of destruction; possibly <captured by Shishak]	
3B	Ir. II	9th-7th	Israelite town	*lmlk* sealings

345

3B	Bab.	6th-5th		early Greek + Seleucid pottery	
4	Arab	7th-11th AD	Crusader fortress * by Saladin	Arab ware	

"Goliath shard" was found in strata 2.[1127]

?: Tel Burna, 4 miles east of Tel Zayit

Strata	Age	Cent.	Description	Unique
	LBIIB	14th	wall	
	Iron IA	13th		
	Iron IB	12th		Philistine bichrome
	Iron IIA	11th	casemate wall and towers of David	
	Iron IIB	10th-9th	fort and loom weights; flagstone pavement	*lmlk* jars
			[no mention of destruction debris; possibly <captured by Shishak]	
	Iron IIC	8th-7th	silos, olive oil press; wall burned ^ by Sennacherib?	
	Persian	5th-4th	stone houses	

Tel Burna is just a couple miles from Beth-Guvrin, and ". . . a settlement called Labana was situated at that time [of Medeba Map] near Beth-Govrin,"[1128] and a place called Horvat Livnim is nearby, so it is often associated with Libnah.

Victory Relief's Possible Lost Cities Conquered by Shishak/Sheshonk IIa

Lost# S. Beth-Shemesh ('house of the sun'): Tel Beth-Shemesh/Tell Rumeileh

Strata	Age	Cent.	Description	Unique
VII	LBI	17th	2-storey house	Mycenean + Cypriot ware
VI	LBII	16th	Patricians' houses with wooden columns	
V	Ir IA	15th	Wall, gate + 2 towers, Philistine ware, *^Seti I?	City I {Mackenzie}
IVa	Ir IA	14th	Bichrome ware, Ugarit tablet, *^ by RamIII	City II
IVb	Ir IB	13th	Copper workshop, Caananite alphabet ostracon, coated cisterns	
-(IIIa)	Ir IC	12th	Israelite transitional pottery and silos	
III(b)	Ir IIA	11th	Olive oil presses; unwalled Judean city	City III
IIa	Ir IIB	10th	royal city, casemate repair, TPB stables, resevoir *^ by Shishak	
IIb-c	Ir II	9th	unfortified village, oil + grape presses, dyeing	* by TPIII
Ia	Ir II	8th-7th	royal jar seals, * by Senacherib in 712 BC	rock-cut resevoir
Ib	Roman – Byzantine		medieval pottery	2nd cent. BC coins

[Philistine cities entered Iron Age earlier than Israelite cities.]

> "The Iron Age I levels at these sites (Tel Batash Stratum V, Tel Beth-Shemesh Stratum III, and Gezer Strata XIII-XI) contain a pottery assemblage similar to that of Ekron Strata VI-V: local Iron Age I pottery that developed from the Late Bronze Age Canaanite tradition mixed with a certain amount of Philistine bichrome ware."[1129]

1127 http://faculty.biu.ac.il/~maeira/goliath.html
1128 *Encyclopedia of Archaeological Excavations in the Holy Land, Volume IV*, Exploration Society of Jerusalem and Prentice Hall, 1975, p. 1024
1129 Coogan, Michael, *et al.*, editors, *Scripture and Other Artifacts: Essays on the Bible and Archaeology in*

Appendix A

". . . red-slipped and hand-burnished pottery . . . known throughout Israelite territory during the time of David and Solomon . . . correlates Timnah Stratum IV with Tell Beit Mirsim Strata B3, Beth-Shemesh Strata IIA, Gezer Strata VIII, Lachish Strata V, and Tell Qasile Strata IX-VIII."[1130]

"Destruction of Timnah Stratum IV and perhaps Beth-Shemesh Stratum IIa occurred during this invasion [of Shishak]."[1131]

Lost# Gezer ('portion'): Tell Jezer/Tell Gezer; between Jerusalem and Tel Aviv

Strata	Age	Cent.	Description	Unique
XXVI	EBIA	24th	unfortified village, hearths	Cream ware
XXV	EBIB	23rd	cave-dwellings, stone jars w/ grain, grindstones	
XXIV	EBIIA	22nd	population increased, buildings	
XXIII	EBIIB	22nd	town expanded, pottery; then abandoned	
XXII	EBIII	21st	resettled; then abandoned	1 Khirbet Kerak shard
	EBIV-MBI	20th		
XXI	MBIIA	19th	large city, homes w/ courtyards + platered floors + cisterns; granary acropolis, 12th dynasty statuette with name of "Heqab"	
XX	MBIIB	19th		
XIX	MBIIC	18th	wall, tower, 3-chamber gate, glacis; a high place with 10 liths	
XVIII	MBIII	18th	high place w/ 10 monoliths, plastered glacis, little Egyptian pottery	
XVII	LBIA	17th	storage jars w/ grain; *^ by Thutmose III	
XVI	LBIB	16th	palace complex, outer wall, (water system?); *quake? Amarna glass	
XV	LBIIB	15th	homes dif' orientation *^by Merenptah; Merenptah plaque + pectoral	
XIV	IronIA	14th	No MycIIIC; "post-destruction period"	
XIII	IronIA	14th	Philistine town; granary, acropolis #5 * by Sea P.; few Philistine bichrome	
XII	IronIA	13th	new fine homes w/ courtyards, granary rebuilt; acropolis #4 *^ by quake?	
XI	IronIB	13th	another settlement, acropolis #3 * by ?	
X	IronIB	12th	rebuilt acropolis #2	Philistine bichrome ware
IX	IronIC	11th	remodeled acropolis #1 *destroyed by Osorkon I as gift to Solomon	
VIII	IronIIA	10th	Solomonic gate and ashlar casemate wall; Gezer calendar, Baal altar *destroyed by Shishak	
VII	IronIIB	9th	gate rebuilt, sparse occupation	
VI	IronIIC	8th	*^destroyed by Tiglath-Pileser III	
V	IronIIC	7th	gate rebuilt and resettled, *lmlk* sealings, Neo-Assyrian tablets *^ by Neb.	
IV	Persian	5th-4th	Persian pottery, silver vessels	
III	Greek	3rd-2nd	*Yehud* and *Yeruselayim* sealings	
II	Hasmonean		coins * by ?	
I	Roman		coins	

A Hyksos scarab (#IAA1974.187) belonging to "Taz-re" was found at Gezer.

Honor of Philip J. King, Westminister John Knox press, 1994, p. 251
1130 Ibid., p. 253
1131 Ibid., p. 256

Lost# BeerSheba ('well of the oath'): Tell Beer-Sheva/Tell es-Saba

Strata	Age	Cent.	Description
	MBI	20th	shards, deep well
IX	Iron IA	14th	silo, pits, and huts
VIII	Iron IB	13th	pits and stone houses
VII	Iron IC	12th	Israelite 4-room houses, enclosed settlement, watchtowers
VI	Iron IIA	11th	Negev administrative center (royal city according to Holladay)
V	Iron IIB	10th	4-chamber gate, fortress, palace, brick on stone walls, glacis, fosse, water shaft, stables, temple, 4-horned altar; *^destroyed by Shishak
IV	Iron IIB	9th	stones for altar reused in wall; cistern system *destroyed by earthquake
III	Iron IIB	8th	casemate wall, gate, stables, storehouses; *^destroyed by Sennacherib
II	Iron IIC	7th	ashlar casemate wall, glacis, limestone altars, 4-room houses
I	Iron IIC	6th	fort, millo; then abandoned (exiled by Nebuchadnezzar's force?)
	Persian	5th-4th	40 Aramaic ostraca some with Artaxerxes III
	Herodian	1st	bathhouse
	Roman	2nd-3rd AD	fortress, which continued until early Muslim 7th AD

In stratum II were a Hebrew ostracon, a large storage jar with "*lmlk* Zif" with a 4-winged scarab, and a cylinder seal from the son of Hadad-ezer.[1132]

Lost# En-Rimmon: Tell Halif/Tell el-Khuweilifeh, 10 miles northeast of Beersheba

Strata	Age	Cent.	Description
XIX-XVII		24th	improved adjacent caves for burial
XVI	EBI	23rd	village, then abandoned in EBII
XV	EBII	22nd	fortified with wall, tower, and glacis, then *^destroyed w/ 3.5m ash
XIV	EBIIIA	21st	rebuilt town without a wall
XIII	EBIIIB	21st	
XII	EBIV	20th	
	MB	19th	(adjacent caves 4-5 contain MB flints & MBII bowls)
XI	LBIA	18th	Hyksos-type scarabs
X	LBIB	17th	Egyptian-style residence; then * "massive destruction" by Thutmose III
IX	LBIIA	16th	partial resettlement
VIII	LBIIB	15th	mud-brick platform with stone-lined storage pits
VII	Iron I	14th	Philistine pottery and stone-lined grain pits
VIC	Iron II	10th	arrowheads and sling stones *^destroyed by Shishak
VIB	Iron II	9th-8th	textile production: loom weights *destroyed by Senacherib
VIA	Iron III	7th	*^destroyed by Babylonians, then abandoned (exiled)
V	Perisan		
IV	Greek		
III	Roman/Byzantine		
II-I	Islamic		

[1132] *Encyclopedia of Archaeological Excavations in the Holy Land, Volume IV*, Exploration Society of Jerusalem and Prentice Hall, 1975, p. 165

"Stratum VIB, parts of which were preceded by Stratum VIC that is dated to the 9th century BCE, contains remains of destroyed structures covered with a thick layer of ash produced by a fire hot enough to calcify the mud bricks. This fire also helped preserve organic matters that became charred or carbonized. That the fire was a result of a military action is evident by the numerous arrowheads, sling stones, and remains of other weapons uncovered in the destruction context. Since the end came fast, most of the contents of the structures remained *in situ* (in place) and we get a freeze-frame picture of life at the point just before the destruction took place. Had the inhabitants had the time to leave the place leisurely, they would have removed much of the contents. Furthermore, Stratum VIA, which was inhabited possibly by refugees from Stratum VIB, was abandoned in haste with the contents of the structures also left intact behind. The way these two strata reached their end enables us to reconstruct life as it was just before the demise of the town. Now we know that a major occupation of the local inhabitants was textile production, as seen from the large number of clay loom weights and other tools."[1133]

Ramat Matred, 4 miles SW of Avdat in Negev

Strata	Age	Cent.	Description
	IronI-IIA	11th-10th	farming + ranching town, one cluster of homes w/ pillars at door enclosed by a fence; silos + paved areas * by Shishak

Timnah ('portion'): Tel Batash, near Gath (Tel Miqne)

Strata	Age	Cent.	Description	Unique
	EBI	23rd	pit huts, pottery	
	EBII-III	22nd-21st		
	MBI-II	20th-19th	pits, pottery, long barrow burial	Hyksos scarab
VII	LBIIA			
VI	LBIIB	15th	Philistine city	
V	IronI-IIA	14th-11th	< by David in 1062 BC	
IV	IronIIA	10th	royal city, (TPB stables?) * by Shishak	"ben Hanan" bowl
III	IronIIB	9th-8th	massive fortifications + gate (Uzziah);	4-wing *lmlk* jars
II	IronIII	7th	2-wing *lmlk* jars (Hezekiah)	
I				

Ader ('flock') in Moab: 4.5 miles NE of Karak

Strata	Age	Cent.	Description	Unique
III	EBIV	21st		
II	MBI	20th	town built with clay bricks	*^ by ?
I	MBIIA	late 20th	Canaanite temple and menhirs; brick walls on stone foundations	
	IronII	11th - 10th	sherds	*^ by Shishak
	Roman		Nabatean sherds	

1133 Borowski, Oded, "Tell Halif," Middle Eastern and South Asian Studies at Emory University, May 2010 http://www.bibleinterp.com/articles/halif357921.shtml

Pharaohs of the Bible

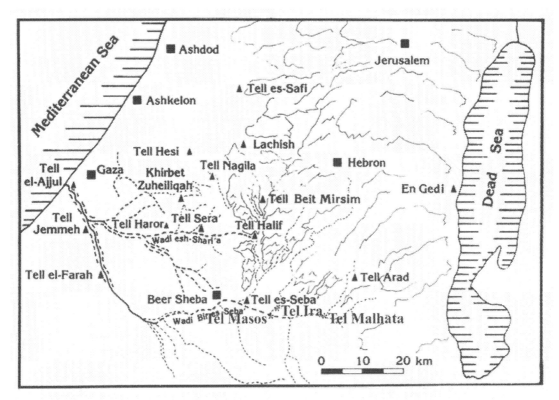

?: Tel Ira, now Khirbet Gharreh, between Beersheba and Arad

Strata	Age	Cent.	Description	Unique
IX	EBIII	21st	town with pottery sherds near bedrock, then abandoned	
VIII	Iron II	11th	town with pottery	
VII	Iron II	10th	solid city wall with 35 meters of casemate wall, 6-chamber gate, glaces, towers, stone revetment, admin. bldg.,	*by Shishak
VI	Iron II	9th-7th	fortifications rebuilt and strengthened; [unpopulated during Babylonian exile]	*^by Nebuchadnezzar
V	Persian		small town	2 Aramaic ostraca
IV	Greek		some new buildings (from Ptolemy I to Hyrcanus I), then abandoned	
III	Roman		small Jewish town	
II	Byzantine		highly populated	
I	Islamic		small town	

A scarab was found on the surface of the tell, but dated to 7th century stratum VI.‖ Next . . .

*And the children of the Kenite, Moses' father in law, went up out of the city of palm trees with the children of Judah into the wilderness of Judah, which lies in the <u>south of **Arad**</u>; and they went and dwelled among the people. And Judah went with Simeon his brother, and they slew the Canaanites that inhabited Zephath, and utterly destroyed it. And the name of the city was called **Hormah**. (Judges 1:16-17)*

Appendix A

The Kenites of Midian (east of Gulf of Aqaba) first dwelled among the Canaanites south of Arad, and tells in the area contain 'Midianite bowls'. The "wilderness of Judah" was not conquered all at once. Eventually the tribes of Judah and Simeon attacked Zephath and completely destroyed it.

In Kempinski's 1978 article on Tel Masos he wrote, "Settlement period was abandoned around 980-970 B.C." Later in the same article he wrote, "The pottery finds point to the destruction of the settlement at the beginning of the 10th century, possibly around 990-980, the beginning of David's reign in Jerusalem." Though I agree with the dating near 970 BC, I disagree it had anything to do with king David. Kempinski also noted that the people of Tel Masos then moved to Tel Ira. Because of the Midianite bowls and 12th century destruction, Kempinski thought Tel Masos was likely Zapheth which was renamed Hormah ('destruction'). I would expect the first two Hormahs of Moses' time (1490-52 BC, Numbers 14:45; 21:3) to be located in the Arabah near Seir (Deut. 1:44). I would expect a destruction layer during Joshua's campaign (1451 BC) for the new Hormah which was previously called Zephath (Judges 1:17), but none is recorded. Tel Masos is not Zephath.

? Tel Masos (6 hectares) on road to Hebron, 12km east of Beersheba (NOT Hormah)

Strata	Age	Cent.	Description	Unique
	EBI	23rd	flint tools, pit huts	
	MBI	20th	Canaanite mud-brick fortress	* by Hyksos?
	MB	19th	Hyksos fort + glacis	
	LB	17th	square-shaped houses	
			[If it's Hormah, where's the destruction layer?]	
IIIB	Iron IA	15th	'Israelite' ovens; simple homes w/ courtyards	
IIIA	Iron IA	14th	cattle, unburnished red slip	Seti II (1394-1388) scarab
IIB	Iron IB	13th	fortress, lg. public bldg., 4-room houses	
IIA	Iron IC	12th	stables, temple * by quake?	Bichrome, Midianite bowls
IB	Iron IIA	11th	fortress + tower, TPB stables, 4-room houses = Arad XII	
IA	Iron IIB	10th	abandoned "about 980-970 BC" (for Tel Ira) prior to *<Shishak	
pre-I	Iron IIC	7th	small fortress * by Nebuchadnezzar II	

Jacob-El (trading city of Yaqub-har)?: Tell Malhata/el-Milh, 7.5 miles SW of Tel Arad

Strata	Age	Cent.	Description	Unique
1A	EBIB	23rd	settlement	sherds and flints
1B	EBII	22nd	larger settlement, abandoned	
2A	MBI	20th	Hyksos stone millo + plastered glacis	
2B	MBIIA	19th	1m thick outer wall with rooms atop rampart	
2C	MBIIB-C	18th-17th	*^ by Thutmose III	White Slip V Cypriot ware
	LB		no settlement	
3A	IronIIA	11th-10th	TPB stables, 4m thick wall with terraced glacis *^ by Shishak	
3B	IronIIB	late 10th	unwalled town with fireplaces	
3C	IronIII	7th	sq.-pillared stables, rosette jar sealing; *by Neb.; Judean + Edomite pottery	

During the Iron Age, Tell Malhata was the largest fortified Israelite settlement in Beersheba valley (prior to Tel Ira and Aroer). Jacob-El was also captured by Thutmose III and Rameses II.

Pharaohs of the Bible

Lost#?: Tall Zira'a/Tell Zera'a, 4.5 km south-west of Gadara in northern Jordan

Strata	Age	Cent.	Description
	EBIV	21st	2.2m high city wall
	MBI	20th	At least two strata, habitation, test trench on the western slope
	MBIIA	19th	
MBIIB-C		18th	
	LB	17th	City wall, water channel
	LB	17th-16th	Casemate wall, gate, tower with sanctuary, water channels, 3 homes, 2 palaces, 28 cylinder seals, silver pendant, scarabs, Egyptian faience Mycenaen and Cypriot wares *^ by Thutmose III
	IrnI	15th-14th	4-room house + courtyard house, pit silos, huts, stables
	IrnII	13th-12th	Fortified city, "zigzag wall", buildings, metal & textile workshops
	IrnII	11th-10th	Textile workshop, olive oil storage, dif' houses *^ by Shishak
	Greek		pits
	Roman		pits
	Byzantine+	1st - 7th AD	Large fortified city; Villa rustica

Lost#? Achshaph ('bewitched'): Kafr Yasif, near Acre

Strata	Age	Cent.	Description
13	LBI	18th-17th	town * by Thutmose III
12	IronIA	15th-14th	town * by Sea Peoples (1310 BC)
11	IronIC	13th-12th	town
10	IronIIA	11th	
9	IronIIB	10th	* by Shishak
8	IronIIC	9th	
7	IronIIC	8th	
6	IronIIC	7th	(exiled by Nebuchadnezzar II?)

Shihor-Libnath ('dark'-'white'): Tell Abu Hawam at Kishon River harbor, near Haifa

Strata	Age	Cent.	Description	Unique
VA	LB	16th	fishing village, abandoned	
VB	LB	15th	fortified wall, gov. home, Canaanite temple	*^ by Seti I
VC	LB	14th	Mycenaen IIIa-b and Cypriote, * Rameses III,	Rameses II cartouche
IVA	IronIB	13th	2-room homes with enclosed court	
IVB	IronIC	12th-11th	improvements in buildings	*^by David
IIIA	IronII	11th-10th	massive ashlar walls	Samarian and Greek Geometric II-I ware
IIIB	IronII	10th	building additions and improvements	*by Shishak
IIA	IronII	9th	small fortified town reused part of walls	
IIB	IronII	8th	additions and repairs, Tyrian coins	*by Assyrians?
I	Persian – Byzantine, then abandoned			

Hamilton dated stratum III between the early 11th century (1100 BC) and the last quarter of the 10th century (925 BC).[1134]

1134 Hamilton, R. W., Excavations at Tell Abu Hawam (1935), *QDAP*, 4, pp. 5-8

Appendix A

Lost#? Dor ('generation'): Tel Dor, 8 miles north of Caesarea on coast

Strata	Age	Cent.	Description	Unique
	MBIIC	18th		
	LBI	17th	town founded	*^by Thutmose III
	LBIIA-B	16th - 15th	large city	*^ by Tjekker
	IrIA-C	14th - 12th	Sea People city sea wall, smithy, bakery, fishery	Philistine + Cypriot ware
9	IronIIA	11th	< by David; structures, glacis, 4-chamber gate	Greek imports
8b	IronIIB	10th	built up by Solomon (< by Shishak?)	Greek imports
8a	IronIIC	9th	Assyrian vassal, ashlar blocks	
	IronIIC	8th		< by TPIII
	Persian		fortress	
	Greek		fortress	
	Hasmonian		minted coins	

Lost#? Socoh {N} ('bushy' or 'entwined'): Tel Zeror, 12.5 miles south of Dor

Strata	Age	Cent.	Description	Unique
	MBI	early 20th	town, large stone slab graves	
	MBIIA	late 20th	4.5m city brick wall on stone with 2-chamber tower	
	MBIIA	early 19th	ramp and coated moat to hold water	
	MBIIB	late 19th	very prosperous	
	MBIII	18th	gap of occupation	
	LBI	17th	palace and public building; abandoned (Zrar)	* by Thutmose III,
	LBIIA	16th	wall rebuilt, coppersmiths' quarter (Tjekker?)	Cypriot pottery
	LBIIB	15th	pit and stone-lined graves, Cypriot ware	< by Joshua
	IronIA-C	14th-12th	4-room Israelite houses, pits, and pottery	
	IronIIA-B	11th-10th	casemate wall, mud-brick citadel, storehouses	* by Shishak
	IronIIC	9th-8th	4-room houses rebuilt, stone-lined cisterns	* by Tiglath-Pileser III
				l-smk (El -support) inscription
	Bab.	6th	resettled	
	Persian	5th-4th	pottery	
	Greek	3rd-2nd	farmhouse, round watchtower	
	Byz. - Arab		village	

Seven miles north of Tel Zeror is Tel Mevorakh at the junction of the Sharon plain and the Carmel coast and Nahal Tanninim (Crocodile River). Northwest of Tel Mevorakh a 10th century BC shaft tomb was discovered which contained Red Burnished Phoenician and Cypro-Phoenician wares.[1135] Its stratum XI temple may have Aegean influence along with chocolate on white ware.

? Tel Mevorakh (15 strata), near Dor

Strata	Age	Cent.	Description	Unique
XV	MBIIA	20th	first town; no fortifications	
XIV	MBIIB	19th	Egyptian mud-brick fortress, millo + glacis	Hyksos sealing
XIII	MBIIC	18th	continued in use	Cypriot ware

1135 http://www.archaeowiki.org/Tel_Mevorakh

Pharaohs of the Bible

XII	LBIA	17th	Aegean-style rectangular brick temple with lime floor		* Thutmose III
XI	LBIB	17th	new rectangular bldg on stone pavement		
X	LBIIA	16th	sanctuary w/ lime floor and plastered bench		2 Mitanni-like cylinder seals
			faience disks, ring with palmette		Cypriot White-Slip milk bowls
			bronze cymbals, bronze snake like at Timnah and Hathor		
IX	IronIA	15th	debris of another Canaanite wayside sanctuary		* ?
VIII	IronIIA	11th	Solomonic casemate wall, Admin. complex w/ lime floor		
			Bichrome, Cypriot, Red burnished, White Painted wares		
VII	IronIIB	10th	casemate wall and large building		*^ by Shishak
VI	IronIIC	9th	Judean rosette sealings		* ?
V		8th			* ?
IV		7th			
III	Bab.	6th			

Zaphon ('northward'): Tell es-Sa'idiyeh, on E bank of Jordan 30 miles east of Samaria

Strata	Age	Cent.	Description	Unique
	EB		town	
	LB		tomb#101 electrum pendants + toggle pins; tomb#102 ivory, scarab, bronze	
	IronIA	15th	town < by Joshua	
	IronIB	14th	stone + mud-brick walls concealing stairs to spring at base of mound	
V	IronIIA	10th	town	*^ by Shishak
IV	IronIIB	9th-8th	10 mud-brick homes on stone, 3.5m thick city wall, temple + altar	
				* by Sennacherib
III	IronIIB	7th	rebuilt, exiled by Nebuchadnezzar II	
II	Bab.	6th	12 mud-brick homes on stone foundations	
I	Bab.	5th	threshing floors + granary bins	
3	Persian	4th	palace, limestone incense burner	
2	Greek	3rd	fortress	
1	Roman		watchtower, 2 plastered resevoirs	

Geshur capital: Tel Hadar, at Sea of Galilee about five miles north of Tel en Gev

Strata	Age	Cent.	Description	Unique
VI	IronIC	12th		
V	IronIIA	11th		
IV	IronIIB	10th	storehouses, TPB *^destroyed by Shishak	Greek lebes
III		9th		
II		8th	basalt concentric defensive walls 10-12 ft thick, topped with brick	
			lime-plastered grain storage bldg., citadel, TPB-stables *^Sennacherib?	
I	IronII	6th	outer wall, houses, barracks, paved courtyards and streets; exiled by Neb.	

Tel Hadar IV had a rectangular above-ground granary similar to some in Egypt and Nubia. The destruction of Tel Hadar IV is set at 980 BC, at the latest, by its excavators Beck and Yadin in their final report.[1136] Of course, I'd place Tel Hadar IV's destruction at 970 BC by Shishak.

1136 Fantalkin, Alexander, "Low Chronology and Greek Proto geometric and Geometric Pottery

Appendix A

? Tel en Gev, on the eastern shore of Lake Galilee in Geshur (now Golan Heights)

Strata   Age   Cent.   Description   Unique
J-Va-b   Iron II 11th-10th   TPB's with stone foundation   * by Shishak
J-IV   Iron II 9th - 8th   TPB-stables
J-III   Persian   pits dug into Iron Age strata
J-II   Greek   large buildings, one with flagstone-paved floor; large pit
J-I   Roman   lime-kilns

The Iron Age: large building, casemate wall with towers, burnt brick, potsherds dating to the ninth–eighth centuries BCE. The outer walls of the large building were over 1m wide and the southwestern part was lined with ashlars. The TPB's date of construction is not clear.

Lost#? Tel Shikmona, 1.3 km SW of Carmel cape

Strata Age   Cent.   Description   Unique
        MBIIB   late 19th
        MBIII   18th   tomb with **Yaqub-har scarab** (excavator dated tomb to MBIIB)
        LBI   17th   bronze + silver objects off-shore
        LBII   16th-15th   Seti I bulla
        IronII   11th-10th   Town A, casemate wall and palace   * by Shishak
        IronIIC   9th-8th   Town B, 3 oil presses   * by Tiglath-Pileser III
                  late 8th   Town C, storerooms and a workshop   * by Sennacherib
        IronIII   7th   Town D   * by Nebuchadnezzar II
        Bab.   6th   Babylonian exile gap
P   Persian   6th-5th   terraces, stone-paved streets, courtyard homes   * by ?
PB   late 4th   Phoenican fortress, perfume shop   * by Alexander's general
H   Greek   3rd-2nd   new fortress , amphora w/ "year 180 of Seleucid era"
R   Roman   1st-3rd AD   new fortress destroyed previous one, plastered pools
B   Byz.   4th-7th   villa + houses   *quake in 4th, new town * in 7th
A   Arab   7th   building

Lost#? Tel Zayit/ Tell Zeitah (6 acres), 5 miles north of Lachish on Wadi Guvrin

Strata Age   Cent.   Description   Unique
        MBIIC   18th   pottery
        LBI   17th   village   Egyptian imports
        LBIIA   16th   faience bowl
        LBIIB   15th   city mud-brick wall   *^ by Joshua 19th or 20th dyn. scarab
        IronI   late 15th
        IronIBC   14th-12th
        IronIIA   11th-10th   wine and vinegar production, amphorae *^ by Shishak
        IronIIB   10th-9th   *^ by ?   ostracon abecediary
        IronIIC   8th   floors   *^ by Sennacherib
        Roman   3rd AD   stone acropolis which lasted until the Crusades
        Muslim   7th   to the Crusades 10th

in the Southern Levant," *LEVANT* 33, 2001, p. 118

"The excavation at Tel Zayit, then, is helping to clarify the historical picture for the borderland region between Judah and Philistia during the Iron Age IIA-B periods. Stratigraphically connected remains have emerged from the tenth through the eighth centuries BCE, and during this 300-year period the site was destroyed by fire near the end of each century."[1137]

Lost# Ashkelon ('a weighing place'): Khirbet Asqalan on Mediterranean coast

Strata	Age	Cent.	Description	Unique
A	EBI	23rd	huts, silos, tools of bone and flint	
B	EBII	22nd	*, then break in occupation	
C	MB	20th	massive embankments, temple	silver calf, Assyrian seal
D	LB	15th	*destroyed by Israelites; then sandy dark brown earth layer	
Vc	Iron I	14th	new port of 50-60 ha, monochrome	no pigs *^ by Merenptah
Vb	Iron I	14th-12th	*^retaken by Philistines (1310), bichrome	pigs
Va	Iron IIA	11th	Phoenician pottery	*^ by David
VIb	Iron IIB	10th	*^ by Shishak, then a Philistine town again	
VIa	Iron III	9th-8th	captured by Assyrians	
VIIb	Iron III	7th	*destroyed by Nebuchadnezzar II	
	Persian	5th	ashlar big buildings and warehouses	Phoenician inscriptions
VIIa	Greek	4th-2nd	villas, colonade, and theater	Egyptian gods gain status
VIIIc	Roman	2nd-4th AD	forum and basilica	
VIIIb	Byz.	5Th-6th	bathhouse, church, and synagogue	
VIIIa	Muslim	7th - 9th	* by Mamluk	

-Other Israelite Cities which Shishak did Not conquer, but others did

Gerar: Tel Haror

Strata	Age	Cent.	Description
			Egyptian vassal and MycIIIB
K3+B7			*destroyed by Israelites
			Israelite city with MycIIIC
B4-B2	IronI		Monochrome and Bichrome in use

Tell Esdar, midway between Beersheba and Dimona

Strata	Age	Cent.	Description
IVb	EBI	23rd	silos + threshing floors, flint axes, painted pottery, agate pendant
IVa	EBII	22nd	lage fan scrapers, jar rims
III	IronIBC	13th-12th	Israelite home in a circle facing in, stone jars * by Amalekites
II	IronIIA	11th	3-room farmhouse with stone floors and silos
I	Rom.-Byz.		potsherds and terraces

1137 Tappy, Ron E., http://www.zeitah.net/overview.html

Appendix A

Tel Michal (Khirbet Makmish)

Strata	Age	Cent.	Description	Unique
XVII	MBIIB	19th	platform, brick millo, glacis, buildings	Amenemhet III sealing
			*destroyed by earthquake	Hyksos scarabs
XVI	LBI	16th	millo, fort, houses * by ?	Cypriot ware
XV	LBII	15th	millo, rampart; abandoned in 14th century	
XIV	IronII	11th	2 temples with benches, 1 high place	Phoenician influence
XIII	IronII	10th	then abandoned	2 long wine-presses
XII	IronII	9th	resettled, then abandoned in the 8th century	
XI	Persian	6th	trading post, fort, barracks, silos	
X-IX	late	5th	houses, temple	
VIII-VII	early	5th	kilns, wine-presses	
VI	late	4th	fort, silos; then *destroyed and abandoned	
V	Greek	3rd	fortress, houses, large wine-press, silos	coins of Ptolemy I-III *destroyed
IV		2nd	Seleucid control	
III-II	Roman	1st - 1st	large fortress and lighthouse, then abandoned	
I	Islamic	8th AD		

Bethel? ('house of El'): Beitin, 10.5 miles north of Jerusalem at major crossroads

Strata	Age	Cent.	Description	Unique
{originally}	EBII	22nd	village, abandoned	
{MBI}	MBIIA	19th	occupied continuously from now on	
{MBIIA}	MBIII	18th	rebuilding near the springs	
{MBIIB}	LBIA	17th	3.5m thick wall + rhomboid gate, sanctuary; serpents on jars *^TIII	
{MBIII}	LBIB	16th	new city and west wall; abandoned ?	
{LBII}	IronIA-B	14th-13th		
	IronIC	12th		
	IronIIA	11th-9th	South Arabian clay seal (due to Solomon's incense trade)	
	IronIIB	8th-6th		
	Persian	5th		
	Greek	4th-3rd		
	Roman	2nd	NE city gate *destroyed; new gate and cisterns built	
	Herodian	1st	garrisons	
	Byz.	2nd-5th AD	resevoir and church	

Jarmuth ('heights', Khirbet el Yarmuk): Tell Jarmuth, near Beth-Shemesh

Strata	Age	Cent.	Description	Unique
VII	EBII-III	22nd - 21st		Khirbet Kerak ware
VI	LBII	14th		
V	Iron I	13th	Israelite	
IV	Iron I	12th	Philistine large kiln	
III	Iron I	11th	*destroyed by Saul	
II	Iron II		Byzantine	

Pharaohs of the Bible

Ophel ('hill', 'mound', or 'stronghold'): Afula

Strata	Age	Cent.	Description		Unique
X	EBI	24th	stone-lined granary pits		Gray-burnish ware
IX	EBI	23rd	brick wall on stone foundation		Band slip
VIII	EBIII	22nd			Khirbet Kerak ware
VII	EBIV	21st	8 building complex, 2 ovens	* by ?	folded ledge baubles
VI	MBI	20th	3 pottery kilns		
V	MBIIB	19th	38 graves most with Hyksos scarabs		Tell el-Yehudiyeh ware
IV	LBII	16th	many graves in virgin soil		Mycenean and Cypriot
IIIB	IronIA	15th	brick walls on stone foundation		just Cypriot ware
IIIA	IronIB	13th-11th	Philistine granary and kilns		* by Saul and David
preIII	IronIIA	11th	pottery kiln		Samaria ware
II	Roman	2nd-4th AD	Roman coffins		
I	Crusader	11th-13th AD	2 cisterns		

N. Aphek ('hold back'): Tel Afek/Tel Ras el-'Ain, north of Mt. Carmel

Strata	Age	Cent.	Description	Unique
(area	EBIV	21st	Palace I, massive wall	
X)	MBIIA	20th	Palace II, masonry graves; *^ by ?	13th dyn. scarab; Khabur ware
16	MBIIB	19th	Palace III	
15	MBIIC	18th-17th	* by Thutmose III	
14	LBIB	17th	Palace IV	
13	LBIIA	16th	Palace V	
12	LBIIB	15th-13th	Egyptian Palace VI and residency, (winepresses in area A) *^ by Sea Peoples	scarabs of Rameses II and IV
11	IronIB	13th	Sea People town (1310 BC)	Cypro-Minoan Linear Script
10	IronIC	12th		
9	IronIIA	11th	captured by David	
8	IronIIB	10th	Israelite town	
7	IronIIB	9th		
6	IronIIC	8th		
	Greek		city expanded northwards towards the springs	
	Roman		ashlar mausoleum *^ by ?	
	Byzntine		wall and lime pit	
	Crusader		two-storey fortress	

?: Tell 'Aitun/Tel 'Eton, 3 km north of Beit Mirsim (Debir)

Strata	Age	Cent.	Description	
	EB		first town, sherds	
	MB		town	
	LB		rock-cut tombs, lots of jar rims	
	IronI		sparse	< by Joshua
	IronII		major town	
	IronII	8th	town	* by Sennacherib, and abandoned

Appendix A

Persian-Greek town

Jokneam ('people lament'): Tell Yokneam/Qeinum/Kaimun {vital pass to Dor}

Strata	Age	Cent.	Description	Unique
	EBA		pottery sherds	Khirbet Kerak ware
	MBA		pottery sherds	
	LBIA	18th	city expanded	
	LBIB	17th - 16th	<conquered by Thutmose III	
	LBIIA	15th	captured by Joshua	
XIX	LBIIB	14th	*destroyed by Rameses III	
XVIII		13th - 12th		
XVII	Iron I	11th	*destroyed by David	C14 date 1005-925 BC
XVI-XV				
XIV			fortified Israelite city with Phoenician trade	
XIII	Iron II			
XII				
XI			royal city	

The highest average Carbon14 transition date for Iron IB (king David) to Iron II (king Solomon) in Israel was 950 BC,[1138] but all the high outliers were removed.

(Laish) Dan: Tell el-Qadi/Tel Dan

Strata	Age	Cent.	Description	Unique
	EBI	23rd	settled	
	EBII	22nd	town	
	EBIII	21st	large city with stone wall; abandoned (stones used in following millo)	
	MBIIA 19th		millo and rampart (filled with whole vessels) coated with clay plaster	
	MBIIB 19th-17th		houses with cooking vessels	* by Thutmose III
V	IronIA 15th		many vessels	* by tribe of Dan
IV	IronIA-C 14th - 11th		3m thick city wall w/ 2 towers	* by Ben-Hadad
III	IronIIA 10th		limestone sanctuary with bench and statue base; fine masonry acropolis built by Jeroboam I	
II	IronIIB 9th-8th		large building w/ 300 juglets, inscription *l'ms* (Amaz/iah?) *Sennacherib	
I	IronIIB 7th-6th		Phoenician inscription "belonging to Baal-Pelet"	

Chinnereth ('harp'-shaped)/Genneseret: Tel Kinrot on west shore of Galilee Sea

Strata	Age	Cent.	Description	Unique
X	EBI-II	23rd	city	
IX	EBII	21st	fortified city	Red-polished pottery
VIII	MBIIB	19th	fortified town, glacis *?	(surface find?) scarab of Queen Tiye
VII	LBI	17th	rebuilt	fertility goddess torso and cylinder seal

---

1138 Sharon, Ilan, "Report on the First Stage of the Iron Age Dating Project in Israel: Supporting a Low Chronology," RadioCarbon, Vol. 49, No. 1, 2007, pp. 2 and 22

VI	IronIA	15th	12m thick city wall * Quake?	Philistine bichrome ware
V	IronIA	14th	rebuilt, sealing of Egyptian healing god Reshef; Phoenician fine ware *^	
IV	IronIA	13th	squatters, then abandoned	
III	Iron II		2-TPB stable, 2-chamber gate and towers, fortress, grain storage	
II	Iron II		repairs made *^TPIII	bronze male god with conical hat
I	Iron II		town	Egyptian blue lion-bowl

Beth-Haccerem ('house of vineyards'): Ramat Rahel, between Jerusalem + Bethlehem

Strata	Age	Cent.	Description	Unique
		9th	terraced vineyards; ashlar base casemate wall	
Vb		8th	small citadel	dozens of *lmlk* sealings w/ 2+4 wings
Va		7th	3.5m thick wall, fortified citadel + palace	Assyrian Palace ware
			Jehoiakim's city * by Sennacherib	
IVb	Persian-Greek		Perisan and Hasmonean sealings	
IVa	Herodian		ossuaries * by Romans in 70 AD, then abandoned 200 years	
III	Roman		bathhouse and villa	
II	Byzantine		Kathisma church and monastery	
I	Islamic			

Stratum Va sealing inscription "('to Elijaqim steward of Yochin [Jehoiachin]'), which is identical with those found at Tell Beit Mirsim and Beth-Shemesh."[1139]

Tel Erani/Tell Sheik el-'Areini (Tel Gat), about 10 km NW of Lachish:
a fortress city of Solomon and Rehoboam

Strata	Age	Cent.	Description	Unique
	EBI	23rd	fortified town	serekh portion
X	IronIIB	10th	fort, casemate wall + glacis fortifications in areas A + G; lime pit	
IX	IronIIC	9th	gateway square, stone foundation fort, white-washed mud plaster	
VIII	IronIII	8th	courtyard buildings	
VII		8th - 7th	baked-brick wall, pebble paved entrance;	graffito '*lyhz*'
			2 inner courtyard buildings *^ by Sennacherib	
VI		mid 7th	4-room Israeli mud-brick homes with pebble foundations	
			amphorae handles 'to the king from Hebron' w/ 4-winged scarab below	
V		late 7th	3 large bldgs w/ pebble-paved courtyards, 1 for industry, 2 oblong ovens,	
			burnished *lmlk* bowls	
IV		6th	ovens and rooms [gap of 70 years (Babylonian exile 606-636 BC)]	
III	Persian	5th	silos	
II	Persian	4th	beaten-earth pavement and late Israelite pottery	
I	Greek	3rd - 2nd	sparse occupation, then thick ash *^ ?	

1139 *Encyclopedia of Archaeological Excavations in the Holy Land, Volume IV*, Exploration Society of Jerusalem and Prentice Hall, 1975, p. 1006

Appendix A

Ekron ('uprooted' - emigration): Tell el-Hesi

City	Age	Cent.	Description	Unique
	EBIII	21st	bronze vessels, spearhead, adzes	crescent-shaped ax blade
XIII	MBII	19th	City I glacis, wall and tower	*^
XII	MBIII	18th	City II rebuilt; kiln with slag	*^
XI	LBI	17th - 15th	City III; Amarna-like clay tablet	*^ (thick ash layer) by Joshua
X	LBII	15th - 12th	Israelite's City IV w/ strong citadel	scarabs and cylinder seals
IX	IronII	11th	City V massive wall + towers; TPB-stables	
VIII	IronII	10th - 9th	City VI Rehoboam's fortifications 7.5m thick bldg.; *lmlk* sealings	
VII	IronII	8th	City VII erosion prevention terraces	*^ by Tiglath-Pileser III
VI	IronII	7th	City VIII massive platform	*^ by Nebuchadnezzar II

Ashdod: Tel Ashdod, 2.5 miles inland

Strata	Age	Cent.	Description	Unique
	EB	21st	sherds	
XIX	MBII	20th - 19th	Hyksos fortifications, acropolis	
XVIII	MBIII	18th	foundation of brick wall, glacis and fosse	
XVII	LBIA	17th	bichrome and Cypriot	scarabs
XVI	LBIB	16th	large administration building of fortified brick	Cypriot and Painted ware
XV	LBIIA	late 16th	silos	scarabs and figurines
XIV	LBIIB	early 15th	Egyptian governor's palace,	*^destroyed by Israelites
XIIIb	IronIA	15th-14th	Israelite Pottery workshop Mycenean IIIC-1	
XIIIa	IronIA	14th	high stone foundation	Philistine ware
XII	IronIA	14th-13th	taken by Sea Peoples; ashlar casemate wall, plastered cisterns, "great mother" figurine and Minoan seals	
XI	IronIB	13th-12th	fortress, gate tower, fosse,	Philistine ware
Xb	IronIC	12th-11th	kilns in lower city	* by David
Xa	IronIIA	11th	large administration building; 2 towers and gate	* by ?
IX	IronIIB	10th	large wall with stone foundation and 6 gates and 2 towers	
VIII	IronIII	9th - 8th	small temple, altar, figurines; fragment of basalt	*^Sargon II victory stela
VII	IronIII	7th	potters' quarter; Hebrew inscriptions "[h]phr"	* by Psalmtik I
VI	Bab.	6th		*lmlk* stamp
V	Persian	5th	administration building	*^ by ? Aramaic ostracon
IV	Greek	4th - 2nd	brick foundations and stone walls, Rhodian wine jars	*^ by Hasmoneans
III	Herodian	1st-1st	Terra Siglata and Megarian ware; coin of Antiochus VIII (114 BC)	*^67 AD
II	Roman	3rd-4th	small buildings and workshops	
I	Byz.	5Th - 6th	houses, silos, wine presses; marble slab with Jewish symbols	

"Ashdod XIIIB is attributed to an 'early wave' of Sea Peoples, not the Philistines,"[1140] but I attribute the destruction and takeover to the Israelites.

[1140] Stager, Lawrence, "The Impact of the Sea Peoples in Canaan," *The Archaeology of Society of the Holy Land*, 1995, p. 342

Pharaohs of the Bible

Gath ('winepress'): Tel Miqne (50 acres at Stratum VI; 10 acres at Stratum IV)

Strata	Age	Cent.	Description
	EB		
IX	LB		industrious city *^destroyed
VIII	LB		4 ha Egyptian vassal, trade with Aegean and Anatolia
VII	LBIIB	15th	20 ha Philistine city with workshops, homes, central 'palace', silos, kilns, mudbrick fortifications, and MycIIIC monchrome pottery
VI	IronIA	14th	Philistine bichrome, massive wall and gateway, kilns, shrine (#352)
V	IronIA	13th	Sea Peoples added (1310 BC), Palace-temple complex (#351) 'royal city'
IV	IronIB	12th	temple complex (lg. bldg. #350 pillared hall + benches) * by Samson 1155 [lower city abandoned for a season]
III	IronIIA	11th	small town around #351, David called it a "royal city" (I Samuel 27:5)
II	IronIIB	10th	wall and large tower, massive olive oil industry (115+ olive oil presses)
IC	IronIIB	9th-8th	temple-palace complex #650, city wall + gate (Hezekiah), 2 *lmlk* handles
IB	IronIII	7th	*destroyed by Nebuchadnezzar II
IA	Babyl.	6th	

Na'aman cited the 'Azekah Inscription' in which a Neo-Assyrian king (Sargon II) described the siege of "a royal [city] of the Philistines which H[ezek]iah had captured and strengthened for himself"[1141] which was "surrounded with great [to]wers and exceedingly difficult [its ascent]', with a "palace like a mountain", and a "moat was dug around it".[1142]

Deir el Balah, ten miles SW of Gaza

Strata	Age	Cent.	Description		Unique
IX	LBIIB	15th	houses and 2 potter's kilns	< by Joshua;	Rameses II scarabs
VIII	IronIA	late 15th			
VII	IronIA	14th	Administration building; town "abandoned" by influx of Sea Peoples		
VI	IronIA	late 14th			
V	IronIB	13th			
IV	IronIB	late 13th			
III	IronIC	12th	Philistine bichrome		
II	IronIIA	11th	red-slip		
I	Byz. - Crusaders		pottery and watchtower		

Fifty anthropoid coffins in the cemetery were dated to the 13th century.

Eglon ('calf-like'): Tel Nagila is 15km NE of Tel Gerar and 28 km east of modern Gaza

Strata	Age	Cent.	Description
XIV	EBI	23rd	
XIII	EBII	22nd	tomb
XII	EBIII	21st	pottery

1141 Na'aman, N., "Sennacherib's 'letter to God' on his campaign to Judah", *Bulletin of the American Schools of Oriental Research*, 214, 1974, p. 27
1142 Na'aman, N., "Ekron under the Assyrian and Egyptian Empires", *BASOR* 332, 2003, p. 85

Appendix A

XI	EBIV	21st		
X	MBI-IIA	20th		
IX	MBIIA	20th		
VIII	MBIIB	19th	fortress, wall, gate, glacis, fosse, parallel streets	
VII	MBIIB	19th	ostrich eggshells, Hyksos scarabs	
VI	MBIIC	18th-17th (LBIA) two-line proto-Canaanite inscription		* by Thutmose III
V	LBIIB	15th	town	< by Judahites
IV	Ir.I-IIA	late 10th - 9th	fortress, grain pits, bichrome, pre-*lmlk* jars, and Black on Red ware some Late Philistine Decorated Ware	
III	IronIIB	8th	temple with massebah and storeroom	
II	IronIIC	7th-6th	cooking pots	
I	Islamic	7th AD	stronghold	

Strata VI-XIV are based on very limited information. According to Joshua 10:34-36, Eglon is between Lachish and Hebron.

Khirbet Rabud: Tel Rabud, on Nahal Hevron, 7.5 miles SW of Hebron

Strata	Age	Cent.	Description	Unique
	EBI		first town	tombs and sherds
	MBI			tombs and sherds
	LBI			
	LBIIA		fort and wall	Ush e Saqra burial caves
	LBII			
	LBII			
	LBII			Cypriot + Mycenaen
	IronI	10th	Israelite town; rock-cut cistern	
IIIB	IronIIA	9th	massive 4m thick wall	sherds
IIIA	IronIIB	8th	* by Sennacherib	*lmlk* sealings
IIB-A	IronIIB	7th	wall	
IB	Bab.	6th	*^ by Nebuchadnezzar II	
IA	Bab.	5th	return of exiles – a few homes	
	Roman		watchtower	

Timna Valley in Arabah

Strata	Age	Cent.	Description	Unique
5	EBI	23rd	flint tools, copper smelting, pottery	
4	LBI-IrIA	17th-14th	Hathor temple	Rameses II scarab, faience ringstand of Rameses III

[It was abandoned during Egyptian anarchy 1377-1323 BC, and Midianites moved in and effaced Hathor and worshipped a bronze snake instead.]

3b	IronIB	13th	worship structure I	* by quake; large copper smelting complex
3a	IronIC	12th	worship structure II	* by quake; then Egyptians left for good
2	IronIIA	11th	Midianite pottery and small temple (possibly used by Solomon)	
1	Roman	1st AD	Roman sanctuary and pottery	

Beth-Yerah (Khirbet el Kerak), south end of Sea of Galilee

Strata	Age	Cent.	Description	Unique
I	EBI	24th	pits of roofed pit homes	
II	EBI	23rd	rectangular houses w/ courtyards paved w/ basalt slabs	
III	EBII	22nd	mud-brick wall 8m thick w/ basalt gates	
IVA	EBIII	21st	rectangular bldgs w/ circular silos, basalt homes	Khirbet Kerak ware
IVB	EBIV	21st	^* ?, then rebuilt	
IVC	MBI	20th	potter's workshop	
IVD	MBII	20th	grave	
	Greek	3rd-2nd	1300m basalt wall topped with brick w/ square and circular towers	
	Roman	1st-3rd AD	fort and bathhouse w/ drainage system	
	Byz.	4Th - 6th	church and synagogue	
	Muslim	7th +	building	

I include this city because Khirbet Kerak Ware originated with it and is cited elsewhere. Some view the Khirbet Kerak Ware as that of caucasian immigrants to the area. Sarit Paz calls them Early Transcaucasians (ETC) migrants, and found they came as family groups and also brought portable hearths or andirons, and a different home architecture.[1143] Paz also discovered that Beth-Yerah was only partially abandoned by its original occupants, as is noted at several other sites. This could be viewed as God's commands during the Peleg period of the Ice Age to different family groups within a town to stay or to leave, or the refusal of some families to leave.

-Other Israelite Cities

Azor: Yazur, 3.5 miles from Jaffa, on road from Jaffa to Jerusalem

Strata	Age	Cent.	Description	Unique
9-8	EBIA	24th	town, stone buildings	ossuary tombs
7	EBIB	23rd		tombs w/o occuaries
6	EBII	22nd	hearths and pottery	
5	EBIII	21st	brief gap in occupation	
4	EBIV	late 21st	new settlement	
3	MBI	20th	ceiling collapse (quake?)	
2	MBII	19th	Hyksos pottery and 21 scarabs	horses and humans buried together
1	IronIA	15th		Cypriot ware in tombs
	IronIA	14th	Philistine ware and pit graves	19th-20th dynasty scarab of Hopi
	IronIB	13th	burials in large pottery jars	
	IronIC	12th	burials in brick coffins	Philistine ware
	IronIIA	11th	(< by David) new people group who cremate and put ashes in jars	
	IronIIB	10th	Israelite burial jars in stone-fenced generational family plots, scarabs Egyptian amulet; Cypriot and Phoenician ware	
	IronIII	9th - 8th	copper smelting with 'pinched rims'	
	IronIII	7th - 6th	26th dynasty scaraboid of Negroid head with a prancing horse on the base	

1143 Paz, Sarit, "A Home Away from Home?: The Settlement of Early Transcaucasian Migrants at Tel Bet Yerah," *Tel Aviv*, Vol. 36, 2009, pp. 196-216

Appendix A

Azekah ('tilled'): Tel Azekah/Tell Zakariya, now Azeqa; 5.5 miles north of Beit Guvrin

Strata	Age	Cent.	Description
A	Canaanite	17th-15th	scarabs of Thutmose III and Amenhotep II
B	early Israelite	15th-11th	plastered floors; 2-winged *lmlk* jars
C	late Israelite	10th-6th	(Rehoboam's) ashlar fortress, 6 towers; 4-winged *lmlk* jars
D	Seleucid	4th-1st	rock-hewn tombs

The personal seal "belonging to Saran, son of Abima'as" was found there.

Mount Yeruham, 18.5 miles SSE of Beersheba

Strata	Age	Cent.	Description	Unique
II	MBIA	early 20th	ranching + farm town with animal pens, kiln, scrapers, + sickles	
I	MBIIA	late 20th	stone homes and workshops	18 copper ingots

-Other

Karkara: Tell Qarqur in Syria

Strata	Age	Cent.	Description	Unique
20-18	EBI			
17	EBIIa			
16	EBIIb			
15	EBIII			
14	EBIVa		temple *^ ?	
13	EBIVb		*^ ?	
12	MBI		* ?	
11B	MBIIa			
11A	MBIIb-c		* ?	
10B	LBI			
10A	LBII			
9	IronI		* ?	
8	IronII		gateway and casemate walls	*^ ?
7	Persian		* ?	
6	Greek		*^ ?	
5	Roman		* ?	
4	Byzantine			glass pendant w/ Christian symbols
3	Islam		* ?	
2	Ayyubid		* ?	
1	Mamluk			

Pharaohs of the Bible

Cities of Israel and Philistia

APPENDIX B

This appendix contains my notes, computations, and analyses made during my research.

Presuppositions

Comet instigation of Noah's Flood

The entire title of Whiston's book was *From its Original, to the Consummation of All Things, Where the Creation of the World in Six Days, the Universal Deluge, And the General Conflagration, As laid down in the Holy Scriptures, Are Shewn to be perfectly agreeable to Reason and Philosophy*.

In March 2010, scientists concluded after 20 years of research that the Chixulub impactor triggered the mass extinction of the dinosaurs and deposited a layer of iridium. They also debated whether it was one of several pieces of a larger object which hit the earth simultaneously.

According to the Titius-Bode law of 1772, a planet should exist between Mars and Jupiter; this hypothetical planet was dubbed Phaeton, son of Sun in Greek mythology. A dwarf planet, about $1/25^{th}$ of the moon, was discovered and named Ceres. It is the sole spherical object in the asteroid belt, and makes up 1/3 of the mass of the objects in the belt. I postulate that Ceres was the moon of a planet which was there, but was destroyed, and that many of the pieces hit Mars, Earth, Earth's moon, Venus, Mercury, and other pieces were disintegrated by the Sun. One of Phaeton's pieces hit Chixulub. I propose these pieces broke through the toroid water canopy around the Earth which started the rain, and the other pieces compromised the Earth's crust which ruptured the aquifers.

There may even have been a very large piece which was caught by Earth's gravity and orbited around the Earth two or three times before it was sling-shotted out into space. This is the theory of Donald Patten in his book *The Biblical Flood and the Ice Epoch*. Then again, God could have caused the Earth's crust to rupture with one "look", and set off volcanoes with a "touch".

> *He looks on the earth, and it trembles: he touches the hills, and they smoke. (Psalm 104:32)*

Pangaea/'Atlantis' and Magnetic Stripes on Sea Floor

> *And God said, Let the waters under the heaven be gathered together to one place, and let the dry land appear: and it was so. And God called the dry land Earth; and the gathering together of the waters called he Seas: and God saw that it was good. (Genesis 1:9-10)*

The "*dry land*" could have been something like Pangaea. I think it may have been called Adam's land, which in Hebrew is *Adam erets*, which over millenia could sound like 'Atlantis'; an 'island' of great technology which was consumed by a flood.

According to Dr. Brown's hydroplate theory, most magnetic stripes on the sea floor were created in a matter of days during Noah's flood, not millions of years.[1144]

[1144] Brown, Walter, Ph.D., *In The Beginning: Compelling Evidence for Creation and the Flood*, Center for Scientific Creation, www.creationscience.com, 2008, pp. 105-142

Ice Age and Drought of EBI-II, Followed by Abandonment

A geologic study of Nile delta core samples confirmed low Nile flow at the end of the Old Kingdom in 4,000 BC.[1145] Traditionally, the Old Kingdom consists of the 3rd - 6th dynasties, so possibly he found confirmation of the ice age. According to an article's abstract, ". . . there is no convincing EB II presence anywhere on the mound of Megiddo."[1146] Occupants of Megiddo and other towns were commanded by Elohim to move during the Peleg period (2247 BC) of the Ice Age.

Ham

(K)Ham, *khawm*, means 'hot',[1147] not 'black' as some have argued. His name is derived from *khaw-mam'* which is a primitive root meaning "to be hot (literally or figuratively): - inflame self, get (have) heat, be (wax) hot, (be, wax) warm."[1148] It could be that Ham's metabolism made his skin hot, he was born during a hot day, or that he was a cranky baby. It is interesting that *kham-mawn'* means "a sun pillar: - idol, image,"[1149] and that the land of (K)Ham was known for its sun worship.

Jacob's Chronology

1836 BC	Esau and Jacob were born.
1782	Jacob travelled to Harran and began 7 years of service as a bride-price.
1775	Jacob, at age 61, married Leah and Rachel
1774	Reuben born of Leah
1773	Simeon born of Leah
1772	Levi born of Leah
1771	Judah born of Leah
1770	Dan born of Bilhah
1768	Naphtali born of Bilhah
1766	Gad born of Zilpah
1764	Asher born of Zilpah
1757	Issachar born of Leah
1755	Zebulun born of Leah, and Dinah later that year or next
1748	Jacob began service for cattle.
1745	Joseph born of Rachel.
1742	After 6 years service, Jacob's family left Laban.
1742	El Elyon renames Jacob to Israel (prince of El)
1741	Benjamin was born, and Rachel died.
1728	Joseph, at age 17, was taken to Egypt.
1716	Isaac died, aged 180.
1715	Joseph, at thirty, governor of Egypt

1145 Stanley, J. D., Krom, M. D., Cliff, R. A. and Woodward, J. C. (2003), Short contribution: Nile flow failure at the end of the Old Kingdom, Egypt: Strontium isotopic and petrologic evidence. Geoarchaeology, 18:395–402. doi:10.1002/gea.10065 placing the end of the Old Kingdom and this drought around 4,000 BC.

1146 "What happened to Megiddo in the early bronze age II?" *Eres Israel*, 2003, vol. 27, pp. 66-72, 285
1147 Strong's Concordance #2526 derived from #2525 meaning 'hot' or 'warm'.
1148 Ibid., #2552
1149 Ibid., #2535

Appendix B

1706   Benjamin, by age 35, had ten sons.
1706   Jacob and 65 kin moved to Egypt.
1689   Jacob died in Egypt but was buried in Canaan.

This twenty years have I been with you; your ewes and your she goats have not cast their young, and the rams of your flock have I not eaten. . . . Thus have I been twenty years in your house; I served you fourteen years for your two daughters, and six years for your cattle: and you have changed my wages ten times. (Genesis 31:38 and 41)

"*This twenty years*" dwelling with Laban as son-in-law was 1768-1748 BC. The other twenty years of service was for wages: 14 years for daughters (1782-1768 BC) and 6 years for cattle (1748-1742 BC). Jacob spent forty years total near (C)Harran with Terah's relatives (1782-1742 BC).

Biblical "Inconsistencies"

The addition of Kainan in Luke 3:36 is a copying error. Greek copyists were not held to the same high standards as Hebrew copyists of Scripture.

In calculating the day of the Feast of Weeks, according to the Talmud, book 2: "It can happen as R. Shemaiah teaches: Pentecost falls on the fifth, sixth, or seventh of Sivan. How is this possible? In a year when the months of Nissan and Iyar have thirty days each, Pentecost falls on the fifth of Sivan; when they each have twenty-nine days, Pentecost falls on the seventh of Sivan; but when the one has twenty-nine days and the other has thirty days, Pentecost falls on the sixth of Sivan."

Abraham: Birth Order of Terah's Sons

And Terah lived seventy years, and begat Abram, Nahor, and Haran. . . . And the days of Terah were two hundred and five years: and Terah died in Haran. (Genesis 11:26+32)

"Haran was certainly the eldest son of Terah, and he appears to have been born when Terah was about seventy years of age, and his birth was followed in successive periods with those of Nahor his second, and Abram his youngest son. Many have been greatly puzzled with the account here, supposing because Abram is mentioned first, that therefore he was the eldest son of Terah: but he is only put first by way of dignity. An instance of this we have already seen, #Ge 5:32, where Noah is represented as having Shem, Ham, and Japheth in this order of succession; whereas it is evident from other scriptures that Shem was the youngest son, who for dignity is named first, as Abram is here; and Japheth the eldest, named last, as Haran is here. Terah died two hundred and five years old, #Ge 11:32; then Abram departed from Haran when seventy-five years old, #Ge 12:4; therefore <u>Abram was born</u>, not <u>when his father Terah</u> was seventy, but when he <u>was one hundred and thirty</u>." - Clarke's Commentary [Japheth, Shem, Ham]

And he said, Men, brothers, and fathers, listen; The God of glory appeared to our father Abraham, when he was in Mesopotamia, before he dwelled in Charran, And said to him, Get you out of your country, and from your kindred, and come into the land which I shall show you. Then came he out of the land of the Chaldeans, and dwelled in Charran: and from there, when his father was dead, he removed him into this land, wherein you now dwell. (Acts 7:2-4)

369

It could be that Abram left Ur when he was between the ages of 70-75, and that Terah became ill when they reached Charran, and so they dwelt there until Terah died. When Abram was 75 years old, God commanded him to leave Charran for the land He would show him (Gen. 12:1-4).

Joshua 10: Hailstones and the Sun standing still

And the LORD discomfited them before Israel, and slew them with a great slaughter at Gibeon, and chased them along the way that goes up to Bethhoron, and smote them to Azekah, and to Makkedah. And it came to pass, as they fled from before Israel, and were in the going down to Bethhoron, that the LORD cast down great stones from heaven on them to Azekah, and they died: they were more which died with hailstones than they whom the children of Israel slew with the sword. Then spoke Joshua to the LORD in the day when the LORD delivered up the Amorites before the children of Israel, and he said in the sight of Israel, Sun, stand you still [damam] on Gibeon; and you, Moon, in the valley of Ajalon. And the sun stood still [damam], and the moon stayed [amad], until the people had avenged themselves on their enemies. Is not this written in the book of Jasher? So the sun stood still [amad] in the middle of heaven, and hurried not to go down about a whole day. And there was no day like that before it or after it, that the LORD listened to the voice of a man: for the LORD fought for Israel. (Joshua 10:10-14)

Damam means to be dumb, be silent, be still, hold peace, to tarry or wait. *Amad* means to stand, be still, or to tarry. "*Middle of heaven*" means mid-sky or horizon. The Sun rotates once every 27 Earth days. The surface of the Sun is boiling with incredibly loud explosions. The solar wind has a "spiral angle" to its Interplanetary Magnetic Field (IMF) which can effect the Earth's rotation if in its path. So Adam Clarke may have been correct to deduce that Joshua was truly telling the Sun to stop rotating and emitting its solar wind.

"Sun! upon Gibeon be dumb:
And the moon on the vale of Ajalon."

Though in poetic form, Yehoshua's command had the same effect as Yeshua's command upon the Sea of Galilee. "*Master, care you not that we perish? And he arose, and rebuked the wind, and said to the sea, Peace [silence, be dumb], be still [muzzled]. And the wind ceased, and there was a great calm.*" (Mark 4:38c-39) Since Elohim created the heavens and the earth and the laws by which they function, He can manipulate His creation however He wills. When Elohim suspends those laws, it is rightly called a miracle. Elohim may have chosen to make a local time distortion.

> "There is also a tradition of a rupture between the sun-god and the moon-god. This is somewhat similar to the Hebrew tradition in the time of Joshua and of the extended day in which meteorites (fire and brimstone) rained from above, and the Sun and Moon were in irregular motion—again comparable to the Egyptian story of Phaethon, being drawn across the sky in a solar chariot by steeds gone wild."[1150]

1150 Patten, Donald, *The Biblical Flood and the Ice Epoch*, p. 170

Appendix B

Joshua and Jericho

In 1927 the Jordan Rift experienced a strong earthquake, and a large embankment at Adam fell into the Jordan River, damming it and stopping its flow for 20 hours;[1151] something similar perhaps? The city of Jericho had a lower stone revetment wall built upon bedrock and 20 feet high.[1152] Kathleen Kenyon found piles of red mud-bricks piled almost up to the top of the revetment wall, which would have allowed the Israelites to use the rubble as a ramp to go up into the city.[1153] Kenyon uncovered a revetment wall with the first course of red brick still in situ.[1154] There was a glacis between the lower and upper walls, but over time, poor houses were built on the northern part of the glacis. There were also MB houses built outside what became the lower revetment wall.[1155]

An Italian excavation in the early 1900's discovered 9 feet of remaining house walls atop the defensive wall on the north side of Jericho, which correlates with Rahab's house which was not destroyed (Joshua 6:17-25).

> *And they burnt the city with fire, and all that was therein: only the silver, and the gold, and the vessels of brass and of iron, they put into the treasury of the house of the LORD. (Joshua 6:1 repeated in verse 24)*

In Kenyon's excavation report on the fallen walls of Jericho, she wrote:
"The destruction was complete. Walls and floors were blackened or reddened by fire, and every room was filled with fallen bricks, timbers, and household utensils; in most rooms the fallen debris was heavily burnt."[1156]

A piece of charcoal in this destruction debris was dated to 1410 BCE, plus or minus 40 years.[1157] (1410 + 40 = 1450) Thus the 1451 BC campaign of Joshua is very close to the Carbon 14 range.

Kathleen Kenyon excavated at Jericho in the 1950's and determined the city was destroyed in 1550 BC, overturning John Garstang's 1400 BC date for the destruction of the LBA "City IV" when he excavated Jericho only twenty years prior. In the southeast area of Jericho, Garstang had discovered a layer of ash 3-foot thick along with many jars full of charred grain. This demonstrates Jericho was burned after a short siege soon after the barley harvest (Joshua 2:6; 3:15, 6:15),[1158] as a First Fruits burnt offering. Dr. Bryant Wood, an expert in Canaanite Late Bronze pottery, studied the pottery finds of Garstang and Kenyon, and determined the pottery was 15th century and not 14th century. The Canaanite black and red pottery was used during 1450 – 1400 BC, and the bowls with concentric circles on the inside were used during his LBI period of 1550 – 1400 BC according to Dr. Wood. Dr. Wood stated it took half an hour to walk around Tell es-Sultan, and that the upper city

---

1151 Nur, Amos, quoted in "The Stanford Earth Scientist," pull-out section of the *Stanford Observer*, Stanford Univ. News Service, November 1988, p. 5; Joshua 3:15-17
1152 Wood, Bryant Dr., http://www.biblearchaeology.org/post/2008/06/The-Walls-of-Jericho.aspx#Article, in second video lecture
1153 Ibid., Joshua 6:5
1154 Ibid., with a picture of Kenyon standing in front of revetment in west trench
1155 Ibid.
1156 http://www.truthnet.org/biblicalarcheology/6/conquestcanaan.htm
1157 Kenyon, Kathleen, *Jericho 5*, p. 763, sample BM-1790
1158 Wood, Bryant Dr., http://www.biblearchaeology.org/post/2008/06/The-Walls-of-Jericho.aspx#Article

may have housed 2,000 people, and he placed the destruction of Jericho in Spring of 1406 BC.[1159]

"If Wood is correct, then there is evidence at Jericho to support the early date of the exodus."[1160]

John Garstang divided Jericho into "four main epochs":[1161] Neolithic, Early Bronze Age, Middle Bronze Age, and Late Bronze Age (his City IV). His dates were based upon conventional Egyptian chronology. Garstang noted "About 2000 BC the site of Jericho was enclosed by definitive defensive ramparts . . . The area of the city was only about 8 acres."[1162]

> "About 1800 BC, the city of Jericho was re-fortified upon a more ample scale, . . . The area of Jericho now attained its maximum of about 12 acres. . . . The art is that of the Hyksos period . . . Names of Hyksos leaders are found upon seals both in the tombs and the palace area of the city suggested that some of these personages both resided and died there. . . . Quite a number of the jars had been sealed after the fashion of the age, in the name of Hyksos chieftains. . . . The whole system was destroyed 1600 BC by a general conflagration, an event which seemed to coincide with the demolition of the cities ramparts, though the evidence as to the date of the latter case is not so complete as to warrant a definite conclusion."[1163] - John Garstang

Garstang excavated tombs in the cemetery northwest of Jericho and also discovered scarabs of 18th dynasty pharaohs Hatshepsut, Thutmose III, and Amenhotep III as the last pharaoh to control Jericho.[1164] Overall he found "160 scarabs which cover the period of time from the beginning of the Hyksos period down to this Pharaoh's reign,"[1165] being Amenhotep III. According to Kenyon:

> "Burials cease in all the tombs in the northern cemetery at the end of the Middle Bronze Age. There is a similar break in those in the western cemetery. But in the latter area, five were found to contain deposits belonging to the Late Bronze Age."[1166]

Area H north balk diagram shows the palace of Eglon in red after a yellow period of debris.[1167] King Eglon built a small palace (Judges 3:13) on the ruined city of Jericho a few decades after Joshua's death. Dr. Wood concluded:

> "Kenyon was able to identify many different occupational phases during the Bronze Age at Jericho. Middle Bronze III, the last subperiod of Middle Bronze, lasted from about 1650 to 1550 B.C.E. The beginning of the Middle Bronze III phase at Jericho can be fixed quite confidently at Kenyon's Phase 32. From Phase 32 to the end of the life of City IV, Kenyon identified 20 different architectural phases, with evidence that some of

---

1159 Ibid., Dr. Bryant Wood in second video lecture
1160 Hoerth, Alfred, *Archaeology & the Old Testament*, Baker Books, 1998, p. 210
1161 Garstang, John, "Jericho and the Biblical Story" in *Wonders of the Past*, 1937
1162 Ibid.
1163 Ibid.
1164 http://www.biblearchaeology.org/post/2008/05/Did-the-Israelites-Conquer-Jericho-A-New-Look-at-the-Archaeological-Evidence.aspx
1165 Garstang, John, "Jericho and the Biblical Story" in *Wonders of the Past*, 1937
1166 Kenyon, Kathleen, *Archaeology in the Holy Land*, 1985, p. 182
1167 http://www.biblearchaeology.org/post/2008/06/The-Walls-of-Jericho.aspx#Article, Joshua 3:13 Jericho was known as the "city of palm trees" and Joshua 3:20 Eglon's "summer parlor" from which Ehud escaped in Joshua 3:26 and went to the mountains of Ephraim.

these phases lasted for long periods of time. Over the course of the 20 phases there were three major and 12 minor destructions. A fortification tower was rebuilt four times and repaired once, followed by habitation units that were rebuilt seven times. If Kenyon were correct that City IV met its final destruction at the end of the Middle Bronze Period (c. 1550 B.C.E.), then all these 20 phases would have to be squeezed into a mere 100 years of the Middle Bronze III period."[1168]

Though I don't agree with his final analysis, I thank Michael S. Sanders for his fine article and chart on Jericho at Mysteries of the Bible (www.biblemysteries.com).

(Garstang)	Period	Jericho finds
City I	EBI-III	Fortified city with walls rebuilt 16 times
	EBIII-IV	destroyed by quake and fire
City II (8 acres)	MBI	Amorite stronghold
City III (12 acres)	MBII	Hyksos stronghold and trading post influenced by Phoenician culture
Palace I	MBIIC-LBI	destroyed by Thutmose III
Palace II	LBI-II	Egyptian vassal (no wall or fort)
City IV	LBIII	Fortified city with upper and lower walls and glacis between destroyed by fire by Joshua
Outpost	Iron I	Small outpost to which David sends men (II Samuel 10:5)
Palace III	Iron I	Eglon's palace, but no walls (Judges 3:13)
	900 BC	Foundation and gate by Hiel (I Kings 13:34)
	890 BC	School of prophets? (II Kings 2:5)

Joshua and Jebusites of what would become Jerusalem

As for the Jebusites the inhabitants of Jerusalem, the children of Judah could not drive them out; but the Jebusites dwell with the children of Judah at Jerusalem to this day. (Joshua 15:63)

I suggest that Joshua could not drive the Jebusites from the "stronghold of Zion" originally built with massive stones in the Early and Middle Bronze Ages.

> "The excavations at Tell Rumeida uncovered an occupational sequence very similar to that of Jerusalem."[1169]

1168 Wood, Bryant G., "Dating Jericho's Destruction: Bienkowski Is Wrong on All Counts, *Biblical Archaeology Review* 16:05, Sep/Oct 1990
1169 http://en.wikipedia.org/wiki/Tel_Rumeida

"There is also ceramic evidence that the Stepped-Stone Structure's <u>substructural terraces and superstructural mantle are one architectural unit, built at the same time</u>. Shiloh's excavation produced approximately 500 potsherds from the Stepped-Stone Structure, including roughly 100 potsherds from the substructural stone fills, 350 potsherds from the substructural soil fills and 50 potsherds from the rubble core. The composition and character of these ceramic assemblages are identical. The latest of these potsherds date to the transition between the Late Bronze Age II and the Iron Age I, about the 13th-12th century B.C.E."[1170] [the <u>Millo</u> made be the Jebusites]

*And the children of Benjamin did not drive out the **Jebusites** that inhabited Jerusalem; but the Jebusites dwell with the children of Benjamin in Jerusalem to this day. (Judges 1:21)*

*And the king and his men went to Jerusalem to the Jebusites, the inhabitants of the land: . . . Nevertheless David took the strong hold of Zion: the same is the city of David. . . . So David dwelled in the **fort**, and called it the city of David. And David built round about **from Millo** and inward. (II Samuel 5:6-9)*

David did not build the city of David and its "*fort*" but "*called it*" his city after capturing it, and then built a retaining wall and/or a glacis around it.

Judges

Netherlands' archaeologists found a prophecy of "*Balaam, son of Beor*" written in ink on plaster in Deir Alla, Jordan.[1171]

N.K. Sanders wrote *The Sea Peoples: Warriors of the Ancient Mediterranean, 1250 – 1150 BC* published by Thames and Hudson in 1978 and described how they conquered the Hittites of Anatolia and invaded Egypt. One of their tribes was called Peleset (Philistine).

Deir Alla Inscription

Computations of Egyptian Dynasties

First Dynasty

The 1st dynasty ruled from Thinis near Abydos where most of the pharaohs of this dynasty are buried. The Turin King List (TKL) includes the years lived by each pharaoh in the 1st and 2nd dynasties (second column). With the third column, it changes to the regnal years, months, and days; and the age at death. Regnal years from Mizraim/Menes to Djet are from the TKL. The Palermo Stone recorded cattle counts of the 1st - 5th dynasties, as well as some offerings.

2330-2298   Mizraim/Menes (Narmer)
2298-2296   Hor-Aha

1170 *Ten Top Biblical Archaeology Discoveries*, West, Jane Cahill "Jerusalem's Stepped-Stone Structure: Jerusalem in David and Solomon's Time," 2011 Biblical Archaeology Society, pp. 125-126

1171 "Deir Alla Inscription," http://en.wikipedia.org/wiki/Deir_Alla_Inscription, accessed 9/20/10; discovered in 1967 and dated to the 8th century BC.

Appendix B

2296-2284	Djer
2284-2261	Djet
2261-2229	Den (32y, Palermo stone)
2229-2219	Anedjib (TKL, lived 74 years; Palermo stone, reigned 10)
2219-2210	Semenkhet (TKL, lived 72 years; Palermo stone, reigned 9)
2210-2184	Qa'a (TKL, lived 63 years)

Total: 146 years

Second Dynasty

During Nynetjer's reign, Raneb's name was erased several times in Documents 20, 21 and 22.[1172] In an inscription which mentions the *ka*-house of Hotepsekhemwy on a stone vessel (Document 21) from Djoser's Step Pyramid, "the name Nynetjer is written over an erased name."[1173] "The red granite statue of a certain priest named Hetepdief (found in 1888) shows his service under the consecutive reigns of king Hotepsekhemwy, Raneb and Nynetjer respectively since the object bears their three names engraved on its back right shoulder;"[1174] so the erased name must be Raneb. Weneg is attested only by inscriptions on stone vessels found in the Step Pyramid of Djoser and in Tomb S 3014.[1175] Weneg ruled during a divided 2nd Dynasty. Weneg's exact position, as well the identification of his Horus name among those known for the second dynasty kings, has remained uncertain.[1176] But as Jochem Kahl observes:

> "A long-known inscription from Tomb P at Umm el-Qaab (Doc. 22) provides the key to solving some of the problems associated with Weneg. In the inscription the *nsw bjt nb.tj* name Nynetjer faces the opposite direction from the name of Ra'-neb and that of his palace (Fig. II. 2.1) Ra-neb's name is partially erased. Scrutiny of the inscription reveals that the name Nynetjer is written over Weneg. Traces of the plant sign used to write Weneg are discernible, as are the enigmatic strokes to the upper left and right of it (Fig. II 2.2) Thus Nynetjer must have been Weneg's successor, and the original inscription referred to the palace of Horus Ra'-neb and to *nsw bjt nb.tj* Weneg."[1177]

Sekhemib-Perenmaat is the successor of Khasekhemwy based upon the discovery of a fragmentary seal impression of Sekhemib-Perenmaat in the Umm el-Qaab tomb of Khasekhemwy (V, on sack-sealings from rooms 31-33, directly north of the burial chamber) by Gunter Dreyer.[1178]

1172 Jochen Kahl, 'Dynasties 0-2: Hetep-sekhemwy to Netjerykhet. The Succession' in Erik Hornung, Rolf Krauss & David Warburton (editors), *Ancient Egyptian Chronology* (Handbook of Oriental Studies), Brill, 2006, pp. 102-105

1173 Ibid., p. 105

1174 Alessandro Bongioanni & Maria Croce (ed.), *The Treasures of Ancient Egypt*: from the Egyptian Museum in Cairo, Universe Publishing, a division of Ruzzoli Publications Inc., 2003, pp. 30-31

1175 Jean Lauer, *Pyramide* IV.1 pls. V:4, 19: 105, 20: 101-103 and 106-107; IV.2, pp. 50-53

1176 Wolfgang Helck in *Untersuchungen zur Thinitenzeit*, Harrassowitz Verlag, 1987, p. 103. Helck had proposed to identify Weneg with an enigmatic Horus Sa who is known by the mention of his *Ka*-house in inscriptions on stone vessels from the Step Pyramid.

1177 Kahl, Jochen "Dynasties 0-2: Hetep-sekhemwy to Netjerykhet. The Succession" in *Ancient Egyptian Chronology* (Handbook of Oriental Studies), Brill, 2006, pp. 102-103

1178 Dreyer, *MDAIK* 59, 2003, p. 115, pl. 24b

Pharaohs of the Bible

Turin Papyrus

TKL	Name, ruled in Thinis	TKL	Name, ruled in Memphis
II/20	Hotepsekhemy		
II/21	Raneb (Kakaw)	II/23	Weneg (Wadjnes) [erased] (lived 54y)
II/22	Nyetjer (95y; ruled 40y-Palermo Stone)	II/24	Senedj (lived 70y){ruled 20y?}
III/2	Sekhimib-Peremaat [erased] 8y?	II/25	Seth-Peribsen [Aaka] {ruled 17y?}
III/3	Khasekhemwy (lived 40+y, but ruled 18y on Palermo Stone)	III/1	Neferkasokar (reigned 8 years)
		III/2	erased, (reigned 1 year and 8 months)

According to Wikipedia, Khasekhemwy "ended the infighting of the Second dynasty and reunited Egypt." If Khasekhemwy reunited Egypt, then it must have been divided during the 2nd dynasty. I assume his "civil war" was against the intentionally erased (*hudjefa* in TKL III/2) name in Memphis, because Khasekhemwy mentions war against the Nubians and the northerners.[1179] The missing king, named between a 3rd and 7th dynasty king in the Abydos, may fit in TKL III/2 with a reign of 1 year, 8 months and 4 days, dying at age 34. Khasekhemwy may have wiped out this rival. Khasekhemwy Bebti built forts in Nekhen and Abydos, south and north of Thinis respectively.

"...some scholars are of the view that Nimaethap was the daughter of Khasekhemwy, the wife of Pharaoh Sanakht and mother of Djoser. ...There is clear evidence that Djoser arranged the queen's funeral."[1180]

"Nimaethap held the titles of Mother of the King's Children, Mother of the Dual King and Attendant of Horus. In inscriptions dating to the Fourth Dynasty she is referred to as a King's Wife."[1181]

I agree that Nimaethap was Sanakhte's wife, but I think she gave birth to twins or two boys close in succession who shared the same prenomen of Netjerikhet: Djoser and Netiqerty. And that upon Sanakhte's death, he willed both his sons should be kings; one to continue at Thinis (Netiqerty) and one to rule at Memphis (Djoser). Since Djoser reigned 29 years, I give Netiqerty a 30-year reign; and make the 7th dynasty at Thinis concurrent with the 3rd dynasty in Memphis.

Third Dynasty

TKL	Name	Reign	Clarity Name	Reign
III/4	lost	19y	Senakhte	19y
III/5	Djoser-it	19y, 1m	Djoser	29y
III/6	Djoser-ti	6y	Sekhemkhet	7y
III/7	erased	6y	Khaba	6y
III/8	Huni	24 years /// the one who has built Seshem-///	Huni	24y

TKL total of 64 years, but mine is 85 years.

1179 Clayton, Peter, *Chronicle of the Pharaohs*, Thames and Hudson Ltd, 2006 paperback, p. 26
1180 Wikipedia quote based upon Verner, Miroslav, *The Pyramids: The Mystery, Culture and Science of Egypt's Great Monuments*, New York: Grove Press, 2001, p. 105
1181 Wikipedia quote based upon Grajetzki, Wolfram, *Ancient Egyptian Queens: a hieroglyphic dictionary*, London: Golden House, 2005, p. 5

Appendix B

Sanakhte Nebka divided the united Egypt which Khasekhemwy Bebti had gained. The population of Thinis must have been huge after 300 years as the capital of Egypt. Djoser's new capital at Memphis would provide new opportunities for trade. Manetho gave (Netjerykhet) Djoser 29 years, and Wilkinson confirmed he completed 28 years according to the Palermo stone annals.[1182]

Fourth Dynasty

Beneath the south wall of Khufu's great pyramid, two great boats were buried beneath large roofing stones which have Djedefre's throne name and/or horus name on them, and one records his 11th regnal year. The four names following Khafre in position III/12 in TKL were unreadable.

4th - 7th Dynasties

TKL	Name	Reign		Clarity	Name	Reign
III/9	Sneferu	24y	{4th dynasty}		Sneferu	24y
III/10	lost	23y			Khufu	23y
III/11	lost	8y			Djedefre	11y
III/12	Kha[fre]				Khafre	24y
III/13	lost				Baka	2y
III/14	lost	18y (with room for ten glyph)			Menkaure	28y
III/15	lost	4y			Shepsekaf	4y
III/16	lost	2y			Khentkaus I	2y
III/17	[ ]ka[]	7y	{5th dynasty}		Userkaf	7y
III/18	lost	12y			Sahure	12y
III/19	lost				Kaki	10y
III/20	lost	7y			Isi	7y
III/21	lost				Neferefre	1y
III/22	lost	13y			Ini	7y
III/22	Menkauhor	8y			Menkauhor	8y
III/23	Djed	28y			Isesi	28y
III/24	Wenis/Unas	30y			Unas	30y
III/25-27	Summation: Total of the kings beginning with Menes down to [Unas, their years]					
IV/1	lost {6th dynasty}	[ ], 6 months, 21 days			Teti (Saq. St.)	12y
IV/2	lost			(Saq. St.)	Userkare	2y
IV/3	lost	20 years		(25th count)	Pepi I	25y
IV/4	lost	44 years		(Saqqara Stone)	Nemtyemsaf I	13y
IV/5	lost	90 years			Pepi II	44y
IV/6	lost	1 year, 1 month			Nemtyemsaf II	1y
IV/7	lost				Net. Siptah	1y
IV/8	*Ntiqrtj* {7th dynasty}				Netiqerty	30y
IV/9	Neferka				Neferka I	25y
IV/10	Nefer	2 years, 1 month, 1 day			Neferkare II	2y
IV/11	Ibi	4 years, 2 months			Ibi	4y
IV/12	lost	2 years, 1 month, 1 day			Shemai	2y
IV/13	lost	1 year			Khendu	1y

1182 Wilkinson, Toby, *Royal Annals of Ancient Egypt*, pp. 79 and 258

Pharaohs of the Bible

IV/14-15 Summation: /// kings /// 181 years, 6 [months] and 3 days, "erased" 6, total /// kingship
IV/16-17 Summation: [Total of kings beginning with] Menes, their kingship, their years [their ?] "erased", /// 9 months, 16 days, "erased" 6 years; total /// 955 years and 10 days
{955 – 181 = 774 years for 1st - 5th dynasty reign totals in TKL.}
{20+44+90+1+2+2+4+2+1+(12 months) = 166 years for the reigns of the 6th and 7th dynasties. 181.5 – 166 = 15.5 years divided among the three missing reigns of the 6th and 7th.}

TKL III/9-16 contains the 4th dynasty pharaohs, III/17-24 contains the 5th, and IV1/-7 contains the 6th. A supporting fact for 4th and 5th dynasties being concurrent: the Palermo Stone lists an estate belonging to (last pharaoh of 3rd dynasty) Huni's cult during the reign of Neferirkara in the 5th dynasty. Sneferu, first pharaoh of the 4th dynasty, acquired timber from Lebanon. The Palermo Stone stated 40 ships with timber arrived as purchased by Sneferu. Userkaf, first pharaoh of the 5th dynasty, is of unknown lineage. He was the first to build sun temples in Abusir (later called Cairo).

Pharaoh Sahure of the 5th dynasty had a fleet which traded with the eastern Mediterranean. The Bitter Lakes may have been navigational to the Gulf of Suez and into the Red Sea to Punt. A block at Abusir shows king Sahure cultivating two myrrh trees with text he had brought them from Punt.[1183]

Djedefre had a cattle count of 11 years which is given one-to-one correspondence to his regnal years. Khafre, his successor, had a cattle count of 13 years, but is often given a reign of 26 years, doubling the cattle count. The cattle count is not every other year, as is noted in the offset for Pepi I. Senusret III celebrated his jubilee in 1817 which was the 25th year of Pepi I in my chronology.

Pepi I's highest dated document is the Year of the 25th Count, 1st Month of Akhet day [lost] from Hatnub Inscription No.3.[1184] The South Saqqara Stone also confirms that Pepi I's last year was his Year of the 25th Count.[1185] Two copper statues of Pepi I and his son Merenre were found at Hierakonpolis (ancient Nekhen, near Edfu) with a thin copper sheet engraved with "Pepi I, on the first day of the Jubilee."[1186] I suggest the statues were a gift from Pepi I to king Senusret III (Itjtawy) on his 30th year, which were later taken as loot to Hierakonpolis; and that Pepi I only reigned 25 years. Dua-Khety wrote instruction to Pepi I, showing a connection between 6th and 9th dynasties.

Possible Evidence Against My cFIP

". . . long-lived palace courtier *Netry-nesut-pu* explicitly lists this sequence of Old Kingdom kings under whom he served under in his tomb: Radjedef → Khafre → Menkaure → Shepseskaf, and the first three 5th dynasty kings namely Userkaf, Sahure and Neferirkare."[1187] [except that Neferirkare is not listed on page 166 or 167 of *Urk 1*, and there is no mention he served under them; they are just listed on his tomb's lintel]

At the top of page 166 of *Urkunden 1* is a similar king listing without Djedefre: Khafre,

---

1183 Awady, Tarek, "Scenes of the return of Sahure's expedition from Punt" at http://egypt.cuni.cz/OKAA%20Awady.htm
1184 Spalinger, Anthony, Dated Texts of the Old Kingdom, *SAK* 21: 1994, p. 304
1185 Wikipedia and http://xoomer.virgilio.it/francescoraf/hesyra/ssannals.htm
1186 Bongioanni, Alessandro & Croce, Maria (ed.), *The Treasures of Ancient Egypt: From the Egyptian Museum in Cairo*, Universe Publishing, a division of Ruzzoli Publications Inc., 2001, p. 84
1187 O'Mara, P.F., *Manetho and the Turin Canon: A Comparison of Regnal Years*, GM 158 (1997), p. 51
O'Mara's source on *Netry-nesut-pu* is Kurt Sethe's *Urkunden* or *Urk I*, 1933, p. 166

Menkaure, Shepsekaf, Userkaf, and Sahure which came from a Giza pyramid tomb inscription.

From Djedefre/Radjedef to Shepsekaf was 69 years (1930-1861 BC), and from Userkaf to Sahure was 19 years (1972-1953 BC) with a 23 year gap between them in my chronology. Both lists specifically omit Baka (1895-1893 BC) and Khentkaus I (1861-1859 BC) of the 4th dynasty. Both list the kings in dynastic order with the kings from Memphis preceding the kings from Nen-Nesu.

Fifth Dynasty

The 5th dynasty began south of Memphis as offspring of the 4th dynasty. The five names following the [ ]ka[ ] for Userkaf in position III/17 in TKL were unreadable. Niuserre Ini has a Sed Fest scene in his solar temple, but I think it is the one he attended for Khety of the 9th in 1926 BC or for Amenemhat I in 1924 BC. The symbol for ten always precedes symbols for one, and in TKL III/22, three one strokes with a smudge above them follow the year glyphs. The experts say the smudge is a ten glyph, so I will give Niuserre Ini 13 years. TKL III/24 shows Unas with 30 years. Unas had no sons but did have a daughter named Iput, so I propose he established a co-reign with Merikare, son of Queen Khentkaus I, and gave the city a new name (Nen-Nesu to Herakleopolis Magna) to establish a new dynasty; in exchange for his daughter Iput marrying the man who would reign Memphis, Teti I. Unas may have stepped in to rule Memphis after the death of Queen Khentkaus I. Queen Khentkaus I may have had a daughter who married Teti I, Queen Khent (or Khentkaus III) but died early, and so Unas arrived at his solution. This Queen Khentkaus III might be given a reign of three years from after her mother died until she herself died (1859-1856 BC). Queen Khentkaus III may have been blamed for famine and her name expunged from all lists.

Kagemni, the vizer of Unas's successor Teti, began his career under Djedkare Isesi and Unas. Thus, there was a linear transition from the 5th to the 6th dynasty.

Sixth Dynasty

Teti married the daughter of king Unas, thus marrying into royalty. I think he saw Memphis being run by Byblite trade reps, and decided to step in as authority. Several of the 6th dynasty pharaoh reign lengths are found on the South Saqqara Stone which is the lid of a queen's sarcophagus inscribed with annals of the pharaohs of the 6th dynasty from Teti to the early years of Pepi II. Based on its information, the **estimates** are 12 years for Teti, 2-4 years for Userkare, 49-50 years for Pepi I, and 11-13 years for Nemtyemsaf I. The names of the 7 kings of the 6th dynasty pharaohs in the TKL are lost, but some have regnal data. The following regards Pepi I's dates:

"-Wadi Hammamat : 'year after the 18th occasion, 3d month of Shemu, day 27 ...
1st occasion of the Heb Sed'.
-Wadi Maghara (Sinai) : 'year after the 18th occasion, 4th month of Shemu, day 6 ...
1st occasion of the Heb Sed'.
-Hatnub: 'year of the 25th occasion, 1st month of Akhet, day […] …
1st occasion of the Heb Sed.'

This shows the Heb Sed indication doesn't always mean that the festival was celebrated that particular year. It seems to be understood as the mention of a new era, something like a new reign, analogous to the *wHm-ms.wt* events at the Ramesside period. A date of Pepy I's 21st count, 1st month of Pert, day 23 on the tax exemption stela from the entrance of Sneferu's double pyramid cult complex at Dahchur [sic] doesn't mention the Heb Sed."[1188]

I take this to mean that during Pepi I's reign, in his 18th year (1824 BC), one king had a heb sed; and in his 25th year (1817 BC), another king had a heb sed; but that no one had a heb sed in his 21st year (1821 BC). The best candidate for a heb sed in Pepi's 18th year is Sheshi, who would be ending his 50th year (1874-1824 BC). A candidate for a heb sed in Pepi's 25th year is Senusret III ('47-'17).

I think the scribe made an error in TKL IV/4-5, and that IV/5 (attributed to Pepi II) should have been written 'reigned 44y and lived to be 90'.

Weni and the Wawat

Weni was an official whose career spanned the reigns of Teti, Pepi I, and Nemtyemsaf I.

In the 6th dynasty there were Irtjet, Medja, Yam, Wawat, and Kaau Nubians.[1189] Wawat dwelled largely between the first and second cataracts of the Nile. In eastern Sudan there is a namesake town of El Hawat in the Dinder National Park. Mernere Nemtyemsaf I (1810-1787 BC) named Weni governor of a 40 mile stretch of the Nile from Yebu (Aswan) north to Medenyt (Gebelein near Silwa Bahari). The first cataract of the Nile is near Aswan.

> "His majesty sent me to dig five canals in Upper Egypt, and to build three barges and four tow-boats of acacia wood of Wawat. Then the foreign chiefs of Irtjet, Wawat, Yam, and Medja cut the timber for them. I did it all in one year. Floated, they were loaded with very large granite blocks for the pyramid 'Mernere-appears-in-splendor'. Indeed I made a saving for the palace with all these five canals. As King Mernere who lives forever is august, exalted, and mighty more than any god, so everything came about in accordance with the ordinance commanded by his ka."[1190]

Though the area to the east of Weni's nome is barren now, it must have led to forests of acacia wood at the time, and so canals were dug to float the trees to where they could be planed and fashioned into barges and boats. The canals may have connected to the Kalabsha-wadi Al Arab. Nemtyemsaf I built his pyramid at Saqqara.

> "When his majesty took action against the Aamu (Asiatic) Sand-dwellers, his majesty made an army of many tens of thousands from all of Upper Egypt: from Yebu in the south to Medenyt in the north; from Lower Egypt: from all of the Two-Sides-of-the-House and from Sedjer and Khen-sedjru; and from <u>Irtjet-Nubians, Medja-Nubians, Yam-Nubians, Wawat-Nubians, Kaau-Nubians</u>; and from Tjemeh-land." - Weni

6th and 12th dynasty possible connection with Weni

Antefiqer was vizier under Amenemhat I of the 12th dynasty. On a rock inscription at Wadi el Hudi dated to year 20 (+ x) of Amenemhat I, Antefiqer noted the coming of Weni, an assistant treasurer, to collect amethyst.[1191] This could be Weni of the 6th dynasty.

1188 JD at http://egyptologist.org/discus/messages/24/4273.html?1033131628
1189 Weni's autobiography from his tomb at Abydos now at the Cairo Museum #1435.
1190 Breasted, James Henry, *Ancient Record of Egypt*, part I, p. 293ff autobiography of Weni
1191 Grajetzki, Wolfram, *Court Officials of the Egyptian Middle Kingdom*, London, 2009, p. 30

Appendix B

6th and 11th dynasty connection

The Sakkara List has Pepi II followed by Montuhotep II who united much of Egypt. Early in his reign, Montuhotep II had inscribed at Deir el-Ballas, "Wawat and the Oasis, I annexed them to Upper Egypt. I drove out the re[bellious (?*btkw*?)]."[1192]

Teaching for King Merykare

Sixth dynasty followed the Fourth dynasty in Memphis. Seventh dynasty in Thinis was contemporary with the Third dynasty in Memphis. Eighth dynasty followed the Seventh dynasty in Thinis. Ninth dynasty began with Khety of Asyut. He built himself a palace in Tell el-Dabᶜa where the earliest foundation has inscribed "the door of the two roads of Khety".[1193] Khety of the 9th was the author of *Teaching for King Merykara* for his grandson. The following translation was by William Ward in *Egypt and the East Mediterranean World 2200-1900 B.C.*. {comments are mine}.

Section II: Summary of Conditions in the North
81 He who becomes lord in a city arises with troubled heart because of the Delta, *Ht-smw* to *Smb3k*,
82 its southern boundary at the Two-fishes Canal.
   The entire west is friendly toward me as far as the coastal flatlands. It works
83 for itself (thought) it gives *mr*-wood and one sees juniper which they give to us.
   (But) the east is 'rich in **bowmen**' {from footnote 101}
84 and their tribute {'is lacking': fn 102} The middle Delta and everyone in it is topsy-turvy
   (so that) the administrative districts are becoming important
85 and one honors (them) more than me.

Section III: Instructions for Reorganizing the Middle (?) Delta
85 Behold [the land] which they harmed should be made into districts and
   all important citizens . . . (so that) the sovereignty of one
86 is in the hands of ten men. Magistrate(s) should be appointed who provide
   [revenue for] you and a reckoning of all taxes. The {*wab*-'priest': fn 109}
   shall be provided with fields and work for you as one people.
87 They will never become disaffected thereby.
   The Nile will not fail for you in that it does not come. The revenue of the Delta is in your hand.

My Notes on *Teaching for King Merykara* Section II-III
   Looking at 81-82: Since Khety mentions a southern boundary north of Cairo, the other two would most likely be the western and eastern ports which could either be sunken or inland now.
   "It is one of the world's largest river deltas—from Alexandria in the west to Port Said in
   the east, it covers some 240 km of Mediterranean coastline—and is a rich agricultural
   region. From north to south the delta is approximately 160 km in length. The Delta
   begins slightly down-river from Cairo." -Wikipedia

1192 (Fischer 1964: 114), Catherine Hubschmann, "Who Inhabited Dakhleh Oasis? Searching for an Oasis Identity in Pharaonic Egypt," http://pia-journal.co.uk/article/view/pia.341/52
1193 Bietak, Manfred, *Avaris and Piramesse: Archaeological Exploration in the Eastern Nile Delta,* Oxford University Press, 1979-1986, p. 7

The westernmost branch of the Nile delta was originally called Herakleotic (now, Canopic), and so I suggest the westernmost port city which Khety established for trade was at the mouth of that branch; and the other is the port on the Pelusiac branch called Herakleopolis Parva.

It is possible that Sneferu placed Khety in charge of delta imports and exports. Khety of the 9th dynasty ruled the western delta successfully. I propose Khety established one of his non-royal generals, Ameny, to secure the eastern delta and its trading port. I suggest Ameny hired Nubian "bowmen" to protect the eastern delta from the native 'Asiatics' living there. Then after Ameny established himself, he declared himself pharaoh Amenemhat I and sent out propaganda that he would build a much better wall than Sneferu's. Though Ameny's mother was from Upper Egypt, I think his father lived near the Fayyum, where the 12th dynasty established their base, though they kept their presence in the eastern delta until mid-reign of Amenemhat II (from 1950-1870 BC). Hence the administrator had become more important than Khety (lines 84-85), and he had lost the tribute of the eastern delta. Those in the middle of the delta didn't know whose side to take.

85-86 "... (so that) the sovereignty of one {'unique one' fn 107} is in the hands of ten men."

Therefore, Khety warns Merikare to divide the power of the 'unique one' (Ameny, in the eastern delta) and divide the district among ten men, so as to receive his tribute from them.

Section IV: {Khety's} Outpost in the Eastern Delta
88 The mooring-post has been driven in the district which I made
    on the east of the limits of *Hbnw* at
89 {*W3t-Hr*} Ways-of-Horus, people with citizens, filled with the choicest
    people of the whole land ['to oppose' fn 115 is a guess] to protect those
90 with them. Let me see a valiant one who can surpass it! Let him accomplish
    more than I have done [lest I be] shamed with a feeble heir.

My Notes on *Teaching for King Merykara* Section IV:

Could the mooring-post on the east limits of *Hbnw* along the Ways-of-Horus be ancient Tjaru/Siles? One and a half miles east of Kantara is Tell Abu Sefeh which may be ancient Tjaru/Siles which the 19th dynasty built upon. Or *Hbnw* could be Hebua several km NE of Tell Abu Sefeh. I think *Hbnw* was the name of the new district.

Teaching for King Merykara Section V: Digression: The Nature of the Asiatics and {Khety's} Initial Skirmishes with Them

91 But this moreover is said of the foreigners. Lo, the wretched Asiatic;
    his homeland {lit. 'the place where he is': fn 117} is difficult, troubled with water,
92 hidden with may trees, the roads thereof dangerous because of mountains.
    He does not dwell in one place; a will-o'-the-wisp.
93 who travels about on his feet. {nomadi Shashu} He has been fighting since the time of Horus;
    he neither conquers nor is he conquered.
94 he does not announce the day of fighting like a thief whom a group repulses. But as I live
95 and as I shall exist! These foreigners were like a sealed wall which opened
    [immediately] when I pro[ceeded] against it.
96 I caused the Delta to strike them; I captured their men, I seized their cattle

Appendix B

97 to the disgust of the Asiatics toward Egypt. Do not trouble yourself about him
   (for) the Asiatic is a crocodile on
98 his river-bank; he will snatch at a single person but will not seize a town of many inhabitants.

My Notes on *Teaching for King Merykara* Section V:

Some 'Asiatics' were Shashu bedouin who used gorilla tactics when raiding supplies. Other 'Asiatics' were likely descendants of Caphtor, Mizraim's son, who are later called Keftiu; and they had every right to dwell in the Nile delta. Though the east delta Asiatics would defend themselves when attacked, they would not instigate a battle; which was very Egyptian. Egyptians hired mercenaries like Nubians to do their fighting for them.

CAPHTOR WAS Located on Eastern NILE DELTA

"... the Genesis record gives the commonsense and verifiable place of the Caphtorim's settlement as Egypt, or Mizraim where the name of the Caphtorim was rendered 'Keftiu' in a record that is conventionally dated to ca 2200 BC.... Furthermore, Josephus relates the involvement and subsequent defeat of the Caphtorim (whom he names the Cephtorim) in the Ethiopic War, a conflagration that was confined to the Nile delta, and which did not, as far as we know, involve the isles of the sea. Moreover, Jeremiah 47:4 describes the Philistines as the '*remnant of the country of Caphtor*' ... That Caphtor's descendants were mainland dwellers is also confirmed in the Assyrian inscriptions in which they are named as the Kaptara; and in the Ugaritic inscriptions as the 'kptr'"[1194]

Kothar wa-Khasis is Hebrew for 'skillful and wise', a Canaanite god whose other name meant 'deft with both hands'; a craftsman and metalworker. He created two magic weapons to aid Baal to defeat Yam (the sea, often represented by a snake). Kothar's abode is in Egypt, which in Ugarit is h.k.p.t ("hikaptah") derived from the Egyptian for "the house of the ka of Ptah", and is referred to as 'kptr' (Caphtor) in a Ugaritic poem in which Kothar builds Baal a lavish palace and OPENs its windows to receive rain upon the land. Ptah is the Egyptian god responsible for crafts, whose name means "the Opener". Kothar's double abode in Egypt and Syria linked by the sea alludes to the sea trade at the time. -Wikipedia

Since the Caphtor were familiar with the sea, most of them fled to islands, primarily Cyprus during the Ethiopic War. I think when Ahhotep II opened trade with Crete and Cyprus and discovered the Keftiu, she hired them to do the artwork on the walls for the government palaces of Egypt's trading post cities. When the Aegean volcanoes made the islands uninhabitable, the Keftiu returned to their homeland and received permission from Rameses III to dwell along the coast of Canaan as a buffer to the Hittites.

"Representations of Keftiu are known in a number of Theban tombs from the reign of Hatshepsut/early Tuthmosis III onwards." (Bietak in review of *A Test of Time* 2004)

Teaching for King Merykara Section VI: Instructions for Fortifying the Eastern Delta
99 Dig a canal until it is un[hindered] Flood its half as far as Like Timsah {*Km-wr*}.

1194 Cooper, Bill, *After the Flood*, New Wine Press, 1995

Behold it is in the life-line of the foreigners.
100 its ramparts are warlike, its warriors many. The people in it are able to bear arms as well as
101 the free householders. The area of Memphis numbers 10,000 men consisting of
free citizens without its taxes.
102 Magistrates have been in it since the time of the Residence.
The borders are firmly established, its bulwarks strong.
103 Many northerners flood it as far as the Delta, paying taxes of barley with the status of freeman.
104 ... Behold it is the doorway [for entering the] Delta. They have made a canal to
105 Heracleopolis {Parva}. Numerous citizens are a comfort.
Beware lest the followers of an enemy move about (freely);
106 Those who are on guard grow old in years.

My Notes on Section VI:

The 'Asiatics'/Keftiu had been pushed away from the Pelusiac's fresh water by Khety. If Lake Timsah was their fresh-water supply, then Merikare built a canal from Lake Timsah to Tjaru/Sile at Tell Abu Sefeh on the opposite side of Ballah Lake, it would create a north-south barrier against east-west traffic, and also siphon off their fresh water and possibly act as a siege against their fort at Lake Timsah. Tjaru/Sile was the gateway to the Delta. Heracleopolis Parva was maybe 20 miles from Tjaru/Sile, and Khety already provided it with fresh water via canal. I have Khety of the 9th dynasty reigning from 1956-1886 BC, so faithful men he appointed at these port garrisons have become old with him, and an enemy might enter in and discover this weakness, so he warns his son.

Merikare of the 9th dynasty was concurrent with the end of Intef I; this mixes the 9th and 10th dynasties. The author of *Teaching for King Merykara* had a connection to a Khety who ruled in Asyut. But he was not Meribre or Wahkare, for neither fought against Thinis or Maki; so this Khety author must have been the founder of the Heracleopolitan dynasty.

Khety's Lament
127 Egypt fought in the necropolis,
128 destroying tombs in vengeful destruction.
129 I did the like, and the like happened,
130 as is done to one who strays from the path of the god ...
131 Do not deal evilly with the Southland,
132 You know what the residence foretold about it. {reference to Prophecy of Neferty?}
133 [As this happened so that may happen.]
134 (But) they have not transgressed like they said!
135 I attacked Thinis and Maki, opposite its southern border at Tawet.
136 I engulfed it like a flood !
137 King Mer(ib)re, the justified, had not done this,
138 (so) be merciful on account of this [to the encumbered].
139 [Make peace], renew the treaties.
140 No river lets itself be hidden.
141 It is good to work for the future.
142 You stand well with the Southland,
143 they come to You bearing tribute, with gifts.

Regarding Thinis, a city named Tunis is just north of Sohag, and Maki/Akhim is below Tunis opposite the Nile from Sohag. These are all roughly 45 miles south of Asyut. I have made Khety of the 9th dynasty the destroyer of the tombs and these cities, and the author of these instructions in which he now laments how he is getting tribute from the "Southland".

7th - 10th Dynasties using Turin (TKL) and Abydos (ABL) King Lists

The Abydos King List is located on the wall of Seti I and consists of 3 rows of 38 cartouches on each row, but the third row merely repeats Seti I's name. Reigns were not included. The list omits the 13th-17th dynasties and Hatshepsut, Akhenaten, Smenkhkare, Tutankhamen, and Ay.

TKL	Name	ABL#	Name
IV/8	Netiqerty [Netjerkare/Nitocris?], 30y?	40	Netjerikare
IV/9	Menkare (Neferka I), 25y?	41	Menkare
IV/10	Neferkare II (Nefer), 2y, 1m, 1d	42	Neferkare II
IV/11	Ibi [two tens erased] 4y, 2m, 1d	43	Neferkare Neby III
IV/12	lost, reigned 2y, 1m, 1d	44	Djedkare Shemai
IV/13	lost, reigned 1 year	45	Neferkare Khendu IV
IV/14-17	summations		8th dynasty
		46	Merenhor
		47	Sneferka [Neferkamin I]
10th dynasty in Asyut (no reign lengths)		9th dynasty in H. Magna (no reign lengths)	
IV/18	lost [likely, Khety of 9th]	48	Nikare
IV/19	lost [likely, Meryhathor of 10th]	49	Neferkare Tereru [VII]
IV/20	Neferkare [V of 10th]	50	Neferkahor
IV/21	Khety (Meribre) [I of 10th]	51	Neferkare Pepiseneb [VIII]
IV/22	Serenh . . . [of 10th]	52	Sneferka Anu [Neferkamin II]
IV/23	lost [likely, Wahkare Khety II of 10th]	53	Kaukara
IV/24	Mer . . . [Merikare of 9th ?]	54	Neferkaure [II]
IV/25	Shed . . . [Khuy of 10th ?]	55	Neferkauhor
IV/26	H . . . [of 10th]	56	Neferirkare [II]
V/1-9	lost [likely Abydos #48-56]		
V/10	Summation: Total of kings being 18		

The 7th and 8th dynasties ruled in Thinis and may have been protectors of the necropolis at Abydos. The 8th dynasty was followed by the Thinis and Abydos dynasties. The TKL omits most of the 9th dynasty. "Khuy" means 'protector', and may have been a title rather than a name. He was followed by Shed . . . who possibly had a brother or son whose name began with 'H'. The 12th dynasty likely saw the Herakleopolitan dynasty (9th/10th) as an extension of their own. There is no Neferkare VI in my chronology.

Pharaohs of the Bible

Seventh Dynasty

I place the 7th dynasty in Thinis contemporary with the 3rd dynasty in Memphis. The 7th dynasty was immediately followed by the 8th dynasty in Thinis. Manetho gave Neferkare I a reign of 25 years. The 7th dynasty contained Neferkares I-IV.

Netjerikare, to whom I give a 20 year reign
Menkare (Neferka)/Neferkare I, to whom Manetho gave a 25 year reign
Neferkare II reigned 2 years
Neferka Neby III reigned 4 years
Djedkare Shemai reigned 2 years
Neferkare Khendu IV reigned 1 year

Eighth Dynasty

The 8th dynasty continued the rule of the 7th dynasty in Thinis. The 8th dynasty's distinction is that it is concurrent with other dynasties in my cFIP. It is followed by the Abydos dynasty. There is no regnal data for this dynasty except for Qakare Ibi at IV/11 in the Turin King List which has 4 clear strokes and two faded areas for ten glyphs. The reigns of the others are my best guesses.

Merenhor, to whom I give 5 years
Sneferka [Neferkamin I] reigned 2 years
Qakare Ibi reigned 24 years and built a small pyramid about one mile south of Djoser's complex
Khuiqer (temple doorway),[1195] to whom I give 5 years
Snaib (stela), to whom I give 2 years
Pantjeny (stela), to whom I give 2 years
Wepwawemsaf (stela), to whom I give 2 years

Ryholt placed Khuiqer in the FIP,[1196] which is where his "Abydos dynasty" belongs. Ryholt noted, ". . . the Turin King-list proceeds chronologically throughout, except that contemporary dynasties are recorded one at a time in order not to mix kings of different dynasties . . ." Since I propose the 13th dynasty (columns VI and VII in TKL) placed in Thinis the rulers above in italics, those rulers would have to be written in a later column, which I suggest was column XI.

Thinis (T-13th) and Abydos (A-14th) Dynasties

Thinis Dynasty placed by Early 13th dynasty in FIP

TKL	Name
XI/10-14	lost [possibly Khuiqer, Snaib, Pantjeny, Wepwawemsaf, and one other]
XI/15	clearly gives a summation of 5 kings

TKL lines 10-14 inclusive provide space for names of 5 kings. Though von Beckerath suggested

---

1195 Leahy, A., "A Protective Measure at Abydos in the Thirteenth Dynasty," *JSTOR*, vol 75, 1989, pp. 41-60
1196 Ryholt, K.S.B., *The Political Situation in Egypt during the Second Intermediate Period*, 1997, p. 163

the summation should be emended to '(15)',[1197] I don't see any room for the 'ten' glyph. There are three kings not listed on the TKL who are attested by crude stela at Abydos: Sekhemreneferkhaw Wepwawemsaf, Sekhemrekhutawy Pantjeny, and Menkhawre Snaaib. *Pantjeny* means 'he of Thinis', and Ryholt includes them in his "Abydos Dynasty" of known "local Abydos (or Thinis)"[1198] kings. Since their prenomens are similar to 13th dynasty kings, I think early 13th dynasty kings placed them (Khuiqer, and one other) in Thinis at the end of the 8th dynasty to continue trade and administration.

Thinis (Tunis) and Abydos (El Araba el Madfuna near el Balyana) are about 45 miles apart on the west side of the Nile. Thinis had been the ancient capital of Egypt since 2330 BC, and its port may have become blocked with silt, so the ancient Egyptian capital was moved closer to its ancient necropolis in Abydos. The 14th dynasty recognized the need for a better port for distribution of goods and sent representatives to Abydos.

Abydos Dynasty placed by 14th dynasty during cFIP and early cSIP

TKL	Name	TKL	Name
XI/16	(Woser...re)	XI/27-29	3 lost
XI/17	(Woser...re)	XI/30	(...heb?re)
XI/18-25	8 lost	XI/31	(...webenre)
XI/26	(...hebre)		

I think the dynasty lists were divided geographically foremost, and chronologically as best as possible. Therefore I suggest the remainder of the 16+ kings of the Abydos dynasty were placed there by kings of the 14th dynasty. The prenomen Woser...re is akin to the prenomen of NubWoserre Y'ammu. The prenomens of the latter group, ...hebre and ...webenre, are akin to Maaibre Sheshi.

So I separate Ryholt's "Abydos Dynasty" into those of Thinis (with stela at Abydos as the lost names in TKL XI/10-14) who finished the Thinite dynasty at the request of the 13th dynasty, and those named in TKL XI/16-31 who were sent to facilitate distribution at Abydos by the 14th dynasty.

Ninth and Tenth Dynasties

Founder of the 9th dynasty was Khety. Khety's sons were Meribre Khety I and Wahkare Khety II, and his grandson was Merikare. The 9th dynasty began with Khety's amazing trade routes which included a station at Tell el-Dabᶜa. The 10th dynasty began in Asyut but moved north during the famine because Ankhtifi seized Khuy's nome. Ankhtifi allied himself with Neferkare VII, and his tomb referred to "Ka-nefer-Re". Ankhtifi's tomb also noted people were so famished they were eating their own children.[1199] The 9th and 10th dynasties were intertwined. There is no regnal data for these dynasties, and I have made my best estimates based upon the spacing and number of pharaohs.

       Delta
       Khety of 9th, 70y?

1197 Von Bekerath, Jurgen, "2. Zwishenzeit," *Archiv für Orientforschung*, 1964, pp. 194-195
1198 Ryholt, K.S.B., *The Political Situation in Egypt during the Second Intermediate Period*, 1997, p. 163
1199 http://en.wikipedia.org/wiki/Ankhtifi

10th in Asyut	9th in Herakleopolis Magna	9th in H. Magna cont.
Meryhathor, 15y?	Nikare, 20y?	Sneferka Anu, 10y?
Neferkare V, 3y?		Kaukara, 10y?
Meribre Khety I, 10y?		Neferkaure II, 5y?
Senenh... (Setut), 3y		Neferkauhor, 5y?
Wahkare Khety II, 9y?	Merikare, 5y?	Neferirkare II, 5y?
Khuy, 5y?	Neferkare Tereru VII, 11y?	(end of 9th dynasy in
Shed..., 10y?	Neferkahor, 15y?	Montuhotep II's 30th year)
H..., 10y?	Neferkare Pepiseneb VIII, 5y?	
Wankhare Khety III, 10y?		
Nebkaure Khety IV, 10y? (end of 10th dyn. in Montuhotep II's 14th yr)		

"... in his fourteenth year, described in contemporary inscriptions as 'the year of the crime of Thinis' (the nome which included the holy city of Abydos). It seems that Khety (a Heracleopolitan king of the Ninth and Tenth Dynasty) had regained control of Abydos (damaging part of the old necropolis in the process) and set his sights on the rest of Upper Egypt. Montuhotep II responded by launching an offensive during which he took control of Abydos, Asyut and Heracleopolis (the home of the Ninth and Tenth Dynasty kings)." -Ancient Egypt Online[1200]

I think Montuhotep II only gained Abydos and Asyut from Nebkaure Khety IV in 1801 BC, though the last two Khety's may have also ruled Heracleopolis. It's possible Sneferka Anu (Neferkamin II) stopped Montuhotep from taking Heracleopolis Magna.

9th - 11th Dynasties

"The text describes it thus: Neferkare, in alliance with the nomarchs Hotep and Ankhtify, tried to destroy the power of the Theban princes in Upper Egypt. Given by Ankhtify the job of deposing and substituting for the prince of Edfu, Jui, allied with Intef I (of the contemporary 11th dynasty), in Thebes. Ankhtify, with the help of the prince of Elephantine, attacked the governor of Thebes and his ally the prince of Qift. But the operations were finally suspended, given that the country was paralyzed by a period of drought and famine."[1201] [Jui is Khuy]

"After the death of the nomarch Ankhtifi, Intef II was able to unite all the southern nomes down to the First Cataract."[1202]

Ankhtifi fought against Neferkare VII of the 9th and Intef I and Intef II of the 11th dynasties.

1200 http://www.ancientegyptonline.co.uk/montuhotep2.html
1201 Wikipedia on Neferkare III who is also numbered VII, VII, or IX
1202 Wikipedia on Intef II

Eleventh Dynasty

The 11th dynasty began when a nomarch of Thebes,[1203] Mentuhotep I, claimed to rule all of Upper Egypt at the end of cFIP when the Abydos dynasty came to an end. Between 1889-1878 BC, I think Montuhotep I campaigned against Nubia. Senusret I last fought Nubia in his 18th year (1916 BC), and the next time the 12th dynasty thought to bolster their authority in Nubia was in Senusret II's 3rd year (1855 BC), 61 years later. Montuhotep I inscribed the following in El-Deir, rightly describing the multiplicity of kings during his reign and the lack of 12th dynasty oversight in Nubia:

> ". . . [from] Wawat [in Nubia] and the Oasis . . . I drove out the troublemakers in them. I annexed them to Upper Egypt. There is no [Egyptian] king whom they served in his time . . ."[1204]

What is especially interesting is how Nubians from one tribe would readily join the Egyptians to fight Nubians of other tribes. Such was the case of Nubian Tjehemau.

> "Inscription which Tjehemau made. Year of smiting the foreign land of south: I began to fight [as a mercenary for the Egyptians] in the reign of Nebhepetre [Montuhotep I] in the army, when it [the Egyptian army] went south to Buhen. My son went down with me towards the king [to offer our service as mercenaries]. He [the king] traversed the entire land, for he planned to exterminate the **A'amu** of Djaty [in southern Wawat]. (ITM 11-20)"[1205] (Nebhepetre is Montuhotep II in my chronology.)

Djaty is *D3ty*, and just a couple miles from Kerma, Kush (just south of the third cataract) is the town of Dagarti. Buhen is just north of the second cataract in Nubia. The *A'amu* were 'foreigners', regardless of if they came from Asia or Nubia. Therefore, **I deduce the A'amu of the 14th dynasty were from tribes in Nubia and Kush, not Asia.**

> According to Ryholt, ". . . kings of the dissident Theban dynasty, the Eleventh Dynasty, also did not adopt a complete royal titulary as a manner of course."[1206]

That's because the 11th dynasty was not the major power in Egypt at the time; the second half of the 12th dynasty was still large and in charge. The Saqqara king list hints at the importance of the 12th dynasty during the divided cFIP and cSIP by listing only the pharaohs' names of the 12th dynasty in reverse order, and not listing the 7th - 10th dynasties or the 13th - 17th dynasties, and only listing Montuhotep II and III in the 11th dynasty.[1207] The 11th and 15th dynasties did not use full royal titulary unless a pharaoh had conquered and reunited significant portions of Egypt like Montuhotep II and Apepi (and Khayan).

The Thinite nome (#8) revolted during the fourteenth year of Montuhotep II (1801 BC) which correlates to the famine caused by high Nile floods between the 20th and 24th years of the reign of Amenemhat III (1807 and 1803 BC) in my chronology. Montuhotep II subdued the Thinite nome but had to spend the next decade subduing Nubia and securing his southern border before expanding

---

1203 According to Thutmose III's 'Hall of Ancestors' monument in Karnak
1204 Hamblin, William J., *Warfare in the Ancient Near East to 1600 BC*, Routledge, NY, 2006, p. 383
1205 Ibid., p. 383
1206 Ryholt, K.S.B., *The Political Situation in Egypt during the Second Intermediate Period*, 1997, p. 124
1207 "Comparing King Lists," Pharaonic Times at http://hieroglyphs.wordpress.com/tag/saqqara-tablet/

Pharaohs of the Bible

northwards. I have Montuhotep II completely subjugating nomes #18 and #19 of Herakleopolis (along with nomes #1-17) by his 39th year. Montuhotep II may have even fought in Canaan. One of Montuhotep II's generals, Intef, has a painting of his soldiers attacking an Asiatic fortress,[1208] which I think is Sharuhen, the major fort and trading post of the 15th dynasty during Apepi's campaigns.

To avoid confusion, the Intefs are as follows: (Sehertawy) Intef I, (Wahankh) Intef II, and (Nakjtnebtepnefer) Intef III of the 11th dynasty; there is no Intef IV, (Sehetepkare) Intef V is of the 13th dynasty, (Sekhemre-Wepmaat) Intef VI and (Nubkheperre) Intef VII are of the 16th dynasty, and (Sekhemre-Heruhirmaat) Intef VIII is of the 17th dynasty.

11th Dynasty Regnal Years

TKL	Name	TKL Reign	Clarity Reign
V/11	Heading: The kings . . .		
V/12	(Wah/Kah . . .) [Montuhotep I]		11y
V/13	lost [Intef I]		22y co-reign
V/14	(...n...) [(Wahankh) Intef II]	[ ] 49 [ ]	49y co-reign
V/15	lost [Intef III]	[ ] 8 [ ]	1y, 8 months
V/16	(Nebkherure) [Montuhotep II]	51 years	51y
V/17	(S-ankh-n-kh-ptah) [Montuhotep III]	12 [ ]	3y, ?m, 12 days
V/18	Summation: /// 6 kings, making /// years /// [erased?] 7, total 143		

49 + 8 + 51 + 12 = 120. 143 – 120 = 23 years could be divided between the first two kings in the list, though Wikipedia says its 16 years to be divided;[1209] but since so much has been lost, we really don't know what numbers the scribe was adding up. Manetho states that the Eleventh Dynasty consisted of sixteen kings based in Thebes, who reigned for a total of forty-three years. Montuhotep I is described as a nomarch by Thutmose III, and Intef I was the first to call himself a pharaoh which was contested by Ankhtifi of Mo'alla, who was nomarch of Hierkonopolis (#3). Intef I gained acquisition of three nomes by the end of his reign, which meant military battles, so he was wise to make his brother a co-regent. Intef II fought Ankhtifi and gained nome #3. Intefs I and II were brothers who each fought Ankhtifi, and were buried in a rock-cut tomb next to each other.[1210]

> "The tomb had a large trapezoidal courtyard, with a chapel at the eastern end. This chapel may have been intended to serve the same purpose as a valley temple. According to a Ramesside inscription, a pyramid was part of the funerary complex, but no remains of the pyramid have been found. The Abbott Papyrus mentions that the pyramid was 'crushed down upon' the tomb. A stela mentioning the king's dogs was said to be set up before the tomb. A stela mentioning a dog named Beha was discovered, but it was found near the offering chapel, and there is doubt if there was really ever a pyramid." -Wikipedia (Intef II)

Since Intef I and II were brothers and both fought Ankhtifi during the second Biblical drought, I give them a long co-reign. Intef III only restored a ruined tomb in Aswan, so I give him 1 year and 8 months rounded to 2 years. All the glyphs for Montuhotep III's prenomen Sankha are present, and only lack the closing cartouche, and then there is a long space before the strokes for 12 which I

1208 Grajetzki, Wolfram, *Court Officials of the Egyptian Middle Kingdom*, Duckworth, 2009, p. 102, fig. 44
1209 Wikipedia Intef I article
1210 http://www.ancientegyptonline.co.uk/intefII.html

conjecture are for days; and so I'm attributing only three years to him since his own mortuary temple was not finished. My 11th dynasty totals 128 years (1889 – 1761 BC).

Twelfth Dynasty

"In 1950, Richard A. Parker concluded, after a detailed study of the astronomical and other evidence, that the Twelfth Dynasty ruled for 206 years, from 1991 to 1786 BCE. . . . In the past decade, a series of studies have appeared which challenge Parker's conclusions and lower the dates for the Twelfth Dynasty by over half a century. This research is based primarily on exhaustive studies of the astronomical evidence, . . . The new dates proposed for the Twelfth Dynasty are 1937-1759 BCE. . . . Some adjustments have had to be made in the matter of co-regencies and the lengths of individual reigns. It seems most likely that the Twelfth Dynasty ruled for 178 years, from 1963-1786 BCE (Kitchen 1989), and these are the dates I am now using. It must be emphasized, however, that even these absolute dates are approximate . . . for Canaanite archaeological phases, the scarab evidence indicates the . . . Middle Bronze I began some time before the Twelfth Dynasty, ca. 2000 BCE, Middle Bronze II began toward the end of that dynasty, ca. 1800/1750 BCE, Middle Bronze III began ca. 1650 BCE, the so-called Hyksos Age."[1211] - William Ward

Based on an astronomical sighting from an unnamed city, "The high/low dates . . . of the Twelfth Dynasty (7th regnal-year of Senwosret III) are 1872 B.C. and 1830 B.C.;"[1212] whereas my date is 1840 BC. My span for the 12th dynasty is from 1954 to 1772 BC concurrent with many other dynasties of my cFIP and cSIP. Some scholars note that the architecture of Amenemhat's monuments and pyramids "revert" back to the 6th dynasty; whereas in my chronology, the 12th dynasty precedes and then is contemporary with the 6th dynasty.

TKL	Name	Reign	‖	Clarity Name	Reign
V/19	[Kings] of **the Residence Itjtawy**				
V/20	[Sehete]p-ib-[re]			Amenemhat I	30y
V/21	[Kheper]-ka-[re]	45 years, [ ] months		Senusret I	45y
V/22	lost	[beginning of a ten stroke]		Amenemhat II	38y
V/23	lost	1[9] years		Senusret II	19y
V/24	lost	30 years		Amenemhat III	48y
V/25	lost	40 years		Senusret III	39y
VI/1	Maakherure	9 years, 3 months, 27 days		Amenemhat IV	9y
VI/2	Sobeknefe[ru]re	3 years, 10 months, 24 days		NeferuSobek	4y
VI/3	Total of kings of the Residence [Itjtawy], 8 [kings],				232
	making a total of **213** years, 1 month and 17 days				

45 + 19 + 30 + 40 + 9 + 4 = 147. **213** – 147 = 66, averaging 33y each for Amenemhat I + II

The 12th Dynasty reigned 182 years from 1954-1772 BC in Clarity chronology.

1211 Ward, William, "Beetles in Stone: The Egyptian Scarab," *The Biblical Archaeologist*, Vol. 57, No. 4 (Dec., 1994), p. 199, Published by The American Schools of Oriental Research
1212 Ryholt, p. 184

Amenemhat I 30; his 30th year = 10th year of Senusret
Senusret/Sesostris I 45; his 44th year = 2nd year of Amenemhat II
Amenemhat II 38
Senusret II 19; his 3rd year = 35th year of Amenemhat II
Senusret III 30; his 20th year = 1st year of Amenemhat III
Amenemhat III 48; papyrus with regnal year 46
Amenemhat IV 9; his 1st year = year 46 of Amenemhat III

I think the years of TKL V/24 and V/25 were switched. "Obsomer (1995) . . . makes a strong case that Sesostris I was not a co-regent at either end of his reign . . . shows that Sesostris I reigned into a 46th year, whereas Kitchen allots him 45 years;"[1213] I agree with Kitchen here. A scarab and a dedication inscription contain the names of both Senusret II and III,[1214] so I suggest an 8 year co-regency which enables Senusret III's heb-sed festival to be held in 1817 BC in the 25th year of Pepi I.

Along with Wegner, I think the year 39 hieratic control note on a white limestone block from Senusret III's mortuary temple belonged to him.[1215] The first heb-sed festival was celebrated after 30 years of rule, and subsequent ones every three years afterwards. A papyrus of Senusret III's first heb-sed festival (1817 BC) was discovered, and the completion of his mortuary temple may have been part of his celebrating a subsequent one (1814 BC).

The introduction to the *Prophecy of Neferty* concerned Sneferu at his palace in Memphis. In my chronology Sneferu reigned from 1965-1953 BC, and Amenemhat I began to reign in 1954 BC. Ameny was already a nomarch of the eastern delta under Khety during Sneferu's reign.

Prophecy of Neferty to Sneferu {with my comments in parentheses}

It happened that the Power of the dual king Sneferu was potent in the entire land ...
{from 1977-1973, Sneferu was the last king of a united Egypt (two lands) until 1720 BC}
the council of the Residence {Memphis} entered the Palace . . . for the audience. ...
the sealer who was beside him {an official with a scarab seal}
'Hurry and bring me the council of the Residence ...
and they were on their stomachs in the presence of His Power ...
seek out for me a son of yours who is wise ... who will tell me some fine words ...

Then His Power, ... said 'Come then, Neferty, friend, Tell me some fine words, choice phrases to entertain My Power at hearing them.'
And the lector Neferty said, '(on) what has happened, or what is to happen, O sovereign?'
So His Power, ... said, 'on what is to happen, for today is already happened and gone'.

[1213] Manning, Sturt, *A Test of Time: The Volcano of Thera and the chronology and history of the Aegean and east Mediterranean in the mid second millennium B.C.*, Oxbow Books, 1999, p. 375

[1214] Murnane, William J., "Ancient Egyptian Coregencies," *Studies in Ancient Oriental Civilization* (SAOC) 40, The Oriental Institute of the University of Chicago, 1977, p. 9

[1215] Wegner, Josef, "The Nature and Chronology of the Senwosret III–Amenemhat III Regnal Succession: Some Considerations based on new evidence from the Mortuary Temple of Senwosret III at Abydos," *JNES* 55, Vol.4, (1996), p. 251

Appendix B

And he stretched out his hand to the chest of writing equipment, and took out a papyrus roll and
writing palette, and prepared to write down what the lector Neferty would say . . .
{Sneferu wrote down Neferty's words:}

He {Neferty} gathered his thoughts on the events in the land,
he recalled the turmoil of the East, the rampage of Asiatics with their forces,
disrupting the hearts of those at harvest, seizing those yoked in ploughing.
{PAST: Prior to cFIP, the Asiatics stole Egypt's share (taxes) during the harvest. Since Egypt's
capital was in Thinis and the delta was left unprotected.}

Do not tire: look at it before you, Stand up to what is in front of you, {FUTURE}
Look, now, the officials are cast to the ground. What was made is become unmade, ...

This land is destroyed without any to care for it, ...
The sun disk is a being concealed, and will not shine for the people to see,
and no one can live, when the clouds cover it. ... {deluge: 2nd famine}

The river of Egypt is dry, the water is crossed on foot. {drought: 1st famine} ...
Its course is turned into its shore, its sandbank into flood,
The place of water into what should be the place of the shore. {river course changes}
The south wind does battle with the north wind, {tornadoes?}
So that the sky will lack the single wind. {change of jet stream?}
Alien birds will give birth in the pool of the Delta. {migration changes}
It has made a nest on the (Delta) fringes, even approaching people out of **famine**.

Utterly destroyed are those (times) of happiness at those basin lakes, {drought: 3rd famine}
with men set to slitting fish, overflowing with fish and fowl. {El-Ballah Lakes and others dry up}
All happiness has departed, flung down in the land of hardship,
from those (weights) of supplies of the Asiatics who are throughout the land. {Hyksos}
Men of violence have emerged in the East, Asiatics are coming down into Egypt, {Apepi}
The fortresses are lost {in delta and Nubia}, another is beside, {Memphis} who will not be heard. ...
The herds of foreign lands will drink from the rivers of Egypt {Joseph & children of Jacob?}
They will be refreshed on their shores, for want of any to drive them back. ...
Weapons of war will be taken up, as the land lives in turmoil. {17^{th} dyn. against 15th Hyksos} ...
No mourning will be observed today - the heart is turned entirely to itself. {the exodus?} ...
The land is laid waste, even though law is decreed for it, {YHWH's 10 plagues, not man's doing}
Destruction is a fact - ruin is reality. ...
A man's property is taken from him, and given to the outsider. ... {Hebrews spoiled the Egyptians}
Goods are given out only hatefully, to silence the mouth of the speaker. ...

The land is poor, but rich in directors, {the anarchy between 19th and 20th dynasties?}
It lies ruined, but its labours are great. The harvest is small, ...

393

Pharaohs of the Bible

Let me show you the land in turmoil; the powerless is now powerful, ...
and let me show you the lower made the upper, {Dynasty 21A surpassing Dynasty 21} ...
People live in the necropolis, {tomb robbers of 20th dynasty}
and the humble will acquire great wealth until uproar breaks out. {trials of tomb robbers}
It is the vagabonds who can eat bread, the labourers who enforce labour.
The Province of the Sun-god can no longer be the birth place of any god. {tombs are no longer safe}

There is a king who will come from the south {returning to Sneferu's immediate future}
Ameny true of voice is his name. {Amenemhat I of 12th dynasty}
He is the son of a woman of the Land of the Bow, he is a child of the Heartland of Nekhen.
He will take up the White Crown, he will raise up the Red Crown,
he will unite the Two Mighty Goddesses, he will appease the Two Lord Gods with what they desire.
The field circuit is in his grasp, the oar in the jump.

Rejoice O people of his time The son of a man will make his name for eternity and everlasting time.
Those who fall into evil, or plan treason, they will be overthrown on themselves for fear of him,
the Asiatics will fall at his slaughter, the Libyans will fall at his fire,
the rebels at his force, the evil-hearted at his majesty.
The rising cobra who is in the palace will overpower the evil-hearted for him.

He will build the <u>Walls of the Ruler</u> . . . to prevent the Asiatics from coming down into Egypt
if they request water in the proper manner, to let their flocks drink. {1st famine - drought}
Right is returned to its place, and evil is expelled.
Rejoice whoever will see, whoever will live in the following of the king.
The wise man will pour water for me, when he sees what I have said come to pass.
{end of prophecy}

    Yahweh gave several kings warnings of what was to come, and Sneferu may have received a true prophecy. Ameny did build the "Walls of the Ruler", and much more to defend against *Amu*. Amenemhat I campaigned against Nubia in his 29th year (1925 BC), and likely built a fort at Semna, Kerma, and Halfa. Senusret I campaigned against Nubia in his 18th year (1916 BC), and may have built other forts like Buhen and Iqben (possibly the island near Mirgissa). In Senusret II's 3rd year (equal to Amenemhat II's 35th year of 1855 BC), a stela of the officer Hapu recorded an inspection of the fortresses in Wawat (Nubia). Senusret III campaigned against Nubia in his 8th, 10th, 16th, and 19th years (1839- 1828 BC), and rebuilt Amenemhat I's fort in Semna and added a couple more there, at Uronarti and elsewhere. Semna East, Semna West, and Uronarti are built of the same materials. Semna West later had temples honoring Senusret III built by Thutmose I, II, and III. Hatshepsut's name was replaced with Thutmose II. Amenophis II and Taharka later built temples there.[1216] Women's items in homes near forts might mean families were stationed for several years.[1217]

1216 Reisner, G. A., "Ancient Egyptian Forts at Semna and Uronarti," *Bulletin of the Museum of Fine Arts*, Volume XXVII, Boston, October 1929, Number 163, pp. 64-75
1217 Ibid.

Appendix B

Amenemhat III and Proto-Hebraic influence of mine-workers in Sinai

[During the 3rd dynasty about 2040 BC, a ligatured script of quickly written clustered signs, known as hieratic, was developed by Imhotep.[1218] Several hieratic symbols are almost identical to the Hebrew letters of beth, gamlu, he, mem, and 'ayin.[1219]]

"The first true alphabet was developed by Semitic people . . . between 1800 and 1300 BC."[1220]

Amenemhat III (1827-1779 BC) began his reign a few years before Djehuty started his reign. Keel dates one of Amenemhat III's unique scarabs to the 13th dynasty.[1221] It is unique because it has a human hieroglyph determinative in a Canaanite style called protosinaitic script found mostly near the copper and turquoise mines of Sinai. The laborers of the mines fused Egyptian hieroglyphs with some Hebrew letters, and some short-cuts of their own, and made scarab-seals for Egyptian dignitaries in the Delta and abroad. People in Syria liked their ideas and created a cuneiform version called Ugaritic.[1222] Byblos, on the Syrian coast, may have influenced these miners in the way they wrote the name Hathor, the goddess of turquoise, with a Horus bird and an angle instead of a falcon in a square.[1223] The protosinaitic script is found on a Sinai stela dated to Amenemhat III's 23rd year, at Wadi Magharah dated to Amenemhat III's 42nd year, and the mines of Serabit el Khadim in Amenemhat III's 45th year.[1224]

On a stele at the temple of Hathor, Amenemhat IV recorded he was accompanied by the Ruler of Retjenu to the copper mines on his expedition to the Sinai,[1225] which may have been Apophis in my chronology. "On the Second Stela, Kamose refers to Apophis as a 'chieftain of Retjenu'. Retjenu is traditionally identified as an area covering Sinai and Canaan south of Lebanon."[1226] Yet not one seal of Apophis has been found in Canaan, so maybe Retjenu during the cSIP was limited to the Sinai and Sharuhen/Tell el-Ajjul which was just south of Gaza. Ryholt wrote "It is noteworthy that errors abound on royal seals of the Fifteenth Dynasty, whereas they are quite rare on the far more numerous seals . . . of the Fourteenth Dynasty." Most 15th dynasty scarabs were made of steatite/soapstone which was mined in Upper Egypt by the 16th and 17th dynasties.[1227] But the palace at Knossos had a steatite libation table,[1228] so the Phoenician Hyksos may have had their trade partners from Crete make their scarabs instead of the Canaanite workers in the Sinai.

A Keftiu offering was placed beneath the wall at Tell el-Dab^{c}a's palace compound with the large silos at the time of Ahmose and Joseph (named the bread of life man). *Wadj wer* "great green" of the Nile Delta is the god of the Keftiu who holds an ankh and a loaf.

"Of importance to the chronology may be a foundation deposit under a wall of this

---

1218 Baines, *Literacy*, p. 577
1219 Goedicke, Hans, "A Bamah at the First Cataract," *Time-lines in honor of Bietak* Vol. 2, 2006, p. 119-127
1220 Voigtlander, Katherine and Lewis, Karen, *The Alphabet Makers*, Institute of Linguistics, 1990, p. 8
1221 Goldwasser, Orly, "Canaanites Reading Hieroglyphs: Horus is Hathor? - The Invention of the Alphabet in Sinai," 2006, p.148, footnote 146
1222 Goldwasser, Orly, "Canaanites . . . The Invention of the Alphabet in Sinai," 2006, pp. 152-153
1223 Ibid., p. 124
1224 Ibid., pp. 129, 137, 144
1225 Ryholt, K.S.B., *The Political Situation in Egypt during the Second Intermediate Period*, 1997, p. 115
1226 Ibid., p. 131
1227 Ibid., p. 174, and p. 159 fn583 "According to Fuchs (LA, V, 1271-1274) steatite is found in the Eastern Desert from Wadi Attala (which branches off from Wadi Hammamat) in the north to Wadi Halfa (Nubia) in the south."
1228 Hogan, C. Michael, "Knossos Fieldnotes", *The Modern Antiquarian*, 2007

compound (L 1057). It contained a bowl and clay model items, such as hoes, baskets, mortars, sieves, a <u>loaf of bread</u> and especially a chunk of meat with a <u>hieratic</u> ink inscription (Reg. 8741) (Figs. 8, 9)."[1229] - Bietak {emphasis mine}

From Egyptian hieractic and Canaanite protosinaitic came the north Semitic alphabet known as Phoenician from which the early Aramaic alphabets of Hebrew and Arabic were birthed.

12th and 13th Dynasty Links

Some 13th dynasty kings were buried in 12th dynasty pyramid complexes. Lady Sonbtisi, maternal grandmother of 13th dynasty kings, was buried in 12th dynasty complex of Amenemhat I.[1230] Ryholt wrote "Many officials are also attested in Nubia through graffiti and rock-inscriptions, but it is difficult to determine whether a text is of Twelfth or Thirteenth Dynasty date."[1231]

12th and 13th Dynasty Synchronism of Neferusobek and Siharnedjheritef

Sobekneferu/Neferusobek, was claimed by Manetho to be daughter of Amenemhat III. But Amenemhat III is only depicted with his daughter Neferuptah at Medinet Maadi, and only she is buried in a small pyramid next to his. Whereas Senusret I and his sister-wife had daughters named Neferuptah and Neferusobek. According to Ryholt, the name Neferusobek is on the base of a statue of a king's daughter in Gezer and on a bowl at the pyramid complex of Senusret I in Lisht.[1232] So I suggest Neferusobek was the daughter of Senusret I, not Amenemhat III.

Avaris/Tell el-Dabᶜa

In 1941 AD Labib Habachi found a statue of HotepibRe Amu[1233] SaHornedjheryotef (13th) with three statues of queen Sobeknofre in a sanctuary near the palace at F/I, d/1.[1234] Ryholt placed Siharnedjheritef as the sixth king of the 13th dynasty (I place him as his father Qemaw's representative in the Nile delta). Senusret I's daughter Neferusobek represented him at Lisht and the delta to direct trade. Clarity chronology for the reign of Ameny-Qemaw is 1931-1925 BC, so his son, Siharnedjheritef ruled in the delta about the same time. Siharnedjheritef and Neferusobek may even have met in the Nile delta. The reign of Senusret I (1934-1889 BC) with his daughter Neferusobek ruling within his reign (c.1914-1910 BC) fits with Clarity chronology 1880-1870 BC for Tell el-Dabᶜa F/I, d/1 in which one Siharnedjheritef statue and three of Neferusobek's statues were found. These conclusions are also supported by the mace inscribed with Hotepibre, the prenomen of Siharnedjheritef, found at Ebla in the tomb of the "Lord of the Goats" which was dated to the nineteenth and eighteenth centuries BC of the Middle Bronze Age.[1235]

1229 Bietak, Manfred; Marinatos, Nanno; Palivou, Clairy *Taureador Scenes in Tell el-Dabᶜa (Avaris) and Knossos,* Austrian Academy of Sciences Press, 2007, p. 18
1230 Ryholt, K.S.B., *The Political Situation in Egypt during the Second Intermediate Period*, 1997, p. 83
1231 Ibid., p. 92, footnote 297
1232 Ryholt, K.S.B., *The Political Situation in Egypt during the Second Intermediate Period*, 1997, p. 213
1233 Ryholt argued that the 'Amu' before Siharnedjheritef has been misread to mean 'Asiatic' in 1998 article "Hotepibre, a Supposed Asiatic King in Egypt with Relations in Ebla".
1234 Bietak, Manfred, *Avaris* 1996, p. 30 with fn Habachi 1954, pp. 458-70, plates VI and IX.
1235 Suriano, Matthew J., *The Politics of Dead Kings: Dynastic Ancestors in the Book of Kings and Ancient Israel*, Germany, 2010, pp. 59-60

Appendix B

Nile Records at 2nd Cataract Semna East (Kumma) and Semna West

Written Name	Pharaoh of dynasty #	Regnal Year	Clarity Year BC	Clarity History [my suggestions]
Sekhemkare	Sonbef of 13th	3 + 4	1936 -35	
Nerikare	(Nerikare) 13th	1	1932	
Neferusobek	Neferusobek 12th	3	1911	Oversaw trade in delta and Nubia
Sekhemre-khutawy	Sobekhotep II of 13th	1 to 4	1910 - 1907	
Nimaatre	Amenemhat III of 12th		*1828	Low Nile; Senusret III retreated
		1	1827	Unknown position
		5 to 7	1822-20	Unknown positions
		9	1818	Below average flood
		14 + 15	1813-12	Average floods
		20	1807	High above average flood
		22 - 24	1805-03	High above average floods
			*1800	[High flood and Wawat attack]
		30 - 32	1797-95	High above average floods
			*1795	High flood [and Kerma attack]
		33	1794	Unknown, but built Kerma wall
		36	1791	Unknown position
		37	1790	Slightly above average flood
		40	1787	Average flood
		41 + 43	1786- '84	Slightly above average floods
Makherre	Amenemhat IV of 12th	5 to 7	1776 - 1774	Unknown positions

12th and 13th Dynasty Synchronism of Nile Records at 2nd Cataract

At Semna East, also called Kumma, there were 18 inscriptions (2 unknown) of high Nile water levels; at Semna West there were 9 more: 19 for Amenemhat III, 1 for Amenemhat IV, 1 for NeferuSobek, and 4 for Sekhemrekhutawy (who could be Sobekhotep II or Khabaw, since Khabaw has hundreds of seals at Uronarti). In 1929 AD, only one of the Semna West inscriptions was in its original position; the Nile's undercutting of the cliff caused the other inscriptions to fall from their positions. The enlarged western channel meant that the Nile there would never again reach the 25 foot mark during Amenemhat III's 23rd year.[1236] During the 1960's, the remaining *in situ* inscriptions at Kumma were cut out and taken to the gardens of the Sudan National Museum,[1237] and the name Nerikare was added; and later Sekhemkare.[1238] The inscription for Sekhemrekhutawy's 3rd year included the fact that Renseneb was the commander of Semna West at the time. This commander may have become king Renseneb (TKL, VI/16). NeferuSobek's third year Nile record is physically close to those of Sekhemrekhutawy, Sekhemkare, and Nerikare; the first three kings of the 13th dynasty according to Ryholt, supporting her placement in early cFIP.[1239] Since Sekhemkare's Nile record was in his 4th regnal year, that eliminates Sekhemkare Amenemhat V who only reigned three.

6th, 12th, 13th and 16th Dynasty Synchronism of Nubia & Kerma Attacks

Sixth dynasty official Weni (c.1845-1800 BC), who served Teti, Pepi I, and Nemtyemsaf I, described how the land and people of Wawat were kept subdued and subservient to Egypt. I suggest Wawat, Nubia was under Egyptian control until the Wawat attacked in 1800 BC.

Nile Level Records on cliffs at Semna

In year 29 of Amenemhat I (1925 BC), he subdued the people of Wawat. He and his sons built forts at the second cataract of the Nile over 300 miles from Thebes at Mirgissa and Semna, with the largest fort at Buhen built by Senusret III. But in the 19th year of Senusret III (**1828** BC), low Nile levels caused them to abandon the campaign and retreat from Nubia.[1240] **1828** – 1800 = 28 years for the hostile Wawat people to plan an attack, and take advantage of Upper Egypt's devastation by years of high flooding. At Semna for Amenemhat III there were 14 Nile level records which were found *in situ* on the cliff, and 16 which were found at its base. The average flood level at the second cataract was 19 meters at the beginning of Amenemhat III's reign (1827-1808 BC). The years *in situ* close to average flood levels were 9, 14, 15, 37, 40, 41, and 43. But between his 20th and 32nd years (1807-1795 BC), the Nile flood levels spiked close to 21 meters four times out of his six *in situ* records.[1241] I suggest based upon the inscriptions of famine, flood, and foreign attack by Neferhotep III and Montuhotepi in their shared year of 1800 BC, that it was a high flood year in which the Wawat attacked. Prior to 1800 BC neither military nor resource excursions into Nubia were recorded during the reign of Amenemhat III. He was too busy building dykes and canals to try to control the finicky Nile. Finally, in Amenemhat's 33rd year (<u>1794</u> BC), he travelled to Kerma to erect a (*senbet*) border wall and a granite stela which noted it took 35,300 bricks to build it.[1242] This was in response to the recent Kerma attack in 1800 BC.

In my chronology 1801 BC was the 14th year of Montuhotep II when the Thinite nome rebelled possibly due to the high floods and subsequent famine. Hearing of unrest in the Theban dynasty may have encouraged the Wawat to attack (1800) from the south while they were busy in the north.

According to Wikipedia, "Pepi I's reign was marked by aggressive expansion into Nubia . . ."

1236 Ibid.
1237 Yvanez, Elsa, "Rock Inscriptions from Semna and Kumma: Epigraphic Study," Khartoum, 2010, p. 2
1238 Ryholt, K.S.B., *The Political Situation in Egypt during the Second Intermediate Period*, 1997, p. 315-18
1239 Ryholt, K.S.B., *The Political Situation in Egypt during the Second Intermediate Period*, 1997, p. 320
1240 *The Oxford History of Ancient Egypt*, (ed. Ian Shaw), Oxford University Press, 2003, p. 155
1241 Rohl, David, *Pharaohs and Kings: A Biblical Quest*, 1995, pp. 335-340; see his chart on page 340
1242 Vilbell, Dominique, "The Cultural Significance of Iconographic and Epigraphic Data Found in the Kingdom of Kerma," Ninth International Conference for Nubian Studies, Boston, 1998, p. 2

Possibly thinking Pepi I had subdued the Nubians, when Nemtyemsaf I began to reign (1817 BC), he appointed Weni, an official (not a military man), as the first governor of all Upper Egypt. I suggest that in 1800 BC the 'amu (foreigners) from Wawat attacked Thebes during the first high flood, and Neferhotep III recorded it at Karnak along with the famine because his city of Thebes "was sunk". Neferhotep III may have died in this attack, because his successor, Montuhotepi, stated in his stela that he was "one who acts as king" while his army appeared like "crocodiles on the flood";[1243] an apt portrayal of men in armor wading through waist-deep flood waters.

1800 – 1795 = 5 years, which is long enough for Kerma/Kush to plan and carry out their own attack, but I think they first captured the Nubian forts[1244] and learned from the Wawat to attack during a high flood when the Egyptians could not maneuver passed the cataracts upstream yet the Kushites could send their fleet downstream. I also think the Kushites learned they would need allies to truly be effective. The first and last *in situ* records of high floods were in Amenemhat III's 20th and 32nd years (1807-1795 BC), and I suggest the Kerma/Kush attacked Egypt in 1795 BC.

Kerma Attack of Thebes (1795 BC)

Ryholt wrote, "There are some indications that the Kushites made raids on Elephantine during this period, and at least one, possibly conducted by the Kushite ruler buried in Tumulus X at Kerma, seems to have taken place during the late Thirteenth Dynasty."[1245] Bruce Williams of Chicago excavated graves (tumulus) in Sudan (ancient Kerma was it's capital). Kerma Tumulus X contained a statuette of Sobeknakht II and imported Tell el-Yahudiyeh pottery of the same kind as at Tell el-Dab^{c}a strata E/3 and E/2; in earlier Tumulus III, an alabaster jar with the name of Sobeknakht I or II was found.[1246] Sobeknakht I was known to have had a mayoralty of El-Kab in year 1 of King Nebiriau I of the 16th dynasty. [A statuette of (Khahotepre) Sobkhotep VI was found in Tumulus X.] So first, let's date the rule of Sobeknakht II as governor of El Kab, who recorded the Kerma attack.

"The Cairo Juridical Stela dates to Year 1 of his reign when the father of Sobeknakht II — Sobeknakht I — purchased the office of Governorate of El-Kab from Kebsi. Kebsi was the son of Governor (later Vizier) Aymeru and grandson of Aya who was appointed Vizier in Year 1 of King Merhotepre Ini of the 13th Dynasty. This suggests that the owner of the richly decorated tomb T10 at El-Kab was Sobeknakht II. Accordingly, if Sobeknakht I first purchased his office in Year 1 of Nebiriau I's reign — who is given a reign of 26 years by the Turin King List— his son would have been king [*sic*, governor] during the final years of Nebiriau I, Nebiriau II and probably Seuserenre Bebiahkh (who is given 12 years by the Turin Canon)."[1247]

I suggest roughly 25 years per Egyptian generation, and there were 3 X 25 = 75 years between Aya's appointment as Ini's vizier in Ini's first year and Sobknakt II becoming governor of El-Kab. In Clarity Chronology, Merhotepre Ini's first year was 1891 BC and Nebiriau I's reign was 1799-1773

1243 Wilkinson, Toby, *The Rise and Fall of Ancient Egypt*, Random House Pub., NY, 2010, pp. 181-182
1244 Ibid., p. 182. At Buhen, Ka wrote, "I was a brave servant of the ruler of Kush."
1245 Ryholt, K.S.B., *The Political Situation in Egypt during the Second Intermediate Period*, 1997, p. 77
1246 Bietak, Manfred, *Avaris and Piramesse: Archaeological Exploration in the Eastern Nile Delta*, Oxford University Press, 1979-1986, p.234. Also Ryholt, p. 162, fn 591 "Besides the seals [of Nebiriau I], a vessel inscribed for a Governor of El-Kab named Sobknakht has been found in Kerma Tumulus III dating to the Late SIP." Thus dating the Kerma attacks of Thebes to the reign of Nebiriau I.
1247 Wikipedia on Nebiryraw I

BC; thus 1891 − 75 = 1816 with seventeen years to spare until Nebiriau I's 1st year. So in my chronology Sobeknakht II could have been governor of El Kab from the very beginning of Nebiriau I's reign. According to the high Nile records of Amenemhat III and when he erected the Kerma boundary wall, the likeliest date for the Kerma attack was 1795 BC. From 1799 to 1795 gives four years for Sobeknakht II to build and furnish his tomb.

Sobeknakht II, governor of El Kab, was an eyewitness to a military attack on southern Egypt and wrote about the incursion on the walls of his tomb (T10).

"Listen you, who are alive upon earth ... Kush came ... aroused along his length, he having stirred up the tribes of Wawat ... the land of Punt and the Medjaw ..." It describes the decisive role played by "the might of the great one, Nekhbet", the vulture-goddess of El Kab, as "strong of heart against the Nubians, who were burnt through fire", while the "chief of the nomads fell through the blast of her flame".[1248]

There was a capital of Kerma at the third cataract around which an empire had formed unto the fifth cataract called Kerma and also Kush/Cush. Wawat was on the eastern side of the Nile between the first and second cataracts. The Medjaw/Medjay were a warrior tribe of Nubia, possibly on the western side of the Nile. Punt (Yemen) was the south-western Arabian Peninsula whose ships may have traded with the Wawat and gained their trust and alliance. El Kab (Nekheb) was about 20 miles south of Thebes.

"The discovery explains why Egyptian treasures, including statues, stelae and an elegant alabaster vessel found in the royal tomb at **Kerma**, were buried in Kushite tombs: they were war trophies. Mr. Davies said: "That has never been properly explained before. Now it makes sense. It's the key that unlocks the information. Now we know they were looted trophies, symbols of these kings' power over the Egyptians. Each of the four main kings of Kush brought back looted treasures." The alabaster vessel is contemporary with the latter part of the 17th Dynasty. It bears a funerary text "for the spirit of the Governor, Hereditary Prince of Nekheb, **Sobeknakht**". Now it is clear that it was looted from Sobeknakht's tomb, or an associated workshop, by the Kushite forces and taken back to Kerma, where it was buried in the precincts of the tomb of the Kushite king who had led or inspired the invasion."[1249]

"Davies stated that this vessel proves that during the invasion Sobeknakht's tomb was already prepared for the old governor's death. Relatedly, early studies on the inscription revealed that it was a late addition to the tomb, as it was painted in red on the outer

---

1248 Alberge, Dayla, "Tomb Reveals Ancient Egypt's Humiliating Secret", *The Times* (London), July 28, 2003
1249 Ibid.

chamber, which, according to the Ancient Egyptian taboo, made it untouchable. Davies added that as the tomb's decorations were completely finished by the time of the Kushite attack the corridor between the two chambers was the only space left to record such an event."[1250]

The tomb artist Sedjemnetjeru is noted in Sobeknakht's tomb in El Kab and in Horemkhauef's tomb across the Nile at Hieraconpolis.[1251]

"Horus, avenger of his father, gave me a commission to the **Residence**, to fetch (thence) Horus of Nekhen together with his mother, Isis . . . He appointed me as commander of a ship and crew because he knew me to be a competent official of his temple, vigilant concerning his assignments. Then I fared downstream with good dispatch and I drew forth Horus of Nekhen in (my) hands together with his mother, this goddess, from the good office of **Itjtawy in the presence of the king himself**."[1252] -- Horemkhauef on stela at his Hieraconpolis' tomb

Horemkhauef's wife was Sobeknacht (f) who is dated to the late 13th dynasty as 'one adorning the king'.[1253] The 13th and 16th dynasty nomarchs recognized the real Residence of power was in Itjtawy with the 12th dynasty pharaohs. Thus we have a synchronism of the appointment of Sobeknakht II linked to 13th dynasty pharaoh Ini and 16th dynasty pharaoh Nebiriau I, and one of Sobeknakht II's contemporaries recognizing the real power stems from the 12th dynasty pharaohs at the 'residence' of Itjtawy. Ryholt stated ". . . two sources which can be dated to the very end of the [13th] dynasty strongly suggest that the royal residence was still located at *it-t3wy* at Memphis. One is the stela of King Sankhptahi . . . The other is a stela from Edfu on which the priest Haremkhawef recounts that he travelled north to *it-t3wy* to fetch a statue of Horus 'in the presence of the king himself.'"[1254]

Itjtawy was also called Lisht during the cSIP. Ryholt also wrote ". . . Lisht may still have played a political role during the early Fifteenth Dynasty," and the 16th dynasty vizier "Sobka/Bebi is attested by two scarab-seals, one of which was found at Lisht."[1255] Tentatively, we also have the 6th dynasty subduing Wawat until about 1800 BC when the Nile became too unpredictable and then the Kushites joining with other Nubian warriors and Punt to attack Thebes and El Kab in 1795 BC.

Kahun Papyrus IV

Among the papyri found at Lahun is one called Kahun IV. Papyrus Kahun IV is an itemized list of a lector-priest's large household dated to year 1 of Sekhemre-Khutawy (which could be Sobekhotep II or possibly Khabaw who has many seals at Uronarti). Regarding a son and daughter, the papyrus mentions a "year 40" which most attribute to Amenemhat III. The Nile records at second cataract were made during the reigns of Amenemhat III, Amenemhat IV, NeferuSobek, a Sekhemrekhutawy, a Sekhemkare, and a Nerikare; the first four were reported in 1929, Nerikare in

---

1250 Vivian Davies interview, "El Kab's Hidden Treasure," *Al-Ahram*, 31 July - 6 August 2003, Issue No. 649 at http://weekly.ahram.org.eg/2003/649/he1.htm
1251 Grajetzki, Wolfram, *Court Officials of the Egyptian Middle Kingdom*, London, 2009, p. 121
1252 Shaw, Ian, *The Oxford history of ancient Egypt*, p. 186
1253 Grajetzki, Wolfram, *Court Officials of the Egyptian Middle Kingdom*, London, 2009, p. 158
1254 Ryholt, K.S.B., *The Political Situation in Egypt during the Second Intermediate Period*, 1997, p. 79
1255 Ibid., p. 260

1960's, and Sekhemkare later.[1256]

Scarab Groups of Tufnell and Ward

Based upon the accepted linear transition of dynasties one after the other, Tufnell and Ward classified nine groups of scarabs found in archaeological contexts: FIP of $7^{th} - 10^{th}$ dynasties (class I.1) → 11th (I.2) → early 12th (I.3) → early to mid 12th (II) → mid to late 12th (IIA) → late 12th (III) → 13th and 14th (IV) → 15th (V) → early 18th (VI). Ward noted, "In Period VI (earlier Eighteenth Dynasty), for as yet unexplained reasons, several early typological features that had gone out of use suddenly reappear."[1257] In Clarity chronology, the 12th dynasty is the leader of my cFIP (4th, 5th, end of 7th, 8th, 9th and 10th, early 12th, Theban 13th, Kushite 14th, and Hyksos pre-15th dynasties) and most of my cSIP (6th, 9th, 10th, 11th, rest of 12th, 13th, Kushite 14th, Hyksos 15th, 16th and 17th dynasties). I would eliminate the mystical reappearance by rearranging these scarab groups, thus: I.1 and I.3 and IV → II → I.2 and IIA → III and V → VI.

Thirteenth Dynasty

Ryholt wrote, "As regards the royal family, the royal residence, and administrative patterns, the Thirteenth Dynasty was initially nothing but an extension of the Twelfth Dynasty . . ."[1258] Several of the early 13th dynasty rulers were sons of Ameny/Amenemhat I, possibly by a wife or consort other than Neferitatjenen (with whom he had four other children): Sonbef, Sobekhotep I, Qemaw, and Ranseneb. The first two named themselves sons of Amenemhat, but since a new, non-royal (in Elephantine?), took the name Amenemhat (V) prior to Qemaw's rule, Qemaw called himself son of Ameny to point to Amenemhat I who likely sent his sons to protect Egypt's southern border.

The heading for the 13th dynasty in the Turin King List is "/// Kings /// who came after /// the King of [Upper and] Lower Egypt [Sehet]epibre, may he live, prosper and be healthy."[1259] (The /// = lacuna, and [ ] for restoration of lacuna.) It is very clear that the 13th dynasty kings came right after (Sehetepibre) Amenemhat I, with most being his sons, and was concurrent with the 12th dynasty.

Though the 13th dynasty kings placed several monuments and stelae at Karnak (Thebes east), I think its initial location may have been Madamud (7 km north of Thebes) due to their temple works there (Wegaf, Seth I, and Sobekhotep II; and Sobekemsaf II of the 17th). I think the Turin King List is generally chronological with groups of kings according to various locations and affiliations. I've placed most of those who ruled in Thebes in the first half of the 13th dynasty: Sonbef, Nerikare, Neferhotep I, Sobekhotep I, Qemaw, Sobekhotep II, Khendjer, Aya, and Ini. Amenemhat VI is son of Intef, son of Ameny; so I placed him after Amenemhat V, who likely ruled in Elephantine. I am ascribing the Roman numeral I to the first Sobekhotep in the list (Khaankare) Sobekhotep I, and the next is (Sekhemre Khutawy) Sobekhotep II; whereas Ryholt reverses the numbering.

> "Ankhu is known from several monuments dating to the reigns of the 13th Dynasty kings Khendjer and Sobekhotep II, attesting that he served several kings. Ankhu appears in the Papyrus Boulaq 18 as the head of the court officials. The papyrus is dated to the reign of Sobekhotep II and mentions Queen Aya." - Wikipedia

---

1256 Ryholt, K.S.B., *The Political Situation in Egypt during the Second Intermediate Period*, 1997, p. 315
1257 Ward, William, "Beetles in Stone: The Egyptian Scarab," *The Biblical Archaeologist*, Vol. 57, No. 4 (Dec., 1994), The American Schools of Oriental Research, p. 195 in text beneath classification chart
1258 Ryholt, K.S.B., *The Political Situation in Egypt during the Second Intermediate Period*, 1997, p. 296
1259 Kinnaer, Jacques, "Turin Kinglist" translation at http://www.ancient-egypt.org/index.html

Appendix B

Based upon Papyrus Boulaq 18, I am keeping (Sekhemre Khutawy) Sobekhotep II in his position just before Kendjer, and not exchanging him with Wegaf as Ryholt did. To avoid confusion, the others are (SekhemreSewadjtawy) Sobekhotep III, (Khaneferre) Sobekhotep IV, (Merhotepre) Sobekhotep V, (Khahotepre) Sobekhotep VI, and (Merkaure) Sobekhotep VII of the 13th dynasty; and (Sekhemre Seusertawy) Sobekhotep VIII of the 16th dynasty.

I am using Ryholt's placement of the Turin King List papyrus fragments, but Gardiner's Roman numerals for the columns.[1260] Prenomens are placed into parentheses, and if location of rule is known it is placed after the word 'in'; but if location is questionable yet artifacts found there, a '?' follows. Most rulers of less than a year do not appear in my overall chronology chart, nor do several others due to space limitations. Several 13th dynasty kings are placed in the chart as close as possible to their known links with other dynasties, while others are squeezed into random open spaces. For example, Ryholt suggests Monthhotep/Montuhotep V should be placed soon after the reign of King Djehuty and Queen Montuhotep of the 16th dynasty.[1261]

13th Dynasty Kings in the Turin King List [with additions]

TKL	Name	Reign
VI/5	(Khutawire) Wegaf	2 y, 3 mo, 24 d
VI/6	(Sekhemre) Sonbef in Thebes	
VI/6	[room for (Nerikare) in Thebes]	6 years
VI/7	Amenemhat V in Elephantine?	3 years
VI/7	[room for Ameny-Qemaw in Thebes]	
VI/8	(SeHotepibre) [Amu]Siharnedjheritef in delta	[at least 1 year]
VI/9	Jewefni	
VI/10	Amenemhat VI in (Qina) el-Mahamid Qibli?	. . . 23d fragment
VI/11	(Semenkare) Nebnun	. . . 24d fragment
VI/12	(Sehotepibre) Horus:Sewesekhtawy	. . . 27d fragment
VI/13	(Sewadjkare)	. . . 13d fragment
[Ryholt Seb]	at (Qina) el-Mahamid Qibli	
VI/14	(Nedjemibre)	7[y]
VI/15	Sobekhotep[re] I, son of . . .	. . . 2
VI/16	Ranisonb/Renseneb in Thebes?	4 months only
VI/17	Hor I [coregency with Khabaw]	. . . 7 [months?]
[Ryholt Kay]	at (Qina) el-Mahamid Qibli	
[Ryholt (Sekhemrekhutawy) Horus: Khabaw, likely Sobek[1262] in Nubia?]		
[Ryholt (...kare, likely Hotepkare[1263]) Horus:Djedkheperew in Nubia?]		
VI/18	(Sedjefakare) Amenemhat VII in el-Mahamid Qibli?	
VI/19	(Sekhemrekhutawy) Sobekhotep II in Thebes	
VI/20	Khendjer in Thebes, then delta at Athribis	[5y, 4 mo, 15 d][1264]

1260 Ryholt, K.S.B., *The Political Situation in Egypt during the Second Intermediate Period*, 1997, p. 71
1261 Ibid., p. 237
1262 Ibid., Ryholt, based upon seals p. 401
1263 Ibid., p. 403
1264 Ibid., pp. 193-195 from dated block of his pyramid complex

403

Pharaohs of the Bible

VI/21	Imyremeshaw	. . . 4 fragment
VI/22	Intef V in Medinet Madi (near Faiyum)?	. . . 3 or 4 fragment
VI/23	Seth I in Madamud (7 km north of Thebes)?	. . . 6 fragment
VI/24	(SekhemreSewadjtawy) Sobekhotep III in Sehel?	4 y, 2 mo . . .
VI/25	Neferhotep I in Heliopolis?	11 y, 1 mo
VI/26	Sihathor [co-regent] in Heliopolis?	. . . 3 days
VI/27	(Khaneferre) Sobekhotep IV in Heliopolis?	
VII/1	(Khahotepre) Sobekhotep VI	4 y, 8 mo, 29 d
VII/2	Ibiaw in el-Mahamid Qibli?	10 y, 8 mo, 28 d
VII/3	Aya in Thebes	23 y, 8 mo, 28 d
VII/4	(Merhotepre) Sobekhotep V	2 y, 2 mo, 9 d
VII/5	Sewadjtu	3 y, 1 mo
VII/6	(Merskemre) Ined	3y, ?, ?
VII/7	(Swadjkare) Hori	5 y, ?, 8 d
VII/8	(Merkaure) Sobekhotep VII	2 y, ?, 4 d
VII/9	lost, possibly (Mershepsesre) Ini in Thebes	. . . 11 days
VII/10-12	lost, possibly (Sewahenre) Senebmiu[1265] in Thebes?	. . . 3 days
VII/13	(no prenomen) Dedumose? [son of Sobekhotep IV, V, or VI][1266]	
VII/14	(. . . maatre) Ibi	
VII/15	(. . . webenre) Hor II	
VII/16	(Mer...re) [Ryholt-possibly (Mereskhemre) Neferhotep II]	
VII/17	[Ryholt-(Merkheperre)] (...enre) Senebmiu?	
VII/18-19	lost, possibly (Sekhaenre)	
VII/20	[Ryholt-(Sewedmare) Montuhotep V]	
VII/21	[Ryholt-(...mosre)]	
VII/22	(Merkheperre)	
VII/23	[Ryholt-(. . . benre) Hor...] (Merkare)	
VII/24	(Se...kare)	
VII/25	[Ryholt-(Seheqenre) Sankhptahi]	
VII/26	(....re)	
VII/27	(Se...enre) [possibly (Sekhaenre) . . . . . s, a female][1267]	

Other artifacts provide the following regnal years: 5 for Sonbef, 4 for Sobekhotep I, 5 for Khendjer, and 9 for Sobekhotep IV,[1268] and 4 for Seth I. Ryholt wrote, "Amenemhet VII has been tentatively estimated at 6 years since he is relatively well-attested, and Sobkhotep IV has been assigned an independent reign of 10 years since he is the best attested king of the entire Second Intermediate Period."[1269]

1265 Ryholt, K.S.B., *The Political Situation in Egypt during the Second Intermediate Period*, 1997, p.72 fn213 "It may be noted that an official temp. Sonbmijew had a canopic chest which contained the same text as the canopic chest of king Djehuty of the early Sixteenth Dynasty . . ."
1266 Ibid., p. 262
1267 Ryholt, K.S.B., *The Political Situation in Egypt during the Second Intermediate Period*, 1997, p. 359
1268 Ryholt, K.S.B., *The Political Situation in Egypt during the Second Intermediate Period*, 1997, p. 193
1269 Ibid., p. 196, fn 693

Appendix B

An architrave has partial names of Hor and Khabaw together in a way often used to demonstrate coregency.[1270] Hotepibre's statue was found at Qantir near Avaris in a secondary context. Ryholt argues it was possibly moved by Apophis from Memphis,[1271] but it could have been moved from Thebes by Qemaw or his son. Ryholt proposed (Merneferre Ay) Aya's pyramid is one of the unnamed ones in the Memphis necropolis; and that Aya's pyramidion was transported to Qantir during the 15th dynasty,[1272] likely by Apophis.

"Ryholt (1997:72) argues for not less than 57 Thirteenth Dynasty 'kings'. One suggestion is that a strong vizierate (created under Sesostris III) took charge and ruled through largely puppet pharaohs (hence so many, and most with very short reigns)."[1273]

"Since subsequent 13th Dynasty kings after Merneferre Ay in the Turin Canon list are attested only (if at all) from the monuments, inscriptions, and so on from upper Egypt, this has prompted some to argue that the 13th Dynasty perhaps moved to, and limped on at, Thebes."[1274]

Not just Senusret III, but all the pharaohs of the 12th dynasty sent underling pharaohs to the delta, Thebes, and Nubia to oversee food and other shipments and building projects. There may be some clues in the different scarab designs used for various areas and projects. Sobekhotep III wrote clearly on his stelae and seals that he was not a royal descendant; and Neferhotep I, Sihathor, Sobekhotep IV, and Sobekhotep V did the same.[1275] Those subordinate to the 12th dynasty pharaohs knew the real power was at Itjtawy. Ryholt agrees, ". . . the main capital in the Thirteenth Dynasty was still Itjtawy in the North, near the modern village of el-Lisht."[1276]

Sekhemkare Khutawy (Sobekhotep II) is first pharaoh of 13th dynasty in Nubia. I conjecture that Qemaw sent his son Hernejheryotef/Siharnedjheritef Hotepibre to the delta (then under Khety's rule of 9th dynasty) to oversee shipments to and from Thebes, and that is why a mace with Hotepibre was found in Ebla.

"This king had extensive connections with northern Syria. A sceptre in the shape of a ceremonial club with his name, found in a contemporary royal tomb called by the excavator the 'tomb of the Lord of the Goats' in Ebla, was most probably a diplomatic gift."[1277]

1270 Ryholt, K.S.B., *The Political Situation in Egypt during the Second Intermediate Period*, 1997, p. 318
1271 Ryholt, 1997 fn on page 214
1272 Ibid., pp. 80-82
1273 Manning, Sturt, *A Test of Time: The Volcano of Thera and the chronology and history of the Aegean and east Mediterranean in the mid second millennium B.C.*, Oxbow Books, 1999, p. 404
1274 Ibid., p. 405
1275 Ryholt, K.S.B., *The Political Situation in Egypt during the Second Intermediate Period*, CNI Publications 20, Museum Tusculanum Press, 1997, pp. 298-299
1276 Wikipedia in an article on Neferhotep I
1277 Bietak, Manfred, *Avaris* 1996, p.30 fn Matthiae 1980, 50-62; Scandone Matthiae 1979 and 1982

Queen Ini, wife of King Aya, and Nubian-Kerman Trade

King Aya's spouse was Queen Ini, who is attested by 21 scarab-seals (two of which were found in Kerma) datable to the 13th dynasty.[1278] Ryholt wrote, ". . . the number of seals would indicate that Queen Ini presided over a domain that required considerable administration and thus must have been of some considerable size. . . . an impression from a seal of Queen Ini was found in Nubia as far south as Kerma, the Kushite residence. The sealing was found in one of two shafts used as dumps, which contained about 800 sealings including several inscribed for contemporary kings of the Fourteenth Dynasty. No seals or sealings of Thirteenth Dynasty kings have been found at Kerma."[1279] Queen Ini may have been Nubian or Kushite, or had other ties which made her the best candidate to assume authority of Egypt's trade with the southern lands.

13th and 14th dynasty Sealings at Kerma

Reisner found 800 sealings in shafts (garbage pits) Z3 and Z4 in the Lower Defufa at Kerma. The bottom 50 cm of 400 cm shaft Z3 were untouched by fire where four sealings of Sheshi (1874-1821), one of Sekhaenre (Yakbimu, 1934-1894), and one of Queen Ini (spouse of king Aya of 13th dynasty, 1915-1891), were found. Shaft Z4 was untouched by fire, but the depth at which the one seal of Yaqub-Har was found was not given.[1280]

12th and 13th dynasty Sculptures at Kerma in Late SIP

"A group of sculptures of Twelfth and Thirteenth Dynasty date have been found in Late SIP contexts in Nubia, especially at Kerma."[1281] A statuette of Khahotepre Sobkhotep (VI) was found in tumulus X,[1282] so he must have ruled prior to the Kerma attack in 1795 BC. The 13th dynasty has many monuments in Elephantine. "There are some indications that the Kushites made raids on Elephantine during this period, and at least one, possibly conducted by the Kushite ruler buried in Tumulus X at Kerma, seems to have taken place during the late Thirteenth Dynasty."[1283]

13th and 14th dynasty cooperation in Trade

Ryholt wrote, "Archaeologically, it is clear that Tell-el-Dabᶜa, Tell Farasha, and Tell el-Naskhuta were part of the Fourteenth Dynasty because of the significant Canaanite cultural traits (MB II/a-b) at the settlements and necropolises of these sites contemporary with the Thirteenth Dynasty."[1284] Ryholt also wrote ". . . Fourteenth Dynasty officials were even buried within the Egyptians forts in Nubia, suggesting that they may have operated from these forts alongside officials of the Thirteenth Dynasty."[1285]

1278 Ryholt, 1997, pp. 234-5 and p. 38 fn 98
1279 Ryholt, K.S.B., *The Political Situation in Egypt during the Second Intermediate Period*, 1997, p. 235
1280 Ibid., pp. 113-114 with Clarity Chronology dates inserted
1281 Ibid., p. 141
1282 Ibid., p. 353
1283 Ibid., p. 77
1284 Ryholt, K.S.B., *The Political Situation in Egypt during the Second Intermediate Period*, 1997, p. 103
1285 Ibid., p. 112

Appendix B

13th and 14th dynasty Sealings in Uronarti fortress in Nubia

According to Ryholt, ". . . Sheshi, was contemporary with Djedkheperew of the early Thirteenth Dynasty."[1286] The Uronarti fortress divulged over 4,000 seals of Djedkheperew and Khabaw (both being their Horus names). In granary room #157, one sealing of Khabaw, seven sealings of Djedkheperew, and one sealing of (Maaibre) Sheshi were found together. "Being found in a contemporary context with their seal-impressions, it provides an invaluable synchronism between the Thirteenth and Fourteenth Dynasties. . . . It may be noted that all the royal impressions of the Thirteenth Dynasty contain the Horus-name of the kings in question, whereas that of Sheshi contains his prenomen."[1287] [A fragmentary sealing at the site has a clear "Canaanite Second Intermediate Period origin" of a formula used for early 18th dynasty kings.[1288]]

Djehuty

"One of Ibiaw's sons became the father-in-law of King Djehuty of the early Sixteenth Dynasty, and accordingly the family stretches over the final years of the Thirteenth Dynasty."[1289] A stela of Senebhanef, son of vizier Ibiau is dated to the reign of 13th dynasty king Ibiau. Senebhanef also became a vizier, and is attested on the coffin of his daughter Montuhotep who had married king Djehuty of the 14th (and 16th) dynasties.[1290] Queen Montuhotep's coffin has been dated to the 11th, 12th, 13th, 16th, and 17th dynasties;[1291] and, except for the 17th dynasty, I agree with all the rest.

Another synchronism is that of matching text on canopic chests of a 13th dynasty official named Sonbmijew/Senebmiu with king Djehuty.[1292] Montuhotep V has an early version of the Book of the Dead on his coffin, as does Queen Montuhotep, spouse of King Djehuty. "This suggests that King Monthhotep should be fixed chronologically close to Djehuty of the Sixteenth Dynasty."[1293]

12th-17th Dynasties

During Amenemhat III's 9th year is the only non-royal Nile level inscription by the Semna commandant.[1294] Sobekhotep VIII left a stela dated to his 4th year describing how he waded through the flood waters with the workmen at the temple in Karnak;[1295] and I propose this flood's inscription was lost and occurred during Amenemhat III's 13th year (1814 BC), which would have been the third year of Sobekhotep VIII (1817-1801 BC). Rahotep restored the Karnak temples after the floods from the 20th to the 32nd years of Amenemhat III.

1286 Ryholt, K.S.B., *The Political Situation in Egypt during the Second Intermediate Period*, 1997, pp. 75, and 198-199
1287 Ibid., p. 322
1288 Ben-Tor, Daphna, *Scarabs, Chronology, and Interconnections*, Academic Press Fribourg, 2007, p. 47
1289 Ryholt, p.77, fn 228
1290 Grajetzki, Wolfram, *Court Officials of the Egyptian Middle Kingdom*, London, 2009, p. 40
1291 Van Diik, Jacobus, "A Late Middle Kingdom Parallel for the incipit of Book of the Dead Chapter 22," *The Bulletin of the Australian Centre for Egyptology* 18 (2007), pp. 54–56
1292 Ryholt, p. 72, fn 213
1293 Ryholt, p. 237
1294 Reisner, G. A., "Ancient Egyptian Forts at Semna and Uronarti," *Bulletin of the Museum of Fine Arts*, Volume XXVII, Boston, October 1929, Number 163, p. 75
1295 Hibachi, 1974, p. 210

Pharaohs of the Bible

Tell el-Ajjul with Clarity Dates

City/Palace	date BC by	Canaanite Age	*Dyn.* Important Object
3/I	1940	MB II C (III)	14th, 6 meter deep fosse
2A/I	1840	Chariot horses in tomb	15th, Sheshi scarab (14th) and Neferhotep I (13th) and 16 dynasty scarabs
2/II	1764 *Montuhotep II	LB (Bronze) I	15th, Apepi scarab
1/III	1720 *Ahmose I	LB I	*early 18th*
1/IV	1670 <Thutmose III	LB II A	jar of Hatshepsut & Thutmose III
1/V	1473 <Rameses II	I (Iron) A	Rameses II

I place general Intef of Montuhotep II attacking City 2 of Tell el-Ajjul in 1765-1764 BC at the end of Montuhotep II's reign and the beginning of Apepi's.

"The 14th Dynasty seals from Tell el-Ajjul (Ryholt 1997:106 n.356) can be seen as dating from City 3 through to the construction of City 2 (Kempinski 1983:140-141). Kempinski in his 1983 book regarded king Sheshi of the 14th Dynasty as marking more or less the end of City 3 and Palace I (since a scarab of Sheshi was found in the construction fill of City 2). In his 1993 study (in Stern 1993:52-53) he allows Palace I to run on to the time of Khyan. Kempinski (1983:225) dates Sheshi and the close of City 3 c.1670/60BC, whereas Ryholt (1997:200) places Sheshi c.1745-1705BC. Either way, city 2 begins by, or in, the earlier 17th century BC. On the latest assessment, Palace II would commence around 1600BC. The latest scarab evidence from the City 2 destruction belongs to Apophis (Kempinski 1983:138), hence City 2 may be considered as ending about the close of his reign, or slightly later (sack of Ahmose)."[1296]

Fourteenth Dynasty

According to the Late Ramesside Letters (see Appendix C), priests were dispatched to Arjo (Yar), Ethiopia which is roughly 350 miles SE of Khartoum, Sudan. Kenya and the current Massai tribes are 400 miles further south. Based upon central east-African shield similarity to 14th dynasty seals and the fact that a fellow Nubian called other Nubian tribes A'amu (foreigners) and Ahmose Pen-Nekheb captured a Nubian among the Amu-Kehek; I deduce the Amu/A'amu/Ammu of the 14th dynasty were from tribes in Nubia or Kush, not Asia; and that Amenemhat I of the 12th dynasty called the first overseer 'Ammu.

Foreigners would only establish trade with those carrying seals with a name in a cartouche. Most of these 14th dynasty 'kings' worked under Sheshi around the Mediterranean and throughout Egypt and Nubia to oversee trade using Sheshi's seal. Sheshi's seals are found from Saqqara to Dongola, between the third and fourth cataract, in thirty cities along the Nile.[1297] Sheshi's queen was a Kushite queen. If Sheshi was also Kushite, maybe he sent some of his 'kings' to start the lineage of the "King's Son of Kush" as trading partners, while others with Semitic names were sent to Canaan.

1296 Manning, Sturt, *A Test of Time*, Oxbow Books, 1999, p. 184, footnote 899
1297 Ryholt, K.S.B., *The Political Situation in Egypt during the Second Intermediate Period*, 1997, CNI Publications 20, Museum Tusculanum Press, p. 107

Appendix B

Based upon Ward's scarab studies, "Four kings have been identified as predecessors of Sheshi through the seriation: Yakbimu, Ya'ammu, Qareh and 'Ammu."[1298] The Turin King List does not have room to list these names at the end of column seven, I think, because they were not considered real kings, and did not put their names in a cartouche. There is room for one name at VII/29 which I think would have been Sheshi. The 14th dynasty was primarily a non-Egyptian military protection force of Egyptian trade. "Neither Horus, Nebty, or Golden Falcon name is attested for any of the kings of the Fourteenth Dynasty . . ."[1299] None of them have monuments until Sheshi began to rule like a pharaoh. Though Ryholt stated, ". . . there is reason to believe that Yakbim might have founded the dissident Fourteenth Dynasty . . .,"[1300] he did not explain the reason. Since Yakbimu had three scarabs as a prince, I place Yakbimu as the son of 'Ammu. A king named y-k-b-'-r-b, who has two seals very similar to Yakbimu's,[1301] may have served as a representative during Yabkimu's reign.

Ryholt wrote, ". . . seals attested for the Fourteenth Dynasty [are] close to a thousand . . . ," and ". . . the use of private name seals was extremely limited, being restricted to the treasurer . . . The numerous seals attested for certain treasurers strongly suggest that these were used by an entire class of officials, just as those of the king."[1302] Ryholt added, "The five kings seem to have ruled altogether for about a century . . .,"[1303] though I think it was closer to 130 years. Ryholt made estimates of regnal length based upon number of seals, and then adjusted them upward as follows: 25 years for Yakbim, 10 years for Ya'ammu, 10 years for Qareh, 15 years for 'Ammu, and 40 years for Sheshi.[1304] For the first four kings, I estimate roughly ten years for thirty seals; but since that would give Sheshi a 130 year reign, I've given him about half that.

Seals	Years	Name	Reign BC
62	20y	(Ahotepre) 'Ammu	1954-1934
122	40y	(Sekhaenre) Yakbimu, 3 as prince	1934-1894
26	10y	(Nubwoserre) Ya'ammu	1894-1884
30	10y	(Khawoserre) Qareh	1884-1874
396	53y	(Maaibre) Sheshi	1874-1821
3 as king		(Asehre) Nehesy, 27 as prince	1821-1820

Fourteenth Dynasty in Turin King List

When looking at conventional chronologies, some dismiss the existence of a 14th dynasty, though the Turin King List does name Nehesy as its final king, and has space for one prior name, like Sheshi, who was the first to place his name in a cartouche. These were the only two 'pharaohs' of the dynasty, while the sixty following lines for names in the TKL were most likely trade emissaries who served from one to four years during the duration of this dynasty. Ryholt noted ". . . numerous Fourteenth Dynasty seals found abroad, most of which come from burials, may be taken as an

---

1298 Ibid., p. 49
1299 Ryholt, K.S.B., *The Political Situation in Egypt during the Second Intermediate Period*, 1997, p. 125
1300 Ibid., p. 251
1301 Ryholt, p. 102, footnote 340
1302 Ryholt, K.S.B., *The Political Situation in Egypt during the Second Intermediate Period*, 1997, p. 109
1303 Ryholt, K.S.B., *The Political Situation in Egypt during the Second Intermediate Period*, 1997, p. 299
1304 Ibid., pp. 199-200

Pharaohs of the Bible

indication of officials permanently stationed abroad to maintain trade routes for the crown."[1305] I agree and propose one of those TKL lost names below may have been found as Nebhotepenre on a scarab at Tel Kabri in Canaan beneath its MB IIA-B 'palace' structure.

TKL	Name	Reign
VII/29	lost [likely, (Maaibre) Sheshi]	
VIII/1	(Asehre) Nehesy	?, ?, 3 days
VIII/2	(Khatjere)	[a few months – Ryholt p.300]
VIII/3	(Nebfawtre)	1 year, 5 mo, 15 days
VIII/4	(Sehibre)	3 years, ? mo, 1 day
VIII/5	(Merdjefare)	3 years
VIII/6	(Sewadjkare)	1 year
VIII/7	(Nebdjafare)	1 year
VIII/8	(Webenre)	
VIII/9	lost	
VIII/10	(...djefawre)	4 years
VIII/11	(...webenre)	3 years
VIII/12	(Awtibre)	?, ?, 18 days
VIII/13	(Heribre)	?, ?, 29 days
VIII/14	(Nebsenre)	?, 5 mo , 20 days
VIII/15	(. . . re)	?, ?, 21 days
VIII/16	(Sekheperenre)	2 years
VIII/17	(Djedkherewre)	2 years, ?, 5 days
VIII/18	(Sankhibre)	?, ?, 19 days
VIII/19	(Kanefertem...re)	?, ?, 18 days
VIII/20	(Sekhem...re)	
VIII/21	(Kakemure)	
VIII/22	(Neferibre)	
VIII/23	(I...re)	
VIII/24	(Khatkare)	
VIII/25	(Aakare)	
VIII/26	(Semenenre) Hapu...	
VIII/27	(Djedkare)	
VIII/28	(...kare) Babmun/Bebenum	
VIII/29	(…......ptah)	
VIII/30	lost	
IX/1-6	lost	
IX/7	(Senefer...re)	
IX/8	(Men...re)	
IX/9	(Djed...re)	
IX/10-13	lost	
IX/14	(Inenk...)	
IX/15	('I-n...)	

[1305] Ryholt, K.S.B., *The Political Situation in Egypt during the Second Intermediate Period*, pp. 84-85

Appendix B

IX/16	('I-p...)		
IX/17	(Hab)		
IX/18	(Sa)		
IX/19	(Hepu)		
IX/20	(Shemsu)		
IX/21	(Meni)		
IX/22	(Werqa...)		
IX/23-24	lost		
IX/25	(...ka)		
IX/26	(...ka)	[Ryholt-10 years]	
IX/27	lost	[Ryholt-40 years]	
IX/28	(...ren) Hepu		
IX/29	(...ka) Nebnanatti		
IX/30	(...ka) Bebnem		
IX/31	lost	6 days?	

Ryholt adds unplaced 14th dynasty kings (to be put after Babnum): Nuya, Sheneh, Shenshek, Wazad, Yakerab, and prenomen Khamure.[1306] My thanks to Belgian Egyptologist Jacques Kinnaer who has put an enormous amount of information, especially the Turin King List, on the internet.[1307] Nehesy's son, Djehuty, is not recorded with the 14th dynasty because Salitis ran him out of Avaris, and Djehuty continued south and took over the 16th dynasty. Djehuty is recorded in TKL XI/1.

Tel Kabri

Tel Kabri is north of Haifa and Nahariya, and "is less than 5 km. From the Mediterranean coast . . ." providing ". . . easy access to the Mediterranean Sea for fishing and commerce."[1308] The following is based upon Kempinski's book, *Tel Kabri: The 1986-1993 Excavation Seasons*.[1309]

Stratum	Period	Area
1	Ottoman	E
2	LBA – Iron Age	E
3a-b	MB IIB	B, C, D
4	MB IIA	B, C, D
5	MB IIA	B, C
	MB I	cemetery
6	EB III	rampart -isolated sherds found in the rampart debris
7	EB II	B
8	EB II	B
9	EB Ib	B
10	EB Ia	B
11	EB Ia	B
12	Late Neolithic	B

1306 Ryholt, K.S.B., *The Political Situation in Egypt during the Second Intermediate Period*, 1997, p. 99
1307 Kinnaer, Jacques, "Turin Kinglist" at http://www.ancient-egypt.org/index.html
1308 Kempinski, Aharon, *Tel Kabri: The 1986-1993 Excavation Seasons,* Emery and Claire Yass Publications in Archaeology, Tel Aviv, 2002, p. 7
1309 Ibid., p. 5

Description of Tomb 1105 dug into stratum 12: "Mixed in with the dense layer of stones that covered the tomb were many sherds and flint tools of both EB IA and Late Neolithic periods."[1310] Strata 11 and 10: "The existence of floors with EB IA pottery in Strata 11 and 10 indicates that this phase covered a considerable period of time."[1311] Stratum 9; structure 1057, floor 992: "A seal impression with a human figure raising its arms standing next to a building was found on a storage jar sherd . . . The structures have been dated on the basis of the architectural, ceramic and lithic finds to the EB IB."[1312] "Stratum 8 structures . . . were built with a massive stone base; the walls . . . were faced with large chalk fieldstones . . . floors were made of lime plaster . . . ."[1313] Stratum 6 ? is based upon "isolated sherds found in the rampart debris," and the rampart is built on top of Tomb 503.[1314] Stratum 5 is the rampart?: "Tomb 503 is firmly dated to the early MB IIA, and was sealed by the rampart fill."[1315] But since EBIII sherds of stratum 6 were found in the rampart debris, it is strange that the cist grave of tomb 503 is "firmly dated to the early MB IIA" unless it is solely being dated by the pottery. Stratum 4 contained "a considerable amount of Cypriote ware . . ."[1316] and is called the pre-palace stratum.

"The two pre-palace (Stratum 4) floors exposed in Hall 611 were simple crushed chalk floors."[1317] Hall 611 was later painted with Minoan frescoes.[1318] "The structure that was uncovered in this area was in use for about 200 years, during which time its internal plan was modified."[1319] This Stratum 3 structure, which had a courtyard and an industrial section, also had infant jar burials beneath its floors in Tombs 504 and 420, and in Tomb 448 which had 3 scarabs dating within XIIIth – XVth dynasties which had been "tied to the forehead" of three infant skulls.[1320] Thus, I suggest the MBIIA-B period must be about 200 years, though in my generalized chart it only lasts 175 years. All three scarabs have signs of Egyptian royalty, though no cartouches, as during the 14th Dynasty. The names on these scarabs may be some of the missing names in columns VIII and IX of the TKL:

". . . nine hieroglyphs . . . *hpr*, a bar and an ^{c}*nh*. It is symmetrically flanked by . . .
dd, *nb*, and a probable *h3t*,"

"A *hpr* sign above a *h^c* sign is flanked by two *nfr* signs."

". . . the hieroglyphs *sw*, *m* and an angular sign . . .
generally thought to be the hieroglyph *ntr* . . ."[1321]

1310 Kempinski, Aharon, *Tel Kabri: The 1986-1993 Excavation Seasons,* Emery and Claire Yass Publications in Archaeology, Tel Aviv, 2002, p. 19 Though his chart shows a gap between strata 11 and 12, Tomb 1105 evidenced no gap.
1311 Ibid., p. 23, chapter written by Na^{c}ama Scheftelowitz. In Clarity time EB I lasted 120 years.
1312 Ibid., p. 25, chapter written by Na^{c}ama Scheftelowitz
1313 Ibid., p. 25, chapter written by Na^{c}ama Scheftelowitz
1314 Ibid., p. 49, Fig. 4.40 shows strata lines #2-4, #5 atop rampart, tomb 503 below, by Aharon Kempinski
1315 Kempinski, Aharon, *Tel Kabri: The 1986-1993 Excavation Seasons,* Emery and Claire Yass Publications in Archaeology, Tel Aviv, 2002, p. 39, chapter written by Aharon Kempinski
1316 Ibid., p. 49, chapter written by Aharon Kempinski
1317 Ibid., p. 68, Area C chapter written by Aharon Kempinski
1318 Ibid., pp. 254-298, chapter written by Barbara and Wolf-Deitrich Niemeier
1319 Ibid., p. 46
1320 Ibid., p. 47
1321 Kempinski, Aharon, *Tel Kabri: The 1986-1993 Excavation Seasons,* Emery and Claire Yass Publications in Archaeology, Tel Aviv, 2002, pp. 319-321, chapter by Yosef Mizrachy

Appendix B

These three scarabs were found in Area C at Tel Kabri. In Area B, Stratum 7, were MB pit graves Tomb 984 (over Structure 922) and Tomb 902 (under Structure 900). Tomb 902 held a minimum of 33 individuals and 10 scarabs were found: two contained the name *ykbmw*, one circular conoid depicted a lynx like an Asian caracal or African serval, and one scarab was set in a ring. The cartouche of the ring scarab is surrounded by 8 scrolls and a rope motif. The glyphs in the cartouche are *htp*, ͨ, *n*, *r*, ͨ, and *nb*.[1322] Possibly for the prenomen Nebhotepenre, another official of the 14th dynasty. Tomb 984 was masonry-built and had three burial phases spanning MBIIA-B according to the ceramics.[1323] It did not contain scarabs, but did have a unique Syrian cylinder seal which is dated to the first half of the 18th century BCE:[1324] Two griffins divided by interlocking swirls on right of cylinder seal facing a man in a long skirt who is holding a branch above an ankh symbol and looking toward two robed figures facing each other with bent arms touching each other and pointing toward a star (of Ishtar in typical Babylonian worship); and below the bent elbows is a 'walking tower' opposite the large ankh. All three humans are wearing masks over their eyes, and have feathers, like the griffins, instead of hair. Griffins and Ishtar worship were prevalent during Hatshepsut's reign.

TEL KABRI STRATUM ACCORDING TO CLARITY

Stratum	Period	Area	Objects	Dynasty
1	Ottoman	E	Ottoman pottery	
2	LBA – Iron Age	E	ash layer	18ff
3a	MB IIC	B, C, D	Minoan frescoes	6,9,11,15-17
3b	MB IIB	B, C, D	13th-15th scarabs	6, 9-16
4	MB IIA	B, C, D	pre-palace/fortress	4,5,9-10,12-14
5	MB IIA	B, C	rampart	4,5,A,9,12-14
6	MB IIA	rampart	sherds, Tomb 503	4,5,8,9,12-14
7	MB I	B	Structures 900+922	4,5,7,9,12,14
8	EB IV	B	lime plaster	3,7
9	EB III	B	spindle whorls	2
10	EB II	B	curved wall	2
11	EB I	B	infant jar burials	1
12	Late Neolithic	B	Tomb 1105	0

Because Yakbimu's scarabs were found in tombs of Stratum 7 structures (which I have placed during MB I), that would put his reign early in my cFIP. I think Amenemhat I placed Kushite warriors in Avaris as the 14th dynasty to oversee trade, and according to my dates on Tell el-Dabͨa's levels, Amenemhat I began building his temple/palace at Avaris at general phase N/2-3, soon after he came to power in 1954 BC. Kushites and Nubians continued at Avaris until Salitis kicked them out.

During the transition from the 14th to the 15th dynasties at Tell el-Dabͨa in Area A, Stratum E/2, Nubian scarabs and a similar Canaanite infant burial practice were found.[1325] "The burial of children

---

1322 Kempinski, Aharon, *Tel Kabri: The 1986-1993*, p. 333, Fig. 9.3:5, chapter by Yosef Mizrachy
1323 Ibid., pp. 32-33
1324 Ibid., p. 344 Fig. 9.12, chapter by Yosef Mizrachy
1325 Bietak, Manfred, *Avaris and Priamesse: Archaeological Exploration in the Eastern Nile Delta,* Oxford University Press, 1979-1986

under the age of two years was generally within the houses beneath the floor. They were placed in amphorae. Each amphora would have contained a single child."[1326]

Pre-15th Dynasty

The pre-15th dynasty representatives of Byblos in Memphis and the delta until 1820 BC:

TKL	Name
X/1	I . . .
X/2	Seth . . . (II)
X/3	Sunu . . .
X/4	Hor . . .
X/5-6	lost
X/7	Nib . . . (Nob . . .)
X/8	Mer?en?
X/9	(Penensetensepet)
X/10	Shepesu (Kheretheb)
X/11	(Khut . . . hemet)
X/12	lost
X/13	lost summation?

Fifteenth Dynasty

According to Ryholt, "Contemporary with the Fifteenth Dynasty, we may place the following events: (1) an overlap with the end of the Thirteenth Dynasty until the Fifteenth Dynasty conquest of its residence at Memphis, (2) the entire Sixteenth Dynasty, (3) the Fifteenth Dynasty conquest and subsequent occupation of Thebes, (4) the entire Seventeenth Dynasty, and finally (5) an overlap with the beginning of the Eighteenth Dynasty which lasted until Ahmose's conquest of Avaris."[1327] I agree with all his points except #3; my 15th dynasty never conquered nor occupied Thebes.

The 15th dynasty was an extension of the pre-15th dynasty from Byblos. The main 15th dynasty begins with Salitis in the Turin King List at X/14, but none of the names are complete until the final king, Khamudi, in X/20.

TKL	Name	Reign
X/14	lost [Salitis]	?, ?, 3 days
X/15	lost [Beon]	?, 8 mo, 3 days
X/16	lost [Sakir-Har]	
X/17	lost [Khayan]	40 years
X/18	lost [Apophis with other prenomen: Neb-Khepesh-Re, A-Qenen-Re, or A-User-Re?]	
X/19	lost [Apophis]	33 years [Rhind Mathematical Papyrus]
X/20	Khamudi	11 years [Rhind Mathematical Papyrus, at Heliopolis' capture]
X/21	summation of 6 Hyksos who ruled 108 years[1328]	

1326 Booth, Charlotte, *The Hyksos Period in Egypt,* Shire Publications Ltd, UK, 2005, p. 34
1327 Ryholt, K.S.B., *The Political Situation in Egypt during the Second Intermediate Period*, 1997, p. 188
1328 Gardiner, *Royal Canon*, p. 17 The 100 glyph is clear; others are not.

Appendix B

15th Dynasty Scarabs from Tell el-Ajjul (Sharuhen)

At Tell el-Ajjul, Horizon 6, scarab N95 was found. It has five glyphs in CBABC order with A = *w3d*, B = *nfr*, and C = ʿ-like sign. Similar scarabs were found at Tell el-Farah South, Tell el-Yahudiyeh, Esna, Qurta, and Aniba.[1329] At Horizon 7, scarab N98 was found. "The ureai have a branch-like inner pattern and the falcon in a fine net pattern. Such representations certainly do not occur before the 15th dynasty. At Tell el-Dabʿa they are not recorded until the 2nd half of the 15th dynasty. A similar is to be found at Tell el-Dabʿa in Str. D/3 . . . The back and the side view are identical. However, the three-figure composition stands on a crocodile in this case."[1330]

"The two scarabs, A00T10H6L191N95 and A00T4H7L210N98, although they are a bad chronological indicator for a certain phase, are dated to late Middle Bronze Age IIB–early Middle Bronze Age IIC according to Mlinar (Appendix to this report). Mlinar reports that this date is supported by the slender shape of the cowroid N95 (cf. also KEEL 1995: 78). She also reports that the falcon (or owl?) flanked by two snakes in scarab N98 is a representation which does not occur before the 15th Dynasty. The latter is restricted to the second half of the 15th Dynasty at Tell el-Dabʿa. Both scarabs were very likely made in southern Palestine. This claim is supported by the ungainly, angular signs of N95 which point to a seal cutter who is ignorant of hieroglyphic writing. N98 is an unusual large scarab (24.5 × 17.5 × 10 mm), which was very likely manufactured at Tell el-ʿAjjul itself: 10 out of 29 parallels with falcons/owls flanked by two snakes are from Tell el-ʿAjjul and were very likely made by the same seal cutter. Preliminary date: Middle Bronze Age IIC / Late Cypriote IA1 / Second Intermediate Period, late."[1331]

At Tell el-Ajjul in Tomb 198, scarab N97 was found. "The bee with the L-shaped crown can be rated as an exceptional piece. The L-shaped crown with other signs appears relatively frequently, namely 32 X. Its prevalence extends from Taanach to Nubia. No geographical concentration is traceable. At Tell el-Dabʿa it is recorded only once in Str. E/1 . . . and once in a secondary deposit. However, it is assumed that this type of representation of the crown was a creation of the Palestinian area and was prepared even earlier, perhaps as early as the end of the 13th Dynasty: e.g. in Tel Aviv, Rishon Lezziyon, Megiddo and Lachish and one piece from Tell el-ʿAjjul. In Nubia the majority of the L-shaped crowns occur in contexts from the 18th Dynasty."[1332]

Bietak found Nubian scarabs at Tell el-Dabʿa Stratum E/2. I suggest E/2 was when Salitis conquered Avaris and ended the 14th dynasty. So scarab N97 could have been one of the earliest 15th dynasty scarabs. Sharuhen became the port/fort of great importance to the 15th dynasty as one of their main suppliers, and the Canaanites even began producing scarabs in association with them. Formerly, Sharuhen/Tell el-Ajjul had been a major trading partner with the 14th dynasty. Ryholt wrote, "In Canaan, it may be noted that Tell el-Ajjul is the site where most seals of Fourteenth Dynasty kings and treasurers have been found (16 seals)."[1333]

1329 Fischer, Peter, *et al.*, "Tell El-Ajjul 2000 Second Season Preliminary Report," in *Egypt and the Levant XII*, 2002, pp. 145-146 scarab section by Christa Mlinar
1330 Ibid., p. 149
1331 Ibid., p. 134 (I underlined for clarity.)
1332 Ibid., p. 146 scarab section by Christa Mlinar
1333 Ryholt, K.S.B., *The Political Situation in Egypt during the Second Intermediate Period*, 1997, p. 115

End of the 15th Dynasty

Ryholt wrote, "No royal burials of the Fifteenth Dynasty are known . . ."[1334] and "On the Second Stela, Kamose refers to Apophis as a 'chieftain of Retjenu'. Retjenu is traditionally identified as an area covering Sinai and Canaan south of Lebanon."[1335] In his 22nd year Ahmose I placed oxen he acquired in Bashan of northern Canaan to work in Tura's quarry. This was after a 3-year siege of Sharuhen in southern Canaan; thus Ahmose must have conquered Avaris in his 18th or 19th year.[1336] I place the destruction of Avaris and the end of Khamudi's reign in 1720 BC which is the 18th year of Ahmose's reign beginning from a one year co-reign with his brother, Kamose in 1738 BC.

Synchronisms for 12th and 15th Dynasties through TeY Ware

"Early archaeologists linked the presence of the so-called 'Tell-el-Yahudieh' pottery (first found in Egypt and later discovered throughout the Levant) to the presence of the Hyksos. . . . it is possible to explain the distribution of the pottery as a result of commerce between Egypt and the Levant, . . . some examples of this ware have been found in Dynasty Twelve contexts at Buhen (in Nubia), el-Lisht, and tombs number one and two at Byblos (which are clearly datable to the reigns of the Dynasty Twelve kings Amenemhat III and Amenemhat IV)."[1337]

Sixteenth Dynasty

Just as the 15th dynasty had a pre-15th dynasty before a charismatic military leader arose, the same is true for the 16th dynasty. The pre-16th dynasty was comprised of five lost kings including Zeket..., Ar..., and ...nia... prior to Djehuty, and its summation is incomplete (X/30). I suggest the 13th dynasty established the pre-16th and 16th dynasties to shore up their southern boundary. Djehuty had the red crown of LE, where he ruled briefly, on an UE Edfu stela; and his queen Montuhotep, likely from Nubia, wore the white crown of UE. Neferhotep III is the "first" pharaoh depicted wearing the blue war (khepresh) crown.[1338] Neferhotep III and Montuhotepi (Mentuhotep VI) were only in control of Thebes.

The 16th dynasty specifically ruled El-Kab and Edfu. Two scarabs of Nebiriau I found in Lisht might show peaceful trade with the 12th dynasty during his reign. Nebiriau II has nothing but an axe with his name on it. Bebi-Ankh has a stela and a rock inscription. Montemsaf has one inscription at Edfu.

1334 Ryholt, K.S.B., *The Political Situation in Egypt during the Second Intermediate Period*, 1997, p. 138

1335 Ibid., p. 131

1336 Thomas Schneider, *The Relative Chronology of the Middle Kingdom and the Hyksos Period (Dyns. 12-17)* in Erik Hornung, Rolf Krauss & David Warburton (editors), Ancient Egyptian Chronology (Handbook of Oriental Studies), Brill: 2006, pp. 194-195

1337 Freed, John, "The Size of the Hyksos "Empire" (Part I)," posted on his blog on Friday, May 29, 2009. His footnote: "Enberg, R. "Hyksos Reconsidered", pp. 26-28. See also Hayes' comments in Scepter, vol. II, p. 12 where he agrees with the present author that Tell-el-Yahudieh ware does not indicate the presence of the Hyksos."

1338 Cairo stela 20799, also on Cairo stela JE59635

TKL	Name	Reign length
X/22	lost heading or name	
X/23	lost	
X/24	lost	
X/25	Zeket...	
X/26	Ar...	
X/29	...nia...	
X/30	incomplete summation	
XI/1	(Sekhem...re) Djehuty	3y
XI/2	(Sekhem...re) Sobekhotep VIII	16y; he has a year 4 stela.
XI/3	(Sekhemre) Neferhotep III	1y
XI/4	(Sankhenre) Montuhotepi	1y (also known as Montuhotep VI)
XI/5	(Sewadjenre) Nebiriau/Nebiryraw I	26y
XI/6	(Nebiretawe)	
XI/7	(Semenre) Nebiriau/Nebiryraw II	
XI/8	(Seuserre) Bebiankh	12y
XI/9	(Shekemre) Shedwaset	

The last readable name of the 16th dynasty is (Shekemre) Shedwaset at XI/9. This is followed by the five kings of the Thinite dynasty and the 16+ kings of the Abydos dynasty. There are no 17th dynasty king names on the TKL.

The TKL lists four rulers, after the listed end of the 16th dynasty, who were located at Edfu: (Djedankhre) Montemsaf, (Djedhotepre) Dudimose I, (Djedneferre) Dudimose II, and (Seneferibre) Senusret IV. Since they were not listed with the 16th dynasty, they may have considered themselves a separate Edfu dynasty, and could be considered a post-16th dynasty.

I suggest Nubkherre Intef VI alluded to the multiplicity of kings in Egypt when he wrote a decree against a traitor in Coptos that "as for any king or any ruler who shall be merciful to him, he shall not wear the white crown, he shall not wear the red crown . . ."[1339]

12th through 17th dynasties Synchronisms

According to Ryholt, outside of the Theban vicinity of the 16th dynasty, only royal seals of Nebiriau I have been discovered "at Lisht in the north and at Gennari, Faras and Mirgissa in Nubia." He continued, ". . . Lisht may still have played a political role during the early Fifteenth Dynasty." Ryholt concluded, that the archaeological context of Nebiriau I's Nubian seals ". . . may indicate the presence of permanently stationed officials in Nubia along the lines of officials during the Fourteenth Dynasty. . . . Besides the seals, a vessel inscribed for a Governor of El-Kab named Sobknakht has been found in Kerma Tumulus III dating to the Late SIP."[1340]

"Kitchen assumed that the 17th Dynasty either immediately followed the whole of the 13th Dynasty, or, alternatively, that it began during the 13th Dynasty, no earlier than Merneferre Ay, and perhaps after Dedumose II. He saw the start of the 17th Dynasty as effectively contemporary with the start of the 15th Dynasty in the Delta."[1341]

1339 Breasted, James, *Ancient Records of Egypt volume 1*, University of Chicago Press, 1906, p. 341
1340 Ryholt, K.S.B., *The Political Situation in Egypt during the Second Intermediate Period*, 1997, p. 162
1341 Manning, Sturt, *A Test of Time*, Oxbow Books, 1999, p. 409

Pharaohs of the Bible

My 17th dynasty began during the latter half of the 13th dynasty 100 years after Merneferre Aya, and continues on after Dedumose II of the 16th dynasty. My 16th dynasty ruled south of Thebes, primarily at El-Kab and Edfu in the second and third nomes.

> "However, Ryholt (1997) makes a strong case for the view that the 16th Dynasty was not some irrelevant regional grouping. Instead, Ryholt proposes that the 16th Dynasty ruled at Thebes following the end of the 13th Dynasty (a case could be made for an overlap), until a proposed conquest of Thebes by the Hyksos 15th Dynasty – the latter proposal however lacks evidence and is speculative/questionable. On this model, the 17th Dynasty is the post-conquest new dynasty at Thebes."[1342]

The average flood level during the reigns of 12th dynasty pharaohs Sobekneferu (1914-1910 BC) to the beginning of Amenemhat III (1827 BC) was 19 meters at the second cataract, which would have fully irrigated farm lands along the Nile. But between the 20th and 32nd years of the reign of Amenemhat III (1807 and 1795 BC), the Nile flood levels spiked close to 21 meters four times out of his six remaining records.[1343] Sobekhotep VIII of the 13th dynasty recorded the flooding of the Karnak temples. [In the 1840's, archaeologist Karl Lepsius noted the flood levels at the second cataract were nearly 12 meters above the low-water mark; he did not take into consideration that the western cliffs near the Semna fort had been undermined, allowing for greater breadth of the Nile to pass.[1344]] Rahotep (1761-1757 BC) restored the enclosure walls of the Karnak temple after the floods during Amenemhat III's reign. During the 17th dynasty there was a garrison of soldiers at Abydos "designated *i'wyt*, which was also the term to designate garrisons stationed in Nubia during the Twelfth and Thirteenth dynasties."[1345] This term alludes to these dynasties being contemporary.

Seventeenth Dynasty

My 17th dynasty was post-conquest of Montuhotep II and his death in 1761 BC. Montuhotep II reunited Upper and Middle Egypt, but Montuhotep III who succeeded him was not as strong. I conjecture that Rahotep ruled nome #3 of Hierakonopolis and El-Kab; and during the weak rule of Montuhotep III, Rahotep took over nomes #4-8 as well. At the beginning of the *Quarrel with Apophis*, Seqenre Tao is referred to as the nomarch/chieftain (*yar*) and king in the "Southern City",[1346] which Ryholt assumes to be Thebes,[1347] but I think refers to Denderah. Tao likely moved to Denderah, the pharaonic nome (#6) and built his palace there, since his son Ahmose dwelt there. According to Ryholt, "In a damaged passage of the Unwetterstele, it is said that Ahmose dwelled (*hms*) at *s df3-t3wy* in the neighbourhood of Dendera."[1348]

> "The main source that has been used to reconstruct the order of the other kings dating to the Seventeenth Dynasty is Pap. Abbott. . . . but it cannot be used to reconstruct the

---

1342 Manning, Sturt, *A Test of Time*, Oxbow Books, 1999, p. 410
1343 Rohl, David, *Pharaohs and Kings: A Biblical Quest*, 1995, pp. 335-340
1344 Reisner, G. A., "Ancient Egyptian Forts at Semna and Uronarti," *Bulletin of the Museum of Fine Arts*, Volume XXVII, Boston, October 1929, Number 163, p. 68
1345 Ibid., p. 171
1346 Ryholt, K.S.B., *The Political Situation in Egypt during the Second Intermediate Period*, 1997, p. 176
1347 Ibid., p. 176
1348 Ryholt, *The Political Situation in Egypt during the Second Intermediate Period*, 1997, p. 174, fn 625

order of kings within the Seventeenth Dynasty . . ."[1349] - Ryholt

I am following Ryholt's order, but I've placed the Antef/Intef kings serving under Sobekemsaf I (possibly simultaneously) instead of having their own unique reigns.

Clarity 17th Dynasty began during the end of my cSIP
1761-1757 (Sekhenre Wahkhaw) Rahotep
1757-1754 (Sekhemre Shedtawy) Sobekemsaf I
        2y during father's reign (Sekhemre Wepmaat) Intef V
        5y began in father's reign (Nubkheperre) Intef VI
        1y (Sekhemre Herhermaat) Intef VII
1754-1747 (Sekhemre Wadjkhaw) Sobekemsaf II
1747-1746 (Senakhtenre) Ahmose [formerly Tao I]
1746-1742 (Seqenenre) Tao [formerly Tao II]
1742-1738 (Wadjkheperre) Kamose

Sobekemsaf II had a rock inscription of his quarrying activity at Gebel Zeit which named Minemhet as the governor of Koptos, whom Intef VII also named in his Koptos decree.[1350] He also has statues in Karnak and Abydos.

During the 17th dynasty the Egyptians recognized they were sandwiched between the Nubians south of Elephantine, and the Asiatics in the delta. Senakhtenre Ahmose, the elder, maintained nomes #1-8, but he lost his campaign against the Hyksos. Kamose has a stela and rock inscriptions in Nubia, and recruited Nubian soldiers in his attack against the Hyksos. "According to the Second Stela of Kamose, at the start of his reign the Seventeenth Dynasty comprised the territory from Elephantine in the south to Cusae in the north."[1351] Cusae (#14 nome) is roughly thirty miles north of Asyut (#13 nome). By the end of the 17th dynasty, they had secured the four southernmost nomes of the territory of the old Herakleopolitan dynasty. The Second Stela of Kamose goes on to state the Cynolpolite nome #17 is in his possession in his third regnal year, and that Apophis was encamped at Atfih in nome #21. Thus Kamose had conquered and plundered territories previously controlled by the king at Avaris, but not Avaris itself.

Early Eighteenth Dynasty
1738-1712   Ahmose I, reunited Egypt in 1720
1712-1702   Amenhotep I with Ahmose-Nefetari, mother-regent
1702-1688   Amenhotep I

Ahmose I campaigned in Nubia, and extended the boundaries of Egypt to the Second Cataract. He left a commander in charge at Buhen. After the first campaign of Ahmose I in Nubia, a Nubian named Aata rebelled but was defeated. Then Tetian, an anti-Theban Egyptian, gathered rebels in Nubia, and was also defeated. Ahmose restored Egyptian rule over Nubia from a new administrative center established at Buhen. Yet his son would also have to fight against the Nubian Bowmen.

1349 Ryholt, K.S.B., *The Political Situation in Egypt during the Second Intermediate Period*, 1997, p. 169
1350 Ibid., p. 174
1351 Ryholt, K., *The Political Situation in Egypt during the Second Intermediate Period*, 1997, pp. 171-172

Pharaohs of the Bible

After the death of his mother, Amenhotep I decided to expand Egypt's borders further into Nubia and Kush. He raided it for gold, cattle, and people. I assume Egypt's southern border was at Buhen prior to Amenhotep's first campaign.

> "Then I conveyed King Djeserkare, the justified, when he sailed south to Kush, to enlarge the borders of Egypt. His majesty smote that Nubian Bowmen in the midst of his army. They were carried off in fetters, none missing, the fleeing destroyed as if they had never been. . . . Then his people and his cattle were pursued, and I carried off a living captive and presented him to his majesty. I brought his majesty back to Egypt in two days from 'Upper Well,' and was rewarded with gold."
> - tomb inscription of Amasis/Ahmose, son of Baba

"In antiquity, the average speed sailing up-river was between 40 and 70 kms per day."[1352] So if Amenhotep I was travelling down-river from Nubia towards Egypt, he might be able to travel 100 kms per day. 'Upper Well' was *iteru* + sky,[1353] possibly alluding to 'head waters' or the primary city of Kerma near the third cataract. It's about 200 kms from Kerma to Buhen at the second cataract. Thus in two days they could have arrived at Buhen. During the rebellion near Buhen, general Ahmose Pen-Nekheb ". . . captured a Nubian alive. When the king returned to the north he engaged in a fierce conflict with some people called Amu-kehek, or Amu-neb-hek."[1354] This may have been people near 'Abka, Sudan on the opposite side of the Nile from Wadi Haifa.

First Half of Eighteenth Dynasty

1688-1674	Thutmose I, 14 years (Manetho is 12y 9m, but latest monument is 9y)
1674-1672	Thutmose II, 2y (only 1st year is attested) (Hatshepsut counts regnal years)
	Thutmose III possibly born in 1675 BC, and declared successor in 1672 BC.
1672-1651	Hatshepsut (with Thutmose III), 21y total, (Manetho gives 21y 9m, but only 7y attested in Senemut's tomb)
1651-1618	Thutmose III (last 4 as co-reign), 54 total, his last campaign in 50th year (1622 BC) when he declares Amenhotep II as his successor before going to war.
1622-1596	Amenhotep II (first 4 as co-reign)

I calculate the 54 year reign of Thutmose III from 1672 BC when he was designated heir apparent as a toddler; thus he spent his childhood under Hatshepsut's reign.

> ". . . Hatshepsut celebrated her jubilee in her year 16 as 30 years from the death of her father, Tuthmosis I, and thus 30 years after she became 'heiress', seems the most plausible construction of the evidence . . ."[1355] [But there's a better one.]

1352 http://www.reshafim.org.il/ad/egypt/timelines/topics/means_of_transportation.htm#rem12

1353 Budge, Sir Ernest A. W., *The Egyptian Sudan: its history and monuments,* volume 1, J. B. Lippincott Company, Philadelphia, 1907, p. 565

1354 Ibid., p. 565 continues - "The Amu-kehek were vanquished, and, as we know that Amehhotep I conquered a number of Asiatic foes, we may ASSUME that they were among them." Hence all Amu became Asiatics.

1355 Manning, Sturt, *A Test of Time: The Volcano of Thera and the chronology and history of the Aegean and east Mediterranean in the mid second millennium B.C.*, Oxbow Books, 1999, p. 400

Appendix B

Counting Hatshepsut's regnal years from 1674 BC makes 1658 her 16th year, which would be the 30th year from the beginning of her father's reign. She may have felt she helped her father greatly, possibly with aiding Ineni in his great building projects at Karnak. She specifically dedicated her great obelisk to her father. She also dedicated to Khnum a red granite statue of Thutmose II wearing a Sed festival robe and white crown for her brother in honor of her father.

Hatshepsut's Thera Bo Eruption and Other Eruptions

In 1987 Manfred Bietak wrote, ". . . the more recent high chronology for the Santorini (Thera) explosion at about 1628 BC, based on radiocarbon and dendrochronology . . ."[1356] In 2003, Bietak wrote, ". . . the results obtained for the excavated samples agree with the present dating range of the Minoan eruption between 1650 and 1450 B.C." The later date was being supported by ash in Greenland ice cores. But in November, 2003, new data attributed the Greenland ice core volcanic eruption of 1645 +/- 7 BC to an Alaskan eruption.[1357] Though there is some validity to ice core dates, scientists believe "the seasonal character of the dating parameters have only changed little over the past 10,000 years."[1358] 1645 + 6 = 1651 BC, my date for the Thera Bo eruption.

"Neutron Activation Analysis . . . indicate that the pumice originated from the explosion of the volcano of Santorini. Its chronological context at Tell el-Dab^{c}a within a single restricted stratum of the New Kingdom dates it to sometime after the reign of Ahmose and before that of Thutmose III."[1359] {Clarity Chronology between 1712-1618 BC} Thus, an eruption occurred during the reign of Hatshepsut; and I place that eruption in 1651 BC.

Evolutionary scientists date Thera's Lower Pumice at Cape Thera (CT/Bu) to 200,000 BC, Middle Pumice II (BmII) to 100,000 BC, Middle Pumice I (BmI) to 21,000 BC, and the Minoan eruption Upper Pumice (Bo) to about 1600 BC.[1360] Since then, scientists reported Thera had only one other eruption in 197 BC, and nine more afterwards up to 1950 A.D..

Clarity Chronology of Thera's Eruptions
Lower Pumice (Bu) – likely at end of Noah's flood
Middle Pumice II (BmII) – during an early dynasty
Middle Pumice I (BmI) – during an early dynasty
Upper Pumice (Bo) – 1651 BC which ended Hatshepsut's reign

In "The Preliminary Chronology of Tell el-Ajjul," with eight Horizons from stratum H8-H1, Peter Fischer described numerous samples of pumice found in levels H1-H5, but found none in older H6-H8.[1361] Forty-eight samples of pumice from Tell el-Ajjul were analyzed by NAA; half of which

---

1356 Bietak, Manfred, *Avaris, The Capital of the Hyksos: Recent Excavations at Tell el Dab^{c}a*, British Museum Press, London, 1996, p. 76 based on Warren 1987; Warren and Hankey 1989, pp. 140-141
1357 Keenan, Douglas J., "Volcanic ash retrieved from the GRIP ice core is not from Thera," *Geochemistry G3 Volume 4, Number 11*, November 2003, pp. 1-8
1358 Hammer, C.U., and Clausen, H.B., "Thera and the Aegean World III," *Proceedings of the Third International Congress, Santorini, Greece, Volume Three: Chronology,* September 1989, pp. 174-178
1359 Bietak, Manfred, *Avaris, The Capital of the Hyksos: Recent Excavations at Tell el Dab^{c}a*, British Museum Press, London, 1996, p. 78
1360 Francaviglia, V. and Sabatino, B. Di., *Thera and the Aegean World III*, 1989, pp. 29-52
1361 Fischer, Peter M., "The Preliminary Chronology of Tell el-Ajjul: Results of the Renewed Excavations in 1999 and 2000," *The Synchronisation of Civilisations in the Eastern Mediterranean in the Second Millennium B.C. II*, Osterreichische Akademie der Wissenschaften Wien, 2003, pp. 263 and 266

came from level H5. "Forty-five, or more than 95%, of all pumice samples come from the 'Minoan' eruption of Thera which corresponds to Upper pumice (Bo). Two samples can clearly be related to the Caldera Pumice eruptions on the Aegean island of **Nisyros** (maximum 24 ky B.P.: Limburg and Vaekamp 1991). One sample comes from the 'Preminoan' eruption of Thera which represent the result of an earlier eruption sequence deposited between 100 to 203 ky B.P. (Druitt *et al.* 1999)."[1362] {ky = thousand years and B.P. = Before Present}

Eruptions from Nisyros: http://www.volcanodiscovery.com/volcanoes/greece/nisyros.html

1881-1887 - hydrothermic explosions of the crater "Micros Polyvotis"
1500 - hydrothermic explosions
1000-2000 B.C. - hydrothermic explosions of the crater "Stefanos"
5000-10,000 B.C. - hydrothermic eruptions of the Kaminakia craters
15,000-10,000 B.C. - building of postcalderic volcano domes
15,000 B.C. - effusive eruption of the central caldera of Nisyros ("Upper pumice")
25,000 B.C. - effusive eruption of the central caldera of Nisyros ("Lower pumice")

40,000-30,000 B.C. - effusive eruption ("Kira-Formation")
150,000 B.C. - first submarine eruptions

I would place the oldest volcanic eruptions at Noah's flood and the Upper caldera eruptions of Nisyros during the ensuing 100 years. The Nisyros pumice was found at Tell el-Ajjul Level H2, which Fischer determined to be mid-18th Dynasty[1363] (stating that Tell el-Hebwa's placement between the reigns of Thutmose IV to Amenhotep III was too low).[1364] Fisher found no pumice in H6-H8 which he places in the Middle Bronze Age.

Santorini/Thera Ancient Eruption History
(Data is from http://www.decadevolcano.net/santorini/eruptionsummary.htm)
[ky = 1,000 years B.C.]
2,000 – 600 ky Eruption of early submarine centres of Akrotiri
528 ky   Construction of Peristeria 1 core complex
496 ky   Extrusion of domes and flows of Peristeria 2
480-308 ky   Eruption of lavas of Peristeria 3
299 ky   Extrusion of the andesites of Cape Alai
                             Cape Therma 1 eruption
                             Cape Therma 2 eruption
257 ky   Extrusion of rhyodacites of Cape Alonaki + NE Thera
                             Cape Therma 3 eruption
203 ky   Lower Pumice 1 eruption
180 ky   Lower Pumice 2 eruption
170-60 ky   Cape Thera eruption
60 ky   Middle Pumice eruption

1362 Ibid, pp. 267-270
1363 Fischer, Ibid., p. 289 chart
1364 Fischer, Ibid., pp. 270 and 287

Appendix B

60-50 ky	Vourvoulos eruption
60-40 ky	Upper Scoriae 1 eruption
40 ky	Upper Scoriae 2 eruption
21 ky	**Cape Riva eruption**
6-3 ky	Minoan eruption (updated to 1640 BC)

Fischer found **Cape Riva** eruption pumice in tomb L205 at Tell el-Ajjul which spans the 15th - 18th dynasties. {Clarity chronology approx. 1800-1500 BC} Fischer's 48 pumice samples were a part of the "Thera Ashes" study which did not differentiate between preMinoan and Minoan eruptions of Santorini/Thera. An olive tree on Santorini was buried alive in the upright position by tephra deposits. In 2006 Friedrick "wiggle-matched the Carbon 14 dates of the tree rings" and determined the olive tree was 1627-1600 BC when it died.[1365] Friedrick's Carbon 14 dating "wiggle-match" is wrong as shown by Manning.[1366]

Each eruption from each volcano has a unique chemical fingerprint which scientists add up to equal 100% of the tephra examined, with most of the tephra metals hovering around 1% of the total. According to the 2003 "Thera Ashes" study:

> "The use of the term tephra layer should be restricted to strata consisting predominately of tephra (>50%). In Cypriote soil samples only a disperse tephra content was detected. In samples from Ebla and Megiddo no particles were found. The Turkish drill cores (Ova Golu, Amuq and Golbasi) showed no tephra content. The sample from Delfinos/Crete contained a substantial layer of coarse Minoan ash. . . . One sample from Tell el-Dabᶜa could not be related to an Aegean volcanic source."[1367]

> "Our database comprises presently 3 eruption cycles at Milos, 6 at Santorini, 2 at Nisyros, 2 at Giali and 1 at Kos (all Greece). Additionally, there are also included 6 of the biggest Kappadokian eruptions in Turkey."[1368] - Max Bichler

Page 13 of "Thera Ashes" displays graphs with shaded areas of the "natural variation range of the original deposits" for eruptions from four different Aegean volcanoes. Of the four, the shaded area of Santorini Bo remains closest to 1% for all chemicals; whereas Nisyros caldera pumice contains more Calcium, Barium, and Tantalum; Giali main pumice contained more Potassium, Rubidium, Anitmony, Calcium, Barium, and Tantalum; and Kos plateau tuff pumice contained more Potassium, Manganese, Rubidium, and Tantalum. Santorini/Thera and Nisyros also share a high amount of Chromium and Arsenic, so they are quite difficult to tell apart; though Nisyros tends to

---

1365 Bruins, H, et al., "The Minoan Santorini Eruption and Tsunami Deposits in Palaikastro (Crete): Dating by Geology, Archaeology, C14, and Egyptian Chronology," *Radiocarbon*, vol 51, No 2, 2009, p. 408

1366 Manning, Sturt, "No Systematic Early Bias to Mediterranean 14C Ages: Radiocarbon Measurements from Tree-ring and Air Samples Provide Tight Limits to Age Offsets", *Radiocarbon*, Vol 44, Nr 3, 2002, pp. 739–754 by the Arizona Board of Regents on behalf of the University of Arizona

1367 Max Bichler, Martin Exler, Claudia Peltz and Susanne Saminger; "Thera Ashes," *The Synchronisation of Civilisations in the Eastern Mediterranean in the Second Millennium B.C. II,* Österreichische Akademie der Wissenschaften Wien, 2003, p. 12

1368 Personal correspondence http://baheyeldin.com/science/pumice-on-mediterranean-coast.html

have higher Arsenic levels than Thera.[1369] Fischer noted, ". . . the distinction of other, chemically rather similar eruption products of other volcanic sources such as Kos, Gyali, Nisyros and Milos (i.e. the southern Hellenic volcanic island are) has been demonstrated in earlier studies (e.g. Pelts *et al.* 1999; Bichler *et al.*)."[1370]

During the Bichler study of the various B.C. Thera/Santorini eruptions, the chemical fingerprints were so close, they had to graph the ratios of five elements to help them make a distinction between the eruptions.

> "Usually pumices can be assigned to their source volcano by the 25 element distribution pattern. In very tricky cases – the distinction of compositionally highly similar eruptions of one volcano – it was found to be helpful to plot the ratios of some elements. A typical example are the preminoan rhyolithic eruption cycles of Santorini. Figure 5 shows the ratios of the elements Eu, Ta, Th, Ba and Hf found in pumice produced by the Lower Pumice eruptions Bu1 and Bu2 (ca 200ky), the Middle Pumice Tuff Bm (ca 100ky), the Cape Riva Tuff (ca 21ky) and the Minoan eruption (ca 3,6ky)."[1371] {I did not copy Figure 5.}

> "From the beginning of excavations in 1967, the Greek archaeologist Spiridon Marinatos noted that the city had undergone a first destruction, due to an earthquake, before the eruption, as some of the buried objects were ruins, whereas a volcano alone may have left them intact. At almost the same time, the site of Aghia Irini on Kea was also destroyed by an earthquake. One thing is certain: after the eruption, Minoan imports stopped coming into Aghia Irini (VIII), to be replaced by Mycenaean imports." -Wikipedia

On a volcanic signal chart based upon ice-cores, there were 6 eruptions greater than Krakatoa between 1700-1450 BC, and 3 more grouped together around 1427 BC.[1372] I think the group of three caused Rameses III trouble with the Sea Peoples seeking new homelands, but it was in 1310 BC.

> "The Canaanite jar from Thera (Fig. 2) is very similar to the MB IIB jars from Kabri tomb 498 (Fig. 1). Other parallels for the Thera example come from the MB IIB layers XI and X at Megiddo (Loud 1948, Pl. 35 no. 2, 42 no. 4, 43 no. 1; Kempinski 1983, Pl. 9 no. T 143) and the MB II stratum 3 of Hazor Area C (Yadin *et al.* 1960, 89-90, Pl. CXIV, 1-6)."[1373] {I did not copy Fig. 1 or Fig. 2.}

1369 Bichler, Max, *et al.*, "Thera Ashes," *The Synchronisation of Civilisations in the Eastern Mediterranean in the Second Millennium B.C. II,* Osterreichische Akademie der Wissenschaften Wien, 2003, p. 18
1370 Fischer, Peter M., "The Preliminary Chronology of Tell el-Ajjul: Results of the Renewed Excavations in 1999 and 2000," *The Synchronisation of Civilisations in the Eastern Mediterranean in the Second Millennium B.C. II,* Osterreichische Akademie der Wissenschaften Wien, 2003, p. 267
1371 Bichler, M., *et al.*, "NAA-applications in cosmology, archaeology and palaeontology" on internet
1372 Manning, Sturt, *A Test of Time: The Volcano of Thera and the chronology and history of the Aegean and east Mediterranean in the mid second millennium B.C.*, Oxbow Books, 1999, p. 277. 5 of the 6 possibly accounted for on p. 282: "Avellino in Italy, Aniakchak II in Alaska, the Mount St. Helens Yn tephra eruption in western USA, Avachinsky in Kamchatka, and the Nissyros volcano (Yiali) in the Aegean"
1373 Niemeier, W.D., "Thera and the Aegean World III" Volume Three: Chronology" *Proceedings of the Third International Congress*, Santorini, Greece, 3-9 September 1989, pp. 120-126

Appendix B

Tomb 498 was a large well-made tomb holding at least 23 individuals, hundreds of Middle Bronze containers, and 14 scarabs from the 13th - 15th dynasties.[1374]

Second half Eighteenth Dynasty

1596-1588   Thutmose IV
1588-1550   Amenhotep III (co-reign 1 year)
1551-1534   Amenhotep IV/Akhenaten
1534-1531   Smenkhkare (3 years of olive oil from Ahkhkheprure from Armana)
1531-1530   Nefertiti/Neferneferuaten
1534-1524   Tutankhamun (usurped years after Akhenaten, and is first attested in year 4)
1524-1520   Ay
1520-1493   Horemheb (or possibly not until 1492)

Thutmose IV

Hatshepsut began a tradition of celebrating a heb-sed festival for a father who did not survive to his 30th year of rule. Thutmose IV commemorated what would have been the jubilee of his father, Amenhotep II, four years after his father's death by wearing a gold shebiru in remembrance of him.

Horemheb

The inscription of Mes which gives Horemheb a reign of 58-59 years was an attempt to eliminate Akhenaten's heresy by starting Horemheb's reign at the beginning of Akhenaten's. The transition from Horemheb's capital to Rameses' I new capital in Pi-Rameses in the Nile Delta may have taken a little longer than normal succession.

Horemheb appointed Rameses I as his successor sometime in 1493 BC, so there may be a few months of co-reign. Rameses I has a Year 2 II Peret day 20 (Louvre C57) stela which ordered provisions for the Temple of Ptah within the fortress of Buhen, so he reigned at least 17 months using I Akhet 1 as the civil new year for counting regnal years.

Nineteenth Dynasty

Here is a quote from a 4th century astronomer named Theon:
> "On the 100th year of the era of Diocletian, concerning the rising of the Dog, because of the pattern we received from the era of Menophres to the end of the age of Augustus the total of the elapsed years was 1605."

If Augustus refers to the first emperor Caesar Augustus who reigned from 27 BC to 14 AD; then 1605 – 14 = 1591, and if we subtract 100, we arrive at 1491, the date of the exodus. But that's a lot of 'ifs'. Much has been written about Egyptian astronomy and the rising of Sothis/Sirius, the 'dog star'. Egypt's "fixed dates" of the ascensions of Thuthmose III in 1479 BC and Rameses II in 1279 BC are just wrong. After reviewing the dearth of Egyptian papyri and inscriptions, Otto Neugebauer wrote, "Egypt has no place in a work on the history of mathematical astronomy."[1375]

1374 Kempinski, Aharon, *Tel Kabri: The 1986-1993 Excavation Seasons*, Tel Aviv, 2002, pp. 52, 321-330
1375 Neugebauer, Otto, *The Exact Sciences in Antiquity*, New York, Dover Publishers, 1969

Pharaohs of the Bible

Canals of Seti I

Ameneman wrote the following letter regarding the life of the Egyptian peasant farmer.
". . . Next the unfortunate wretch is seized, bound, and carried off by force to work on the **canals**; his wife is bound, his children are stripped. . . ."[1376]

To gain access from the Nile to the Red Sea, an east-west canal from the Pelusiac branch to Lake Timsah was constructed along the natural Wadi Tumilat, possibly by Senusret II.[1377] Though Lake Timsah may have naturally connected to the Bitter Lakes to the south and unto the Gulf of Suez in the past, by this time it too needed canals. To the north of Lake Timsah was Lake Ballah and its wetlands which offered a short connection to the Mediterranean Sea.

"French cartographers discovered the remnants of an ancient north-south canal running past the east side of Lake Timsah and ending near the north end of the Great Bitter Lake in the second half of the 19th century."[1378]

At Karnak, Seti I recorded his first campaign in three reliefs. The central one depicts victorious Seti returning with captives passed fortresses. Al-Ayedi noted,

"They are shown about to enter Egypt across a water-way or a canal, running north-south, whose water is infested with **crocodiles** and its banks lined by reeds and swamps, characterizing a fresh-water environment. The accompanying text refers to it as *T3-dnit*, 'the dividing canal' or 'the **canal**'. The reeds continue to the border of the reliefs, into another body of water which has a barren shore and contains marine species. This body of water represents the salt water of the Mediterranean. One of the depicted Egyptian-style fortresses straddles a bridge over the water-way, while a smaller one guards the road to the east. The bridge fortress is named 'the fortress of Tharu'. The other one, guarding the road, is named *t3 'tp3m3i*, 'the dwelling of the lion', which was reachable by boat from the fortress 'Tharu'."[1379]

1376 Lenormant, Francois, *A manual of the ancient history of the East to the commencement of the Median wars*, Lippincott, 1871, p. 258
1377 Wikipedia article on the Suez Canal
1378 Carte hydrographique de l'Basse Egypte et d'une partie de l'Isthme de Suez (1855, 1882). Volume 87, Paris, p. 803
1379 Al-Ayedi, Abdul Rahman, "Tharu: The Starting Point on the 'Ways of Horus'," his thesis, 2000, p. 23-24

It could be that the north-south canal was marginally functional when Seti I began his reign, but that the east-west canal desperately needed some dredging before he could use it to salvage the chariots from the Gulf of Aqaba. Tharu was likely the fortress at Tell Hebua I.[1380] Between Tell Hebua I and II is a depression which once held water, and contained a crocodile skeleton.[1381] The 'dwelling of the lion' was not likely the 'mansion of the lion' built by Amenemhat III at Tell el-Borg, but Tell Hebua II built upon the Hyksos' ruins.[1382]

High Priest Bakenkhonsu I

1504	born
1491-1480	under Seti I (11y from age 13)
1488-1484	Amun wab priest (4y)
1484-1472	prophet of Amun (12y)
1472-1457	3rd prophet of Amun
1457-1441	2nd prophet of Amun
1441-1414	1st prophet of Amun (27y)
1414 (age 90)	died in last year of Rameses II

Campaigns of Rameses II (1480-1414 BC)

1478	Sherden sea pirates captured in Nile delta
1476	took Amurru (Djahi), and left 3 stelae between Beirut and Byblos; Shabtuna
1475	lost battle of Qadesh, so Hittites infiltrated Canaan and Syria
1473	retook Syria, attacked Jerusalem and Jericho; and took Moab and Edom, and Heshbon, Damascus, Kumidi, and Upi
1472	took Ashkelon, Beth-Anath, Salem, Merom and Acre; took Depur and Tunip
1471	BethShean
1458	quelled Nubia

Cities taken by Rameses II according to other monuments and annals: Altaku, Apheq?, Arrapkha?, Arzawa, Assyria?, Geba, Hamath, Isy, Jacob-El, Keftiu?, Kiriath-Anab, Lullu, Migdol?, Papkhi, Pella, Rosh-Kadesh, Shankhar, Takhshi, Tyre?, Ullaza, Uzu, and Yanoam.

Many people theorize that the *Admonitions of Ipuwer* concern the aftermath of the exodus. The copy of the papyrus was made during the New Kingdom, but it may hearken back to another time.

Selections of "Admonitions of Ipuwer" with {my annotations}

I

The bird [catchers] have drawn up in line of battle [. . . the inhabitants] of the Delta carry shields. Confusion [. . .] another. Come and conquer; {Delta is under attack?}

the tribes of the desert have become Egyptians everywhere {in order to get food}

the land is full of confederates, and a man goes to plough with his shield. {Food needs protection.}

1380 Sharp, Alastair, "Sinai fort may hold clues to ancient Egypt defenses", May 7, 2009; http://www.reuters.com/article/idUSTRE5465N120090507 accessed 8/17/10
1381 Al-Ayedi, Abdul Rahman, "Tharu: The Starting Point on the 'Ways of Horus'," his thesis, 2000, p. 95
1382 Ibid., p. 163

Indeed, the Nile overflows, yet none plough for it. {It wasn't initially caused by a drought.}
Indeed, the women are barren and none conceive. {Malnutrition stops menses.}

II
Indeed, [hearts] are violent, {Lack of food causes riots of desperation.}
pestilence is throughout the land, {Disease follows malnutrition;}
blood is everywhere, death is not lacking, {followed by mass deaths,}
Indeed, many dead are buried in the river; the stream is a sepulcher {no strength to bury}
Indeed, the river is blood, yet men drink of it. Men shrink from human beings and thirst after water. {After fouling the Nile with diseased bodies, the water is not potable.}
Squalor is throughout the land, and there are none indeed whose clothes are white in these times.
      {Clean water is needed for clean clothes.}
Every town says: "Let us suppress the powerful among us."
      {Nobles were unable to keep food production stable. Lack of food makes everyone equal.}
Indeed, gates, columns and walls are burnt up, while the hall of the palace stands firm and endures. Indeed, the ship of [the southerners] has broken up; towns are destroyed and Upper Egypt has become an empty waste. {Upper Egypt is abandoned as people head to Saqqara food fortress.}

III
Indeed, the desert is throughout the land, {The famine included drought.}
barbarians (foreign bowmen) from abroad have come to Egypt. {Foreigners come for food}
Indeed, men arrive [. . .] and indeed, there are no Egyptians anywhere.
{not enough Egyptians to fight foreigners}
    Indeed, gold and lapis lazuli, silver and turquoise, carnelian and amethyst, Ibhet-stone and [. . .] are strung on the necks of maidservants. Good things are throughout the land, (yet) housewives say: "Oh that we had something to eat!" {Food is more valuable than precious stones.}
    Indeed, the builders [of pyramids have become] cultivators, and those who were in the sacred bark are now yoked [to it]. {Class structure crumbled as everyone sought to survive. Ahmose's pyramid complex was the last to be built. No more Hebrew slaves, so Egyptians are enslaved.}

    None shall indeed sail northward to Byblos today; what shall we do for cedar trees for our mummies, and with the produce of which priests are buried and with the oil of which [chiefs] are embalmed as far as Keftiu? {no more luxuries of Byblos' cedar and Cretan oil}
      They come no more; {People wanted food, not luxury items.}
      gold is lacking [. . .] {The Nubian supply line was broken;}
      and materials for every kind of craft have come to an end. {Men need food to work in mines.}
      The [. . .] of the palace is despoiled.
    How often do people of the oases come with their festival spices, mats, and skins, with fresh rdmt-plants, grease of birds . . .? {People of the oases still had food, and likely stayed away.}
      Lacking are grain, charcoal, irtyw-fruit, m'w-wood, nwt-wood, and brushwood.
    And every foreign land [comes]! That is our fate and that is our happiness! What can we do about it? All is ruin! {Egypt provided during famines of the past, and so foreigners come.}

Appendix B

IV
Those who were Egyptians [have become] foreigners and are thrust aside.
Indeed, hair [has fallen out] for everybody, {an effect of malnutrition}
and the man of rank can no longer be distinguished from him who is nobody.
Indeed, [. . .] because of noise; noise is not [. . .] in years of noise, and there is no end [of] noise. {noise of revolt/tumult}
Indeed, the children of princes are dashed against walls, and the children of the neck are laid out on the high ground. {People kill those they held responsible to provide food and maat.}
Indeed, the Delta in its entirety will not be hidden, and Lower Egypt puts trust in trodden roads. {Egypt can't hide the fact that it has food, and trusts people will come and go peacefully.}
What can one do? No [. . .] exist anywhere, and men say: "Perdition to the secret place!" Behold, it is in the hands of those who do not know it like those who know it. {Is the 'secret place' Djoser's comples with its many underground passageways?}
The desert dwellers are skilled in the crafts of the Delta.
There are no remedies for it; noblewomen suffer like maidservants, {incurable diseases erupt}
Indeed, trees are felled and branches are stripped off. {The deforestation of Egypt}

V
Indeed, magnates are hungry and perishing,
[Is it] by sprinkling for Ptah and taking [. . .]? Why do you give to him?
There is no reaching him. It is misery which you give to him.
Indeed, the hot-tempered man says: "If I knew where God is, then I would serve Him." {The Egyptian gods have failed the people; so they may be seeking the true God.}
Indeed, all animals, their hearts weep; cattle moan because of the state of the land. {The animals are also going hungry.}
Indeed, terror kills; the frightened man opposes what is done against your enemies.
Moreover, the few are pleased, while the rest are . . . {Few are satisfied; most are fearful.}
Indeed, the ways are [. . .], the roads are watched; men sit in the bushes until the benighted traveler comes in order to plunder his burden, and what is upon him is taken away. He is belabored with blows of a stick and murdered. {People resort to theft and murder.}

VI
Indeed, [men eat] herbage and wash [it] down with water; neither fruit nor herbage can be found [for] the birds, and [. . .] is taken away from the mouth of the pig. No face is bright which you have [. . .] for me through hunger.
Indeed, everywhere barley has perished and men are stripped of clothes, spice, and oil; everyone says: "There is none." The storehouse is empty and its keeper is stretched on the ground; a happy state of affairs! . . .Would that I had raised my voice at that moment, that it might have saved me from the pain in which I am. {Possibly he saw the store owner slain, and wishes he were dead as well.}
Indeed, public offices are opened and their inventories are taken away; the serf has become an owner of serfs. The corn of Egypt is common property. {City silos first established by Joseph (Gen. 41:48) were now stolen from.}
Indeed, the laws of the council chamber are thrown out; indeed, men walk on them in public

places, and poor men break them up in the streets. {Normal laws do not function during famine.}

Indeed, the great council-chamber is a popular resort, and poor men come and go to the Great Mansions.

VII

Behold, the fire has gone up on high, and its burning goes forth against the enemies of the land. Behold, things have been done which have not happened for a long time past; the king has been deposed by the rabble. {Was there a king after Tausret who's name has been erased?}

Behold, he who was buried as a falcon [is devoid] of biers, and what the pyramid concealed has become empty. {Storage of dried foods and wood beneath Djoser's pyramid were found and taken.}

Behold, it has befallen that the land has been deprived of the kingship by a few lawless men. Behold, men have fallen into rebellion against the Uraeus, the [. . .] of Re, even **she** who makes the Two Lands content. {Chancellor Bay and his Asiatic traitors. **Tausret**}

Behold, the secret of the land whose limits were unknown is divulged, and the Residence is thrown down in a moment. {Qantir destruction level?}

Behold, Egypt is fallen to pouring of water, and he who poured water on the ground has carried off the strong man in misery. {Priests fighting warriors?}

Behold, the Serpent is taken from its hole, and the secrets of the Kings of Upper and Lower Egypt are divulged. {The secrets of Egypt?}

Behold, the Residence is afraid because of want, and [men go about] unopposed to stir up strife. {There aren't enough 'police' to protect the food and the people.}

Behold, the land has knotted itself up with confederacies, and the coward takes the brave man's property. {When government systems no longer work, people make up their own.}

Behold, the Serpent [. . .] the dead: he who could not make a sarcophagus for himself is now the possessor of a tomb.

Behold, the possessor of wealth now spends the night thirsty, while he who once begged his dregs for himself is now the possessor of overflowing bowls.

Behold, the possessors of robes are now in rags, while he who could not weave for himself is now a possessor of fine linen. {Fortunes have turned.}

Behold, he who could not build a boat for himself is now the possessor of a fleet; their erstwhile owner looks at them, but they are not his. {The spoils go to the strong.}

VIII

Behold, he who had no loaf is now the owner of a barn, and his storehouse is provided with the goods of another.

Behold, a man is happy eating his food. Consume your goods in gladness and unhindered, for it is good for a man to eat his food; God commands it for him whom He has favored [. . .]. [Behold, he who did not know] his god now offers to him with incense of another [who is] not known [to him]. {a change of religion?}

Behold, he who could not slaughter for himself now slaughters bulls, and he who did not know how to carve now sees [. . .]. {To survive, people had to learn new skills.}

[Behold,] the chiefs of the land flee; there is no purpose for them because of want. The lord of [. . .].   priests transgress with the cattle of the poor [. . .] {Priests are eating the gods' offerings instead of burning them.}

Appendix B

IX
Behold, he who had no grain is now the owner of granaries, and he who had to fetch loan-corn for himself is now one who issues it.

Behold, the strong men of the land, the condition of the people is not reported [to them]. All is ruin! {Breakdown of communication}

[Behold, he who once recorded] the harvest now knows nothing about it, while he who never ploughed [for himself is now the owner of corn; the reaping] takes place but is not reported. The scribe [sits in his office], but his hands [are idle] in it. {People are growing crops for themselves; not paying taxes.}

X
Destroyed is [. . .] their food is taken from them [. . . through] fear of his terror. {"his" = 'tax-gatherer'}

He is captured laden with goods and [all his property] is taken away. {non-payment being criminal}

Destroyed is the doing of that for which men are sent by retainers in the service of their masters; they have no readiness. Behold, they are five men, and they say: "Go on the road you know, for we have arrived." {Brute-force has replaced civil authority.}

Lower Egypt weeps; the king's storehouse is the common property of everyone,

and the entire palace is without its revenues. {Normal taxes can't be collected during a famine.}

Destroy the enemies of the august Residence, splendid of magistrates [. . .] in it like [. . .]; indeed, the Governor of the City goes unescorted.

XI
Remember to observe regulations, to fix dates correctly, and to remove him who enters on the priestly office in impurity of body, for that is doing it wrongfully, it is destruction of the heart [. . .] the day which precedes eternity, the months [. . .] years are known. [. . .] lack of people; come [. . .] Re who commands [. . .] worshipping him [. . .] West until [. . .] are diminished [. . .].

{Restoration of worship of old gods.}

Behold, why does he seek to fashion [men . . .]? The frightened man is not distinguished from the violent one. Remember: The things to remember are the duties of the priests, first among them the pharaoh as High Priest, to their gods. In accordance with the magical thinking of the day (and which still persists among many believers) the meticulous fulfillment of duties brings with it the favour of the gods and thus the well-being of the pious.

XII
He brings coolness upon heat; men say: "He is the herdsman of mankind, and there is no evil in his heart." Though his herds are few, yet he spends a day to collect them, their hearts being on fire. Would that he had perceived their nature in the first generation; then he would have imposed obstacles, he would have stretched out his arm against them, he would have destroyed their herds and their heritage. {This king may have brought in a mercenary group who turned his heart against his own people.}

Combat has gone forth, and he who should be a redresser of evils is one who commits them; neither do men act as pilot in their hour of duty. Where is he today? Is he asleep? Behold, his power is not seen. If we had been fed, I would not have found you, I would not have been summoned in vain; "Aggression against it means pain of heart" is a saying on the lips of everyone. The land has not fallen [. . .] the statues are burned and their tombs destroyed [. . .] Authority, knowledge, and truth are with you, yet confusion is what you set throughout the land, also the noise of tumult. Behold, one deals harm to another, for men conform to what you have commanded. If three men travel on the road, they are found to be only two, for the many kill the few.

{Ipuwer looks in vain for the power of pharaoh to set things right.}

XIII

You have told lies, and the land is a weed which destroys men, and none can count on life.

All these years are strife, and a man is murdered on his housetop even though he was vigilant in his gate lodge. Is he brave and saves himself? It means he will live.

When men send a servant for humble folk, he goes on the road until he sees the flood; the road is washed out and he stands worried. What is on him is taken away, he is belabored with blows of a stick and wrongfully slain. Oh that you could taste a little of the misery of it!

{Ipuwer wants the pharaoh to share his pain. Drought was followed by flooding.}

It is [indeed] good [. . .] dignities for them, and the roads are passable. It is indeed good when the hands of men build pyramids, when ponds are dug and plantations of the trees of the gods are made. {Ipuwer longed for the Egypt of old.}

It is indeed good when men are drunk; they drink and their hearts are happy.

XIV

It is indeed good when fine linen is spread out on New Year's Day [. . .] on the bank; when fine linen is spread out and cloaks are on the ground. {Did pharaoh cancel New Year's Day celebration? Or was there just not enough food to have one?}

The overseer of [. . .] the trees, the poor [. . . . . .] in their midst like Asiatics [. . .]. Men [. . .] the state thereof; they have come to an end of themselves; none can be found to stand up and protect themselves [. . .]. {Ipuwer expresses hatred of Asiatics, like the Hebrews.}

Everyone fights for his sister and saves his own skin. Is it Nubians? Then will we guard ourselves; warriors are made many in order to ward off foreigners. Is it Libyans? Then we will turn away. The Medjay are pleased with Egypt.

{Maybe Ipuwer wants Nubians and Libyans to fight the Asiatics.}

XV

How comes it that every man kills his brother? The troops whom we marshaled for ourselves have turned into foreigners and have taken to ravaging.

{Instead, their foreign police force turned on them.}

What has come to pass through it is informing the Asiatics of the state of the land; all the desert folk are possessed with the fear of it. {Ipuwer's fear of Egypt being taken over by Asiatics.}

XVI

What Ipuwer said when he addressed the Majesty of the Lord of All: {pharaoh?}

[. . .] all herds. It means that ignorance of it is what is pleasing to the heart. You have done what was good in their hearts and you have nourished the people with it. They cover their faces through fear of the morrow.

Appendix B

Twentieth Dynasty

Info on O. Chicago 12073 states 18 years elapsed between 17th year of Rameses III (1301) and 3rd year of Rameses IV (1283). 1301 – 1283 = 18 years.

1322-1318   Setnakhte (4y attested by quartz stela belonging to the HPA Bakenkhunsu)
1318-1286   Rameses III (died 1 ½ months into 32nd year)
1286-1279   Rameses IV (7y attested; P. Turin Indictment indicates death thereafter)
1279-1275   Rameses V (4y attested, but then may have died of smallpox)
1275-1266   Rameses VI (8y attested, 9y by Turin Accounting Papyrus 1907+1908)
1266-1258   Rameses VII (7y attested, 8y argued by Eyre in P. Turin 1883 + 2095)
1258-1256   Rameses VIII (1y attested, 2y inferred by calendar)
1256-1237   Rameses IX (19y exactly according to legal documents)
1237-1228   Rameses X (9y attested)
1228-1199   Rameses XI (27y attested, 29y in Book of Sothis; no Sed festival was held)

Rameses IV sent an expedition to Nubia and had a map made of the area, now called the Turin Papyrus Map.

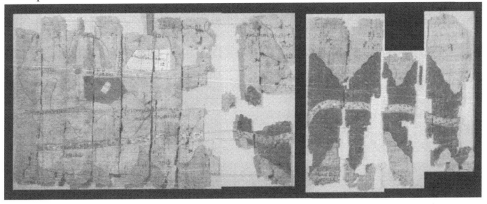

In the Turin Accounting Papyrus, 1907 and 1908 are dated to year 7 of Rameses' VII reign (1259 BC) and stated that 11 full years passed from year 5 of Ramesses VI (1270 BC) to year 7 of his reign. 1270 – 1259 = 11 years

Volcanic Eruptions during reign of Rameses III

Volcanoes today have multiple eruptions decades or hundreds of years apart; so is the case with Thera. The scientists who reported Thera had nine eruptions from 1 to 1950 A.D., concluded "We found that almost all of the known eruptions of Santorini were preceded, accompanied and/or followed by at least one tectonic shock in the proximity of the volcano, within a circle with a radius of a few hundred kilometers and within a time-period usually less than one year. We conclude therefore that the same had to happen at the time of the Minoan eruption as well."[1383]

The Greenland ice core ash which dated the Theran eruption to 1645 BC and caused great controversy in the world of Egyptology was later shown to be that of the volcano of Aliakchak in

---

1383 Komlos, G., *et al.*, *Thera and the Aegean World I*, 1978, pp. 97-107

Alaska in 2003 BC;[1384] therefore its date is now meaningless. In 1942 AD eight WWII fighter planes crashed in Greenland and were located in 1988 AD, and six years later a privately funded team spent four months retrieving one P-38 through 268 feet of ice.[1385] So during 50 years, 268 feet of ice accumulated which averages to a little over 5 feet of ice per year. So most ice core data is useless for dating. I place the Minoan series of eruptions at the end of the reign of Hatshepsut. One of the other Cycladic island volcanoes erupted in 1313 BC (Rameses III's 5th year), and another eruption in 1310 BC (Rameses III's 8th year) to account for the influx of the Sea Peoples.

Solution to End of 20th Dynasty and Beginning of 21st

At the great temple in Abu Simbel are two hieratic graffiti: one by Panaho who was a scribe to the viceroys of Nubia and to both Wentawat and Ramessesnakht; and the other by the "charioteer at the Residence" son of Wentawat.[1386] Wentaw(u)at served as KSOK during the reign of Ramesses IX, described as follows:

> "King's son of Kush, overseer of the Gold Lands of Amen-Re King of the Gods, Head of the stable of the Court. First of His Majesty (i.e. charioteer), Door-opener. Steward of Amun at Khnum-Weset. High-Priest of Amun of Khnum-Weset, or of Ramesses"[1387]

Piankh became KSOK and general after Wentawuat died in the 18th or 19th year of Ramesses IX. Piankh also served Rameses X and up to the 11th year of Rameses XI. During the reign of Rameses XI, Piankh also became HPA at Thebes. When Piankh died, Herihor became HPA and general, and Panhesy served as KSOK during years 12-17 of Rameses XI; afterwards, Herihor also became KSOK. From the 9th year of Rameses IX to the 29th year of Rameses XI, Dhutmose was a scribe of the necropolis. When Dhutmose became chief scribe in the 17th year of Rameses IX, he elevated his son or brother Butehamon to serve as necropolis scribe with him. Butehamon continued in his service through the reigns of Herihor and Pinedjem I. [For charts see page 438, and for Late Ramesside Letters see Appendix C.]

Twenty-First Dynasty

The 21st dynasty in Tanis was concurrent with the HPA's ruling as kings in Thebes, which is designated as Dynasty 21A. I accept Wenamun's report during "year five" as Herihor's year prior to his taking the title of pharaoh in the latter part of his 6th regnal year (since there are two coffin dockets in his 6th year with Pinedjem as HPA). Since Smendes and Tentamun are already functioning as treasurers in Tanis in the report, I place Smendes in Tanis the year prior (1995 BC). Because I give Herihor 30 years based upon evidence he celebrated his heb-sed festival, that would mean Smendes served Herihor for at least 26 years as treasurer.

Pinedjem served Herihor as HPA, with the first attested regnal year being 6 with two reburial documents, one being for Amenhotep I. This confirms that Herihor declared himself to be pharaoh

---

1384 Pearce, N., *et al.*, "Reinterpretation of Greenland Ice-core data recognizes the presence of Late Holocene Aniakchak Tephra (Alaska)," in print in the Proceedings of the SCIEM 2000 Euro-conference, May 28-June 1, 2003 in Vienna.
1385 According to articles from *The New York Times* and AboveTopSecret.com
1386 Peden, Alexander J., *Graffiti of Pharaonic Egypt*, 2001, pp. 132-133
1387 Reisner, George A., "The Viceroys of Ethiopia (Continued)," *The Journal of Egyptian Archaeology*, 1920 http://euler.slu.edu/~bart/egyptianhtml/kings%20and%20Queens/Viceroy_of_Kush_(or_Nubia).html

Appendix B

in year six after Wenamun's year five. HPA Pinedjem's last attested reburial documents (for Seti I and Ramesses II) were in Herihor's 15th year.[1388] Then as king Pinedjem I, he wrote a reburial document in his own regnal year 8. His son, HPA Masaharta, wrote a document in king Pinedjem's 16th year for a second reburial of Amenhotep I.[1389] HPA Masaharta has Merytamun's linen's documented to regnal year 18.[1390] Linens for years 19 to 21 have no name associated with them, and as you'll read below, a year 18 and 19 is associated with Masaharta; so I give Masaharta 19 years and Djedkhonsefankh 2 years as HPA serving their father king Pinedjem I.

Butehamon served king Herihor: "Years 10, 11, 12, 13 of an unspecified ruler, but in company with Pinudjem I as high priest, in a series of Theban graffiti."[1391] "A further, unpublished, grafitto apparently associates a Year 16, the high priest Masaharta, and Butehamun's son Ankhefenamun."[1392] I suggest the "Year 16" was of Pinedjem I.

Menkheperre has bricks and linens ascribed to him solely as HPA for various years up to 48, but he also has bricks with his cartouche as king at el-Hibeh, Medamud, and Gebelein. King Menkheperre also has his name in a cartouche in several inscriptions at the quarry in Wadi Hammamat.[1393] Menkheperre has two separate year 49 inscriptions at Thebes and Kom Ombo;[1394] so I attribute 49 years to Menkheperre as king and HPA.

I agree with Karl Jansen-Winkeln that Theban stela and monuments of Menkheperre's regnal years 48 and 49 have been incorrectly associated with Psusennes I. Psusennes I's claim to fame is building the enclosure wall around the Tanis temple to Amun, Mut, and Khonsu by reusing building materials from Avaris and Piramesse as well as from older dynasties all over the delta. Psusennes I has several other minor artifacts from the delta in addition to his usurped sarcophagi and coffin, so Manetho's attribution of 46 years is acceptable.

My thanks to Andrzej Niwinski and his research on the yellow anthropomorphic coffins of the 21st dynasty and his subsequent chronology chart.[1395] A non-gilded coffin (#333) of Nebhepet, Butehamon's son, had tags with the twentieth and twenty-first years of a king, and a year 16 Masaharta "unpublished graffito".[1396] "On linen around the mummy of Meritamun was found an inscription ordering its restoration in year 18 and a second inscription recording that the restoration had been accomplished in year 19"[1397] which are usually ascribed to Masaharta.[1398] The leather tag ('mummy brace') on #86 and #96 had names of Pinudjem II and Amenemope, so they were concurrent. The tag on #104 gives year 48 of Menkheperre and year one of someone else who Niwinski suggested was Amenemope. Coffin #152 had tags of Amenemope and Smendes II. He documented the gilded coffin (#316) of Nauny, a daughter of Pinedjem I. Another non-gilded coffin (#100), which was usurped by one of the many Henuttawys, had a tag with Menkheperre's name in a

---

1388 Ritner, Robert K., *The Libyan Anarchy*, Society of Biblical Literature, Atlanta, 2009, p. 115
1389 Kitchen, K. A., *The Third Intermediate Period in Egypt*, Aris & Phillips LTD, England, 1973, p. 412
1390 Ellis, Ralph, *Solomon, Pharaoh of Egypt*, 2002, p. 353
1391 Kitchen, K.A., *The Third Intermediate Period in Egypt*, 1973, p. 38 also Spiegelberg footnote
1392 Ibid., p. 38 based on footnote 160
1393 Goff, Beatrice, *Symbols of Ancient Egypt in the Late Period*, Mouton Publishers, 1979, p. 64
1394 Kitchen, K. A., *The Third Intermediate Period in Egypt*, England, 1996, p. 421 and 573
1395 Niwinski, Andrzej, *21st Dynasty Coffins from Thebes: Chronological and Typological Studies*, 1988, Table VI
1396 Kitchen, K. A., *The Third Intermediate Period in Egypt*, Aris & Phillips LTD, England, 1973, p. 38
1397 Goff, Beatrice, *Symbols of Ancient Egypt in the Late Period*, Mouton Publishers, 1979, p. 56
1398 Ellis, Ralph, *Solomon, Pharaoh of Egypt*, 2002, p. 353

cartouche as does #126. Gilded coffins became a target for gold-seekers, and they were often meticulously stripped. Those who could afford gilding were of the royal Theban family.

From Niwinski's research, royal family members can be deduced by gilded coffins. Menkheperre's wife, Istemkheb, and daughter Meritamun are exceptions; and Istemkheb's coffin was usurped from a prior dynasty. Niwinski noted the superior gilding and inlays of coffins of Pinedjem I (#73, though his coffin was a re-used rishi-coffin of Thutmose I), his wife Henuttawy (#71), and his sister Nodjmet (#72). The coffins of family members of Pinedjem I and II were originally located in Deir el-Bahari, whereas the coffins of family members of Menkheperre were moved there from Bab el-Gauss in antiquity, so sometimes the tag of the king who reburied them was affixed, as in the case of #124 which was tagged by Siamun in years 8 and 10, but the older linens had the name of Amenemope and the newer linen had the name of Pinudjem II. The following are gilded yellow coffins numbered by Niwinski in his 1988 book *21st Dynasty Coffins from Thebes: Chronological and Typological Studies*:

No.	Name and relationship	Details
44	Henuttawy C, daughter of Menkheperre	
79	Esamun	Tag of Psusennes
83	Hori, son of Menkheperre+[ ]hetepi	Linen of Pinedjem II
84	Gautseshen B, granddaughter of Menkheperre	
89	Menkheperre B, grandson through Tjanefer	
92	Gautseshen, daughter of Menkheperre	Tag of Amenemope
99	Esy	Tag of Psusennes II
125	Pennesuttawy	Tag of HPA Menkheperre in a cartouche
142	Tjanefer, son of Menkheperre+Istemkheb	Tag of Pinedjem II
143	Tausatre	Tag of Pinedjem
144	Herituben, grand-daughter of Menkheperre	Psusennes II tag ; Siamun's linen and bandages of Pinudjem II
146	Henuttawy B, daughter of Pinedjem I	Tag of HPA Menkheperre in a cartouche

Burial/Reburial Attestations:
6th year 2nd fall month; HPA Herihor reburial coffin dockets on Seti I and Rameses II[1399]
6th year (of king Herihor) 3rd [linen] and 4th [coffin] winter months by HPA Pinedjem[1400]
15th year of HPA Pinudjem linen reburial notice on Rameses II
1st year of king Pinudjem I on linen of Nodjmet[1401]
8th year of king Pinudjem I on inscription across breast of Ahmose I[1402]
16th year king Pinudjem inscription of HPA Masaharta ordering reburial of Amenhotep I
18th year king Pinudjem on linen of HPA Masaharta[1403]
Regnal years 19-21 without a name, I attribute to king Pinudjem I

[1399] Ritner, Robert K., *The Libyan Anarchy*, Society of Biblical Literature, Atlanta, 2009, p. 100
[1400] Ibid., p. 115
[1401] Goff, Beatrice, *Symbols of Ancient Egypt in the Late Period*, Mouton Publishers, 1979, p. 57
[1402] Ibid., pp. 56-57
[1403] Ritner, Robert K., *The Libyan Anarchy*, Society of Biblical Literature, Atlanta, 2009, p. 115

Appendix B

Reburial of Seti I in 6th year of HPA Menkheperre on linen[1404]
Linen on mummy of 48th year of HPA Menkheperre
Menkheperre year 48 linen with year 1 of another king, most likely Amenemope
(Hor-Pasebakhaenniut) Psusennes' I throne name is Akheperre Setepenamun.
(Hor-Pasebakhaenniut) Psusennes' II throne name is Tyetkheperre Setepenre.

Mummy tags on #79, #80, #99 and #144 have the name Pasebakhaenniut. Coffin #80 was usurped and used for Makare, the daughter of Pinedjem II, so the tag must have been written by Psusennes II. Coffin #144 is for a chantress of Amun named Herytwebkht which may be the long version of Harweben, a daughter of Pinedjem II whose "bandalettes" were dedicated in year 8,[1405] most likely of his own reign; and the tags were then dedicated by Psusennes II. On coffin #99 king Pasebakhaemut is adoring Khonsu.[1406] Psusennes II likely wrote on all four mummy tags.

HPA Pinedjem has years 6 and 15 attested, which I assume are Herihor's regnal years. Pinedjem I became king after Herihor's death. King Pinedjem I has regnal years 1, 8, 16, and 18 attested, and HPA Masaharta has years 18 and 19 attested, and linens for years 19, 20, and 21 have no name; so I give HPA Pinedjem 24 years serving Herihor and king Pinedjem I 21 regnal years during the first 19 of which HPA Masaharta served him followed by 2 years in which HPA Djedkhonsefankh served Pinedjem I.

John Taylor noted the coffins of Tanite kings often had "corrupt writing" and "the phrase 'may he give water (etc.)' does not generally occur at Thebes or elsewhere in the south."[1407] These distinctives separate dynasty 21 from 21A coffins. Taylor noted that though El-Hibeh was controlled by Thebes during the 21st dynasty, predominantly northern style coffins were buried there.[1408]

Using the genealogy table of the 21st dynasty of Menkheperre from the roof of Khonsu temple combined with the genealogy for the 22nd dynasty from the Memphis Serapeum stela of Pasenhor,[1409] "Grdseloff established . . . the order of these two men . . ., for a priest in Memphis, who lived in the Twenty-second Dynasty, made a list of the priests of Ptah in which the priest of the time of Psusennes is said to be the son of the priest of the time of Neferkare."[1410]

"Tjanefer, as Wente has shown, was fourth prophet of Amun in year 40, when
Menkheperre visited a series of temples in the Theban area. By the sixth year of
Siamun he had been promoted to second prophet of Amun."[1411]

1404 Goff, Beatrice, *Symbols of Ancient Egypt in the Late Period*, Mouton Publishers, 1979, p. 63
1405 Goff, Beatrice, *Symbols of Ancient Egypt in the Late Period*, Mouton Publishers, 1979, p. 82
1406 Ibid.
1407 Taylor, John H., "Coffins as Evidence for a 'North-South Divide'," *The Libyan Period in Egypt*,
    Nederlands Institute, 2009, p. 392
1408 Ibid., p. 398
1409 Ritner, Robert K., *The Libyan Anarchy*, Society of Biblical Literature, Atlanta, 2009, pp. 16 and 21
1410 Goff, Beatrice, *Symbols of Ancient Egypt in the Late Period*, Mouton Publishers, 1979, p. 69
1411 Ibid., p. 76

Pinedjem II Inscription in his own year 14

"The pertinent inscription is a limestone fragment from Karnak which reads: 'Pinedjem, son of Menkheperre, year 14, 4th month of summer, 5th day of [his] Majesty, 'I------(this fragmentary name in a cartouche).' . . . [Young] sees in the "I,' which is all that is preserved of Osochor's name, an epithet attached to his name, perhaps 'Beloved of Amun' ('I[*mn-mr*]), so common with royal names of this period."[1412]

Stela Information

I attribute "regnal year 25" of the 'banishment stela' to Menkheperre. The Large Dakhla stela was engraved in the 5th regnal year of Sheshonk I. It regards water rights, and the fact that only one well was registered to Weben-Re, not two, in the 19th year of Psusennes. I attribute regnal year 19 of Psusennes in the Large Dakhla stela to Psusennes I.

Clarity Chronology Detail of High Priests and 21st Dynasty 147 years

Thebes

HPA Herihor 5y + 25y king = 30y total KSOK	Pinedjem I King 21y [y1, 8, 16 attested] [y19-21 linens]	King Menkheperre 49y, (son of Pinedjem I and Henuttawy)	Smendes II 2y	Pinedjem II 22y	Psusennes III 23y takes control of Tanis after 9y as Pusennes II
Pinedjem HPA [y6-15 attest] w/ Masaharta as 2nd prophet	Masaharta 19y [y 16-18 attested] Djedkhonsefankh 2y	HPA Menkheperre and king for 49 years [y48 linen]	Smendes II 2y	Pinedjem II 22y	Psusennes III 23y takes control of Tanis after 9y as Pusennes II
Chief scribes Butehamon + Ankhfenamun	Chief scribes Butehamon + Ankhefenamun	General Menkheperre 49y			[Psusennes y23 = y3 of Sheshonk]

Butehamon served "Years 10, 11, 12, 13 of an unspecified ruler, but in company with Pinudjem I as high priest, in a series of Theban graffiti." - K.A. Kitchen, *The Third Intermediate Period*, 1973; p. 38 also Spiegelberg footnote. "A further, unpublished, grafitto apparently associates a Year 16, the high priest Masaharta, and Butehamun's son Ankhefenamun." - Ibid., p. 38 based on footnote 160. Years 10-13 and 16 could be of Herihor or Pinedjem I.

Tanis

| Smendes, 26y treasurer [y5 Herihor Wenamun] | Smendes, king, 23y [UE quarry stela in y22 or y23] | (Neferkare) Amenemnisut 4years [co-reign] King Psusennes I 46y (42y alone) [y19 on large Dakhla stela] | 9y Amenemope | 6y Osorkon [y2] | "Pharaoh" Siamun 19y [y17 attested] | Psusennes II 14y |

1412 Ibid., p. 78

Appendix B

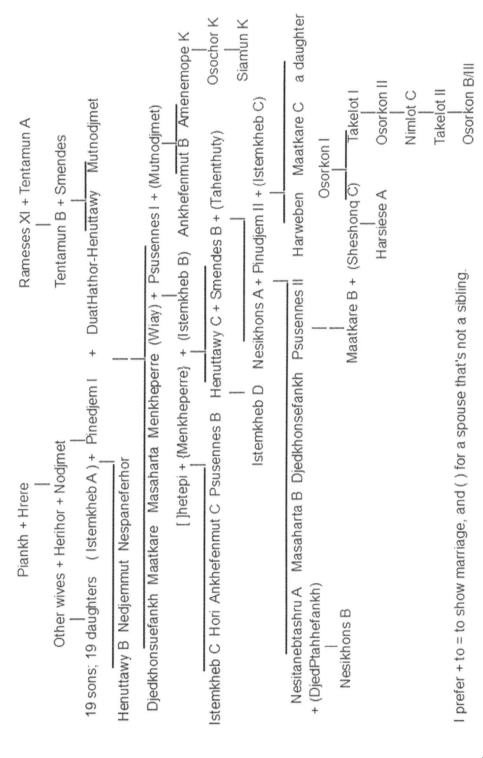

Pharaohs of the Bible

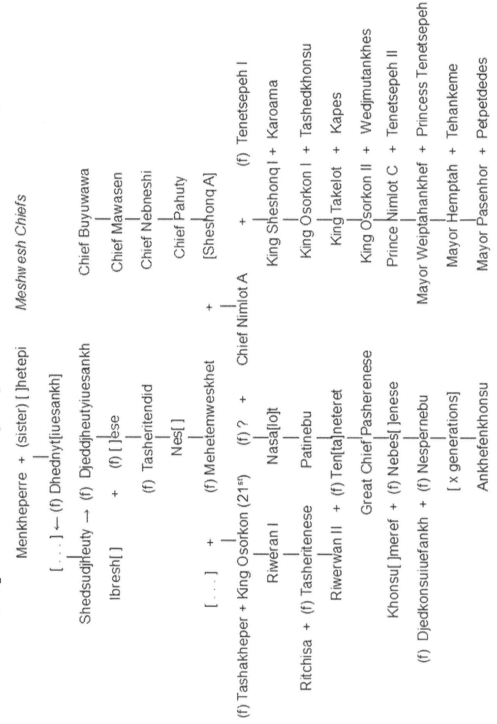

Appendix B

Karnak Nile Level Texts KNLT (Karnak Quay Texts)

In 1896 AD Legrain recorded and numbered the 45 inundation level inscriptions on the west face of the Karnak temple quay. These Karnak Nile Level Texts are often abbreviated as KNLT or NLT. The baseline, or zero mark, for the measurements (in meters) was the pavement of the hypostyle hall. Sometimes, as in year 12 of Sheshonk III and year 6 of Taharqa, a first measurement is surpassed by a second measurement. Since year 12 of Sheshonk III records two above zero levels, the year 12 below zero level of KNLT #24 can not belong to Sheshonk III, and so I ascribe it to Takelot II. I accept that HPA's often used their own regnal years. I suggest that Sheshonk III was a young son of Osorkon I's old age. In order to match Pedubast I's NLT's with Sheshonk III's NLT's, Takelot II had to count his regnal years from his time as HPA Takelot F in 935 BC in my chronology. My following order is based upon the translations on pages 34-44 in Ritner's *The Libyan Anarchy*.

#	Regnal year(s) and name(s)	Nile level
1	Year 6 of Sheshonk (I)	+0.07m
2	Year 12 of Sekhemkheperre Setepenre Osorkon (I)	+0.09m
20	Year __ of HPA Iuwelot, son of Osorkon Meriamun (I)	+0.67m
21	[Year __ of HPA Iuwelo]t, son of Osorkon Meriamun (I)	+0.10m
16	Year 5 of HPA Iuwelot, son of Osorkon Meriamun (I)	+0.16m
17	Year 8 of HPA Smendes (C), son of Osorkon Meriamun (I)	-0.38m
18	Year 14 of HPA Smendes (C), son of Osorkon Meriamun (I)	-0.52m
19	Year __ of HPA Smendes (C), son of Osorkon Meriamun (I)	(lowest) -0.92m
24*	Year 12 {of Takelot II}, which is year 5 of Usermaatre Setepenreamun Pedubast Si-Ese (I) by Harsiese (B)	-0.15m
23	Year 6 of king Usermaatre Setepenreamun Sheshonk (III), by HPA Harsiese (B)	+0.09m
8	Year 12 of king Usermaatre Setepenreamun (Sheshonk III), son of Osorkon Meriamun (I)	+0.15m
9	Year 12 of king Usermaatre Setepenreamun (Sheshonk III), son of Osorkon Meriamun (I)	+0.25m
10	Year [1]3 of king Usermaatre Setepenreamun (Sheshonk III), . . .	-0.19m
26*	Year 16 of king Pedubast (I) which is year 2 of king Iuput (I)	-0.33m
11	Year 21 of king Usermaatre Setepenreamun (Sheshonk III), son of Osorkon Meriamun (I)	-0.27m
12	Year 22 of king Usermaatre Setepenreamun (Sheshonk III), son of Osorkon Meriamun (I)	-0.29m
28	Year 18 of king Pedubast (I) by HPA [Harsi]ese (B)	-0.435m
27	Year 19 of king Pedubast (I) by HPA Harsi[ese] (B)	-0.18m
14	Year 29 of king Usermaatre Setepenreamun (Sheshonk III)	-0.26m
15	[Year __ of king Usermaat]re [Setepenre]a[mun (Sheshonk III),] son of [Osorkon Meriamun]	-0.345m

29	Year 23 of king Pedubast (I) by HPA Takelot (B)	-0.42m
22	Year 39 of king Usermaatre Setepenreamun Sheshonk (III) Si-Bast, by HPA Osorkon (B)	+0.30m
3	Year 5 of Hedjkheperre Setepenre Sheshonk Si-Ese (VIa)	-0.21m
5	Year 3 of king Usermaatre Setepenreamun Osorkon (III) Si-Ese, whose mother is queen [Kamama]	+0.785m
6	Year 5 of king Usermaatre Setepenreamun Osorkon (III), whose mother is queen Kamama	+0.185m
7	Year 6 of king Usermaatre Setepenreamun Osorkon (III), whose mother is queen Kamama	+0.15m
13*	Year 28 of king Usermaatre Setepenreamun Osorkon (III) Si-Ese, ruler of Thebes, which is year 5 of his son [Usermaat]re Setep[enreamun] Takelot (III) Si-Ese, ruler of Thebes	+0.715m
4	Year 6 of king Takelot (III) Si-Ese, whose mother was Tentsai	-0.355m
25	Year 6 of Usermaatre Meriamun Sheshonk (VI) by HPA Takelot (D)	+0.23m
30	Year 2 of king [Sha]bako	+0.29m
31	Year 4 of king Shabako	+0.23m
32	Year __ of king Shabako	+0.04m
33	Year 3 of king Shebitku	+0.04m
34	Year 6 of king Taharqa	(highest) +0.84m
35	Year 6 of king Khunefertumre Taharqa	+0.77m
36	Year 7 of king Khunefertumre Taharqa, and council in charge of the flood	+0.28m
37	Year 8 of king Khunefertumre Taharqa, and council in charge of the flood	+0.28m
38	Year 9 of king Taharqa	+0.28m
39	Year 10 of king Wahibre Psametik (I), and council in charge of the flood	+0.46m
40	Year 11 of king [Wahib]re Psametik (I), and council in charge of the flood	+0.285m
41	Year 17 of king Wahibre Psametik (I), and council in charge of the flood	+0.155m
42	Year 19 of king Wahibre Psametik (I), and council in charge of the flood	+0.25m
43	Year 3 of king . . .	-0.185m
44	Year 6 of king __ and HPA . . .	-0.24m
45	Year 15 [+ x] of king . . .	-0.32m

"In Nile level record no. 23, dated to regnal year 6 of Shoshenq III Harsiese B is mentioned as High Priest of Amun,"[1413] noted Broekman, who also suggests NLT #14 should be assigned to Osorkon II based upon paleographic evidence. Since my chronology has Sheshonk III succeeding Osorkon II, I suggest both NLT #14 and #15 belonged to Sheshonk III. "Harsiese B was the genuine

---

1413 Broekman, Gerard, "Takelot III and the End of the 23rd Dynasty," *The Libyan Period in Egypt*, Netherlands, 2009, p. 99

Appendix B

High Priest of Amun who is attested in office late in Osorkon II's reign, in the regnal year 6 of Shoshenq III and in regnal years 18 and 19 of Pedubast I, according to Jansen-Winkeln."[1414]

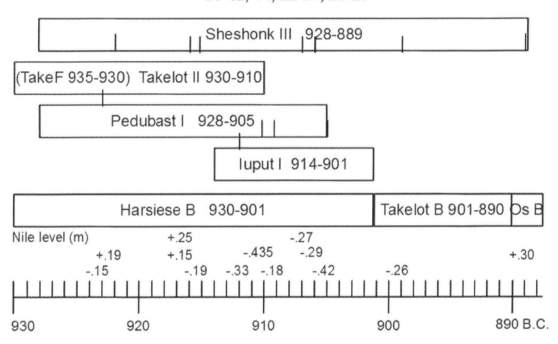

Takelot F was the son of Nimlot C and the grandson of Osorkon II. High Priest Takelot F became Takelot II in the latter years of Osorkon II. I suggest Takelot II counted his regnal years from when he was high priest Takelot F.

> "Takelot F, the son and successor of the High Priest of Amun Nimlot C, served for a period of time under Osorkon II as a High Priest of Amun before he proclaimed himself as king Takelot II in the final 3 Years of Osorkon II's reign. This situation is attested by the relief scenes on the walls of Temple J at Karnak which was dedicated by Takelot F – in his position as High Priest – to Osorkon II, who is depicted as the celebrant and king."[1415]

Hor IX built Temple J at Karnak with the help of HPA Takelot F for Osorkon II in that king's later years. Hor IX served Pedubast I and has a statue with his name in a cartouche in his tomb. "Since Shoshenq VI's prenomen is inscribed on Hor IX's funerary cones, this indicates that Hor IX outlived Pedubast I and made his funeral arrangements under Shoshenq VI instead."[1416]

1414 "Harsiese A" Wikipedia
1415 Aston, JEA 75, p. 147 from http://www.nationmaster.com/encyclopedia/Takelot-II
1416 Davies & MacAdam, *A Corpus of Inscribed Egyptian Funerary Cones*, 1957, pp. 25-26

King David

King David's millo at Jerusalem may have been discovered initially by Kathleen Kenyon and labelled as "lower massive terrace 10th century" at the base of the "city of David" beneath 12th century "terraces".[1417] These "terraces" may have been called "*stairs*" by Nehemiah. "Stair" is *ma'alah* in Hebrew (from *ma'aleh*, a platform or ascent), meaning elevation, a step or grade mark: things that come up, go up; stair, step, or storey.

> . . . *and the wall of the pool of Siloah by the king's garden, and to the* **stairs** *that go down from the city of David. (Nehemiah 3:15d)*

> *And at the fountain gate, which was over against them, they went up by the* **stairs** *of the city of David, at the going up of the wall, above the house of David, even to the water gate eastward. (Nehemiah 12:37)*

Zobah was an area first noted as having several kings in I Samuel 14:47. Zobah is 'Subutu' in Assyrian, and it was north of Damascus.[1418]

> *David smote also Hadadezer, the son of Rehob, king of Zobah, as he went to recover his border at the river Euphrates. (II Samuel 8:3)*

King David may have organized his thirty mighty men according to Egyptian military protocol. The word "captains" is used in I Chron. 11:1-3; 12:23-40 and II Samuel 5:1-3.

> **Captains** - The word שָׁלִישׁ *shâlîysh*, literally "third or thirtieth," may represent an Egyptian title. The king had about him a council of thirty, each of whom bore a title, Mapu, a "thirty man." The word occurs frequently in the Books of Kings. David seems to have organized the Shalishim as a distinct corps (see 2Sa_23:8 Hebrew), retaining the old name, and adopting the Egyptian system. A meaning of the word derived from "the third," i. e., "the chief of three warriors in a chariot".[1419]

The chariot had a driver, a shield-bearer, and an archer. It is the archer who is the "third" and if he led ten chariots, then he was the captain of 30 men. See II Samuel 23:16-39 on David's 30 mighty men and the famous three.

"An ordinary day's march for the Roman army consisted of 15-18 miles done in 7 of our hours (or 5 of the Roman summer hours)."[1420] If we give David's army 15 miles a day for three days (I Samuel 29:1-3, 30:1; or 45 miles) to return to Ziklag from Aphek, that brings us to Sderot; but with 18 miles for a total of 54 miles, we come to Tell es-Sera near Rahat.

According to I Samuel 27:6-7, David dwelt at Ziklag for 1 year and four months. Since his attacking the Amalekites unto Shur must have occurred in 1055 BC coinciding with Saul's final battles with the Philistines, David lived at Ziklag from late 1057 BC.

1417 Steiner, Margaret, editor, Excavations by Kathleen M. Kenyon in Jerusalem 1961-1967, volume III, Sheffield Academic Press Ltd., 2001, p. 28

1418 Free, Joseph P., *Archaeology and Bible History*, Zondervan, 1992, p. 136

1419 Barnes' Commentary

1420 Hamper, Rich, http://www.therthdimension.org/AncientRome/Roman_Army/On_the_March/on_the_march.htm

Appendix B

Ziklag: Tell Sera'/esh-Shariah on wadi Sharia (Gerar), 12 miles NW of Beersheba[1421]

Strata	Age	Cent.	Description	Unique
	EB		sherds	
	MBI		sherds	
	MBIII		sherds (Areas A, A-I, B)	
XII	LBI	17th		
XI	LBII	16th		
X	LBIII	15th	bldg. w/ plastered stone drain	Mycenaen + Cypriot ware
IX-A	IronIA	14th	Gov. residency w/ cedar beams and 19th dynasty scarabs	
IX-B	IronIB	13th	Egyptian bldg, hieratic bowl inscription	Egyptian pottery + faience
IX-C	IronIC	12th	sanctuary; ostraca of taxes	*^ by Philistines
VIII	IronIIA	11th	Philistine pottery with no monochrome, fortress	*^ Amalekites
VII	IronIIB	10th- 9th	Israelite city; ashlar casemate wall	
VI	IronIII	8th-7th	long storeroom, Assyrian citadel	*^ by Nebuchadnezzar II
V	Persian	5th-4th	brick-lined silo, grain pits	Attic ware
IV	Greek	3rd-1st		
III	Roman	1st AD	villa w/ frescoes, bathhouse, large watchtower	
II	Byzantine	4th-6th	Church with mosaic floor; plastered pool	
I	Islamic	7th	floors	

Stratum IX had a bowl with "'year 22', apparently of Rameses III."[1422] Stratum VIII noted: ". . . the tenth century B.C. Houses were sunk into a thick layer of ash, which belonged to a series of large storage pits of the eleventh century B.C.. The pottery repertoire of stratum VIII includes typical late Philistine sherds . . ."[1423]

The mud-brick walls of strata IX and VII were built upon kurkar foundations. Stratum VII had well-planned buildings: public storehouses, and private 4-room houses with white plaster and paved courtyards. Stratum VII has "four or five phases of rebuilding."[1424]

"Ziklag, and Bethmarcaboth, and Hazarsusah, And Bethlebaoth, and Sharuhen" (Joshua 19:5-6)

Ziklag means 'winding', possibly of the wadi winding around it. *Bethmarcaboth* means 'house of the chariots', and *Hazarsusah* means 'village of cavalry'. *Bethlebaoth* means 'house of lionesses'. *Sharuhen* means 'place of refuge'. So I suggest that a chariot city and a city for cavalry will be found between Tell Sera' (Ziklag) and Tell el-Ajjul (Sharuhen).

Regarding David's 3 and 7 years of famine

The Tishri year 1052-1051 BC was a jubilee year. The fourth sabbath year from that jubilee [1052 – (4 X 7) = 1024] was the Tishri year 1024-1023. To reconcile II Samuel 24:13 (7 years) and I

1421 And 5 miles east of Tel Haror
1422 *Encyclopedia of Archaeological Excavations in the Holy Land, Volume IV*, Exploration Society of Jerusalem and Prentice Hall, 1975, p. 1065
1423 Ibid., p. 1064
1424 Ibid., p. 1063

Chron. 21:12 (3 years), I include the sabbatical Tishri year 1024-1023 BC as the first year of no sowing prior to the counting of first three years of famine in 1023-1020 to provide a total of four. From Samuel's view, the famine was from 1024-1017. The Tishri year 1017-1016 was also a sabbath year; and Adonijah and Solomon both had coronations of sorts the next year (1015 BC).

King Solomon

"Archaeological discoveries show us, however, that precisely during the period 1100-900, when the kingdom of Israel was being built up, the 'weak and inglorious twenty-first dynasty' was ruling in Egypt, Assyria had gone into a period of decline, and the Hittite Empire in Asia Minor had come to an end, and the glory of the Mycenaeans had disappeared in Greece. There was a power vacuum in the Mediterranean world and the Near East. Thus God in his providence overruled so that *Solomon ruled over all kingdoms from the River to the land of the Philistines, as far as the border of Egypt* (I Kings 4:21)."[1425]

Tell el-Kheleifeh is 500 yards from the shore of the Gulf of Aqaba. The site was an acre and a half surrounded by a wall originally 9 feet wide and 25 feet high with a triple gate.[1426] It included a smelting and refining area according to Glueck.

An inscribed clay stamp from South Arabia (Sheba) used to seal bags of frankincense and myrrh was found at Bethel.[1427] *Tarshish* means 'metal refinery' in Phoenician.[1428] Shikmona was one of Solomon's harbor cities, and had "four-roomed houses, oil presses, and a variety of artifacts dating from the tenth century."[1429]

Twenty-Second Dynasty

Manetho according to Africanus:
The Twenty-second Dynasty consisted of nine kings of Bubastus.
1. Sesonchis, for 21 years.
2. Osorthon, for 15 years.
3. 4, 5. Three other kings, for 25 [29] years.
6. Takelothis, for 13 years.
7, 8, 9. Three other kings, for 42 years. Total, 120

A leather tag of Osorkon I (without a year) was attached to the mummy of priest Nakhtefmut. Its linen bandages of the third layer of wrapping were of "year 3", and its linen bandages of the fifth layer of wrapping were of "year 33".[1430] This mummy could have been wrapped in year 3 (1021 BC) of HPA Sheshonk C, and then further wrapped in year 33 (989 BC) of Osorkon I in a reburial. Since Osorkon's renewal of heb-sed inscription at Karnak "strongly suggests that Osorkon I reigned into

---

1425 Free, Joseph P., *Archaeology and Bible History*, Zondervan, 1992, p. 141
1426 Free, Joseph P., *Archaeology and Bible History*, Zondervan, 1992, p. 143
1427 Van Beek, G.W., *BASOR*, October, 1958
1428 Cornfeld, Gaalyah, *Archaeology of the Bible: book by book*, Harper and Row, 1976, p. 110
1429 Ibid., p. 111
1430 Ritner, Robert K., *The Libyan Anarchy*, Society of Biblical Literature, Atlanta, 2009, pp. 262-263

Appendix B

his thirty-fourth year,"[1431] then Sheshonk I's renewal of heb-sed inscription at Karnak[1432] should also attribute to him at least 33 years.

I think Manetho's three other kings were all sons named Sheshonk from Hedjkheperre Sheshonk I and three different wifes: Heqakheperre Sheshonk IIa to Karoama, Tuthkeperre Sheshonk IIb to Patareshnes, and Maakheperre Sheshonk IIc to an unknown consort. High Priest of Amun, Sheshonk C, was the son of Osorkon I and Maatkare. Usermaatre Sheshonk Sibast/Siese III, Hedjkheperre Sheshonk IV, Usermaatre Meriamun Sheshonk VI, and Hedjkheperre Sheshonk SiEse VIa have unknown parentage. Pami was the father of Aakheperre Sheshonk V.

Ussher placed Hadad's return to Edom and Solomon's marriage to the daughter of pharaoh in 1014 BC whereas I place the first in 1010 BC and the latter in 1007 BC. Ussher placed Jeroboam fleeing to Shishak in 978 BC based upon his knowledge of Egyptian chronology at the time; the date may be correct, but Ussher's Egyptian chronology was not.

Sheshonk I

By Sheshonk I's regnal year five, his son Iuput was already in position of high priest of Amun in Thebes according to the Deir el-Bahari cache Interment of Djedptahiuefankh.[1433] So though he only called himself the "great chief of Ma" in his second regnal year, I think Psusennes II died near the end of the next year for Sheshonk to get Iuput positioned in Thebes; so I give Sheshonk I and Psusennes II an overlap of just three years.

Gebel es-Silsilah Stela

This was a massive stela cut into the sandstone cliff almost 3 meters high by 2.5 meters wide with 57 columns of text. It mentioned heb-sed festival three times, and stated that the building of the heb-sed court (along with the pylons, colonnade, doors, and statues) was the main purpose in Sheshonk's "regnal year 21, second month of summer, on this day while his majesty was in residence at . . . Re-Horachty."[1434] Sheshonk I was clearly preparing for his 30th year jubilee celebration 9 years in advance, so he likely knew about how long it would take to complete such a task. In the latter years of Ramesses II, Re-Horachty was used to describe Piramesses.[1435] Since the stela recorded Re-Horachty, as Sheshonk's residence, calling his reliefs the Bubastite Portal is a misnomer.

According to a 2008 study, with modern tools and power it takes 0.217 million BTU's[1436] to quarry one ton of sandstone.[1437] That's just to cut it out of the earth, and does not include finishing, processing, or transporting it. In the early 1900's at the Excelsior Stone Quarry of sandstone, "The 10 ton blocks were cut so that they could be transported to Las Vegas using the 'Big Devil Wagon'. This frightful locomotive-like behemoth could haul 20 tons of cut stone on a single trip. The odd looking contraption also burned about 400 gallons of crude oil per day."[1438] Quarrying and

---

1431 Aston, David A., "Takeloth II Revisited," *The Libyan Period in Egypt*, Netherlands, 2009, p. 7, fn 60
1432 Ritner, Robert K., *The Libyan Anarchy*, Society of Biblical Literature, Atlanta, 2009, p. 196
1433 Ritner, Robert K., *The Libyan Anarchy*, Society of Biblical Literature, Atlanta, 2009, pp. 178-179
1434 Ritner, Robert K., *The Libyan Anarchy*, Society of Biblical Literature, Atlanta, 2009, pp. 187-193
1435 Ibid., p. 192 footnote #14
1436 A BTU is a British Thermal Unit equivalent to the energy it takes to heat one pound of water.
1437 "Sandstone Quarrying and Processing: A Life-Cycle Inventory - A Report," Prepared for The Natural Stone Council Prepared by University of Tennessee Center for Clean Products, August 2008
1438 http://www.sunsetcities.com/Red-Rock-Canyon/sandstonequarry00.html

Pharaohs of the Bible

transporting sandstone takes a lot of energy.

Sheshonk's heb-sed court "was located between the first and second pylon. The court enclosed the Sety II shrine and the northern section of the Ramesses III temple. The court was lined on its northern and southern sides with sandstone papyrus bud columns."[1439] The following is from a modern Missouri quarry website:

> "As a small 2 acre quarry, we hand-cut about 300 tons in a year. . . . Twenty cubic feet of sandstone weighs about 1.25ton (2500 lbs). . . . A 20 ft long 2 feet high wall that is stacked 1 foot deep = 20ft x 2 ft x 1 ft = 40 cu ft."[1440]

The completed heb-sed court measured 82 meters by 101 meters (269 X 331 feet), and the western gate had an opening of 17.70m (58 ft) and a total height of 27.50m (90 ft).[1441] I don't know the wall thickness of the court; but with just a one foot depth 6,423.75 tons of sandstone would be needed, which may have taken the ancient Egyptians at least four years to quarry.

The Gebel es-Silsilah quarry was located 40 miles north of Elephantine and 90 miles south of Thebes. To transport 6,000 tons of sandstone to the work site would have taken at least a year, and to dress and to place the blocks may have taken another year. Seven scenes of Sheshonk I and his son Iuput "depicted on an equal scale"[1442] were completed at Karnak along with over ninety lines of hieroglyphs (not counting the 130+ captured city names), possibly taking another year. 4 + 1 + 1 + 1 = 7 year minimum, not accounting for losses of time due to accidents, weather, war, etc.. On the eastern pilaster is inscribed, "First occasion (of) repeating the jubilee . . .;"[1443] thus, Sheshonk I reached his 33rd regnal year. This completed and moderately decorated jubilee court and gate attest to the long life of Sheshonk I, and not a sudden death during construction.

Sheshonk I won victories in Sinai, Nubia, Phoenicia, Syria, and Aegean

Sheshonk I's victory relief at El-Hibeh only has one row beginning "The western oasis, the eastern desert,"[1444] which are on either side of Thebes (though the west oases extend to the Fayyum). Sheshonk's victory stela at Karnak recorded that his soldiers had been killed, and Sheshonk slaughtered those that killed them "ashore on the bank of the Bitter Lakes"[1445] which are on the western side of the Sinai Peninsula. These Bedouin (and Nubians) who "had fallen into the practice of attacking [his] boundaries"[1446] were noted in one of the central scenes of he and Iuput at Karnak "Smiting the chiefs of the Nubian tribesmen, of all inaccessible foreign lands, of all the lands of the Phoenicians, and foreign lands of the Asiatic back-country."[1447] The easily accessible land of Canaan is not mentioned (except for Megiddo), likely because Sheshonk witnessed David's military might. After Sheshonk I regained the loyalty of the wealthy cities of Phoenicia, he made a show of force at Megiddo and placed his stela there to exact trade tribute, and then proceeded northeast.

1439 http://www.sunsetcities.com/Red-Rock-Canyon/sandstonequarry00.html
1440 "hand-cut" with power tools instead of a dozer   http://www.blackriverstone.com/stone_questions.html
1441 http://dlib.etc.ucla.edu/projects/Karnak/feature/ShoshenqICourt
1442 Ritner, Robert. K., *The Libyan Anarchy*, Society of Biblical Literature, 2009, p. 193
1443 Ibid., p. 196
1444 Ritner, Robert K., *The Libyan Anarchy*, Society of Biblical Literature, Atlanta, 2009, p. 222
1445 Ibid., p. 218
1446 Ibid., p. 202 lines 6-7
1447 Ritner, Robert K., *The Libyan Anarchy*, Society of Biblical Literature, Atlanta, 2009, p. 201

Appendix B

Sheshonk I likely went through the Aramaean land of Rehob to the city of Hamath, and continued marching inland to regain fealty from the cities of the upper Euphrates and Tigris rivers.

Amun's speech on Sheshonk I's victory relief at Karnak concludes:

"Every country that has come without number – Your Majesty has destroyed them in the completion of a moment. I have struck for you those who rebelled against you, suppressing for you the Asiatics. The armies of **Mitanni** – I have slain those belonging to them beneath your sandals."[1448]

Both Thutmose III and Rameses II fought the Mitanni. In Clarity Chronology, Suppiluliuma I conquered the Mitanni, and he sent EA #41 to Akhenaten (1551-1534 BC), yet the Mitanni were allowed to be vassal kings for another hundred years. The inclusion of "Mitanni" in Sheshonk's victory relief at Karnak has been a conundrum, but it is just a translation issue.

The Egyptian word translated Mitanni is *Nhrn* referring to Aram-**Naharim** which means "Aram **two rivers**" and refers to the Aramaeans of the upper Euphrates and Tirgris rivers who had carved out space for themselves near the Assyrians (descended from Shem's son, Asshur). Tiglath Pileser I fought Aramaeans about 100 years prior to Sheshonk I's attack. Both kings Saul and David fought in Aram-Zobah on the road through Damascus, and king David made it to the Euphrates.[1449]

"And the children of Ammon came out, and put the battle in array at the entering in of the gate: and the Syrians [Aram] of Zoba, and of Rehob, and Ishtob, and Maacah, were by themselves in the field." (II Samuel 10:8)

"So they went up, and searched the land from the wilderness of Zin unto Rehob, as men come to Hamath" (Numbers 13:21)

A couple cities named Rehob exist in the south, but the Aramaeans lived in the land of Rehob (now Rechaiya) which contained the road to Hamath. Ishtob is the land of Tob.

Sheshonk I slew the armies of "two rivers," yet none of those city names are listed on the Karnak victory wall. Cities #3, 7, 8 refer to Nubia, who are referenced in one of the central scenes of Sheshonk I and Iuput.

"Smiting the chiefs of the Nubian tribesmen, of all inaccessible foreign lands, of all the lands of the Phoenicians, and foreign lands of the Asiatic back-country."[1450]

In this inscription instead of "two rivers" (*Nhrn*), Sheshonk I referred to the "Asiatic back-country" (*phw.w St.[t]*) which was another 100-200 miles northeast of Hamath. The statue given to Abi-Baal is evidence that Sheshonk I subdued Byblos whose ancient name was Gubla which may be

---

1448 Ibid., p. 204 lines 22d – 24a with *Amu* being translated 'Asiatics'
1449 I Samuel 14:47 and II Samuel 10 respectively
1450 Ritner, Robert K., *The Libyan Anarchy*, Society of Biblical Literature, Atlanta, 2009, p. 201

Pharaohs of the Bible

G3[d(t?)] #11 in his list with Megiddo #12 and *Rbyt* (Beth-Rehob?) finishing the row at #13. But I conclude the rest of the cities on the victory relief were conquered by someone else who actually led a campaign against Israel. Merenptah mentioned "Israel", but Sheshonk I never named it.

In Sheshonk's victory relief is the following text next to the image of the goddess of Thebes:

"Recitation by Thebes the Victorious, Lady of the strong arm, Mistress of all foreign lands. Recitation: 'Thus I have given to you all lands and all inaccessible foreign countries, the Nubian tribesmen of Lower Nubia'. Recitation: 'Thus I have given to you all foreign lands, the Asiatic back-country, the Aegean islands, to [. . .]' Recitation: 'as the father commanded.'"[1451]

Sheshonk I led a campaign to the Aegean islands (Haunebut) to make them submit to Egypt's trade tariffs once again as they did under queen Ahhotep II (1730-1692 BC). Another inscription on the relief[1452] described how Sheshonk I forced countries to submit to Egypt.

". . . since I have burned for you [all] foreign lands who were ignorant of Egypt and who had fallen into the practice of attacking [your] boundaries, and I have caused their heads to be cut off."[1453]

So I would expect decapitated bodies and burnt strata of cities around 1040 BC (Iron IIA) in western Sinai, Nubia, Phoenicia (especially near Byblos), Syria (Naharin), and the Aegean islands.

Incongruities of the Karnak Victory Relief

Iuput's description in several scenes throughout the jubilee court reads, "First Prophet of Amun-Re, king of the gods, great general and leader Iuput . . .;"[1454] hence I conjecture general Iuput was between Amun and Sheshonk I at the center of the army facing front.

The original group of captives or soldiers were standing with recurve bows in the furthest hand and a "vial of oil" (?) in the closest hand. On top of that the central group of three sets of seven bearded men facing left and right are standing with one arm raised in praise. The left headbands may be Canaanite mercenaries, and the right helmets may be Cretan mercenaries.

Philistine and Canaanite

Helmet on vase from Knossos, Crete

Mercenary bowmen honoring Sheshonk I and Iuput

1451 Ritner, Robert K., *The Libyan Anarchy*, Society of Biblical Literature, Atlanta, 2009, p. 205
1452 Digital Egypt photo at http://dlib.etc.ucla.edu/projects/Karnak/resource/BubastitePortal/1515
1453 Ibid., p. 202

450

Appendix B

In the center of these male groups, Iuput A was facing front with both arms crossing his chest holding objects.[1455] His left elbow makes the first male appear to be female. Names in the bottom right were Sharudad, Raphia, Laban, Ain-Goren ('well of threshing floor'), and Ham. Raphia was a city south of Gaza, Laban may be a city near the Gulf of Aqaba.[1456] Tell Goren is Ein-Gedi, so maybe there is a connection.

Amun$_v$ Sheshonk$_v$

woman^ ^Iuput

The small woman beneath Amun, goddess of Thebes, is holding something like an arrow or spoon in her right hand, and a stick (the top of which no longer remains) in her right hand.[1457] The image of Sheshonk I wearing the white crown is barely visible, but upon close inspection, the Chicago Epigraphic Survey determined it was "modelled in gypsum on the stone".[1458] Iuput's head is missing. I would like an art expert to clarify which carvings were first and last. These incongruities suggest this wall was usurped by someone after Sheshonk I, like his son, Sheshonk IIa.

"A forensic examination of Shoshenq II's body by Dr. Douglas Derry, the head of Cairo Museum's anatomy department, reveals that he was a man in his fifties when he died."[1459] If Sheshonk IIa was born in 1022 BC, and died in 970 BC, that is 52 years. Dr. Derry wrote that Sheshonk IIa died of a massive septic infection in a head wound.[1460] I suggest this head wound was

---

1454 Ritner, Robert K., *The Libyan Anarchy*, Society of Biblical Literature, Atlanta, 2009, pp. 196-200
1455 Digital Egypt photo at
http://dlib.etc.ucla.edu/projects/Karnak/assets/media/resources/BubastitePortal/highres/100_0868.jpg
1456 Deuteronomy 1:1
1457 Digital Egypt photo at http://dlib.etc.ucla.edu/projects/Karnak/resource/BubastitePortal/1527
1458 Kitchen, Kenneth A., *The Third Intermediate Period in Egypt*, England, 1973, p. 73, fn #357
1459 Wikipedia based upon Douglas E. Derry, "Note on the Remains of Shashanq," *Annales du Service des Antiquités de l'Égypte* 39, 1939, pp. 549-551
1460 Douglas E. Derry, "Note on the Remains of Shashanq," *Annales du Service des Antiquités de l'Égypte* 39,

451

inflicted during his campaign in Canaan, that he died shortly after his return with Jerusalem's treasures, and was afforded a grand burial in a silver coffin with a gold mask and placed in the tomb of Psusennes I. I suggest that before his death he ordered his campaign to be engraved next to his father's victory relief in Karnak, possibly even wanting to attribute them to his father in some way. There were several empty walls available in the court, and maybe the instructions were unclear, so that the list of cities conquered by Sheshonk IIa were squeezed into the left side of Sheshonk I's victory relief across from the glistening representation of Sheshonk I in gypsum. Possibly the artisan reworked most of Iuput out of the relief before Sheshonk IIa died and the project came to a halt.

"The Egyptian king referred to as Shishak is conventionally equated with Sheshonk I ... chooses to ignore the valid criticism of James *et al.* (1992:127) that there are other alternatives, and that there are problems with the Sheshonk I candidacy ... James *et al.* James (1991:229-231) and Rohl (1995) plausibly question this assumption ... there is another Sheshonk (II) in close proximity who might also be a candidate."[1461] The problem stems from acceptance of Thiele's dates (1983:80).[1462]

I agree with Manning that a Sheshonk II is a better candidate for Shishak, and that Thiele's dates have caused problems. Since Heqakheperre Sheshonk IIa died from an infected head wound from battle and was honored with a gold face mask and silver coffin, he is the best candidate for Shishak. Found on Sheshonk IIa's mummy was a jeweled pectoral inscribed with "Sheshonk, Great Chief of the Ma" which belonged to his father Sheshonk I before he was king.

At Sheshonk's temple to Amun at el-Hibeh, the pillar scene in the first pillared hall has the following inscription:

"King offers floral collar and two pectorals to Horus."[1463]

This is followed by an inscription under Horus.

"To you I have given all life, stability, and dominion appearance upon the throne of Horus, [who leads the living.]"[1464]

Could Horus refer to a promise that Sheshonk IIa, the child of Sheshonk I's old age, would rule? Is that why the mummy of Sheshonk IIa contained the pectoral of Sheshonk I? Did king David retake Goshen and Avaris, forcing Sheshonk I to travel to far-off lands to establish trade?

Twenty-Second and Twenty-Third Dynasties

King Hedjkheperre Setepenre Takelot I is attested by a Year 9 stela from Bubastis, and so I only give him a nine year reign. I chose 9 years for Sheshonk IIa, and 5 years each for Sheshonks IIb-c.

The following regnal years were listed with corroborating physical evidence (with dashes to a probable year) by David Aston in *The Libyan Period in Egypt*.[1465] I give my probable years from my notes following.

1939, pp. 549–551

1461 Manning, Sturt, *A Test of Time: The Volcano of Thera and the chronology and history of the Aegean and east Mediterranean in the mid second millennium B.C.*, Oxbow Books, 1999, p. 378

1462 Ibid.

1463 Ritner, Robert K., *The Libyan Anarchy*, Society of Biblical Literature, Atlanta, 2009, p. 223

1464 Ibid.

1465 Aston, David A., "The Chronologies of Dynasties 22 and 23," *The Libyan Period in Egypt*, Nederlands Institute, 2009, pp. 6-7

Appendix B

	Ashton		Clarity
P6	y5	Iny	
	y12	Iuput I	13y
	y21	Iuput II	21y
	y33-34	Osorkon I	34y
p7	y23-29	Osorkon II	32y
	y28	Osorkon III	29y
	y7	Pamiu	
	y23	Pedubast Sibast	23y
	y23	Pedubast Siese	23y
	y10	Peftjauawybast	
	y21	Shoshenq I	33y
	y39	Shoshenq III	39y
	y10	Shoshenq IV	15y
	y37	Shoshenq V	38y
	y6	Shoshenq VI	6y
	y5	Shoshenq VIa	5y
	y9	Takelot I	9y
	y25	Takelot II	25y (first 5 as HPA)
	y13	Takelot III	14y

22nd Dynasty in Tanis was concurrent with 23rd Dynasty king and/or [HPA] in Thebes.

Sheshonk I (Hedjkheperre) 21y
            [Psusennes II for 4 years until Sheshonk's son, Iuput A] 12y
Osorkon I (Sekhemkheperre Setepenre) 34 or 35y   [*Sheshonk C*] 24-30y
Takelot I (Hedjkheperre) 9y-10y   [*Iuwelot*] [*Smendes III*]
Manetho gave 25y total for Sheshonks IIa-c
Sheshonk IIa (Heqakheperre) 9y
Sheshonk IIb (Tutkheperre) 5y
Sheshonk IIc (Maatkheperre) 5y
Osorkon II (Sekhemkheperre) 30y-32y   *Har SiEse A* 7-10y
Sheshonk III (Usermaatre Setepenre/amun) 39y   [*Harsiese B*] 14-30y
  years 22-29 of Sheshonk III are followed by years 11-24 of Takelot II's 25 years

"Harsiese A died before the twelfth regnal year of Osorkon II."[1466]

I plan an in-depth analysis of the TIP in volume 2 of *Pharaohs of the Bible*.

1466 http://en.wikipedia.org/wiki/Harsiese_B

Pharaohs of the Bible

APPENDIX C

This appendix contains my Late Ramesside Letters chart and my time-lines.

Clarity Order and Chronology of Late Ramesside Letters

Q for Quoting a previous letter within new letter; R for Response to a previous letter; TW=Thebes West; TE=Thebes East; MH=Medinet Habu; { } is not in text but my idea

#	From	To	Others	About	year
46	(mentions chief taxing master)	"Great official"-ThebesW	Efnamon, your eldest brother. Esamon. Henuttawi wants humor.	I was in the house when you were born. Should you become vizier . . .	y1 Ram IX
42		Henuttawi, chantress-Thebes	Scribe Esamenope; field cultivation, copper, calf	"I am summoned before Pharaoh." Palace	y2 Ram IX
37	Henuttawi-Thebes.	Esamenope-"don't worry about your father." Hori. Menmaarenakht overseer of granaries + treasury	Scribes Pentahunakht &Saroy; oipe-measure for emmer appraised; fishermen taking 2.5 khar each. Prenuemef case against father. Paunesh general takes men with oil from Thoth fort to MH	She provided own grain offerings. <u>Grain in sealed chest</u> with Paseny. Wab-priest Espamedushepes Ship loaded with salt + goods from north. vizier + bread rations	**Y2** "year 2" of Ram IX
12	[Dhutmose] Tjaroy-MH & and army scribe Pentahunakht	Deputy Hori, (returned to) Thebes East (near Ne)	7 Men of Necropolis in Ne: Pennestitawi, Neferamon, Horimose, **Wenamon**, Panakhtenope, Amenhotep, Kadjadja to be brought west to MH	No Meshwesh attack yet. Place 7 men under <u>scribe Butehamon</u> with Pakhor+Audjar =9 Have you paid the pilot?	y3 of Ram IX
47	("tell the Ombite")	<u>Es</u>[amenope]-ThebesW, oversees distributing grain to workmen	Essobek, your scribe. vizir. scribe Efnamon; *watchman* **Wenamon**; *doorkeepers* Khonsmose and Dhutmose (not Tjaroy)	Get to work! *Give grain* to men confined and workers lest they be idle, lest they fix blame on you.	y5 of Ram IX
33	(mentions chief taxing master)		Mayor of west of Ne, **Paweraa**; Eshor, son of Efnamon and Esmut	Men appointed to cultivate new land of Perdjadja; son of Omer	y9 Ram IX

#	From	To	Others	About	year
36	Esamenope-south (notes chief taxing master CTM)	Chantress Mutenope-ThebesW	Deputy of temple, Esobek; for CTM, Sobeksankh & Sekhayeniot cut wood and clear brush	Plant fruit trees; Penhapi; deben and 5 kite for 15 weapons Onery makes	
32	[general] Piankh-	controllers-ThebesW	Join with chief taxing master and build wall.	Wall in pasturage. {need a stonemason?}	y10 RIX
38	Herere, principle of the harem-Elephantine	Peseg-ThebesW troop commander	This is the second request.	"Give them rations" of grain from "it" {chest?}.	y10 Ram IX
40	**Paiankh**-Nubia	Peseg-ThebesW		{possibly: do whatever my wife, Herere, says}	y10 RIX
39	Herere, chantress-Elephantine	Peseg-ThebesW troop commander	This is third request now backed by her husband's (Piank's) letter.	"look after the men" give rations of grain	y10 Ram IX
19	General	Tjaroy-ThebesW	Why have rations stopped? [feed the warriors or beware]	Have Akhmenu give bread rations to Meshwesh nearby	y10 Ram IX
22	General-south. scribe Pentahunakht	Tjaroy-ThebesW papyrus rolls	W/ Pentahunakht resolve matter of Akhmenu	"assemble men"-*rations* "give *coppersmith* job"	y10 Ram IX
	Dhutmose (Tjaroy) is sent		on first expedition to	Nubia (Yar, Ethiopia)	
29	Butehamon-ThebeW	Shedsuhor-Nubia	Shedsuhor is troop commander	Assist weak Tjaroy on journey never taken b4	y10 RIX
43	[Butehamon+ Shedemdua]-ThebeW Deir el-Medina	[Shedsuhor]-Nubia; thru Akhmenu + Hadnakht	Q"When Hemesheri was here I sent you a letter." I wrote twice; they didn't get to you.	Pilot Tjaroy in boat; look after him and be his man	y10 Ram IX
13	Amenopen-sakht, TW the *stonemason*	Dhutmose-Nubia	QD: "Send Amenhotep, I await him." "I look after this Butehamon."	Cultivable land, barge to ground; **Piankh** 'haven't sent one letter'	y10 Ram IX

Appendix C

#	From	To	Others	About	year
5	Dhutmose-Yar D is sick, and asked for prayer. (messenger Esamon)	Bute+Shede-Thebes clear brush; trees on 3 riparian plots "take water to Amun" also in #3	Donkeys to Medjay Chief Sermontu to get field grain to boat; wood to my house, *stone patchwork*. herdsman Esamon' oxen. "Paykamen, my brother" Tapeses+Paturaa	Wab-priest Pentahu-nakht will supervise boat transport. Smaragdus vessels; Attend Hemesheri & Khonsmose' daughter. Clothe housemen. 3 garments from Pakhor	y11 Ram IX
30	Pharaoh's general-Nubia	Workmen+ Butehamon+ Kar-TW	Tjaroy+Shedsuhor "have reached me". Bute+Kar get copper from Heramen to give to Tutuy+Hori+2	Fetch chariot poles. Five servants are yours, don't give Heamenpenaf any; receive from Herere	y11 Ram IX
14	Amenhotep, prophet-Thebes	Dhutmose-Yar	Hemesheri's daughter: fine (R#5); "general, your lord"	Quotes that he attends Butehamon+Shedem "danger removed"	y11 RIX
51	Dhutmose-	(partial)	It is for payment . . .		
6	Dhutmose-Yar	Bute+Hemesh eri-TW	Chantresses Baky +Shedemdua	"I am alive. I am well." "bring me back alive"	y11 RIX
15	Amenhotep, prophet-Thebes	Dhutmose-Yar;taken by Nubians	Butehamon prays + *offers water* on your behalf. to give advice	"Stay on the boat!" it protects you "Write in your own hand"	y12 Ram IX
25	Dhutmose-Nubia	controller-ThebesW	Son of Amenpanufe – crew 3 deben of silver to pay for violate Hadnakht; work w/ [Shed]suhor, son of mine	"Give the money to Hori" **I won't delay**; have written testimony	Y17-18 Ram IX
	Dhutmose is	called back	to Thebes when Amen-	hotep is suppressed.	y18
23	Hekanufe is 2nd prophet [Nubia?]	Tjerta (Tjaroy)-ThebesW	"servant of the general Penhershefi" [Hemesheri is Hek's wife]	Don't cease writing to me about your condition.	y19 Ram IX
24	Hekanufe 2nd prophet	Tjuroy (Tjaroy)TW	Hemesheri is alive and well; Penhershefi	Write thru anybody who comes northward.	y19 RIX
26	Ne, Mayor-ThebesE	Dhutmose -ThebesW	Troop commander says harvest spoils from neglect	Workman says he was beaten. - send to me	y19 Ram IX
27	Panufenufe-ThebesE	Dhutmose Tjaroy-TW	Treasury scribe, prophet of Sobek, matter of Kassu	Don't make a claim against Sobek; hear case	y19 RIX

Pharaohs of the Bible

#	From	To	Others	About	year
48	-ThebesW	Dhutmose-	Grain vizier registering "this damage"	Determine loss, store all that's found	y19 RIX
17	Singer of general-south	Dhutmose+ Heme+Shed	"singer of General, Pentahures"	Requests sending letters thru messengers	y19 RIX
21	general-Nubia Pentahunakht Kenkhum	Tjaroy-ThebesW	General's scribe Kenkhum and controller Payshuuben W/ Nuteme throw two medjay into Nile by night	"How shall pharaoh reach Nubia? Of whom is pharaoh superior still?" barge, send gold	y1 of Ram X
34	general-Nubia	Payshuuben-ThebesW	W/ Nuteme +Tjaroy throw 2 medjay into Nile	"Do not let anybody of the land find out."	y1 RX
35	General-south Kenykhum	Nuteme/Nodj-met harem ThebesW	W/ Nuteme +Tjaroy throw 2 medjay into Nile by nite	"I have noted all matters which you have written."	y1 Ram X
20	general-south	Tjaroy-ThebesW	"You know this journey which I'm going to make"	Send cloth and rags for bandages for soldiers	y9 RX
28	workmen+Bute+Kar-TW written 9days via Hadnakht, the Medjay	[Pi]ankh-Nubia HPA letter sent by Hori retrieved by Butehamon	KSOK, overseer granaries+ pharaoh's troops; Piankh's workmen *Amenpanufe* + Heramenpenaf; Tjaroy inspector to tombs	Demands clothes -wife? Uncover debris from foremost tomb; transport boat was sunk; brought back men from Ne	y1 Ram XI
18	general-south	Tjaroy-ThebesW	I've noted all matters about which you wrote.	"I have accomplished all commissions"Q#28	y1 RXI
	Piankh going	N to Thebes.	Dhutmose going South to	meet him in Elephantine.	
4	Dhutmose-Edfu to fort Elephantine Nubia (rebellion)	Bute+Shedemdua-TW "another matter" Butehamon + Hermenpenaf	Workmen Amenhotep, Ese, Hermenpenaf, Bak-amon; scribe Kenkhnum "tell *Amenpanufe* to write letter to let man receive it" warden Penpawenher	Feed soldiers, send oil to delta, attend Khonsmose' daughter and Shedemdua Superior [Piankh] saying "I will go up to meet **Panehsi**"	y1 Ram XI
31	Singer Pentahures-Elephant	Butehamon-ThebesW	Confidant Akhmenu, craftsman, Hemesheri chantress Tuia, scribe Hori	Look after kids and father. Have spear and confections made; receive Taymedjay	y1 of Ram XI

Appendix C

#	From	To	Others	About	year
3	Dhutmose-Yar "when I returned" gold	Butehamon-ThebesW	Tainuteme and Paadjadja I. "take water to Amun" bread-rations	Attend Shedemdua and Hemesheri Plant grain and vegies.	y2 Ram XI
45	? M. Habu-ThebesW	Dhutmose-Nubia; "2nd expedition"	Send thru Pentahunakht, general's scribe.	You've sent 3 letters to Bute, but none to me.	y3 Ram XI
2	Dhutmose-Yar hills "up" "write to me"	Bute+Shedemdua-ThebesW	Workmen Amenhotep, Kas Bakeamon, Henuaa Takamene, Sedsumut; scribe Khenkhnum relay	Herere with Piankh in Elephantine. welfare of Hemesheri; letters up with Elephantine men	y4 of RXI
49	-ThebesW	[Piank-Nubia]	General. After you left Ne daughter of slave-woman	She is to be brought back.	y5 RXI
1	Dhutmose-Yar ill when arrived	Butehamon-ThebesW	Chief workmen Bakenmut, Amennakht; Heramenpenaf guardian Kadere, Pakhor	Protect Shedemdua from fieldmen. D sent several letters, but received none.	y5 of Ram XI
27 A	Dhutmose	controller-ThebesW	Guardian of mine shall collect remainder	Illness; "you shall make for him"	y6 RX
50	Dhutmose-Nubia	Butehamon+Shedemdua-ThebesW (Quoted in #16)	Young Takamene, Scribes Meniunufe+Amenhotep Shedsumut, Tainuteme, Tapeses, Medjay Kasy. "I will not be silent about it."	You haven't written me about 17 spears and coppersmith Hori's job. You have not sent boat bearing general's name.	y6 of Ram XI
10	Dhutmose-	**Karoy**+Bute-ThebesW	Another matter from Scribe Khenkhnum – Hemesheri "write your condition"	Wrote about spears prior to your letter. Give Hori copper for spears, not $.	y6 of Ram XI
7	Dhutmose-Yar	Guardian **Kar**-ThebeW	Chantress Tauhenu Dhutmose is sick.	Attend Shedemdua; prevent another wrong	y7 RXI
44	Shedemdua-Thebes	Dhutmose-Yar	*Coppersmiths* brought before vizier. Tabake (her)	Wax mouths of vessels of smaragdus. foreigner	y7 Ram XI
11	Heramenpenaf-TW	Dhutmose	Write about your condition "presence of the general"	Look for Amenkeni	y7 Ram XI

Pharaohs of the Bible

#	From	To	Others	About	year
9	Dhutmose-**Yar** Sick, but beer and good news	Butehamon + Shedemdua + Hemesheri-ThebesW	Medjay Kas-weaver. Send Medjay Hadnakht (Sherden Hori); scribe Horsheri; ass of Nofreti, <u>Iunufe's son</u>	4 spears + balance-Hori for guardian **Kar**. Chariot donkeys. Documents; "my superior" **abandoned**	**y 10** Rameses XI
16	Butehamon + Shedemdua-Thebes	Dhutmose-Nubia "hills" "water" Q#5	Workman Heramenpenaf Payshuuben gets spears <u>son of Iunufe</u>, Hemesheri	"I wrote spears letter to guardian **Karoy** in Ne." R#50 Medjays Kasy(Q#9)+Kahnakht	y10 of Ram XI
8	Butehamon-Thebes	Dhutmose-Yar	Heramenpenaf, Amenopenakht, *Amenpanufe*; Pentahures (Q#17)-	Quotes grain+vegie#3. Quotes 17 spears #9 to **Kar**(oy). Q#2-"writing about your condition"	y10 of Ram XI
41	Bakenkhons-TE general's scribe and Dikonsiry	Ankhef-ThebesW Necropolis scribe	Don't listen to words of opposition Bakenkhons is wab-priest of king's food [Herihor]	"You wrote in opposition to this false testimony" "be firm with these 16 bread-rations"	20+ year later

Q for Quoting a previous letter within new letter; R for Response to a previous letter; TW=Thebes West; TE=Thebes East; MH=Medinet Habu; { } is not in text but my idea

Appendix C

CLARITY TIME-LINES

SHEM

Shem

Pre-flood Pangaea (Adam's Land) 2448-2348 (flood lasted one year)	Greater Armenia 2347-2307?	Northern Levant? 2307?-2244?	Canaan? 2244?-2050?

Pharaohs in Thinis

Mizraim (1st) 2330-2298	Hor-Aha 2y	Djer+ Djet 2296-2261	Den (1st) 2261-2229	Anedjib + Semerkhet + Qa'a 2229-2184	2nd Dyn. 2184-2062

Shem

Egypt 2050?-2002?	China 2002?-1919?

Pharaohs in Memphis

Sanakhte (3rd) 2062-2043 (in Thinis)	Djoser (3rd) 2043-2014	Sekhem-khet (3rd) 2014-2007	Khaba (3rd) 2007-2001	Huni (3rd) 2001-1977	Snefuru (4th) 1977-1953	Khufu (4th) 1953-1930	Djedefre (4th) 1930-1919

Shem

China 1919?-1852?	Canaan 1852?-1846

Pharaohs in Memphis

Khafe (4th) 1919-1895	Baka (4th) 1895-1893	Menkaure (4th) 1893-1865	Shepsekaf (4th) 1865-1861	Khentkaus I (4th) 1861-1859	I.... (pre-15th) 1860-1856	Seth II (pre-15th) 1856-1854	Teti (6th) 1856-1844

Pharaohs of the Bible

The Patriarchs

ABRAHAM
Abram/Abraham

Ur 1996-1923				Charran 1922	Egypt 1921-1919	Canaan 1919-1859
Pharaohs in Memphis						
Huni (3rd) 2001-1977	Sneferu (4th) 1977-1953	Khufu (4th) 1953-1930	Djedefre (4th) 1930-1919		Khafre (4th) 1919-1895	Baka – Khentkaus I 1895-1859 (4th)

Abram/Abraham

Canaan 1859-1821		
Pharaohs in Memphis		
I . . . (p15) 1860-1856	Teti (6th) 1856-1844	Pepi I (6th) 1842-1817

JACOB
Jacob/Israel

Canaan 1836-1782									(C)Harran 1782-1742	Canaan 1742-1706	Goshen, Egypt 1706-1689
Pharaohs in the Nile delta											
Sheshi (14th) 1874-1821	Salitis (15th) 1820-1815	Beon (15th) 1815-1810	Sakir -Har 1810-1805	Khyan (15th) 1805-1765	Apepi (15th) 1765-1731	Khamudi (15th) 1731-1720	Ahmose I (18th) 1720-1712	Ahmen-hotep I+ Nefertari 1712-1702	Ahmen-hotep I (18th) 1702-1688		

462

Appendix C

JOSEPH

Joseph

Canaan	Egypt
1745-1728	1728-1635

Pharaohs in the Nile delta

| Apepi I (15th) 1765-1731 | Khamudi (15th) 1731-1720 | Ahmose I (18th) 1720-1712 | Amenhotep I (18th) 1712-1688 | Thutmose I (18th) 1688-1674 | Thutmose II 1774-1772 | Hatshepsut (18th) 1772-1651 | Thutmose III (18th) 1651-1618 |

MOSES

Moses

| Egypt 1571-1531 | Midian 1531-1491 In 1491 Moses returned to Egypt to lead the exodus out of Egypt. | Camps 1491 | Kadesh-barnea 1490-1449 | Camps '49-'51 |

Egypt's Pharaohs

| Amenhotep III (18th) 1588-1550 | Amenhotep IV Akhenaten 1551-1534 | Smenkhkare 1534-1531 | Nefertiti 1531-1530 | Tutankhamun 1534-1524 | Ay 1524-1520 | Horemheb 1520-1493 | Rameses I 1493-1491 (19th) | Seti I 1491-1480 | Rameses II 1480-1414 |

JOSHUA

Joshua

| Egypt 1536-1491 | Camps 1491 | Kadesh-barnea 1490-1449 | Camps 1449-1451 | Canaan battles 1451-1444 | Tribal Israel 1444-1426 |

Egypt's Pharaohs

| Akhenaten 1551-1534 (18th) | Smenkhkare 1534-1531 | Nefertiti 1531-1530 | Tutankhamun 1534-1524 | Ay 1524-1520 | Horemheb 1520-1493 | Rameses I 1493-1491 (19th) | Seti I 1491-1480 | Rameses II 1480-1414 |

463

Israel's Judges

Israel

Elders 1426-1409	Othniel 1409-1369		Ehud 1369-1349		Deborah 1339-1299
			Shamgar 1366-1340	Barak and Jael 1338	
	40 years land rests (Judges 3:11)		(Judges 3:30 and 5:31)		40 years land rests
				1351-1271 fords of Jordan 80y of rest	

Oppressor

Aramaens 1417-1409		Jabin of Hazor 1358-1338	
		Eglon of Moab 1369-1351	Philistines 1350? - 1340

Egypt

Rameses II 1480-1414	Marenptah 1414-1394	Seti II 1394-1388	Merenptah Siptah 1388-1381	Tausret 1381-1378	anarchy 1378-1323	Setnakht 1322-1318	Rameses III 1318-1286
		Amenmesse 1394-1390					

In 1313 and 1310 BC major volcanic eruptions in the Aegean Sea caused "Sea Peoples" to seek new homelands.

Appendix B

Israel's Judges

Israel

	Gideon 1291-1251		Tola 1251-1228	Jair 1228-1206	Jepthah 1206-1200	Ibzan 1200-1193	Elon 1193-1183	Abdon 1183-1175	Samson 1175-1155	Eli 1155-1115
	40y land rests (Jg.8:28)									
		Abimelech ruled Shechem for 3y								

Oppressor

Midianites 1298-1291			Philistines 1224-1206		Philistines 1195-1155
Amalekites			Ammonites		

Egypt

Rameses III 1318-1286	Ram. IV 1286-1279	Ram. V 1279-1275	Ram. VI 1275-1266	Ram. VII 1266-1258	Ram VIII 1258-1256	Ram. IX 1256-1237	Ram. X 1237-1228	Rameses XI 1228-1199	Herihor 1199-1169	Pinedjem I 1169-1148

Samuel preached during Philistine oppression from 1115 to 1095 BC when God routed Israel's enemies. Then Samuel anointed Saul king, but Samuel continued to judge in Israel until a few years before king Saul died.

Clarity Chronology Detail-A of the end of 20th Dynasty

Thebes

Pharaoh	Rameses IX up to 9th year	Rameses IX 10th year	Rameses IX 11th 12th years	RamesesIX 14th - 16th years	RamesesIX 17th - 18th years	Rameses IX 19th year, and he died	Rameses X 1st year (Mayer Papyri)
Vizier	Khamwese	Khamwese	Khamwese	Nibmarenacht 14-16	Khamwese (went to Byblos?)	Nibmarenacht 19th year	
HPA High Priest of Amun	Ramessesnakht, who dies	Amenhotep (rewarded for Karnak)	Amenhotep	Amenhotep	Amenhotep suppressed 9 months	Nesuamon	Nesuamon
2nd prophet	Amenhotep	Nesuamon	Hekanufe	Penhershefi	Nesuamon	Hekanufe	
KSOK Viceroy to Kush/Nubia	Wentawuat	Wentawuat	Wentawuat	Wentawuat	Wentawuat	Piankh	Piankh
Chief scribes of Necropolis	Esamon & Dhutmose	Esamon & Dhutmose	Efnamon & Dhutmose	Khaemhedj &Dhutmose	Dhutmose& Butehamon	Dhutmose & Butehamon	Dhutmose & Butehamon
Mayor of Thebes east	Paser	Paser	Paser				
Mayor of Thebes west	Paweraa	Paweraa	Paweraa	Paweraa		Psmennakht	
Nubian			Panehsy	Panehsy	Panehsy	Panehsy	Panehsy

Clarity Chronology Detail-B of end of 20th Dynasty

Thebes

Pharaoh	Rameses X up to 2nd year	RamesesX 9th year, dies	Rameses XI 1st year	Rameses XI 7th year	Rameses XI 11th year	Rameses XI 12th year	Rameses XI 19th year	Rameses XI 29th year, dies
Vizier	Nibmarenacht				Piankh		Herihor	Herihor
HPA High Priest of Amun	Nesuamon	Nesuamon	Piankh	Piankh 7th	Piankh	Herihor, Piankh's son-in-law	Herihor	Herihor
General	Piankh	Piankh	Piankh	Piankh	Piankh	Herihor	Herihor	Herihor
KSOK Viceroy to Kush/Nubia	Piankh	Piankh	Piankh	Piankh 7th-11th y	Piankh 11th y Piankh dies	Panehsy 12th -17th y (Turin P.)	Herihor	Herihor
Chief scribes of Necropolis	Dhutmose & Butehamon	Dhutmose & Butehamon	Khaemhedj & Butehamon	Khaemhedj & Buteham	Dhutmose & Butehamon	Dhutmose & Butehamon	Dhutmose & Butehamon	Dhutmose & Butehamon
Nubian	Panehsy	Panehsy	Panehsy	Panehsy	Panehsy		Panehsy	Panehsy

". . . by year 7 of the repetition of births, the high priest named in an item of correspondence is Piankh."
(*The Third Intermediate Period in Egypt* by Nick Thom, April 2008, p. 4)

Appendix B

Clarity Chronology Detail of High Priests and 21st Dynasty 147 years

Thebes

HPA Herihor 5y + 25y king = 30y total KSOK	Pinedjem I King 21y [y1, 8, 16 attested] [y19-21 linens]	King Menkheperre 49y, (son of Pinedjem I and Henuttawy)	Smendes II 2y	Pinedjem II 22y	Psusennes III 23y takes control of Tanis after 9y as Pusennes II
Pinedjem HPA [y6-15 attest] w/ Masaharta as 2nd prophet	Masaharta 19y [y 16-18 attested] Djedkhonsefankh 2y	HPA Menkheperre and king for 49 years [y48 linen]	Smendes II 2y	Pinedjem II 22y	Psusennes III 23y takes control of Tanis after 9y as Pusennes II
Chief scribes Butehamon + Ankhfenamun	Chief scribes Butehamon + Ankhfenamun	General Menkheperre 49y			[Psusennes y23 = y3 of Sheshonk]

Butehamon served "Years 10, 11, 12, 13 of an unspecified ruler, but in company with Pinudjem I as high priest, in a series of Theban graffiti." - K.A. Kitchen, *The Third Intermediate Period*, 1973; p. 38 also Spiegelberg footnote. "A further, unpublished, grafitto apparently associates a Year 16, the high priest Masaharta, and Butehamun's son Ankhefenamun." - Ibid., p. 38 based on footnote 160. Years 10-13 and 16 could be of Herihor or Pinedjem I.

Tanis

Smendes, 26y treasurer [y5 Herihor Wenamun]	Smendes, king, 23y [UE quarry stela in y22 or y23]	(Neferkare) Amenemnisut 4years [co-reign] King Psusennes I 46y (42y alone) [y19 on large Dakhla stela]	9y Amen-emope	6y Osor-kon [y2]	"Pharaoh" Siamun 19y [y17 attested]	Psusennes II 14y

467

Pharaohs of the Bible

Clarity Chronology of High Priests (21A) and 21st Dynasty during Israel's Judges

Pharaoh Tanis	Smendes, as treasurer	Smendes I 1169-1146	Psusennes I 1146-1100 Amenemnisut 1146-1142	Amenemope 1100-1091
HP-king Thebes	Herihor 1199-1169	Pinedjem I 1169-1148	Menkheperre 1148-1099	Smendes II 1099-1097

Israel Judge	Ibzan 1200-1193	Elon 1193-1183	Abdon 1183-1175	Samson 1175-1155	Eli 1155-1115	Samuel 1115-1095

As-syria	Ashur-nirari III 1203-1197	Enlil-kudurri-usur 1197-1192	Ninurta-apal-Ekur 1192-1179	Ashur-Dan I 1179-1133	2 kings 1133	Ashur-resh-ishi I 1133-1115	Tiglath-Pileser I 1115-1076

Clarity Chronology of High Priests and 21st Dynasty during the Kingdom of Israel

LE=Lower Egypt (Delta); ME=Middle Egypt; UE=Upper Egypt (Thebes)

LE king	Osorkon 1091-85	Siamun 1085-66	Psusennes II 1066-1052	Sheshonk I 1055-1022	Osorkon I 1022-988	Takelot I 988-979	Sheshonk IIa 979-970
ME				Nimlot B, general	Shedsunefertem		
UE king	Pinedjem II 1097-1075	Psusennes III (II) 1075-1052					
HPA Thebes	Pinedjem II 1097-1075	Psusennes III (II) 1075-1052	Iuput A 1052-1024		Sheshonk C 1024-994	Iuwelot 994-984	Smendes C 984-970

Israel	Saul 1095-1055	David 1055-1015	Solomon 1015-975
		Ishbosheth 1055-1053	

Syria (Damascus)						Hezion	Tabrimon
Assyria	Tiglath-Pileser I 1115-1076	Asharidapal-Ekur 1076-1074	Ashur-bel-kala 1074-1056	Eriba Adad II 1056-1054	Shamshi Adad IV 1054-1050	Ashur-nasir-pal I 1050-1031	Shalmaneser II 1031-1019	Ashur-nirari IV 1019-1013	Ashur-rabi II 1013-972

Appendix B

Clarity Chronology of Egypt during Divided Kingdom of Israel and Judah

LE=Lower Egypt (Delta); ME=Middle Egypt; UE=Upper Egypt (Thebes)

King of Israel	Jeroboam I 975-954			Nadab 954-953	Baasha 953-930	Elah 930-929	Omri 929-918	Ahab 918-897 Ahaziah 898-896		Joram 896-884	
King of Judah	Rehoboam 975-958		Abijah 958-955	Asa 955-914				Jehoshaphat 914-889		Jehoram 889-885	Ahaziah 885-884

LE king	Sheshonk IIa 979-970	Sheshonk IIb 970-965	Sheshonk IIc 965-960	Osorkon II 960-928			Sheshonk III 928-889			Sheshonk IV 889-874	
ME	HPA's in north also			Nimlot C			Takelot II (935) 930-910		Thutemhat	Os B	Nimlot III	Djehutiemhat
UE king		Smendes III 970-950			HarSiEse I 950-928			Pedubast I SiEse 928-905	Iuput I (co-reign) 914-901		
HPA		Smendes C 970-960	HarSiEse A 960-950	..dju.. 950-935	Takelot F 935-930	HarSiEse B 930-901			Takelot B 901-890	Osorkon B 890-871 *Sheshonk VIa* 886-881	

Syria	Hadad 980-916				Ben-Hadad I 916-885	
Assyria	Ashurreshishi II 972-967	Tiglath-Pileser II 967-935	Ashur-Dan II 935-912	Adad-nirari II 912-891	Tukulti-Ninurta II 891-884	

Pharaohs of the Bible

Clarity Chronology of Egypt during Divided Kingdom of Israel and Judah

LE=Lower Egypt (Delta); ME=Middle Egypt; UE=Upper Egypt (Thebes)

King of Israel	Jehu 884-856	Jehoahaz 856-839	Jehoash 841-825	Jeroboam II 825-784	{no ruler} 784-773	Zechariah +Shallum 7 months	Menahem 773-761	Pekahiah 761-759
King of Judah	Athaliah 884-878	Joash 878-839	Amaziah 839-810	Uzziah 810-759				

From Ussher's Chronology: 770 Manahem bribed (1000 talents of silver) Pul (Ashur Dan) to depart. 776 1ˢᵗ Olympiad

Syria	Hazael 885-845	Ben-Hadad II 845-833					
Assyria	Ashur-nasir-pal II 884-859	Shalmaneser III 859-824 {Qarqar 853}	Shamshi Adad V 824-811	Shammuramat 811-808	Adad-nirari III 811-783	Shalmaneser IV 783-773 *solar eclipse 791*	Ashur-Dan III 773-755 {solar eclipse 763}

LE king	Pami 874-863	Osorkon 3 863-834	*Sheshonk V* 834-796	Sheshonk 6 796-790	Osorkon 4 790-772	Tefnakte I 787-759	
UE *HPA* king	Osorkon B 890-871 *Sheshonk VIa* 886-881	*Takelot C* 866-840	Takelot III 840-826	Pedubast II SiBast 826-788 *Takelot D* 826-811			Piye 35y total 780-760
Theban priestess		Shepenupet I 863-834	Amenirdas I 834-811	Shepenupet II 811-			

Cush		Alara 864-834	Kashta 834-811			Piye 780-745	

Appendix B

Clarity Chronology of Israel and Judah sent into Exile

LE=Lower Egypt (Delta); ME=Middle Egypt; UE=Upper Egypt (Thebes)

King of Israel	Pekah 759-739	{anarchy} 739-730	Hoshea 730-721 king So	*Assyrian exile*				
King of Judah	Jotham 759-742	Ahaz 742-726	Hezekiah 726-698		Manasseh 698-643	Amon 643-641	Josiah 641-610	

| Assyria/ Babylon | Ashur-nirari V 755-745 | Tiglath-Pileser III 745-727 Nabonasar 747-731 | Shalmaneser V 727-722 *Took away Samaria* | Sargon II 722-705 Merodach-Baladan 722-709 | Sennacherib 717-681 Sennacherib 688-681 | Esarh addon 681-668 | Ashurbanipal 668-627 *sacked Thebes* Ashuretil-ilani | Nabopol assar 625-605 |

Tanis			Sethos -Herodits			678-676 no king	Psamtik I 663-624	Necho II 624-605
Sais king	Backenrenef 759-743	Padinemti 741-718	Tefnakhte II 718-702	Nekauba 702-688	Necho I 688-678	Psammetichus I 15y (provincial) from 20th y of Manasseh. +39y=54		
UE king	Piye 35y total 760-745	Shabako 16y 745-729	Shebitju 16y 729-713	Taharqa 26y 713-687	Tantamani 687-678	12 kings 678-663	Psammetichus I 663-624; -605 Necho II	

From Ussher's Chronology:
728 Shalmaneser invaded; Hoshea became tributary. 725 Hoshea revolted. 724 Assyrian invasion. 721 Samaria taken.

Clarity Chronology of Judah sent into Exile and Solomon's Temple Destroyed

King of Judah	Jehoahaz (3 mnth)	Jehoiakim 610-599		Jehoiachin (3 months)	Zedekiah 599-588	*Babylonian exile 606-536*

| Babylon | Nabopolassar 625-605 | Nebuchadnezzar II 607-562 (20 months viceroy, 43 years sole king   - Eusibius) |

LE king	Necho II 624-595	Psamtik II 595-589	Hophra 589-570	Amasis 570-526	Psamtik III
UE king		Necho II 605-595			

Made in the USA
Charleston, SC
01 August 2012